CONQUERING THE VALLEY

Stonewall Jackson
at Port Republic

Robert K. Krick

William Morrow and Company, Inc.
New York

It is the policy of William Morrow and Company, Inc., and its imprints and affiliates, recognizing the importance of preserving what has been written, to print the books we publish on acid-free paper, and we exert our best efforts to that end.

Library of Congress Cataloging-in-Publication Data

Krick, Robert K.
  Conquering the valley: Stonewall Jackson at Port Republic / Robert K. Krick.
    p.   cm.
  Includes bibliographical references and index.
  ISBN 0-688-11282-X
  1. Shenandoah Valley Campaign, 1862.   2. Jackson, Stonewall, 1824–1863
I. Title.
E473.7.K74   1996
973.7'32—dc20   95-36392
                                                                            CIP

Printed in the United States of America

First Edition

1   2   3   4   5   6   7   8   9   10

BOOK DESIGN BY KAY SCHUCKHART

CONTENTS

Contents

The battles at Port Republic and Cross Keys—the triumphant culmination of Stonewall Jackson's Shenandoah Valley campaign—were among the most important of the Civil War. In a strategy that will always be remembered as a military classic, the general took advantage of the Valley's unique geography to launch his attacks. The result: decisive victories that abruptly revitalized the fighting spirit of the South and brought hope to the floundering Confederate States of America. *Conquering the Valley* brings to life the dramatic events of June 8 and 9, 1862, when one stern general's remarkable conquests indelibly marked his place in Civil War history.

Drawn from eyewitness accounts, private diaries, and intimate letters, this fascinating work takes the reader minute-by-minute through two significant Civil War battles. Robert K. Krick, author of *Stonewall Jackson at Cedar Mountain*, uses newly discovered sources to paint a vivid picture of conflict, both in battle and in everyday life.

Here is the story of men fighting for hearth and home, the only Americans in our national past who have literally fought in their own backyards, in sight of their wives and children, to protect their freedoms. Krick's focus on the final battles—at times involving only a few score men scrambling through the streets of a tiny Valley hamlet, some in pursuit of Jackson and others hoping to protect him—makes for electrifying reading.

Stonewall Jackson's near capture by the enemy sparks the text with intrigue and excitement. The dour and uncommunicative general found his niche in wartime battle, and the unique personalities of Jackson's peers—both friends and foes—provide

(continued on back flap)

Conquering the Valley

PREFACE

ore than 125 years ago General Thomas J. Jackson, then known within only a narrow circle and no more than moderately admired even within that orbit, clawed his way to center stage in Virginia's Shenandoah Valley. Within the ten weeks ending on June 9, 1862, "Stonewall" Jackson made a lasting impact on the American Civil War—and on the broader course of American history. As late as June 7, despite a dazzling succession of marches and triumphs, Jackson's ultimate victory remained uncertain. During the 8th and 9th he fought twice in quick succession against two Federal armies, winning battles at both Cross Keys and Port Republic. This dramatic, triumphant crowning achievement ended a campaign that at once assumed legendary dimensions. Jackson and the Shenandoah Valley have ever since been synonymous in American consciousness. His campaign there continues to fascinate new generations of military historians and general students of the war.

Before Stonewall Jackson won in the Valley, the Confederate nation appeared to have a life expectancy numbered in months, if not weeks. After a succession of unleavened disasters all across its frontiers, the new country faced in the spring of 1862 a mammoth invading army that besieged its capital city of Richmond. Jackson's second front in the Valley anchored opposite him a Northern force far larger than his own numbers, reducing the odds against Richmond. When Stonewall soundly thrashed his enemies in the Valley, it freed him to hurry across the Blue Ridge Mountains to assist in lifting the siege of Richmond. As a Virginian wrote at the time, the two-day battle was "one of those peculiar contests which act upon events around them, as the keystone acts upon the arch. With Jackson beaten here, Richmond, humanly speaking, was lost, and with it Virginia. With Jackson victorious, Richmond and Virginia were saved."

Cross Keys and Port Republic are fascinating subjects even aside from the broad effect they had on the course of the war at large. As the climax of Jackson's first major campaign, they vividly illustrate his growth as a leader. The stern general exhibited more tenacity than adroitness in tactical situations in these battles; but when presented with a bitterly difficult choice, Jackson calmly made a decision that few other generals would have considered, earning a mighty victory as a result.

Even more than as a laboratory for examining Stonewall Jackson, the two battles serve as a riveting setting for observing mid-nineteenth-century American civilian-soldiers at war. Alfred North Whitehead has aptly said, "We think in generalities, but we live in detail. To make the past live, we must perceive it in detail in addition to thinking of it in generalities." The flood of writing about Civil War topics includes a great deal more that is general than is specific. A number of monumental battle studies exist, and many more personal narratives—memoirs, diaries, and letter collections. Relatively few books, however, examine battles in both tactical and human detail, attempting to limn the experiences of discernible individuals in the midst of combat (as the English historian John Keegan has challenged military writers to do). Cross Keys and Port Republic offer the opportunity to attempt that dual historical narrative. Despite the battles' far-flung impact, the numbers engaged were small enough to allow detailed attention to individual experiences without losing the tactical flow. Similar detail for Jackson's last battle, Chancellorsville— extrapolating from the relative strengths and losses of the armies— would yield nearly a dozen volumes the size of this book.

A fascinating subtheme of the Valley Campaign is the story of men fighting for their own homes and hearths. Confederates are the only Americans in our national past who have literally fought on a large scale in their own yards and fields, in sight of their wives and children, to resist invasion (except on a few narrow fronts briefly, such as during 1814). The phenomenon of local resistance to far larger invading forces recurs throughout history—for instance by the

Waldenses butchered in fifteenth-, sixteenth-, and seventeenth-century Europe.

I wrote this book because no monograph of any sort exists about Cross Keys and Port Republic, not even a bad one. Two good books about the campaign as a whole discuss the battles, as do several biographies, histories of units and armies, and survey histories. No one, however, has examined the two days of fighting in detail, either as a tactical and operational military event or as a cataclysmic human experience affecting about 25,000 Americans. In unraveling precisely what happened, I discovered that some of the generally circulated assumptions about the battles simply are erroneous. Even more frequently, I found answers to questions no one had asked before because there had not been adequate background information to frame them.

My intended result is an account that unravels, with as much precision as can be attained after the passage of a century and a quarter, what happened at the climax of Stonewall Jackson's Valley Campaign. The book is intended not only for students of that mysterious, fascinating Virginian, and of the war upon which he made such immense impact, but also for anyone interested in the American experience. It will serve, I hope, as a memorial to the men of both sides who faced mortal combat in Virginia's lovely Valley that long-ago June—both those who fell and those who survived apparently unscathed.

**Stonewall Jackson's
superiority over his foes
grew in part out of a
clenched-jaw
purpose that rode
roughshod over
obstacles.**

CHAPTER 1

THE VALLEY CAMPAIGN

When Stonewall Jackson awakened in Port Republic on the morning of June 8, 1862, he anticipated enjoying a day of much-needed rest. Both the army and its commander had reached a state of abject exhaustion while eluding Federal pursuers on muddy roads during the past ten days. One of Jackson's aides declared frankly in a letter that the legendary general was "completely broken down." Because June 8 was a Sunday, the extraordinarily pious Stonewall no doubt looked forward eagerly to worship and rest on the Sabbath.

The sun rose that morning at 4:45. By the time it had crawled above the adjacent Blue Ridge Mountains, Jackson was ready for a mounted tour of his army's front. Major Robert Lewis Dabney, his chief of staff and a Presbyterian minister, was putting the final touches on a sermon designed for delivery to assembled officers and troops. Aides and supernumeraries moved lazily through the camps. Sue Kemper, the eleven-year-old granddaughter of Jackson's hosts, lounged on her front porch and observed with interest the young men of an inexperienced Confederate artillery battery gathered on the side lawn. Two dozen infantrymen, the only battle-ready soldiers near headquarters, stood casual guard on an adjacent riverbank. Two little girls of the Maupin family watched eagerly from a perch atop the fence around their yard a block from headquarters, hoping for a glimpse of the famous general visiting their neighborhood. Officers with the freedom to circulate in town flirted with older girls.

Suddenly, inexplicably, the placid scene exploded with frightening speed and impact. Unseen Ohio artillery pieces belched shells at point-blank range from just across the river. Indiana infantry supported the cannon from a nearby knoll. Federal cavalry splashed into the river and boiled across into the streets of town. Confederate cavalry screening the area obviously had failed to accomplish their simple mission, and Jackson's army faced a perilous surprise. The general himself was apparently trapped by the raiders. As he mounted a horse and spurred into the streets of the village, Stonewall Jackson was heading for his closest shave of the war.

❅ ❅ ❅ ❅

The Federals who so completely surprised Stonewall Jackson at Port Republic on June 8 were ushering in the final act of a military drama that had been sweeping across Virginia's Shenandoah Valley for the preceding eleven weeks. As recently as June 1, Jackson's troops had been precariously situated in the midst of an apparent trap, with every indication that the campaign might end in failure. The impact of such a failure upon Southern fortunes might well have been irreversible.

In March of 1862 the fledgling Confederate States of America stood on the brink of extinction. After a brave beginning and some initial successes, the seceded Southern states had met a series of reverses. Momentum from the heady Confederate triumph eight months earlier at the First Battle of Manassas (Northerners called it Bull Run) had dissipated during an uncomfortable months-long period of inaction. Combined naval and land forces carried the Union flag into Tennessee early in 1862 on the strength of victories at Fort Henry and Fort Donelson. Louisiana lay vulnerable to Northerners intent on taking New Orleans. Worst of all, a mighty invading army under General George B. McClellan inched ponderously up Virginia's peninsula toward Richmond, besieging the capital city of both the state and the Confederacy.

Time and events had tarnished the bright prospects of most of the South's early heroes. The dispirited civilian populace looked frantically for some hopeful signs. If the Confederate nation was to survive into a second year, victories and leaders were badly needed, and soon.

Thomas J. "Stonewall" Jackson and fewer than 4,000 soldiers held a precarious perch in the lower Shenandoah Valley in March, but not even the most sanguine Southern jingoist could project an important role for them. The men were too few, and were facing too many a well-armed foe, to excite any expectations; and their leader was better known for his eccentricities and his uneven record as a prewar professor at Virginia Military Institute than for any military attainments.

Despite an unpromising beginning and the lack of any apparent potential for accomplishment, the awkward professor turned the war on its ear during three months in that spring of 1862, and made history with a campaign that will always be studied as a military classic. Stonewall Jackson's name conjures up the Valley to anyone with even a passing acquaintance with American history, and the Valley brings Jackson to mind—an association destined to last in legend beyond other Civil War campaigns involving far more numbers.

From late March until mid-May, Jackson patiently used passive devices to thwart Federal might while he prepared to strike. Aided and abetted by Robert E. Lee (an apparent failure in his brief field efforts to date, now serving as a relatively powerless bureaucrat in Richmond), Jackson hoarded friendly units that came within his grasp and studied maps of the Valley that he had commissioned.

The Valley itself offered substantial advantages to an outnumbered but determined commander. The lovely Shenandoah River proved more formidable than beautiful to an invading force faced with crossing its two widely separated forks. Between the arms of the river loomed mighty Massanutten Mountain, fifty miles of rocky bulwark passable from east to west by road at only a single point. As a bemused Vermonter wrote home to his family, "The Shenandoah Valley is a queer place, and it will not submit to the ordinary rules of military tactics. Operations are carried on here that Caesar or Napoleon never dreamed of. Either army can surround the other, and I believe they both can do it at the same time."[1]

Jackson fought only twice during the first nine weeks of his campaign, then four times more in a closing flurry that unfolded in just over two weeks. On March 23 at Kernstown, his tiny army pitched into a large Federal force to make sure that it did not leave the Valley and head toward the beleaguered Confederates east of the mountains. Kernstown lay just south of Winchester, which for two weeks had been the hub of Federal operations. Jackson's usually reliable intelligence source—local cavalry notable for bravery but not for discipline—misled him on March 23 about enemy strength and intentions. As a result of that flawed information, the general displayed unwarranted aggressiveness that led to a near disaster tactically. He disengaged with difficulty and retreated southward, having suffered more casualties than he had inflicted. When an uninhibited private of his egalitarian army impertinently asked Jackson about the results of the day, the army commander snapped, "I think I may say I am satisfied, sir!" In spite of the near disaster, the general did indeed have reason for satisfaction: he had fulfilled his assigned strategic imperative by holding Federal attention in the Valley.[2]

The enemy force that followed Jackson south up the Valley (since the rivers in the Valley flow generally north, that direction is "down," and "up" is south) in late March soon ran into a new Confederate line strengthened by natural obstacles. In mid-April, Jackson fell back farther south and ensconced himself in the impenetrable mountain fastness of Swift Run Gap in the Blue Ridge. His toehold in the Valley at that point gave the general the chance to threaten any enemy detachment that attempted to move across his front. During this hiatus Jackson diligently augmented his strength by applying the new Confederate conscript law—the first national military draft in American history—in the region around him. In the process he quelled a mutiny by force of arms and also struck a bargain with pacifist Dunkards and Mennonites that allowed them to discharge noncombatant functions. Arming the freshly minted soldiers posed additional problems.

Stonewall fought at McDowell (nearly 150 miles southwest of Kernstown) in the rugged mountains of Highland County on May 8 as much for the purpose of strengthening his own army as to hurt his foe. Confederate general Edward "Alleghany" Johnson had been west of the Valley in the mountains long enough to absorb a nom de guerre from them. The few thousand men under Johnson had been fending off a much larger Northern force commanded by the famous western explorer John C. Frémont—"the Pathfinder." Jackson left his stronghold at Swift Run Gap at the beginning of May and guilefully marched east, out of the Valley and toward Richmond. Beyond the mountains he put his men on trains and rapidly shuttled them back into the Valley, then west toward Johnson's position. Near dusk on May 8 the combined Southern detachments fought a bitter, confused engagement in dense thickets atop a high hill outside McDowell. Although Jackson again lost more men than his opponent (nearly twice as many), when the gunfire died away he had achieved his goal. Frémont's Yankees scampered north through the mountains and took themselves out of the war for nearly a month. That left Jackson free to assimilate Johnson's men into his expanding army.

With Frémont out of the picture and his own force growing in strength, Jackson could begin to think about taking the initiative. To accomplish all that he hoped to do, though, the general needed even more troops. For weeks he had been playing a careful hand with his superiors in Richmond in an effort to add to his army the division just east of the Blue Ridge commanded by General Richard S. Ewell. The delicate command situation at the Confederate capital included Jackson's nominal superior, Joseph E. Johnston and Robert E. Lee, who at this point held little real authority as a glorified military secretary to President Jefferson Davis. Lee was sympathetic with Jackson's audacious designs and eager for him to have Ewell's troops to help achieve them. Johnston's equivocal nature left him uncertain about that and other matters, but with an emphasis on stodgy caution at all times.

During the second and third weeks of May, Jackson waged a frustrating telegraphic struggle for control of Ewell's reinforcements.[3] At the same time he methodically blocked mountain passes behind Frémont to protect that flank, and exerted much effort in bemusing the Federal force in the Valley under Nathaniel P. Banks. Jackson finally won the contest for use of Ewell's troops by virtue of his strong will. He took responsibility for ordering that general and his men into the Valley on the basis of a narrowly constructed view of the meaning of some outdated orders from Richmond. When Ewell joined Jackson on May 21, his numbers nearly doubled Stonewall's strength, to a total of about 16,000.

The era of dodging and patience ended with a resounding crash on May 23 when Stonewall Jackson surged down the flank of the Blue Ridge and destroyed a Federal detachment at Front Royal, a dozen miles east of the primary Union stronghold at Strasburg. The months of preparation had allowed Jackson to set a stage on which he now at last could reveal himself as a dazzling offensive fighter. His coup at Front Royal put Stonewall in excellent position to race northwestward to Winchester before his enemies at Strasburg could reach that essential base in their rear. Jackson has been criticized by some historians for not winning the race to Winchester—for not even running that race. The general's overriding strategic imperative, however, remained precisely what it had been two months earlier in this same vicinity: he must not allow the Federals to move east over the mountains. A dash to Winchester would have opened to Banks and his Northerners the reasonable option of crossing in Jackson's wake through the gaps due east of Front Royal. At Kernstown on March 23, Stonewall's careful attention to priorities had involved him in a tactical buffeting. At Front Royal on May 23–24 the same considerations left Jackson with a triumph somewhat circumscribed in scope.

When Banks recognized his plight and he and his men dashed for Winchester, Jackson finally was free to unleash his veterans in pursuit. Banks inevitably won the race under the circumstances, but he could not hold Winchester. Confederates intoxicated by victory in a region that was home to many of them, and freed at last from months of cautious maneuvering, stormed the enemy line in the outskirts of Winchester early on May 25 and shattered it. General Richard Taylor's Louisiana regiments—which were quickly becoming Jackson's favorite shock troops—charged steadily across a broad, open hillside into the heart of the Federal position and routed the Yankees in one of the war's most dramatic and successful frontal assaults. Jackson galloped into the midst of his triumphant soldiers, waved his hat over his head with glee, and shouted, "Very good! Now let's holler." The men already were hollering, of course, and when they recovered from their shock at seeing the undemonstrative Jackson in the grip of high passion, they hurried in pursuit of the fleeing foe.

The close pursuit lasted for hours; pursuit on a broader scale continued for most of a week. Jackson pushed his columns northward and northeastward toward the Potomac and Shenandoah. The

Shenandoah Valley seemed to threaten Washington even more acutely than it actually did. Confederates apparently poised for new adventures on the Potomac upriver from Washington seemed to embody an ominous danger for the capital. In fact, Jackson could not long hold his advanced position; his gesture toward Washington was a completely hollow one. Posing the threat was what Stonewall needed to do. To the delight of Southern strategists, the threat accomplished precisely what Jackson and Lee had hoped it would. Their enemies responded anxiously, deflecting resources away from the threatened Richmond theater and toward the Valley.[4]

Federal political and military leaders dispatched columns on several tangents in an effort to entrap the suddenly famous Jackson. During the first days of June the Confederates marched huge distances southward to escape the snare. The Valley's friendly topography helped them, as did torrential rains that turned rivers into even more formidable barriers. By June 5 the Northern pursuit had resolved itself into two columns pushing south on either side of Massanutten Mountain.

By the first week of June the campaign's salient features were well established: Confederates marching to the point of exhaustion; occasional sudden lunges by Jackson; high Southern morale and trust in the army commander; and a wearying combination of terrain and weather that affected both armies.

Jackson's burgeoning fame made him the cynosure of all eyes whenever he dashed through the army. The troops were much taken by his lack of ostentation. A Louisianian was one of many surprised by the legend's unprepossessing looks, describing Stonewall as "a very ordinary looking person, riding . . . like a house on fire . . . who looked to me like a Jew pedlar." An anonymous Alabama journalist left a detailed account of Jackson's appearance later in the year:

> He is of medium size and height, weighs about one hundred and forty-five or fifty pounds; has dark, not black, hair. . . . His complexion is rather pale, and his features, when at rest, are destitute of expression. . . . One who should meet him on the road, would be apt to take him for a quiet farmer . . . , or, better still, for a country schoolmaster, who, though all unused to the saddle, has undertaken to ride over to a neighboring patron's house on Saturday, and was meanwhile engaged in some difficult mathematical calculation as he jogged along.[5]

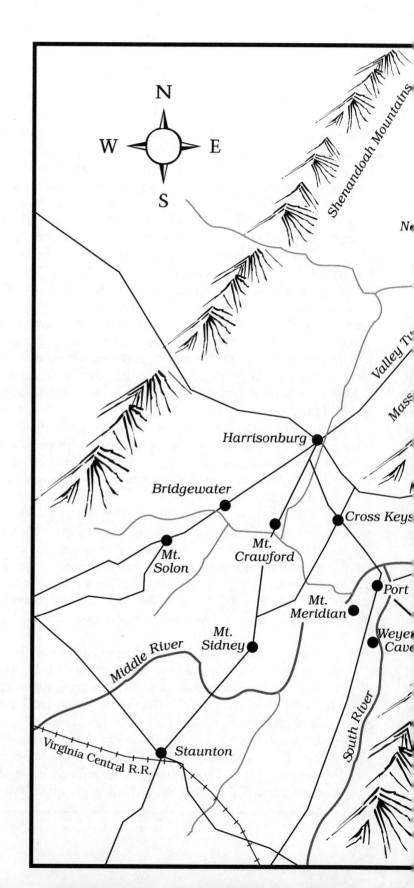

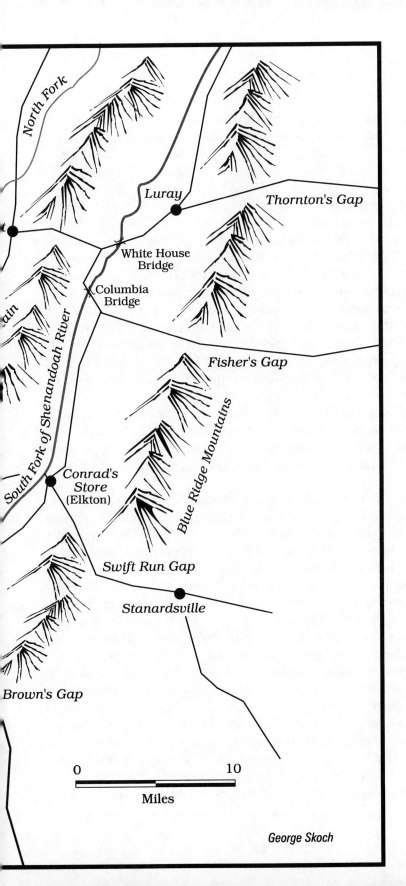

George Skoch

One of Jackson's staff officers limned the general from close and regular observation. "Jackson was in face prematurely old," the staffer wrote in a private forum. "His face was rather sharp than handsome, his lips thin and often blue & bloodless, showing the effect of the dyspepsia he had suffered from for so long a time." The general's horsemanship was skillful but graceless: "He was an excellent rider but a more awkward & ungraceful one never sat a horse."[6]

Confederates relished Jackson's religious devotion and his stoic acceptance of the hardships he shared with the troops obeying his stern dictates. A Maryland cavalry officer recalled riding behind the army commander during the early June movement up the Valley during "a violent thunder gust" during which "the rain poured in torrents." The Marylander unfurled a rubber poncho in a vain attempt to cope with the downpour. Jackson ignored the water completely. His old forage cap with a high crown did little to protect him, but the general "never made the slightest motion to show he was even aware it was raining, and I saw the water running in a stream down his back." The same observer remarked on Jackson's piety, evinced among other ways by a habit of praying in battle, "his right arm raised at the elbow, the indexing finger pointing straight up; at intervals he would raise his arm to full length for an instant, and then lower it."[7]

Jackson's two main foils, James Shields and John C. Frémont, had little of the Confederate leader's skill or determination. Shields had been born in Ireland, came to the United States as a teenager, and was in his early fifties in 1862. He was well-read, largely self-educated, a brilliant public speaker, and a veteran of Mexican War brigade command. The lawyer-politician feuded bitterly with Abraham Lincoln when both were Illinois politicians, but later they became friends. President Lincoln valued the support of Shields in part because he was one of the preeminent Irish-Americans in the land.[8]

Carl Schurz, a prominent German-American Federal general destined for great postwar prominence, described John Frémont as "a man of middle stature, elegant build, muscular and elastic, dark hair and beard slightly streaked with gray, a broad forehead, a keen eye, fine, regular features." Given Frémont's uneven reputation, Schurz was surprised that he could not discern at first glance "much of the charlatan in him." He did, however, confirm the widely spread stories about the "unusual 'style' " at Frémont's headquarters, which was overrun with Hungarian aides-de-camp and featured much ostentation in the manner of European military establishments.[9] As the first-ever candidate for president (in 1856) of the now all-powerful Republican Party, Frémont enjoyed an impeccably solid political base.

Stonewall Jackson's superiority over his foes grew in part out of a clenched-jaw purpose that rode roughshod over obstacles. That single-minded demeanor, combined with secrecy that approached a fetish, made Jackson a spectacularly difficult superior officer. Several important subordinates bridled under his inflexible style. On May 13, General Ewell bewailed his fate in a letter to a relative, calling Jackson "that enthusiastic fanatic," and concluding that "there seems no head here at all, though there is room for one or two." That same week the army's able quartermaster officer, Major John A. Harman, told his brother in a letter that he was sick of "mismanagement" resulting from Jackson's "incompetency." General Charles S. Winder, commanding Jackson's own old Stonewall Brigade, writhed under his chief's rigid attitudes, writing in his diary that the army commander's marching habits were "insane."[10]

The most intense and noticeable of Jackson's conflicts with his subordinates came in his relationship with cavalry chief Turner Ashby. Jackson had cause to be pleased with the colonel's reconnaissance skills, with the single notable exception of at Kernstown, but was horrified at Ashby's indifference to organization and discipline in his command. At the end of April Colonel Ashby sent his resignation in through Congressman A. R. Boteler, who was friendly with both of the principals. Ashby declared, "I cannot be longer of service here," due to indignities heaped upon him by Jackson. "I feel bold to announce the fact without a fear of being considered vain," Ashby asserted, "that for the last two months I have saved the army of the Valley from being utterly destroyed." The cavalryman's efforts elicited no support from Jackson; in fact they were "embarrassed by the want of such information from him . . . [making] my duty much more arduous." Ashby saw the army collapsing. "The impressed Militia [sic]" were all deserting, and men held to infantry service instead of being allowed to join Ashby's ill-disciplined cavalry were doing the same.[11]

Before Boteler received Ashby's emotional missive, the crisis had been resolved. In the words of a staff officer, it was "settled for the present by General Jackson backing square down . . . but I am afraid there will be no good feeling in the future." The ugly quarrel prompted Quartermaster Harman to write on April 27: "Jackson is a

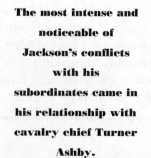

The most intense and
noticeable of
Jackson's conflicts
with his
subordinates came in
his relationship with
cavalry chief Turner
Ashby.

strange man. . . . As sure as you and I live Jackson is a cracked man and the sequel will show it." The sequel of course showed no such thing. By the end of the Cross Keys and Port Republic epoch, Ewell and Harman would admit as much. Ashby and Winder did not live long enough to repent of their poor prophecies.[12]

Confederates of lower ranks remained comfortably ignorant of the high-level friction. Almost to a man, those who wrote of their experiences luxuriated in the reflected glory of their general, whose fame they shared as the campaign wended its way toward legendary status. Most of them were beginning to think that Jackson might be invincible, which meant that they would be too. A soldier in the Stonewall Brigade who was especially irate about Yankee mistreatment of civilians declared, "I dont hesitate to say that whip them we can and whip them we will." An officer in the same command dwelt longingly on his desire to enter the ministry, but meanwhile, he admitted, "My life is now given to the army. . . . I am not fond of the army. Indeed many things in it are hateful to me; but nothing is so much so as the invader of my native soil."[13]

One of Jackson's staff wrote derisively of the boasting by Frémont and Shields that filtered across the line. The Yankees seemed especially fond of the phrase "bag him," when referring to plans to corner Stonewall. William Pouncey of the 15th Alabama wrote home in good humor of the enemy's efforts: "Old Linckon called out all of his malishigs, but the funnyest part of it was, when we were up at 'Harpers Ferry' the Yankies surrounded us and we had to fight our way back!" That sort of experience of course assumed a cheerful patina only in secure hindsight.[14]

Confederate staff officer John Esten Cooke ran across one cavalryman with a decidedly different attitude toward the enemy. After a sharp skirmish between mounted men of both sides late in the campaign, the officer spotted a trooper sitting at the foot of a tree. He yelled at the laggard to hurry up. "I can't go." "What do you mean?" "I have just killed my brother . . . and I don't feel as if I could fight any more." The disconsolate Confederate had cut down a mounted enemy and only recognized as his target fell that the foe was his brother.[15]

Some of the Federals pursuing Jackson no doubt had the good sense to worry about what would happen if he caught them, but most imbibed the optimism spouted by their headquarters. When Yankees followed their prey through New Market, citizens heard a drummer in the passing column beating a tattoo and chanting: "Jackson in a funnel, Jackson in a funnel, Got him in a funnel sure." A member of the 75th Ohio in that same column admitted some confusion throughout the campaign: "movements in the valey are strange. First we drive the Rebels up and they drive us back, then we drive them up again and then fall back. I dont understand what it means." The Buckeye was not alone.[16]

During the first week of June, weather bedeviled the Unionist pursuers far more than Jackson did. Four decades later, an extraordinarily wet spring of 1901 prompted Southern farmers to put that season in perspective. They concluded "that it was nothing compared to the second year of the war," which "was the wettest within living memory." A nearby weather station recorded on June 4 more than 50 percent of the average rainfall expected for the entire month during a normal year. Comments in the weather ledger for June's first week include "sharp lightning & thunder"; "rained all night"; "rainy since 7 p.m."; and "drizzle off & on all day." Temperatures remained unseasonably cool, with an average recorded low of 65 and recorded highs on June 5 and 6 of 71 and 70 degrees.[17]

The downpours raised the level of the rivers that were serving Jackson as moats and turned the pursuers' roads into muddy sloughs. An Ohioan marching east of Massanutten Mountain noted that his campsite was "all afloat" and movement was impossible. His 29th Ohio wasted thirteen miles countermarching in search of unburned bridges and fordable torrents. General Robert H. Milroy, who enjoyed far more camping amenities than most Federals, grumbled of being drenched for days on end, "wet to the skin, my boots full of water." "Both officers and men . . . have been compelled to lay out," he complained, "exposed to all kinds of weather day and night . . . without a change of clothes."[18]

Confederates faced precisely the same weather and roads, but with two crucial distinctions: they used the roads first, before they had been churned into impassable morasses; and as the defensive force they happily accepted the status quo imposed by limited mobility. Gray-clad soldiers slogging through the mess doubtless took little solace from such considerations. Ordnance officer William Allan of Jackson's headquarters went two days without sleep while struggling with muddy roads. By then he could hardly stay on his horse. A large dose of peach brandy supplied by a cavalry major invigorated Allan for a time and enabled him to ride groggily into Woodstock. He found some of the staff awaiting dinner at the Clinedinsts' home and joined them. Before the meal arrived, however, Allan "slid down off my chair and fell asleep on the floor." Efforts to revive the exhausted officer failed, so his mates just went on with supper over his body and left him on the dining room floor all night.[19]

An Alabama soldier in the soggy column concluded that his mates "were equal or superior to horses on the march. . . . We waded the Shenandoah river, the water coming up to our necks and quite cold." Lieutenant George P. Ring of the 6th Louisiana told his wife of the hardships: "You cannot think darling how much we have suffered. . . . two thirds of the time it rained evry night. . . . our sleep did us little good. . . . my sleep was not very profound." Ring and his comrades were always hungry, too, surviving on a single meal a day, and that only bread and meat. Even that pittance was of poor quality. The 8th Louisiana called its bivouac of June 3 "Camp Bad Crackers," because the hardtack issue was so rotten, one wrote, that "we could *scarcely* eat them." A Rockbridge County, Virginia, artillerist named Tom Wade beseeched his family to come to his aid with a shipment of "something to eat in the shape of cakes & something sweet, old preserves or any thing of the sort" to supplement his diet of leathery beef.[20]

The tattered, if victorious, troops following Stonewall Jackson made a striking contrast to the prettily outfitted men who had begun the campaign. Years later Sam Moore commented on the differences he had noticed as a nine-year-old mid-Valley youngster:

> When they first passed through . . . on their way to Winchester, they appeared newly equipped, with handsome flags flying and every indication in bearing and movements of high spirits. As they returned, the men looked weary and worn. What remained of their flags were hanging around the staves, badly torn and tattered and riddled with bullet holes. The ranks were badly thinned and the men . . . were no longer fresh and gay and resplendent in their new uniforms. These were dust-stained, and in some cases even marked with blood. The men scarcely seemed able to drag themselves along.[21]

Stonewall Jackson's marching regimen was stern enough to have left his troops dragging even without the vagaries of weather and inadequate food supplies. His provost had promulgated a rigid set of marching orders in mid-May that revealed just how meticulous the general was about such things. Canteens must be filled before the march began; regiments must leave camp with unfurled colors and music until the colonel ordered "route step"; for the same period, the troops must carry arms and "march as though they were on drill"; when approaching a halt, the same formal system applied for the final approach march; anyone leaving ranks "in cases of necessity" must leave his musket with the main column, carried by someone else; brigade commanders must regularly align themselves to review their marching troops; a ten-minute halt was dictated each hour, with arms stacked; and one hour was the designated lunch stop "about 12 or 1." Skeptics wondered, no doubt, about halting to eat nonexistent food.[22]

These minute strictures and many others revealed Stonewall Jackson's rigid sense of precision, which at the same time was one of his primary military virtues and the cause of incessant friction with more casual subordinates. "I am still in the land of the living," Tom Wade wrote at the end of the campaign, "but dont know how long I will be if 'old Jack' keeps us running about as much as he has done lately." Wade admitted frankly that he would have fallen out on the roadside during the march but for the fear of capture by pursuing Yankees. In early June Irby Scott of the 12th Georgia claimed that his regiment had "not been stationary two days since . . . the 6th of March." Scott's company had dwindled from 70 to 26 during the campaign and finished with neither officers nor noncommissioned officers present.[23]

Before the war ended, the Valley was destined to be one of the most thoroughly brutalized regions in the country's history, but in May 1862 it had no notion of the horrors that lay ahead. On the last day of the month, Harrisonburg's city council passed an hygienically oriented ordinance establishing a $5 fine for anyone who hitched "a horse or mule to the fence near the Big Spring." Within days animals and men would be running amok all over the Valley town. Citizens soon learned to fear and loathe the immigrant troops, collectively termed "Dutch" (i.e., Germans), of Louis Blenker's division of Frémont's army. "No more despicable creatures ever disgraced a uniform," a Valley boy wrote. When word later filtered back about the drowning of a number of men of that division in a river crossing, the mistreated civilians could "only wish the quota had been larger."

Even General Ewell mentioned the miscreants of that division in reporting with atypical relish on the casualties he had inflicted.[24]

The Federal high command recognized the depredations and at times sought, generally without effect, to control them. General Milroy wrote: "The dutch brigades are composed of the most infernal robbers, plunder[er]s and thieves. . . . our army is disgraced by them. . . . The officers . . . encourage and share the plunder with them." Frémont issued a general order deploring "the many disorders and excesses and wanton outrages." To counter the evil he issued strict orders, including one directing that no man might leave camp even to bathe without a noncommissioned officer along. Frémont also issued an order that anyone entering a private house should be executed; there is no known record of it having been enforced. An Ohioan named Ladley had kin in the Valley and sympathized with their plight, but a man named Culp from the same state grumbled fiercely about the suffering imposed on his regiment by "the idiotic orders preventing the burning of fence rails, the killing of hogs, chickens and cattle." Culp disdained these orders as "wonderful specimens of the 'kid glove policy' advocated during the early part of the Rebellion," but had the good fortune to see later stages of the war when such nonsense was abandoned.[25]

Mistreatment by the invaders of course redoubled civilian support for Confederate units. One of Jackson's men remembered fondly how he was "captured by force of arms by a bevy of young ladies and held fast until my Haversack was filled with good things." Local residents later recalled Jackson's Valley Campaign with pride as the high point of the war in their vicinity. Despite the difficulties they experienced at the hands of Blenker's bravos, the citizenry did not suffer anything like what was in store for them in 1864. The fondness for Jackson engendered by his prowess tended to embellish memories of having seen him.[26]

Yankees, Rebels, and civilians were witnessing the prelude to the climactic final acts of the Valley Campaign during the first week of June. By the 6th the contending forces were drawing near to the fields where the ultimate decision would be reached.

Grieving soldiers laid
their leader's
body in the front
room of the Frank
Kemper house in the
lower end of
town. There the
ladies of the
village prepared
Ashby for burial. One of
them placed a rose
over the spot on his chest
where the fatal round
had torn his
uniform.

CHAPTER 2

THE APPROACH TO

PORT REPUBLIC

The first five days of June 1862 unfolded in a welter of rain, marching, and uncertainty for Jackson and his retiring army. On June 1 he wriggled through the narrowest bottleneck of the campaign, holding aside Federals closing in from either direction on his route through Strasburg. Both enemy forces were closer to Strasburg than was the midpoint of Jackson's marching army that day, but he feinted boldly in both directions and squeaked through. Then Frémont's Yankees chased Jackson southward along the west side of Massanutten Mountain and Shields's column pushed south on the east of that massive feature.

In herding his troops and his captured spoils southward, Jackson had special need of cavalry screening as his final rear guard. The general's well-founded uncertainty about Turner Ashby's capacity to lead large units had led him to place General George H. "Maryland" Steuart in command of a sizable portion of his mounted strength. Steuart had some prewar experience with the cavalry arm, but had horribly bungled a big opportunity at its head at Winchester on May 25 by ridiculous insistence on orders through channels. Jackson only learned his lesson about Steuart sluggishly. After the Marylander mishandled another responsibility near Woodstock on June 2, cavalry colonels Thomas T. Munford and Thomas S. Flournoy complained loudly enough to convince Stonewall to put Ashby back in overall command. The result, Munford recalled, "was more congenial to all the parties."[1]

Stonewall Jackson and his staff rode for about four hours through a torrential downpour on June 2 and went to bed soaking wet. The next night they camped in the yard of the big brick Rice house near New Market, and a freshet sweeping through that bivouac literally floated things out of the general's tent. On the morning of June 4, Jackson finally overcame his reluctance to make headquarters in private dwellings and went into the house of the Strayer family. The Strayer women learned of Jackson's enthusiasm for lemonade and made him a jugful. The empty pitcher, of course, became a virtual religious icon ever after.[2]

From a pleasantly dry chamber at Strayer's, Jackson planned and schemed. Movement farther south would deprive him of the towering protection of Massanutten Mountain on his left, but it also offered new opportunities. Twice during the day the general called his skilled topographic engineer Jedediah Hotchkiss to his side to inquire "about the country in the vicinity of Port Republic, the topography, etc." Finally he ordered Hotchkiss to draw him a map of the environs of Port Republic. Jackson's chosen option evidently was coming into focus. To further his plans, he sent Hotchkiss off at ten P.M. on the 4th, with a flag signalman in tow, to climb to the southern tip of Massanutten. From that aerie 1,600 feet above the Valley floor, known locally as Peaked Mountain, they could keep an eye on the progress of Shields's Yankees. To retard that enemy column, Jackson also undertook to burn the bridges in its path near Luray and Conrad's Store.[3]

Bridging the swollen streams in Jackson's own zone proved to be difficult. The North River near Harrisonburg was the highest it had been in a quarter century and "extremely rapid." It was easy to see that no temporary bridge was practicable. Somehow the Confederates must push a long train of sick and wounded men across it, together with a vast quantity of captured matériel. Energetic pioneer troops—as engineer detachments were called—built two boats out of scrap lumber and began ferrying sick and wounded across the torrent early on June 5. Captain Claiborne R. Mason was the driving force behind the successful ferrying operation. This grizzled veteran builder, who was disdainful of regular engineers and their "pictures," would be of crucial importance to Jackson's plans three days later. His ferry eventually moved not only the medical cases across the river, but also a huge ordnance train and every bit of the army's captured pelf. Meanwhile other detachments managed to bridge other streams athwart the road to Port Republic.[4]

By the end of June 5 the army's entire array of trains had crossed North River and moved on toward Staunton. Jackson's profane and highly efficient chief quartermaster, Major John A. Harman, had been determined, if pessimistic. During the 5th he had written to his brother, "If I get through this safely General Jackson must either relieve me or reduce the train. I will not be worked so any longer." That night John Harman collapsed in the aftermath of the ordeal. "Nature could stand it no longer," he reported the next day. "I had to knock under."[5]

Back in Richmond, Robert E. Lee was eagerly seeking ways to help further Jackson's aims. Lee had taken command of the Army of Northern Virginia only on June 1, but his earlier role at the War Department had kept him fully abreast of details from the Valley. On June 5 Lee wrote to Secretary of War George W. Randolph, proposing to send reinforcements across the mountains to Jackson. With them Stonewall might sweep north once again and spread further confusion in the enemy's ranks, Lee thought: "as he is a good soldier, I expect him to do it." Lee also sent messages to Staunton urging the post commander there "to collect all the troops in that vicinity, raise the community, magnify their numbers, and march down the valley. . . . It will shake Shields and make him pause." General Lee's suggestions were impractical at the time, but they foreshadowed the fabulous collaboration he and Jackson were destined to inaugurate before the end of June.[6]

Frémont's pursuit had been hampered by weather and roads, of course, but even so he did not display any excess of zeal. One of Jackson's staff told his mother that Frémont "had not been exactly pushing us, yet following pretty closely." The Yankee general's maladroit staff contributed to the delays. Early on June 4, one of them spied a Rebel battery across the river near Mount Jackson. He hurried some Ohio cannon into position "in hot haste," trained its guns, and opened fire. The Southern artillery, a disgusted Ohioan wrote, "proved to be six innocent rail heaps, which his eye had clothed with the panoply of war."[7]

Across Massanutten Mountain, Shields's column moved no more rapidly than Frémont's despite the absence of Confederate opposition. Those Yankees faced several unbridged crossings of booming streams and rivers, in some instances because their enemies had burned the bridges. Shields started up the Luray Valley, as the subvalley east of Massanutten is called, on June 1 and covered ten miles that day. He moved fifteen more miles on June 2. After dark on June 3 Shields sent a detachment south on a seventeen-mile forced march to protect a bridge. After all night on the rain-swept, muddy road, the weary Federals saw the bridge's burned timbers floating past them on the river. They spent the day marooned by high water in a camp that was "all afloat." On the 5th a large detail built a bridge, and part of Shields's army crossed it. An advance column pressed on toward Port Republic under Colonel S. S. Carroll, but another portion of Shields's force made a fruitless thirteen-mile march on June 6 that looped northward then back south to its starting point.[8]

Jackson's mapmaker Jed Hotchkiss spent June 5 climbing Massanutten Mountain, establishing a signal station there, and then scrambling back down the steep slope. Hotchkiss did not even hold a commission from the general, performing the invaluable cartographic services that won him great renown as a civilian employee throughout the war. That evening Hotchkiss found Stonewall Jackson and his headquarters encamped one mile east of Harrisonburg on the road to Port Republic. The general had picked Port Republic and its surrounding streams as the best point from which to work his will upon the two armies chasing him.[9]

The village toward which Jackson was heading was an old place with roots in the river confluence at its eastern edge. A German named Jacob Stover recorded a deed of five thousand acres including the town site in 1733—listing every barnyard animal as a head of household ready to settle on a claim. He then sold smaller chunks and made a great deal of money. In 1745 one Henry Downs bought the site where the village would grow and soon built a mill. That same year the road Stonewall Jackson would use 117 years later was laid out, connecting Downs with Swift Run Gap. An 1802 Virginia Assembly act established Port Republic as a town. That year it contained fifty-two lots that sold for about $200 each. Methodism took hold as the religion at Port (as locals called the village), circuit rider Francis Asbury visiting to preach each year and getting a new suit of clothes as his annual reward. Less religious settlers soon gave Port a reputation for "fights and rowdy atmosphere."[10]

Port Republic's heyday came in the 1820s, when the Shenandoah was made navigable for flat-bottomed boats. Flotillas of awkward scows called "gundalows," about nine feet wide and up to ninety feet long, carried the rich produce of the Valley downstream to market. The village became a warehousing center for agriculture of all kinds and for pig iron from mountain furnaces. In 1835 Port had thirty dwelling houses, one church, one common school, two stores, a host of commercial buildings, and a population of 160. By the 1850s the town had one or more each of shops, mills, factories, tanneries, warehouses, harness shops, saddlers, shoemakers, cabinet makers, foundries, sawmills, flour mills, woolen mills, machine shops, and contractors. The most distinguished feature in Port was John Dundore's tannery, started in 1816, which was famous for fine-grade leather. Dundore fancied himself a regional aristocrat (he became "purse proud," it was said), affected expensive trappings, and "aped the manner of the English aristocracy," but eventually died poor.[11]

Surrounding Rockingham County harvested immense fields of crops from fertile, well-drained soil. In 1850 the county produced more wheat and hay than any other county in Virginia. It also grew a substantial tobacco crop. The county's population in 1820 numbered 14,784. Ten years later the total had grown to 20,683, "a large portion . . . of German origin." Three decades later, on the eve of the Civil War, population had increased only to 23,408, of whom 532 were free blacks and 2,387 were slaves.[12]

Civilians around Cross Keys and Port Republic enjoyed a degree of insulation from the secession frenzy sweeping more populous centers as war neared. Fannie Kemper, who lived near Cross Keys, wrote mostly about apples and produce in a February 1861 letter, but in June her correspondence echoed terror about coming events: "My darling old man has to start to the war. . . . I am almost crazy. . . . Dr. Webb has to go too, and Nealie is on her head. There is no one left in this neighborhood except Mr. Van Leer, and he aint much in a fight." Some six dozen of the inhabitants of Port took up arms.

The local chapter of the Sons of Temperance—the most notable local social organization—included about eighty adult males, of whom fifteen saw Confederate service. Most of the region's young men went into the 10th Virginia Infantry or the 1st Virginia Cavalry; others belonged to the 33rd Infantry, Chew's Battery, or the 6th Cavalry. At least five men from Port were killed in action during the war and many others suffered wounds.[13]

Valley demography ensured some division of opinion about the war in the region. The village itself was almost unanimously Confederate. Mennonite and Brethren families were unswervingly pacifist, however, no matter what the provocations. Most of them lived west of the Valley Turnpike. Some of the mountaineers in the Blue Ridge east of Port were pro-Union, a few even joining Federal units to fight against their neighbors. John H. Layman, Jr., was conscripted into service in June 1862 at the age of thirty-four and assigned to the local 10th Virginia Infantry. Less than two months later Layman was shot to death for desertion.[14]

Inevitably a few citizens sought to play both ends against the proverbial middle. Foundry owner John Francis Lewis succeeded admirably at that game. "When the occasion demanded," a local observed, "he would declare himself a loyal citizen of the United States." His primary occupation during the war, however, was manufacturing iron for the Confederacy. William S. Downs attempted the same balancing act. He made leather in Port Republic for Confederate military use, procuring hides under military protection and winning exemption from conscription as crucial to a war industry; but he also evinced Yankee tendencies when convenient. He was spotted in a tête-à-tête with a Union cavalryman during the June 8, 1862, raid. Fellow tradesman and equivocator John Lewis used his influence to bail Downs out when Northern raiders were about to hang him in 1864, and after the war certified Downs as deserving war reparations as a loyal Unionist.[15]

Citizens of all persuasions saw war close up for the first time when Stonewall Jackson marched past at the beginning of May 1862 en route over the Blue Ridge on a feint. Muddy roads turned that march into a nightmare for both troops and civilians. Eventually detachments assigned to move supplies bought lumber in the village—3,364 feet of it—and 88 pounds of nails to build boats and float their freight down the river. Now, a month later, the roads were even wetter and the soldiers were coming back in earnest. Jackson, Frémont, and Shields were converging on Port Republic.[16]

When Turner Ashby rode through Harrisonburg early on June 6 with the Confederate rear guard, he had been a general for less than two weeks. Jackson had reinstated Colonel Ashby's command after the failed experiment with Steuart, but opposed the promotion in a pointed letter to his favorite congressman. "I would gladly favor it," Jackson declared, "if he were a good disciplinarian, but he has such bad discipline and attaches so little importance to drill, that I would regard it as a calamity to see him promoted." The army commander insisted that he would "always take pleasure in doing all I can for his advancement consistent with the interest of the Public Service." Two other generals under Jackson, who already had been promoted against his wishes, prompted him to exclaim, "When will political appointments cease?" The answer of course was never, but it is hard to blame Stonewall for complaining.[17]

Valley civilians shared none of Jackson's qualms about their local favorite. As he rode through Harrisonburg, Emily Pence (age forty-nine) sent Ashby a bouquet. Emily would have echoed the admiring portrait of a contemporary who described Ashby as

> one of the picturesque characters of the war. Five feet seven or eight inches, weighed about a hundred pounds, his complexion was as swarthy as an Arab's, his hair and beard very black, thick and strong. The latter grew close up under his eyes, so his face was covered by a thick, strong, rather coarse hair, not very long, but very abundant. . . . He told me that he had been under fire for sixty consecutive days. . . . But he found no inconvenience from it. "I eat a few apples, drink some spring water, and draw up my swordbelt a hole or two tighter, and I'm all right. It's just as good as eating."[18]

Emily would have been scandalized by a Yankee description of Ashby written that same week by a Cincinnatian who had met him before the war. Ashby had achieved enshrinement in the Yankee pantheon of villains:

> [Ashby] was totally uncultivated, and had as bad a face as I ever remember to have seen on mortal man. It was one of those

faces which . . . [proves] the doctrine of total depravity. He was . . . of a complexion darker than that of many a mulatto, his face pimply, and his expression as if all the bad juices of the earth had contrived to lodge in his blood. His forehead was low and receding. . . . [He] is formidable—not in brains or fore-sight—but in recklessness and malignity.[19]

Federals followed Ashby's rear guard into Harrisonburg at about one o'clock on a clear, warm afternoon. They had marched before six that morning and had received reports that Jackson was bearing off to the southeast toward Port Republic. Emily Pence's sister Mary Yancey watched with disdain as the enemy dashed in, "Hooping and hollowing and in full gallop." Some of the Federals, in addition to "waveing thier Swords and whooping," fired their weapons in excite-ment. Whether intentionally or not, one of them shot civilian William Gay through the side just above his hip. Northern infantry continued to arrive during the afternoon, and Yankees of all arms went to work on smokehouses and other such targets. "We have got Jackson now," the Virginian populace heard their foe boasting. "We have him in the jug and all we have to do is to put the stopper in."[20]

Confederate artillery emplaced on high ground southeast of town, with the 1st Maryland Infantry for support, discouraged further Federal advances. One local Valley boy knocked a bold Yankee off his horse at the south end of town from a range of six hundred yards with a well-aimed rifle round. When these deterrents had produced two hours of quiet, the Confederates moved about four miles south-eastward toward Cross Keys, then retraced their steps to within two miles of Harrisonburg. There Turner Ashby was preparing an ambus-cade for his noisiest enemy.[21]

Colonel Sir Percy Wyndham was an English adventurer who commanded the 1st New Jersey Cavalry. A chaplain who met him called Wyndham a "military dandy of the first water, with long curls, and a profusion of gold lace." He had fought afoot in France at age fifteen, served with the French navy, then the British army, then in Italy (whence came his knighthood). Despite a grating tendency to pomposity, Wyndham proved capable of his command, turning a weak regiment into a good one. Among his boasts, Southerners be-lieved, was the vain assurance that he would whip the vaunted Rebel Turner Ashby.[22]

To essay that task Wyndham led nearly 400 men of his own

regiment out of Harrisonburg on the afternoon of the 6th, accompanied by bits of three other cavalry regiments—the 6th Ohio, 4th New York, and 1st Pennsylvania. The troopers cantered out on the Port Republic road until they spied a line of Southern horsemen drawn up beyond a stream. Wyndham ordered a full-blown charge without bothering to reconnoiter the situation. Confederates in ample numbers boiled out of nearby thickets and routed the Jerseymen and their allies. *New York Times* correspondent Charles H. Webb, who was riding in the center of the cavalcade, admitted that "such an utter scene of rout and demoralization as then ensued I never before witnessed." The journalist called the fleeing men "a precious set of cowards . . . to have bought your worthless existences by sacrificing the lives of our comrades and the honor of the flag." General R. H. Milroy, back in Harrisonburg, wondered why Frémont had not sent assistance to Wyndham's battered command. "We were all anxious to go," Milroy asserted.[23]

Ashby expressed disgust that the enemy had fled after so weak a showing. The general led the Confederate charge in the highest spirits. "Fences were cleared which at any other time would have been thought impossible," one account declared. When the pursuit approached Federal reserves, the enemy loosed volleys that flew harmlessly overhead. Ashby noticed some of his men ducking when the bullets hissed close. He laughed and shouted, "No use to dodge Boys they will not one in ten thousand hit you." In fact the Confederates suffered a handful of casualties, including a severe wound to Major John Shackleford Green, a forty-five-year-old farmer from Rappahannock County who was commanding the 6th Virginia Cavalry. Nevertheless the Confederates inflicted far more damage than they incurred, and came away with a captured Yankee flag and 63 prisoners.[24]

The most noticeable of the captives was an irate Colonel Wyndham. The huge Englishman had spurred his horse ahead of most of his men and there ran afoul of Confederates who corralled him and sent him to the rear. Years later several Virginia veterans quarreled bitterly in the public press over who deserved the credit, some on their own behalf, others in support of comrades too modest to fight about the matter. The likeliest candidate was Sergeant Holmes Conrad, a six-footer with gray eyes and black hair who belonged to a company of what would become the 7th Virginia Cavalry. One good witness insisted that no one captured the foreigner, that Wyndham disgustedly dismounted when his troops fled, came forward, and turned over his sword, saying "I will not command such cowards!"[25]

A Virginia infantryman who saw Wyndham heading toward the Confederate rear recalled, "I . . . never saw so much embarrasment in a prisoner's face and actions." A Mississippian wrote, "He was the worst chagrined man that was ever seen." Another observer saw the big man riding behind a small Louisiana soldier on horseback and "in a furious passion at being called by the jocose Marylanders a 'Yankee'—a word he hated." When Ashby appeared nearby, Southerners "wanted to cheer him for capturing a live Englishman from Great Britain," but the general shushed them.[26]

By the time Wyndham started his captive ride toward Port Republic, Jackson had established his headquarters at the western edge of the village. He chose the lovely home of Dr. George Whitfield Kemper, Sr., for his base of operations. Kemper's house, Madison Hall, had been built by 1800 by John Madison, a cousin of the president, on a knoll where in earliest times a rude fort had provided protection against Indians. By a first wife, Dr. Kemper had eight children. Two of them, William Meade and George Bezaleel, served in the 10th Virginia of Jackson's army; both would be killed later in the war. Adelaide Wayne Kemper, the second child of a new marriage, was three months old when Jackson arrived at her home.[27]

From his comfortable new billet above the strategic river confluence, Stonewall Jackson considered his options. Jed Hotchkiss had gone back toward Peaked Mountain and stayed in touch with a signalman there, so the general had a good idea of Federal progress on both fronts. He was surprisingly pessimistic about accomplishing anything further. Stonewall's first thought was of keeping Shields and Frémont apart; or he was willing to go over the mountains to Richmond, he said in a communiqué to the capital, and could be on a train the second day of movement. Jackson asked for key indicators about when to make such a move. The general glumly (and wrongly) concluded on June 6 that his enemies would give him no further openings in the Valley: "At present I do not see that I can do much more than rest my command and devote its time to drilling."[28]

Unfortunately for Turner Ashby, the cavalry clash that bagged Wyndham did not end rearguard fighting for the day. When his defeated advance guard staggered back into Harrisonburg, Frémont ordered out General George D. Bayard with fresh cavalry to watch the

Rebels but forbade any further advance. Bayard, however, succumbed to the blandishments of Colonel T. L. Kane, who commanded a Pennsylvania infantry battalion called the Bucktail Rifles. The Bucktails, many of whom wore the tail of a deer on their hats, had been attached to a cavalry brigade, even though afoot, so they were a sturdy set of fellows. Kane thought it essential to go out and collect friendly wounded, lest the entire army be demoralized. By the time Bayard noticed Confederate infantry moving toward Kane, it was too late to recall him. Musketry began whistling past correspondent Charles Webb, who described the noise as akin to holding a large bee then "opening your hand a little to let him buzz, and then suddenly shutting off his music into a sharp fiz-z-z-z." The artillery rounds that began pounding in seemed to Webb like "a winged coach-and-four coming to carry you bodily to the devil." Civilians listening anxiously on their porches in town heard the same sounds; they also could hear men screaming.[29]

The Confederates shooting at the Pennsylvania Bucktails were infantrymen whom Turner Ashby had pushed forward to entrap just such a sortie. Circumstances temporarily made the Bucktails the ambushers. Ashby left Colonel Thomas T. Munford in command of the Southern cavalry, together with two or three artillery pieces, along the road. He personally led the 58th Virginia Infantry, followed by the 1st Maryland, up into the woods to the right to flank any enemy force heading out from Harrisonburg. Munford's men, all but a few carefully placed under cover, would tumble out of the woods and charge the routed prey once Ashby had unhinged the Yankee line. Munford later claimed that he had warned Ashby: "Genl you have done a handsome thing already. Do you think they will be as easily fooled again? His reply was. . . . I am tired [of] being *crowded* and will make them stop it after today."[30]

Ashby's route took him through a densely wooded thicket that opened on a field that sloped upward, a part of the farm of Joseph Good. The Bucktails arrived at the far woodline just in time to take position behind a convenient fence. The 58th Virginia and 1st Maryland were moving in columns about fifty yards apart, rather than in long attack lines. The Bucktails had an oblique aiming angle that made their fire tell especially well. Both sides were surprised by the moment of encounter and concluded that they had been ambushed. One of the Pennsylvanians wrote, "the rebels fired uppon us for they wer in ambush[.] we took cover behind the Trees & went at them Indian fashion." Confederates suddenly under fire felt that they had been the party stumbling into a deadfall.[31]

The 58th Virginia was closest to the Bucktails and bore the brunt of their fire. Ashby put himself at the regiment's head, with the 1st Maryland to his left, and encouraged the Virginians as they "poured volley after volley into the thicket, that glowed with the shining musket barrels of the . . . Bucktails." The 58th recoiled from the fire and the Marylanders rushed into the fray. They too felt the galling fire from their right flank. The exchange of fire seemed to a cavalry observer to last for an hour, but it doubtless continued for only a small fraction of that time.[32]

In response to the flanking fire, the 1st Maryland performed the difficult maneuver of changing its front by pivoting through a ninety-degree turn. A volley that struck during that delicate moment hit more than a score of the Marylanders. One of the Pennsylvanians described the impact vividly: "we pi[c]ked them off *like pigeons*." Once realigned the 1st Maryland swept determinedly toward the Federal fence, following Colonel Bradley T. Johnson in the thickening twilight. J.E.H. Post of Baltimore admired how sturdily the foe resisted the charge. The "Yankees never flinched till we got within ten feet of them," he wrote, "and then away they went and we brought them down by dozens." Bucktail A. M. Crapsey admitted that after their initial success, he and his mates "had to *run run* for life for they . . . wer like to capture us & we had to run through an open field & we had showers of bullets sent after us[.] the rebels wer within 5 rods of me when I climed the fence." Marylander John Gill recalled with feeling that "it was a charge that those who participated in it will never forget." Two days later General Ewell would order the Marylanders to affix captured bucktails to the regimental colors.[33]

Meanwhile Ashby's carefully crafted cavalry trap on the road to his left could accomplish little. The artillery with the cavalry opened fire as soon as Ashby's infantry fight erupted. The guns hurled shells into the Unionist ranks, scattering enemy soldiers in dismay. Colonel Munford could tell that the roar of musketry was not dwindling into the distance, so he knew that Ashby had his hands full.[34]

The most consequential result of this fight, far more important than fleeting advantages in ground gained or other casualties inflicted by either side, was the death of Turner Ashby at the height of the action. A Federal bullet killed the general's horse near the front of the 58th Virginia, but he landed on his feet and began waving his sword and firing his pistol at the troublesome enemy woodline. Almost at once an enemy round slammed into Ashby's side, passing through his body and out his chest on the other side. The Shenandoah Valley's favorite cavalryman died instantly and without a sound.[35]

Calm retrospect allows us to recognize Turner Ashby's shortcomings, some of them painfully flagrant, in discipline and organization. Most of his subordinates and contemporaries, however, idolized the dashing cavalier as representative of highly prized Southern manly virtues. A reliable cavalry officer went so far as to declare that "at that time Ashby was deeper down in the affections of the Valley army than Jackson," though he admitted that a bit more time changed those sentiments dramatically. An infantryman writing within hours of the event declared, "a gloom was cast over the whole army. . . . I consider that we lost more by his fall than we had gained during the whole campaign." Within a few weeks one of Ashby's companies had raised from their meager pay more than $500 for a monument to the dead hero and placed the funds in the hands of Captain John Calvin Shoup—himself destined to be killed in his native Valley two years hence. Even enemies admired the dashing Confederate leader. A Federal surgeon with Frémont reported seeing "tears, at his loss, roll down the hardy cheeks of Federal soldiers" with whom Ashby had had chivalrous dealings.[36]

High-ranking Confederates paid broad tributes to Ashby in private forums unaffected by the need for tact. General Ewell told Colonel Munford that he had "the highest admiration for Ashby." Ewell, an old dragoon from prewar days himself, envied Ashby the freedom of mounted service and longed for such a command himself, away from "being cramped as I am, and never know what is to be done." Colonel William L. Jackson, Stonewall's cousin and a member of his staff, wrote of Ashby on June 8: "He was a great man in his particular line, and his loss cannot well be supplied. I have seen him in battle and he seemed to possess a magnetic influence over his men. . . . In ordinary life he was not regarded as a man of talents, but as a scout, and as a ranger, and in battle as a leader, he was a genius."[37]

Stonewall Jackson never had cause to repent of his analysis of Ashby's inadequacies, but he soon would regret the loss of the cavalry leader's personal control—such as it was—of his ill-organized companies. The army commander met the fruits of Ashby's final great success, in the form of Percy Wyndham, before news trickled down the road of the general's subsequent death. Wyndham finished his humiliating ride to Port Republic late in the afternoon. A Valley militiaman standing guard in town pointed the cavalcade escorting Wyndham toward the headquarters flag flying in front of Madison Hall. Jackson first met with the captive, however, in the hotel on Main Street. A village lad who overheard their conversation reported that Stonewall inquired why Wyndham had come to fight Confederates when most Englishmen of stature were pro-Southern. Sir Percy replied "that Ashby had become so famous, that he had joined the Union Army with the intention of capturing or killing him." Wyndham eventually was transferred to headquarters at Madison Hall, gave his parole, and slept on the floor.[38]

Turner Ashby's corpse was borne to Port Republic across a horse in front of one of his men past General Ewell's headquarters; a staff officer saw the accompanying cavalry column "crying, most of them, like children." When word reached Jackson, he paced the floor of his room at Madison Hall "for some time, in deep sorrow, greatly moved by the sad news." Grieving soldiers laid their leader's body in the front room of the Frank Kemper house in the lower end of town. There the ladies of the village prepared Ashby for burial. One of them placed a rose over the spot on his chest where the fatal round had torn his uniform. Someone took a picture of Ashby, the only such photo extant of a Confederate general killed in action; the flower is evident in the print.[39]

After the ladies had finished their dolorous chore, General Jackson paid his final respects. A soldier who ducked in to see Ashby's corpse came face-to-face with Jackson and hurriedly backed out of the room. The next morning Ashby's remains were placed in the village chapel until midday. Then a funeral cortege wound its way up the east side of South River to Waynesboro and thence over the Blue Ridge to Charlottesville. A black charger followed the ambulance, his leather gear trimmed in mourning and the general's sword buckled to the saddle. The dead man's original company escorted the body. As this imposing procession made its way through the camps, long lines of officers and men turned out on the roadside and uncovered their heads in a salute. When the procession came upon a group of Yankee prisoners along the road, they too took off their caps and stood in respectful silence while the hearse passed.[40]

Comrades gathered up the other Confederates killed near Harrisonburg and buried them that night in the cemetery across from Union Church at Cross Keys in a spot that would itself be a hotly contested battlefield within hours. A detail from the 1st Maryland dug a large single grave, wrapped their dead comrades in blankets, and covered them with earth. "Theirs was the burial they would have most wished—a Soldier's burial," Private Washington Hands opined. Most of the Southerners wounded in Ashby's battle made it to friendly lines by mounting behind cavalrymen and enduring an agonizing ride to Port Republic. General Ewell remained at the rear until all of the injured were cared for. He visited the men too badly hurt to be removed and divided the contents of his purse among them. Then the general assigned rearguard duties to a portion of the 2nd Virginia Cavalry and headed toward Cross Keys.[41]

Other Confederates scavenged the battlefield, where they found steel breastplates worn by Federals. One of these novel protective devices had a hole through it. The Southerners viewed them as somehow not proper. They were more offended by what they thought was evidence of illicit explosive bullets. Men responsible for channeling Yankee prisoners to the rear fed them first and fraternized in a fashion that belied the savagery just past. Both sides went to rest that night convinced of their enemy's intentions to continue the fight on the morrow. A Mississippian under Ewell told his diary that "the enemy seem to be pressing on with unusual courage," but at the same time expressed "the most unwavering faith" in Jackson. New York journalist Charles Webb had just become convinced that the Confederates were extremely good soldiers and he had been slow to recognize it. By contrast, Webb feared, "no small proportion of our men intend to be soldiers without actually exposing their lives to the precarious chances of war."[42]

Stonewall Jackson's army eagerly embraced the opportunity to rest from its labors during most of Saturday, June 7. In the preceding thirty-five days it had marched 250 miles and won three battles and countless skirmishes. "Wearied as we were by several hundred miles of forced marches," one of them wrote, "the quiet and rest of the camp were very much enjoyed." Lieutenant James L. Dinwiddie of the Charlottesville Artillery, who was destined to play a crucial role in the next morning's emergency, told his wife on the 7th that he was physically "weary worn and broken," but with "spirit . . . undiminished." Another artillerist speculated that the soldiers' quiet demeanor reflected "their deep regret for the loss of Gen Ashby, and feeling him to be an irreparable loss to his command."[43]

The more reflective men recuperating in Southern bivouacs worried about the army's situation. Lieutenant George P. Ring of the 6th Louisiana expected all day long to be called out "to either retreat or fight." The once-eager regiment had now seen fighting and marching "a little more than they wished for." "No one knows anything of Stonewall Jackson's ideas," Ring declared on June 7. The problem facing the army did not seem easily manageable. "Men whispered by the watch-fire, with bated breath: 'Jackson is surrounded,' " admitted the general's admiring staffer, R. L. Dabney. "Our eyes, then beclouded with apprehension, confused, saw no light." A Louisianian writing after the war remembered thinking that the vicinity for miles around Port Republic was redolent of danger, destiny, "wildness and romance." Jackson's reaction to the things that so worried his army was characteristically calm. The peril did not confuse Stonewall, or render him uneasy and unsure. He distinguished the decisive points and formed a workable conclusion.[44]

Little that happened on either enemy front bothered Jackson or his weary army on June 7. Frémont sent out General R. H. Milroy at two P.M. with a mixed command to advance down the Port Republic road toward Cross Keys. Milroy found the road "very bad." He picked up Federal wounded from the two Ashby fights and sent them back, then moved southward a few more miles. Most of the column saw no Confederates, but Milroy's advance guard engaged in some desultory skirmishing. Ewell encamped at Jackson's direction on June 7 around Union Church and southeastward on what would be on the morrow the battlefield of Cross Keys. Civilians in the area spotted a few Yankees skulking through the woods, but nothing came of it before Milroy headed back toward Harrisonburg, arriving there about ten P.M.[45]

Ewell's troops relished the quiet of June 7 and marveled at the gorgeous weather. Jackson's orders to Ewell to halt "for one day at least" were couched in language that made clear his intention to fight if pressed. The 15th Alabama, picketing around Union Church on Ewell's left front, was not molested at all. Other units in every direction moved short distances to good camping locations but in essence did nothing of military significance. As the 21st North Carolina straggled casually toward a bivouac, some of the Tarheels noticed General Ewell approaching from their rear. "He was alone riding in a walk and [in] his habit[ual] way on such occasions," Eli S. Coble recalled, "a little forward in the saddle and to the right hand side & with his face down and gazing intently in the road as though he was looking for something." A Carolinian named Jesse Montgomery was picking his teeth as Ewell cantered past, apparently oblivious to the soldiers in the road. Montgomery caught his eye, however, and Ewell belabored him for straggling. Montgomery complained that he was moving slowly because he was hungry; but the general rejected the argument: "you are not hungry; you have had something to eat[.] You are picking your teeth. Hurry up to your command." Thus trapped, Montgomery could make no reply, and his comrades "had the run on him." Their teasing had a short play. Jesse died in battle two months later at the age of twenty.[46]

Federals of Shields's advance guard were moving south toward Jackson's other front with more expedition and purpose than Frémont displayed. Shields himself was hanging back near Luray because Confederate deserters had bedazzled him with a ludicrous tale that General James Longstreet and 10,000 Southern reinforcements were headed for that location. He sent forward General Erastus B. Tyler on June 7, however, and Tyler reached Naked Creek early that evening after a march of about fifteen miles that had begun at eight A.M. Tyler's men had a terrible time on the road, "completely worn out . . . [and] completely disgusted. . . . Things have got in a terrible Snarl." At particularly muddy spots, double and triple teams were required to extricate artillery and wagons, even with infantrymen adding their strength to the effort. Tyler's men would have gone hungry had they not stolen food from civilian homes along the roadside.[47]

Shields's forward element, the brigade of Colonel S. S. Carroll, was nearly a day's march ahead of Tyler. Carroll's men marched for Port Republic soon after five P.M. on the same sodden, muddy roads that bedeviled Tyler. A disgusted artillery officer called the roads "lakes of liquid mud." Some mules sank into the gumbo until only their long ears protruded. To add to the misery, the contents of an artillery ammunition chest inexplicably exploded, scattering missiles in every direction. Amazingly, no one was seriously hurt. Carroll's men halted for a grimy rest during the night, but would press forward before sunup.[48]

Confederate units went into camp all around Port Republic, separated into distinct locations by its three rivers, all unaware of Carroll's approach. Rockingham County's own boys of the 10th Virginia bivouacked just beyond North River in woods overlooking the bridge into town. The rest of the 10th's brigade and the Stonewall Brigade were nearby. Significantly—and accidentally—the untried cannoneers of the Charlottesville Artillery were encamped around Jackson's headquarters. One section of the battery had gone about two miles upstream to Weyer's Cave, but then was ordered back closer to Port Republic. A misunderstanding destined to have important results kept the Charlottesville guns near headquarters. Orders to "occupy Kemper's Hill" had prompted the unit's officers to move to near Dr. Kemper's house. The army's artillery chief had intended to position them above the bridge on the knoll on the left bank of North River, which someone told him bore the name of Kemper's Hill. When the confusion came to light it was nearly midnight and too late to adjust the campsite.[49]

Stonewall Jackson had spent June 7 preparing for any Federal initiative that the morning might reveal. Jed Hotchkiss remained in touch all day with his signalman atop Peaked Mountain. An artillerist in the army noted with curiosity how the signal flag waved "with a jerky fluttering nearly all day." The army commander enjoyed some well-earned, if brief, rest during the day. His best staff officer, Sandie Pendleton, admitted on the 7th that he himself was "sadly in need of" some sleep. Jackson, who always needed a solid ration of rest, was "completely broken down." When the general roused himself and rode into town he was a curiosity for townspeople. Two little Maupin girls, who lived just below Madison Hall in town, had heard so much about the famous man that he was like a fairy-tale figure to them. Laura Maupin and her sister hung over their fence awaiting a glimpse. When Jackson appeared on the Kemper porch, the girls ran to the far end of their lot and saw their hero ride past. When the general met one of the Kempers who needed permission to go downstream toward the Yankees, he threw a leg across the pommel of his saddle and wrote out a pass.[50]

Back in Richmond that day, Robert E. Lee pondered how to help Jackson and whom to put in Ashby's vacated post. He rejected several suggested replacements in a letter to the secretary of war, and concluded that his nephew Fitzhugh Lee could not "carry with him Ashby's men." As to helping Stonewall Jackson, however, Lee wrote with feeling: "We must aid a gallant man if we perish."[51]

Ashby's leaderless cavalry watched Jackson closely when he appeared on horseback, wanting to see signs of his reaction to Ashby's death. They saw only his familiar "inscrutable look . . . the face that never changed, either in the glory of triumph or the gloom of defeat." One trooper made bold to inquire of Jackson where he was going to fight the Yankees. With a slight smile, the general responded, "We'll fight them in Brown's Gap." When intelligence reached Jackson that Shields had some troops drawing nigh, he sent two cavalry companies downstream on the right bank of the Shenandoah to verify the news and gather information. Captain George W. Myers led one of the companies and Captain Emanuel Sipe headed the other. Sipe was thirty-one years old and a native of Rockingham County. Since he had been lieutenant colonel of a local militia regiment, he should certainly have known his way around and been well motivated to protect his native heath.[52]

At about dusk a courier rode up to headquarters and reported enemy advancing from Frémont's front. This was Milroy's impotent roundtrip march. Jackson immediately ordered up his horse and mounted to ride across his front on a reconnaissance accompanied by a bevy of staff officers. He returned by about nine P.M., sent a dispatch by courier to General Ewell with instructions for the morning of June 8, and went to bed. He had chosen his position well. The two pursuing Federal columns could not support one another without driving Jackson from his strong central location. Should he suffer a reverse of any sort, Stonewall enjoyed easy access to a readily defended mountain stronghold around nearby Brown's Gap. The safety of Richmond might hinge on the results of a test, but Jackson had every reason to be confident. He did not know that the cavalry he had thrown downstream were incapable, after losing Ashby, of even the most rudimentary screening functions.[53]

Stonewall Jackson was at his headquarters at the western end of town, together with a handful of staff officers.

STONEWALL JACKSON HOUSE

CHAPTER 3

STONEWALL JACKSON

BETRAYED BY

INDOLENT CAVALRY

F
ew spots on earth can compare with the Shenandoah Valley on a springtime morning for rich pastoral beauty. Dawn arrived over the tiny village of Port Republic on June 8 with a splendor familiar to local residents but pleasantly startling to most of the thousands of soldiers visiting the region. Confederates enjoying a hiatus from weeks of wet marching and hard fighting blithely assumed that the day offered a chance to refresh themselves. Stonewall Jackson hoped that this favorite day of the week, a much-beloved Sabbath, would yield blessings from divine services throughout his army. Federals who had been pushing through a muddy darkness for hours welcomed the sunrise even more eagerly than did their resting foes, but they fully intended to destroy the calm of the pretty morning.

Colonel Samuel Sprigg Carroll led the advance guard of Union troops that pushed wearily south during the night of June 7–8 on the wretched road leading from Conrad's Store toward Port Republic. Carroll was well educated and reasonably experienced in military matters despite being only twenty-nine years old. He had entered West Point in 1852 from the District of Columbia and graduated— barely—four years later, ranking forty-fourth among forty-eight graduates in the Class of 1856. Fitzhugh Lee, the rambunctious nephew of Robert E. Lee, finished forty-fifth in the same class. The two young men also stood near one another at the bottom of the institution's deportment rolls. Carroll and Fitz Lee underwent valuable postgraduate seasoning on the violent western frontier during the late 1850s. Despite his dreadful academic record, Sprigg Carroll would carve a long and distinguished career in the postwar army. At dawn on June 8 he faced a day that would be among his most famous Civil War experiences. It certainly would be the most controversial.[1]

Carroll commanded a temporary brigade. His own regiment, the 8th Ohio, was not present. Federal organization was rather amorphous in Shields's advance, but Carroll controlled four infantry regiments and a detachment of about 150 men of the 1st Virginia (Union) Cavalry. The cavalrymen and the 7th Indiana Infantry made up the bulk of Carroll's flying column. Captain Lucius N. Robinson's artillery company (Battery L, 1st Ohio Light Artillery) supplied Carroll with some important firepower. The 1st Virginia (Union) Infantry moved close behind the rest. A member of that regiment recalled the difficulties of a march made "without sleep and without [food], unwashed, unkempt, and tired. Through swamps and forests the trail led. . . . How the artillery kept up . . . is hard to say." Robinson and his Ohio men did keep up somehow, and played a crucial role when fighting erupted. All of Carroll's Federals would have agreed with one of their number who wrote that the men were "urged forward almost beyond the powers of endurance of the strongest."[2]

The 7th Indiana, which bore a pivotal responsibility as the leading infantry element, moved toward battle in a spirit of discontent bordering on mutiny. An anonymous letter from the regiment dated June 6 expressed outrage about being overworked. The grumbler blamed Colonel James Gavin because he "does not object to it occasionally." Rumor had it that Lieutenant Colonel John F. Cheek, "the favorite of both officers and men—and the man who should be Colonel," was about to resign in disgust. The fed-up letter writer suggested that the 7th Indiana would simply disobey the next order to march, "and if it is a disgrace to refuse to obey such orders (as the Colonel says it is) why the Old Seventh will be disgraced—that is all."[3]

Despite their petulant attitude, the men of the 7th Indiana did obey the order to march when it came late on June 7, perhaps prodded by the prospect of action. One hint that business was at hand came in the form of orders "to take all the men who had shoes on their feet . . . (a majority of them were practically barefoot,) and make quick time" in the direction of Port Republic. The cavalry detachment in front engaged in "feeling our way along through the mud and darkness," one of the mounted men recalled. The Indiana soldiers followed gingerly. They found that "the road a main part of the way was along the river bottoms and in some places close to its banks, where the slightest misstep would throw one over the bank and into the water—an incident of not unfrequent occurrence."[4]

Anticipating battle at last, one of them wrote: "Like to the spirits of the damned," the 7th theretofore had been "roaming through the valleys and clambering over the mountains. . . . We have footed and counter-footed a distance of over four hundred and fifty miles." Chasing Stonewall Jackson entailed strenuous labors. Catching him at last might make it all worthwhile. After a few more difficult miles, Carroll called a three-hour halt about six miles from Port Republic. Some lucky Indianans found shelter in a barn, but most of the infantry lay down outdoors in the mud.[5]

During the rest break, Carroll received some intimation of the prize and the challenge that awaited him at the end of his march. He had sent scouts forward in the darkness to investigate Jackson's strength and positions. Had Confederate cavalry been more attentive to their screening assignment, the curious Federals could have ascertained little of importance. Southerners believed fervently that the scouts who worked for the Yankees were disloyal local men, "renegade spies" who told Carroll "of affairs at Port Republic, and whom he had for guides. . . ." Whoever the prowlers were, the indolent post-Ashby cavalry did not interrupt their outing. Carroll's scouts returned with information about Jackson's trains and the relative handful of defenders near them.[6] It is clear from later developments that this first intelligence reaching Carroll actually was not very detailed, but enough to provide reason to forge ahead toward Port Republic.

It took the weary Unionists an hour or more to shake themselves into marching alignment and resume the advance near four A.M. The infantry marching order remained unchanged: the 7th Indiana, then the 1st Virginia (Union), and finally the 84th and 110th Pennsylvania. One of the men calculated that by the time they reached their destination, the night march had covered twelve miles.[7]

Carroll's hundred and a half cavalrymen continued to lead the way. Once the little mounted force moved from its night camp, a recently immigrated Irishman attached to Shields's staff exerted his strong personality to control its actions. Myles W. Keogh, age twenty-two (he had cheated by a year on his age in army paperwork, hoping to appear more mature), had been serving in the Papal Guard in Rome at the outbreak of the war. His friend Daniel J. Keily, a thirty-two-year-old veteran of the British navy and of the Irish Battalion in papal service, had been variously decorated by the pope. The two men of like background decided early in 1862 to come to North America to see the world's biggest war. They arrived in New York Harbor on April 1, 1862, and almost instantly managed to draw commissions as staff captains and assignments to the congenial duty of serving with countryman James Shields. With a few weeks of experience behind them, both men would be distinguished in daring endeavors on June 8 and 9.[8] (Captain Keogh is one of the most famous names at that rank in the history of the U.S. Army because he was killed commanding one of George A. Custer's companies at the Little Big Horn in 1876.)

Ranking officers of the 1st Virginia (Union) Cavalry accompanied the advance guard, and Colonel Carroll was in near proximity; but contemporary witnesses said that Myles Keogh actually led the detachment during the final six miles to Port Republic. The Northern column continued to face a daunting succession of muddy and flooded spots in the road. A soldier in the 7th Indiana remembered slogging through several more "streams and swamps in the timber" before nearing Port Republic. The rigors of the road caused Colonel Carroll's mount to founder, and he was forced to borrow an artillery officer's horse, named Bogus, in order to continue. At about six A.M. the cavalry advance halted a mile or so below the village. The van of the 7th Indiana soon caught up and waited behind their mounted comrades. Officers ordered the infantrymen to load their muskets in recognition of the near proximity of armed enemy.[9]

Carroll and his fellow officers set about looking for detailed information and examining their options. Stonewall Jackson had devel-

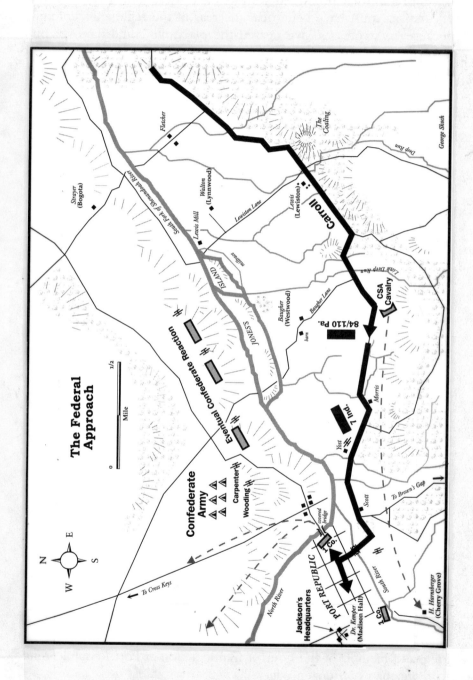

The Federal Approach

oped an aura that prompted wariness and awe. John Hadley of the 7th Indiana must have been near the rear of the regiment's column, because he wrote, "As we neared the place we could discover but little sighns of the enemy." Billy Davis of the same regiment, however, "could see Jackson's troops and trains across the river." Even in the regiment behind the 7th a soldier noted that he was "in site of the enemee."[10]

The relaxed Confederates attracting all this earnest attention remained remarkably ignorant of it. Their instinctive but misplaced trust in the late Ashby's cavalry lulled them into a near-fatal sleep. As a result Sprigg Carroll was able to reconnoiter the Southern position without interruption, and then able to position his troops at leisure, aided by a dense early morning fog. When the mist cleared a bit, a staff officer (almost certainly Keogh) took Sergeant Francis M. Cunningham of the 1st Virginia (Union) Cavalry and another trooper for a closer look. "We dashed up the road at a lively gallop almost to the town," marveled Cunningham, "and wheeled quickly about and back again without seeing any force or anything else." Wherever Jackson's cavalry was (and no firm answer offers), it was operating far short of any military norm on that morning—and even farther below the exacting standards of stern Stonewall.[11]

Carroll soon learned what he needed to know. As he later reported to his superiors, Carroll "found the enemy's train parked on the other side of the [river], with a large quantity of beef cattle herded near by, and the town held by a small force of cavalry only." This confirmed the promising if vague reports that had reached him at the midnight rest camp six miles below Port Republic. Carroll gleefully looked up the commander of his artillery detachment, Captain Lucius N. Robinson, and imparted the good news. "Captain," Carroll said excitedly, "my scouts have come in and report that there are no troops over in town except a cattle guard and train." He proposed to "go over and knock Hell out of them before the rebel army could come up."[12]

An Ohio artillery sergeant standing next to Captain Robinson during this exchange would play a prominent role in the next hour's drama, then become among its most important chroniclers after the war. Sergeant James Gildea was twenty-seven years old in 1862 and had served with Robinson's Battery for several months. His careful longhand memoir of the hour of frantic action at Port Republic runs to more than two dozen pages.[13]

Sergeant Gildea's account of Colonel Carroll's optimistic report goes beyond the good news about lightly guarded spoils of war. The sergeant also offers an extremely important bit of evidence about Carroll's instructions concerning the Port Republic bridge, which would become the day's cause célèbre. Gildea testifies that in discussing plans for a dash into the village, the colonel warned Robinson "that he had received an order from Gen. McDowell through Shields not to burn the bridge but to hold it at all Hazards until our army came up."[14] Later, Shields and others would dishonestly claim that Carroll had been ordered to burn the span.

Sprigg Carroll and Bogus galloped away from the meeting with artillerist Robinson to coordinate simultaneous preparations by the Unionist cavalry and infantry. The colonel decided to split the four Ohio guns into two 2-gun sections. One joined the mounted detachment that headed for a point opposite the middle of Port Republic. Carroll sought a good position for the other section where it could bring the ends of the bridge under fire. He found what he wanted in a modest eminence called Yost's Hill, the home of Mrs. Yost, above the right bank of the Shenandoah River a few hundred yards downstream from the confluence that formed that stream.[15]

In his official report, Carroll described the advantages of the location: "I chose the most commanding position I could find, about half a mile from the bridge, and planted there two pieces of artillery to command the ends of the same." One of the infantrymen of the 7th Indiana who lay behind the guns in support called Yost's Hill "a rise of ground." The Federal troops spread themselves among Mrs. Yost's "farm house and other buildings and in plain View from the ridges on the opposite side of the river." Confederates occupying those ridges in plain view remained comfortably ignorant of what was developing across from them.[16]

The considerable body of infantry available to the Federal raiders was ill-suited for the initial opportunity at hand. Circumstances called for a dash into the lightly guarded village by the cavalry and some artillery, supported by the rest of the artillery firing from a secure position protected by the river. If Carroll could capture the bridge, as he had been instructed, then his infantry would be essential to hold the prize. Meanwhile most of the foot soldiers waited wearily. Only a portion of the 7th Indiana actively supported Robinson's two guns in Mrs. Yost's yard. The rest stood at the front of the infantry column, awaiting word to move forward again. Some of the regiment's companies did not load their guns until after firing had erupted in town. Colonel Joseph Thoburn's men of the 1st Virginia (Union) spread into the level wheatfields and cornfields on either side of the main road behind the 7th Indiana. The terrain gave them comfortable resting places, but little real shelter should Confederate artillery pay them any attention.[17]

Robinson's cannon would signal the opening of the attack, but Carroll's 150 cavalrymen would splash into town to do the important close-in work. Colonel Carroll ordered Major Benjamin F. Chamberlain, who commanded the three-company detachment, to cross the South River into the village and then "rush down and take possession of the bridge." Myles Keogh went along; he seemed to observers to direct the most vivid moments of the raid. The men Chamberlain and Keogh led were not well armed by Civil War standards. They carried sabers and "old flintlock horse pistols altered to percussion, with a portable shoulder stock." The eagerly observant James Gildea went with one of the two guns accompanying the cavalry raiders. The mixed force marched upstream beyond the confluence for about one hundred yards and settled into an orchard opposite the South River ford. Robinson's two guns unlimbered there. To their amazement, all of the hostile preparations in full view of the far bank went unnoticed: "Every thing was quiet in the town."[18]

Thousands of complacent Confederates lounged unaware, within easy gunshot. Most of them were spread out over the rolling country across the North River from Port Republic, in the broad angle of the North River and the Shenandoah. Ample Southern artillery stood quiet and unlimbered, the crews encamped back from the river. William Humphreys of Carpenter's Battery was awake but relaxing, confidently expecting another day of well-earned rest. Clarence Fonerden of the same unit remembered that "we were lolling lazily all over the grassy fields, and . . . our horses were leisurely grazing about with their harness on."[19]

Infantry stretched for three miles northward toward Cross Keys. Taylor's Louisiana Brigade was farthest away, in a camp closer to Cross Keys than to Port Republic. Colonel John M. Patton's small brigade was within a mile of the bridge. One of Patton's soldiers wrote that morning, "we will be bound to have another fight today or tomorrow." In the event, there would be a fight each day. The two closest units were General Charles S. Winder's famous Stonewall Brigade and General William B. Taliaferro's brigade of Virginia regiments. Winder's unit had been Jackson's first command. Ever since, it had formed a rock-solid core for his army—the general's own palace guard. Marylander Winder had been disliked by his soldiers at first because he replaced, on Jackson's orders and through no fault of his own, a popular Virginian, General Richard B. Garnett, at the head of the brigade. Jackson had harshly (and evidently unjustly) brought charges against Garnett early that spring. Winder was a solid professional, however, and steadily won the respect of those below, around, and above him. His stern discipline bothered some subordinates but delighted the inflexible Jackson.[20]

On the other hand, Winder was deeply disgusted by the army commander's rigid behavior and indifference to common courtesy. He had reached the end of his tolerance for mistreatment, Winder decided, during that first week of June. He jotted in his diary late on June 7, "growing disgusted with Jackson." Winder arose early on the 8th and determined to take action to end his unhappy association with Stonewall. His diary entry that morning read: "wrote note to Genl Jackson requesting to leave his command." Winder in fact never escaped his bête noire, and died at Jackson's side two months and one day later. When Carroll's artillery fire called the Confederates to battle stations, Winder was in his camp, perhaps preparing to carry his ultimatum to Jackson. Lieutenant McHenry Howard of Winder's staff was employing the apparent respite on this pleasant morning to rearrange his meager wardrobe. "I had taken my little store of clothing out of my carpet bag," he remembered, "and had it lying around me as I knelt" at the moment that the alarm was raised.[21]

The camp of Taliaferro's Brigade spread across the crest of the hill just above the bridge that soon would become the focus of all eyes. Taliaferro was alone at the top of Stonewall Jackson's lengthy blacklist, in large part because of an insubordinate encounter in January, so his proximity cannot have been for congenial reasons. One of the brigade's three regiments, the 10th Virginia Infantry, drew six of its ten companies from surrounding Rockingham County. Port Republic obviously was home territory for a number of the men now guarding it from Northern invasion.[22]

Perhaps because of its local roots, the 10th was on a looser rein than Taliaferro's other regiments. John W. Fravel of the 10th was one of "a great many of the men [who] went down to the river to wash their clothes and go in bathing." Fravel had just finished cleaning mud and black-powder grime from his rifle when the startling fire erupted. Joseph F. Kauffman of the 10th felt less industrious. "This was a beautiful morning," he recalled, "and we were all lying down and expected to have a good day's rest."[23]

Fortunately for the unwary Confederates, General Taliaferro did not share Stonewall Jackson's religious ardor. He wrote later: "Believing that 'cleanliness is next to godliness,' and in the conservative effect of the army regulations . . . I ordered my regiments and batteries to assemble for inspection, instead of for church." James W. Orr recalled that his 37th Virginia "was in line for inspection" when artillery firing shocked them. Church services had been scheduled to follow this military ritual, despite Taliaferro's cavalier comments about his priorities. In fact, Adjutant J. H. Wood of the 37th (the regiment closest to the bridge) was reading the orders for divine services to the assembled ranks when noise from Federal intruders startled the formation.[24]

Stonewall Jackson was at his headquarters at the western end of town, together with a handful of staff officers. On that side of the river with him the general had only three companies of infantry— fewer than one hundred men. At the critical opening moments of the surprise attack, the vast array of strength across the North River would be useless to the general. Colonel James Walkinshaw Allen of the 2nd Virginia Infantry had sent the three companies into town on picket duty, but himself remained across the river with his main command. Allen had been on the Virginia Military Institute staff with Jackson before the war, and perhaps knew the punctilious army commander well enough to see an advantage in staying as far away as possible.[25]

One of Allen's three companies accomplished nothing whatsoever. It disappeared at the crisis so adroitly that no one mentioned seeing it go. A second company was strewn along the right bank of the North River at the mouth of the covered bridge. Among the pickets at the bridge was Corporal Cleon Moore, a twenty-one-year-old schoolteacher from near Winchester. Moore joined his mates in reveling in the "bright, pleasant" morning: "The country looked beautiful . . . clothed in the verdure of early summer." Moore and his compatriots saw "no indication of the enemy's advance, and we looked forward to spending a quiet, restful day." Those of the detachment not formally assigned to posts had taken off their military equipment and begun fishing in the river. Others frolicked boisterously.

The 2nd Virginia pickets benefited from the near proximity of

Port Republic's single hotel. The crude, low, log building stood on the north side of Main Street one block west of the bridge. Moore and his friends had eaten their breakfast there, relishing a repast of fried chicken and buckwheat cakes. That unusual early morning fare they "deemed a luxury . . . after our arduous campaign." They had also arranged with the landlord for an even better meal for midday dinner. That enticing prospect, Moore wrote sorrowfully, "we only enjoyed in anticipation."[26]

The soldiers of Colonel Allen's third small company in the village were destined to become the most important two dozen men in the Confederacy for a few exciting minutes. Captain Samuel Johnston Cramer Moore had led them into town on the afternoon of the 7th under orders to picket at the village end of the upper ford on the South River, which was located within short musketry range of Jackson's headquarters. The captain's orders "indicated the necessity for unusual vigilance." Moore, a lawyer from Berryville nearing his thirty-sixth birthday, had no prewar military training or experience. He would display, however, ample reserves of determination and tenacity.

Captain Moore's detachment consisted of two lieutenants, one sergeant, and twenty-one men. A foundry—Moore called it "the blacksmith shop"—not far from the ford provided a convenient squad room and rallying point. The captain split the two dozen men into three groups of eight, with a lieutenant or a sergeant to command each. One group remained at the ford at all times, rotating back to the foundry on a regular schedule. The night passed quietly. Moore slept on the floor of the shop next to his sergeant, John R. Nunn, who was feeling "exceedingly unwell." At daybreak Nunn's suffering drove Moore to grant him permission to go into town to find a bed, since, the sergeant recalled, "every thing was then perfectly quiet, and no indication of the approach of the enemy." Nunn found a kind family and a comfortable bed, but would not enjoy it long.[27]

A few Confederate officers were also loose in town. Local citizens recalled that "the Beau Brummels among [Jackson's] staff and army officers were ingratiating themselves into the favor of the belles of the town." Jackson's chief surgeon, Dr. Hunter Holmes McGuire, had strolled down the slope from headquarters into the village on the serious business of checking on wounded men in his charge. Casualties from the June 6 fight and from subsequent skirmishing had been housed in the Methodist Church midway down the village. On the evening of the 7th, the doctor had ordered ambulances to report to the church to pick up such of the wounded as could be moved. When McGuire reached the church he found several ambulances and wagons obediently backed up to the front steps, ready to load their suffering cargo.[28]

As mentioned earlier Stonewall Jackson was housed that morning in Madison Hall, the spacious hilltop home of Dr. George Whitfield Kemper. Jackson's host was seventy-four years old and had been for years one of the village's most prominent citizens. The general was always enormously fond of "the pious ladies" with whom he came in contact when quartered with civilians, exhibiting a "childlike fondness, almost tenderness" toward them. This of course "singularly endeared him to these gray-haired matrons," an observer noted, "and he repaid their attentions with a respect and deference which was beautiful to behold." No doubt the general had struck up this familiar religious harmony with the Kemper women after two days at the site.[29]

Dr. Kemper's granddaughter Sue, age eleven, was living with her grandparents because her mother had died. Sue was sitting on the front porch of Madison Hall that Sunday morning, quietly watching the activities of some young artillerists gathered under a big tree in her grandfather's yard. When Stonewall Jackson strode by her at the beginning of the morning's excitement, he made an impression on Sue that she talked about for the rest of her many days—which stretched several decades into a new century.[30]

The field behind Madison Hall teemed with wagons, baggage, trains, cattle, and the other impedimenta of a large and mobile army. They constituted a lure that Colonel Carroll could hardly ignore. Major John A. Harman, Jackson's profane and able chief quartermaster, had put his entire field establishment in this location. It seemed to be far behind the front and therefore safe from danger. The clutter in the field also included captured Federal property and some prisoners of war. Those of Jackson's staff who could not be accommodated in the main house had pitched tents in the same field or in the yard. According to Jackson's interim cavalry commander (Colonel Thomas T. Munford, who was near Cross Keys and not with the screening companies), both the 6th and 7th Virginia Cavalry were "protecting the baggage train" on the village side of the river. Wherever they were, they would make precisely no impact. The atmosphere in the packed field was bucolic. William Allan, underutilized as an ordnance clerk, was in the field that morning; he later became a successful corps ordnance chief and among the most distinguished of Confederate historians. "It was a perfectly splendid day," Allan wrote. "We were in a beautiful camp and after a hard campaign, so we were late and took our leisure about breakfast." (The high was about 70 degrees and the low about 60.)[31]

Across the road in another field Allan could see more men and horses encamped in a shallow depression. They belonged to a brand-new artillery battery that had only recently reached the army. Captain James McDowell Carrington's Charlottesville Artillery would fight well for three years of the war. On this day, however, its men and guns had never been in battle. The unit was as raw as it possibly could be. Confederate good fortune had dropped the Charlottesville boys in this apparent backwash. The novice artillerists had arrived near Kemper's on the afternoon of June 7 and promptly swarmed over the neighborhood. Some bathed in the river. Others traveled south to play tourist at Weyer's Cave.[32]

One of Captain Carrington's gunners was eighteen-year-old John Gibson Herndon, who happened to be a great-nephew of Dr. Kemper. Despite being a kinsman of the battery's temporary landlord, Private Herndon did not find out until the morning of the 8th that Stonewall Jackson's headquarters was in the house "and that we were his guard." That guardianship, of course, had not been intended by anyone. The Charlottesville boys arose leisurely on June 8, reveled in the "bright and calm" of the morning, and ate their breakfasts. After the meal, Lieutenant James L. Dinwiddie sat down on a mess chest and wrote a note to his wife, then opened his New Testament for morning devotions. Private Wilbur F. Davis retired to his tent with his messmates. There the soldiers "were making ourselves easy," Davis recalled, as they talked over the prospects for the day. The amateur strategists agreed that a battle might well develop across the front, but it surely would be "some miles from us."[33]

Stonewall Jackson's personal staff lounged around the Kemper house and its yard. Lieutenant Henry Kyd Douglas, a gregarious and somewhat vain young aide, was tending to his horse. He welcomed "the absolute quiet" of the morning "after so many of noisy activity." When Douglas heard orders going out for the troops to spend the day in camp while chaplains held services, he presumed that this Sunday would be calm. Lieutenant Edward Willis lay abed, stricken with fever and chills. He had determined not to accompany Jackson and his entourage when they rode out to look over the lines that morning. Breakfast waited beside Ned Willis's sickbed in the event that his appetite returned.[34]

Jed Hotchkiss was sick too. This most famous member of Jackson's staff had been bearing an immense workload for weeks without adequate sleep. By his own diagnosis, "The result of this over-work was a violent attack of headache during the night of the 7th." The general's mapmaker joined Ned Willis in asking for sick leave when Jackson stirred about in preparation for his morning ride. Hotchkiss retired to his tent, which was pitched in Kemper's front yard, looking down the slope toward the upper ford where Captain Moore's two dozen men were quietly doing their duty.[35]

The Reverend Dr. Robert Lewis Dabney, Jackson's dour and maladroit chief of staff, performed in a fashion that morning that left him convinced he had saved the army. Because no one agreed with him, an embittered Dabney would attempt to stir controversy over the events of June 8 for the rest of his life. Dabney started the morning in his role as preacher. After breakfast he asked Jackson "whether there would be military operations on that day." The general answered: "No, you know I always try to keep the sabbath, if the enemy will let me. I want you to preach this morning, in the Stonewall brigade. I wish to attend myself." Under that charge, Dabney retired to his tent, which was pitched in the Kemper orchard, "and lay on my pallet, preparing my sermon." His horse grazed loose nearby.[36]

Jackson planned to attend church with his old brigade, but first he needed to examine the position of the troops around Port Republic and then ride on to Cross Keys to consult with Ewell. In his official report, Jackson mentioned what he knew of the enemy on the morning of June 8. Frémont was "near Harrisonburg." Shields "was moving up the east side of the South Fork," and "was then at Conrad's Store, some 15 miles below Port Republic, my position being about equal distance from both hostile armies." The Confederate units around Port Republic, Jackson reported, "were immediately under my own eye . . . on the high ground north of the village." Jackson had gathered such of his staff as were not ill or engaged in sermon-writing chores, to accompany him on a reconnaissance aimed at improving his knowledge of both armies' locations, when Colonel Carroll's Federals snatched the initiative from him.[37]

The last moment of calm for Jackson's thousands of relaxed Confederates expired at about eight-thirty A.M. Men looking back through the subsequent tumult timed its beginning from "very soon after sunrise" to as late as ten A.M. The usually reliable Jedediah Hotchkiss reported that late hour. The great majority of the estimates, however, fall between eight and nine o'clock. General Winder, whose diary habitually reported times faithfully to the nearest quarter hour, declared that the uproar broke out at "about 8.30 A.M."[38]

That Jackson's army could have been so thoroughly surprised seemed at the time, and still seems in retrospect, absolutely astonishing. Stonewall's fame was based in large measure on achieving just such surprises against his enemy. Never before or afterward was he the victim of anything of the sort. The fault rested squarely, as we shall see, on his inept cavalry, which had been wretchedly administered but ably led by Turner Ashby during the campaign. With Ashby thirty-six hours dead, his grieving men had lost the paste that had held them together and had covered up their dreadful shortcomings in organization and company-level leadership.

Colonel Thomas T. Munford, who struggled manfully but in vain as Ashby's temporary replacement, supplied a careful apologia in his official report. The weather had been dreadful for weeks. Macadamized roads in the Valley, especially the Valley Turnpike, had played havoc with unshod or poorly shod animals. The army provided little grain and no salt, leaving the horses obliged to exist "mostly on young grass." Jackson of course demanded cavalry duty that was virtually "eternal, day and night. We were under fire twenty-six days out of thirty." In a letter to his family, Munford wrote of long days in which the men had not a bite to eat. He told his home people what he dared not write in an official report that might give aid and comfort to the enemy: that his command included "at least one thousand horses that are rendered unfit for duty by excessive work." Despite it all, Munford concluded with a burst of optimism, "the men are cheerful and bright."[39]

Using the cavalry at hand, Jackson had taken appropriate steps to avoid being surprised by Shields. At about midnight word had reached him (from whom it is not clear) that Federals were on the road downstream from Port Republic. These Yankees of course were Carroll's men, at that hour in the rest camp six miles from town. Jackson ordered Lieutenant Douglas to send cavalry to watch them. Douglas directed two companies in that direction, "with orders to go until they met their [Union] pickets and report the locality by courier, to drive in the pickets, ascertain the position of the leading column and promptly report." Another company remained around the town, ostensibly on special alert. The three cavalry units were commanded by Captains George W. Myers, John J. Chipley, and Emanuel Sipe. Jackson would issue a blistering condemnation of Myers and Chipley in the aftermath of the action.[40]

Some of the mounted Southerners sent downstream came back before the crisis, having seen Yankees, but they evidently did not fulfill their simple primary mission of telling headquarters about what they had learned. Cleon Moore of the bridge guard at the east end of town watched some Southern cavalrymen come up the river "in a brisk trot." They paused long enough to tell the handful of infantrymen "that the enemy was advancing in force on the eastern side of the river." The infantry typically—and appropriately in the case of this cavalry detachment—"jocularly remarked that they had better hurry up and get out of danger and they took the advice without any coaxing." The horsemen did just that, heading upstream.[41] Perhaps in their demoralized state the cavalry band rationalized that talking to some infantry pickets constituted reporting what they knew.

Unlike Chipley's and Myers's men, Emanuel Sipe's company had done about what was expected of it. Sometime on the morning of the 8th—the note bears no time, nor even date—Sipe sent back important news: "The enemy have had a scout of 20 near the bridge this morning at Port Republic. On our approach they fell back. We pursued them, but did not see the scout at all." At the time that Sipe scribbled his note (probably a bit before six A.M.), the Federal advance was "just below General Lewis'." Jackson obviously received this vital intelligence after some delay. It doubtless was what prompted him to plan to ride out from headquarters soon after breakfast, because his brilliant young aide Sandie Pendleton sent the dispatch to Ewell with this endorsement: "The general commanding directs me to inclose this dispatch, just received. He is going down in person to see into it, but requests that you will not advance your pickets until you hear further from him."[42]

Stonewall Jackson and his staff officers had no difficulty deciding where to assess blame for the fiasco. Major Harman snarled, "The cavalry . . . behaved very shamefully." In the same vein, Jed Hotchkiss wrote disgustedly that the friendly cavalry "took to its heels and went off towards Brown's Gap, leaving the river road . . . entirely open." Sympathetic Colonel Munford admitted that his two companies "disgraced themselves by running." Jackson pulled no punches in explaining the affair. Abandoning the stilted language normal in his official reports, Stonewall seethed as he described the "disgraceful disorder" of Myers's company and the manner in which Chipley's men "shamefully fled." Not content with that stern declaration, Jackson took the unusual step of issuing a general orders on June 17 to reemphasize his displeasure: "It is the painful duty of the Comdg Gen. to announce to the Army that on the 8th Inst. when in the Providence of God our arms were so signally crowned with success, Capt. G. W. Myers & Capt. Chipley & their commands, at the mere approach of the enemy fled from anticipated danger, regardless of the fate of the gallant Army they so disgracefully deserted."[43]

Assigning blame lay in the unimaginable future at eight-thirty on the morning of June 8—a luxury available to survivors. Jackson and the several score Confederates in the village of Port Republic had no certainty that they would be among that fortunate number at the frantic moment when suddenly Yankees seemed to be everywhere. Colonel Carroll's carefully set stage exploded into action when his artillery opened fire. The conventional picture painted over the years by historians describing the raid on Port Republic has made the Federal cavalry dash concurrent with the artillery barrage. Carroll would have been much more successful, particularly in corralling Jackson and his headquarters, had that been the case. The artillery fire actually preceded the cavalry across the river by enough minutes to give the Confederates some reaction time. A local historian summarized the Federal predicament when he concluded that they had "unexpectedly surprised themselves by surprising Jackson."[44]

Captain Robinson and Sergeant Gildea and their Ohio artillerists commenced firing into Port Republic at point-blank range across the South River before the other two guns of the same battery were ready on Yost's Hill. Robinson's opening round flew not in the direction of the bridge, but rather "at some buildings reported [to be] a guard house." The shell could hardly miss at that range. It plunged right through the roof of the target building and of course "roused everyone." The Yankee gunners "could see them run in every direction." Excited but specious rumor in the Federal army insisted that the building had been jammed with hundreds of Northern prisoners, including three spies about to be hanged, who escaped when their guards fled.[45]

Not long after the two Ohio guns along South River fired into town, Robinson's two guns on Yost's Hill opened as well. Their targets were Confederates around both ends of the bridge across North River. Southerners scurried first for cover, then to respond. As a 7th Indiana infantryman crouched on Yost's Hill wrote, "the fight was on."[46]

After the artillery near South River had fired quite a few uncontested rounds, it clearly was time for the Federal cavalry to get into town (with hindsight, it obviously was *past* time). Crossing South River proved to be more difficult than had been contemplated, even though little or no hostile fire interfered with the effort. The immense rainfall of the past week had swollen both rivers to dangerous levels. Fortunately for the Yankee cavalry, the dynamics of the nearby confluence at the lower end of town kept South River from racing at high speed. North River's current dominated that of the smaller stream, so South River backed up in a quiet eddy. It was deep but not nearly as swift as North River or the confluent Shenandoah River. No bridge had ever been built across South River (the first would be constructed in 1885, the second in 1955). Once the cavalrymen negotiated South River, they would be able to use "a slab bridge," as one Yankee called it, that spanned the millrace running along the southern edge of most of the village.[47]

Carroll's orders to dash into town foundered for a time on the question of leadership. Major Chamberlain, the ranking line officer, chose this inopportune moment to be thrown from his mount and injured. Carroll sent Captain Earle S. Goodrich, who was on temporary duty with him, "to urge the cavalry forward immediately." With prompting from Goodrich and leadership by example from the daring Myles Keogh, the Yankee cavalry approached the flooded river. Carroll meanwhile noticed Confederates clustering around the crucial North River bridge. He was afraid they would burn it, so directed the Ohio guns to disperse them with artillery fire.[48]

Troopers of the 1st Virginia (Union) Cavalry looking at South River as an obstacle found little comfort in the fact that it was not quite as fast as the other two rivers a few hundred yards away. One of them described it as "booming high." When it became apparent that there was no bridge, "nobody seemed to want to be the first fellow over" through the murky and unknown waters. Sergeant Frank Cunningham "could see rebels running out of town and across the bridge over North River." As far as the sergeant could tell, no one fired a single shot at the raiders. Cunningham sat astride a big brown stallion and his comrade Sergeant Ebichousen ("a big Dutch sergeant") rode a fine mare that was a good swimmer. The two noncommissioned officers did their duty. They plunged in and to their surprise crossed "without much trouble." The rest soon followed and all made the crossing successfully.[49]

Cunningham, Ebichousen, and their more timid followers reached the north shore at the crossing point known in times of ordinary flow as the middle ford. The horsemen splashed out of the water onto an island of sorts in the back yard of the Palmer house. They crossed the slab bridge over the millrace and headed north for Main Street. Frank Cunningham noticed as he rode through town such evidences of civilian activity as a metal wheel rim heating over a fire. When the raiders reached Main Street they could see Confederates fleeing in every direction but southward—they were headed across the North River bridge, north into fields beyond town, and west up the road beyond Madison Hall.[50]

Lucius Robinson, James Gildea, and their men faced the formidable task of following the cavalry across South River. They had to drag two guns through the water with them, keeping the ammunition in limber chests and caissons dry in the process. Gildea recalled that South River "was Swoolen from the rains of the week past and ran like a mill race." How they got the two guns and their ammunition across successfully remains a mystery. Sergeant Gildea recounted most of his experiences in minute detail but threw no light on the crossing. Apparently Cunningham's "without much trouble" indicated the potential for fording with more ease than expected for both arms. The two Ohio guns clattered across the slab bridge over the millrace and continued due north to the rendezvous point at the corner of Main Street.[51]

Colonel Carroll had plunged into South River ahead of his artillery and "came dashing in" to Main Street to take control of his task force as it reassembled there. By the time the artillery arrived at Main Street, Colonel Carroll was interrogating an important prisoner. Colonel Stapleton Crutchfield, Jackson's chief of artillery, had not been able to elude the Yankee cavalry. The Confederates visible scampering in all directions prompted Carroll to point his force in two opposite directions. Carroll decided to leave one gun at the Main Street intersection, facing west to command the upper end of town under Captain Robinson's direct command. The other he sent a few blocks east to the North River bridge. Carroll's cavalry also split into the two directions. A handful dashed for the bridge. The majority moved toward the west end of town in hopes of capturing, or at least stampeding, the Confederate supply train and cattle herds. Carroll situated himself between the guns, near the east end of town.[52]

Unionist cavalry and artillery would find excitement in both directions. Those moving toward the North River bridge were heading for the highest drama, because in postmortems the span became the focus of interest; furthermore, Stonewall Jackson was in that direction in person. Colonel Carroll's first gesture came the moment he dashed up to the Main Street intersection. He ordered Sergeant Frank Cunningham to take another sergeant and two corporals through the covered bridge, ride to the top of the hill beyond it, "make an observation, and return as soon as possible." From the perspective of a man with his own neck at risk, Cunningham called this a "foolhardy piece of business," since "any one could see that there were lots of rebels" over there—which was precisely what Carroll needed to know.[53]

This first Federal move to the bridge drove the last Southerners in the east end of town across it. Carroll reported pushing some Confederate cavalry, no number specified, over the bridge. An infantryman watching from Yost's Hill thought that only about a half-dozen Rebels, and only one of them mounted, scurried through and scattered over the hills. In a dispatch to Shields later that morning, Carroll described his gesture across North River as being "in pursuit" of a retreating force.[54]

Frank Cunningham and his tiny party went to the top of the bluff beyond the bridge without any difficulty. No one seemed to be paying them any attention. Once they reached the crest, however, the cavalrymen had to retire quickly. "How we got back," the sergeant wrote bitterly, "I suppose the good Lord knows, but I don't." Confederate bullets wounded two of his comrades and mortally wounded the third's horse. Cunningham escaped unscathed, but he admitted being "scared when the bullets were flying thick about me." The Yankees spotted four Confederates crouched under a tree and dashed toward them, firing the inaccurate altered carbines they were carrying. Three of the Southerners ran away to safety, but scouts captured the fourth. As Cunningham attempted to force the captive up behind him on his horse Confederates seemed to spring up from the hillside around him. Leaving the briefly captive Rebel behind, the Yankee sergeant dashed for the river, lying flat on his horse's back. All four men pounded through the bridge to momentary safety.[55]

By this time James Gildea and an Ohio artillery piece had arrived to guard the southern end of the bridge. When Captain Robinson remained with the gun facing west down Main Street, he directed Sergeant Gildea to go east to the bridge in charge of Sergeant Lee T. Beatty's fieldpiece. As the Ohioans moved in that direction, they heard the chilling sound of dozens of Confederate drums beating "the long roll"—the steady, staccato drumbeat that was a universal call to arms in an emergency. It sounded to them as though the sound came from "every direction so you would think there was a drummer at every tree." Just short of the bridge Gildea noted "a large circle of fire in front of a blacksmith shope." Port Republic had been preparing for a busy day of helping its friends in the army with their refitting needs. Gildea knew that he could have used the fire to burn the bridge with the greatest of ease, but he also knew from Carroll's conversation in his presence that saving the bridge was the order of the day. He later mused, in a manner familiar to many a sergeant from many an era, "but I was there not to disobey orders."[56]

❈ ❈ ❈ ❈

Carroll had set the stage, but Jackson had an ample supply of players to strut upon it. In effecting his hair's-breadth escape and coordinating the Confederate rally that finally stymied Carroll's raid, Stonewall Jackson played his most dramatic personal role of the entire war. Before telling that story, however, the burning question of Carroll and the bridge deserves unraveling. Were his orders to save or to burn the bridge? Should he have burned it while he could? Did some Federals attempt to light it on fire, and if so did Carroll know of it?

Although the bridge over the booming North River seemed to be an indispensable element of life in southeastern Rockingham County, the span was in fact relatively new in 1862. A lottery held in the county in 1832 to build a bridge in that location evidently failed, since two decades later the river remained unspanned. In 1852 a subscription drive among inconvenienced local residents succeeded. The funds bought "trees 50 feet Long," according to surviving records. One John Beckone finished the structure in 1854, so when most of America had occasion to discuss it, the bridge was only eight years old. Even so, one of the last Confederates who crossed the river on its planks on June 9, 1862, called it "the crazy old bridge," implying a state of deterioration. Perhaps he was referring to the considerable battle damage in evidence by then; or maybe he was deriding all of the military attention it had drawn. Although there has been some historical uncertainty about the nature of the famous structure, it unquestionably was a covered bridge. A North Carolinian who used the bridge wrote simply, it was "a wooden structure roofed over."[57]

Colonel Carroll received firm, written, specific orders not to burn the bridge, but rather to save it. Fortunately the colonel had the foresight to save them. The order from General Shields, dated June 4, read: "You must go forward . . . to *save the bridge* at Port Republic" (emphasis added). What James Gildea and Lucius Robinson heard from Carroll on the morning of June 8, just before they advanced to action, was a reiteration of that simple directive. The colonel obviously still considered himself bound by his orders "not to burn the bridge but to hold it all Hazards," as Gildea recorded them.[58]

One of the mysteries of June 8 is whether Federals temporarily set the bridge on fire during their brief tenure as its masters. Several Confederates and Federals accepted ignition as a fact. A member of the Stonewall Brigade writing at the time declared that the Federals clearly "attempted to burn it," and referred to Carroll's detachment as "the bridge-burning column." A North Carolina officer who was at Cross Keys wrote within the week, obviously on the basis of word in the army, that the Yankees "drove our guard away & set fire to the Bridge" before Jackson "had the Fire put out & drove them back."[59]

At least four accounts by Federal infantrymen, three of whom were watching from nearby Yost's Hill, report that a fire was started. A member of the 7th Indiana wrote that mounted Yankees swarming around the bridge found that "it had been fired" and had the flames "promptly extinguished," implying that worried Confederates might have been the arsonists. Another Indiana writer credited Myles Keogh with setting fire to the bridge and regretted that Carroll "heard what had been done [and] ordered the fire put out." A member of the Unionist Virginia infantry regiment at Yost's Hill reported that some cavalrymen piled straw inside the bridge "and fired it"; but "before the fire had caught, orders were given to stay the burning and hold it at all hazards,—fatal mistake." John H. Burton of the 7th Ohio was some miles to the rear. By the time he heard the story it had expanded in the best tradition of rumors to the point that Carroll supposedly had ordered "the flames to be extinguished three times after it had been set on fire as often."[60]

A primary source that has been overlooked by most students of the battle is difficult to explain. Lieutenant D. R. Timmons, commanding a detachment of pioneers from Ohio, declared in matter-of-fact fashion that he had been sent with Colonel Carroll expressly to burn the bridge! He reported three days later to his superior officer what happened: "According to your orders I prepared to burn the bridge at Port Republic and stationed the pioneers awaiting orders. Colonel Carroll went across the bridge. On his return he gave no orders. Soon the rebel cavalry dashed upon the bridge, and I ordered the men to fire it. The rebels put out the fire." An accompanying document from Shields's staff emphasized the mission—on the same day that Shields ordered Carroll, in writing, to *save* the bridge.[61]

It is possible that the Timmons document was part of a conspiracy—that it was fabricated by Shields and his friends to cover up a decision that backfired badly. The report and the endorsement are worded in suspiciously pat style. Furthermore, Timmons's narrative contains at least two flagrant errors: Carroll certainly did not cross the bridge, nor did any Confederate cavalry dash onto the structure during the crisis. The Southerners who raced across the span to retrieve it were part of a regiment of what any observer could tell at a glance was infantry. A more likely explanation is that Timmons really did accompany the column prepared to burn the bridge if that was ordered. In the excitement he presumed that Cunningham or other Federals who crossed the bridge were Carroll; then he scurried for cover sooner than he was willing to admit and did not see what species of Confederates crossed the bridge. Whether he lied about the incipient fire must remain debatable.

If Yankees did light the bridge, however briefly, or attempt to do so, why did James Gildea not know of it? In two independent accounts, which have been cited frequently throughout this chapter, Gildea reported several salient facts: he heard Colonel Carroll tell Captain Robinson to save the bridge; he noticed means for igniting a blaze in a handy blacksmith's fire, but knew that he must obey contrary orders; he remained in the very mouth of the bridge until Confederates surged onto the far end (see the next chapter); he reported the morning's events in thorough detail; and he mentioned neither a fire nor any gestures toward setting one.

It is barely possible to imagine a series of events that encompasses most of the evidence. Military affairs always abound in confusion, even when surprise is not a factor. An element that aggravated the confusion in this case was the prompt, universal recognition that the Federals *should* have burned the bridge. Within days, if not hours, thousands of men of all ranks on both sides knew that Jackson would have been in serious trouble had the bridge gone down. As one of Jackson's staff wrote to another, citing a third, "fortunately, the enemy's commander had no sense (Crutchfield [who had talked with Carroll while a prisoner] thought him drunk)."[62]

The unkind and inaccurate suggestion about Carroll's sobriety came from a pompous officer who believed that no one else could match his own moral splendor. Carroll actually was not intoxicated, but disgruntled Unionists retreating down the Valley were willing to say that and more about him. Their unbalanced invective generated a haze of wild talk that further complicates attempts to find the truth. Charles Bard of the 7th Ohio summarized Port Republic to his girlfriend as a potentially successful venture, "but the commander of our force was intoxicated and did not burn the Bridge."[63]

One of the infantrymen in Carroll's column described the colonel's military style in a revealing passage. Carroll "was a strict disciplinarian" who predictably "was not over acceptible to the free-born, rolicking American volunteer, who had up to that time been accustomed to doing almost as he pleased." The stern-visaged veteran of hard-bitten frontier service as a Regular, who peered suspiciously at volunteer soldiers from behind a set of scraggly mutton-chop whiskers, did not inspire confidence. The lack of confidence made possible a widespread belief in the army that Carroll was capable of disobeying crucial orders. It also left soldiers swearing that the colonel had "won for himself the execration of the whole army" for behavior that would have been readily forgiven in a more popular and sympathetic figure.[64]

Fortunately for Carroll's reputation, the army had cause to be even more disgusted with Shields. The regimental historian of the 7th Indiana described with relish the outcome of an attempt by Shields to complain about the bridge episode. The senior officer "at once began upbraiding" the colonel "for not having burned the bridge, 'as ordered.'" Carroll drew from his pocket the written orders from Shields and read from them the strict admonition to save the bridge from destruction. "The General at once wheeled his horse," according to the appreciative Hoosier narrator, "and rode off." An article in the New York *Tribune* on June 18 stoutly defended Carroll, declaring firmly that he "was not ordered to burn the bridge. . . . On the contrary he was ordered by Gen. Shields to save the bridge."[65]

Again and again contemporary commentary described actions as revolving around the bridge, even though it was in truth only a tactical focal point for a few minutes on the first morning. Within ten days, for instance, a newspaper as far away as Canandaigua, New York, was describing Captain Keogh as a hero because he had fought near the now-notorious bridge. A similar report reached a Georgian who was being held captive in Washington. Stories circulating in Washington also imagined the bridge as the central landmark on June 9, during a fight two miles away. "Our forces tried to reach the bridge repeatedly to destroy it," according to that inaccurate account.[66]

Veterans retreating down the Valley were blaming Carroll "for not burning the bridge, for if he had done this, Fremont could have caught them." With that delicious might-have-been to heighten their dejection, blue-clad soldiers vanquished in the battles groaned and muttered. The fleeting moment of opportunity loomed with infinitely more clarity after the event than during its minuscule original life.[67]

The considerable, if conflicting, testimony suggests that the Truth About The Bridge is that: Shields ordered Carroll to save it; in case destruction became necessary, a detachment ready to attempt that went along; in the frenzied excitement as events unfolded, no one had much chance to think about burning, and surely no time to accomplish it; if some individuals did start an unsuccessful fire, it lasted very briefly and no one in Federal authority knew that they had lit it.

Dr. Hunter Holmes McGuire of Jackson's staff rode up and down the line of ambulances threatening to shoot the first man who left. To the dismay of the pious Jackson, McGuire was "exhausting his vocabulary of profanity" in his exhortations.

CHAPTER 4

A VILLAGE FULL OF

YANKEES

As Stonewall Jackson prepared to ride toward Cross Keys, two excited cavalrymen brought fragmentary reports about approaching danger. The general and some of his staff were on the porch or nearby when a trooper dashed up and shouted excited news about an enemy force across the river and downstream. The aroused youngster did not make much sense, however, with his "very indefinite" report, so the officers sent him back to seek better information. As the fellow galloped away and before he disappeared from view, a cavalry officer raced up to say that Federals now were in sight of the village.[1]

Captain Moore sensed the stirring excitement at his post in the foundry near the upper ford. Then a cavalryman hurried into the foundry yard and clattered to a stop near the captain. Although he was only sixteen years old, Henry D. Kerfoot already had served more than a year in Moore's infantry company before transferring to the 6th Virginia Cavalry. When Kerfoot told Moore of encountering enemy near at hand, the captain knew that he could trust his former subordinate. Henry and his horse had splashed through South River with Yankee cavalry shooting at his back, though they did not follow him immediately. Moore's first thought was to deliver the word to Jackson. He ordered Kerfoot to ride the few yards to the Kemper house to do that, then quickly began forming his score or so of reserve infantry. Henry Kerfoot found Jackson on the porch at Kemper's. The messenger, one of the youngest boys in the Confederate army, saluted his legendary general and blurted out the bad news. Jackson accepted the report "without excitement or change of countenance" and said simply—typically—to Kerfoot: "Well, sir, go back and fight them." The lad did just that, returning to fight beside his former captain, Samuel Moore.[2]

The inexperienced soldiers of the Charlottesville Artillery nervously watched Jackson's headquarters from afar when the first stirrings of excitement began. Charles H. Harman, the unit's quartermaster sergeant, had been out since before sunup in quest of forage. The sergeant galloped back to camp, slid to a halt, and blurted out that the Yankees were coming. Captain Carrington glanced toward Madison Hall for confirmation, but saw some of the headquarters people lolling about, unconcerned. The captain presumed that Harman was needlessly excited and sent him back about his business. Harman returned almost at once even more aroused; Carrington sent him away again. When the frustrated sergeant quickly and angrily returned to camp for a third time, knowing full well what he had seen, his captain finally found confirmation: Jackson and his companions were rushing for their mounts and racing away.[3]

Several of the general's staff who did not actually accompany him, and other knowledgeable army memoirists, reported that Stonewall was already astride his horse. Captain G. Campbell Brown of Ewell's staff heard that Jackson "was only saved by the accident of being on horseback." A leading local historian judged that the general was just "riding down into the village" when Federal fire erupted. William Allan judiciously—and perhaps accurately—hedged his estimate by suggesting that Jackson had "probably received the first intimation of the approach of the Fed. cavalry . . . before leaving," even if no shots had yet been fired.[4]

Jedediah Hotchkiss straddled the question of whether his chief had mounted before the crisis exploded. In his invaluable contemporary diary, Jed wrote that "the General and a portion of the staff were on the point of going over to the army across North River." Once firing started, by the Hotchkiss diary version, Jackson "started down toward it, on foot, as his horse was not ready, and went into the town." In describing the moment years later, Hotchkiss concluded somewhat differently that "Jackson and the staff and escort [had] mounted and started" before the first shots. The mapmaker and diarist was not an eyewitness, having missed participating by the space of a few yards and a few moments, which probably accounts for his mild uncertainty.[5]

The witness best situated to observe Stonewall Jackson's behavior as he attempted to leave Madison Hall was Henry Kyd Douglas. The young aide had his horse saddled and tied to a fence near the house when the sudden "hustling for horses" began. Jackson's own horse, his famous Little Sorrel, was inconveniently far away in a distant corner of the field. Douglas was disdainful of most of the general's mounts, grumbling that Jackson "never had a decent looking horse during the war." One was "gaunt and grim"; another was "a stupid brute & the troops 'cussed' him all along the line." Little Sorrel, though, seemed to Douglas to be "a remarkable little horse. Such endurance I have *never* seen in horse flesh." The faithful beast was about to earn its feed, if the orderly scurrying to catch it could do so in time.[6]

Seeing his horse so far away, and Douglas's conveniently saddled and at hand, Jackson leaped on the closer mount and "started to ride off," shouting over his shoulder that the aide should ride Little Sorrel. Then something prompted the general to reconsider. Perhaps the switch struck him as incongruous and unchivalrous. More likely, Jackson's rigid riding habits made him uncomfortable on a strange animal. He jumped down from Douglas's mount when an orderly hurriedly brought Little Sorrel to him, then sprinted away.[7]

Jackson left the Madison Hall yard in an understandable hurry. Eleven-year-old Sue, the Kemper granddaughter, described the general's trip from porch to horseback as made "hurriedly." His departure once astride Little Sorrel, Sue told a local historian about 1910, was "at a brisk gait." In an account she gave a newspaperman about the same time, Sue reported that Jackson "rode rapidly away." Lieutenant Dinwiddie of the Charlottesville Artillery described the general's pace as "gallop[ing] away furiously," and Dabney, who was around the corner of the house, wrote of how in "mad haste, Jackson leap[ed] into the saddle."[8]

Even amid the alarums, Stonewall's gallop through the village was momentarily held up by an encounter with his staff surgeon, Dr. Hunter Holmes McGuire, at the church midway down Main Street. Port Republic Methodist Church was the only sanctuary in town. In 1862 the pastor was one G. V. Leech. The building that Jackson approached was only eight years old.[9]

Without knowing of the approaching emergency, McGuire had gone to the church to arrange for moving his sick and wounded charges sheltered there southwest to Staunton by ambulances and wagons. Long windows that came down to the floor of the church (whose front faced south, toward Water Street) made moving the wounded easier; some of them could be lifted through the windows without having to be carried out the narrow hallway and door. A few of McGuire's patients were housed across Main Street in one of the Bateman buildings. Provost guards under Captain John Avis (of whom more later) helped load the injured soldiers.[10]

Hunter McGuire had not been supervising the loading long when Robinson's guns opened fire from the orchard across South River. Sergeant Gildea thought that his opening rounds struck a guardhouse; McGuire knew that they struck the church. The Confederate physician thought that the first five or six shots were aimed right at the steeple. Perhaps the Ohio gunners who saw the steeple through the trees presumed that it marked a courthouse or other public building. One or two rounds hit the steeple squarely "and sent down," McGuire recalled, "over the drivers and horses a shower of broken shingles." The teamsters gave signs of wavering. To hold them to their task, McGuire wrote, "I . . . was riding up and down the line of ambulances threatening to shoot the first man who left."[11]

By his own account, Hunter McGuire "in order to enforce my commands was using some profane language." A thirteen-year-old village boy, William C. Harper, watched McGuire excitedly as the medical officer rode urgently among the ambulances on a beautiful blaze-faced horse with white legs and feet, loudly "exhausting his vocabulary of profanity" on the drivers. Just then a new element entered the tableau in the pious person of T. J. Jackson.[12]

Jackson of course admired his surgeon's bravery and efforts, but the language he could not approve or ignore, even in the present crisis. McGuire recalled that the first he knew of the presence of his commander came when "I felt somebody touch me on the shoulder, and looking around, found it was Gen. Jackson, who had . . . ridden on down the main street of the village until he came to the church." The general asked mildly, "Doctor, dont you think you can manage these men without swearing?" Taken aback by the unexpected admonition in the midst of surprise and crisis, McGuire did the only thing he could do: "I told him I would try."[13]

Stonewall Jackson had used up all of the leeway available to him. By now the interval during which the Yankees had opened artillery fire and prepared to cross South River had evaporated. Enemy cavalrymen were on their way into the streets; it was time for Jackson to leave. "Immediately after" delivering his sermonette, McGuire recalled, Jackson "left me [and] went rapidly down towards the bridge, reaching it just in time."[14]

The bridge and the safety that it represented stood only three long blocks from the church. Confederate officers watching anxiously from several directions saw their famous general thundering toward the span. Cleon Moore of the little guard detachment posted at the west end of the bridge had the closest contact with Jackson. When the shelling started, Moore saw that much of it was aimed at the bridge. He decided to seek a safer route out of town. The corporal angled through the village toward South River. From the bank he could see lots of mounted Yankees. "They were using their carbines very freely," Moore recalled. He added drolly, "knowing that I could not successfully attack alone a regiment of cavalry, I returned to the main street of the town." As soon as Corporal Moore reached Main Street between the church and the bridge, he saw Stonewall Jackson bearing down on him, "riding as fast as his horse could carry him . . . and going toward the bridge." The young soldier "pointed, as he passed, in the direction the enemy was advancing." As Jackson galloped past, Moore wrote, "shells were bursting in and around the town and confusion reigned supreme."[15]

There is no evidence that any Federal cavalryman recognized Jackson as he scampered past them, either as they watched from across South River or as they dashed into the streets. Lieutenant John Timberlake of Carrington's Battery was hurrying through town at the same time, going in the opposite direction to rejoin his unit. Timberlake judged that the Yankee cavalry in its random advance "probably didn't notice Jackson specially," but to worried Confederates it seemed that the enemy must recognize the prize. Jed Hotchkiss, watching from near Madison Hall, concluded that "this attacking party had turned its attention to Jackson and his followers, who had just about that time gotten well into the streets of Port Republic, and made a rush for them." The enemy rush, whether random or focused, swept like lightning through the streets. Even Dr. Dabney, an inveterate Yankee-hater and -detractor, gave them due credit. "Right briskly did those invaders (bold, quick men, for Yankees,) occupy the village," he wrote.[16]

Stonewall Jackson did not pause as he approached the North River, even though "shells were bursting in the bridge and making the splinters fly." Cleon Moore watched with bated breath as the general thundered "at a full gallop through the bridge . . . I expected to see him killed." A few minutes earlier, Moore had avoided that avenue of escape for himself because it "seemed . . . like committing suicide." Midway through the covered structure Jackson met Captain Alexander M. Garber of the army's quartermaster trains. As the two officers passed at midstream, a shell fired from Yost's Hill crashed through the wood just above their heads and continued up the river. Sandy Garber took the shell as an omen and decided to follow his general's example. He reined up, turned, and dashed away from the village after Jackson. Cleon Moore was surprised and delighted a few moments later to see Stonewall Jackson clatter off the far end of the span and gallop up the opposite bluff.[17]

As soon as he reached the relative safety of the bluffs above the river, Jackson turned his attention to straightening out the mess into which his army had suddenly been plunged. He sent his cousin, Colonel William L. Jackson, and Lieutenant J. Keith Boswell of his staff in opposite directions along the left bank of North River to gauge the extent of the Federal incursion. Boswell rode upstream and looked diagonally back into town, where he could see enemy horsemen swarming in all directions. Colonel Jackson went toward the confluence, and had firsthand evidence of the situation when Yankees fired on him from the east end of town and through the bridge itself. Any doubt that a raid in force had struck Port Republic had by now disappeared.[18]

General Jackson's narrow escape margin soon had the army's rumor mills in full cry. An apocryphal tale that spread through the Confederate ranks within hours claimed that Stonewall's route had been blocked by a Unionist cannon and crew before he could reach

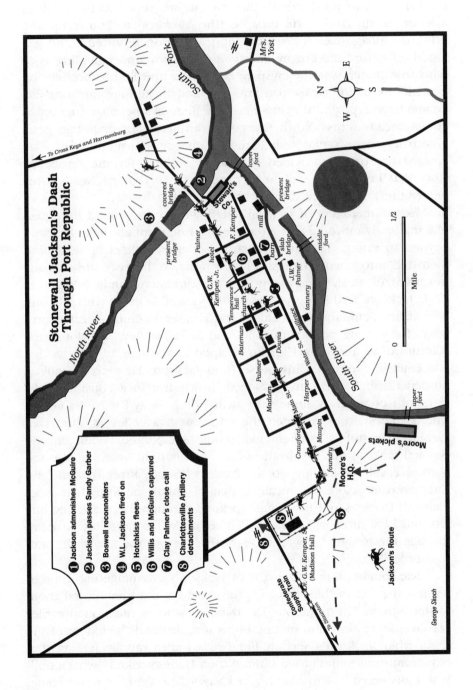

Stonewall Jackson's Dash Through Port Republic

To Cross Keys and Harrisonburg

North River

South Fork

Mrs. Yost

covered bridge

present bridge

Stewart's Co.

lower ford

present bridge

Palmer

hotel

F. Kemper

mill

G. W. Kemper, Jr.

Temperance Hall

church

barn

slab bridge

middle ford

Bateman

Downs

J.W. Palmer

tannery

Palmer

Water St.

millrace

Harper

Madden

Main St.

South River

Crawford

Maupin

upper ford

foundry

Moore's H.Q.

Moore's pickets

Confederate Supply Train
T. G. W. Kemper, Sr.
(Madison Hall)

To Staunton

Jackson's Route

George Skoch

N / E / S / W

Mile
0   1/2   Mile

① Jackson admonishes McGuire
② Jackson passes Sandy Garber
③ Boswell reconnoiters
④ W.L. Jackson fired on
⑤ Hotchkiss flees
⑥ Willis and McGuire captured
⑦ Clay Palmer's close call
⑧ Charlottesville Artillery detachments

the bridge. A medical aide in the 4th Virginia repeated the myth in a letter on the 10th: "He ordered [the Yankees] to limber up and bring the piece over the river," John Apperson reported, "and galloped off before the enemy had time to get any understanding as to who the officer was." Newspapers all over the South gleefully reported this bit of Jacksonian trickery, and incautious historical accounts have repeated it ever since. The general's peculiar attempt to communicate across North River with artillerists of uncertain pedigree (they were Yankees, as it turned out) several minutes after he crossed the bridge provided the vague outlines for the erroneous story that became legend. In fact Jackson had crossed North River before the first Yankee cannon had reached it.[19]

Eleven members of Jackson's staff who were around headquarters that early morning also attempted to ride through the village and beyond to safety. The front four did so; three others close behind them fell into enemy hands; and the four at the rear turned back toward Madison Hall and escaped in that direction. Sandie Pendleton, W. L. Jackson, Kyd Douglas, and Keith Boswell kept up with Jackson; Ned Willis, Stapleton Crutchfield, and Hunter McGuire became prisoners for varying periods of time; and R. L. Dabney, Jed Hotchkiss, William Allan, and John Harman escaped to the rear.[20]

Once he retrieved his horse from Jackson, Lieutenant Douglas hurtled through town at top speed. In a letter to a cousin, he declared: "I escaped by some very swift riding, & as I waved adieu to [the Yankees], they returned the salute with a volley of shot from carbine & pistol." The lieutenant could see Sandie Pendleton and General Jackson not far ahead of him. To his right he could also see Yankee cavalry splashing up the banks of South River toward him. They were so close, he recalled, that "I could see into their faces plainly." Douglas and his mount sprinted through the spattering bullets and kept after Jackson and Pendleton. When he followed them through the bridge, Douglas thought that he was the last of the staff to escape.[21]

The four staffers at the rear of Jackson's entourage had time to witness the fate of their three captured mates, and they turned about to find safety. The pompous Dr. Dabney, who as mentioned earlier was preparing a sermon outline in his tent, learned the extent of the crisis when Jackson's servant Jim Lewis began rapidly jerking tent pins from the ground around him. When Dabney asked "what's up," Lewis answered: "Why don't you know? The Yankees done come, and the General . . . gone across de riber, fast as he horses legs can carry him." Dabney exchanged his Bible for a pistol and told Lewis to catch and saddle his horse. Lewis refused: General Jackson had told him to have the tents and baggage headed to the rear within five minutes, and he intended to do it. Dabney mounted on his own and rode to the front of Madison Hall.[22]

Jed Hotchkiss only learned of the danger in his tent when a "volley of musketry" came tearing through the canvas. When he rushed outside, Hotchkiss could see Federal cavalry crossing South River. After shouting to the teamsters and servants to strike the tents and load the wagons, the mapmaker caught his horse and scampered back out of range. Hotchkiss continued upstream, by his own unembarrassed account, "quite rapidly" along with a stream of flying horses, wagons, and men. He continued all the way to Weyer's Cave and spent the rest of the day there nursing the bad headache that earlier had excused him from service. Hotchkiss would miss the chance to record the most dramatic battle action in his detailed diary entries.[23]

Major John A. Harman had been at home in Staunton on a brief leave but returned to Jackson early on the 9th. Rather than ride all the way down to the Port Republic bridge, the hardy Harman decided to take a shortcut to the wagon trains that were his responsibility. He plunged into North River, swollen, turbulent, and filled with floating trees though it was, and swam to the right bank. Harman probably had no time to change from his dripping clothes before having to flee the enemy cavalry. He escaped to westward, in a contemporary letter crediting the enemy with having "come in the boldest manner."[24]

At the first fire, William Allan saw men racing west beyond Madison Hall. Teamsters at once began frantically hitching up their wagons and pulling into the road "in great excitement." Allan saw to the prompt loading of his headquarters wagon and ordered it off to the rear. When he turned to where his horse was tied to a nearby fence, he remembered that his saddle was in the departed wagon. Rather than ride bareback, Allan decided he would plunge into the big wheat field running down to South River the moment the Federal cavalry turned the corner. Presumably the mounted men would chase the tempting wagon train as their primary target. The enemy never quite reached that corner, so Allan was safe, if ineffectual, as he stood poised for flight into the wheat.[25]

The three unlucky members of Stonewall Jackson's staff who were captured met that fate within feet and moments of one another. Hunter McGuire's capture resulted from zealous performance of duty. As Jackson rode away after counseling McGuire about his language, the faithful surgeon directed his train of six ambulances and two wagons onto Main Street. McGuire then headed toward the bridge, "expecting to meet Gen. Jackson," he wrote later. He quickly noticed "a great commotion in the street about the bridge, but thought it was some of our cavalry who had been on picket, and were driven in." The mounted men were trying to form into line for a charge as McGuire rode innocently toward them. The cavalrymen were Yankees, of course, and they demanded the doctor's surrender. Someone asked McGuire whether he would give his parole not to attempt to escape; he refused to answer. Minutes later he was riding unwillingly with his enemies in a charge toward Madison Hall.[26]

Poor Ned Willis started the morning feeling dreadful and finished it in durance vile. As the twenty-one-year-old Georgian lay listlessly abed in the Kemper house, he recalled, "I heard the thundering of the artillery not a half mile off." That roused him enough to stagger feverishly out of bed and dress hurriedly, "though I was so weak I could hardly stand." As Lieutenant Willis awaited his horse on the front porch, he teasingly asked the little Kemper granddaughter "which she would rather see a prisoner, General Jackson, or I." Once mounted, the sick aide made his way down the slope into the village. There he found a disorderly mass of women and children intermixed with a handful of fleeing Southern soldiers. After vainly attempting to rally the armed men among the fugitives, Willis rode on toward the bridge. He saw more cavalry in that vicinity and determined to rally them by force if necessary. The lieutenant drew his pistol and spurred toward the mounted line, only to discover at close range that they were Yankees. They did not shoot at Willis, so he pretended to join their ranks. His gray coat soon betrayed him, and a Unionist waved a sword over his head to emphasize a demand for surrender.[27]

Colonel Stapleton Crutchfield also fell captive as he attempted to reach the bridge. His captors at once took the Confederate officer to Colonel Carroll. The Yankee commander was too busy to pay much attention to Crutchfield, but ordered him to remain near under charge of an enlisted trooper. He watched with mounting trepidation as a Northern scout galloped up from the west end of town and shouted: "Colonel, you have just got Jackson's whole baggage train."

"Where is it?" "Just up yonder, in full sight across that old farm. . . . Hundreds of wagons and no troops." Carroll jubilantly ordered the majority of his cavalry to head to that end of town to gather the prize. In recounting his experience, Crutchfield told Jed Hotchkiss that "his heart went down to the bottom of his breeches pockets. He knew his own whole ordnance train was there, nearest the town of any; his new white wagon sheets most miserably conspicuous." He watched "in despair" as the Yankees moved westward on their mission.[28]

The unsung Confederate heroes of the struggle in the village were Captain John Avis and his small provost detachment. Although they received relatively little notice, Avis's provost guard and the adjacent 2nd Virginia detachment near the bridge actually faced the first fire. Some of them fired the initial answering shots, aimed across South River and obliquely beyond the confluence toward Yost's Hill.[29]

Captain Charles H. Stewart, a thirty-year-old former clerk from near Winchester, commanded the bridge guard. His first positive notice of the attack came when a shell smashed squarely through the superstructure of the bridge. Other shells followed in rapid succession. Stewart's men bore the first few well, but were outraged when one crashed into the hotel where they had arranged for a sumptuous midday meal. One of the men cried out in anger, "that spoils our dinner!"[30]

Stewart immediately dispatched a messenger to Captain Avis, "asking for instructions." John Avis had commanded a company in the Stonewall Brigade until April. He was well known to Stewart's men for that reason and because he was from their home county. On June 8 Avis had been assigned as "the provost-marshal of the town." (In July, Avis would assume command of a special provost company in nearby Staunton, perhaps on the basis of his performance on June 8.) The messenger from Stewart to Avis dashed back with orders to hold on "as long as possible"—only to find that meanwhile Stewart had slipped across the bridge with all of the detachment that he could round up. Shells were exploding in and around the bridge, and "the whole town was in a great uproar."[31]

Captain Avis and his handful of men feverishly labored to help Dr. McGuire load his sick and wounded men and get them on the road, then protect them along their route out of danger. The captain seemed to an observer to be the hero of the hour for his cool demeanor. Among Avis's other responsibilities were the Yankee prisoners in town. They caused no special trouble, but prisoners' faces "beamed with delight" at Confederate consternation and the apparent prospect of imminent release. By the time the 2nd Virginia messenger reached Avis the second time and reported the defection of Stewart and his party, the captain was so frantically involved with the ambulance train that he could pay little attention to the deteriorating situation back near the bridge.[32]

The citizens of Port (as mentioned earlier, "Port" is what the locals have always called their home village—not "the Port") faced a terrifying few minutes of chaos when Carroll's raiders so suddenly appeared. The first to run into trouble was James A. Maupin, who lived just down the slope from Madison Hall. At seventeen, Jim was close to military age (he would join the Confederate army later in the year). He had ridden out that morning in search of his family's strayed milch cow. He crossed the river and headed north toward Lewiston, where he spotted Carroll's Yankee force. In his own words, Jim "had not gone far before I learned that safety lay in the opposite direction."[33]

Most of Jim Maupin's neighbors learned of their danger just as their Confederate defenders did—when Federal shells suddenly burst among them. Everyone outdoors scurried for the illusive shelter of frame homes far from impervious to artillery fire. One shell pierced the roof above the kitchen of the Crawford house at the west end of town. Miss Cassie Crawford was making soap in a big iron kettle on her stove and the shell landed squarely in the vessel. Considering the timing of this homely chore, Cassie "seems not to have been an observer of Sunday," a local historian commented dryly. Fortunately the projectile did not explode. Even so, it thoroughly "ringed the floor and walls with soft soap"; and it left Miss Crawford with a story worth repeating for the rest of her life.[34]

Two or three shells landed in John Harper's barn, a few feet from the Crawford residence. A Harper boy and his chum survived a memorable close call as they watched the excitement out of an attic window in the hotel not far from the bridge. William Harper nervously asked Charles Lee, whose family owned the hotel, what he would do if a shell struck the building. With the bravado of youth, Charles insisted that he would maintain his perch. Almost at once a shell crashed into the gable next to the window and tore on through the roof. Both boys scampered to the stairway to get away. In his hurry, Charles fell down the steps but emerged unscathed.[35]

At least two civilians played active roles. William S. Downs, the prominent local man who straddled the political fence when it was not convenient to be an overt Yankee sympathizer, came out into the street in front of his house to talk in friendly fashion with a raider. Harry Maupin of the 6th Virginia Cavalry saw them from his position about four hundred yards away at the far western end of Main Street and fired a shot—either at the Yankee or the civilian collaborator. The bullet "whistled by in the narrow space between the two," Maupin's sister reported with apparent regret. Citizen I. B. Sheets, obviously of more loyal bent than Downs, broke out a private firearm and fired it at the invading force. Later in the war when Port came under Federal control, Northern authorities shipped Sheets off to prison at Fort Delaware for his efforts at local defense.[36]

The shelling did not last long, but it quickly convinced most of the civilians that they should flee. Their panicked flight produced scenes that "would have melted a heart of stone," one onlooker wrote. Lieutenant James Dinwiddie of the Charlottesville Artillery described the terrified exodus to his wife four days later: "Women & children poured out of town in droves during the cannonade. I met several beautiful young girls with their clothes up around their waists and running for life to the woods and ravines." Behavior that immodest in the Victorian era was an indication of unrestrained chaos. Dinwiddie continued his vivid narrative: "Mothers with staring eyes streaming with tears, clasped their little babes in their arms, and besought me to take them to a place of safety." After the lieutenant helped the terrified mothers, "their looks of gratitude were worth crowns of gold. . . . It brings tear to my eyes to think of them."[37]

Teenager Clay Palmer survived the closest personal call experienced by a Port civilian. As the attack struck, the boy had just pulled his family's rockaway carriage out of their barn, which stood on the river side of the millrace right next to the slab bridge over that narrow waterway. Young Palmer left the rockaway on the edge of the bridge while he went for a horse to hitch to it. When the uproar started, Clay crawled into the haymow and peered out the door to see what was happening. Carroll's troopers clattered up to the bridge, which was their only corridor over the millrace and into town, but the rockaway blocked them. Several Federals leaped down and shoved the light carriage over into the race. Palmer watched the destruction of his vehicle with horror. Worse followed: one of the Yankees saw him peering out of the loft and snapped a shot in his direction. The bullet missed. Clay dove into the hay, burrowed under cover, and remained quietly out of harm's way.[38]

While Clay Palmer avoided harm and the women and children ran shrieking out of town, Captain Sam Moore and his two dozen men prepared to play a pivotal role. Unlike most soldiers in town, Moore thought he heard a smattering of musketry downstream before the artillery opened. Together with virtually every other participant, Sam was certain that the opening rounds screamed directly over his own position. Henry Kerfoot's news that mounted Yankees were crossing South River down near the confluence was hardly surprising after the introductory noise. While Kerfoot continued to Madison Hall to report to Jackson, the captain sought to organize his handful of infantrymen.[39]

Captain Moore's first measure was to order the fourteen men with him at the foundry reserve post to form into line. He had with him Lieutenants James H. O'Bannon and Charles A. Marshall, and Sergeant J. R. Nunn. The other portion of his company, under a third lieutenant, remained far out of reach on the other side of North River. Moore quickly sent word to the eight men guarding the upper ford of South River, about one hundred yards southeast of the foundry, to fall back on their supports. The upper ford no longer had any significance, with Yankees swarming across downstream. As Moore knit the ford guards into his line back at the foundry, he found two men missing. They were "recent conscripts," he wrote later, who "had never been under fire . . . and availed themselves of the opportunity to escape up the river bank." The deserters took with them nearly 10 percent of Moore's firepower.[40]

Sam Moore led his tiny army to the rear for about two hundred yards. There his ready eye saw the potential military value of the high ground sloping up from the west end of town toward Madison Hall. If the Yankees were to overrun headquarters and the rich trove of supplies behind it, they would have to move west down a long, open street. Then, unless they abandoned the road, they would have to swerve to their right and climb diagonally up the slope. In the process, they would expose a vulnerable left flank to fire from the Kemper yard and be climbing a hill toward still another right-angle turn. Moore pushed his men past the Kemper yard to its northeastern corner and positioned them behind "one of those substantial stone fences, built of rather large pieces of native blue limestone, [which] furnished to men kneeling behind it considerable protection and a strong rest for their guns." A wooden fence atop the stones provided further protection when knocked down and added to the rude defensive work. Moore's position, he noted with satisfaction, "placed me near Head Quarters, in a position between the enemy and our Ordnance train, and . . . enabled me to command the approach from the village."[41]

When his men had settled into position, Captain Moore told them to lie down behind the fence and then delivered a short speech. "I ordered them . . . when the enemy appeared in our front, each one to pick his man, but not to fire until the order was given," Moore recalled. He suggested that the fate of the army rested on their few muskets. Moore closed with a histrionic touch: "the time has come when we must drive back the enemy or die!" Between the sounds of approaching gunfire and horses and Moore's fiery stump oratory, "the moment was a most anxious one." The anxious men did not have long to wait.[42]

Stalking around the Kemper knoll near Moore, convinced that he was decisively involved, was the Reverend Dr. Dabney. After abandoning his sermon notes and strapping on a pistol, the dour preacher had headed into the chaotic yard. He ran across a few infantrymen, who told him they belonged to a 2nd Virginia Infantry picket under Captain Moore. Dabney assumed that the man who answered him was Moore, and tried to tell him what to do. The soldier either ignored the staff officer or did not understand him. In either case the infantry went on to do as they were told by their duly constituted leaders. Dabney came away from the brief colloquy erroneously convinced that he had crafted an infantry defense for the knoll.[43]

The untested boys of the Charlottesville Artillery lolling around and behind the Kemper house made up the only organized military unit other than Sam Moore's in the vicinity of headquarters. The battery had six cannon more or less ready for service. Its two 3-inch rifles were modern weapons with long range. The other four guns did not measure up to 1862 artillery standards. Carrington's two 10-pounder iron howitzers and two 6-pounder smoothbores were, he knew, "rather hard specimens . . . even at that time"; but, the captain said later, "still they did some pretty good service." A hundred or so mounted Yankees were about to see the first example of that good work.[44]

The boys of the battery had seen no service at all. Lieutenants James Dinwiddie and John Timberlake were the only two men in the

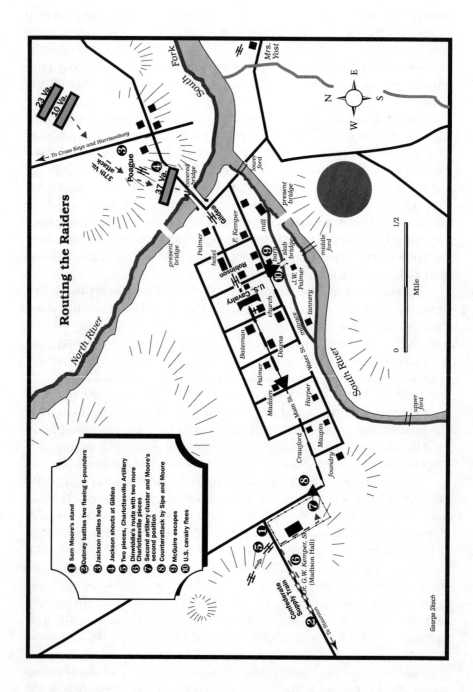

Routing the Raiders

Legend:

① Sam Moore's stand
② Dabney battles two fleeing 6-pounders
③ Jackson rallies help
④ Jackson shouts at Gildea
⑤ Two pieces, Charlottesville Artillery
⑥ Dimwiddie's route with two more Charlottesville pieces
⑦ Second artillery cluster and Moore's second position
⑧ Counterattack by Sipe and Moore
⑨ McGuire escapes
⑩ U.S. cavalry flees

To Cross Keys and Harrisonburg

23 Va.
10 Va.

South Fork

Poague
37th Va. attack
37 Va.
covered bridge

Mrs. Yost

N
E
S
W

present bridge

North River

Gildea

Palmer
hotel
F. Kemper
mill
Robinson
U.S. Cavalry
church
Bateman
Downs
J.W. Palmer
millrace
tannery
barn
slab bridge
present bridge
lower ford
middle ford

Madden
Palmer
Main St.
Harper
Water St.
Maupin
Crawford
foundry

South River
upper ford

Confederate Supply Train
Lt. G.W. Kemper, Sr. (Madison Hall)
To Simmons

0   Mile   1/2

George Skoch

battery who had ever been in action. "Captain Carrington at that time hardly knew how to load a cannon," Dinwiddie recalled, "but he was brave and thoughtful." The antiquated guns had just reached the company within the week. The tyro artillerists had not drilled with them even once, nor "made a single maneuver on the field." Timberlake and Dinwiddie kept the battery following Jackson on the endless marches of early June. At night in camp the two seasoned lieutenants "taught the men how to load and fire," Dinwiddie remembered, "and that was all the knowledge of artillery which they possessed."[45]

Captain Carrington had received an earlier alert than most at the west end of town because his quartermaster sergeant, Charles H. Harman, had ridden back from duties elsewhere with a warning. Carrington had rejected the news because army headquarters had shown no signs of excitement. The captain had noticed Jackson himself on foot in the yard. Harman had run across comrades in town and had given them warnings they had believed. He told Leroy W. Cox to help round up battery members and get them back to camp; Yankees were only a few minutes away. Cox dashed back to camp, riding bareback on a big dappled gray he had been watering.[46]

When events finally convinced James Carrington of the imminent emergency, he ordered the battery bugler to sound the alarm to "Limber up in short order." Cox galloped into a chaotic campsite. "I found everything in confusion," the youngster recalled, "the men hitching up and a general breaking up of camp." Lieutenant James Dinwiddie found the panicky reaction of his green subordinates amusing—"a very funny scene. Such confusion worse confounded I hardly ever saw before." Once started toward the rear, "some did not stop 'till they were arrested in Staunton by the Provost Marshall," Dinwiddie noted disgustedly. Terror infected both the enlisted troops and some of the company's black supernumeraries. Other men in each category stood firm and soon would pose a sturdy barricade squarely in Carroll's path.[47]

The battery's two seasoned officers, Timberlake and Dinwiddie, attempted without much success to restore order. Many of the men believed that they had been ordered to escape—"to hitch up and fall back . . . as rapidly as possible." Captain Carrington unconvincingly declared much later that he had ordered four of the six guns to retire for short, specified distances. Private Wilbur F. Davis provided an apt analysis of the atmosphere when he wrote that "some [were] ordering one thing—some another." The piece to which Davis was assigned served as a momentary rallying point for a few mounted Confederates. When the horsemen almost immediately resumed their flight, Davis and his mates limbered up their gun and joined the rout. "We were ourselves almost in panic," the cannoneer admitted. "So off we dashed, the drivers whipping their horses to a rapid trot and we running alongside."[48]

The Reverend Dr. Dabney helped to stabilize the artillery situation, though less than he later claimed. Captain Carrington's first contact with Dabney came when the staff officer "came back a good deal excited, and reported . . . that Gen. Jackson had been captured, he thought, with his entire staff except himself." That alarmist and inaccurate account inflamed the excitement among the artillery boys and hastened their steps rearward. Dabney spotted two little six-pounders disappearing up the pike toward Staunton and spurred after them. The galloping parson managed to catch up with the rear of the party and halt it. Then he sent one of the detachment ahead to stop the leading gun, which Carrington was accompanying. As Dabney remembered the scene, Carrington was "astonished and somewhat indignant at being stopped in his retreat until I told him who I was, and what I wanted." Then the two officers turned the two guns around in the road (it must have been a trying maneuver in the midst of flying wagons and refugees) and started back. Dabney and Carrington eventually would emplace their small bronze pieces in the southeastern corner of the Kemper yard and participate in the final act of the morning's drama.[49]

Meanwhile Lieutenant Dinwiddie had abandoned his role as a sympathetic and amused observer of the rout and had begun playing a crucial part in stemming it. He and Timberlake promptly and efficiently rolled one gun by hand to the northeast corner of the yard, where Moore was preparing his few infantrymen behind the stone fence. Another cannon soon joined them at the corner. While wagons jammed both lanes of the pike toward the rear as far as the eye could see, the two lieutenants calmly prepared to stay where they were and resist the unknown strength of their attackers. Hurriedly the men remaining with the lieutenants pulled down "every other corner of the worm fence" at the corner and made barricades from the rails.[50]

Timberlake stayed on at the northeast corner of the Kemper yard while Dinwiddie hurried west to help turn around the rest of the battery. Although he was only twenty-two years old, John Henry Timberlake had an impressive military background. He had received military training at the school of Colonel John Bowie Strange, who would die at the head of a Virginia regiment in September 1862. Timberlake's cousin, Hilary P. Jones, soon would become a Confederate artillery colonel. The young lieutenant's most impressive credential was that he had been elected at the age of twenty as colonel of an Albemarle militia regiment. "He had," an admiring contemporary wrote, "remarkable military aptitude for his years." The joint efforts of the two lieutenants were uncoordinated, as might be expected in the confusion. Timberlake thought that he had performed "without orders from anyone, or hint or suggestion." Each man probably centered his independent exertions on pushing one of the two pieces into position.[51]

As Sam Moore, Dr. Dabney, and several artillery officers strove valiantly to knit together a defense, Stonewall Jackson pursued the same goal from the relative safety he had reached beyond North River. The general dispatched aides toward the strong Southern units encamped not far northeast of the bridge, then worriedly followed in person. He bumped into a squad of the 6th Virginia Cavalry just above the bridge and ordered its captain to resist any Yankee advance beyond the bridge. Henry Clay Clement, a twenty-two-year-old private who had been in Jackson's presence often while serving as a courier, noticed with astonishment that the stern general smiled as he talked to the captain. Perhaps Stonewall was recounting his undignified flight.[52]

Captain William T. Poague, commander of the Rockbridge Artillery, knew Jackson well. Both men were from Lexington, Virginia, and the battery had served with Jackson from his early days in brigade command. Poague saw not amusement but excitement on his neighbor's face when the general reached the Rockbridge command, which was close to the bridge and on the left of the road. "I never saw Jackson as much stirred up at any other time," the artillerist recalled. As he galloped past his hometown battery, Jackson, "addressing no one in particular," yelled: "Have the guns hitched up, have the guns hitched up!" Poague could hear the general as he passed on toward nearby infantry shouting: "Have the long roll beat, have the long roll beat!"[53]

One of Poague's men admitted in a letter to his mother that "A scene of the utmost confusion ensued." A soldier in an adjacent battery put a somewhat better face on the reaction when he wrote with understatement, "Some confusion had ensued." A few of the artillerists had reacted casually to the opening explosions, "thinking an *old load* was being fired off by some of our own men." The delusion was short-lived. Men chased down excited horses and hurriedly hitched them to limbers. Jackson soon dashed back past the busy Rockbridge Artillery camp on his way to the bluff above the bridge, which lay only some four hundred yards away. He "snapped out" another order to Poague: "Captain, have your battery ready at once." The battery commander assured him that it nearly was, and Jackson replied: "Good, I will be with you presently." Poague followed the general almost immediately with the first gun ready to move.[54]

Stonewall Jackson was not fond of General William B. Taliaferro because of disciplinary encounters, but he was delighted to have that subordinate's infantry close at hand. Just beyond Poague's camp the army commander came upon the 37th Virginia standing for inspection. Taliaferro had himself been "just in the act of shoving his arms through" the sleeves of a shirt when the first artillery round exploded. He told an acquaintance that he had "put on [his] shirt quicker than man ever put on shirt before." Not long after he had hurriedly dressed and run out among his troops, Taliaferro met Jackson "spurring up the road." Taliaferro thought that Stonewall "was not excited—he never was, and never, under any circumstances that I am aware of, lost his presence of mind or yielded to panicky influences." When he recalled the event in later years, Taliaferro could not remember that Jackson issued any orders. The need to head for the bridge was obvious.[55]

A soldier of the 10th Virginia busily cleaning up in the river remembered being startled by the double "boom! boom!" that signaled Carroll's onset. Another man from the 10th wrote in his diary, "the first thing we knew they were firing into our camp." Federal gunners actually aimed at the bridge, but at all points of the horizon soldiers felt that hostile ordnance was searching especially for them. Part of the 37th received special advance warning. Captain H. C. Wood had been in the village when the first stirrings of trouble began and he hurried breathlessly to the 37th's colonel to alert him. The regiment started promptly through a wheat field toward the bluff above the bridge.[56]

Stonewall Jackson's gallop through the camps took him as far north as his eponymous brigade. An aide at the brigade's headquarters had quickly started packing when he heard the cannon fire. A colleague asked why. "Well," the packer replied, "it's Sunday and you hear that shot." Despite Jackson's well-known piety, he seemed always to fight on the first day of the week. "The army fully believed," insisted General Winder's aide, "that Jackson would rather fight on Sunday than on any other day."[57]

Some time after artillery firing first startled John Apperson of the Stonewall Brigade's 4th Virginia, he saw Jackson riding past. The general was alone. As he passed, Stonewall called to his veterans, "Get your guns and cartridge boxes." He rode on to General Winder's tent, where that disgruntled subordinate had just written his terse note intended to get him away from Jackson's unpleasant control. The emergency overrode that concern. When Jackson ordered Winder to send a regiment to the bridge "in double-quick time," the brigadier dispatched the 2nd Virginia. It formed "in a short time" and set out toward the firing, weapons in hand.[58]

Colonel John M. Patton's small brigade lay next beyond Winder's camp. Jackson had rallied more than enough support by the time he reached the Stonewall Brigade, so he did not continue north beyond Winder's tent. Either couriers or good sense prompted Patton to prepare to move anyway. His units quickly struck camp, loaded wagons, and took to the road. They would arrive only in time for the engagement's aftermath.[59]

Jackson spurred Little Sorrel back toward the bridge. He reached the bluff on the river's left bank before the first reinforcements arrived, although the leading gun of the Rockbridge Artillery rumbled into position not far behind. The general spotted horsemen milling around the village end of the span and yelled loudly at them. One of his staff thought that Jackson ordered them to come over the bridge, on the assumption that they were Confederates; another heard that his chief's cry had been "Go away from that bridge. Go away from that bridge." The horsemen, however, could not hear anything above the noise of battle and the roaring water. The troopers were Yankees, of course. Presently they wheeled and rode off. A few moments later an artillery piece unlimbered near the mouth of the bridge and Jackson repeated his confused, or at least confusing, performance with this new audience.[60]

The threatening gun belonged to a crew under Jim Gildea, the Ohio sergeant who left a wonderfully detailed narrative of his exciting experiences in and near Port Republic. Captain Lucius Robinson had somehow muscled a six-pounder gun and a twelve-pounder howitzer through swollen South River. Robinson stayed with the gun that remained on Main Street about opposite the millrace bridge that had been the Yankee corridor into Port Republic. Jackson and Southerners near him watched Gildea's horses and the other gun move through the lower end of town and turn into the lane leading to the bridge. The crew, who moved steadily and quietly, were dressed in blue overcoats.[61]

The cannoneers unlimbered the piece next to the left side of the bridge's mouth and pointed it across the river. Gildea tied his horse across the street then joined the crew. When he reached the gun, the sergeant found it aimed vaguely toward the crest of the opposite ridge. The Ohioans quickly loaded their cannon. Just at that moment several mounted men came across the top of the bluffs and into view. The enticing targets at point-blank range were Stonewall Jackson and his entourage, who had been watching from the reverse slope. Gildea did not know who the strangers were, of course, but he knew that he could hit them easily at that range. One of the mounted men gesticulated forcefully toward Gildea and his men and obviously was shouting orders at them: Stonewall Jackson was reprising his performance of a few minutes earlier with Federal cavalry who had been in the same spot. North River's noisy water made Jackson's efforts as useless as they had been before. As Gildea later wrote, "what he said we could not distinguish."[62]

Sergeant Gildea grabbed the elevating screw under the breech of his gun and began cranking it down to raise the muzzle. Unfortunately for the Northern war effort, as Gildea zeroed in on his target, Captain Robinson rode up to check on things. He saw his sergeant's intentions and yelled, "Jim don't fire there, that is our own men." Frank Cunningham and a few other Unionist cavalry had been to that side of the river and apparently Lucius Robinson knew it. When Gildea insisted that his targets were Rebels, the captain said to wait until he could dash back a few blocks and get advice or orders from Colonel Carroll. A few minutes later, Gildea heard Carroll himself shout across the distance, "Give them Hell Sergeant."[63]

From Jackson's side of the river the situation looked every bit as confusing as it did to Captain Robinson. Either mistaken again about the identity of the soldiers or encouraged by the success of his recent shouts at the cavalry, Jackson decided to ride over the crest into full view and repeat his attempt to shout across the river. As Gildea and his men aimed their cannon at him, Jackson "rose in his stirrups and called out loudly, 'Bring that gun over here!'" As was his custom in battle, Jackson repeated his exhortation several times. Kyd Douglas and Keith Boswell of the general's staff were certain that Gildea's men were Yankees, and they watched in horror as the South's most successful general risked his life over something of no real consequence. Confederates in overwhelming numbers would reach the bridge within a few minutes. They would rectify the situation no matter what happened meanwhile.[64]

Confederate confusion over the blue-coated gunners grew out of two circumstances. One Southerner on the bluff noted that "still we were confident they were our own men, as three-fourths of us wore captured overcoats." Captain Poague, whose Rockbridge Artillery was just arriving, contributed to Jackson's uncertainty by mentioning that the Charlottesville Artillery had brand-new uniforms something like those in view. Poague and Jackson could not know that many of the Charlottesville boys were fleeing and the rest were trying desperately to hold on in the Kemper yard. As Poague and a subordinate remembered the affair, Jackson actually began by thinking that Gildea's crew were Yankees until the Virginians talked him out of it. It was in order to cut through the nettlesome uncertainty that Jackson trotted over the crest and started yelling.[65]

The Yankees temporized just barely long enough to save Jackson from the consequence of his rashness. As Carroll bellowed "Give them Hell Sergeant" to Gildea, the sergeant could see that Jackson "had discovered his mistake and was making fast time over the crest," moving so rapidly that Gildea "could not get the range quick enough to follow him." In the excitement, some Confederates looking on thought that Gildea fired before Jackson discerned his Northern identity, but missed. Gildea knew better. He had had Jackson over his sights for long, tense minutes, but was under orders not to shoot him. After Jackson scurried over the top of the bluff, Gildea honored Carroll's order by unleashing his canister round—more than two-dozen iron balls flung smoothbore, as though from a shotgun—at the empty stage where Jackson had been.[66]

Jackson's scamper over the crest and Gildea's canister charge opened a new stage of the battle at the eastern edge of the village. With the general safe and reinforcements pouring to his aid, the Yankee hold on the bridge could not last long. Meanwhile, the crackle of musketry and unexpected artillery discharges on the western end of Port Republic let Stonewall Jackson know that the handful of Confederates there were making a valiant attempt to check Carroll's progress toward the wagon trains.

When Captain Samuel
J. C. Moore could
wait no longer, he
bellowed "FIRE!" at the
top of his lungs. Two
dozen lead bullets
poured toward the
mass of cavalry in
the lane.

CHAPTER 5

ROUTING THE RAIDERS

S prigg Carroll and his Unionist raiders reached their high tide soon after they chased Stonewall Jackson through the bridge. Colonel Carroll had reveled in the good news reaching him about Jackson's vulnerable trains and camps behind Madison Hall. From his vantage point as a prisoner standing near Carroll, Confederate colonel Stapleton Crutchfield had cringed at the same news. As Jim Gildea's gun and the Ohioans of its crew headed toward the bridge, the other Federal cannon in town remained on Main Street and pointed vaguely toward its west end. Most of Carroll's cavalry lined up four abreast and trotted slowly up Main Street toward the lucrative goal of unguarded Confederate wagons and supplies.

Captain Sam Moore and his two dozen hardy soldiers (the two

faint-hearted conscripts had already run away) awaited the Yankees behind the stone fence and stacks of wooden rails opposite the northeast corner of the Kemper yard. One of the waiting Confederates was John Nunn. Moore had allowed Nunn to find a hospitable civilian bed in town the night before because he was very sick. The excitement in the streets prompted Nunn to hurry back to his unit. He arrived just as Moore had formed his men for the move to the corner where they would make their stand. Nunn fell in at the front of the company and marched with it.[1]

The Virginians did not have long to wait after they selected spots behind the stones where they had pulled down some of the rails topping the fence. Near them artillerymen were manhandling first one and then another of the Charlottesville Artillery guns into position. Before the cannon were ready, Carroll's cavalry column came into view. Southern musketry would have to suffice for at least a few more minutes. Moore was relieved to see that the force moving toward him seemed neither confident nor in a hurry. They "moved cautiously," he recalled, "in a walk." On the other hand, there were more of them than he liked. The massed Yankees looked "like a regiment of cavalry," numbering "at least three hundred." They actually numbered no more than one third that many, and probably fewer; but Moore's quick, wide-eyed glance showed him accurately enough that he was outnumbered by several multiples.[2]

Citizen soldiers—and Civil War armies were made up of them—almost never managed to suppress the urge to fire too soon when crouching in ambush. Nevertheless, Sam Moore's firm admonitions to hold fire for a concerted volley somehow worked in this instance. The Yankees turned right at the dead end of Main Street and started up the slope four abreast toward Moore's little knoll. That many mounted men jammed the narrow lane to its limits. When Moore could wait no longer, he bellowed "FIRE!" at the top of his lungs. Two dozen lead bullets poured toward the mass of cavalry in the lane. They obviously could not have hit more than two dozen targets, but as such things go, probably did not hit a half dozen. Moore thought that this "most effective" volley "emptied many a saddle, and produced great confusion in their ranks." Years later the captain told his son that "it seemed to him that every gun emptied a saddle" as the Northerners "reeled back."[3]

About the confusion there could be no doubt. John Nunn called the fire "a well directed volley . . . which checked them," but said nothing about enemy casualties. Another contemporary described the Federal recoil as "scampering back." Terrified horses with empty saddles tore past and through Moore's position, but no mounted enemies reached the top of the hill. The tangle of horseflesh and men in the road was indescribable. Moore's fire had "hurled the head of the column back upon the men in their rear." Turning that many men and mounts on the narrow road would have been a recipe for chaos even without bullets raining down on them.[4]

At least a few Southern cavalrymen clung briefly to Moore's knot of resistance. An artillerist roaming the vicinity spotted "2 or 3 . . . near this fence firing their pistols." One of them was shooting so wildly that the young cannoneer asked him "to let me have his pistol, saying I would get one at every crack." The fellow made no reply, fired a few more shots randomly into the air, then fled.[5]

Four Confederates reported on Moore's volley as interested and surprised, but impotent, observers. Colonel Stapleton Crutchfield stood at Carroll's side as the Unionist cavalry rode away from them "at a gentle trot." The Confederate colonel watched "with sickening desperation" as the head of the column turned right and disappeared from view. To his amazed delight, "a ringing little volley of rifles" crashed as though out of nowhere and the Yankees recoiled.[6]

Although Crutchfield did not notice them, nor did they spot each other, two of his mates on Jackson's staff went forward unwillingly as prisoners of the attacking Yankees. Ned Willis described in a letter home how Moore's infantrymen "drove us (Yankees) back, to my delight, though the balls whistled in rather close proximity to my head, and many a Yankee bit the dust." Hunter McGuire had the misfortune to be nudged close to the front of the advance by the Yankee trooper who was guarding him. He recalled: "I went along with them in the charge, and was among the front line when Capt. Moore fired into them and emptied a good many saddles. When he fired, the Yankees went back for some distance." McGuire later learned that Moore only had about twenty men firing, but to his delighted ears on June 8, the surprising volley "sounded to me as if he had a thousand." The Yankee guarding McGuire and riding next to him "fell from his horse, I suppose shot," the doctor reported without any discernible remorse. In the confusion a few minutes later, Dr. McGuire escaped through the chaotic streets to safety.[7]

The fire that so threatened McGuire did not sound like much to the more distant William Allan. McGuire's fellow staff officer was

91

poised to dash into the tall wheat behind Madison Hall and hide from the Yankee raiders when the surprising volley rang out. To Allan's practiced ear the crash was not loud enough to indicate substantial resistance. Colonel Carroll estimated the volume of fire as Allan did and was sure he could overcome it. Carroll and his staff scrambled in the streets to rally their cavalry and send them back again. Moore's men had reloaded as rapidly as trembling hands could manipulate cartridge box flaps, cartridges, ramrods, and primer caps. Instead of waiting for a renewed assault and another volley opportunity, Moore turned them loose to load and fire at will. Yankees brought their carbines into play and returned fire "in a desultory way." Moore's Virginians continued "to fire as fast as they could load, [and] the confusion of the enemy was increased."[8]

To the relief of Moore's little band, the two friendly cannon in their vicinity by this time were nearly ready to fire. Captain Moore described the arrival of the guns relative to the first cavalry repulse as "about this time," and "at once"; John Nunn's phrase was "very quickly." The cannons' spot behind the stone and rail fence was just to Moore's right, or west. The infantry men noticed from the corners of their eyes that the Charlottesville boys were laboring mightily to nudge their cannon into position by hand. Most of the battery horses had scattered, and in any case the tight position would not have accommodated horse-drawn positioning right at the fence.[9]

Lieutenant James Dinwiddie noticed with relief that after the first shock, "the men . . . soon became calm, at least those who remained." That solid remnant obeyed Dinwiddie's orders to prepare for action. Other artillerists scrambled across the fields to catch the panic-stricken horses. Dinwiddie soon left under orders to corral the fleeing guns of his own section. He would face further adventures in catching them and then using them against Carroll's raiders from another position.[10]

The second gun coming up on Moore's right had nearly joined the flight to the rear. Private Leroy Cox had run up to Lieutenant John Timberlake and pleaded, "For God's sake don't let us leave without firing a shot. If we do we will be captured." Timberlake, who would be one of the day's heroes, "seemed to grow at least 6 inches" at the challenge. He drew his sidearm, stood up in his stirrups, and ordered the gun toward the crucial corner.

Private Ira Gardner, riding the outside lead horse, turned its head back toward the front. His companion on the front wheel horse, a strapping Irish conscript, decided that enlightened self-interest called him elsewhere and raced away on foot. Without a moment's hesitation, Edmund Drew "jumped on in his place and drove the horses to the . . . turn in the road." Drew performed his brave exploit without the least obligation to do so; he was a black man employed by the battery as a barber, with no combat obligation.

Drew and Private Gardner pushed the team as close as possible to the turn in the road where Moore was making his stand. Cox and Privates Samuel Shreve and Julius Goodin helped to unlimber the piece, an iron howitzer, then looked for some canister with which to load it. They found none and had to settle for an explosive shell. Julius Goodin stuffed the round into the muzzle and Cox rammed it home. The four soldiers and their barber were ready for Carroll's next attack. They did not have long to wait.[11]

Leroy Cox barely had time to affix a lanyard to the friction primer in preparation for firing. Before anyone could attempt to adjust the height of the muzzle with the screw at the breech, Yankee cavalry clattered into view. This time they did not use the cautious walking gait of their earlier advance, but "rode furiously" up the road directly at the Confederates. The gun next to Cox and Drew and their mates did have some canister in its limber chest. Its gunners had excitedly jammed three rounds into their piece. Then the Yankees were upon them, within "half pistol range." The canister scythed through the mounted ranks, but Cox's shell did more harm to the remnants of fence near him than to the enemy. Moore's infantry also contributed its best to the effort, firing from sheltered fence corners just to the left of the cannon. The effect of this combined fire was gratifying: the enemy "at once fell back around the turn in the road." Targets had disappeared from view long before the newly minted gunners could reload.[12]

Prisoner-of-war Stapleton Crutchfield had been astounded to hear the first Confederate volley. He watched with concern as Carroll circulated among the repulsed troopers and "angrily ordered them to reform and advance." Crutchfield was also amazed to hear the roar of two artillery pieces as the Yankees rode up the slope past Madison Hall the second time. It seemed to him "as if they had fired from the sky. . . . where on earth did those guns come from? Did I not place all the batteries? Don't I know they are all on the north side of the river?" Jackson's chief of artillery obviously had lost track of his newest reinforcements. He looked on delightedly as the horsemen, having been surprised once again, "came scampering down the street, with canister shot richochetting about the horses' heels." Another Confederate declared somewhat extravagantly that the two guns had "cleared the streets with showers of cannister."[13]

Carroll's artillery piece along Main Street near the hotel responded to the sound of hostile cannon by throwing a few shells toward the Confederate knoll. One smashed several limbs from a big hickory tree at the corner without doing any real harm. The two Charlottesville guns fired at least one counterbattery round in return, but would have no more opportunities to shoot at cavalry at close range.[14]

The focal point for Confederate defense shifted after Carroll's first two cavalry charges. Several officers had manufactured a new artillery cluster, with different guns, southeast of the Kemper house, and Sam Moore was about to shift his infantry to protect the guns there. John Nunn was stating simple truth when he wrote proudly: "The stand taken by our Company . . . saved from capture and destruction Genl Jackson's baggage and ordnance train." Moore acknowledged the pivotal and timely support of the guns, "without which . . . the cavalry would have ridden over my little squad." The captain had had no idea who they were during the crisis, but applauded their performance. "Although the men of the battery had never been under fire before they behaved like veterans," he wrote. "I have ever since been proud of Carrington's battery, for its gallant conduct on that day."[15]

Meanwhile, Lieutenant James Dinwiddie had chased down his own section to halt its retreat. When he caught up with the fleeing teams, the lieutenant had to draw his pistol and point it at the drivers to persuade them to obey his orders and turn back. The Reverend Dr. Dabney came up to the halted detachment with Captain Carrington and directed that officer to follow him back toward Kemper's with the two guns best supplied with ammunition.[16]

Dinwiddie shepherded the two teams and crews back down the road almost to Moore's vital corner. About two hundred yards short of the corner he turned them south into a private lane leading across the back of the house. From behind the southwest corner of Madison Hall the guns turned east for a few more yards and set up in a hollow there. Lieutenant Timberlake soon joined Dinwiddie, Carrington, and Dabney; so did Lieutenants Cochran and Bibb of the battery. Unlike the hurried artillery defense at Moore's corner, where key partici-

pants had been a sixteen-year-old boy and an ostensibly noncombatant black barber, this new artillery effort would be supervised by
more than enough officers.[17]

Sam Moore recognized that the center of gravity of the defense
was shifting a few yards south to the western terminus of Main Street.
To adjust to the changed situation, he led his men down to help
out, "in high spirits at their success." Captain Carrington saw this
reinforcement arrive and called Moore "as cool and brave a man as
was ever seen." Carrington thought that the infantrymen all looked
like youngsters. Moore positioned his boys and their muskets "on
the left and a little in rear of the artillery."[18]

Although the position in the yard's southeastern corner commanded the entire length of Main Street, a fence blocked the gun
muzzles and screened the view. The gunners could see over the
obstacle from rising ground not far in their rear. The fence consisted
of vertical posts with four planks nailed horizontally to them. Carrington proposed tearing away the planks, but Dabney stopped him. The
staffer, by his own immodest account, was thinking "with lightning
quickness." He calculated that the old boards were too thin and
brittle to interfere with artillery fired through them. Furthermore,
Dabney claimed, "I knew that mine must be a game of bluff mainly,
and this screen would make the surprise more useful." If the Yankee
commander in town could readily observe the slender Confederate
strength, he "would see at once that the thing . . . to do was to dash
on and ride down my gunners."[19]

Dabney's claims of preeminence in the defense of Port Republic's west end put on weight as the years passed. He eventually
painted himself as the wise and prescient force that restored order
from chaos. At the time, however, Moore and his infantry paid him
no attention whatsoever. When Dabney later asserted that he was
"the ranking officer of the line that morning," he betrayed his casual
ignorance of military organization. Dabney was not a line officer at
all. In his postwar accounts, Moore pointed out cogently that had he
noticed Dabney, he would not have obeyed him: "a staff officer is
the agent and mouth piece of his commander . . . and when he is
so situated that he cannot communicate with his commander, his
occupation and authority are gone." Dabney himself had been recklessly spreading the tale that Jackson was a prisoner.[20]

Curiously—and significantly—Dabney's own long letter to his
wife summarizing the events of June 8 made absolutely no mention

The pompous Dr. R. L. Dabney's claims of preeminence in the defense of Port Republic's west end put on weight as the years passed. At the time, however, Captain Moore and his infantry paid Dabney no attention whatsoever.

of any role he played around headquarters. It described his upset stomach and criticized Stonewall Jackson sharply (among other things, incredibly, for being a "poor disciplinarian") but ignored the events that years later seemed to Dabney to have thrust him to center stage.[21]

Sometime during the struggle the last two of Carrington's guns came back toward the front. They had no ammunition, and in any case the two guns already in place were "all that could be used for the narrowness of the street down which we had to fire," gunner Wilbur F. Davis recalled. Davis faced a serious problem as he prepared his piece for action. It was his duty to affix the lanyard to the friction primer and then pull it crisply at the order to fire. In the hubbub, the lanyard had been jostled out of its spot on the limber. One of the drivers loaned his whip to Wilbur and the youngster tied the tip of the whip to the primer's ring. In that crudely rigged fashion Davis's gun awaited its first-ever firing in battle.[22]

The Yankee cavalry who had ridden twice toward the upper corner had lost some of their poise by this time. Some Confederates behind the fence never had a sense that the enemy advanced again in organized fashion. Stapleton Crutchfield, still a prisoner, could see the final effort better. He watched as Carroll by frantic exertion rallied the cavalry once more and made them "advance more rapidly" than before. Carrington had been worried about firing canister down the street. "We were afraid that Jackson and his staff had been captured, and were with this cavalry and might be killed," Carrington remembered. Carroll's shouted order to his men to charge ended the hesitation. Dabney "waited until the column got at close quarters, then I let drive both guns." Moore's infantrymen added their staccato musketry to the deep bass of the cannon.[23]

Simultaneously with the surge of Carroll's cavalry up Main Street, the Federal cannon in the street near the hotel fired toward the west end of town. Some of Carrington's men thought that that fire triggered their own response. All of them later swore that both Federal guns had shot at them, having heard two enemy guns without knowing that Gildea's fire all went the other way. Wilbur Davis saw a puff at the far end of the street, and then a shell crashed through a small frame outbuilding within a few yards of him. Another round exploded just in front of the Charlottesville guns. A third seemed to Dabney to be heading straight for the gun crews, so he "shouted to the young men to fall down." After it screamed past they went back to work. Henry Clay Page, gunner at one of the pieces, hit an enemy limber or carriage in front of the hotel with his second shot and knocked a wheel off. Soon thereafter Page was severely wounded. Confederate guns on Jackson's side of North River also fired against the Federal pieces in town.[24]

The Charlottesville guns poured a variety of rounds down Main Street. Carrington recalled using "one or two shells and several rounds of canister." Most Confederates who wrote of the experience used some form of the word "sweep" to describe what they did. Lieutenant Dinwiddie put it vividly: "We filled the guns nearly to the muzzle with canisters, and swept the street like a broom."[25]

Having things mostly their own way seemed fine to the novice soldiers. Dabney wrote fondly of the boys' performance: "The scene . . . would have been laughable had it not been so serious. There was no drill and no idea among the young gentlemen, of subordination and silence, every fellow of them was talking and suggesting. But they were brave." As Wilbur Davis's gun limped through its maiden action, awkwardly using a whip as its lanyard, it ran into further complications. The rammer staff had been run over in the gun's rough ride, breaking off the sponge end. Marshall Burgoyne, a Louisiana Irishman who would soon be arrested for having deserted from Dick Taylor's Brigade, had the duty of ramming powder and rounds down the muzzle. Without the sponge to swab out the piece, each firing increased the chance of a premature discharge from unextinguished sparks. Davis reported admiringly that D. H. Boyden took over from the reluctant Burgoyne. Boyden performed his chore in gingerly fashion, "trying to manage to lose as little as possible of his arms—if the gun sh[oul]d go off while he was at it." The brave replacement survived the day and the war to become an Episcopal minister.[26]

The effect of all of this Confederate fire was to make Main Street an untenable position for Carroll. Sam Moore could see Unionist officers "engaged in rallying and reforming" for another try, but the battery "soon cleared the street of them." A Yankee officer dashed up to Carroll and told him, in Stapleton Crutchfield's hearing: "the scout was mistaken. There is a whole park of artillery up there supported by infantry." Crutchfield had watched anxiously as the cavalry "came back pell-mell" through the rain of canister. As the guns "thundered on," the captive colonel recalled, "the whole regiment melted off into the side alleys, where [Carroll's] curses and blows failed to rally them."[27]

Crutchfield soon saw a personal opportunity in the confusion. The fire blistering the street drove Carroll and his aides into the perpendicular side street leading back to the millrace bridge and South River. To avoid the fire, Carroll ducked into a house on the side street with Crutchfield in tow. The Southerner kept right on going through the house and out its rear door.

Most of the Federal cavalry soon bunched up on Water Street. There they were out of Carrington's firing lane and close to a retreat route across South River. The Charlottesville Artillery slowed its fire when targets vanished, then ceased firing completely when they spied friendly infantry pouring down the bluffs toward the North River bridge.[28]

Sam Moore capped his memorable morning by looking for a means to drive the wavering Federals out of town. A cavalry company under Captain Emanuel Sipe had arrived nearby at a gallop just as Carrington's guns opened fire. In a "hurried consultation," Sipe and Moore agreed to move down into the village in tandem to clean it out. The artillery fire had waned in the absence of targets, so Sipe led off right down Main Street. Moore promised to protect his rear against any Yankee cavalry that might still be lurking on side streets.

The two little detachments had not gotten far before they heard the shrill Rebel yell from the throats of Confederate infantry boiling across the North River bridge. To avoid running straight into friendly fire, Moore swung left into a side street and then pointed his muskets back in the direction of South River. By that time the street fighting was over. Carrington's two guns busily "shelled around very loosely everywhere we thought a Federal soldier might be lurking" near and beyond South River. Dabney ran across another stray cavalry detachment, under Captain Samuel B. Myers, and sent it into the village to help round up prisoners and horses. That, Dabney concluded, "closed the battle of Kemper's Lawn."[29]

Confederate success at the west edge of town had resulted from three separate stands by a mixture of defenders. At the other end of Port Republic, Carroll's raiders faced expulsion in a single climactic episode.

Jackson's earliest support on the bluffs of the left bank of North River came from the artillery camped closest to the threatened point.

Batteries under Wooding, Carpenter, and Poague all rolled rapidly forward. Much of their attention focused on Yost's Hill, whence Federals were hurling shells with great vigor. Jackson sought to use the first gun up, a Parrott rifle belonging to Poague's Rockbridge Artillery, against Gildea's piece at the mouth of the bridge. The general personally herded the Parrott rifled cannon through a field of wheat atop the bluff to a point opposite Gildea. Captain Poague reported firing two shots at the Yankee gun and implied that they drove it away. A less sanguine gunner admitted that the difference in elevation thwarted the effort: "We . . . could not depress our gun sufficiently for a good aim."[30]

Close behind Poague and the other batteries came General William B. Taliaferro's Brigade. The 37th Virginia Infantry led the way, followed by the 10th and the 23rd. A series of staff officers and then Stonewall Jackson in person had ordered Taliaferro to hurry. The coincidental assembly of the 37th for inspection made it possible for Taliaferro to obey, he reported, "without an instant's delay."[31]

Colonel Samuel Vance Fulkerson rode at the head of the 37th as it hurried forward. The colonel had been one of the first signers of a mutinous complaint about Jackson during the past winter, but Stonewall still thought very highly of him; perhaps he did not know about the signature. Jackson valued Fulkerson's competent control of his southwestern Virginia men. When the inept Captain J. F. McElhenney had proposed a few weeks before to "go home and fill up my company," Fulkerson evenly responded, "No, Mac, you go home and stay *there*!" The thirty-nine-year-old lawyer and judge was such "a great favorite with the General" that Stonewall's "eyes filled with tears" when he heard of Fulkerson's death in battle less than three weeks after Port Republic. Jackson wrote to one of the dead man's kin: "he was highly prised by me you may rest confident."[32] On the morning of June 8, Fulkerson had the chance to perform bravely under the eye of his patron.

Despite his prompt departure for the front, General Taliaferro had his brigade moving only "very slowly" through the fields as it drew near the bluff, according to an eyewitness. As Taliaferro reached the crest somewhat upstream from the bridge, the whole scene of conflict opened before him like a relief map. He could see that "some cavalry and two field pieces, had penetrated the town, and that a piece was planted at the mouth of the bridge, commanding its entrance and the whole distance through it." The piece pointing right into the bridge (which was Gildea's, of course) could not hit the 37th until the regiment came right across that narrow focus. Shells hurtling in from Yost's Hill did pose some danger, but most of them went wildly overhead and up North River.[33]

Jackson rode eagerly up to his favorite colonel and tersely ordered Fulkerson to "Charge right through colonel, charge right through." Stonewall's behavior was far less characteristic than his speech. He not only took off his cap and swung it around his head: the taciturn Jackson even uttered "a low cheer" before wheeling and riding on down the column. A soldier in the ranks heard Jackson encouraging the men to "Attack at once." Another saw the general wave his cap over his head again and shout: "CHARGE THE BRIDGE! CHARGE THE BRIDGE! CHARGE THE BRIDGE!" Taliaferro, whom Jackson disliked as much as he liked Fulkerson, reported that the army commander's more restrained instructions to him were "to charge across the bridge, capture the piece, and occupy the town."[34]

Perhaps to reach the covered bridge without coming under the gun's muzzle until the last minute, or perhaps simply because it was the closest route in a straight line, Jackson directed Fulkerson obliquely down the slope to approach the bridge from its upstream side. The general disdained spending the time to wheel the 37th from column into line as the regiment poured down the slope at an angle. Instead, "with a tone and mien of inexpressible authority," Stonewall ordered the 37th "to deliver one round upon the enemy's artillerists, and then rush through the bridge upon them with the bayonet."[35]

Jim Gildea's Ohio gun crew saw the 37th appear over the crest carrying its muskets at "right shoulder shift." The Virginians hurriedly brought their pieces around to bear and fired. It seemed to Gildea that the Confederates fired from the hip without aiming at all. "If they had not been Excited and taken aim," Gildea estimated convincingly, "I do not think that any of us would have got away." The hurried infantry volley hurt the Yankees, albeit not nearly as much as several hundred bullets should have done. The noisy fire spooked all of the artillery horses. Gildea's animals were facing to the rear, and they ran off in that direction with the limber chest, taking with them the reserve ammunition. The team dragged its lead driver, Charles W. Shaw, along to the rear as he clung desperately to his mount's head.

A Southern bullet hit Ohioan Frank Piles in the forehead as he inserted a friction primer into the cannon preparatory to firing. Gildea caught Piles as he fell and took the lanyard from his hand. The bullet had administered Piles "a glancing lick which plowed a groove up his crown." Gildea sent his bleeding crewman to the rear on horseback with an escort.

Sergeant Gildea now found to his disgust that all but two of his crew had fled. Corporals William Carey and Patrick Burns loyally stuck to their gun. The three men used a handspike to manhandle the piece right into the bridge, on the notion that "the sides would protect us except in front." Upon examining their resources the gunners discovered that they had precisely one friction primer among them. That meant that they could fire only a single round. Gildea had Carey ram down an extra canister round atop the one already in the gun. The sergeant then urged his subordinates to head for the rear. One man could set off one round without endangering the rest.

Carey and Burns stoutly refused to leave, pointing out that if Gildea fell they represented extra chances to get the shot away. "We stand or fall together," Carey insisted. Captain Lucius Robinson dashed into the tense tableau with entirely sensible orders to pull the gun out of the bridge and retreat with it: "Jim get that gun away, we have got to fall back." Gildea pointed out that he could not move the piece without the horses. Furthermore, if he left, the massing enemy would cross unscathed and capture everyone in town. Robinson accepted the sacrificial logic and hurried off to attempt to save his cannon near the hotel.

Jim Gildea completed his lonely preparations by affixing the lanyard to the primer in the vent. He passed the lanyard through the wheel so he could keep direct tension on it, then knelt down on his left knee and propped an arm on the wheel. Gildea watched a mounted officer aligning his troops. "In a few minutes, he turned, and his men having formed into column" began the attack that Gildea, Carey, and Burns had been dreading.

The bridge, Gildea recalled, "was a double span" of two abutments and a center pier, "and was about 250 feet long." The Ohioan waited for what seemed like an eternity as the Confederates came screaming through the covered structure at him. He thought that they had "gained the center," or at least "had got pretty well in the bridge" before he gave in to the urge to pull the lanyard. Standing from his crouch and leaning away from the gun, Gildea exerted "a steady pull" on the lanyard until the gun fired. Then "with out waiting to see the effect of the shot," the three men bolted and ran for their lives. They reached the cross lane leading to South River "in short time" and headed for safety at full tilt.

Gildea's hard-earned shot should have butchered several Confederates, perhaps even several dozen of them. The two canister rounds contained more than fifty 1-inch iron balls. Incredibly, however, after going to such risk to get off the round, Gildea had purposely not aimed it at the charging Southerners. Under the aberrant notion that his cannon could damage or destroy the bridge, he had "not aimed at the men, but diagonally across the bridge, with a view to weakening the timbers, and thus . . . prevent" Fulkerson's crossing. In another account Gildea explained that "the gun was not pointed straight into the bridge but quartering, with the intention of weakening the timbers and to ricochet the shots." A number of families in southwestern Virginia had cause to be grateful for Gildea's errant judgment.[36]

The Confederate infantry volley that had seemed so daunting to Gildea, but which hit only one gunner, actually came from only one tenth of the 37th Virginia. General Taliaferro had pulled the last of the regiment's companies from line "to deliver its fire upon the opposite bridge-head" so that the rest of the 37th could attack without deploying out of column and into line. Amid the noise coming from all points of the compass, men on both sides could be forgiven for accounting the company's fire "a terrific volley."[37]

Colonel Sam Fulkerson sat on his horse for a moment to gather himself for the charge, resting a revolver in one hand on his thigh. Then he shouted "Battalion, Forward, Rout Step, March," and led the way far ahead of the nearest subordinate. Taliaferro's official report described Fulkerson's deportment as "the utmost gallantry." The more reserved Jackson applied the same adjective to the regiment, but he also must have been proud of his favorite colonel's showing.[38]

The Confederates trotting directly into the muzzle of a loaded cannon displayed even more bravery than did the handful of men waiting to shoot it at them. Fulkerson surely would have been mutilated by canister aimed down the long axis of the bridge, and so would numbers of his followers. It is hardly surprising that a Confederate source thought that the length of the bridge was 450 feet, nearly twice as long as Gildea's estimate. Some Southerners also presumed that the dreaded fire that came at them constituted more than one shot, or even several discharged "rapidly." General Taliaferro concluded that the gun in the bridge never did fire. Others correctly called the single shot. They all could agree with the observer who said: "The wonder is that [Fulkerson's] regiment was not decimated." The actual loss by one estimate was two men wounded. At least one officer in the 37th discerned through the smoke and fire that the canister, as Gildea had intended, "took effect in the sides of the bridge."[39]

The 37th's brave plunge through the bridge probably occupied no more than a minute on the clock, though time seemed to stand still for the men awaiting the slicing canister balls. They screeched "a yell that rent the air" as they faced their fate. That "mighty yell" echoing off the bridge walls served the useful purpose of alerting Sam Moore and Emanuel Sipe to the state of affairs as they drove concurrently into Port Republic from the other end. W. E. Holland of the 37th vividly remembered the "high parapets" of the bridge looming over him as he ran.[40]

The men at the head of the 37th's column burst out of the bridge with intense relief, only to face a new threat: mistaken fire from men of their own regiment. In the excitement and confusion, soldiers at the tail of the regiment mistook their mates beyond the bridge for enemy and opened fire on them. A Rockbridge Artillery cannoneer looking on saw "a little fellow stoop, and, resting his rifle on his knee, take a long aim and fire. Fortunately, they shot no better at their own men than they did at the enemy, as not a man was touched." Attempts to shoot down horses of the escaping enemy cannon were equally ineffectual.[41]

As Fulkerson charged, the devout Stonewall Jackson solicited divine help. Jackson "drew up his horse," a contemporary biographer wrote, "and, dropping the reins upon his neck, raised both his hands toward the heavens while the fire of battle in his face changed into a look of reverential awe." Surely Someone deserved credit for inducing Jim Gildea to shoot at walls instead of soldiers.[42]

Two regiments followed the 37th through the bridge. The 10th Virginia, with its sizable contingent of local boys, would be well suited to rooting Yankee stragglers out of the streets. In fact, had that unit most familiar with the village been in the lead, it might have trapped more of Carroll's raiders. Lieutenant Colonel E.T.H. Warren, a peacetime lawyer in nearby Harrisonburg, led the 10th over the river "close on [the] heels" of the 37th. Fulkerson's regiment had moved slowly part of the way, but the 10th "made triple-quick time" on its march. The men saw Jackson just short of the bridge and, his prayer apparently finished, the general ordered them to fire and advance. Behind the 10th came the 23rd Virginia. It too met Stonewall, who shouted, "Give it to them boys."[43]

Nothing but mopping up remained to be done in the village. The 37th dashed past Gildea's now-silent six-pounder and tore through the streets in pursuit of any bluecoats the men could see. Supposing that the lower ford, near the confluence, was the only way out of town, most of the 37th flowed in that direction. By the time the 37th reached South River it had captured a number of Federals, but the Confederates could also see others swimming away out of reach. When Lieutenant Charles T. Duncan noticed Yankees in numbers farther upstream, he quickly carried as much of the 37th as he could gather together in that direction and opened fire on them. Duncan and his men were too late to cut off the enemy, but they inflicted casualties upon them.[44]

The thrust of the 37th was headed directly toward Sam Moore and Emanuel Sipe and their victorious Confederate detachments pouring into town from Madison Hall. James Orr of the 37th spotted the friendly troops. "I never knew where they came from," Orr mused later, but to his delight, "by the time we arrived . . . they had whipped the enemy and routed them." Moore felt the same way about taking part in the fighting in town. He wrote that the Virginians who rushed the bridge had cleaned out the streets "before we could get up to take part with them." The letdown that both Southern groups felt resulted from the fact that their simultaneous victories at opposite ends of Port Republic left a vacuum in mid-village through which Carroll's troops had fled in desperation.[45]

Although organization had vanished, and control with it, Confederates easily flooded Port Republic and swept it clean. Local boys from the 10th Virginia poked through haylofts and stables familiar from youth and dragged out Yankee prisoners. Fittingly, two of old Dr. Kemper's sons were among the first Confederates to sprint the length of the streets of Port. A few Southerners splashed into South River in pursuit of the fleeing foe. Beyond the river they scoured the woods for Federals, "bringing them in out of the brush, three or four or a half-dozen in a bunch." James Orr called this exhilarating phase of the battle "the chase and the fun."[46]

Yankee cavalrymen and cannoneers scurrying toward safety found neither exhilaration nor fun in the endeavor. Their share of those sensations had come and gone during the preceding half hour. From Carroll's vantage point in mid-village, the changing tide became evident in steady sequence. The Federal colonel remained hopeful even after Sam Moore's delaying volley and the opening rounds from Carrington's first pair of guns. Carroll had just ordered a cavalry captain to "charge and give them hell!" when he spotted the head of the 37th Virginia curl over the crest above the bridge. At that daunting sight, an uncharitable Northern trooper wrote of the colonel, "he changed his mind and disappeared." In Carroll's view, his cavalrymen were the ones overwhelmed by the sight of Fulkerson's charging Rebels. As the colonel stood at the intersection on Main Street, he "suddenly perceived the enemy's infantry emerging from the woods a short distance from the bridge and dashing down upon it at a run." The cavalry at once "broke and ran in every direction by which they could secure a retreat." Shields quoted Carroll as saying, "the cavalry fled [at] the first fire."[47]

Confederates advancing resolutely from both directions supplied ample reason for both commander and trooper to get out of town. Carroll's prompt order to the two guns to leave at once produced limited results. Gildea's was stranded at the bridge. Captain Lucius Robinson herded his other piece out of town and across the river. In avoiding the fire-swept main road, however, Robinson followed fleeing Northern cavalry into some woods just across the river. The carriage became so ensnarled there that he had to abandon the gun after a perfunctory attempt to hide it.[48]

While Robinson managed to get one gun across the river before hopelessly entangling it, his brother was less fortunate. Lieutenant Charles H. Robinson left his post near the hotel to join Gildea and his men, who had just fired into the bridge and then run toward South River. The lieutenant lost his way as he dodged through yards and alleys, was wounded, and fell into Confederate hands. Carroll did the two Robinsons full justice in his report, referring to "the noble manner in which they stuck to their pieces after they were deserted by their cavalry support," and calling Charles a "gallant young officer."[49]

The routed Unionists flooding toward South River used every available cross street as they scattered "in every direction." Numbers of them headed at once for Water Street, no matter how far east or west of the millrace bridge they might be. Main Street became untenable the moment that Carrington's guns blew down the fence at its western end. The mounted men on Water Street hurried west or east—mostly east—to the cross street near Palmer's store. Turning onto the millrace bridge, the fugitives thundered past Clay Palmer's overturned rockaway carriage and then plunged into South River. Fugitives who retreated on Main Street came together at the essential cross street, next to the Sons of Temperance Hall. There they "huddled together in a very uneasy condition" for a brief spell before dashing south to the river.[50]

Sergeant James Gildea and his two stalwart subordinates had scampered away from the bridge after touching off their one mighty, if ineffectual, blast of canister. The sergeant's horse was tied just across the street, but he did not risk the time to get the animal. They passed the gruesome corpse of one of Gildea's closest friends, Sergeant Christopher Houtchins, who had been cleanly beheaded by a shell. A Virginian who passed the same spot moments later and had never yet seen a dead man at close range remembered Houtchins as "a terrible sight" that remained "photographed vividly in my mind." Gildea and his mates caught up with their own limber and Captain Robinson's piece at the millrace bridge. The quicker cavalry had beaten them through the bottleneck, tearing up the simple slab bridge as they churned across it.[51]

The Ohio gunners completed a crude repair just as Gildea ran up, and the artillery vehicles bounced across toward South River. Men clustered atop all of the horses, hung onto the limber chest, and even straddled the cannon. When the artillery horses pulled their burden into the stream, Gildea faced the necessity of jumping in and crossing what looked like about sixty feet of water. He had never learned to swim, but, he recalled, "no with standing, I plunged in head foremost, and made [it] half way across before I came to the surface." All around him, "the water was boiling from the hail of bullets" fired by Southerners who had dashed up to the riverbank. Gildea quickly plunged below the surface again and flailed his way toward the right bank. When he came up for air the second time he could feel the bottom beneath his feet.

Jim Gildea's comrades riding on the horses and vehicles had galloped out of sight into the woods by this time, leaving the sergeant feeling very much alone. He was sure that every Rebel in Virginia had a bead on his back as he tried to "slip up the bank." As Gildea dug a foot into the slippery bank the leg collapsed. A bullet had smashed into his right thigh a few inches below the groin. Adrenaline alone enabled him to lunge up the muddy slope and dodge behind a large sycamore tree. There he found a friend, Salathiel Millirons, and asked for his help. When Millirons glanced back across South River and saw Southern cavalry pounding down the lane toward the bank, he abandoned his comrade and sprinted away toward safety.

The wounded Ohio gunner stumbled across an abandoned handspike and used it as an ersatz crutch to hobble into some nearby woods. Although the leg hurt and was bleeding "freely," Gildea stubbornly kept moving away from the river under cover of the woods. He heard the distinctive cheering of Federal infantry, then the thunder of Confederate guns in reply; the noises came from a brief Northern stand near Yost's Hill. Gildea continued his painful trek until he was beyond the reach of Southern artillery, then turned left and pushed downstream in search of friends. Two straggling cavalrymen finally gave Gildea a ride, after suspiciously pointing pistols at him. A gray-clad rider who approached the three men proved to be a Northern spy who had broken loose from captivity at Port. The man still sported a severed handcuff on each wrist. The spy's skill at escape clearly exceeded his spying prowess: he claimed to have learned that Longstreet had just joined Jackson, bringing Confederate strength in the Valley to precisely 38,000 men.

The motley cluster of cavalrymen, wounded gunner, and inept spy cautiously approached the main Union line forming near Lewiston. Gildea found that his craven friend Millirons had announced his death. As the reassembling cannoneers compared notes, Sergeant Otto D. Foster came in with a captured Confederate trooper. The Southerner had attempted to ride Foster down, but tangled his carbine sling around his neck in the process. Foster drew his big Navy Colt before his attacker could square away his own weapon, and came in with his captive as a trophy.[52]

Jackson's three staff officers who had been Carroll's prisoners took diverse paths amidst the chaotic Federal retreat. After escaping through a house, Stapleton Crutchfield dodged enemy cavalrymen galloping toward the bridge. They had been effective guards for a time, but by now were much more interested in their own safety than in his status.[53]

Hunter McGuire broke free from his captors soon thereafter. His guards pushed McGuire and his horse along with them as they fled onto Water Street. When the party reached the right turn onto the millrace bridge leading to South River, McGuire rode rapidly straight ahead on Water Street. Within a few yards he turned left and, he later wrote, "ran off by a side street and escaped." Two of Dr. Kemper's sons, confidently roaming the familiar streets of their youth, ran into both Crutchfield and McGuire and captured some Yankees at the same time.[54]

Edward Willis could have joined Crutchfield and McGuire had he not foolishly pledged his parole to his captors. He and Sprigg Carroll were old friends from more peaceable times. Carroll "was very glad to see me," Willis remembered, "and his delight, when I told him I was a member of Stonewall's staff, was uncontrollable." Willis accepted Carroll's offer to leave him unguarded on his word of honor not to escape. Willis agreed to that proposal because, he rationalized, he "was being exposed to a very heavy fire." The fact that Willis was weak and sick doubtless contributed to his sensitivity. When Moore and Sipe stormed down off the western knoll, Ned Willis found himself almost alone: "But it was too late; I had given my word, so, with a firm spirit, but a sorrowing heart, I dashed into the river with the Yankee cavalry." Confederates closing in delivered a volley of musketry that seemed like "a perfect sheet of fire . . . saddles were emptied; dead, dying and wounded men and horses floating and sinking as we swam. . . . I expected every minute would be my last." Willis glumly followed the Yankees through the trees then across open ground under heavy shell fire, keeping "a Yankee or two to my left" as a shield. He wound up miles to the rear at the home of a widow named Ergenbright, where friendly Southern women put him to bed.[55]

As the sound of hurrying cavalry faded away south and southeast of Port Republic, participants on both sides would have agreed that they had experienced fighting and excitement enough for one day. Carroll's artillery fire and dash into town, Jackson's hurried escape, desperate rallies by Sam Moore and two different groupings of Carrington's guns, Jackson's personal episode at the bridge, the charge of the 37th Virginia against Gildea's lone gun, the Federal flight out of town—all of that perilous activity and derring-do unfolded in tantalizing sequence before the vitally interested participants. The elapsed real time, however, cannot have been very considerable. William Allan, preparing to hide in the field behind Madison Hall, admitted that the whole affair "occupied a very short time." Jim Gildea did not estimate the total extent of the episode, but knew that once it broke up, it was over "in short time." Federal trooper Frank Cunningham thought that he and his comrades had been in Port "about 30 minutes." A well-balanced Northern account, favorable to Carroll—whose stay in the village would not be underestimated by friends—calculated that he spent no more than twenty minutes on that side of the river.[56]

The whole dazzling affair was of short duration, and resulted in but few casualties. Carroll reported losing forty men during the day, almost all of them in the 7th Indiana near Yost's Hill in an action yet to be described. He completely ignored cavalry losses, and reported only two casualties in Robinson's artillery (Robinson actually lost at least nine men on June 8).[57]

It is impossible to establish how many casualties Carroll's cavalry suffered in the streets of Port. Ned Willis's contemporary mention of empty saddles and bodies floating in South River must carry some weight; so too must McGuire's account of troopers falling around him during the charge he unwillingly joined. On the other hand, a Charlottesville Artillery participant declared, "In the whole skirmish I dont think there was any one hurt." The only blood he saw was on a wounded strawberry roan that black barber Edmund Drew corralled as a reward for his brave conduct. Captain Carrington rode through town and counted fourteen dead horses. In the Charlottesville battery, gunner Henry Clay Page was the only man hit; the wound led to his discharge from service. Daniel Brown ran away during the initial panic and never came back.[58]

The significance of that early morning half-hour lay not in mathematical results, but in subjective ones. Jackson had dodged a situation fraught with potential for disaster. The proud veteran army that followed Jackson received another injection of morale-building confidence. Jed Hotchkiss crowed in his diary what the entire army was thinking: "we drove them howling back—with loss." Near defeat had turned into heady victory.[59]

The staunchest heroes of the half hour were Sam Moore and his two dozen infantrymen of the 2nd Virginia. Moore himself stated the case immodestly when he wrote: "But for the gallant stand . . . against great odds . . . Genl Jackson would most probably have been a prisoner; Captn Carrington's battery would have been surprised and taken before it could have fired a shot, and the ordnance train would have been captured." In forestalling those disasters, "a small detachment of men from Clarke [County], rendered as valuable service to the Confederacy, as was ever rendered by an equal number of men, during the whole . . . war between the States."[60]

Dr. Dabney's endeavors to carve himself a spotlighted niche failed to detract from Moore's heroic record. The same fate awaited the egocentric General W. B. Taliaferro, who rejected credit for all Confederates at the west end of town by comparison to his own 37th Virginia at the bridge. Major John A. Harman, who normally was much more inclined toward carping than applause, summarized the affair: "the gallantry of Capt. Moore's Company from Clarke . . . saved the whole thing."[61]

Relieved Confederates could not long savor their victory. Other enemies promptly required consideration. A steady roar of cannon swelled from the direction of Cross Keys, penetrating the consciousness of Confederates who had for some time been able to worry only about their immediate vicinity. One of Winder's men near the bridge noticed the noise "about the time [we] sent [Carroll] scampering back." By the time Stapleton Crutchfield shook off his captivity and crossed North River to find Jackson, even the partially deaf general had heard the artillery fire from near Cross Keys. Jackson briskly told Crutchfield—no doubt without so much as a word about the colonel's recent ordeal—to look after the artillery about Port Republic. For his part, the army commander eagerly sought further intelligence to help plan for the day. Stonewall Jackson had moved quickly beyond the morning's excitement. He was ready to meet the next challenge with his customary intensity.[62]

**View across North
River into Port Republic
about 1900**

CHAPTER 6

THE POWER OF HIGH

GROUND

AND ARTILLERY

The situation around Port Republic clarified itself as soon as Carroll's survivors cleared South River and galloped away. Confederates once again held everything on the left bank of all three rivers. The swollen waters served as admirable moats, now that Southerners on their banks were tardily alert for trouble. Two Federal guns at Yost's Hill and some infantry supporting them posed the remaining opposition within sight. Jackson's batteries wheeled into a steadily lengthening line on the bluffs in the angle of North River and Shenandoah's South Fork. The two Ohio guns at Yost's Hill faced this menacing force bravely, if briefly. They did so without their captain, who was in the process of losing another of his guns as he fled through the woods near South River.

An advanced portion of the 7th Indiana had reached the Yost's

Hill strong point by the time the two guns there joined in the first fire into Port Republic. The Hoosiers watched with excitement that turned to chagrin as Carroll raised havoc in town, then left in unceremonious haste. During Carroll's incursion, only desultory Confederate fire came back at Yost's Hill, "at intervals, as if merely making a formal resistance." This weak Southern fire seemed to come from "a single gun at long range." The Federals' situation changed for the worse, however, once Jackson's artillery turned its wrath toward Mrs. Yost's house. The Ohio guns could offer no more than feeble resistance once "the enemy directed their whole fire" in return, Samuel List of the 7th Indiana recalled. Another man in the 7th described the result as "quite a lively artillery duel."[1]

The overmatched gunners could accomplish so little that the next few minutes turned into an exchange between Confederate artillery and Federal infantry. At several hundred yards' range—easy for artillery, too long for small arms—the result was literally as well as figuratively one-sided. "The whole transaction looked," to an Indiana soldier crouched under the storm of iron, "like an act of folly or foolhardiness." Billy Davis of the 7th felt helpless: "We were alone and unable to do any thing." John Hadley described the "terrific fire" hurled at the regiment and believed that he could count eighteen enemy cannon shooting at it; Carroll reported the same number.[2]

The deluge of Southern shells seemed particularly bewildering because initial Confederate resistance had been so weak. Most Unionists who wrote of their experiences around Yost's Hill were firmly convinced that they had been victims of a cleverly staged ambush. The Rebel batteries actually had hurriedly concentrated from different locations, but it looked to the Northern targets as though the enemy had been waiting in hiding. A suspicious Pennsylvanian near the rear of Carroll's column insisted that a carefully disguised Southern wagon train across the river actually "consisted of about thirty pieces of artillery with wagon covers." Another Federal reported that the Confederates had been "screened by some wagons and tents so disposed that attention had not been attracted to them up to this time." The same witness described the Southern pieces as "well served, unusually so, the shells falling fast among the men." A well-aimed Confederate shell hit the color-bearer holding the 7th Indiana's flag. Thomas Grogan hurried to pick up the banner. Giving his gun to a wounded man, Grogan shook the flag out in the breeze and bore it proudly during the rest of the day.[3]

Not all of the 7th Indiana had formed on Yost's Hill at the time that the artillery deluge struck. Some of the regiment had pressed on beyond the hill, following Carroll's cavalry with the intention of reinforcing it. A few companies probably had not yet advanced as far west as the hill. The companies strewn all across their front gave the Confederate cannoneers ample targets. The Hoosiers who advanced beyond Yost's Hill were still moving uncertainly forward toward the confused fighting in the village when Carroll's repulse freed Jackson's artillery to look across the rivers. The retreating Unionist cavalry and the front of the advancing 7th Indiana detachment came together opposite the rivers' confluence to form an attractive target for Rebel gunners. One of the foot soldiers glumly recorded the result: "fifteen pieces . . . raking us from all points with shell, grape, and solid shot."[4]

The advanced companies of the 7th Indiana pressed forward briefly but soon saw that their task was hopeless. They faced about and returned whence they had come, passing "again through their fire." John Hadley wrote proudly that they made the retreat "on common time," rather than in an unseemly rush, even though as a result the regiment lost heavily. The only positive result was that the infantrymen served to cover the retreat of Carroll's hard-pressed cavalry.[5]

The companies of the 7th that had supported the two guns on Yost's Hill made no pretense of retiring "on common time." Billy Davis candidly described the retreat as "in double quick," though he insisted that they executed the move "in very good order." Confederates shooting at them of course redoubled their efforts when the Federals broke from cover to retreat. Southern shells crashed into a pile of fence rails stored in Mrs. Yost's yard, sending splinters and wood chunks to join the iron flying among the Indianans. Several were hit by the wooden projectiles.[6]

Those Federals who had not advanced as far as Yost's Hill halted in the increasing artillery fire for a time, under orders. "After standing this fire for a short time," one of them wrote, "the brigade was compelled to fall back out of range." The last two regiments in the column, the 84th and 110th Pennsylvania, never reached the action. A member of the 7th Indiana referred derisively to the Pennsylvanians' "want of nerve," but it is hard to imagine what they could have accomplished nearer to Yost's. Colonel Carroll did not know that his infantry had advanced beyond the hill. As he galloped back with the retreating cavalry raiders, Carroll saw troops east of Yost's falling back, "partially catching the contagion from the panic-stricken cavalry," and correctly presumed they were the advance guard.[7]

While Unionist infantry pushed steadily and in some cases frantically down the road from Port Republic, the two guns from Yost's Hill limbered up and headed the same way. Infantry choking the road proved to be an obstacle. In swinging around them, one gun was "mired in a lake or swamp." The other crashed to a halt when its main limber pole smashed during the wild ride. The Federal flight swarmed around and past the immobilized cannon and raced for the shelter of woods farther downstream. After a short pause to catch breath and reorganize, Carroll's infantry moved more sedately to the heavily wooded hillsides near Lewiston. Looking back on the ordeal, Elliott Winscott thought that the 7th Indiana had been under fire for about an hour and a half, during which metal "seemed to fall around and in our ranks almost as thick as hail in an April shower."[8]

Confederate artillerists naturally enjoyed the results more than their targets; in fact many of their accounts are downright gleeful. The knoll rising above the left banks of North River and the South Fork at the confluence was part of a tiny settlement called New Haven in the early nineteenth century. Some citizens called the high ground Fisher's Hill. Under either name, the area served as an imposing anchor on which Stonewall Jackson quickly built up a strong artillery line.[9]

General Winder accompanied the first Rockbridge Artillery piece toward the bridge. Winder's impulse was to turn it loose toward the noisy enemy pieces on Yost's Hill, even if the fire from that direction was going high and doing little harm. Jackson intercepted Winder and ordered the gun directly toward the bridge. There it played a part in the dramatic vignette that featured Jackson's escape and Gildea's last shot. When more Rockbridge pieces rumbled up, Winder pointed them toward Yost's Hill. Captain Poague had accompanied the first piece with Jackson. After the 37th Virginia poured over the bridge, Poague went in search of his other guns. He found them in position under Winder's guidance directly opposite Yost's Hill. The two Federal guns responded to the heavy Confederate fire with "an irregular fire for some time." Once Poague silenced them, he shifted his fire to the ample infantry targets in sight. To his delight, the Yankees soon retreated "in considerable haste, leaving some of their dead along the road."[10]

Captain George W. Wooding's Danville (Virginia) Artillery took up the challenge from Yost's Hill as soon as Poague's guns did, or perhaps a bit sooner. Wooding's first shot snapped off a Federal flagstaff, apparently that of the 7th Indiana that Thomas Grogan then snatched up and waved aloft. Wooding put a second round into the same spot, then announced that he would hit a particular soldier with the third. An infantryman watching with interest swore that Wooding did as he had boasted, and that each bursting shell seemed to knock down several Federals. General Taliaferro described the battery's "beautiful service . . . the precision and accuracy of its fire, and the terrible execution it effected."[11]

On Poague's and Wooding's left, Confederate batteries stretched downstream in the direction of the Federal retreat. The road paralleling the South Fork gave them ready access to good positions. A staff officer who watched them deploy described the terrain as "high commanding ground which extended like a terrace to the left, parallel with and down the main river." Captain Joseph Carpenter's Alleghany (Virginia) Artillery unlimbered next to Wooding. Carpenter had let all of his horses out to graze that morning, in preparation for a day of rest. He was one of a great many Confederates "very much surprised" by the ruckus at Port Republic, but his men caught and harnessed the horses so rapidly that Carpenter reached the river terrace while the 7th Indiana still was moving forward. The Yankees were "at first very obstinate and appeared determined to move forward," Carpenter reported. A few rounds thrown with precision into the column, however, "soon taught [the Yankees] the importance of the about-face and double-quick in [their] drills." Winder, who came over to make sure that Carpenter knew what to do, noted that "the guns were rapidly and admirably served, pouring a heavy and destructive fire upon the enemy."[12]

Tactical dogma ordinarily dictated infantry support for artillery, but in this case the flooded South Fork between the opponents obviated that need. Nonetheless Winder hurried to distribute his foot soldiers near the cannon. He sent the 5th Virginia to support Poague and the 27th to support Carpenter. When drums in every direction beat "to arms" that morning, Lieutenant Colonel John H. S. Funk of the 5th Virginia had ordered his men away from their cooking fires and into ranks. Despite the obvious emergency afoot, he also had them load the regimental wagons. As a result, they did not reach

Poague until the Federals had abandoned Yost's Hill and fled downstream while Poague lobbed "well-aimed shots into their lines, causing them to retire in much disorder." In his report Funk did nothing to hide his enthusiasm for the harm done to "the insolent invaders." He expressed "but one regret, that we were unable to do more in repulsing these vandals who have polluted our fair valley by their presence." General Winder ordered the 2nd and 4th Virginia of his brigade to hurry even farther downstream, to cover the Confederate artillery that soon began leapfrogging in that direction to keep pace with their retreating targets.[13]

Winder, Poague, Carpenter, and Wooding did not have long to shoot at stationary Federals. "In less than five minutes," one of Carpenter's cannoneers estimated, "we had the satisfaction of seeing their ranks give way & as we poured shells so directly upon them, constant & terrific, every man of 3 or 4 large regiments was seen to break rank and retreat, every man for himself, for dear life. This is the most complete panic I ever saw." Carroll had four infantry regiments at hand, together with his artillery and cavalry, so the several Confederates who estimated that number were accurate.[14]

Infantrymen watching the unimpeded slaughter of their enemy enjoyed the sensation of victory without risk. One of them applauded his artillery colleagues: "I never heard artillery fire so rapid." John Apperson of the 4th Virginia called this "one of the most exciting battle scenes I have yet witnessed. . . . The balls cut through the enemy's regiments and threw the dirt high above them." The Virginian watched brave Federal officers trying "to steady their commands; but it was impossible." The enemy cavalry was mobile enough to avoid some of the artillery fire by riding toward the Blue Ridge on the Brown's Gap road before turning downstream. Even so, Apperson saw "many riderless horses scamper . . . across the field. When the enemy broke, our boys sent [up] a most glorious shout." Some of the cavalry strewed the road shoulders with accoutrements and arms all the way back to Conrad's Store during their flight.[15]

General Winder directed some of the Confederate fire across the river toward Captain Robinson's retreating gun and team that had disappeared into the woods, even though he could not see it through the foliage. The general hoped that fire into that sector might hamper efforts to get the piece away. Winder knew by careful observation that the gun never emerged into view on the road. The next morning, to his delight, Winder found the cannon where Robinson had been forced to abandon it, and two limbers as well.[16]

As fire flashed across the long line of Confederate guns, Winder discovered that their infantry supports were not only serving no purpose ("the enemy could not get at us across the river"), but also faced risk of harm. Soldiers sprawled on the ground "in front of our guns but lower down the declivity," were cringing as sabots from friendly fire crashed among them. These wooden plates, which separated the main round from the powder bag, were skimming out of the cannon and tumbling downhill. Once they moved back to escape the relatively minor irritant posed by the sabots, Confederates watched the rout of their enemies as though from the tiers of an amphitheater.[17]

Federals fleeing northeastward, parallel to and beyond the South Fork, would have passed out of range had not Charles Winder aggressively pursued them on a parallel route. Poague and Wooding apparently did not join in the movement, but Carpenter's Battery raced down the left bank. Captain Carpenter continued "advancing by half battery so long as [the retreating column] was in sight." In other words, he moved one 2-gun section downstream while the other kept up a heavy fire. Once the relocated guns opened, the others leapfrogged past them to open anew. By "moving my pieces," Winder wrote in his diary that night, he had "pounded in a heavy fire as long as within range." Winder, Jackson, and artillery chief Crutchfield thought that the guns advanced about a mile; Carpenter estimated only half that distance. One of Carpenter's men thought that they had pushed the enemy "4 miles from the Bridge & towards where they came from."[18]

The "novel sight" unfolding on the plain across the river, "of a retreating army pursued by two or three batteries . . . and retiring before them in helpless confusion," drew every Confederate eye. Randolph Fairfax of the Rockbridge Artillery watched eagerly. "All the firing was on our side," he wrote, "a kind of fighting which we all agreed was decidedly the most pleasant we had ever tried." Watkins Kearns of the 27th Virginia told his diary: "I have never seen more beautiful practice. Every shot told." Confederate limbers and caissons and guns "galloped over the swelling field . . . to other lofty positions, whence they still commanded the ground occupied by the retreating foe." Captain Hugh A. White of the 4th Virginia reveled in the sight: "We saw them, their guns glistening, their flags and all, and it did us good to see them in such a hurry to get out of our country."[19]

Unionist fugitives finally found peace and quiet when they reached Lewiston and clambered up the wooded hillsides beyond that beautiful country farmstead. As Colonel Crutchfield reported—and Jackson quoted him verbatim in his own report—the enemy "disappeared in the woods around a bend in the road." On the morrow Stonewall Jackson would fight the Battle of Port Republic for possession of precisely that ground; today it was nothing more than some mysterious woods that swallowed up his enemies. Winder's efforts to push artillery downstream did not end when the obvious targets melted into the woods. He sent guns, followed by infantry, to a point directly opposite Lewiston, a cross-country distance of more than two miles from the North River bridge. There they awaited an opportunity to do more damage.[20]

Although Poague's Rockbridge guns had not joined in the initial pursuit, Winder later sent two of them down to near Lewiston "to a position from which to sweep the road if the enemy should again endeavor to advance." The enemy never did. One rifled piece from Captain Wilfred E. Cutshaw's Battery apparently went the farthest downstream. The 1st Virginia Battalion, among the last Confederate infantry units to reach the vicinity, went down the bank with Cutshaw's rifle. When the cannon and its supports drew opposite the Lewis Mill near Lynnwood, they halted. The rifle went right down to the riverbank and unlimbered. The men of the infantry battalion "laid in a hollow nearly in its rear" and waited for something to happen. They saw Federals make a stand against a few Confederate cavalry scouting across the river, but never had a chance to fire themselves. Early in the afternoon the battalion was ordered to Cross Keys, where it would play a role in the final stages of the battle there.[21]

The whole army had been stung by its morning surprise, so Winder went to extreme lengths to avoid any further unexpected Federal advance. He thrust the 2nd and 4th Virginia of his brigade downstream behind Poague and Cutshaw and at the same time sent the 33rd Virginia far out to the northeast as a detached observation party. The 2nd Virginia, under Colonel James W. Allen, had been camped in woods beyond the fields where Jackson had found Winder that morning. As the 2nd arrived near the river, Captain O'Brien of

Winder's staff told Allen to protect the far left, where "a flank movement of the enemy was apprehended." The colonel threw out skirmishers to avoid any surprises (none was awaiting him) and hurried downstream. Beyond Cutshaw and the mill, he sent two companies to the riverbank to watch for trouble. Allen's regiment was understrength because Sam Moore and the other pickets in Port Republic had come from the 2nd Virginia. Even so, he was ready for anything that might attempt to cross. Nothing did, though he waited until after dark. In Winder's disappointed words, "the enemy did not again advance within range of our guns."[22]

Colonel John F. Neff and his 33rd Virginia went even farther afield, moving roughly eastward from position to position, "changing them every few moments." Winder described Neff's mission as being "to repel a flank movement." Neff remained a bit behind the 4th Virginia, which was backing up the 2nd at its riverfront post. One member of the 4th Virginia wrote that, despite the quiet, "we spent a day of indescribable suspense." Subsequently the 33rd was told to guard any possible fording points farther down the South Fork. Late in the day Neff received orders to move back toward the bridge to rejoin his brigade. Later orders returned Neff to the far left and stranded him there, ignored or missed by couriers, for so long that he did not reach the next day's battle.[23]

A single episode interrupted the uneasy calm that had settled over Port Republic by mid-morning. Colonel Philip Daum, Shields's chief of artillery, had arrived near Lewiston and instigated the action. Daum came with the advance elements of General Erastus B. Tyler's reinforcing column, which Shields had urged forward to support Carroll's advance guard. The artillery colonel learned with disgust of the gun of Robinson's Battery stranded in the mud not far east of Mrs. Yost's house. Although the contentious Daum was later forced out of active service, at Port Republic he displayed an energy and spirit of the sort the Union armies badly needed. Captain Dan Keily, the recently imported Irishman, had been seething over the abandoned guns too, since he had helped to superintend them on Yost's Hill. Keily and Daum rounded up eight volunteers from the 7th Indiana and set out on a daring recovery mission.

Confederate artillerists shot at the little party, but it persisted in its labors. The Hoosiers waded into the muddy swamp and tied a prolonge rope to the limber. Four horses hitched together on firm ground took up the slack in the rope and tried to drag the limber and its attached gun out of the sticky mess. The salvage crew "lifted, pulled and pushed" to help the horses "and after several efforts were able to extricate" the vehicles. Billy Davis, who was one of the volunteers, thought that the ordeal lasted more than a half hour. The whole time shells splashed mud and water on the retrieval team.

Daum had not known of the piece abandoned with a broken limber pole, but when he came across it during the outing he brought it in as well. Incredibly, all ten of the Unionists in the party escaped unscathed, though the 7th Indiana had lost forty men earlier. Colonel Daum noted with scorn that while he and the infantrymen recovered the two guns, the "officers, cannoneers, and horses" of the battery to which it belonged "could not be found for four hours afterward." The episode supplied further evidence of the absolute impotence of the Southern cavalry. With friendly artillery dominating the arena from nearby high ground, a dozen moderately resolute horsemen could have denied Daum's party the chance to retrieve the prized cannon.

Dan Keily came away from this adventure with a well-earned reputation for bravery. Carroll wrote informally of Keily's performance: "I do not think I ever saw a more perfect piece of coolness & heroism." His official report praised both Daum and Keily for "indomitable energy and courage." Four days later Colonel Daum called the eight infantry volunteers to headquarters and recorded their names, which appear in his official report. He also "promised each of them a commission when he got to Washington." The historian of the 7th Indiana wrote many years later with wry skepticism: "It has been a long, weary wait for it."[24]

Other than shooting in vain at the diligent little salvage party, Confederates around Port faced nothing more strenuous during the afternoon than coming down from the morning's adrenaline rush. The 37th Virginia returned from its brief chase beyond South River and regrouped near the bridge it had seized. Not far upstream the regiment found "a nice woodland . . . and stacked arms, and it was soon announced that there would be religious services." Now that the threat was past, the local boys of the 10th Virginia occupied Port Republic in the kind of strength that could have repulsed Carroll from the first. The soldiers of the 10th spread in a solid line all along both rivers "and stayed there all day," one of them wrote. Taliaferro urged special caution at the fords of South River. His 23rd Virginia went far upstream to guard a ford in the vicinity of Weyer's Cave.

Late in the day Joe Kauffman of the 10th wrote in his diary as he stood post in the streets of Port Republic: "have been here all day looking for the enemy every moment but they have not made their appearance yet."[25]

Confederate artillery spread out upstream along South River to further ensure the locking of the proverbial barn behind the gone horses. Captain R. P. Chew's horse artillery battery had been camped that morning far enough from Port Republic that it did not arrive until after the crisis had passed. Gunner George Neese remarked aptly that the excitement had come from Yankees "hammering at and threatening Jackson's rear—that is, if he has anything at present that can be properly designated a rear." By early afternoon Chew's men and guns had moved up South River about two miles to Vernon Forge. Later they went another mile to Patterson's Ford. Jed Hotchkiss, somewhat recovered from his fierce headache, positioned Chew there in obedience to orders from General Jackson. With that, the Confederate army had secured its front for more than three miles above Port Republic and more than five miles south of the nearest Yankee.[26]

Jackson also used such cavalry as he could scrape together to picket across the gap yawning between his own right rear and Ewell's left rear at Cross Keys. The army commander called southward some of the troopers of the 2nd and 6th Virginia Cavalry, who had been with Ewell. Some of the assortment of Ashby companies roaming the countryside helped with the picketing and scouting. Captain Edward H. McDonald, who later would serve successfully at higher rank, "spent the day watching them [Yankees]," and probably functioned well. These "few pickets," as a Jackson staff member called them, constituted the only link between the Confederate force at Port Republic and that at Cross Keys. Fortunately General Frémont was not the sort of foe who would probe aggressively to find a soft spot. The two Southern forces stood back-to-back all day long, forming a ragged W of no particular tactical elegance.[27]

Southwest of Port Republic, Confederate staff officers sought to unsnarl the knot into which the trains had tied themselves. As soon as William Allan sensed the repulse of the raiders, he abandoned his notion of hiding in the tall grain and hurried after the fleeing trains. "I rode rapidly several miles," he recalled, "stopping the running wagons . . . and sending them back." Some teams "had gotten too much the start" and Allan never did catch them. One ordnance wagon got as far as the outskirts of Staunton before its horses collapsed. Captain Asher W. Harman began clapping panicked "camp followers etc. . . . into the guard house as fast as they came into town" to squelch the stories they were spreading. When gruff Major John A. Harman heard of the episode he wrote to his brother during the afternoon of the 8th: "the cowardly dogs who carried such a panic to Staunton ought to be arrested." Harman added, ironically, that Asher "ought to send everything off from Staunton as fast as possible"—but without inducing another panic.[28]

Northeast of Port Republic, Federal regiments arrived steadily and piled up behind Lewiston to support Carroll's advance guard. General Tyler's column had marched at four A.M. from Naked Creek. The men of the 7th Ohio had supped on a meager portion of flour and beef the night before, but went entirely without breakfast before the very early march on the 8th. Someone told the 7th that "some hard bread was in waiting, some six miles ahead," so the regiment "cheerfully pressed forward" under the promptings of that false hope.[29]

Tyler's 5th Ohio apparently had a more provident commissary, because it halted after marching four miles and had some breakfast. Then it pressed forward again, "floundering along through mud and water and doing our best to get to the front and lend a hand." The 29th Ohio moved by similar stages, halting about seven A.M. for breakfast after marching five miles. The 29th's halt lasted something more than an hour. Not long after the Ohioans resumed their advance, word came from Sprigg Carroll about his adventures. General Tyler responded by putting his wagon trains behind the infantry and sending the troops "forward with all speed." By his estimate, the column was six miles from Port Republic when it heard from Carroll.[30]

General Tyler hurried on in advance of his infantry and rode up to the vicinity of Lewiston at about two P.M. As the ranking officer in the vicinity, he at once assumed command from Carroll. Tyler must have been chagrined at the condition of the two Pennsylvania regiments, which he met first as he neared Lewiston. Captain James F. Huntington, who would be distinguished at the head of his Ohio battery the next morning, noticed the "badly demoralized condition" of the 84th and 110th Pennsylvania. The Pennsylvanians had avoided any real danger on June 8, but what little they saw was more than enough. They "lined the road as we passed, calling out to our men, 'Don't go up there; you'll all be killed!' " The same men would be conspicuously missing on June 9 when Jackson and Tyler locked in deadly battle around Lewiston. Eleven months later they again exposed Huntington's flank at Chancellorsville.[31]

The infantry in Tyler's column came on steadily in the general's wake. The 29th Ohio reached Lewiston between four and five P.M. Curious Ohioans could readily see activity among their Rebel foemen on the river's left bank. Wagons and ambulances moved along the road east of Port Republic. More ominously, they also could see "a large force of the enemy across the river, could see the artilery glisten in the sunlight." The 5th Ohio marched up at about five P.M. and deployed on the wooded mountainside.[32]

Some of the newly arrived troops pushed upstream to examine the Confederate positions, but most of them simply settled into a vague defensive cluster. The 29th Ohio planted some artillery near the edge of its sheltering woods and waited quietly for dark. When no Southerners challenged them, the men of the 29th gratefully "encamped for the night very tired after marching some 20 miles." Colonel Daum's first thought after salvaging the two guns abandoned near Mrs. Yost's was to ensure the safety of the Federal rear. For that purpose he sent two artillery pieces back downstream to stand guard over potential fording points. With the wily Stonewall Jackson in the neighborhood, it would be hard to be too careful.[33]

Part of the 5th Ohio spent the evening as quietly as the 29th. Colonel S. H. Dunning, commanding the regiment, dismissed the rest of the day after its arrival when he said the 5th "lay on our arms till morning." Frederick Fairfax wrote in his diary that the 5th "lay in the bushes to watch the movements of the Rebels" without incident until dark. Fairfax noted that the regiment fell farther to the rear at dark and he got to sleep about eleven P.M. George Ray of the 5th calculated that the day's march had totaled 25 miles; he was ready for a night of rest.[34]

A detachment from the 5th Ohio sent forward to reconnoiter found considerably more excitement than most of Tyler's troops. Since the Confederates calmly ignored minor Federal movements on the right bank of the rivers, the scouting party had relative freedom of action. James Clarke wrote, "the enemy did not seem to care about us so long as we let the bridge alone during the evening." Clarke and his comrades stealthily moved to a point so near to the Southerners that they could hear conversations between Rebel pickets. A Confederate cavalry patrol rode close enough to the Ohioans' covert "that we could nearly tell the color of their eyes." Clarke thought that his detachment could have shot every one of the enemy, but that "rash mode of proceeding" would have put them in danger of a vengeful reaction. The Ohio scouts prudently held their fire and then "got out of that locality as quick as we could." Clarke later satisfied himself, on the basis of chatting with prisoners, that Stonewall Jackson had been in the passing cavalcade, too plainly dressed to be identified. The famous Confederate leader surely was not in the group that passed near to Clarke: his legendary status as the focus of Northern fears made him seem ubiquitous as well as omnipotent.[35]

While Tyler's men arrived and found bivouac spots, and in a few instances joined Clarke in looking for trouble, Carroll's men reorganized in preparation for more fighting on the morrow. The 7th Indiana attempted to recover from a difficult morning. They listened to the waxing and waning of Confederate artillery fire that came intermittently "all through the day, with no serious consequences." Stragglers from the 7th who had fled into the wooded mountains filtered in all afternoon. Surgeons tended Carroll's casualties, among them Sergeant Jim Gildea. The Indiana regiment's surgeon probed Gildea's wounded leg, then the sergeant's friends cut him a cane in the woods. Gildea made up a bed atop cracker boxes in his battery's wagon train and from that perch watched with interest as reinforcements arrived.[36]

The most important events within the Federal lines on the afternoon of June 8 involved officers deliberating on the proper course of action. Colonel Daum, the feisty chief of artillery (and the Northern equivalent of General Trimble as gadfly-in-residence), urged an immediate attack toward the North River bridge with all available units. In Daum's words, he proposed to make the attempt "at all hazards." How he would get any considerable force across the swollen rivers, now that they were guarded by alert Confederates in large numbers, Daum did not reveal. Tyler saw the impracticability of the thing, but sent out scouting parties such as James Clarke's 5th Ohio group to look for openings. The general concluded that Jackson's river-moated ground would defy 50,000 attackers.[37]

At a council of war, someone suggested massing the artillery "within range of the bridge, and attempt[ing] to batter it down." Tyler rejected the notion as impracticable, which it clearly was. The desirability of destroying the bridge had become apparent on the basis of battle noise echoing down from Cross Keys. Frémont obviously was doing something in that quarter. A dominant strain in the deliberations was uncertainty about Frémont's plans and achievements in the direction of Harrisonburg. Subsequent criticism of Tyler for not falling back to Conrad's Store instead of facing Jackson on June 9 overlooked the need to cooperate, even if only awkwardly and blindly, with Frémont.[38]

The noise of the Battle of Cross Keys made Frémont's proximity and endeavors readily apparent to Tyler. If Frémont should earn any success, Jackson might be in real trouble. Federal artillery on the ridge where Jackson's artillery now stood would control the entire tactical zone. There obviously was no means by which Tyler could get at the Rebels beyond the rivers. Since he could not advance, should he fall back to meet the rest of Shields's force? A dispatch from Shields to the "commandant of post at Port Republic" (Shields being uncertain who would be in charge when the message reached the front) confirmed Tyler's notion to hold fast near Lewiston rather than retreat. After talking with Carroll's officers who knew the ground, Tyler ordered the troops into bivouac. At the same time, Shields was sending a message to Frémont, "urging him to attack them with all his force in their rear at once." The position near Lewiston, which Colonel Daum had selected, seemed to be "the only tenable one in that vicinity." The events of June 9 would demonstrate just how very tenable it was. Soon after dark all of the combined force of Carroll and Tyler was boiling coffee and eating crude dinners in the woods about Lewiston.[39]

When the Yankee host descended on Lewiston, its first impact fell on the civilians who lived and farmed on the beautiful bottomland beside the South Fork. John Francis Lewis, age forty-four, was the most prominent member of the Lewis clan, which owned most of what would be the battlefield of Port Republic. Lewis had represented the region in the 1861 Secession Convention, in which he was the only delegate from the post-1863 boundaries of the state who refused to sign the secession ordinance. Lewis operated the Mount Vernon iron furnace during the war and supplied tons of war matériel to the Confederacy; but after the war he managed to parlay his resistance to secession into an anti-Confederate pose that left him eligible for reparations for damage to his property. (Anyone who had so much as routine dealings with Southern authorities was theoretically a Rebel and ineligible for reimbursement for even the most egregious harm wrought by Unionist soldiers.) After the war Lewis was a U.S. senator under Reconstruction aegis, and twice lieutenant governor of the state.[40]

John Lewis's sixty-eight-year-old father, Samuel Hance Lewis, lived at Lewiston in 1862. Father and son shared operation of extensive holdings that exceeded three thousand acres. The elder Lewis, a nephew of the Revolutionary War hero Andrew Lewis, had built Lewiston in 1820. The Lewises had played host to Stonewall Jackson when the Confederate leader passed that way at the end of April on a march that led to the Battle of McDowell. During that visit, one of the Lewis horses had strayed into Federal country. John secured a pass from Jackson to look for the animal. In reiterating his pure Unionist credentials after the war, however, Lewis insisted that Jackson "did not require me to take any oath, or to make any promises," as though such peculiar behavior might have been expected. To explain away his ironmaking for the Confederacy, Senator Lewis declared after the war: "My Sympathies were with the Federal Government from the beginning." Wicked Confederates "forcibly claimed and took a portion of the product of my Iron Works," he declared disingenuously.[41]

Federals descending on the farmstead of the Unionist, or at least politically resilient, Lewis clan received a pragmatically warm welcome. One of the Lewis slaves (the family evidently was not entirely politically correct) testified in a postwar deposition about Federal attitudes toward John Lewis. "The union soldiers considered & treated him as a Union man," Abram James asserted, "and said they had always heard he was a Union man. . . . They placed a guard around his premises and kept it there until the battle commenced." With permission from the Lewises, Northern quartermasters took corn from a crib to feed the army's horses during the afternoon and night. They eventually removed about seven hundred bushels.

John Lewis sat on the Lewiston porch with Colonel Carroll to watch the proceedings. In a legal document seeking postwar reimbursement, Lewis swore that both Carroll and General Tyler "knowing of their own personal knowledge that [Lewis] was a loyal man," promised immediate payment. "But before this could be done the next morning, a battle began . . . which resulted in the falling back of the Union troops." Lewis "heard Col Dom [a phonetic spelling that shows how Philip Daum's name was spoken] also say he would pay for the Corn." In a remarkably ecumenical gesture for a hard-bitten opponent of the Confederacy, John Lewis employed James Cochran of Culpeper as his lawyer to recoup payment for corn lost on June 8, 1862. Cochran had been a full colonel in the Confederate army, commanding the hard-fighting 14th Virginia Cavalry—but he won the case for Lewis.[42]

W. S. Baugher, whose smaller farm lay just above Lewiston, fared far less well than his more politically adroit neighbor. Tyler's men ruthlessly stripped Baugher's house and farm of horses, saddles, brandy, blankets, cash, and other property, worth $2,369. When he sought a postwar settlement for this thievery, however, his claim was rejected on the basis of disloyalty to the United States. Baugher's crime was being a Confederate collaborator: he had accepted $35 from the quartermaster of the 42nd Virginia Infantry for corn impressed for use of that regiment on May 1, 1862. That same morning John Lewis was playing host to Stonewall Jackson in person for breakfast at Lewiston.[43]

Mrs. Mary E. D. Sipe suffered extensively on the 8th too. Her home, not far downstream from Lewiston, served as camping grounds for the 7th Indiana. Mary's eleven-year-old son George recalled how the Hoosiers burned fences, destroyed the garden and farm crops, and thoroughly trampled the house and its contents. George's mother appealed in desperation to the commander of the 7th, Colonel James Gavin. He responded by routing the vandals from the house and posting sentinels around it. "No officer of our own army could have been more considerate and courteous," George remembered gratefully.[44]

The Lewis family members who lived at Lynnwood, a thousand yards north of Lewiston, remained loyal to their home state during the war and accordingly appreciated the Federal occupation not at all. Lynnwood, built in 1813 by Charles Lewis, an uncle of Samuel Hance Lewis, still stands in 1993. It is one of the most beautiful and beautifully situated houses in the Shenandoah Valley. During the Civil War, Anne Lewis Walton (née Lewis) lived at Lynnwood with Delia Fletcher, a granddaughter of the builder. Anne's husband, Robert Hall Walton, was serving with the Confederate army as chaplain of Phillips's Georgia Legion. To help the women, Anne's uncle Robert Fletcher and his wife Maggie moved out from Harrisonburg with some other family members. Mrs. Walton's sister-in-law Lucy Walton Fletcher corresponded regularly with her Lynnwood kinfolk and recorded their news in her diary. Lucy Fletcher's diary provides much that we know of the impact of war on Lynnwood. That impact would be heavy on June 9.[45]

Another thousand yards north from Lynnwood and across the South Fork stood the third large landmark house in the vicinity, Jacob Strayer's home, Bogota. Strayer's net worth as shown in the 1860 census was a remarkably high $130,500. His household counted nine other Strayers, including five males from 6 to 31 years of age and four females ranging from 16 to 25 years. Because of the proverbial power of the pen, the most historically important Strayer was Clara V., aged nineteen years in the census. Clara's diary of her experiences during the war survives as an invaluable record of civilian life in the Valley at the time.[46]

Clara and her family were startled on the morning of June 8 by the cannon fire a short distance upstream. Although the fire was of modest volume by battle standards, to the young woman's ears it sounded like a "most terrific cannonading that waked the mountain echos that had slept for ages, perhaps had *never* waked before!" The Strayers watched anxiously as gunfire and galloping men gave hints of developments around Port. Then a line of gray-clad skirmishers filtered into their upper fields. These were the outriders of the Confederate units protecting the artillery advance down the left bank of the South Fork. None of Jackson's batteries actually moved into Bogota's yard, but the skirmishers, Clara wrote, "could not resist the temptation of coming to the house to satisfy their hunger." To the Strayers' chagrin, none of their hungry guests knew enough about the fighting to enlighten them concerning its progress.[47]

June 8 must have been one of the worst days in the life of Frances Empsweller of Rockingham County. Her grief stemmed only indirectly from the armed hostilities. Frances's son Noah, a twenty-one-year-old laborer born in the county, belonged to one of Ashby's cavalry companies. Somehow during the day he fell victim to what county records called an "accidental wound." Empsweller's service record reported him "accidentally killed by gunshot." Noah's company was not one of the two damned for poor performance on the 8th, nor the one that dashed into town with Sam Moore's infantry at the climax. Perhaps Noah dropped his carbine and it went off; perhaps he rode carelessly into an overwrought picket after the crisis, when nerves remained highly strung. Whatever the cause, young Empsweller's accidental death on his home ground left Frances to bury him. When Frances filed a death claim with the Confederate government to recover the meager benefits due her, she hired a lawyer because she was illiterate. Happily, Frances's other son in service, Wesley, survived the war in the same regiment that Noah had served, and lived until 1905.[48]

After its stirring beginning, Thomas J. Jackson's June 8 leveled off for a time into the Sabbath calm he desired. According to a member of the 37th Virginia, Dabney finally did have an opportunity to preach the sermon he had been contemplating when interrupted by Carroll's guns. Near the regiment's camp, which evidently was north of the center of town, the soldiers gathered in the open. "Gen. Jackson sat on a large log," James Orr recalled, "and I sat in ten or twelve feet of him and observed him closely throughout the sermon." Orr learned that Jackson lived up to the piety attributed to him in legend: "He was as devout and paid as good attention to the sermon as if no ripple had ever crossed his placid brow, or [as if] he [had n]ever fired a shot or caused one to be fired to disturb the peace."[49]

Later in the day Jackson heard details of the defense of the village from his subordinates. Hunter McGuire reported in self-deprecating fashion on his exploits, which in retrospect included comic overtones. Jackson "laughed at something ridiculous in my account," McGuire wrote, so the surgeon added "as an excuse for running away from the Yankees . . . 'You know General, I never liked the cavalry anyhow.' " By his own account, the generally humorless Dr. Dabney concluded his report to Jackson "with this statement in the way of burlesque; 'So General, the affair was quite regular and scientific, employing all three arms of the service, artillery, infantry and cavalry, in their proper relations.' Where at he laughed like a gleeful child."[50]

Someone told Stonewall how much he owed to Sam Moore's little band, and the general had occasion to thank them in public during the day. The 2nd Virginia captain and his men marched past Jackson as he sat by the road on horseback. Moore saluted and Stonewall responded, "Well done, captain." Sam Moore cherished the moment for the rest of his life. James Dinwiddie of the Charlottesville Artillery had a similar encounter. The lieutenant was sitting on shattered remnants of the fence in front of the final position of his guns when Jackson rode past. Stonewall examined the riddled fence and said, "That may have been a raw battery, but they knew how to fire at the right height, and they did grand work to-day."[51]

One Jackson legend is supposed to date from Port Republic. A soldier in the Stonewall Brigade, so the story goes, said to a companion: "I wish these Yankees were in hell." "I don't," the second man

Cross Keys battlefield in 1994, looking south of east. Mill Creek runs from right to left through the middle of the view, at the base of the heavily wooded ridge. Mrs. Pence's house is in the left middle distance, below the ridge. Trimble's slaughter of the 8th New York took place beyond Mrs. Pence's place.

responded, "for if they were, old Jack would be within half a mile of them, with the Stonewall Brigade in front!" A Confederate staff officer narrating this byplay insisted that someone had repeated it to Jackson, who had laughed at the story.[52]

Between two armies as he was, Jackson left most of the decisions involving Frémont to Dick Ewell at Cross Keys. About nine A.M. hurried, worried orders had reached Ewell to send his "best Brigade to Port Republic." Since Dick Taylor's clearly was the largest and likely was the best as well, Ewell sent Jackson's messenger on to the Louisianian. The courier reached Taylor "in hot haste" with orders to move "double-quick to Port Republic." Taylor knew that "such a message from Jackson meant business." After a rapid march that exhausted even those skilled and mobile shock troops, further orders halted them. They had marched to within two miles of the bridge, but meanwhile the bobtail defense knitted together in the village had met the crisis.[53] Taylor's lunge southward toward Port Republic would not be repeated that day; instead troops from that sector would move north toward the much heavier action at Cross Keys.

Jackson made one trip to Cross Keys, which is reported elsewhere in this narrative. During it he ran across Taylor's Brigade in the road and helped to direct the Louisianians forward. For much of the day, though, Stonewall remained quietly in the village of Port Republic. Early in the afternoon the general and his aides joined General Winder "on the south side of the road and a short distance west of the Port Republic bridge"; in other words, where Carroll had posted himself during the morning raid. For several hours Jackson stayed right there. Lieutenant McHenry Howard of Winder's staff heard him say "in an undertone to . . . Dabney (. . . appointed by him to the wonder of many and the ridicule of some), 'Major, wouldn't it be a blessed thing if God would give us a glorious victory today?' " As he spoke the wish, Jackson's face held "an expression like that of a child hoping to receive some favor." Most of the time the general stood "silent, with his cap bent down over his eyes and looking towards the ground."[54]

So far as Winder's staff officer saw from his adjacent perch, only two messengers from Cross Keys interrupted Jackson's phlegmatic afternoon wait. Neither of them reported anything of substance. Lieutenant Howard was astounded, therefore, when Jackson presently roused himself and "in his crisp, curt voice" ordered Sandie Pendleton to write a note of exhortation to Ewell. The note was to announce the defeat of the enemy at all points and to urge that Ewell's Confederates press them vigorously. Howard was on horseback at the moment and his friend Pendleton used the shoulder of the lieutenant's mount to lay the paper against. Jackson had not been to Cross Keys for hours. Everyone could hear firing from that quarter, indicating a hard-fought battle, but no particular inference could be drawn from the noise; in any event, Jackson was half deaf. The episode was typical of Jacksonian behavior that built and burnished the legendary aura that clung to the general's eccentric brow.[55]

Robert L. Dabney, innocent of military training and sense as he was, began to worry about enemy intentions: would Shields not press them around Port Republic to help Frémont? Dabney finally approached Jackson to ask him whether they should expect Shields to attack again during the day. Jackson "turned upon me," Dabney wrote, "as though vexed with my obtuseness, with brows knit, and waving his clenched fist towards the commanding positions of the artillery," cited the cannon as his unbreachable bulwark. "No sir! No!" Jackson said firmly. "He cannot do it; I should tear him to pieces." As he almost invariably was when he understood the ground, Jackson was exactly right.[56]

Across the Blue Ridge near Richmond, Robert E. Lee was thinking of Stonewall Jackson on June 8. He was beginning his second week in command of the Army of Northern Virginia. Jackson and Lee would become an incomparable tandem in weeks to come, but they had not yet worked directly together. In a foretaste of their superb collaboration, Lee indited a communiqué to Jackson on the 8th that exactly fit the circumstances. Lee expressed the hope that the Valley commander could find an effective means to confound the Yankees in his district and slip over the mountains to help lift the siege of Richmond. "But," Lee concluded significantly, "should an opportunity occur for striking the enemy a successful blow do not let it escape you." Although Jackson would not receive this apposite advice until at least June 10, on the day that Lee wrote it, Stonewall was already doing just what his leader in Richmond called for.[57]

As darkness spread across Port Republic on the evening of June 8, Stonewall Jackson concluded one of the most unusual days of his career. The morning had exploded in close, frenzied combat, then quieted into a period of waiting that stretched for hours. If he looked back at the results in the vicinity of the village—and he probably did not, being not much given to either retrospection or introspection—

Jackson must have recognized that he had escaped the consequences of some lazy troop dispositions. In the words of Campbell Brown of Ewell's staff, "Gen Jn queerly enough, as it seems now, had moved no troops across the River and was only saved by . . . accident."[58] Jackson knew how poorly organized Ashby's cavalry was; he had been ardently combating the evil for months. Hindsight showed how foolish it was to leave all of the infantry isolated by a swollen river from headquarters and the trains. Foresight ought to have shown the same thing. Jackson showed on the 8th that he was lucky, as well as good.

During June 8 the Confederate army in the Valley also demonstrated that it had leaders and soldiers capable of winning battles without Stonewall Jackson's personal direction. During the hours that Jackson focused most of his attention on affairs at Port Republic, five brigades and several batteries under General Dick Ewell had soundly thrashed Frémont's Federals at Cross Keys.

A SERVICE INTERRUPTED.

**Soon word came that Frémont was advancing.
The men abandoned the open-air church
service, grabbed their weapons, and made a
metamorphosis from worshipers to soldiers
in a matter of moments.**

CHAPTER 7

FRÉMONT LUMBERS

INTO ACTION

As Stonewall Jackson escaped nimbly across the North River bridge, General John C. Frémont was moving ponderously from Harrisonburg toward the Confederate position near Cross Keys. By the time Southern artillery had established dominance over the vicinity of Port Republic, Jackson and his troops could hear the noise of battle swelling steadily beyond the northern horizon where Ewell stood across Frémont's path.

Frémont had arranged for the advance with considerable precision and detail. A written order instructed the pioneer detachments of his force and all "ax-men of every regiment" to depart at five A.M. on June 8, fifteen minutes after sunrise. Cavalry and infantry were to depart in specified sequence from the camps around Harrisonburg, one brigade every fifteen minutes, until by six-forty-five the "General brigade train" could fall into line at the end of the column.[1] Frémont was hopelessly optimistic in expecting full brigades to move into column on a narrow and muddy road within fifteen minutes, but at least the Pathfinder was projecting the energy and verve so necessary to Federal hopes of corralling the elusive Jackson.

The agility of the advancing column suffered from Frémont's ill-advised order of march. Each regiment was to move with its ambulances in the line, as was appropriate under the circumstances; but each unit also had instructions to carry with it enough wagons to convey cooking utensils. That nonchalant arrangement, reminiscent of Frémont's days of peacetime exploration, slowed the advance considerably. Bayard's Brigade of cavalry remained behind to guard luggage and protect the rear.[2] Jackson's omnipresent legions might materialize in any direction at any time; one could not be too careful. Frémont's rate of march probably did not affect the ensuing battles substantially. Had the opening rounds at Cross Keys come an hour earlier than they did, though, it is easy to imagine even the unflappable Stonewall Jackson somewhat bewildered by a simultaneous onslaught from two directions.

The Northern army uncoiled from its camps and formed in the road with banners flying under the early light of a beautiful day. Cluseret's tiny brigade joined the ax-wielding pioneers at the point. The 4th New York Cavalry spread a cloud of mounted men across the advance. Milroy's Brigade, the fifth element in Frémont's published alignment, went in motion on schedule at six A.M. according to an artillerist assigned to the unit. Schenck's Brigade, however, did not move until seven or seven-thirty, according to two diarists in its ranks. Schenck's men had been down the road on the reconnaissance the day before. One of them noted in his journal as they departed, with ardor he may have regretted a few hours later, "Expected to be in a fight to day, unless Enemy had *Skedaddled* again." Bohlen's Brigade did not even appear in Frémont's orders. Someone finally noticed the oversight, and Bohlen received his orders by the time all but two of the other brigades were supposed to be in motion.[3]

As the Yankees marched out of Harrisonburg, one of them noted how "the women gazed at us . . . their eyes streaming with tears, for it was their own husbands and sons and brothers that we were to meet in mortal combat." Another interpretation might be that the tears were tears of joy, prompted by the fact that the thugs generously sprinkled through Frémont's ranks finally were going to make war on someone bearing arms. The man who noticed the tears admitted without discernible anguish that Northern foragers had not been inclined to "confine themselves to the legitimate object" of their foraging.[4]

Frémont's strength cannot be established definitively. Tracts arguing about numbers and losses became a cottage industry on both sides of the Potomac after the war without generating nearly as much light as they did heat. A member of Frémont's staff with good credentials for honesty, and ample cause to know whereof he spoke, estimated it at 10,500. The proudest men in the whole array were the Pennsylvania Bucktails. Those hardy infantrymen, who had performed ably in the June 6 encounter that killed Turner Ashby, had been attached for some time to Bayard's cavalry. After wearily keeping pace with their mounted comrades through thick and thin, the Bucktails now could boast as they left Harrisonburg that they had outmarched the horses. Bayard's cavalrymen remained behind while the Bucktail remnant—"still reported to be in condition!"—marched off to battle attached to Stahel's Brigade.[5]

Frémont's advance encountered only token resistance as it moved down the Port Republic Road toward its intersection with the Keezletown Road. Two companies of the 2nd Virginia Cavalry perfunctorily harassed the invaders and delayed them for brief intervals. The commander of the Virginians was Captain William Fountain Graves, a twenty-nine-year-old farmer and miller from Bedford County. An Ohioan in Milroy's Brigade wrote in his diary that Confederate pickets resisted steadily, "disputing every step," so that the Federals even had to deploy artillery at times. The wagon trains intermingled with infantry brigades and certainly tangled the advance further whenever even mild opposition developed. Bohlen's Brigade, which had been omitted from the original order, now received instructions to hurry forward. Bohlen swung around the ambulances and wagons clotting the road as he strained to obey.[6]

When the van of Frémont's army reached the Keezletown Road, most of the regiments turned right and advanced southwest toward Union Church and the tiny settlement of Cross Keys. Colonel Albert Tracy of Frémont's staff noted that it was about eight A.M. when "the crack of rifles at our front" signaled the first infantry contact. The 8th Virginia (Union) of Cluseret's Brigade held the advance and fired the opening rounds toward Southern pickets of the 15th Alabama. One of Milroy's men timed the first fire at eight A.M.; three others said eight-thirty. Two Confederate reminiscences use nine A.M. as the opening hour. Civilians living near the battlefield agreed with the later time.[7]

As the Northern army moved into the area, frightened civilians came under fire, and some of them fled. A tavern and store at Cross Keys gave its name to the neighborhood. The long, rectangular wooden building had been built about 1800. The pair of large crossed keys hanging above its door were adopted from a bookstore in London, according to local lore. As early as 1804 a postmaster named Hancock operated the United States mails from the building. Rodham Kemper moved to Cross Keys in 1823 and ran the store until his death in 1845. His widow, Ann, aged seventy, was in residence when the war approached her home that June morning. She and her kin left early in the day because "the balls fell so near the house they were afraid to remain." The nearby homes of Dr. Joseph B. Webb and William Van Lear also came under fire.[8]

Many of the civilians who found themselves unwitting participants in battle supported the cause of Southern independence; but a number held views ranging from pro-Union sentiment to the more common neutrality of confirmed pacifists. Some antiwar Dunkard and Mennonite settlers sought to avoid identification with either of the warring camps. Families of those faiths lived thickly in these latitudes and west of the Valley Turnpike, but some occupied farmsteads near Cross Keys. Farther south and east, near Port Republic, they were not so common. Their careful behavior and principled actions of course did almost nothing to protect them from the hobnailed boot of war. The banditry that savaged the Valley in the fall of 1864 afflicted people of all stations. When David Pence and John Armentrout of Cross Keys filed claims with the victorious Federal government for losses to Federal troops, clerks scoured captured Confederate records and rejected the claims because both men had accepted money from Southern commissary officers who had confiscated their corn.[9]

The Alabamians waiting for Frémont held high ground around Union Church. The small brick building stood in a grove of stately oaks not far from the Keezletown Road. It was destined to see hard duty as an aiming point for artillery and then as a hospital. A visitor soon after the war declared that "Its interior was a ruin, and its walls showed many scars of heavy shot and shell." Until that bright Sunday morning, however, only rumors of war had reached its gates. A Confederate cavalryman who rode into the yard not long before the

Union Church, a small
brick bulding,
stood in a grove of
stately oaks not
far from the
Keezletown Road.
It was destined to see
hard duty as an
aiming point for
artillery and then as a
hospital.

enemy approached saw ranking officers inside. As the horseman dismounted, "a shell came hissing over the church, and burst a short way beyond," quickly emptying the church.[10]

A small cemetery just across the road east of the church was destined to play a role in the opening skirmish. In 1862 it included at least a few dozen graves. Two stones dated 1822 survive today. Some of the Valley boys fighting in the June 8–9 battles would eventually be buried at Union Church when they died as old veterans (one of them in 1913). Mrs. S. Fannie Wilson's tombstone, erected at her death in 1940, gives a birth date in April 1862.

As Frémont approached, the 15th Alabama stood alone well to the left front of General Ewell's amorphous position. Most of his strength lay a mile to the southeast. The only Confederates farther left were some cavalry and artillery several miles to the west, near Mount Crawford. The commander of that force described his mission as being "to prevent a cavalry flank movement on Jackson's trains at Port Republic." The small detachment was situated well outside the Cross Keys tactical zone.[11]

The 15th assumed a line of battle early that morning north of the Keezletown Road. The right of the regiment reached to the road. The grove of large trees around the church extended across the road; the Alabamians gratefully took advantage of its cover. Because the undergrowth had been cleared away, the defenders of the hilltop easily could see down to the church and out into the open. Colonel James Cantey, the forty-three-year-old planter and politician who commanded the regiment, soon decided to deploy two of his ten companies in front of the main line as skirmishers. General Trimble later complained that lax performance by Confederate cavalry necessitated using the infantry for this screening duty. Company A was one of the two companies that went forward, because it was equipped with Mississippi rifles capable of better performance than most of the 15th's armaments. Lieutenant Colonel John Fletcher Treutlen, grandson of a Georgia governor, led the two companies out on picket.[12]

Desultory firing echoed across country to the vicinity of the church during the early morning hours. Troops with the main body of the 15th Alabama knew from "the way that the Couriers and staff officers were dashing around [that] an attack was momentarily expected." Treutlen's little detachment of skirmishers came under attack "all at once," and the exchange quickly "got pretty lively," one of the Alabamians wrote. Having accomplished the assigned purpose of giving early warning of the enemy's arrival, Lieutenant Colonel Treutlen pulled his men back to the main line. Their friends watched the return of the skirmishers with bated breath. The men paused when they reached the cemetery, "frequently taking shelter behind a tomb-stone long enough to fire and load." A lieutenant from Company A lingered at the rear too long and fell into enemy hands.[13]

Meanwhile the rest of the 15th Alabama had sidled rightward to a position centered on Union Church. Now that the skirmishers had revealed the extent of the Federal threat, the 15th obviously needed to move south toward friendly forces. The Confederates awaited their enemies near the church "along the crest of a little hill with a gradual slope and open field in our front." Colonel Cantey and his soldiers, most of whom had seen little or no combat, did not have long to wait. Ben Martin of Company E later recalled "how funny we looked." The raw soldiers were nothing but "a lot of farmer boys who had never been out of sight of home before, with heavy knapsacks strapped on their backs, looking more like a lot of old-time foot peddlers than soldiers." Unmilitary though he and his mates seemed in retrospect, Ben always remembered the morning vividly because it was here that he "fired my first shot at a bluecoat."[14]

As the Alabama pickets settled back into the regiment's main lines, the advancing Federals paused on the far edge of the open space near the cemetery, almost as though hesitating to begin the battle. "A deathly stillness prevailed" in the ranks of the green Southern unit, one of its members recalled, "while we were waiting for the Yankees to come in reach, for we were anxious to get a shot." Colonel Cantey had just ordered his riflemen to "Cap your pieces"— putting a small brass percussion cap under the hammer in readiness for firing—when the Northern advance came into view. The enemy soldiers materialized at the edge of a woods in a thin skirmish line about one hundred yards away.[15]

General Isaac R. Trimble, Cantey's superior and brigade commander, reported officially that the 15th Alabama punished the Federal advance "by a destructive fire from the church, the grave-yard, and the woods." Trimble, who was not at the scene, declared that this stout resistance checked the Yankees so decisively that they could not pursue the 15th. Trimble's proud report, however, errs in both of its primary claims. "The men were anxious to fire," one of their captains wrote, "and I could hear the click, click, click of locks along the line" as the men cocked their weapons. Instead of ordering the regiment to deliver a volley, however, Cantey suddenly gave the command "By right of companies to the rear into column; double-quick, march!" Off went the Alabama regiment to the rear without even emptying its loaded muskets at the foe.[16]

The 15th Alabama had accomplished its assignment by developing Frémont's advance; but some of the regiment's officers questioned the validity of Cantey's decision to leave so soon and so precipitately. The Federals seized the opportunity to declare in the public press, after the disasters that befell them the next two days, that they had daringly captured the Confederate camps to open the battle. In his official report General Ewell noted the claim and wrote in rebuttal: "The camp-fires left by the regiment—no tents or anything else—were the camps from which the enemy report to have driven us." The "gallant resistance" of the 15th, Ewell declared, "enabl[ed] me to take position at leisure."[17]

William C. Oates, the feisty young (he was twenty-eight) captain of Company G, complained bitterly about Cantey's retreat. Oates, who did not like Cantey much anyway, later became colonel of the regiment and then governor of Alabama. He was accustomed to saying precisely what he thought; at Cross Keys he thought that Cantey flinched. Oates grumbled that the regiment fled from "nothing that I could see but a line of skirmishers in hot pursuit." An enlisted man in the regiment wrote: "Cantey rode to the right . . . when he saw just over the hill a brigade of Yankees in line of battle marching past our right flank. Had they known our position they could have changed front . . . and had us completely at their mercy, for an attack from that direction would have caused considerable confusion." Trimble accepted Cantey's version, reporting that the Alabamians "narrowly escaped being cut entirely off." Oates grudgingly cited Cantey's report and added with palpable skepticism, "I did not see that regiment; but the colonel . . . no doubt saw it." Even had there been a couple of regiments over the hill, Oates was ready to fight them. Later the 15th handled two or more regiments on numerous occasions. "But," Oates concluded with a modicum of charity, "it was a new business with us then."[18] Cantey clearly should have put up at least some token resistance to make his disengagement more effective. If nothing else, he ought to have unleashed the single crashing volley that his regiment had prepared. At the cost of a few seconds he could have given pursuers pause, even if none of the lead touched them.

The retreat turned into an unpleasant and costly experience because of Cantey's hurried departure. The men of the 15th Alabama scampered a full mile southward, losing cohesion at each step of the way. Much of their route lay through wheat fields. Colonel Cantey was so eager to find shelter that he led the way on his horse. "One could see the wheat heads flying on either side as we ran," one of the retreating men wrote. "The Yanks could take deliberate aim while we were fleeing. I felt like the frogs in the pond when the boys were rocking them. 'It was fun for the boys, but death to the frogs.'" The humming bullets outstripped the speed of the fastest runner. "Zip! Zip! Zip! came their bullets. Whap! and down went Bill Toney [a nineteen-year-old sergeant and 'one of the brightest and best boys in the regiment'] of Co. K, mortally wounded." Jim Trawick of Company G stumbled when a bullet hit him in the head, but he staggered to his feet and later found that the ball had smashed his hat and hat band without breaking any skin.[19]

The flight of the 15th foundered when it ran against a tall, strong rail fence. Brave Alabamians dashed ahead to throw down the horizontal rails. Some parts of the line ran into two or even three fences; every man who participated in the race southward mentioned at least one. The big knapsacks that the men still carried made their vaults over the fences difficult. Soon they would learn to carry only a modest handful of personal gear rolled up in a blanket, but on June 8, one of them remembered, "I know that we did look funny going over that rail fence with those big knapsacks on our backs." Company officers restored some degree of order once the fences were past. General Trimble, always ready to report events in the best possible light, insisted that Cantey's move came off "in good order," though Northern troops were "within long gun-shot range" on both sides.[20]

Trimble dismissed the loss in the 15th as "trifling," but in fact for a withdrawal of this sort the regiment suffered too heavily. Enemy bullets killed Lieutenant Wesley B. Mills of Company E as well as Sergeant Toney. Several others fell wounded. The return of casualties for the regiment does not differentiate between this morning affair and the unit's later adventures, so the precise loss cannot be identified; but the casualties almost surely could have been avoided had Colonel Cantey managed the retirement with calm deliberation.[21]

The novice soldiers also lost heavily in property during the retreat. They soon would have recognized the need to discard stuffed knapsacks when faced with field operations, but to lose them to the enemy was galling. "The most of those knapsacks were left in that

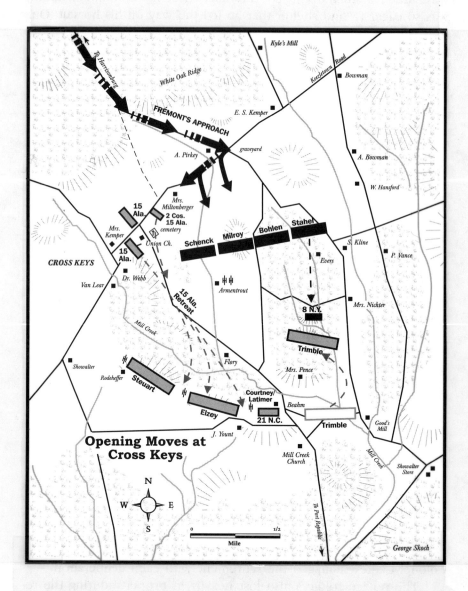

To Harrisonburg

Kyle's Mill

Keezletown Road

Bowman

White Oak Ridge

E. S. Kemper

FRÉMONT'S APPROACH

A. Bowman

A. Pirkey

graveyard

W. Hansford

Mrs. Miltonberger

15 Ala.

2 Cos. 15 Ala.

Mrs. Kemper

cemetery

Union Ch.

Schenck   Milroy   Bohlen   Stahel

S. Kline

15 Ala.

P. Vance

CROSS KEYS

Dr. Webb

Evers

Van Lear

15 Ala. Retreat

Armentrout

8 N.Y.

Mrs. Nichter

Mill Creek

Trimble

Showalter

Flory

Mrs. Pence

Rodeheffer

Steuart

Elzey

Courtney/ Latimer

Beahm

Good's Mill

21 N.C.

Trimble

J. Yount

Opening Moves at Cross Keys

Mill Creek Church

Mill Creek

Showalter Store

N
W   E
S

0   1/2

Mile

To Port Republic

George Skoch

field," one of the 15th wrote, "at least, I left mine there." William Pouncey of Company E sent a chagrined letter to the homefolks: "They came too large A force for our regiment and we had to retreat back to our forces and we were so near . . . rundown; we cut loose our knapsacks and left them; and that left us all without Clothes, only what we had on." Pouncey pleaded for a shipment of clothes from home and swore that he had learned his lesson: "if the Yankies get it—they will get me with it!"[22]

The panicky flight of the 15th Alabama ended in safety for most of its participants because friends in large numbers awaited them at the end of their retreat. Confederates on high ground behind Mill Creek hurried to help. The Courtney Artillery, a Virginia unit, dashed to a position near where the Alabamians were headed and unlimbered its guns. Ben Culpepper, one of the hurrying Alabama boys, recalled the welcome sensation of hearing the friendly artillery open. "It seems to me we ran a mile or more. I know I was completely exhausted when to our joy we found General Ewell had sent a battery to the crest of the hill and open[e]d on the enemy." James M. Rhodes, at thirty-eight a dinosaur in the eyes of the young soldiers around him, ran panting and gasping beside Culpepper. When the first round "belched out" unannounced over their heads, "Rhodes hollered just as loud as he could with what breath he had—something it would not do to repeat." Regaining his poise, and recognizing the effect the artillery support would achieve, Rhodes turned and shouted toward his pursuers, "Now damn you, I guess you will stop." The worn out Alabama troops fell in behind the battery. Before much time had passed General Trimble moved them eastward toward a position that would offer opportunity for easy revenge.[23]

Although the actions of the 15th Alabama had caused its members some discomfort, the effect served Ewell's purposes well. The skirmishing at Union Church had lasted "long enough to let us get position at leisure." The position that the Confederates occupied at "leisure" took advantage of both terrain and ground cover. Ewell described its features succinctly: "The general features of the ground were a valley and rivulet in my front, woods on both flanks, and a field of some hundreds of acres where the road crossed the center of my line, my side of the valley being more defined and commanding the other." A Northern newspaperman looking across the same ground from the opposite perspective wrote: "The ground . . . is gently undulating, covered with woods and wheat, or clover fields, alternating with marshy streamlets, ravines and hollows, interspersed with occasional farm-houses, and a badly frightened people."[24]

Ewell's "rivulet" was Mill Creek, which flowed neither wide nor deep. A determined individual could cross the stream without major inconvenience. A regiment, however, would lose alignment and cohesion in the process, especially if under fire. The steep bluff rising on the south bank of Mill Creek gave the Confederates a sturdy bulwark from which to fight, with the stream serving as a moat. Woods crowning much of the ridge behind the creek offered cover to the defenders. Short of turning the entire position, it is hard to imagine any attacker driving away a force of even modest strength by advancing through the tactical zone in front of Mill Creek Ridge. Federal attempts during the day would seem feeble and futile because of the strength of Ewell's ground.

The primary road on the battlefield bisected the Confederate ridge near its center as it ran from Harrisonburg to Port Republic. Just after crossing Mill Creek and climbing the ridge the road passed the Dunkards' small wooden Mill Creek Church, which stood next to a graveyard that had at least one burial as early as 1849. The cemetery later came to be the resting place for a number of Confederate veterans, including one who died while a prisoner of war a few months after the battle.[25] Because of its location, Mill Creek Church became the most widely recognized landmark on the Cross Keys battlefield despite being outside the area of major engagement.

A member of Stonewall Jackson's staff writing of the vicinity remarked on "the bright waters and . . . green pastures and park-like forests." After a return visit to Cross Keys in 1881, a veteran of the battle wrote: "It is one of the prettiest battlefields nature ever made."[26] The environs of Cross Keys and Port Republic remain in the 1990s one of the loveliest spots in Virginia's picturesque Valley.

Southern soldiers fighting under the devout Stonewall Jackson had come to expect, with a mixture of perverse logic and empirical reflection, that their leader would fight on Sunday rather than keep his Sabbath holy. A Virginian encamped near Mill Creek Church wrote that on June 8 "we were ready again for our usual Sabbath exercises, and Fremont was on hand with his congregation." The men of the 25th Virginia had gathered at seven-thirty A.M. for a sermon delivered by the Reverend George B. Taylor, their regimental chaplain. Taylor was making his points by enumeration and had just reached "Thirdly" when the noise of musketry from the 15th Alabama's outpost reached his audience's ears. Soon word came that Frémont was advancing. The men abandoned the service, grabbed their weapons, and made a metamorphosis from worshipers to soldiers in a matter of moments.[27]

The soldiers of the 12th Georgia were also having church. Their "beloved chaplain," Asa Monroe Marshall, had most of the men enthralled when a youngster in the audience whispered to a mate in "the most profane language." Van Buren Clark, who overheard the whisper, shuddered and thought to himself, "poor fellow, you know not how soon you may be launched into eternity. Sure enough, before the services were fully over, we were called into battle." The profane boy, Gibson Garrad Mahone, soon suffered a fate that earned his impious language mention in the memoirs of several members of his regiment.[28]

The Confederates who headed for the front from their camps and church services filed into position on the ridge above Mill Creek about 5,000 strong. The largest brigade in Ewell's command, the efficient Louisiana troops under General Richard Taylor, had been sent back toward the excitement at Port Republic at about nine A.M. When Taylor returned he would swell Ewell's strength considerably, but he would play only a small role in events at Cross Keys. By the time the 15th Alabama came puffing up the ridge at about ten A.M., the line had taken shape. Ewell deployed Steuart's Brigade on the left; Elzey's in rear of the center, supporting the artillery massed there near the main road, in front of Mill Creek Church; and Trimble's to the right of the road. Ewell intended to shift Elzey as needed, "to strengthen either wing," but in the event most of the latter's troops remained in the center all day long. Taylor's eventual return made his brigade the logical element for maneuver and reinforcement.[29]

The woods crowning the Confederate ridge dominated the thinking of both sides, even more than the commanding elevation. Ewell insisted, surprisingly, that his center "was weak, having open ground in front, where the enemy was not expected." The Federals shared Ewell's impression that wooded ground implied defensive strength. A New Yorker looking toward the Southern stronghold described emphatically the impact of the woods on the attackers: "The enemy . . . lay in ambush in the wood and behind fences. . . . In choosing this position, Jackson showed a sylvan science that should entitle him to wear an oak leaf for an epaulette, as General of the Woods." Men have a horror, the Northerner declared, of venturing into "dark, gloomy paths, where it is known that a foe lurks." A Confederate observer noted that the woods served Southern purposes perfectly, being "penetrable even by a column of artillery, in many places, but yet affording excellent cover for sharpshooters."[30]

Ewell, in sharp contrast to Jackson's command style, always sought advice from his subordinates. General Arnold Elzey helped Ewell select the line to defend—an easy task given the nature of the ground—and Ewell said simply and graciously in his official report that "the credit of selecting the position is due to General Elzey." Trimble noted that Ewell also consulted with him "at about 10 o'clock to examine the ground most desirable for defense." The secretive Jackson would not have dreamed of such a proceeding. Local citizens gloated inaccurately soon after the war about the strength of the Confederate ridge and told a visiting journalist that Jackson deserved the credit. "The wisdom and forecast of General Jackson had selected this battle ground at least eight or ten days before the fight came off. At all events the engineers were at the Cross Keys surveying and mysteriously looking about over the face of the country at least a week before Fremont 'caught' Jackson at this point."[31]

The mysterious advance guard that prompted local people to attribute prescience to Jackson probably consisted of Jedediah Hotchkiss or his helpers, who in fact were scouting the entire countryside on business more strategical than tactical. By the end of the Valley Campaign, however, no speculation about Jackson's powers and prowess seemed beyond reason.

Because the ridge wound its way disproportionately far to the Confederate left, and bent farther to the front in that direction, Ewell's left lay well forward of his right and also farther from Mill Creek Church. The left reached nearly to the Keezletown Road near Union Church once the line solidified. Had it been so situated when the 15th Alabama fell back, the regiment's retreat would best have gone west instead of south. The high open space where the road bisected the ridge served as an aerie—a formidable one, Ewell's disclaimer notwithstanding—from which Southern artillery could sweep the field. The Courtney Artillery, which had proved such a relief to the 15th Alabama, set up there in the open, but covered to some degree by the crest of the hill. Another battery "was under the hill in reserve—& the supporting Reg't lay halfway down the southern slope."[32]

That supporting regiment was the 21st North Carolina. Eli S. Coble of the 21st recalled marching toward the position under beautiful skies, "a lovely morning, fair, not a cloud to be seen." Coble's regiment was "up near the brow of the . . . hill," with its extreme right exactly on the road. Together with everyone else who ever saw him, Coble spoke warmly of Lieutenant Joseph White Latimer, the artillerist commanding the battery in front of the Tarheels. Latimer was only eighteen years old, but had attended the Virginia Military Institute and was widely recognized as, in Coble's words, a "cheery noble spirited boy Captain." Another infantryman said of Latimer: "I believe he is the very best Arty. Capt. . . . & I know we have worse Generals by far than he wd. make." Soldiers of the division to which the "small & slight" Latimer was attached often cheered him as he passed, "a distinction they conferred on very few." This brilliant, popular youngster would be the guiding spirit of the Confederate artillery at Cross Keys all day long on June 8.[33]

Among the troops who filed past the center en route to Ewell's left were the men of the 1st Maryland. The Marylanders had fought stoutly on June 6 against the Pennsylvania Bucktails at the time that Ashby went down. Many of the men had confiscated the bucktails sported by Pennsylvanians whom they had captured, and stuck them on their own caps as souvenirs. Dick Ewell noticed the display as the 1st Maryland marched past him and called over Colonel Bradley T. Johnson. "Colonel, you must carry a bucktail on your colors as your trophy," the general said, "for you won it on Friday." The colonel borrowed the nearest bucktail, which perched on the head of a long-legged boy named Ryan. "Tie it to the head of the colors yourself," Johnson told Ryan, "and your trophy shall be the trophy of the regiment." The martial moment became one of the fondest memories of the Maryland unit, which soon disbanded at the end of its year's enlistment, and in fact one of Confederate Maryland's proudest traditions.[34]

The Confederate line to the right of the artillery knoll and the main road initially followed the same ridge that held the rest of Ewell's line. Trimble and his brigade occupied a very abrupt hillock there covered with pine trees. Most of the line ran through hardwood forests, so Trimble could refer with clarity to his position as "the pine hill." Trimble did not occupy the forward crest, instead placing his regiments "somewhat retired from the front" in a staggered formation that faded away toward the rear. The aggressive Trimble at once left his brigade in line and reconnoitered to his front hoping to find a better position. He would not find a location better suited to standing on the defensive anywhere near Mill Creek—but Trimble's goal, as usual with him, was to locate offensive action wherever it might be found.[35]

While Ewell's infantry regiments settled into position on their commanding ridge, his cavalry undertook the screening function that constituted its primary defensive role. Colonel Thomas T. Munford held titular command of the cavalry on the field, although most of the disorganized companies that had followed Ashby had no thought of yielding fealty to a strange officer; even Ashby's fond and gentle hold on them had been tenuous at best. Munford did have on hand portions of the 2nd and 6th Virginia Cavalry regiments that were accustomed to doing what colonels told them to do. These picketed on the right of the Confederate position all the way out to "the McGaheysville road." A number of roads meandered toward that village on Massanutten's southeastern toe. Munford's sphere of influence extended well beyond what would soon become the battle zone.[36]

A battalion of seasoned horsemen from northern Virginia who styled themselves "the Comanches" served Ewell's headquarters as guards, couriers, and provost detachment. The general sent out Captain Frank Myers of the Comanches with another trooper to scout in the same direction that Munford was operating. Ewell clearly was uncomfortable about that flank.[37] It is easy to see why. The heart of his defense lay where the road crossed the ridge, where he had emplanted the powerful artillery cluster. The infantry line ran fully twice as far to the left as to the right. The truncated main line on the right made the general uneasy about its security.

With the line set and battle drawing near, Southerners of all ranks must have contemplated their situation with some amazement. One Marylander on Ewell's left remarked upon the novel sensation that many surely felt. He recalled the "singular spectacle of two [Confederate] armies standing back to back, facing a foe in front and rear, & but three miles apart."[38]

Richard S. Ewell commanded the Cross Keys half of the back-to-back Confederate formation in splendid isolation. He had become comfortable doing precisely as Jackson told him in recent weeks, an arrangement that suited both men. Now Jackson left him to his own devices for the first time. Stonewall remained riveted near Port Republic for most of this day, except during one brief visit to Ewell's front.

Whether Ewell welcomed the unaccustomed independence can be doubted. Campbell Brown, who soon would become the general's stepson, wrote home to his mother—Ewell's intended—at about this time to complain of his chief's tendency to avoid asserting himself. Brown superciliously told his doting mother of "one defect in the temper" of General Ewell, and professed to know that the entire Ewell clan shared it. The deadly flaw was that, "having formed an idea that his advice will be ungraciously received & perhaps his interference rebuffed, he refuses to interpose in any way." Mrs. Brown herself held dreadful sway over Dick Ewell, so Campbell's concluding admonition that she must never "say a word to him about . . . any such thing as this" was completely disingenuous.[39] Strength of will aside, Ewell was very much a soldier. He would wield the discretion thrust upon him with calm competence on June 8.

Blue-clad soldiers filing into position behind the crests of the ridges and hillocks opposite Ewell could see at a glance the strength of the Southern position. An artillerist from Ohio (most of the Yankees hailed from the Midwest) described the daunting sight of Confederates "occupying an amphitheater of hills from which twice Fremont's force could not have dislodged him." On the other hand, the endless pursuit under wretched conditions clearly had come to an end. Another Ohioan gloried in the chance to close at last with the elusive foe who had led them on such a weary chase. "The day had now come which [we] had sought for about 16 days," the infantryman wrote. He and his mates in the 25th Ohio had endured "intolerable suffering and exposure." Now, "reduced by exposure, fatigue and sickness to half" its original strength, the 25th Ohio was eager to fight a more tangible foe.[40]

When General Frémont and his entourage crossed White Oak Ridge, which parallels the Keezletown Road, they saw smoke from dozens of Confederate campfires on the Mill Creek Ridge more than a mile to their front. As he reached what the locals call Perkey's Crossroads and turned right onto the Keezletown Road, the Northern leader probably was resolved to press the issue. He must have been starved for information. While Ewell knew precisely whence help could reach him—from the incomparably reliable Jackson—Frémont had only the vaguest notion about the meaning of the firing he heard from the south. Whether he would find friends and support remained problematic. Ewell suffered from no such doubts. In that atmosphere the Federals looked over the stern options facing them.[41]

Albert Tracy of Frémont's staff described how the Confederate line appeared. The headquarters party had responded to the sound of firing that accompanied the retreat of the 15th Alabama by hurrying forward. The cavalcade "drove in their spurs, and galloped in the direction of the firing." Frémont and his friends dashed past the long, clotted column and splashed through mud puddles. Two shells that landed near them as they approached the field—probably fired by the Courtney Artillery as it repulsed the pursuers of the 15th Alabama—smothered themselves in the mud and did no harm. The Southern position looming before Frémont and Tracy and the others when they emerged on what would be the battlefield was, Tracy wrote, situated on "an elevation upon the opposite side of a hollow considerably broken, and, in parts, wooded . . . upon a somewhat precipitous ridge, beyond a stream, with a marshy flat at the hither side."[42]

The crescent ridge before the Federals stood out so clearly that they thought they could understand it at a glance. The Confederate left, reaching up to near Union Church, seemed most immediately threatening. Tracy described it as "curving somewhat, inclined towards us." In responding to that apparent threat, Frémont made a mistake. He advanced his own left to parallel Ewell's ridge between Mill Creek Church and Union Church. That caused the Federal left, on the eastern end of the field, to be somewhat exposed. A Confederate participant who would become a historian of the campaign after the war summarized the result: "This movement, which was boldly and skillfully executed, brought [Frémont's] whole line into a dangerous position, which he, apparently, did not comprehend in his ignorance of the topographic conditions of the field, but it gave Ewell an opportunity to detach Trimble's brigade from his right, move it through a forest, and reform it opposite Fremont's left."[43] The resulting action in that corner of the field would decide the Battle of Cross Keys.

Since launching the active phase of his campaign at Kernstown on March 23, Stonewall Jackson had marched hundreds of miles and fought battles and skirmishes all along the way. Although his army never had numbered more than 17,000 muskets, and had been pursued by three times that many enemy troops, Jackson invariably had put superior numbers into action when battles erupted—until June 8. Only at Cross Keys did tactical strength favor Northern arms. The Northern commander had twice as many men under his control as did Ewell. Frémont's great opportunity had arrived.[44]

CHAPTER 8

THE ROAR OF

ARTILLERY

Tactical doctrine called for identifying a defensive position by advancing skirmishers against it. Frémont's subordinate commanders did that as they approached the formidable Confederate ridge. "The enemy felt along my front with skirmishers," Ewell reported, "and shortly after posted his artillery, chiefly opposite mine." A Southern officer who watched the tentative approach expressed surprise at its timid character. During the tense encounters of the past weeks Federal skirmishers and advance units "had proved bold and enterprising," but now they "yielded to the slightest pressure." The Southern observer concluded that the presence of the maladroit Frémont "had a benumbing influence on his troops."[1]

General Robert H. Milroy approached the action in a far from diffident mood, at least by his own account. Milroy's ardor would make him one of the most loathed men in the Valley the following year because of draconian orders he issued about treatment of civilians. At Cross Keys, Milroy wrote to his wife, he "dashed on ahead of my Bgd. as soon as I heard the thunder of battle ahead—was shown the place where I was to form—I had hurried on my artillery (3 batteries) . . . I immediately threw them into position."[2]

Colonel Anselm Albert and Lieutenant Colonel John Pilsen of Frémont's staff bore the primary responsibility for aligning the Federal troops. Pilsen posted the artillery "along the crests of a species of intermediate minor elevations." General Robert C. Schenck's Brigade went to the Federal far right; Milroy's dash took him to the right center; General Henry Bohlen took position on the left center with his brigade; and General Julius Stahel's Brigade had the misfortune to wind up on Frémont's exposed left. Frémont's vague notion was, one of his staff wrote, "in the main . . . to turn the rebels at their right or strategic flank."[3] There was nothing wrong with the concept generally, but executing it from his own most vulnerable point was a fatal mistake.

The Courtney Artillery had been in position near the main road since firing to cover the hurried return of the 15th Alabama. Ewell built an artillery mass around the guns as the Federal threat grew in strength. Elzey's Brigade supported the main artillery cluster from nearby ground that provided shelter. The woods on either flank looked inviting to Elzey's men, but their duty held them in the open fields, crouching behind the crests of the uneven ridge. The broad expanse of open ground commanded by the Southern artillery's muzzles offered a splendid field of fire.[4]

Elzey's men could not move forward of the cannon as skirmishers because the bare terrain offered them no cover. Farther to Ewell's left the wooded ground provided an entirely different battle setting. The Confederates posted fewer artillery pieces there because of the limited vantage points. The infantrymen of General George H. "Maryland" Steuart's Brigade, however, could ply their deadly trade more effectively. Steuart's 58th Virginia lay down in the woods. His 52nd Virginia remained a bit farther to the rear, ready to react to crises or opportunities. The brigade's other regiment, the 44th Virginia, pushed ahead and to the left to provide forward protection. Half of the 44th went straight ahead into "the wood near our most advanced battery on the left." Thirty-eight-year-old Major Norvell Cobb, who commanded that detachment, had been a prosperous hotelkeeper in Farmville before the war. The other half of the regiment advanced far leftward, to the vicinity of the main road near Cross Keys, under the command of Captain Thomas Roy Buckner. Captain Buckner was twenty-five, educated at the University of Virginia, and one of eighteen children in a Caroline County family. No Southerner held a more precarious position at Cross Keys than Buckner, but a quiescent Federal command blithely ignored the tender Confederate left most of the day.[5]

The artillery arrayed on the opposing hills did not wait for a formal signal to open fire with a grand, synchronized volley. Individual batteries began to belch flame and smoke and iron, and soon the cacophony shook the ground and battered the senses of men caught in its midst. Within minutes after the artillery duel began, it reached a deafening crescendo—and held the note for an hour or more. The timing of the opening of the artillery exchange does not matter greatly of itself; but as a benchmark related to other actions, both at Cross Keys and within hearing at Port Republic, the time needs to be approximated. The hour most often cited by participants was ten A.M, but one Confederate specified nine A.M., and Campbell Brown insisted that the time was eleven A.M. A reasonable estimate is that Courtney first fired near ten, with the main duel swelling by about ten-thirty. Supporting that notion is the Federal statement that Lieutenant Colonel Pilsen put the batteries into operation over a period of about one-half hour, and Ewell's report that "About 10 o'clock the enemy felt along my front with skirmishers, and shortly after posted his artillery."[6]

Joining the Courtney Artillery at the focus of the firestorm were the 2nd Rockbridge Artillery, a Virginia battery commanded by Captain John A. M. Lusk; the Baltimore Light Artillery, under Captain John B. Brockenbrough; and the Lee Artillery of Virginia, led by Captain Charles I. Raine. The four batteries mustered at least sixteen guns. They fired from "the reverse of the hills, a little behind the crest, where the cannoneers were protected from all missiles which came horizontally." Not all missiles were so accommodating in their trajectory, of course, but the advantage was an enormous one. The "lively cannonading" that ensued became "for a time . . . very brisk," according to a Southern officer, "then we got the upper hand." The

Federals brought in more and more pieces as they managed to press past the muddy bottlenecks in the road, but the Confederates retained the advantage.[7]

General Ewell thought that his artillery performed admirably, though "exposed to a terrible storm of shot and shell." Writing a week after the battle, presumably on the basis of comments from prisoners or Northern newspapers, Ewell boasted: "The enemy testifies to the efficiency of [the Confederate batteries'] fire." The general "was well satisfied with them all," but especially lauded Courtney's and Brockenbrough's batteries. Ewell paid those two a warm compliment: "I can testify to their efficiency." Courtney's brilliant lieutenant, J. W. Latimer, won kudos from Trimble. The general brevetted Latimer to captain—an action he had no authority to take, but the War Department soon validated the rank. One of the most famous gunners of the Confederacy was on his way to the status of a legend—and to his death before he reached his twentieth birthday.[8]

None of the indignities that war imposes on infantry is more disheartening than lying helpless under artillery fire without any way to fight back. Three companies of 21st North Carolina Infantry faced that unhappy lot as they huddled behind the guns while Latimer distinguished himself. The regimental commander had the good sense to put only that token force at the heart of the maelstrom, keeping the rest of the 21st nearby but under better shelter and "in a manner out of it." Eli Coble was one of the unfortunate men in the front line. He could see the hostile cannon shooting at him, grouped near the main road not far from the Armentrout house. Coble identified the missiles hurled toward him as a mixture of explosive shells and solid shot: "the shots came in rapid succession." "The conflict," Private Coble declared, "was terrific."[9]

The 16th Mississippi Infantry of Trimble's Brigade spent some time just across the road from Coble's position. The 16th was destined to become a sturdy, veteran unit. On June 8, however, it had not yet seen any heavy combat and had come under hostile fire for the first time only two weeks before. A volunteer in the 16th who came from a Mississippi Indian tribe found out about artillery in company with the rest of the regiment. When he heard the first cannon fire, the man "was badly frightened and started back the other way" (as did many another soldier, of course). When a second round roared over him, though, the Confederate Indian "came back and said that there was as much danger in the rear as there was at the front, so he decided to stay," and became one of the most reliable soldiers in the 16th Mississippi.[10]

Among the most interested Southerners watching the artillery duel were civilians who looked on from afar, in safety but also in worried ignorance of its progress. Families near Harrisonburg climbed the highest elevations and watched from a distance as the battle unfolded. "We did not go to church that day," one of them wrote. "I don't know whether there was any church or not." At that distance they could make little sense of developments; but they knew if the action receded from them, their friends and defenders would be retreating. Because the winds in that region customarily blow from the southwest, the spectators could not even hear the roar that seemed deafening to the soldiers fighting in its midst. "We could not hear," an onlooker recalled, "but could see the smoke flying from the cannon."[11]

At the Federal rear, where Frémont attempted to control his force from, the intensity of the artillery fight could be gauged by the way its roar steadily increased. In Colonel Tracy's words, "the low and sullen roar of the enemy's guns, as heard at first above the hills," quickly rose to a "positive thunder—in which our own batteries now joined with a vim of detonation not surpassed." When musketry mixed its crackling fire into the deadly chorus (ineffectually at this point in the action), "the rattling and din upon all sides seemed positively devilish." One Northerner thought the Confederates had paced off distances: "Jackson knew the country well, and having the range, he worked his guns with wonderful precision."[12]

Because the Confederate line curved away from his positions to the southeast, Frémont's left did not participate in the artillery fire to any great extent. A New York gunner stationed there listened with professional interest to "the heavy thunder of the cannon," and suddenly remembered the striking incongruity that the day was Pentecost Sunday. To the New Yorker's right, near and west of the main road, artillery attached to Milroy's Brigade carried the heaviest burden for Frémont's army. Their best position was near the Armentrout house, directly opposite Latimer and the four batteries on Mill Creek Ridge. The Armentrout house has been gone for almost a century, but a big old school building on the crest in that vicinity serves as the most widely visible landmark on the battlefield today.[13]

Milroy had hustled his batteries forward in person. "I immediately threw them into position," the general wrote his wife, "but the enemy batteries opened on mine . . . before we could get ready for firing and threw the shot and shell over so rapidly—but my batteries silenced theirs in 15 minutes after they commenced." An Ohio man working Milroy's guns did not join in the general's ludicrous claim that the Confederate pieces had been silenced, but he did notice that Southern marksmanship deteriorated after a time. "At first their shot came howling close to our ears and plowing the ground at our feet, but the rebel gunners soon got to shooting wild, clear over our heads." A soldier in Milroy's 25th Ohio, supporting the artillery, complained that "shells were bursting on all sides" as they went over the batteries.[14]

The artillery fire on the Federal right and the Confederate left did not rage as hotly as in the center because of the wooded ground. Even so, projectiles crashing through the trees and around buildings in this neighborhood wounded men and terrified civilians. As journalist C. H. Webb paused on horseback near Union Church, a cannonball "came bursting through the graveyard fence" a few feet from him. With that impetus, Webb rode past the church headed farther to the rear. Another shell "tearing through the limbs of the trees, nearly over my head," hurried him on his way. Webb went to Cross Keys tavern, not far west of the church, and found there "three intelligent females [Mrs. Kemper and her charges], a baby and a timid army Chaplain, all about equally alarmed for their safety." The civilians and the chaplain decided to find safer ground. By the time Webb rode back to Union Church, fifteen or twenty wounded Federals had been gathered there for treatment. Confederate artillery was finding its targets.[15]

For Isaac Trimble, inaction under enemy fire was intolerable. Even before he moved his brigade onto the steep bluff to the right of the road, Trimble had been looking to the right front, toward ground from which he could better get at the enemy. He saw there "a wooded hill running nearly parallel to our line of battle." Moving that far forward of the main line, and a little eastward from the road as well, posed some risks. Trimble thought that the gap he would leave on his left rear, back toward Mill Creek and the artillery heights, could be protected with sweeping artillery fire. His right in the new position had strong tactical security in the form of "a ravine and densely-wooded hill." He could protect it further with an infantry detachment. Any doubts about this bold maneuver vanished when cavalry captain Frank Myers, returning from his reconnaissance, told

Trimble that the scouts had spied a heavy Union column advancing in that vicinity. He "at once" moved two of his regiments toward the new position.[16]

Trimble's Brigade included four regiments—the 21st Georgia, 16th Mississippi, 15th Alabama, and 21st North Carolina. The Carolinians overlapped the road and the artillery cluster next to it, so Trimble could not readily move them away. Historians have been confused by accounts of Trimble's fight written by North Carolinians, since his Carolina regiment remained behind to support the artillery on the ridge near Mill Creek Church. The Tarheels with Trimble belonged to a newly formed two-company sharpshooter battalion drawn from the 21st.[17]

The North Carolina battalion, as befitted its sharpshooting and skirmishing specialty, led the way to Trimble's chosen ground. The Georgians and Mississippians followed them. The 15th Alabama, recovered from its morning ordeal, moved at the tail of the column. Trimble of course could not simply push his men down the steep slope near the road. That would have exposed the troops needlessly to an artillery deluge and cost him surprise. The North Carolina battalion was lounging south of Mill Creek Church, hoping for a day of rest, when Trimble ordered the men to loop rightward until they could reach the new position under cover. The Tarheels were to take possession of the north edge of the woods and hold it until Trimble came up with the rest of the brigade. An officer in the 21st Georgia described the approach as being "a circuitous route through the woods."[18]

A Virginia cavalry scout named Fontaine stumbled upon the 16th Mississippi, which was next to last in the column, and noticed that its northward direction was on a line too far west, in danger of being cut off by Federals moving south. The scout told Colonel Carnot Posey of the 16th that he needed to reorient his advance farther eastward, and Posey did so. At once a loud voice demanded, "What is the meaning of this move?" The cavalryman "turned and saw a small man with a naked sword in his hand . . . no insignia of rank . . . but was in his shirt sleeves." The small, noisy apparition was Isaac Trimble, wearing a black hat bedizened with cord and feathers. Posey told the general, "This gentleman says that the enemy is on our left flank." "And who the hell is this gentleman?" Once convinced of Fontaine's legitimacy, Trimble started his own column forward again, saying with convincing sincerity, "we are anxious to meet them."[19]

Trimble had found the 15th Alabama behind the front line and west of the road. He formed the regiment into line and directed it forward as the last of the four units he was moving to his chosen battleground. The Alabamians marched behind the main line for some distance until they picked up the circuitous route that the other regiments had followed.[20]

The troops wending their careful way forward under Trimble's directions passed between two local landmarks that served as points of reference on maps of the area. Since both Good's Mill and the widow Pence's house remain identifiable today, they provide benchmarks useful to modern students of the battle. Samuel Good had founded a tiny village around his mill well before the war. The mill fell prey to Northern arsonists in 1864, but the Good family rebuilt it and operated it well into the twentieth century. Ruins of the old building still stand at the southeastern limit of the battlefield.[21]

On the other (west) side of Trimble's route stood a modest country farmhouse owned by Sarah Pence. The widowed Mrs. Pence no doubt knew that the arrival of armies with banners near her farm portended danger, but she probably was not so pessimistic as to imagine the dire fate in store for her home. By the time the invading Federals retreated from the Pence place two days later, it "was entirely stripped from garret to cellar; in a few words, all was taken. No provisions of any kind were left. Bedding, clothing of every description, wagon and gear, bees, &c." Not long after the battle a sympathetic local man described Mrs. Pence's unhappy fate: "So nearly was this poor widow woman robbed entire, that she has been compelled to leave her house, give up house keeping, and live with her friends and relatives." The Pence house survives today in good condition and is still occupied as a farm dwelling.[22]

East and north of the Pence house Trimble's Brigade found a ready-made deadfall in which to await the advancing Unionists. The little North Carolina battalion settled into the edge of the woods behind a convenient fence. When the rest of the brigade came into sight, the battalion moved ahead across the open field in front as skirmishers.[23] In doing so, the Tarheels conformed to tactical doctrine. They would warn of any enemy advance and they could screen a Confederate attack. Northerners headed for the same point ignored the basic precaution of using skirmishers in advance, and would pay a steep price in blood for their nonchalance.

As the 21st Georgia arrived at Trimble's chosen ground, the

general met the regiment and formed it from marching column into line. Then he ordered the men to lie down behind the strong fence "on the edge of a wood, skirting a clover-field." The 16th Mississippi came up next, with the 15th Alabama bringing up the rear. Trimble put the Mississippians next to the right of the Georgians, but he employed a subterfuge as he emplaced them. The 15th Alabama, destined for Trimble's far right, went up to the fence where the 16th Mississippi was to fight. Trimble then had the Mississippi men "crawl on hands and knees and poke their guns through the fence." When they had reached their positions, the general ostentatiously moved the 15th Alabama away to the right to a point at which it was "concealed from the enemy's view." One of the Alabamians was convinced that this fooled the Federals and led them into the ambush awaiting them. There is no firm evidence on the point, but Trimble's alignment unquestionably resulted in one of the most devastating deadfalls of the war.[24]

The 15th Alabama's move to the right took the regiment to another point on the same fence that protected the front of the 16th Mississippi and the 21st Georgia on its left. The troops marched to their new position under some artillery fire and a smattering of small-arms fire from far-distant Yankees. A member of the 16th Mississippi back at the fence called it a "heavy fire" of shells. The 15th was still a green unit, and the fire unsettled the men. A ball hit Corporal John T. Melvin in the foot, crippling him permanently. Another broke William J. Parish's hand. Parish came back to duty in time to suffer a shattered thigh at Chickamauga. They were the first men in their company who had been hit during the war. The rest of the 15th soon reached its alloted zone and lay down behind the fence. Before much time passed, they would see enemy soldiers over the sights of their muskets.[25]

The right of the 15th Alabama ended Trimble's line in that direction. It was comfortably anchored on the ravine that Trimble had chosen as protection for his right. Beyond the ravine a steep, wooded ridge running perpendicular to the defense's axis provided further protection. The right of the army, however, required stouter security than unmanned terrain, no matter how usefully it was configured. The small cavalry detachments already assigned in that direction would be useless in the face of enemy infantry. To supply the needed security, General Elzey loaned Trimble two regiments, the 13th and 25th Virginia, from his brigade, which was holding Ewell's center with ease. The two Virginia units must have moved out to the far right about concurrently with Trimble's advance, because they were in place before action erupted on the latter's front.[26]

The commander of the 25th Virginia, Lieutenant Colonel Patrick B. Duffy, was not an imposing military leader. Duffy was only twenty-three years old, had been promoted from captain just the month before, came to the army as a merchant from Braxton County, and would resign within a few months. Fortunately, Colonel James A. Walker of the 13th Virginia outranked Duffy and controlled the two-regiment task force protecting the eastern fringes of the battlefield. Walker had attended Virginia Military Institute, where he was expelled bare weeks before graduation in a dispute with that dour and inflexible professor Thomas J. Jackson. The dispute led young Walker to attempt to kill his nemesis with a rock hurled from atop a building. James Walker was an eminently capable officer who would, in ultimate irony, earn the nickname "Stonewall Jim" as a general commanding the famous old brigade of the man he had tried to kill before the war. Lieutenant Colonel James B. Terrill of the 13th, who was also destined to wear the wreath of a Confederate brigadier general, commanded two companies of skirmishers that preceded the detachment. Walker and Terrill and Duffy advanced northward on a line east of Trimble's right, in the vicinity of the Good's Mill Road. The two regiments moved in line without meeting any opposition until they were near the Evers house, north of where Trimble was about to go into action. Trimble clearly had no need to worry about his right flank.[27]

General Trimble's new position looks awkward on a map, unconnected as it was to the main line. That caused concern at headquarters. With hindsight, staff officer Campbell Brown explained the rationale: "To the right of the batteries [on the knoll by the road] the ground . . . was swept by their fire[,] & as Trimble . . . was posted rather in advance of our Centre & also commanded the ground on his left front, it was not thought hazardous to leave an interval of several hundred yards comparatively unguarded." Nor, Brown was able to add after the fact, "did the event prove it so."[28]

Northern regiments were approaching Trimble's carefully selected ambush site even as the Southerners settled into it. General Julius Stahel, with four New York regiments and one from Pennsylvania, moved toward Trimble while General Henry Bohlen followed Stahel with two New York and two Pennsylvania regiments. Both

Union brigades had artillery batteries assigned to them. The 8th New York had the misfortune to serve as Stahel's spearhead. The 27th Pennsylvania followed the New Yorkers in their dangerous advance. Bohlen received orders from division commander General Louis Blenker to support Stahel. A staff officer from Stahel pointed out an elevated point on which Captain Michael Wiedrich's New York Battery was to form. Wiedrich was glad to find good ground from which to fire; he had been tugged from one position to another by high-ranking officers with different notions. To protect the guns, the 58th New York formed on the Federal left and the 74th Pennsylvania went even farther left. Word reached Bohlen that two Confederate regiments were hidden in a wheat field on the left. Someone obviously had spotted Walker's Virginians. Bohlen's other two regiments, the 54th New York and 75th Pennsylvania, caromed from hilltop to hilltop under confusing directions, rather as Wiedrich's Battery had done, until they settled into position near the rest of the brigade.[29]

The actors now were all in position. The curtain came up on the deadly drama of Cross Keys when the 8th New York innocently stepped out into the open field and began to cross it toward 1,500 eagerly waiting muskets leveled against it from Trimble's woodline.

"We hurled such a
storm of 'Buck and
Ball' at them that it
came very near
annihilating their
command." New York
soldiers fell "like
weeds before the cradler.
It was not in men to
stand such fire as that."

CHAPTER 9

THE SLAUGHTER OF

THE 8TH NEW YORK

T he field in front of Trimble's three regiments extended for about two hundred yards to another, thinner "belt of woods" in which Yankees soon began to appear. The men nervously awaiting the opening of the battle later remembered variously that the field contained clover, wheat, or buckwheat. They all agreed that it sloped downward from the Federal woods toward a declivity in mid-field, then rose again to the forest full of Confederates. The Southern line slanted somewhat from a true east-west alignment, running instead on an axis slightly tilted toward a northwest-southeast front. Nominally, however, the attack came from north to south, and the Confederates then counterattacked from south to north.[1]

Participants in the fight agreed that it exploded not long after

Trimble's troops lay down and prepared their defensive position. Ben Culpepper of the 15th Alabama recalled that the Federals advanced "as soon as we were out of the way," which is to say as soon as the 16th Mississippi took over for the 15th Alabama while the latter unit slipped away farther to the right. Captain Oates thought that only "a few moments elapsed." Trimble calculated the interval as being about thirty minutes. The clock hour at which the battle opened remains impossible to establish definitively: estimates range from eleven A.M. to three P.M. It is likely that noon was not long past when the 8th New York stepped into the field.[2]

General Julius Stahel tried to move his entire brigade forward with some cohesion. He left one regiment to support his artillery. Two others, the 41st New York and 27th Pennsylvania, angled away to the right, "into the timber," leaving the 45th New York and the 8th New York headed in the direction of Trimble. The 45th had so little to do with the ensuing combat that Stahel did not even report any casualties for the unit (though it suffered several). That left the 8th all alone as it trudged through the clover down toward the mid-field hollow. There were a few more than five hundred men in the battle line, most of them adoptive sons of New York who had emigrated from Germany.[3]

Since the tactical edge belonged to the defensive force during the Civil War—even without such tremendous advantages of surprise and strong ground as Trimble enjoyed—attacking forces needed a preponderance in numbers to succeed. At Cross Keys the 8th New York attacked against more than twice its own strength. Trimble's Brigade numbered 1,705 men on June 8, but that included the North Carolinians back near the artillery cluster on the main road. Trimble professed to know somehow that he had precisely 1,348 officers and men crouching at the edge of the woods behind the fence.[4]

The handful of North Carolinians posted at the north side of the field saw the New Yorkers coming through the woods and quickly fell back "before a heavy fire." They could tell that the enemy was moving in some force; finding that out was precisely what skirmishers were supposed to accomplish. The Tarheels hurried across the field to the security of the strongly guarded fence on its southern edge. The 8th New York, innocent of the wiles of battle, thought that they had driven away resisting Rebels. The Northerners thought that in advancing into the field, they were in pursuit of fleeing foemen.[5]

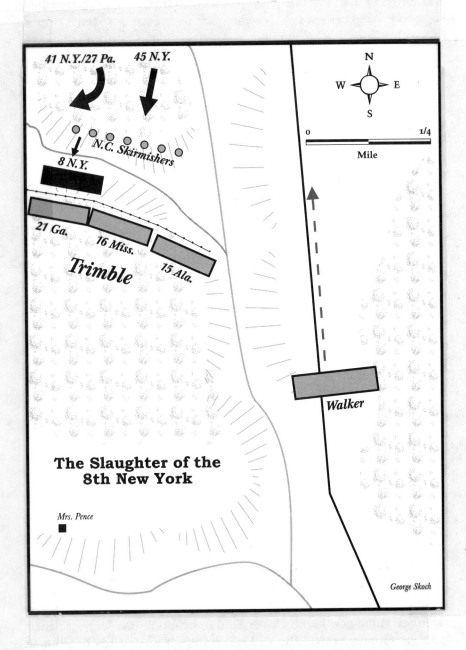

41 N.Y./27 Pa.   45 N.Y.

N.C. Skirmishers

8 N.Y.

21 Ga.

16 Miss.

15 Ala.

Trimble

N
W   E
S

0   1/4
Mile

Walker

**The Slaughter of the
8th New York**

Mrs. Pence

George Skoch

When Trimble's pickets fell gratefully into line behind the fence and looked back whence they had come, they saw an astonishing sight: the Yankees were advancing without even a token skirmish line to lead the way. Confederate skirmishers had performed exactly as they should, but their foe took no note of the procedure. One of the Tarheels marveled that the Federals moved "with no skirmishers in advance." Another wrote: "They were so foolish as . . . to march . . . with no sharp shooters [as skirmishers sometimes were called] in front to locate our position." A Georgian watching the Northerners called his careless foe "the unconscious enemy . . . advancing without a skirmish line." The New Yorkers would get no warning from a few men in front of their main force; all would learn simultaneously what awaited them.[6]

Frémont's inexperienced force included men and units who did know the vital importance of skirmishers, but the 8th New York and its leaders were not among that number. The Pennsylvania Bucktails, who had proved themselves adept, belonged to Stahel's command on this day. One of the Bucktails unkindly attributed the 8th's dreadful technique to the regiment's German composition when he declared, "the Dutch did not know how to fight bush whackers."[7]

Amazed Confederates commented about how skillfully the enemy regiment maintained its alignment as it strode through the grain in double ranks. It was "a beautiful line," a Mississippian recalled. The attacking force "came up briskly, in line of battle," a Carolinian noted, and General Trimble described the advance as moving "in regular order." William McClendon of the 15th Alabama summarized the general Southern perspective when he wrote: "They advanced with such precision, keeping the step, and their line was so well dressed that it was a matter of comment afterwards among our officers, but poor fellows, they did not know what was in store for them behind that fence."[8]

The large hollow in the center of the field hid almost the entire 8th New York from view a few minutes after the regiment started its move south. Because the Confederates were prone behind their fence, the enemy disappeared rather quickly from their range of vision. A Confederate watching them vividly recorded his feelings as he saw the Yankees disappear and then reappear: "The Germans came marching across the clover field in beautiful line, carrying their guns at 'support arms.' The Colonel walk[ed] backwards in front of them, seeing that they preserved a perfect alignment just as though

they were simply drilling. . . . When the Germans got in the hollow
. . . they could not be seen; but when they crossed it and came into
view again, they were within fifty yards of the fence." To A. S. Hamilton of the 21st Georgia, the effect of the hollow made it seem as
though the enemy "charged us over the crest of a ridge."[9]

So many Southerners crowded the fence line waiting for the
chance to unleash their firepower that in many places they had to
be staggered two deep. To increase the cover supplied by the fence
and the woods, some of them stuffed leaves hurriedly gathered from
the woods behind them between the bottom two fence rails. Lying
quietly then, "flat on the ground, with their guns in the bottom crack
of the fence," as one of them wrote, they completed the arrangement
of a perfect deadfall.[10]

The vast majority of the muskets peeping through the leaves and
rails did not pack the deadly wallop or have the extended range of
the rifled weapons with which most of the Civil War would be
fought. Confederate shoulder arms at this stage of the war (and for
an amazing period longer) still included a preponderance of old-
fashioned smoothbore muskets. The firing mechanisms had been altered from crude, flintlock systems, dependent on sparks falling into
raw powder, to the more sophisticated percussion-cap device; but
the unrifled barrels yielded no more range and no more power than
that delivered by the previous century's Revolutionary War pieces.
None of that mattered at short range. The muskets of the 21st Georgia, which would hold center stage in the coming slaughter, had
been loaded not only with round balls, but also with three buckshot
in each load. Some of the Georgians had borrowed shotgun shells
from Southern cavalrymen carrying those close-in weapons, and put
a dozen buckshot into homemade cartridges. Captain James Cooper
Nisbet of the 21st recalled aptly, "It was a mighty destructive weapon
at close range." The 16th Mississippi carried "the old fashion Harpers
Ferry Musket loaded with a ball & three buckshot," and the 15th
Alabama was loaded with similar "Buck and Ball."[11]

The 8th New York was no greener than the majority of the gray-
clad men awaiting it, but the Confederates enjoyed the immense
advantage of being on the defensive. The inevitable edge that went
to the defense was redoubled when green troops were involved.
Lying low and firing on command was a far easier task than moving
in order and maneuvering under fire. Even so, tension ran at fever
pitch down the fence. "The men had their sights drawn and their

fingers on the triggers," one remembered, "and in a quiver of excitement they saw the Germans coming up out of the hollow. . . . Our men had a full, clear view, a lying down rest and an unobstructed range." "There we lay," William McClendon wrote in his memoir, "as a Bengal tiger when he crouches down ready to spring upon his unsuspected prey, each man in deathly silence, with eyes fixed upon the advancing foe. . . . These were almost breathless moments, not a word, not a whisper by the men, only a word of caution was whispered by the officers. See them advancing; keep cool, Alabamians; take good aim, and not fire too high."[12]

The men in the Alabama regiment benefited from the calming presence of Colonel James Cantey. Some of them had doubted his wisdom during the retreat from Union Church that morning, but with heavy gunplay in the offing it was nice to know that the regimental commander had "been in the Mexican war [and] had some idea of what was coming." Cantey had suffered an honorable wound in Mexico. Having a colonel who had been under fire, and even had been hit by it—who had "seen the elephant" in the slang phrase of the war—soothed the tense young men waiting for their own baptism in battle. Colonel Cantey repeatedly told the 15th, "Hold your fire, boys, until you can see the white of their eyes." That battle cry had become famous seven decades before the Mexican War, but it worked again for Cantey.[13]

A few men of the 15th Alabama had fired impulsively at enemy soldiers when they first appeared at the north edge of the field. Cantey "immediately checked" them. The ever-critical Trimble apparently did not notice the early and harmless lapse, since he reported "fine discipline." Colonel John Thomas Mercer of the 21st Georgia took no chances about ensuring fire discipline in his regiment. The handsome thirty-two-year-old graduate of West Point and veteran of frontier service with the U.S. Army simply "sent an order down the line that if any man fired before he gave orders to fire, he would have him shot."[14]

Captain William Oates of the 15th thought that the premature shots actually accomplished some accidental good. When the 8th New York advanced, its center headed for a point well to the left of the Alabamians. Oates suggested that the Yankees might have been seeking to outflank on the west the point from which the scattered volley had come. That seems unlikely, but whatever their motive, the New Yorkers came straight toward Colonel Mercer's regiment.

As Oates put it, they "walked right up to the Twenty-first Georgia." Another eyewitness described how precisely the Northern regiment fronted the 21st: "As the Germans came up out of the hollow, their flag and that of the Georgians exactly confronted each each. This gave the Mississippians an enfilading, or raking fire" from the east, and the Alabamians had an even more sharply oblique fire into the left flank of the 8th New York.[15]

Among the numerous military axioms attributed to Stonewall Jackson is the importance of delivering defensive fire at close range. An intimate of the general's reported that on the eve of the Battle of Cross Keys, Jackson said to Ewell, "Let the Federals get very close before your infantry fires, they won't stand long."[16] Trimble was prepared to fire a devastating volley from very short range indeed, but he was not doing so at the instance of either Ewell or Jackson. His smoothbore weapons made it necessary, and the dip in the ground made it all the more possible. The result no doubt confirmed Jackson's notion.

Just how close the front rank of the 8th New York had come to the Confederate fence before disaster swept its ranks cannot be determined with precision. As is the case with virtually every Civil War objective fact—time, distance, and other such measurements—eyewitnesses estimated unevenly. No Confederate calculated the distance at less than thirty yards; one thought it to be as much as "seventy-five or one hundred." Forty yards is the distance most frequently cited, and fits nicely as an average too. The well-focused Colonel Mercer reasonably enough directed that his men await not a finite yardage, but rather hold their fire "until [the enemy] could be seen from their feet up" as they emerged from the hollow.[17]

The horror of the untested German men following the flag of the 8th New York can only be imagined when, at forty yards distance, "the thickets stirred suddenly with sound and movement [and] southern riflemen rose swiftly on their feet. A sheet of fire ran along their line, followed by a crash that resounded through the woods." A Georgian described the fire as a "volcano more terrible than Vasuvious [sic]." "When the order 'Fire!' rang out from Mercer," one of the colonel's infantryman recalled, "a volley from a thousand guns sounded in the air, and a thousand bullets flew to their deadly work." The spectacle was in fact considerably worse than that, since more than 1,300 muskets delivered their fire and many of them contained four (or even a dozen) projectiles. Mercer's man watched as "the poor Germans fell all across each other in piles" and estimated that he had witnessed "a whole regiment annihilated at a single fire." A member of the 21st writing home to Rome, Georgia, calculated more conservatively that about fifty of the enemy fell dead at the first volley and that that many more were wounded. Then he boasted, less conservatively, that "Our Regiment whipped a whole Brigade."[18]

The 16th Mississippi had as good a shot at the Yankees as did the 21st Georgia. Perhaps it was better, angling as it did into the enemy flank. The Mississippi troops also were out of the likely line of any return fire the shattered enemy might manage to deliver. One of the Mississippians emphasized the "deliberate" nature of his regiment's volley. "So sudden and so unexpected was this, that, seized with terror, they immediately gave away." Another member of the 16th boasted of "a well delivered volley," but then estimated that it only "decimated the 8th New York." Many more than one tenth of the New Yorkers became casualties. A third Mississippian exaggerated in the other direction when he wrote home that "the 16th Regiment . . . cut the 8th New York Regiment all to pieces, there was 700 of them that came into the fight and only about 200 of them that escaped." Without attempting a quantitative estimate, James J. Kirkpatrick told his diary: "Today . . . the 16th Regiment for the first time, made good use of their arms."[19]

The Alabama troops, farthest of the defenders from the focus of the attack, had an even sharper oblique angle of fire into the left flank of the 8th New York. Despite the deadly flanking aspect of their fire, the distance made the 15th Alabama's the least effective musketry aimed at the enemy. With the honest egocentricity that shows through most memoirs, the Alabama men presumed that their volley had been the primary one. William McClendon recalled: "We hurled such a storm of 'Buck and Ball' at them that it came very near annihilating their command." One of his comrades concluded that after nervously awaiting orders, "when we did fire we came near killing and wounding the whole force."[20]

Captain Oates of the Alabama regiment recognized that the 21st Georgia did the most damage. The Georgians, he declared, "just mowed them down in piles at a single volley." Ben Culpepper of the 15th saw most of the war in Virginia at first hand, but after it was over he still remembered the volley into the face of the 8th New York at Cross Keys as the most devastating. "I never saw men double up and fall so fast," Culpepper wrote. The staggered survivors turned and "went so fast down the hill you might have played marbles on their coat-tails."[21]

A citizen living on the battlefield told a reporter soon after the war that the surprise volley leveled the New Yorkers "like weeds before the cradler. It was not in men to stand such fire as that." General Trimble jingoistically trumpeted that his men's "deadly fire . . . dropp[ed] the deluded victims of Northern fanaticism and misrule by scores." On the other hand, Trimble paid a gracious and entirely apt tribute to the unfortunate Federals, "whose gallantry deserved a better fate."[22]

The vivid tableau that had riveted the attention of every Confederate in visual range evaporated at the first volley, hidden by a dense cloud of sulfurous, gray black-powder smoke impenetrable to even the sharpest eye. Battle art (especially that of modern vintage) notwithstanding, close combat during the Civil War offered no extended vistas. A member of the 15th Alabama admitted that "after the first volley we could not see them any more, in consequence of so much smoke. We fired a few rounds at them through the smoke when it was ascertained that they had disappeared from our front, and we were ordered to cease firing." Captain Nisbet of the 21st Georgia also remarked about the stifling "smoke and fog." He remembered firing a total of three rounds before charging over the fence toward the enemy. Another Georgian reported firing "a few volleys." A soldier in the 16th Mississippi recalled that on his part of the line the men fired only a single volley. Charles C. Wight, listening with interest from his position a mile to the west with the 58th Virginia, wrote that the crash of "very heavy" musketry "was not continued very long."[23] The terrifying and deadly experience of the 8th New York under close-range fire cannot have lasted much longer than a minute.

Horrified Federal observers watching from positions north of the 8th New York quailed at the slaughter. A Pennsylvanian wrote of the "murderous fire . . . bringing death and destruction." C. H. Webb of *The New York Times* described how Confederates, "ambushed in the wheat on the edge of the field, behind the fence and in the woods, suddenly revealed themselves by a terrible fire that cut down nearly the whole of the two companies in advance."[24] Had the 8th actually had two companies in advance of the main body, they would indeed have been cut down—but the rest of the regiment would have been better off. In fact, the entire New York unit suffered approximately equally.

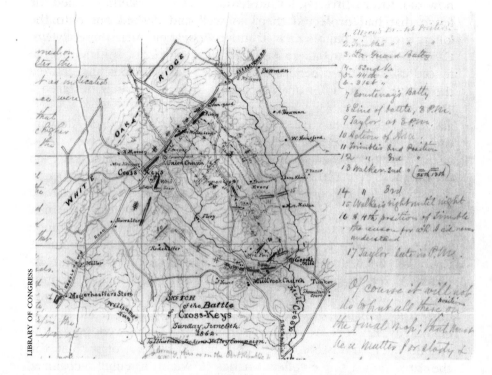

Jedediah Hotchkiss's
manuscript map
of Cross Keys
battlefield

The almost inevitable impulse throughout the Civil War of Confederate defenders who administered a firm repulse was to dash rapidly after the retreating foe, as the victorious Southern infantrymen now did. After delivering a thunderous volley or two they scaled the fence that had protected them so well and dashed out onto the killing ground, screaming the daunting Rebel yell. After three volleys, Captain Nisbet and Georgians all around him "charged over the fence." The men of the 16th Mississippi "sprang to their feet, crossed the fence and advanced firing rapidly and routing them instantly." There can have been little routing left to be done. The New Yorkers already had understandably, necessarily, "fled precipitately" toward the far woods. Those who remained behind because of bravery, indecision, or slight wounds became part of the bag of "a number of prisoners" that the Confederates captured.[25]

The Georgians quickly came across the enemy's battle flag lying on the ground in front of their line. The New York color guard doubtless had been hit by dozens of bullets in its exposed position and dropped the banner not to flee, but to fall dead or wounded. Civil War soldiers viewed their flags with a veneration that approached superstition. The 21st Georgia's trophy on this day came easily, plucked from the ground; most flags captured during the war cost tremendous casualties on both sides, usually in hand-to-hand encounters. Confederates who dashed to the southern lip of the swale drew beads on New Yorkers racing desperately for shelter in the far woods. Even the fiery Trimble, however, quickly recognized that he was not prepared for a major tactical advance. After pursuing for only "a short distance," the general "deemed it prudent" (a word not prominent in his lexicon) to halt his men. "The enemy's rear regiments," Trimble could see, were "halted in the wood on the other side of the valley."[26]

Men of both armies soon would become inured to dreadful scenes of many kinds. In the early-war innocence they still enjoyed in June 1862, the scene of carnage ("a most appalling sight") in front of Trimble's fence stunned them. As he fell back toward the southern woods, Georgian Sidney J. Richardson, age twenty-one, gazed in amazement at the destruction wrought by his regiment's fire. "The dead and wounded yankees was lying on the field as thick as black birds," Sidney told his homefolks. "It was the heardest fighting our army ever had."[27] Richardson would see much more fighting, and harder too, in the next two years, before he himself lay dead in another mound of corpses, near Plymouth, North Carolina.

Correspondent Webb of New York came across the blood-soaked ground where the 8th had suffered about twenty hours after the debacle. His pained description of the scene graphically conveys its ghastly aspect: "The poor fellows lie around . . . in all postures and positions, some on the very spot where they fell, others propped up against the fences where they crawled to die. . . . Many of them lie on their backs with their arms stretched wearily, carelessly out," resembling "men who have thrown themselves on the ground to rest and suddenly sank into slumber." One such corpse looked so relaxed and natural that Webb could hardly believe that the man was dead. Others had died with wild looks on their faces, as though strangling for air.

The scores of wounded New Yorkers made far less noise than Webb had imagined of such circumstances. The most frequent calls were quiet pleas for water. The correspondent noticed that men obviously mortally hurt had no sense that they would die. "To a strong man thus suddenly struck down," he theorized, "it seems impossible that he should die, and his spirit floats away into space while he is thinking of the glory that will redound to him from his scars."[28]

How many men fell victim to the Confederate ambush cannot be calculated precisely. Confederate sources exaggerated the number, and Federal authorities—the only ones who could know with certainty—bent the facts in the other direction. General Ewell claimed to know, when he wrote his report eight days later, that in Trimble's zone "from their own statement they outnumbered us . . . two to one." That figure was accurate and even modest, if it counted Federals opposite the Confederate right to the full depth of their position. The 8th New York, however, faced odds of greater than two to one against it in the tactical arena. Trimble used a similar high-powered multiplier when he reported officially that "on the ground where we first opened fire 290 of the enemy were left dead."[29]

Trimble's figure for Northern dead was about three times too high, but it was not far off the mark for total enemy casualties of all sorts. The official Union return of losses reported 43 dead in the 8th New York, 134 wounded, and 43 prisoners or missing, for a total of 220. A nominal listing of the men in the regiment published by their state after the war reveals much heavier losses. Such enumerations provide the best raw material for checking casualties because they list individuals by name, leaving little room for mistakes or purposeful errors. They usually do not, however, include mention of wounds; that is the case with the New York registers. Tabulation from the New York publication, name by name, of the 8th's Cross Keys losses shows that at least 53 men were killed outright; 27 more died of their wounds; and 24 wounded men and 50 unwounded men became Confederate prisoners. Accepting the official return of 134 wounded men (although it probably is as low as the other categories), yields total losses in the 8th New York of at least 261. The deadly volley and its brief, violent aftermath struck down 80 men killed or mortally wounded and more than 100 men wounded, and resulted in the capture of at least 74 prisoners. Few volleys in the war were more devastating, even though most would be delivered by weapons of far greater range and power.[30]

A familiar refrain in contemporary Southern literature was outrage over the influx of foreigners—a predominant and visible portion of them being Germans—recruited by the North to fight its battles. Some of the reports that circulated about Confederates fighting hordes who could not speak English were exaggerated. The widely reported stereotype of the soldiers of the 8th New York in that regard deserves examination. A member of the 21st Georgia wrote home, "The men we fought were mostly foreign born . . . few of the prisoner[s] could speak English." A Mississippian called the assailants a "German division" and said that prisoners who could speak almost no English "were eager to see the great 'Shackson,' as they called him."[31]

There can be little doubt that the men of the 8th New York were indeed of German stock. In addition to their universal identification by both foes and their comrades, the names of the men clearly display their origins. The New York *Tribune* published a preliminary list of the dead of the regiment on June 19. They included such surnames as Ehler, Gothe, Henkel, Friedmann, Schellhass, Metz, Pauli, Kempf, Franke, Schultz, Kauffman, Heinicke, Wabbenhorst, Schurman, and Schoenheit. In fact, none of the forty-six names on this list of the dead seems clearly non-German.[32]

The German troops in Frémont's army often had been identified as prominent among the scavengers who had been tormenting Valley civilians. The slaughter of a Yankee regiment made up in large part of German soldiery gave distraught Southerners the opportunity for savage exultation. A Richmond newspaper gave voice to common sentiment when it editorialized that the annihilation of the "Eighth New York Dutch regiment" constituted "a just retribution for their excesses in the Valley, by insult, abuse, robbery, and destruction."[33]

Federal reaction to the 8th New York's fiasco focused on the bravery of the men in face of disaster. According to *The New York Times*, "the part taken by Gen. Stah[e]l, and his brigade of Germans, is the theme of general commendation. He has won the popular favor among American as well as foreign officers for his . . . soldierly qualities. He is brave and enthusiastic, and was seen during the day in the thickest of the fight, encouraging and urging on his men." Whether composed of vandals or heroes—or both—the 8th New York had been hard used. A staff officer at army headquarters said a few weeks after the battle "that the loss inflicted on the 8th New York amounted to almost annihilation and that it would be unfit for further service until it had recruited and filled up its decimated ranks."[34] One sixth of the men who had started across the fatal field with the 8th New York had died for their efforts. None of the survivors would ever forget their ordeal.

Confederate losses were of course minimal. Crouched under cover and with surprise on their side, the Southern infantry faced about as little risk as battle conditions ever would offer. It is impossible to segregate the few casualties suffered behind the fence from the larger number the three regiments would incur while carrying out Trimble's adventurous orders over the next few hours. The total reported for all three for the entire day was just more than one hundred, nineteen of them killed. Losses in the 15th Alabama, which accounted for about one half of the total casualties and of the dead, included the sizable number the regiment suffered during its ragged early morning withdrawal from Union Church.[35]

One dead Mississippian, Andrew J. Currie, had been hit by a stray cannonball. Currie had enlisted in Company C of the 16th from the village of Utica, Mississippi. He was the regiment's first man killed in battle. Other losses in the regiment were light wounds, including a flesh wound on Martin Turner's leg. The youngster had skinny legs "and the boys had been telling him that there was no danger of him ever being shot in the legs," according to a waggish comrade. "One of the boys said it must have been a fine bead drawn out that hit him." Achilles Pearson Sparkman, a physician from Pike County, Mississippi, serving in Company E, went down when a bullet passed "entirely through his body . . . so severely injuring him that he never recovered from its effects." That proud language, boasting of an honorable (but evidently exaggerated) wound, comes from an obituary recording Dr. Sparkman's death on June 1, 1913; the doctor had survived it for fifty years and fifty-one weeks.[36]

Confederate soldiers contemplating what they had accomplished in the first serious action they had seen must have been satisfied and relieved. They had passed their first great test, albeit under ideal circumstances. At higher levels, Ewell and Trimble were eager to exploit the advantage. Frémont presumably had learned that he was not facing an impotent rear guard that would be content with retreating toward the artillery fire audible from Port Republic. Trimble calmly took credit for "our handsome success," attributing it to "the judicious position" that he had selected and—more generously—"to the game spirit and eagerness of the men." What none of them could know at the time was that the explosion of fire at Trimble's fence would be the hottest moment in the Battle of Cross Keys. It had drained all of Frémont's initiative.[37]

**Buell's guns and their supporting infantry
dashed out of harm's way just ahead of the
screaming men of the 21st Georgia, who were
led by Colonel John Thomas Mercer.**

CHAPTER 10

TRIMBLE'S ATTACK

After returning from the brief pursuit into the open field, Trimble held his regiments along the line of their original position for about twenty minutes. He was restlessly eager to improve upon the defensive triumph. Some Confederates of overoptimistic temperament thought that the Federals were about to renew their advance and fired across the field. Enemy troops visible in the northern woods actually formed a line and moved into the field according to one Confederate witness, although Trimble did not mention such an advance.[1]

Finding the enemy "not disposed to renew the contest," the general scanned the field in search of something to attack and spied an enemy battery on the Federal left a half mile in front of him. Trimble "promptly decided to make a move from our right flank and try to capture the battery." In his official report the general displayed a defensive tone about his interaction with Ewell on the matter; the subject would later be controversial between them. Just at this stage a messenger arrived from Ewell wanting "to know our success and to ask if I wanted re-enforcements." Trimble replied that he had driven the enemy away and needed no aid, but "thought I could take their battery, and was moving for that purpose." This secondhand communication with his chief obviously could be informational only. Ewell would receive it far too late to have any role in formulating the plan of action.[2]

It is impossible to criticize Trimble for his decision, nor should Ewell have expected to be involved in it without riding to the ground in person at the moment of decision. General Ewell was among the most cordial and cooperative members of the Confederate high command, while Trimble regularly displayed a mean-spirited and selfish mien in his dealings with others. Even more surprising is evidence that Ewell resented the advance. Soon after the war Dick Ewell wrote to a Virginia colonel that Trimble moved forward at Cross Keys "in accordance with his own suggestion . . . to attack with the right flank," but "failed to attack through the left flank." Trimble did attack, though, and quite successfully. What prompted the uncomfortable atmosphere between the two generals remains unclear. They would be in sharper—and more clearly defined—disagreement later in the day.[3]

Trimble's best option for getting at the Federals obviously lay on the eastern edge of the battlefield. Rather than advancing with his leftward regiments, the Confederate leader could best move out on his right under cover, attack the Federal artillery, and unravel the enemy's exposed left flank. That is precisely what he contrived to do. Trimble led the 15th Alabama with fixed bayonets "in person," he reported, "to the right along a ravine, and, unperceived, got upon the enemy's left flank and in his rear, marching up in fine order as on drill." The 16th Mississippi remained behind with orders from the general "to advance rapidly in front as soon as they heard I was hotly engaged." The 16th's opportunity would come soon; but while they waited, the men had the misfortune to come under "a heavy fire of . . . artillery" which they bore "calmly," according to Trimble.[4]

The Alabamians advancing at Trimble's behest did not share his nonchalance about marching "as on drill." They could see activity ahead of them near the left end of the enemy line. This new Federal initiative threatened to outflank the outflankers, it seemed for a time, though in the end nothing came of it. The move down the covering ravine (which was perpendicular to the hollow that had shielded the 8th New York not far to the west) only covered about a quarter of a mile before Trimble faced the need to rearrange his plan. It probably had been amorphous in any case, if in fact he had formed any notion firmer than simply to press ahead. There were Yankees not far to the left, in the woods on the high ground from which the 8th New York had advanced. More could be seen farther north, beyond the first hill. Both enemy groups had artillery in evidence.

Trimble divided the 15th Alabama into two informal "battalions"—a tactical subdivision used primarily as an ad hoc expedient during the Civil War rather than as the organizational building block it became in later wars. General Trimble accompanied Colonel Cantey and the right battalion as it swung farther east under cover of some woods, then north to close with the second Federal line. The left battalion followed Lieutenant Colonel Treutlen sharply leftward against the first enemy force, atop "the hill in the woods." The "recklessly brave old man" commanding the brigade, as a captain called Trimble, surely would have followed the element he deemed most likely to engage in pivotal action.[5] In this case he guessed wrong. Treutlen and his men would find action more quickly, and of hotter temper, on the slopes of "the hill in the woods."

Poised to defend the hill were several segments of Stahel's Brigade. The 8th New York of course had been destroyed. The brigade's four other regiments plus a small detachment of Pennsylvania Bucktails were scattered across the ridges; Louis Schirmer's New York Battery fired from a position somewhat behind the front line; but the focus of Confederate aggression, and of Federal defensive ardor, was Captain Frank Buell's Virginia (Union) Battery of four rifled cannon. The Bucktails and the 27th Pennsylvania lay nearby in supporting positions. The roles of the 39th, 41st, and 45th New York in the fight over Buell's guns are not clear, but certainly were secondary.[6]

The 27th Pennsylvania had come to support the battery before the 8th New York's fight began. The regiment carried about 600 men into battle, a typical regimental strength on both sides. For what seemed like hours they had borne artillery fire, "shot and shell flying thick and fast." The 27th's chronicler concluded proudly that, "though this was their first real engagement, they held the position with the steadiness of veterans."[7]

The Bucktails had advanced right behind their cousins in the 27th under orders to support the battery. The Bucktails numbered only 108 men ready for action, but they were better-seasoned than the much larger regiment. As the Bucktails came out of the woods into view of the Confederate ridge for the first time, shells screamed in and hit one Bucktail and one man in the 27th Pennsylvania. When they dropped into defilade behind a ridge, the shelling stopped. Staying prudently under cover took them too far to the right, though, and "friendly" rounds from the rear flying overhead nudged them back to the left where they belonged. Lying down behind the battery they were to protect was a noisy and frightening business, but not very dangerous. A. M. Crapsey counted the artillery rounds and estimated that "probably 300 Shell & balls passed over us." Only one more man was wounded by all that shelling. The historians of the Bucktails added drolly that a lieutenant "who was also struck, escaped with an injury to his trousers."[8]

The battery, the Bucktails, and the 27th would have to defend their ground against three Confederate attacks. The left battalion of the 15th Alabama swung in from the east on the Federals at an oblique angle. Later the 16th Mississippi and 21st Georgia would come at them from the south. By the time all three Confederate units were committed, the Southerners would enjoy a slender numerical edge—about 1,000 to 800. Attacking in series rather than in concert, however, completely canceled that advantage.

Trimble, who was not at the scene, summarized in a few easy words the fight of the left battalion of the 15th Alabama under Lieutenant Colonel Treutlen. The Confederates "completely surprised the force in their front," he reported, "and drove them by a heavy fire, hotly returned, from behind logs and trees along the wood to westward." The 15th would make some steady progress to westward against outlying Federals, but the driving stopped abruptly before the Alabamians reached Buell's guns. The Yankee captain prepared his pieces for action and then said: "Boys, they've got us, but we will hurt some of them badly before they take my guns." The infantrymen completed their preparations by merely loading their rifles and lying down on the ground.[9]

One of the Bucktails wrote a few days later that a Confederate regiment (the 15th) "tried to flank us & take the Battery but we soon put them to flight." He boasted of inflicting heavy casualties, but admitted that many of his comrades also fell. The most reliable Southern account of the episode estimated that the "gallant fight" by Lieutenant Colonel Treutlen and his battalion as it attacked the wooded knoll lasted "about twenty minutes." Captain Oates of the 15th Alabama could see that the enemy outnumbered the attackers two-to-one. Not surprisingly "the blood was flowing freely" as a result of those odds. Captain Robert Hill commanding Company L was among the 15th's half-dozen dead, and nearly thirty were wounded.[10]

Until that morning, the young men of the 15th Alabama who began climbing over fences and scrambling up the wooded slopes toward Buell's guns had seen almost nothing of war despite having been a full year under arms. Some had faced the sharp skirmish near Union Church, and all of them had scampered back from the church to the main line, more winded and frightened than seriously threatened. Then the regiment had fired at leisure into the 8th New York's ranks.

Going on the offensive was quite another matter, they soon found. As novice soldiers always do, they compared notes about close calls under what seemed to be an inescapable torrent of fire. Bert Lanier had been hit in the foot but somehow escaped injury: "the ball never entered into his foot, it struck him on the Shoe heel, & brused it and burnt a blister!" Mitch Houghton looked up as he scaled a fence and "saw a Yankee take a deliberate aim at me as I straddled the top rail. The bullet buried itself in the rail but did me no harm." George Russell, who was twenty-six, found the experience to be all the war he wanted. His wound at Cross Keys "seems to have satisfied him with the war," his captain wrote, "and he deserted" later in the year. William Fears offered a striking contrast to Russell. The thirty-one-year-old private lost an eye at Cross Keys but came back to the ranks and served loyally to the end of the war.[11]

Several Alabamians fell dead or mortally wounded on the slope below Buell's guns. Corporal W.H.C. Irby, who had enlisted a few months before at the tender age of sixteen, was killed "whilst displaying unusual bravery." The only man hit in one company was Casper W. Boyd, a thirty-year-old farmer from Orion, Alabama. Despite a year in the field, Boyd was still innocent enough to be "shocket by the wicked othes that my fellow soldiers role out." The pious soldier went down with a bullet in his side, but friendly hands carried him to succor and eventually to a hospital in Charlottesville. Boyd wrote home in good spirits from there on June 21: "I have a good kind D[octor] . . . and a lady visits me. . . . I fondly hope to be

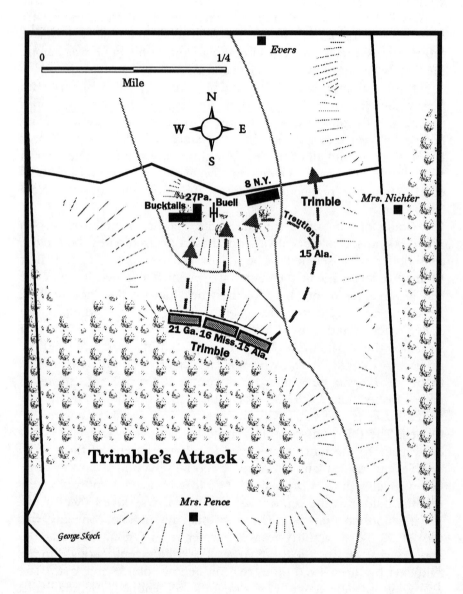

0   1/4

Mile

N
W   E
S

Evers

Mrs. Nichter

8 N.Y.

27Pa.

Bucktails   Buell

Trimble

Treutlen

15 Ala.

21 Ga. 16 Miss. 15 Ala.

Trimble

Trimble's Attack

Mrs. Pence

George Skoch

able to see you." Five days later the lady, a citizen volunteering in the hospital, wrote to Orion with word that Boyd had died soon after surgery probing for the bullet in his side.[12]

The heavy fire coming against the Alabama troops forced Lieutenant Colonel Treutlen to order a withdrawal. The always candid Captain Oates admitted that "a panic seized [the] command, and it retreated in confusion." He insisted, however, that "with few exceptions" the men stopped and re-formed their ranks when they reached the point from which they had started. One man who did not stop was Elijah W. Lingo, age twenty-six, who had been a stalwart in camp, responsible, well-liked—a good man and a good soldier in every regard. In this first heavy action he had seen, Lingo "did not understand that falling back meant to halt at the edge of the woods, and when he got to running he could not halt until he had gone four or five miles. He was not entirely alone, either." When Lingo came back to camp after the battle, he acknowledged having fled, "and was very much mortified and begged to be forgiven." Oates "knew him to be a good man, and neither punished nor reported him." Lingo responded by becoming one of the best soldiers in the regiment. He was promoted to sergeant and served until the end of the war.[13]

Trimble's other two regiments were under orders to advance to the support of the 15th "as soon as they heard" that their friends were engaged. Sounds of unmistakably heated firing had erupted as soon as the 15th Alabama's left battalion attacked. Obeying that prompting, the 16th Mississippi climbed over the fence and moved forward through the field where the wreckage of the 8th New York lay in bloody confusion. The 21st Georgia followed suit. The 16th moved first, however, and faced an irksome situation because its left flank became exposed. Treutlen rounded up most of his Alabamians and sent them forward again about the same time that the 16th Mississippi arrived in front of the Federal position. The focus of the action had moved away from the Alabama men by this time, though, and centered on the Mississippians.[14]

Once over the fence the 16th Mississippi "rushed forward and kept up a rapid fire as it advanced," according to the regiment's historian. It seemed to him, as it always seems to soldiers advancing under artillery fire, that "one of the enemy's batteries . . . seemed to devote its attention" exclusively to his regiment. As the soldiers from the Deep South "fell in with the remainder of the enemy's brigade," to use Trimble's quaint phrase, they found themselves in more trouble on their left flank than they faced from the battery in front. Carnot Posey, the capable commander of the 16th, thought that he detected signs of the Federal guns limbering up to escape. To forestall that he advanced so quickly and far that he passed the 27th Pennsylvania on his flank in the woods. The Yankees promptly "commenced a rapid and destructive fire" against the rear of the vulnerable Mississippians.[15]

General Trimble, always as generous with blame as he was chary with praise, placed the responsibility for this temporary check squarely on Colonel Posey's shoulders. The 16th Mississippi, Trimble reported to Ewell, "omitted to turn up the woods to its left, after the main body of the enemy, thus exposing its men to enfilade fire." In his report the general lauded Colonels Cantey of the 15th Alabama and Mercer of the 21st Georgia, but said nothing in praise of Colonel Posey. To compound the slight, Trimble lavishly praised one of the colonel's subordinates of rank three grades lower. Since Posey would be wounded in the attack, making him an especially apt target for kind words, Trimble's omission surely was significant.[16] It is hard to assess any discredit to Posey for an aggressive move in his first major experience as a combat leader. He went on to win promotion to brigadier general and was mortally wounded at Bristoe Station in October 1863.

Posey and his men fended off the 27th Pennsylvania energetically. They reoriented the regimental front toward the new threat, "firing all the time." "The conflict between these two regiments raged with great spirit," one of the Mississippians wrote. He added generously that "the Pennsylvanians behaved most gallantly." As Posey directed his troops in the smoky confusion, an enemy bullet struck him in the chest. Two of his soldiers described their commander's injury as "wounded in the breast but not seriously," and "slightly wounded in the breast." By the time Posey's wound made the Richmond papers he had become, with patent journalistic license, "badly wounded."[17] The colonel returned to duty with his regiment before many weeks had passed.

Captain James Brown of Company A of the 16th performed with special distinction. The brigade commander credited this ace infantryman and his company with having "killed 12 of the enemy, captured 64, with their arms, and some 25 horses, with their equipments" during "the last few weeks." How much of that impressive record came on the 8th is not of record, but Captain Brown clearly was a warrior.[18]

One of the same regiment's surgeons, on the other hand, drew harsh reviews. Harry Lewis of the 16th wrote home in disgust that some of his wounded friends had died needlessly for want of proper attention. The surgeons "are men or rather *boys* of scarcely no knowledge or experience," Lewis declared bitterly. "Our Asst. Surgeon [James Allston] Groves showed cowardice three times on the field of battle. He could not be found till the battle was over and then away in the rear." Such behavior had "irretrievably disgraced" the doctor; "not one of the Regt. deign to notice him at all."[19]

Heroes and cowards alike would have been in difficulty had not the 21st Georgia hurried forward on the left of the 16th to face the 27th Pennsylvania and lift the pressure. Before the 21st arrived, Federals around the battery had been confident they would win a victory pronounced enough to avenge the 8th New York's losses. Colonel Adolphus Buschbeck of the 27th described the attack of the 16th vividly: "The enemy advanced and charged on the battery with Indian-like yelling, coming within thirty yards of my force." In response his soldiers "charged upon them with a deafening cheer, and succeeded in driving the enemy from the field." Historians of the Bucktails added a bayonet charge to Buschbeck's extravagant claims of a counterattack: "the enemy came charging up the slope, and with a cheer the almost surrounded troops rose and rushed forward to meet them. Using the bayonet with deadly effect they repulsed the attack." Buell allegedly had to implore the Pennsylvania infantry to stand aside because they had interdicted his field of fire.[20] The Federals resisted Posey's attack with fine mettle, but it is unlikely that any of them really used bayonets in the process (Civil War bayonet encounters usually were more figurative than literal) or engaged in counterattacks covering more than a few feet.

The turning point in the struggle around Buell's guns came when the 21st Georgia reached the scene. The Georgians had remained behind, in position next to the 16th Mississippi, when Trimble led the 15th Alabama away to the right. Both of the rear regiments received identical orders: advance straight ahead when gunfire indicated that the Alabamians had become engaged. Why the 16th moved so much sooner than the 21st is hard to fathom. That the time offset was sizable is evident from the details of Colonel Posey's wounding. The commander of the Mississippi regiment had been wounded while at close quarters with the 27th Pennsylvania, at the height of his attack. Yet as the men of the 21st Georgia moved forward "to the aid of the 16th Mississippi . . . at double quick," they "met the litter-bearers taking Colonel Posey . . . to the rear."[21] Judging solely from the timing of the regiments' advances, Colonel Posey deserved more credit than Colonel Mercer of the 21st Georgia—Trimble's implied rebuke notwithstanding. The most reasonable analysis is that both men and both regiments did a good job of coping with the chaos of their first battle experience.

The advance of the 21st Georgia put the regiment just where it was most needed, on the left of the 16th Mississippi and face-to-face with the 27th Pennsylvania in the woods. Had the Georgians been there in the initial attack, as had been intended, the Confederates doubtless would have rolled over the knoll easily. That makes Trimble's calumny against Posey unsupportable. The Georgians not only arrived in an ideal position vis-à-vis friend and foe, they also added enough troops to outnumber the Federals by a slight margin.

The Georgia soldiers found their friends in the 16th "at a disadvantage . . . they were outnumbered" in a fight waged "at a distance." The momentum of their advance gone, the Mississippians were engaging in an exchange of musketry that they probably could not win. The Georgians changed the tide. Confederate accounts from all three regiments of Trimble's Brigade agree that the 27th Pennsylvania and its friends stood unmoved until the 21st Georgia showed up to tilt the balance.[22]

Most of the Federals enjoyed cover provided by woods atop the knoll. That protection, together with the advantage of being on the defensive, made the result of an exchange of fire likely to be favorable for the Northerners. Georgian A. S. Hamilton ruefully described the circumstances: "we in a field and they in timber . . . the musketry was terrific and the artillery deafening." To Hamilton, it understandably "seemed that every battery was in full play" on his regiment "from every point." Tom Hightower of the 21st Georgia wrote home describing how he heard and watched "the balls whistle by our heads as fast and thick as ever I saw hail fall in Georgia." Sidney Richardson had not witnessed much war at first hand yet, but what he saw at Cross Keys prompted him to assert earnestly—if awkwardly—that "it was the heardest fight, every has been fought in Virginia."[23]

The only solution to the Confederate dilemma, short of abandoning the field, was to attack. That formula suited Southern temperaments as well as it suited the situation. The Georgians, and perhaps a few Mississippians who had not lost all of their momentum, advanced rapidly, shouting the familiar Rebel yell. In Captain Nisbet's words, "We charged right over [the 16th Mississippi] into the woods; the Germans broke and we followed, firing and capturing until ordered to stop." Hamilton's part of the line evidently was slower to pick up the charge. He thought things grew "too hot for the 27th, which did not wait to be charged, but 'skedaddled,' leaving the woods strewn with their dead and wounded." Hightower also believed that the Pennsylvanians scampered away without being routed.[24]

The variant descriptions supply a clue to the nature of the event. Nisbet probably fought on the left of the 21st, opposite the most vulnerable part of the 27th Pennsylvania's line, where the Georgians charged to decide the issue. Hightower's account fits in that location too. Hamilton may have been toward the right of the Georgia regiment. Federals who recoiled from his front under the pressure of an attack from their right flank would have looked like they "skedaddled." Captain Oates of the Alabama regiment thought that was what happened. He wrote that his friends on the Confederate left moved "through the woods, and attacked the enemy in flank and drove them from their position in confusion."[25]

Trimble applauded the attack in his official report and boasted that it killed and wounded Yankees in large numbers. General Ewell's report cited Mercer for handling his regiment "with great skill," which the aggressive flank movement certainly displayed. The division commander also apportioned to Colonel Posey some of the credit that Trimble refused to offer.[26]

The battle also displayed the colors of both heroes and knaves in the ranks of the 21st Georgia. Private John Long of Company B pushed out in front of his mates as a skirmisher and behaved so well that General Trimble singled him out for official mention. Long brought in ten prisoners. Five of them he had captured all at once, even though each of the Federals was armed. The doughty private also received credit for shooting a member of General Frémont's staff, almost certainly Captain R. Nicolai Dunka. That officer, a professional soldier from Austria (in keeping with Frémont's European affectations), was shot in the chest while looking for Stahel. Long performed a historical service for posterity when he took from the captain's body a copy of Frémont's order of march that morning. Trimble put the document with his report and it reached print; Federal copies did not survive.[27]

Lieutenant Joseph M. Mack, also of Company B, displayed his bravery in very different fashion. As the lieutenant dashed toward the stubborn Federal line "he paused for a moment to moisten the lips of a dying Federalist, who was imploring water as our men rushed by." A bullet crashed into the lieutenant's upper thigh "while thus humanely engaged," shattering the bone "from end to end." Lieutenant Mack reached the University Hospital in Charlottesville on June 9, more quickly than most wounded found help. Lady volunteers tended him and fed him. Because of the "attractive graces of his personal character," they "vied with one another in their ministrations to him." A special splint that had worked for others gave him some relief for a time, but then intense pain set in. Thirteen days after the bullet hit him, Joe Mack died. An attending physician wrote up the story for Mack's hometown newspaper in Georgia. Mourning women clipped a lock of hair to send with it.[28]

The story of James T. Hawkins of Company H had a markedly different character. He had thoroughly vexed his captain, James C. Nisbet. Hawkins was poorly disciplined and given to looting and lawlessness. In the 21st's brief exposure to combat earlier during the campaign, Hawkins had added cowardly behavior to his unsavory pedigree. Captain Nisbet carefully placed his miscreant subordinate "in a file of three good men, and ordered them to get him into the fight" at Cross Keys.

The captain kept his own eye on Hawkins too, and noticed at once that "when the firing commenced, he started back." Nisbet grabbed Hawkins's collar and ordered him to join the Georgians' firing line, "threatening to shoot him" unless he did his duty. Hawkins whined, "my gun's stopped up." Just then the 21st began its charge and Nisbet had to dash to the head of his company. The assault succeeded so completely that Hawkins saw his chance: "seeing that the enemy was in retreat, [Hawkins] rushed ahead and it was all I could do to keep him from bayoneting the poor Germans who lay before us." Nisbet concluded sadly by observing the universal truth that "there were a few such men in most every company." James Hawkins completed his unsavory career by deserting in the face of the enemy near Antietam Creek in September 1862. He returned to Georgia, joined a Unionist bushwhacker force, and settled the debt with his superior and tormentor by leading the plunder of Captain Nisbet's home and farm.[29]

Lieutenant Kinchen Rambo Foster of the 21st's Company K carried a tiny pistol in his hand. As the attacking Georgians leaped a fence to close with their foe, the pistol discharged and struck James Clay Tate ("a mere boy") in the back. Foster's superior, Captain John B. Akridge, turned hotly on the lieutenant and called on other officers as eyewitnesses. One rejoined, "That can be attended to hereafter; we have plenty of Yanks to fight now, come on!"

After the fighting ended, the Southern officers returned to the matter of poor Jim Tate's wounding. Akridge and an officer who had witnessed the affair found Tate awaiting surgery at a field hospital. They agreed that the tiny .22 caliber pistol bullet eventually extracted from fatty tissue in Tate's back obviously "fit Foster's little pistol." Captain Akridge "gave the atmosphere all around there a bluish tinge. He said Foster was so scared he didn't know his own men from the Yankees; and divers other things." Only the near presence of the enemy and intervention of bystanders prevented a duel on the spot. In the aftermath, an angry Akridge and the frightened Foster had to put up with each other. When Akridge fell mortally wounded at Drewry's Bluff in the spring of 1864, Foster was still around and became the company commander in his stead. Tate survived his unusual ordeal and was among the hardy remnant paroled at Appomattox in 1865.[30]

The irresistible assault by Trimble's Brigade, once all of its components arrived, drove the Federals away but failed to capture the crowning prize, the artillery. Around Buell's guns, the repulse of the 16th Mississippi had bought no noticeable surcease. Almost at once "a new line of attack" appeared (the 21st Georgia, of course), "and the case appeared hopeless." C. H. Webb of *The New York Times* reported that Confederates "pressed around the guns, but the pelting storms of . . . canister" and rifle fire from the Pennsylvania infantry "held them at bay."[31]

The check inflicted on the 16th Mississippi, and the ensuing firefight with the 21st Georgia, prompted Colonel Tracy of Frémont's staff to claim that Stahel "repulsed both by battery and bayonet" two Confederate regiments, "with an almost annihilation of one." Tracy admitted, however, that "in the midst of the bloody work" the Federal force "was nevertheless pushed back" a substantial distance.

General Milroy, no instinctive admirer of the German units, admitted that at least some of his disdain had been misdirected. "A portion of the Germans had evidently fought well," he wrote to his wife, as "was evidenced by the number of dead rebles in front of their position."[32]

Buell's guns and their supporting infantry dashed out of harm's way just ahead of the screaming men of the 21st Georgia. "An opportunity seemed to present itself," wrote the historians of the Bucktails. "The artillery belched forth a murderous flood of [canister] and rapidly limbering up, a dash was made by the imperiled battery and its escort, towards the Union line." A friend watching from the rear acknowledged that the retirement commenced "in some confusion." That confusion was compounded when Union batteries opened fire on the mass of fugitives, assuming them to be advancing Southerners. An irate flag-bearer waved the banner of the 27th Pennsylvania conspicuously until the "friendly" fire ceased. The regiment, the Bucktails, and Buell's Battery finally fetched up safely in the Federal rear.[33]

As Stahel's defensive line dissolved, the remnant of the shattered 8th New York made a brief attempt to lend a hand by advancing on the Confederate right. The idea was a good one, or would have been had not the battalion of the 15th Alabama been lurking near. The soldiers of the 15th had recovered from their earlier repulse during the time that their mates had assailed and finally carried the hilltop. Lieutenant Colonel Treutlen's men launched an "earnest" counterattack and drove the fragments of the 8th New York "pell mell from the field."[34]

The roles of the 27th Pennsylvania, the Bucktails, and Buell's Battery are relatively clear. But what did the rest of Stahel's Brigade accomplish? The 39th, 41st, and 45th New York infantry regiments stood to the Federal right of the heavily engaged portion of the line. Stahel's official return of casualties did not enumerate their losses, including them vaguely in cumulative totals. Jacob Frank of the 41st wrote a few cryptic words in his diary about June 8: "a terrible fight of over 7 hours." New York records show that the three regiments lost at least 16 men killed or mortally wounded, 34 others wounded, and 33 prisoners. That total of 83 casualties falls short of those suffered by the 27th Pennsylvania alone, but still constitutes a considerable toll. No doubt some of them went down under the steady Confederate artillery fire from near Mill Creek Church. Others must have been hit by the left of the 21st Georgia as it drove through the area.[35]

With Buell's Battery and its supports gone, what had been secondary positions farther to the north manned by General Henry Bohlen's Brigade became the new Federal front line. Bohlen had two New York regiments, the 54th and 58th, and two Pennsylvania regiments, the 74th and 75th. Captain Michael Wiedrich's Battery I, 1st New York Light Artillery, was attached to the brigade. These five units had been sifting forward into the vicinity of the Evers house for some time and gradually coalesced into a line. As usual, the artillery served as the hub and focus. Louis Schirmer's Battery joined Wiedrich's in the position, even though it ostensibly belonged to Stahel's Brigade. Schirmer would prove to be more meddlesome than helpful.[36]

When the 58th New York moved forward, Colonel Wladimir Krzyzanowski of the 58th bumped into General Stahel. Bohlen had pointed Krzyzanowski to the right front; Stahel now pointed to the left front, and that's where the 58th went. The Polish colonel wound up in a field of rye, mightily confused, wondering where the enemy was, where his friends were, and what he was to do. The artillery unlimbered and opened fire at long range against Confederate batteries and claimed (without basis) to have silenced them. Krzyzanowski, with atypical modesty, more accurately credited Schirmer's barrage with silencing only "the most deadly of the Southern artillery fire."[37]

Krzyzanowski later claimed that he could see the disaster that befell the 8th New York from his position. It is more likely that the Federal setback he witnessed actually was the loss of Buell's position; talk about the 8th New York fiasco in the same direction would have been prevalent, leading to the confusion. Victorious Confederates moving in Bohlen's direction prompted movement of men from several regiments to protect Wiedrich's guns. Krzyzanowski and his men watched from the shelter of yet another fence at the edge of a copse of woods, "as if . . . viewing a theatrical performance," while Federal fugitives scuttled toward them. The colonel called the scene "strange, unrealistic. . . . Some men running, some walking." When some of the retreating men were mutilated by a shell, others nearby kept trudging along wearily, "seemingly unaware of the tragedies about them."[38]

General Bohlen presumed that the Confederates pushing toward him posed an immediate threat. In fact the 16th Mississippi and 21st

Georgia had almost nothing further to do with the action. By the time they consolidated their captured hilltop and reorganized, the fighting near them would be over. The fact that pursuit did not wash all the way up to the ground held by the 58th gave Bohlen the opportunity to float a grossly exaggerated report that the New Yorkers drove the enemy back "at the point of the bayonet."[39]

When the 74th Pennsylvania neared the combat zone, it formed into a long battle line. After it had waited warily for ten minutes, division commander Blenker came up and expressly ordered two of its companies forward to find the missing 8th New York and protect its wounded. The rest of the regiment was to follow "slowly." The high command had heard reports of bad things happening to the 8th and desperately sought information. Blenker instructed the skirmishers "to be very careful." He also forbade them to fire lest they hit friendly survivors.[40]

The Pennsylvanians, needless to say, ran not into the 8th New York but into Confederates. Major Franz Blessing, who commanded the two advance companies, soon had to ignore Blenker's peremptory orders and begin shooting back at hostile soldiers who were sending bullets into his ranks. He was able to offer convincing evidence about enemies in his front: the Rebels shot down Lieutenant E. von Brandenstein of Blenker's staff, sent along to supervise, and they also killed Blessing's horse. After facing what he described as a heavy volley from twenty yards away, the major and his detachment dashed back to rejoin the 74th under "torrents of musket-balls." The 74th then fell in near Wiedrich's Battery in the stabilizing Federal line.[41]

The 75th Pennsylvania had moved just behind, and even farther left than, its mates of the 74th. As it went tentatively forward in that direction, two companies angled to the right under General Bohlen's direction to supply more support for Wiedrich's Battery. The 75th received the familiar proscription on firing, lest it endanger friends in front. The men of the 75th understood that their mission was to help Stahel; but, the regimental historian reported, "before they could reach Stahel's brigade, it had already retreated." Stahel's units retreated of necessity when Trimble's Mississippians and Georgians obliged them to, not as a result of any misunderstanding of their role vis-à-vis Bohlen's regiments. The 75th fell back as part of the general retirement triggered by Stahel's repulse. Soon it too was part of the aggregation in the vicinity of Wiedrich's cannon.[42]

The final regiment of Bohlen's Brigade, the 54th New York, had been supposed to slide forward off the left and rear of the 75th Pennsylvania. That would have extended the Federal left still farther eastward, and deepened the echeloned arrangement that Bohlen had created. Colonel Eugene A. Kozlay rode ahead of his 54th, however, and decided that what he saw warranted a change of plans. From a convenient hilltop, Kozlay watched the 75th pulling back under "severe" Southern fire and concluded that he could not extend the left rear of a line that had retired. The colonel instead held his regiment in a little valley sheltered from fire. Almost at once orders came for the 54th to fall back to join the rest of the brigade, which then was loosely concentrated near the Evers house and farm buildings.[43]

Both George and Christena Evers were fifty-nine years old in 1860, a farming couple of advancing years and limited means. They lived alone. She was illiterate. The Evers estate, counting both personal property and real estate, totaled only $2,200.[44] Now determined warriors descended on the Evers place, eager to buy temporary possession of it with blood—then move on as though it had no further value.

Colonel James A. Walker had moved skirmishers to a point in "the skirt of the woods near Ever's [sic] house" as part of the initial Confederate movement before the advance of the 8th New York. Bohlen's Brigade had not concentrated there yet, but Walker's Virginians still could see "a large body of the enemy" in the area. The colonel counted enough Federal infantry and artillery to make him uneasy, especially since he had no contact with Trimble to his left and rear. He thought that the Yankees might be moving toward his exposed right, but nothing came of that. Rather than acting in a foolishly aggressive fashion, out on his lonely limb, Walker pulled his men back into the woods and awaited developments.[45]

The next development proved to be the sudden appearance of General Trimble. The general accompanied Colonel Cantey and the right battalion of the 15th Alabama in the direction of the Evers house while the other half of the 15th had gone leftward and started the fight over Buell's guns. Trimble wanted to go after artillery firing at his column. When his few hundred Alabamians approached the enemy battery (which was Wiedrich's), Trimble halted the troops and rode out alone to reconnoiter. He found a vantage point from which he could see Federals in considerable strength swarming around the guns. This, wrote one of the Alabamians, "was too much even for that recklessly brave old man, and he withdrew."[46]

Trimble needed help and knew where to find some close at hand. He rode to the right and looked up Jim Walker. He found the Virginian and "parts of" the 13th and 25th Virginia. Both full regiments actually were present; Trimble probably was being his customarily uncharitable self and deprecating the worth of any unit other than his own. The general promptly ordered Walker "to move on my right through the woods and advance on the enemy in line of battle perpendicularly to his line and in rear of the battery." If Walker could get completely behind the hostile artillery, and attack at right angles to the Federal axis, the enemy position would be untenable. Unfortunately there were too few Confederates on the scene, and too many well-positioned Yankees, to make that kind of textbook attack practicable. Walker reported that Trimble "informed me that he was going forward to charge the enemy's battery, and directed me to advance on his right. This I did."[47] Advancing on Trimble's right was different than looping wide and coming from a ninety-degree tangent into the Federal rear. In doing what he thought he was ordered to do, which was in any case the only reasonable alternative, Walker of course earned Trimble's displeasure.

Walker sent Lieutenant Colonel Terrill forward with skirmishers again. They quickly ran into enemy skirmishers—these Federals were behaving far more prudently than had the 8th New York. Terrill's men brushed them aside with little difficulty, killing and wounding several, and moved steadily until they found Federals in greater strength.[48]

The two Virginia regiments under Walker followed their skirmishers toward the Evers house and barn. When the advance came back and re-formed with the rest of the regiments, the line moved forward smoothly for a time. It struck a high fence and got over it, then moved steadily up a sloping wheat field in the direction of the barn. Because of the confused nature of the ground, and the natural tendency to march at the edge of a westward-slanting woodline, Walker's left crowded in toward the right of Trimble's waiting 15th Alabama detachment. Trimble angrily ordered the colonel to go to the right and, in Walker's words, "to leave the house and barn on my left."[49]

Walker obeyed, of course, but it cost his regiments dearly. Moving away from the enemy exposed a tender flank and rear to deadly fire. A "heavy volley of musketry" raked the 25th Virginia, hitting several men. The 13th Virginia at the same time crossed a crest and

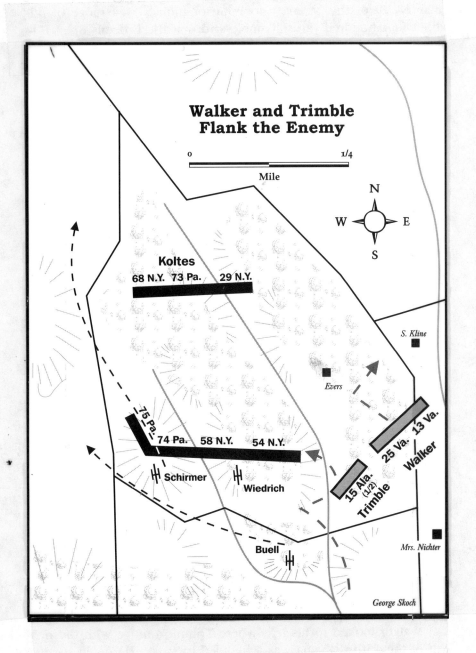

Walker and Trimble
Flank the Enemy

0   1/4
Mile

N
W   E
S

Koltes
68 N.Y.   73 Pa.   29 N.Y.

S. Kline

Evers

75 Pa.

74 Pa.   58 N.Y.   54 N.Y.

25 Va.   13 Va.

Walker

Schirmer   Wiedrich

15 Ala.
(1/2)

Trimble

Buell

Mrs. Nichter

George Skoch

"came into full view" of the enemy artillery and three regiments of infantry, all of that strength looming ominously at a range of only about four hundred yards. Trimble said that the Federals opened on the 13th "with galling effect." Walker described the artillery barrage as "a well-directed and heavy fire with grape." This fire, Walker reported in considerable understatement, "owing to the unexpected nature of the attack, caused some confusion."[50]

One of the men in the 13th Virginia described his experience vividly: "As we rose to the top of this hill, we came face to face with more of the enemy than I had ever seen in one position and with several pieces of artillery, which opened on us with . . . cannister, and small arms which were mowing the wheat about us like a hail storm." From the other end of the cannon barrels, Captain Wiedrich calmly reported firing a few rounds as Confederates appeared in the wheat field in front of him. The histrionic Colonel Krzyzanowski, however, was sure that the fate of free men everywhere hung in the balance. "If the enemy infantry made it as far as the Union artillery batteries they could turn the left flank of Frémont's entire army, threatening it with annihilation or capture," his biographer wrote in summation of the colonel's sentiments. "Only Bohlen's four small regiments [confronting two and one-half smaller Southern ones, we should note] stood between the Southern army and a Northern disaster."[51]

The Virginians of the 25th and 13th (left to right) faced the situation stoutly, and eventually would control it; but they hardly stood on the brink of annihilating Frémont from their huddled firing line. They responded to the fusillades coming against them by advancing fifty yards to the protection of another of the farm fences that sheltered almost every firing line at Cross Keys. Although the fence was "a very strong" one made of posts, so strong that they could not tear it down, its protection was probably more illusory than real. At least it served to keep the line straight. Sergeant Sam Buck thought that the fence's primary impact was that it stymied any further advance. "We could not go forward and would not fall back," he recalled, "so our only alternative was to stand and take it and most nobly did the regiment do it, but most humbly do I now confess, nothing but pride and a sense of duty kept me from running."[52]

Walker looked to his left, where Trimble's move with the right half of the 15th Alabama was scheduled to strike. He could see that Trimble was "detained," so ordered his Virginians to lie down behind the fence and open fire. The colonel's loud but calm orders steadied the troops. "The clarion voice of Walker could be heard," one remembered, over the gunfire and through the gunsmoke. Soon the Confederates settled down to business and the fence line began crackling with musketry. Trimble saw some of this as he looked to his right and applauded with uncharacteristic generosity the Virginians' "steadiness and gallantry."[53]

The outnumbered Southerners fired with enough verve and accuracy to drive Federal gunners from their chores at least twice. Fire came back at them in heavy volume. Walker called it "galling"; enlisted men probably would have been less delicate in euphemism. The 13th had never before been engaged nearly so heavily. Caring for the wounded men presented them with a quandary. Sam Buck's friend Camillus M. Copenhaver fell badly wounded "almost on me" and begged his chum to help him to the rear. Sergeant Buck knew "there was no time for favors then." (Copenhaver, a clever fellow and good soldier, recovered and the two men replayed the same scene at Fredericksburg six months later.) This was Buck's first experience with what became a familiar sight—several fit men helping a wounded soldier to the rear. "I have seen six men carrying one wounded man from the field, often four and always two," the sergeant lamented. "The best way to protect our wounded friends was to do our duty in the line and drive the enemy from them." The temptation to do a good deed that also served enlightened self-interest was irresistible, at Cross Keys and elsewhere.[54]

General Bohlen's role in the exchange of fire on the Evers farm was a minor one. He simply ordered the 74th and 75th Pennsylvania out of the artillery's way. Once he had given "Wiedrich a full sway," the battery "did fearful execution" upon the Rebels, even though Bohlen could see that his enemies enjoyed concealment because of the wheat and the fence. Captain Hubert Dilger's Battery also used canister on the Confederates. Schirmer's Battery withdrew at just the wrong time and did not help much. The 54th New York held to the Federal left, as ordered, and kept up a "severe fire" on any targets that came into sight. Colonel Kozlay of the 54th received enough orders to drive him to distraction, as he recalled drolly in his official report: "through the engagement I received a great many conflicting orders, coming from staff officers unknown to me, which I disobeyed."[55]

Parts of the two Pennsylvania regiments participated in the firefight, though not near the front, Bohlen having pushed them behind Wiedrich. Lieutenant Colonel Hamm of the 74th spoke of "torrents" of Southern fire. The record of one wounded 74th soldier survives in detail. A bullet hit Private Henry Simming of Company F squarely in the skull. Surgeons removed two inches of bone and Simming began a long convalescence. He finally was discharged from a hospital in West Virginia in October 1864. Three months later an examining doctor wrote in Simming's file, "this applicant's mind deranged." In 1868 Simming remained under treatment, though government surgeons—probably under the impetus of a cost-cutting regime—rated his disability "at three-fourths and temporary."[56]

The main body of the 75th had an easy time because Colonel Francis Mahler held it cautiously behind the crest of the ridge. General Blenker later commented harshly on the regiment's performance. Mahler's timidity kept the men out of the heavy fire while awaiting the "moment for action" that the colonel never found. He had earlier sent Companies I and K to support Wiedrich directly, however, and they suffered heavily. The two companies were accustomed to ill fortune. Two months earlier more than fifty men from their ranks had drowned when a boat ferrying them across the Shenandoah River collapsed. Presumably Mahler thought that he was sending the two decimated companies on easier duty when he detached them to join Wiedrich.[57]

Federal fire finally forced Walker's two sturdy regiments to abandon their fence line and slip one hundred yards to the right to gain cover in a body of woods. Bohlen ordered the 75th to the left to increase the pressure, but it arrived just too late to be of use. The 54th New York had already reached the far left, prompted by division commander Blenker. Colonel Kozlay of the 54th was proud of being at the point of decision when Walker retired in "great confusion." The Virginians "began to run," Kozlay reported, and "fled on the other side of the open field." Colonel Krzyzanowski of the 58th New York boasted in a postwar narrative of his own bayonet charge that hurled a horde of Rebels back, saving the Union from destruction— a feat unconfirmed by any observer, which evidently transpired entirely in his own fevered imagination.[58]

Colonel Jim Walker described the relocation to the woods in matter-of-fact prose: "seeing no further good could be accomplished by remaining longer in my position, I moved again by the right flank to the cover of a wood and halted." Trimble attributed the move into the woods to the initial exposure to artillery fire, completely ignoring the stout stand of the 13th and 25th Virginia at the fence line.[59]

Southern civilians huddling in homes suddenly thrust into the midst of battle watched with intense interest as the fighting unfolded. A member of Stonewall Jackson's staff who rode through the battle area a few days later met many civilians impressed by the bravery of the Confederates. That tribute probably centered on Walker's demi-brigade, because its action was the most exposed to civilian view. One set of civilians not far from Cross Keys certainly had its attention focused on Jim Walker. The colonel had roots in Augusta and Rock-ingham counties. His parents and sisters were close enough to hear, "in an agony of trembling apprehension," the guns firing at their family member and his men, without knowing the particulars. A younger sister walked up and down the lane leading to the Valley Turnpike "for the better part of two days, longing for tidings yet dreading to receive them."[60] The Walker family finally received good news about their son.

Although Trimble in his report sniped at Walker by innuendo, the Virginia colonel was one of the most inarguably distinguished Confederates of the day. Walker, for his part, lauded the behavior of the 13th and 25th Virginia, who "were exposed to a terrible fire . . . and behaved to my entire satisfaction." Trimble dismissed Walker's casualties as "small," though in fact Walker lost more men than did Trimble! Jed Hotchkiss, in his careful history of the war in Virginia, later wrote of Walker's "desperate courage"—the strongest enco-mium in his description of Cross Keys. General Ewell recognized Walker's key role. The following January, in recommending his pro-motion to brigadier general, Ewell said: "At Cross Keys Col. Walker with his Regiment, played an important and prominent part keeping back the Enemy and protecting our right flank." Ewell noted that his custom was to recommend "very few promotions," but in Walker's advancement he felt obliged to "heartily concur."[61]

The end of Walker's stand behind the fence came just minutes before the Federal position collapsed and Bohlen's men and guns withdrew. Sergeant Buck presumed that the Yankees had grown un-comfortable about the 13th and 25th Virginia being east of them. The move by the Confederates to their right, although away from the close front of the enemy, placed them even farther beyond the Federal left. Trimble was convinced that he triggered the withdrawal by advancing with the right wing of the 15th Alabama. That detachment had advanced "unperceived, under my direction," Trimble boasted, "to within 300 yards of the battery, then playing rapidly over their [the Alabamians'] heads" on Walker's men. The 16th Mississippi and 21st Georgia by this time had come forward to the vicinity, so Trimble felt strong enough to charge right ahead.[62]

Colonel Cantey and General Trimble pushed their 300 men up the slope toward territory that had been firmly held by several cannon and four regiments of infantry. By Trimble's account the movement, "totally unexpected by the enemy and handsomely carried out[,] . . . completed our success." The Federal battery had limbered up and escaped, its position marked by a ring of dead horses. The failure to capture the guns was not, of course, *Trimble's* fault—"not attributable to unskillful maneuvering," but rather to "one of those accidents" that befall military strategems. Blame ought to be apportioned to *Walker's* clumsiness, and to the 16th Mississippi and others guilty of losing time by "misconstruing my orders." Trimble implied that five minutes' less bumbling by maladroit underlings would have put him in the midst of the battery before it could retire—as though Wiedrich and company had not fallen back in response to pressure.[63]

From the nearby vantage point of the 13th Virginia, it was obvious that the Alabamians were fortunate in moving forward just as the Federals were retiring. Sergeant Buck of the 13th watched in amazement as the regiment marched "calmly by through an orchard, coming out immediately in front of the [Union] line of battle which broke before firing upon them. Whoever was in command of that regiment either knew nothing of the force in front of him or did not know how to put a regiment into action."[64] Everyone engaged on June 8 was relatively new to the deadly endeavor of battle. Buck clearly was right: 300 Alabamians did not drive away all of that artillery and infantry, but rather arrived concurrently with its departure. On the other hand, had Trimble not hurled his little force forward, might Bohlen have attempted to remain? Probably not, because he had lost his artillery support through no fault of his own.

The prime mover in the Federal withdrawal apparently was a mere captain of artillery, Louis Schirmer. Schirmer exercised a narrow seniority over fellow battery commander Wiedrich. The timid Schirmer already had ordered Wiedrich to fall back early in the contest, "against my positive order to remain," Bohlen angrily reported; but Wiedrich soon returned to the front and became the centerpiece of Bohlen's defense. Wiedrich's New Yorkers fired steadily, no one flinching, as the Confederates could attest with dismay. Schirmer left his own battery in the rear and came forward to order Wiedrich back once more. General Bohlen insisted that the guns stay; Schirmer insisted that they retire. The customary result of differing opinions between generals and captains did not result, because a few days earlier General Blenker—Bohlen's superior and the division commander—had told Wiedrich to obey Schirmer![65] This peculiar arrangement, presumably resulting from a feud between the two generals, cost the Federals the position they had ably defended. With the artillery gone, the infantry followed.

The Northerners fell back in reasonably good order and without suffering from any close pursuit. The 75th Pennsylvania, which had been steadily underengaged, "behaved themselves worthy of a better opportunity," according to its colonel. He felt obliged to "deny totally that my regiment ran away, as charged by General Blenker." The 74th Pennsylvania retired only about one hundred yards, and fired several times from behind a fence before Bohlen directed Lieutenant Colonel Hamm to move the regiment back to the northwest, out of action. At army headquarters, word that the 74th had been flanked out of position was credited with being pivotal in Frémont's determination to abandon ground all across his left front.[66]

The 54th New York was dressing its line, preparing to "inflict a more severe chastisement" on the Confederates when orders to withdraw arrived. The regiment did so with no difficulty or confusion, halting after a hundred yards next to the 74th Pennsylvania to await developments. To the excitable Colonel Krzyzanowski, of course, the affair seemed like a veritable Armageddon. He later referred to his regiment's role as "the massacre at Cross Keys," though he reported only seven men killed. Krzyzanowski believed that Confederate masses drove his 58th New York back under "a heavy musketry fire." Regiments of Rebels boiling out of the woods forced him to retire, though carefully and slowly.[67]

For a few minutes the 54th and 74th halted on their new line not far behind the one they had just abandoned. Thinking that he saw another opportunity to capture the artillery prize that had eluded him, Trimble nudged the 15th Alabama and Walker's Virginians forward. "After some minutes' brisk fire by the enemy's sharpshooters," Trimble grumbled, "their entire left wing retreated to their first position" far to the Federal rear. Captain Oates of the Alabama regiment used almost the same language to describe the duration of the final brief encounter: "for a few minutes the engagement became general."[68]

The Northern battery again was Wiedrich's, which had halted long enough to fire a few more salvos. Bohlen and others insisted that the further Federal withdrawal after this final brush was uncontested. "After a few shots the enemy retired," he reported, "and did not molest us any longer." Journalist C. H. Webb declared that the victorious Unionists had "driven the enemy some two miles" and only fell back having "exhausted their own ammunition . . . the enemy showing no signs of pursuing." Many a weary infantryman in blue would have contested those judgments had there been a forum in which to do so. The officers, however, professed to be eager to mix anew with the Rebel foe. Bohlen's regimental commanders, it was said, "simply could not believe" the order to retire.[69]

Among the retiring Federals moved the three-regiment brigade of Colonel John A. Koltes. The 29th New York, 73rd Pennsylvania, and 68th New York (in that order from east to west) had stood quietly behind Bohlen in reserve during the fighting on the Evers farm. Friedrich von Schluembach, a twenty-two-year-old lieutenant in the 29th, carried a German Bible in his pocket. On an endpaper he sketched a map of the regimental alignment of his brigade and Bohlen's. It survives as a vital document—the only known depiction of Union battle positions around the Evers house. The shrieking shells and the rattle of musketry mightily impressed young Friedrich. He wrote "Cross Keys" twice in the margin opposite Luke 19:43, and added the date of the battle. For the benefit of English-speaking infidels who might stumble across his notes, as has in fact happened only recently, Schluembach translated his Cross Keys text: "For the days shall come upon thee, that thine Enemies ['*deine Feinde*'] shall cast a trench about thee, and compass thee round, & keep thee in on Every side."[70]

It is hard to imagine what might have happened to Lieutenant Schluembach to prompt a reaction so stunned. An artillerist under Koltes declared that the brigade retired, "not having fired a shot!" The 29th was on Koltes's far left, and would have been subject to a bit more excitement than the other two regiments had any developed. Koltes reported only one killed for the three regiments combined. The actual losses were only slightly more than that—a level less than minuscule by Civil War standards.[71]

The Confederate equivalents of Koltes's Brigade of passive on-lookers were the cavalry detachments scouting east of the combat zone. Two companies of the 2nd Virginia Cavalry roamed there throughout the afternoon. So did some members of the Comanches battalion assigned to Ewell's headquarters. Confederate foot soldiers, who viewed the galloping cavalrymen as military dilettantes, were given to saying sardonically (and no doubt jealously), "Who ever saw a dead cavalryman?" The Comanches fulfilled that expectation on June 8. Only one man was hit, and he was "touched . . . very slightly, by a bouncing grape shot."[72] The Southern mounted men had no direct impact on the fight against Stahel or Bohlen; but Trimble's maneuvers were not interrupted by any threats from his right, and that was what the cavalry was supposed to ensure.

With Stahel gone and Bohlen and Koltes following him, Trimble stood master of the field in his front. He had, as General Ewell noted in summary, driven the enemy "more than a mile, and remained on his flank ready to make the final attack."[73] The aggressive Marylander had no desire to rest on his laurels. In search of further triumphs he would spend the afternoon and much of the evening hounding Ewell and Jackson for permission to launch his victorious brigade against the Federal mass to his front and left.

Meanwhile battle raged behind Trimble, around the center and left of the Confederate line. Its daunting sound and fury affected individuals on both sides, but nowhere in those sectors did the Battle of Cross Keys develop into decisive close actions such as the three that Trimble had fought and won.

Milroy deployed his
infantry and sent aides
back to bring forward
artillery. "They
soon came," the general
told his wife in a
letter, "and they
commenced preaching to
the rebles in a most
eloquent and striking
manner."

CHAPTER 11

THE FIRE-SWEPT

CONFEDERATE CENTER

While Trimble fought his series of battles, Confederate artillery and its infantry support stood sturdily in the center of the line near Mill Creek Church. For long hours the Courtney Artillery, sparked by its charismatic Lieutenant Latimer, faced northward toward Frémont's position and fired steadily. Courtney's guns had gone into position first, near ten A.M., to protect the returning 15th Alabama skirmishers. For that reason and because of Latimer's dazzling presence, Confederate sources refer to the artillery cluster almost generically as belonging to Courtney. In fact five Southern batteries fired from the rim of the amphitheater, beginning at the main road and running to the left. Two others stood nearby in ready reserve.

John A. M. Lusk's 2nd Rockbridge Artillery was at the front. So were William H. Rice's New Market Artillery, Charles I. Raine's Lee Battery of Lynchburg, and John B. Brockenbrough's Baltimore Light Artillery. William H. Caskie's Hampden Artillery and Wilfred E. Cutshaw's Jackson Artillery were the reserve batteries.[1] Of the seven units, all but Captain Brockenbrough's Marylanders were from Virginia. The Maryland battery stood farthest left of the Confederate artillery. It shared in the action of General George H. Steuart's Brigade in that quarter, so Brockenbrough's experience can be best described in the next chapter, in conjunction with that of the Confederate infantry of the far left.

For about six hours Courtney, Lusk, Rice, and Raine poured shot and shell at the Yankees. In order to maintain a steady drumroll of fire, the Confederates purposely worked their pieces "alternately," a watching infantryman noted; "that is they fired in turn." Eli Coble of the 21st North Carolina looked on with frank admiration as Lieutenant Latimer held the gunners to their dangerous task. A round struck one of Latimer's sergeants in the head, knocking fragments of his skull away. After a time the young lieutenant had to call for help from Coble and his mates, assigning them as volunteers to bring ammunition up to the guns from the caissons parked behind the hill. Latimer "stood two or three steps to the left side of the gun to the left hand," Coble recalled admiringly, "and his cheeks wore a rosey tint, and his face was that of a cheerful soul." The artillerists responded to their leader's example by fighting desperately. At the roar of a Federal artillery discharge, Latimer would sometimes order his men to fall flat on the ground, then they would spring back into action when the searching shells had passed.[2]

Trimble lauded the "heroic conduct" of Latimer and his men, "in holding their position under the incessant fire of four batteries at one time." "The fact that they stood bravely up to their work for over five hours, exhausted all their shot and shell, and continued their fire with canister to the end of the battle, speaks more in their favor than the most labored panegyric," Trimble declared in a labored panegyric. Unfortunately but characteristically the general ignored the artillery fighting next to Courtney and Latimer, leaving the impression—in fact declaring emphatically—that the one battery belonging to his own brigade had stood alone.[3]

Both of Ewell's other brigadier generals (Elzey and Steuart) went down wounded on June 8. Neither filed a report of the battle. As a result, Trimble's self-centered description of the prowess of the bat-

Lieutenant Joseph White Latimer
"stood two or three steps to the
left side of the gun, and his cheeks
wore a rosey tint, and his face was
that of a cheerful soul." Latimer, by
then a major, would be mortally
wounded at Gettysburg before his
twentieth birthday.

tery attached to his own brigade gives even more credit to Courtney and Latimer than the generous portion they deserve. Colonel Stapleton Crutchfield, Jackson's chief of artillery, reached Cross Keys about two-thirty. By then the artillery fight had moved well along toward its conclusion. Crutchfield was wanting in the energy and skill necessary to direct a major component of a field army—especially one led by so zealous a man as Stonewall Jackson. His slothful demeanor had cost Jackson at Front Royal in May, and would affect later affairs too. Arriving at the June 8 hot spot six hours after the first gun fired was a suspiciously casual response to the beckoning of duty.

Nevertheless, Crutchfield's report of what he found when he finally reached Cross Keys serves as an antidote to Trimble's tunnel vision. The colonel mentioned all of the batteries on the line and reported finding them "holding their ground well, and delivering their fire with accuracy and spirit." Raine's guns seemed to be "particularly well and gallantly managed." Charles Raine's horse fell wounded, and the captain pitched in to serve a gun when a shortage of cannoneers developed. His "Lee Battery," as the unit styled itself, lost the most heavily of the Confederate batteries engaged on the ridge.[4]

Crutchfield identified Cutshaw and Caskie as in reserve, but the two companies probably played a role in the fighting. Caskie had at least one casualty, and A. J. Barrow of Cutshaw's Battery wrote in his diary for June 8 that his unit "engaged the enemy . . . and held them back, killing great many of them."[5]

Ewell's cannon served him well from their commanding aerie above Mill Creek. Jennings Cropper Wise, the historian of the army's artillery, summarized the role of the guns clustered near the road: "massed in the center . . . [they] acted more in concert than artillery had hitherto done in the campaign. Their fire was well conducted, with all the advantages of position to which artillery is entitled by a prior selection for the defense of a given point." Wise waxed too enthusiastic, however, when he suggested that this concentration of guns "evidences a growing tendency on the part of Jackson to use his batteries . . . in concert, instead of distributing them here and there on the battlefield . . . thereby dissipating the effect of their fire."[6]

Jackson was indeed honing his tactical skills by means of Valley experience, and he was always especially interested in artillery; but the legendary general had nothing to do with massing Ewell's guns above Mill Creek. Dick Ewell deserved the credit. Even more belonged to Joe Latimer and the few hundred other Confederates who rolled their cannon to the edge of the cliff and stood bravely by them. Massing artillery is a sound concept, but it also makes an easier target for the enemy.

Ewell's artillery did not escape unscathed, although its advantage in elevation provided a considerable edge. The height also neutralized some of the small-arms fire Federals brought to bear on the ridge. Despite their beneficial location, the Virginia batteries suffered. David French Boyd, a Louisianian on General Richard Taylor's staff, noted that Frémont's artillery "was splendidly handled." Unaffected by the usual Southern xenophobia, he thought that was due to the enemy's "expert German officers. I think Fremont's artillery practice at Cross Keys the best I remember during the war."[7]

When Union infantry maneuvered close enough to Mill Creek to bring musketry to bear on the high ground, they chased away for a time Rice's and Raine's batteries. The two captains led their men "to the rear for a short distance" to avoid the infantry fire. After a brief respite, Rice and Raine came back into action and stood firm. Apparently Trimble referred to this temporary withdrawal when he insisted that Courtney had "to contend singly with four batteries of the enemy" after "the battery of . . . Steuart . . . was withdrawn after a severe loss of horses." The battery most closely aligned with Steuart's Brigade was Brockenbrough's, however, and Brockenbrough did not retire. Trimble again was displaying a stark lack of fairness in describing any action not his own. The general did admit to having one Ally: "The most admirable position selected [by Trimble himself, of course] for the battery alone saved it from total destruction, if a special Providence did not guard it from harm."[8] With God and Isaac Trimble on their side—not necessarily in that order—Ewell's gunners had little to fear.

The intensity of enemy fire on the Confederate center is conveyed by the account of Captain G. Campbell Brown. He had carried a message from Ewell to the units on the far left. As Brown returned toward the center, where Ewell commanded from a position near the artillery, the young officer came across a grim vignette. Four cannoneers were bearing to the rear the corpse of a comrade "when a shell struck directly underneath it and exploded in the soft earth, injuring no one but throwing the body to the height of a man's head & prostrating two of the bearers." The two stunned Confederates regained their feet, and the four men "picked up the body again & quietly carried it off."

Brown resumed his ride southeastward and soon came across a youngster trying desperately to get an ordnance wagon out of the range of enemy fire before flying explosives could blow up his load of ammunition. The team's harness had broken and the boy "was working nervously and a little wildly—but pluckily." Captain Brown jumped down to lend a hand "feeling nervous myself," he admitted, envisioning at every moment a shell exploding the wagon's deadly cargo.[9]

The teamster must have been carrying small-arms ammunition, since artillery rounds soon came to be in demand at the front he was leaving. Enemy artillery fire slackened by mid-afternoon, just as Confederate guns ran short of shells. The Courtney Artillery had to withdraw when it emptied its chests. The rest of the batteries in the vicinity told Colonel Crutchfield that they were "getting short." A logistical faux pas threatened the Confederate defense at this critical moment. "The ordnance train," Crutchfield wrote, "had taken a different road from the one intended, and was a considerable distance away." (The colonel's consistent lack of attention to such crucial details repeatedly affected Jackson's operations. Eventually Stonewall would separate ordnance functions from artillery control and give the ordnance responsibility to the brilliant William Allan, who also became a leading postwar historian of the Valley Campaign.)

Nothing much could be done about the ammunition shortage on June 8 under the exigencies of battle. Crutchfield ordered the batteries to slow their rate of fire, which had been more rapid than that of their foe. Now the Virginia batteries conformed to the enemy rate of fire. Before long the Federals ceased firing entirely. Predictably, the fizzling out of the long artillery duel into quiet anticlimax offered both sides the opportunity to claim victory. Crutchfield could boast: "None of our guns or caissons were lost or injured in this affair."[10] The more important result was that no Unionist had come anywhere close to reaching the Confederate position atop Mill Creek Ridge.

❈ ❈ ❈ ❈

General Robert H. Milroy, who held the Federal right center opposite Courtney and his comrades, put his three batteries in position very early in the action. They fired at first from a range too long to have much effect. Milroy soon moved the batteries forward to a better location near the Armentrout house. The general had pushed ahead of his artillery with an infantry force for about half a mile. There Milroy "found a fine position for my artillery in full view of 3 reble batteries." He deployed his infantry in the shelter of a convenient ravine and sent aides back with orders to bring the artillery forward. "They soon came," Milroy told his wife in a letter, "and they commenced preaching to the rebles in a most eloquent and striking manner." Admiring journalist Charles Webb wrote that Milroy aggressively continued "planting his guns each time nearer and nearer the enemy's batteries"; but in fact the relocation to near the Armentrout house was the only substantial artillery advance.[11]

Battery I of the 1st Ohio Light Artillery set up in a copse. To one of the cannoneers it seemed that eight Southern guns focused on his battery alone. "Their shot went shrieking through the trees over our heads," the Ohioan recalled, "tearing ragged holes through large oaks and cutting off great limbs." A gunner of German ancestry who hailed from Cincinnati went down with a mortal wound in his abdomen inflicted by a shell fragment. The billowing muzzle flashes from their own guns set leaves and underbrush on fire. Flames soon began licking up tree trunks and down limbs. Smoke choked the artillerymen and obscured their vision. No doubt the smoke also hid them from Confederate eyes aiming counterbattery fire.[12]

The smoke and fire finally drove Battery I out of the woods to a fresh position on a nearby hillock. When Isaac Gardner of the battery wrote a cryptic note in his diary that night that mentioned "hot fire," he might have been alluding to either Confederate shells or burning woods—perhaps both. Frank Bisel of the 12th Ohio Battery, which also belonged to Milroy, told his diary on June 8 that the 12th "was engaged for six hours" and lost one man killed and several wounded.[13]

In bearing the Confederate fire and returning it diligently, Milroy's batteries accomplished two things. They kept their counterparts in the Southern artillery from completely dominating the field, and they provided a nucleus upon which Milroy tried to build a strong infantry position. Nothing came of Milroy's efforts, but his gunners had done what might reasonably have been expected of them. In the process they caused considerable discomfort to the Confederates, and a few losses.

Despite efforts to keep battery horses under cover, the animals suffered dreadfully during artillery duels. When Federals finally climbed Mill Creek Ridge the next morning, after Ewell had abandoned it, they found dead Southern horses as mute testimony to the accuracy of Northern fire. Milroy noted "large numbers of horses laying around where the reble batteries had been." Correspondent Webb counted twelve dead horses around one Confederate battery, attesting to how Milroy's artillery had delivered its fire "with a precision truly remarkable." He marveled at how Northern guns had torn the soil around where the Confederate artillery stood: "it was furrowed with our shot and shell as with a plow," he wrote.[14]

The artillery of both sides played the role of bridesmaid to the infantry at Cross Keys, as in most Civil War actions. Milroy's hope was to throw his brigade forward under cover of artillery fire and push Ewell off Mill Creek Ridge. He had not the faintest chance of success, other than by a wide turning movement that would maneuver the Confederates away from their dominant ground. Milroy's assault on the afternoon of June 8 was the sort of hopeless gesture often seen during the war's innocent early days.

For such an attempt Robert Milroy had at his disposal only four infantry regiments: the 2nd, 3rd, and 5th Virginia (Union), and the 25th Ohio. They probably brought into action a few more than 2,000 muskets. The regiments first came under fire near Milroy's artillery at its first position, well behind the front. They followed the general to near the Armentrout house, where he called his batteries forward, as described earlier in this chapter. While he contemplated the best way to close with the Confederates atop the ridge, Milroy thoughtfully put his infantry under cover on the reverse slope behind the guns. The soldiers hugged the ground and used one of the ubiquitous Cross Keys fences as further protection. Even so they felt exposed to "the shot and shell [that] flew thick and fast into our lines," one of them wrote.[15]

Milroy had secured Frémont's permission for his initial advance to near the Armentrout house. Beyond that Frémont probably knew little of what transpired until after the battle. Newspaperman Webb found army headquarters "on a gentle eminence, and open ground . . . . in the rear of our line." Reports from the front trickled back to General Frémont at this pleasant spot, "but no part of [the fighting] was to be seen. The musketry was heard in volleys, telling of fearful havoc."[16] (Ewell and his ranking generals by contrast watched their troops from near the front and thus controlled the battle far more directly than Frémont did.)

Robert Milroy was not timid about grasping the initiative that Frémont shunned. He rode forward from the Armentrout artillery cluster "to examine the ground," in search of "the best way of getting my Regiments up where they could use their Minnie [*sic*] Enfield rifles." Milroy came across a ravine that ran southward into another ravine. The first was a small drainage that emptied into Mill Creek. The Mill Creek bottom was Milroy's second ravine, which he described as running "along the foot of the hill on which the reble batteries were situated." Without making a careful reconnaissance— another sign of early war naïveté, akin to that which had put the 8th New York in so much trouble—Milroy "determined to bring my brigade up and deploy at the foot of the hill[,] silence the batteries with my rifles and take them at the point of the bayonet." Without further ado or careful examination of the ground, the general went back and put his regiments to work on his ambitious agenda.[17]

The Federal advance winding downhill toward Mill Creek hugged the shelter of the drainage that carried a little rivulet toward the Flory farm buildings. The serious fighting obviously awaiting them in the bottom would be the first for most of the men. A soulful youth in the 25th Ohio named Thomas Evans recalled his emotions in that trying moment: "Here I was rushing pell mell to probable destruction. I paused. I thought of all whomever I held dear—a mother's and sister's tears will probably be poured out for my life." Evans "trembled with emotion" and prayed. A soldier in the 2nd Virginia (Union) remembered more fear than spiritual anxiety as the advancing men "were treated to the music of the screaming and hissing shells . . . as thick as the leaves." Fortunately for them "the softness of the ground, into which scores of shells sank, saved us from serious injury." The endless rains of the past week, which everyone had damned earnestly as they fell, now proved to be a blessing, as the ground absorbed iron that otherwise would have spread through Milroy's ranks.[18]

Wheat growing thickly around the gully helped to screen Milroy's advance, but it also hid Confederate skirmishers deployed at the base of the ridge. The general moved "caustiously along the ravine leading up to the 2nd but as soon as the head of my columns got within 60 or 70 yards of the 2d ravine we discovered it was full of rebles lying behind a fence in the tall grass almost wholly concealed from view." The Southerners, aided by their friends atop the ridge, "mowed down the head of my column by a deadly fire almost

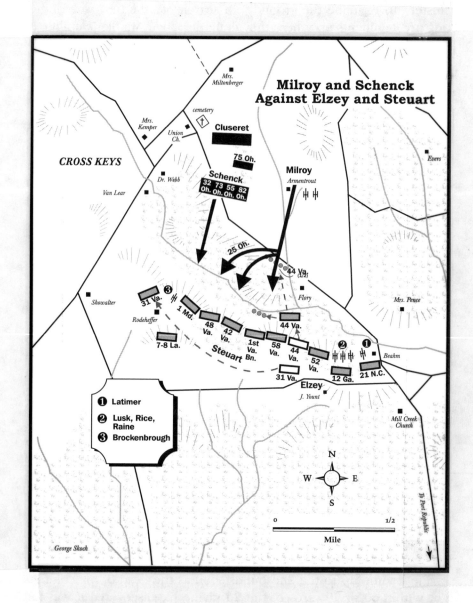

Milroy and Schenck
Against Elzey and Steuart

CROSS KEYS

Mrs. Miltonberger

Mrs. Kemper

cemetery

Union Ch.

Cluseret

75 Oh.

Schenck
32 73 55 82
Oh. Oh. Oh. Oh.

Milroy
Armentrout

Evers

Dr. Webb

Van Lear

25 Oh.

44 Va.
(1/2)

Flory

Mrs. Pence

Showalter

③ 31 Va.

1 Md.

Rodeheffer

48 Va.

42 Va.

44 Va.

7-8 La.

Steuart

1st Va. Bn.

58 Va.

44 Va.

52 Va.

② ①

Beahm

31 Va.

12 Ga.

21 N.C.

Elzey

J. Yount

Mill Creek Church

① Latimer

② Lusk, Rice, Raine

③ Brockenbrough

N
W — E
S

0 ——————— 1/2
Mile

To Port Republic

George Skoch

as fast as they appeared," Milroy recalled sadly. The Federals could not retaliate "with any effect as we could not see them."[19]

Thomas Evans, who had approached battle with such trepidation, found the reality as bad as he had expected. He descended the first ravine into "the deafening roar of musketry and the loud pealing of artillery[,] the bursting of shells, the whiz of . . . cannister." Those noises were less appalling than "the crushing of timber by the dread missiles mingled with the unearthly yells of opposing forces and the moaning of the dying and the screams of the wounded." All of this combined "to chill the blood in my veins," Evans admitted.[20]

A member of Frémont's staff concluded that Milroy, "after a hot bout with a strong line of the enemy's advance people, drove them in," before getting into deeper trouble. In truth the few Confederates on the low ground near Mill Creek were simply doing what Federal attackers foolishly ignored all day: they were fulfilling the basic function of skirmishers, after which they slipped back up the hill into the woods. Now Milroy pushed down out of the first ravine and onto the low ground next to the creek. By the time he shook his advancing line into some semblance of order, it was under heavy fire. Here Milroy's men were parallel to the Federal line behind them, and also to the Confederate line in front of them. As one of them wrote disgustedly, "We were then permitted to witness an exciting artillery duel, which was rendered terrible by the screaming of the horses that were wounded, and far more by the men of the regiment who were shot."[21]

Milroy boldly decided to advance farther, into the Confederate woods to his right front. No doubt the cover looked enticing. This time he sent skirmishers ahead; Milroy was picking up some basics along the way. As soon as those advance soldiers crossed a rise in the ground, out of the protecting wheat, "they rec[eive]d a perfect storm of bullets from the woods which appeared to be full of rebles, but the fol[i]age was so thick we could not see them." The general pushed the rest of his men forward and "opened a tremendous fire into the woods but a deadly fire come out of it and my boys were drop[p]ed by it rapidly." Two bullets hit Milroy's horse Jasper. The animal, blood spurting from its breast, reared and plunged and nearly unseated his rider, who leaped to the ground. Confederate volleys also hit the mounts of the major and the adjutant of the 25th Ohio. Milroy left Jasper for dead and hurriedly sought to find an escape for his regiments.[22]

An officer whom Milroy judged "one of the best captains of the 25th Ohio" went down mortally wounded. Another of the regiment's captains, thirty-seven-year-old James F. Charlesworth, survived the wound he received here, but only narrowly. Because the details of his dreadful ordeal survive, Charlesworth makes an especially graphic example of Civil War wounds and their treatment. A musket ball punched through the captain's abdomen about two inches from his umbilicus, penetrating his sword belt, his clothes, and his entire body. The ball broke the top of the hipbone. The impact felt to Charlesworth something like "an electric shock."

Soon after he was hit the captain fell into merciful unconsciousness. On June 9 hospital stewards carried him about thirty miles to Mount Jackson on a stretcher. Several days later the medical establishment moved Charlesworth on to Winchester, where he arrived "nearly pulseless, his feet and limbs cold, and a clammy sweat covering his body." Until June 20 he received no treatment other than opium and ate nothing but tiny quantities of milk. Starting within hours after the bullet hit Charlesworth, "the contents of the bowels began to discharge through both wounds." They continued to do so until the wounds gradually closed. By then fifteen pieces of the shattered ilium had come out of the openings too. In 1873 Lieutenant Colonel Charlesworth (he was promoted after his wounding) was alive and drawing disability pay—and facing the indignity of having his wounds photographed for public consumption in a government publication. He could get along marginally so long as he was "careful of himself in every way."[23] James Charlesworth must have cringed every time he saw a piece of the romantic battle art in vogue by 1873 (which was not unlike the romantic Civil War art in vogue in the 1990s). His Civil War had not resembled that imagery at all.

Milroy made a final attempt to close with the Confederate line by lunging farther to his right "in order to turn the left flank of the rebles." The 25th Ohio led the way. Some of the Unionist Virginians following the 25th thought the move was to resist Confederates who sought to turn Milroy's right. Milroy and others insisted that the advance teetered on the brink of sweeping success. The 25th Ohio, Milroy reported, "got half in the forest." A soldier behind the 25th described the fight as "a brisk and severe musketry fight . . . with considerable loss to our brigade, and a much heavier one to the opposing forces, who were compelled to give way before the gallantry of our troops."[24]

Correspondent Webb of the *Times* described the Ohio advance as a gallant charge "up the hill where one of the opposing batteries was planted." The Ohioans succeeded in "cutting down the gunners with their fire," Webb wrote. "Had they been supported I think they would have captured a battery. They made the crest of the hill too hot to hold on the part of the enemy and held their position until recalled." A contemporary summary of the battle recounted the Federal advance in glossy terms: "General Milroy, himself in advance of his foremost battery . . . forced the enemy back from point to point, penetrated Jackson's center, and was almost in contact with his guns."[25]

Confederates atop the hill generally were not as ruffled as the Federals were excited, but Milroy's account agreed with Webb's: he only fell back on orders. These came from an aide to Frémont who reached Milroy at his self-proclaimed high tide. "I was never so astonished or thunderstruck in my life," the general wrote to his wife. "I could not believe what the dutchman said and made him repeat it three times." The aide, Milroy noted with disdain, underwent his interrogation while "dodging his head down behind the horse like a duck dodging thunder." As soon as he could, the man "dashed off at break neck speed." Milroy felt ashamed to order his regiments back, so sent staff officers to perform the duty.[26]

The Southern infantrymen who occupied Mill Creek Ridge generally felt more threatened by enemy artillery than by Milroy's soldiers. The main body of the 21st North Carolina remained all day on the left edge of the road where it crossed the ridge, providing support to Courtney's guns posted there. Elzey's Brigade held Ewell's center. Elzey and perhaps Ewell himself, whose headquarters was nearby, probably gave the 21st such direction as it received in Trimble's absence. Essentially the Tarheels and Elzey's men simply had to lie helpless under artillery fire. Fortunately for them, as an officer noted, "The Enemy's shells, pitching over the top of the hill . . . nearly all stopped in the side of [the next hill to the rear], or passing through the treetops struck a few yards back . . . in the woods."[27]

The rest of Elzey's men did not total a large number. Colonel James A. Walker's sterling performance out on Trimble's right included the 13th and 25th Virginia. Both regiments belonged to Elzey. That left him with only the 31st Virginia, the 12th Georgia, and Trimble's orphaned 21st North Carolina. The Georgians remained in reserve all day. They "did not engage the enemy with muskets, but were placed in rear of the artillery to support it," one of them wrote.

"We lay in an open field just behind the cannon during the whole fight."[28]

The 31st Virginia started the day in reserve near the 12th Georgia. At noon Major Joseph H. Chenoweth of the 31st wrote in his diary that "the 31st is supporting the battery which is engaged." (The diary of the twenty-five-year-old major, a graduate and former professor of Virginia Military Institute, is an important source for Cross Keys and Port Republic. Because of his death on June 9, it also is an especially moving document.) One of the enlisted men in the 31st described in similar words the regiment's "position in rear of some of the batteries." Elzey and Ewell evidently had the 31st in mind as their maneuver element, because the regiment "occasionally" moved short distances in both directions to "several positions" around the center. Eventually, at about two-thirty, the generals sent the 31st to bolster the army's farthest flank, to the left of Steuart's Brigade.[29]

The three regiments (and then the two that remained after the 31st moved left) took a pounding from the Federal artillery. Civil War cannon, however, dealt more in sound and fury than in absolute devastation. The noisy and terrifying rounds killed and wounded people when they hit them, but the lack of high-explosive powder and of extensive fragmentation resulted in less damage than seemed likely. A revealing estimate suggests that 10 percent of Civil War battle losses resulted from artillery, while it produced about 90 percent of World War II casualties. Even so, the terror and the casualties were daunting to novice soldiers on both sides at Cross Keys.

Jim Hall of the 31st called the cannonading "the most terrific I ever heard." He and his mates "remained as silent and quiet as if inanimate . . . while the cannon balls like winged devils were flying around us." Hall watched his comrades' reactions. "Some looked pale but calm, their eyes tranquil. The knitted brow and flashing eyes of others, showed the more fiery spirit within."[30]

Major Chenoweth noted an inexplicable lull in the firing shortly after noon, but soon thereafter he wrote in his diary: "This is decidedly the warmest battle with which I have ever had anything to do. The artillery fire is superb, and the musketry is not so slow. . . . The shells fly around us thick & fast." Chenoweth recognized that Mill Creek Ridge dominated the enemy's ground, but admitted that Stonewall Jackson's arrangements across a five-mile front had confused him. "I do not like our position. . . . We may possibly have our flanks turned. . . . Our movements yesterday and today are incomprehensible to me."[31] Chenoweth had been exposed to Jackson's behavior for most of the previous eight years, between VMI and army service, so he can hardly have been surprised to find himself confused by that eccentric genius.

The 21st North Carolina went into position first of the infantry supports and remained to the end. The regiment "was exposed to the effect of the terrific fire," according to the brigade's official report, "but under cover of the hill happily escaped with few casualties." From a view in the ranks, Eli Coble of the 21st estimated the Carolinians' loss at a level fully four times as great as they actually suffered, demonstrating just how deadly the incoming fire seemed.[32]

Coble had a particularly trying day because his imagination tormented him. His spot in the 21st's line was next to a cluster of thin saplings. Before the enemy fire had achieved any real intensity, Coble recalled, "I was seized with an exceeding fear" and a voice "in or near to my breast . . . seemed to say 'you will be killed if you remain here.' " The twenty-seven-year-old soldier told himself to ignore this irrational manifestation, but the "fine still voice" repeated the warning again and again. As the artillery barrage intensified, Coble prayed and contemplated his religious condition, eventually working himself up to such a pitch that he imagined his mother advising him about what to do from beneath her familiar homemade sunbonnet. A huge dead tree not far to the rear looked awfully appealing as a refuge, but pride and the opinion of his peers kept Coble from seeking its protection. Finally a courier came galloping up to the colonel of the 21st. To Coble's immense relief the man's message was: "The General says move your regiment to the right from under fire of that battery." The listening soldiers leaped to their feet before their commander could relay the order and gratefully marched a couple of hundred yards away. As soon as they moved, of course (otherwise Coble would have forgotten the whole thing), in quick succession a Northern shell exploded atop the vacant saplings and then a solid shot smashed them to kindling.[33]

The 12th Georgia's reserve position in an open field behind the batteries left the regiment unable to shoot at anything, but provided no immunity to Federal shelling. "Solid shot, Grape and bombs seemed like they were raining down upon us during the whole action," one of them wrote. A single shell that burst in the midst of the 12th killed or wounded nine men. One casualty was forty-five-year-old Francis Milton Little, who had most of the flesh torn from a shoulder.[34]

Even harder hit was Gibson G. Mahone of Company G. His fate put the cap on the sort of morality play that Americans of Victorian vintage took so much to heart. The eighteen-year-old Mahone was the boy who had cursed profanely that morning during religious services. His part of the line sought shelter behind a rail fence. A deadly shell hit the fence and mangled Mahone's lower body, shattering his legs just above the knees. The boy died not long thereafter, saying "tell them I died with my face towards the damn Yankees." The "them" of the message probably were his grandparents, with whom he had been living. Most of the regiment knew of Mahone's behavior that morning, and attributed the result to the inexorable working of Providence.[35]

What of the pious members of the 12th Georgia? Van Buren Clark, a narrator of Mahone's fate, saw the opposite result at Cross Keys as well. At the same moment that Gibson Mahone went down, a solid shot hurled into the Southern lines whistled within inches of regimental adjutant Dr. George Washington Thomas. The hurtling missile passed between Thomas's bridle reins and his horse's neck. Clark was looking right at Thomas and noted with astonishment, "He did not appear the least excited." Thomas later became regimental surgeon.[36] To complete the catalog of retribution and redemption, it must be noted that Clark did not die until 1921; Adjutant-Surgeon Thomas lived until 1902; and Chaplain Marshall, who delivered the June 8 sermon that Gibson Mahone disdained, lived until 1914.

Confederates who fought near the center of the line commented with more ardor about the artillery they faced than about Milroy's infantry. That resulted to some extent because Milroy's deflections to his right, toward the Confederate left, finally took him into General Steuart's zone. By the time the Federal general made his attempt, only the 12th Georgia and the 21st North Carolina remained near the artillery on the road. The 12th Georgia "did not engage the enemy with muskets," one of them wrote. Musketry crackling just over the ridge, however, prompted one barely literate Georgian to summarize the day in his diary thus: "both small armes and a hevy battle insude At Mill creek church."[37]

The 21st North Carolina saw a bit more of Milroy. General Trimble's report implied that the Tarheels did little infantry fighting. "When the battery was threatened with an infantry force," the general wrote, "this regiment was called and readily took its position to repel the enemy's attack, and stood modestly ready to do its duty as gallantly as heretofore." Gus Clewell of the 21st in a letter home suggested a more active role. The regiment was "in some close places," Clewell said, and eventually took part in a "very severe fight, they outnumbered us but we repulsed them with a heavy loss."[38]

Eli Coble—he of the premonition and the shattered saplings—left the most detailed account of the infantry's role against Milroy. His narrative makes it clear that the artillery did not need much support from Confederate musketry. During the afternoon Lieutenant Latimer warned the colonel of the 21st that the enemy was advancing. Officers called the regiment to attention and prepared to move it forward. Latimer asked that they wait: "Not yet, Colonel, I will give them a few more rounds." The Confederate battery shifted to canister and Northern return fire dropped off appreciably. "Whatever it was our gunners was giving them they give it like they had plenty of it," Coble observed admiringly, "and they were not the kind of fellows who just shot anywhere."

Latimer soon observed Milroy's renewed advance and called, "Colonel, have your men ready the enemy is approaching." As the North Carolinians went forward, the Virginia gunners backed away to give them passage. Coble noticed how begrimed the cannoneers were with black powder as he hurried through the guns. The artillery crews "pulled their caps and waving, cheered us time and again and when we had come up in line with them, the line of one accord bowed to them, and returned the cheering heartily." This stirring exchange of soldierly compliments proved to be the high point of the advance, followed promptly by anticlimax. When the 21st North Carolina "moved on to the top of the ridge . . . the Yankees . . . came up missing." A soldier near Coble complained bitterly about missing the chance to try out his musket.[39]

The briskest exchange of infantry fire involving Confederates atop Mill Creek Ridge would develop farther west, where Steuart's Brigade and its reinforcements awaited Milroy's slanting advance. General Ewell in his report brushed aside the Federal threat with nonchalant language. Campbell Brown of Ewell's staff was equally pointed in describing the unruffled defense of the ridge. The Confederates "repulsed easily the attacks upon them, most weakly pressed as they were," Brown wrote in one narrative. In another he described the "attempted charge on our batteries" as "ridiculous." High ground and ample artillery had settled the issue with the greatest of ease, noisy and sometimes painful hostile fire notwithstanding.[40]

Through the hours of artillery fire and the late flurry of activity caused by Milroy's advance, General Ewell remained near Mill Creek Church and the center of his line. He never strayed far from that vicinity; there was no pressing reason for him to have done so. Brown noted what prompted his chief to choose that vantage point: Ewell "staid nearly all day with the guns in the centre, where he had a view of most of the field."[41]

For several hours Brigadier General Arnold Elzey shared the splendid view with Ewell and also assumed some of the responsibility for running the army. Elzey was an enigmatic forty-five-year-old graduate of West Point born Arnold Elzey Jones who abandoned his common surname to use the more distinctive middle name. A desperate wound put Elzey out of action a few weeks later and reduced his effectiveness throughout the war. On June 8, though, Ewell saw great potential in his subordinate and leaned heavily on him. Elzey deserved "the credit for selecting the position," Ewell declared. "I availed myself frequently during the action of [his] counsel, profiting largely by his known military skill and judgment."[42]

Elzey galloped through the artillery positions, "much exposed" while supervising the batteries' performance personally, "particularly . . . in the center." Early in the action a Northern projectile hit the general's horse and staggered it, but the animal recovered enough to remain in use. Eventually an enemy shell exploded near the energetic officer and a piece killed his sturdy mount. At almost the same moment Elzey went down with a hole in his calf serious enough to make him leave the field on a stretcher. Unfortunately for Elzey, his wound healed quickly enough to allow him to return to duty in about a week, in time to meet with far worse injury near Richmond nineteen days after the Battle of Cross Keys.[43]

The men facing the most daunting prospect on the Confederate center were staff officers. Fighting men made fun of staffers as rear-echelon heroes, what front-line soldiers now call "desk commandos." In this instance, though, aides carrying orders were obliged to brave artillery fire without being able to dodge. As one of them recalled, "in carrying messages . . . the configuration of the ground forced [us] to ride in a certain track."[44]

Randolph Harrison McKim dashed across that fire-swept track to reach Ewell's headquarters. McKim had become a lieutenant on the staff of General George H. Steuart a few weeks earlier, despite being only nineteen years of age. The proud but green lad found Ewell "surrounded by his staff of young officers, well mounted and handsomely equipped." Ewell gave McKim an answer for Steuart, but when the youngster attempted to gallop away, his horse would not budge. The "beautiful black horse" he had borrowed from a quartermaster "positively refused to face the very heavy artillery fire directly in front." McKim had no spurs with which to force the animal to move. Ewell, a warm-hearted but startlingly bluff man, "laughed aloud and said, 'Ha! Ha! a courier without any spurs!' "

McKim was mortified by his commanding general's comment in front of his staff, but he had to accept Ewell's pragmatic advice: "Young man, you will have to go back another way." On the route back to Steuart, McKim found a sympathetic officer who loaned him one spur. So accoutred, the aide headed for further adventures on the left. Perhaps the beautiful black horse had had the right idea in avoiding artillery fire: later in the day McKim's borrowed mount was killed.[45]

Ewell's own staff, which appeared so impressive and handsomely turned out to McKim's eyes, had a busy day on June 8. The general mentioned five of them in his official report. Major James Barbour was a genial fellow and popular in many quarters, although General Jubal Early cashiered him as incompetent in 1864. Lieutenant Colonel John Marshall Jones had been struggling with a drinking problem, but was underemployed at his 1862 rank; he would become a brigadier general before meeting a soldier's death at the Wilderness in May 1864. Volunteer aide Captain Hugh Mortimer Nelson would be dead before the year ended. The other two whom Ewell mentioned both were mixed up in the general's emotional attachment to his betrothed, a strong-willed widow named Lizinka Campbell Brown. Even after he married the woman, Ewell introduced her diffidently as "the widow Brown." Captain George Campbell Brown was her son; Lieutenant Thomas Theodore Turner soon would marry her daughter.[46]

"These officers were much exposed during the day, and were worked hard over an extensive field," Ewell reported. The truth was that Ewell's fiancée so dominated his behavior that the general was afraid to use his staff in an evenhanded fashion. General James Conner, who had nothing at stake in the business, observed with a mixture of amusement and horror that Ewell admitted "that he had never exposed Campbell [to danger] but once, and then was so miserable until he came back, that he did not know what to do." Tom Turner grumbled about Brown's special position, saying of Ewell, "Hang him, he never thinks of my Mother, I suppose." Behind Turner's back, though, another of the staff added: "Turner is safe, but I am in a tight place. Campbell Brown hangs on to his Mother's petticoats, and Turner is engaged to the little Brown girl, and she will prize him up, but I have to fight against the pair." In a letter, General Conner summarized the bizarre affair: "I had a good laugh at them, all in trepidation about the manoeuvering of two women, and one fond, foolish old man. Old Ewell is worse in love than any eighteen year old that you ever saw."[47]

At Cross Keys, General Ewell had his terrifying experience with Brown under fire. He had been using the captain precisely as he should—to carry messages in all directions and to report on the army's condition and progress. Early in the afternoon, as Campbell Brown rode through Elzey's zone, he was astonished to see a column of 75 Federals approaching in good order, marching on the main road. Brown finally deduced that they were prisoners when he spied two Confederates bringing up the rear. The guards complained that "their only trouble was that none of the prisoners understood English!"

When Brown returned to Ewell's headquarters, he learned that his chief had gone farther to the left to examine the line there. As the captain dashed through the artillery curtain in that direction, a shell burst just above his head and a fragment about the size of a man's hand slammed into his right shoulder. The impact knocked Brown from his saddle. He recalled sprawling on the ground, certain that he was dead, thinking "that it was superfluous for a dead man to be trying to get up." Brown eventually explored the wound and discovered that it was not bleeding much. The battered captain climbed to his feet and went after his horse. The animal had hurried on about three hundred yards to join her friends in Ewell's remuda.

Captain Brown managed to catch his mare and mount her without using his numb right arm. When he reported to Ewell, the solicitous general noticed Brown's pale face and learned of his wound. John Jones gave his friend some whiskey from a flask he kept, and Ewell hurried him off to the rear to seek treatment. What Mrs. Brown did to Mr. Ewell over news of her son's close call is not on record. Perhaps the boy's sturdy attitude in a letter to his mother about the wound eased the general's lot. Campbell wrote with dry humor and good-natured deprecation: "I was rather plagued at first for fear my wound would not leave any scar—for it would be a hard case to have to undergo the pain, without bearing the honorable marks of it—but I believe I will have a slight mark to show for it."[48]

The wounded Brown rode slowly back to the vicinity of Mill Creek Church, where he came across Stonewall Jackson, who was just arriving at Cross Keys for an early afternoon visit. With the excitement in the village of Port Republic past, and the Federal raiders driven far away, Jackson rode toward the swelling noise of battle on Ewell's front. Ewell had sent a messenger toward Port Republic with reassuring word that he had the situation well in hand, but Stonewall was eager to see for himself. William Allan and John A. Harman of the general's staff rode to Mill Creek Church at about the same time. A brief visit to the center of Ewell's line revealed what Allan described as "favorable news." The two men sent a dispatch to Staunton to reassure Harman's brother commanding the post there.[49]

The Reverend R. L. Dabney, who apparently did not accompany the general, wrote that Jackson arrived at Cross Keys "a little after mid-day, when the battle was at its height[,] . . . and calmly examined the progress of the struggle." In reality Stonewall Jackson arrived some time after Trimble's repulse of the 8th New York, which must be considered the "height" of the action. Furthermore, Jackson evidently did not go far enough to the front to view much of the fighting in person. Milroy had not yet advanced his infantry, so Jackson could only have seen artillery exchanges. When Brown met Jackson near Mill Creek Church, the general chatted with the captain in the latter's role as Ewell's confidant. Satisfied, he turned back toward Port Republic in company with Brown, who attempted to match the jarring canter of Jackson's sorrel horse. The sorrel's trot struck several observers during the war as an uncomfortable gait. Brown, who quickly felt "unbearable" results in his sore shoulder, would have agreed. He finally mentioned his concealed wound to Jackson and fell behind after the general wished him well "very compassionately."[50]

Stonewall Jackson's brief foray to the neighborhood of Mill Creek Church had almost no impact on what happened at Cross Keys. The general did not meet with Ewell (perhaps because Ewell had gone to his left at this juncture) or with any other ranking officers. Too few soldiers saw him to attribute to his short visit any surge in élan, such as so often followed Jackson's rides along the lines.[51]

Jackson's trip did provide Ewell with strong reinforcements. Dick Taylor's Louisiana Brigade had dashed away from Cross Keys during the furor occasioned by Carroll's raiders. Elzey's Brigade inherited his place in line and subsequently fought from that position. When Taylor's troops had hurriedly covered about half the distance to Port Republic, another officer appeared with orders to halt. The crisis by then had long passed. After the Louisianians had waited in the road for a time, Jackson himself appeared, on his way to Mill Creek Church. The general stopped long enough to give Taylor a firsthand account of his nerve-racking experiences at Port Republic, then continued north, where "the sound of battle . . . thickened." The noise was the combined fire of the artillery duel in the center and Trimble's fight against Federals in the direction of the Evers farm.[52]

Jackson determined that Taylor could do more good back at Cross Keys than at Port Republic, and ordered him to return. When the Louisiana brigade arrived behind his center, Ewell ordered it to stand by in reserve. Eventually he sent part of Taylor's command to the left, where it helped General Steuart. Jackson also ordered the small Virginia brigade under Colonel John M. Patton to move to Ewell's assistance. Patton too wound up on Ewell's left with Steuart before the fighting ended.[53]

Civilians around the Confederate center on June 8 endured their own brand of terror. Abram Flory, age thirty, his wife Barbara, twenty-seven, and a seven-year-old daughter lived on a little farm described in the 1860 census as having neither real property nor personal property sizable enough to record. "The family not having time to leave before the engagement," a local reporter wrote, "were forced to remain in the house while the battle raged around them." The Flory house, part brick and part frame, stood on the edge of the road from Union Church to Mill Creek Church and near the confluence of the drainage that Milroy used to approach Mill Creek.[54]

During the artillery duel the modest house was pierced several times by Yankee cannonballs. Hundreds of rounds of musketry also hit the place from muzzles on both sides of the battle lines. Holes in the building were easier to repair than the immense losses inflicted by Yankees looting unchecked in the aftermath of the battle. The local newspaper calculated the Florys' loss at $3,000 in goods, presumably most of it held as tenants. After the war a member of the family filed a claim against the Federal government for things Frémont's men had taken, including one bay mare, three head of cattle, five hundred pounds of bacon, one carriage, five blankets, six quilts, and seven coverlets. Incredibly, the claim was granted, perhaps because the Florys emphasized humanitarian issues, suggesting that most of the goods "where especially kneeded By the Same troops as the battle of Cross Keys had just been faught."[55]

Henry A. Beahm's house was beautifully situated near Mill Creek, in front of the church. The view northeastward to Massanutten Mountain and in every other direction across the pastoral landscape must have soothed Henry on countless evenings; it remains in 1993 as lovely as any vista in Virginia. On June 8, 1862, however, farmer Beahm's house was in a dreadful location. His house and barn each "were struck a number of times by cannon shot." One Confederate concluded that the firing at the buildings was intentional. "Artillery fire was fierce on both sides, and several houses were quickly destroyed by our joint efforts, for, being finely placed, each was afraid of the other occupying them."[56]

A schoolteacher who lived near the field wrote a heart-wrenching series of diary entries during of battle as she listened to the roar of cannon and the shriek of shells. "Oh! my Father when will this unholy & devastating war be ceased?" she wrote early in the day. Later she added: "Lord stay the hand of our adversaries and let them fall into the pit which their own hands have digged—turn them back merciful God and let not the flower of our country be killed and our citizens robbed of all that they possess." The teacher stopped her narrative when she noticed out her window "a mournful procession . . . bearing to an open grave one who gave his life for his country." The somber scene prompted her to wonder whether "some of the [artillery] reports that I have just heard may have sent some very dear friends of mine to the spirit world." The woman's diary entry for June 8 ended in mid-sentence.[57]

Sketch map of Cross
Keys battlefield
drawn by G. Campbell
Brown of General Ewell's
staff

CHAPTER 12

CONFUSION AND
VICTORY ON EWELL'S
LEFT

The configuration of the ground made the far left of the Confederate line its most vulnerable point. Fortunately for Ewell, stout fighting by his troops kept that tender flank intact against Milroy's advance in that direction and later tentative gestures north of Milroy by Federal brigadier general Robert C. Schenck.

Schenck's timidity contributed to the outcome of the day. The fifty-two-year-old Ohioan had wide experience as a lawyer and congressman, and he brought a big brigade to the field at Cross Keys. But Schenck, like dozens of other political generals, proved incapable of commanding large units effectively. The fatuous Northern insistence—which was echoed on a lesser scale in the South—on seeking a sort of alchemy by turning politicians into generals failed in almost every instance. The system's criminal results can still be counted today in National Cemeteries: it left tens of thousands of dead soldier boys in its wake.

Five strong Ohio regiments made up Schenck's Brigade, with an Ohio battery and an Indiana battery for support. Frémont ordered the Indiana artillery elsewhere soon after its arrival, so the brigade went into action exclusively Ohioan. By their commander's count they numbered nearly 2,500 men. The Federal column had spread from column into line beginning on its left and spreading steadily to its right. Schenck arrived last among the major components of Frémont's army, and wound up farthest right as a result. The general thought it was about one P.M. when he arrived at the crossroads and turned southwest toward Union Church. Schenck received orders to drop off a small detachment of Connecticut cavalry that had been accompanying him. The mounted men would have been useful just then for scouting, but Schenck was obliged to reconnoiter without them. He went forward across country in person to look for a good position, being of course "entirely without knowledge of the ground."[1]

Frémont's instructions to Schenck designated a general area on the army's right wing. The brigade commander turned his troops into the fields toward the right while he examined the choices available for their destination. In his front the Confederate left enjoyed the shelter of woods that screened them and bemused the Federals. Schenck decided to press farther forward than Frémont's vague instructions suggested, in order to use a "more commanding" crest. This enabled him to cover all of "the open ground sloping away" toward the valley in front of the Southern line. Schenck felt concern that his own right was vulnerable to a turning movement, ignoring the far more pertinent reverse conclusion that his right was ideally situated to turn the enemy's left.[2] The commander on Frémont's pivotal right flank was thinking defensively, not offensively!

The Ohioans who headed toward Schenck's chosen ground marched through a series of wheat fields, dodging copses along the way. Confederate artillery firing at long range rained "a pretty severe fire of shell" on the moving column. Surviving accounts written by brigade members complain about the projectiles that whistled past. A soldier in the 55th described how "solid cannon shot from a distant rebel battery came very unpleasantly near." The regiment's colonel shouted in a "shrill voice" for the men to "Lie down!" to avoid the fire. To reduce the size of the target, Schenck split his force. He headed directly toward his goal with the 55th, 73rd, and 82nd Ohio. The 32nd and 75th Ohio covered the artillery while it moved "by a more circuitous route." Despite the excitement, the most pessimistic estimate suggested that the brigade's loss only included "several" casualties.[3]

When Schenck's troops reached the position he had selected for them, he put his battery into action from a point near the right of the brigade line. Captain William L. De Beck's Ohio gunners "commenced shelling the enemy through the woods." One of the supporting infantrymen was so impressed with the performance of the artillery that he wrote years later that this was "the finest artillery duel that I saw during the war, and they were not few." Another reported, with excessive optimism, that De Beck "soon made the Rebels guns quiet in front of us" and even "dismounted two Secesh guns."[4]

The 55th Ohio stood squarely in the center of Schenck's five regiments. Robert Bromley of the 55th noted in his diary that Confederate shells "fell rather thick" around him. The Ohioans took it calmly enough to find an appetite for a hardtack snack while they waited. While they awaited developments, the infantrymen watched a steady parade of "orderlies, aid[e]s and officers" who were "galloping hither and yonder."[5]

Schenck's first gambit with his infantry was to send a handful of men from the 32nd and 73rd Ohio across toward the Confederate woods to his right front. This day's fighting was the regiment's first in precisely a month (since McDowell), while the Confederates facing them had been marching and fighting incessantly during the same period. What combat the 32nd found on June 8 did not amount to much. The company that drew skirmish duty "did not become actively engaged." A few of Schenck's little party ran into Confederate pickets. De Beck tossed a few shells into the woods to help the Northern infantry."[6]

When his paltry skirmish force came back, Schenck pushed most of three regiments in the direction of the wooded Confederate ridge, this time aiming to his left front. The 73rd, 32nd, and 55th Ohio moved forward in line very slowly and tentatively. Schenck boasted cautiously that this gingerly move succeeded in "gradually bringing the concealed line of the rebels to close quarters."[7]

At its peak, this brush with the Confederate left seemed to

Schenck to be a "brisk" small-arms encounter, especially around the position of the 73rd Ohio. The regiment's historian had the good grace to report modestly that the regiment only "skirmished heavily with the enemy," but Private Campbell called his experience "hard fighting." The 73rd lost fewer than a dozen casualties. A member of Frémont's staff dismissed the advance as merely "swinging forward his right" until it "brushed with emphasis the rebels."[8]

If the 73rd Ohio's handful of losses seemed to Schenck to result from a veritable firestorm of action, those units that he did not highlight obviously had a very calm day by battle standards. An official 32nd Ohio document called the battle "a lively skirmish." The regiment's postwar historian wrote that the 32nd and the rest of the brigade "took no active part in the fight of the 8th." A soldier in the 55th Ohio described his experience in nonchalant language: "We lay in the woods about 3 hours moving around with heavy skirmishers in front." A 55th diarist mentioned no movement but called "the firing of Cannon & Musketry quite brisk." One of De Beck's cannoneers behind the infantry wrote in his journal that the Federal right had been "warmly engaged" in a "general engagement."[9]

In reporting on his achievements, Schenck insisted that he had learned just what he needed to know from his forlorn and tentative advances. Whether he was guilty of empty posturing can only be conjectured, although it seems likely. "I believed that the moment for attacking and pressing the rebels successfully . . . had now arrived," Schenck claimed in the soothing glow of hindsight. He put the 32nd Ohio on his right, outside the 73rd, and ordered those two units to lead four regiments in a sweep around the Confederate left. The 75th Ohio would remain alone in the rear to cover De Beck's Battery. Such a move of course was exactly what Schenck should have done. As he prepared (he claimed) to launch the movement, word arrived from Frémont that he must fall back.[10]

A Northern observer confirmed the sense of a lost opportunity. Schenck "had gained favorable ground, well advanced," wrote Alvid E. Lee, "and was about to signal an attack" when the order to withdraw arrived. Schenck was reluctant and sent to Frémont to inquire whether he must retreat at once. Headquarters answered in the affirmative. The Ohio troops fell back "slowly as if on dress parade." They found a strong artillery cluster behind which to rally. Not long after Schenck's Brigade made its initial withdrawal, a courier brought word that Frémont had changed his mind: Schenck could stay at the front if he chose. By then Schenck could see that Milroy had fallen back on his left. It was too late to retrieve the abandoned opportunity.[11]

Another Federal organization, the tiny two-regiment brigade of Colonel G. P. Cluseret, operated in the rear of Frémont's center and right. Somewhere in the vicinity of Schenck's vain strivings Cluseret fought long enough to lose as many men (but still only a handful) from his two regiments as Schenck did from his five. A member of Frémont's staff wrote that Cluseret "maintained himself with skill and perseverance—keeping practically intact his position." That faint praise is nearly all that survives about the colonel's transitory connection with the Battle of Cross Keys.[12] The consequence of the Union's shadowboxing opposite the Confederate left was the loss of Frémont's brightest opportunity for winning a decisive victory. Had Milroy's aggressive thrust been on the right, Ewell would have been hard pressed. The happenstance that put Schenck right of Milroy, instead of the reverse alignment, saved the Confederates a great deal of trouble.

Dick Ewell remained deeply concerned about the northwest fringe of the field. He knew that his position was only vulnerable on the left. Honoring the maxim that a prudent officer should always expect his enemy to do what he *ought* to do, he worried that Frémont would assail the one weak spot. Reinforcing in that direction occupied much of Ewell's afternoon.

The linchpin of the Confederate left was the Baltimore Light Artillery. The Maryland battery had a Virginian in command—a rare combination in an army rife with sectional pride and prejudices. Twenty-six-year-old Captain John Bowyer Brockenbrough ("Brock" is pronounced *broke* and "brough" rhymes with *throw*), known as "Beau," had attended Washington College and the University of Virginia, then practiced law in Lexington. The colonel of an adjacent Southern regiment commented in his official report on "the precision and gallantry with which Captain Brockenbrough served his guns." Return fire from De Beck's Battery and other Federals took a toll on the Maryland gunners and their horses. A Confederate officer described the battery's ordeal: "what they did to the enemy, I don't know, but they were surely knocked into a cocked hat, and nearly, if not quite, every horse was killed." An Ohioan who walked across the position the next morning estimated that he saw twenty dead horses around the battery's location. Human targets in the Southern line suffered from the Federal artillery, though not as heavily. A lieutenant from Maryland had the unusual experience of seeing a speeding rifled artillery round out of the corner of his eye as it hurtled in. The shell "leaped into the midst of a group of men and exploded, killing and wounding several."[13]

A captain whose infantry company supported Beau Brockenbrough's cannoneers wrote in glowing terms of their performance: "Theirs was a most exposed position . . . upon which was concentrated the fire of several of the enemy's batteries. . . . All day long the little battery continued to hurl its shot and shell into the ranks of the enemy. . . . Calmly the officers and men stood to their guns." General Taylor was posted near the Baltimore Light Artillery late in the day and observed its stout behavior. According to battery lore, the Louisiana general presented the Marylanders with guns captured under dramatic circumstances the next day, saying: "from what I saw of you yesterday, I know they will be in good hands."[14]

Bravery, of course, was not universal. A member of General Steuart's staff came across "an artillery man who had taken refuge under the caisson, where he crouched trembling like a leaf. I saw a sergeant . . . point a pistol at his head, saying, 'Come out from under there and do your duty, and you'll have some chance of your life, but if you stay there, by the Eternal, I'll blow your brains out.' " The aide observed this vignette as he rode rapidly past, but could not delay his mission long enough to see the result. Before he had ridden far, the same officer came across another soldier "crouching in terror behind a tree." A solid shot spiraled in, "went through the tree and absolutely decapitated the man!" The officer who observed these instances was of a nature reflective enough to recognize that both men might have done their duty in another instance: "He who, on one particular day and under certain mental or physical conditions, may play the coward, may be steady and true on another day in face of danger."[15]

The boys from Baltimore poured fire across the Mill Creek valley for several hours "with great animation." In fact they fired so rapidly that part of the battery exhausted its ammunition before the afternoon's crisis had passed.[16]

While Beau Brockenbrough and his men served as a focal point for the defense, and as an aiming point for Federal artillery, the decisive military activity would be accomplished by infantrymen. The impressive noise and power of artillery notwithstanding, almost every

Civil War engagement was decided by what infantry could accomplish. Artillery that aided or hindered pivotal infantry endeavors often played an important role, but center stage belonged to men carrying muskets. On the Confederate left at Cross Keys the muskets belonged at first to four regiments of General George H. "Maryland" Steuart's Brigade. Before the end of the day Ewell sent five regiments and a battalion as reinforcements, more than doubling the infantry numbers at his worrisome left flank. Ewell clearly recognized what Schenck could not: the left of the Confederate line was its only vulnerable point.

General Steuart began his vigil by putting his three Virginia regiments into line on the foreslope of the bluff. The 1st Maryland set up farther to the left, adjacent to the knob from which their cousins of the Baltimore Light Artillery fired. The Maryland regiment nominally belonged to Steuart, but at Cross Keys it operated independently most of the time. The colonel of the 1st Maryland, Bradley T. Johnson, wrote an official report on his own. The Marylanders' one-year enlistments had expired during May; since they were volunteers from a state outside the control of the Confederacy, they reasonably enough presumed that the conscript law could not make them into draftees. As soon as the Valley Campaign ended, they would disband. Because of Johnson's independence, and because of the gap between his position and Steuart's main line, the experiences of the two units can best be understood by examining them in sequence.[17]

The 52nd Virginia assumed a position on Steuart's right, closest to the main Confederate artillery cluster but some distance from it. The 44th Virginia and then the 58th stretched the line leftward. The 44th Virginia split into halves and went forward on outpost duty. Before the 44th advanced, all three regiments maintained a line partway down the face of the bluff. A staff officer described them as "lying down on the slope of a hill . . . protected by stumps and the roughness of the ground. Behind them, on and below the crest of the hill, was heavy timber." When the 44th left on its mission, the 52nd and 58th remained behind, no doubt nudging their flanks together a bit to narrow the gap between them.[18]

Charles C. Wight of the 58th Virginia described his regiment's assignment as "the disagreeable duty of supporting a battery," which left the men "exposed for some time to the return fire of the Federal batteries." Wight's experience on the left of Steuart's main line seemed nothing more than "artillery fire and skirmishing . . . for some time." The nature of Milroy's advance and heavier woods in the 58th's vicinity combined to leave the regiment relatively untouched. Its losses were minor, totaling fewer than one fifth as many as those in the nearby 52nd Virginia.[19]

Steuart's right regiment, the 52nd, stayed back when the 44th Virginia went forward. Its experience was far more difficult than the 58th's. Instead of having woods for shelter, the 52nd had to resort to "lying down in the long grass." A passing aide called for a regimental officer and watched with amazement as Major John D. Ross uncoiled from concealment in the grass to his full height. The young major, a twenty-two-year-old graduate of Virginia Military Institute, stood six feet three inches tall. Ross proved to be too large a target; he was wounded, though not dangerously, later in the day.[20]

The ride of staff officer Randolph McKim after his encounter with Major Ross gives an idea of the fire pouring onto the hilltop. McKim galloped through "a perfect hail of shell, cannon-balls, and bullets." It seemed to come from every point of the compass. A solid shot tore under his horse's belly and screamed off to southward. McKim jerked his head in startled reaction, knocking his hat to the ground. He debated whether to stop in the maelstrom to retrieve the lost headgear. "If you get off this horse to pick up that cap," he told himself, "you are a dead man!" But pride won over prudence; McKim could not go back to his general hatless. He survived the recovery mission but always remembered it with terror.[21]

The foot soldiers of the 52nd remained crouching in their inadequate grassy cover. Lieutenant Clinton M. King, a twenty-six-year-old merchant from nearby Waynesboro, was killed on the hillside. His widow and three orphaned children doubtless heard the noise of the round that killed their husband and father, and saw the smoke in the distance, but remained nervously unaware of his fate for hours or days. Another local man, Lieutenant Samuel Paul, went down with a leg "shivered by a shell." The one-legged lieutenant became treasurer of adjacent Augusta County after the war. A similarly crippled veteran of the 52nd, John S. Robson, entitled his published war memoir *How a One-Legged Rebel Lives*. Robson teased his former officer about his good fortune: "I have often thought I would like to be treasurer of something myself—but all the one-legged Rebels can't get their living the same way."[22]

Milroy came toward Steuart's hillside in his first lunge down the Flory ravine before twisting farther toward the Confederate left with his later efforts. John Robson remembered "sustaining and repulsing four distinct charges, each made by fresh troops; but they were mostly Dutch, and we fought them to the best advantage." As usual, defenders egocentrically viewed every enemy movement as aimed toward them personally. At least some members of the 52nd were able to shoot at Milroy's men from behind sheltering trees. The left of the regiment probably shifted left into the woods as the fighting moved in that direction. Casualties in the 52nd were distributed with a capriciousness typical of battle trends. Four men were killed and 27 more were wounded. Companies G and K had between them two killed and 13 wounded, absorbing one half of the regiment's losses among only 20 percent of its strength.[23]

The 44th Virginia carried only about 125 men into action on June 8. Perhaps Steuart chose the regiment for skirmish duty because it was so understrength. Instead of leaving it with a short stretch of the main line, the general had Colonel William C. Scott split his little command and move forward. Captain Thomas R. Buckner, he of the seventeen siblings, led half of the regiment into the bottom, across Mill Creek, and up to the road paralleling the creek in the general vicinity of the Flory house. The five dozen Virginians waiting there when Milroy came down the ravine were the ogres Milroy reported hiding in the grass. Buckner's few soldiers could not do more than check Milroy briefly, which was just what skirmish duty required. The detachment, Colonel Scott reported, "being too weak to defend itself," fell back and rejoined the rest of the 44th on the Confederate side of the creek.[24]

Before Milroy directed his attention farther to the Confederate left, he followed the 44th's skirmishers into the stream bottom. The reunited 44th exchanged "a few rounds" with the enemy. Major Norvell Cobb then led a spirited counterattack against some of the Federals who had incautiously pushed too far forward. The Virginians attacked with fixed bayonets, in keeping with a popular tradition that rarely actually occurred in Civil War battles. Colonel Scott reported that Cobb's men killed "several" Yankees, including one dispatched "with the bayonet," and captured five prisoners. In the satisfied words of Benjamin A. Jones of the 44th, "We gave them a decent thrashing . . . and drove them from the field." As Milroy altered his axis of attack to strike farther to their left, the 44th played a minor if eager role in repulsing those additional enemy advances.[25]

General Steuart supervised the operations of his three Virginia regiments from an observation post atop the bluff. For several hours of artillery firing and through at least some of the infantry fighting, the general maintained control of affairs in his front. Then he fell prey to the Federal iron scouring the Southern positions. Two members of his staff, including Captain Frank Bond, had lost horses killed during the afternoon. When Steuart told Bond to ride to the base of the hill to order Colonel Scott of the 44th to report to headquarters, the captain did not relish his assignment. Bond reached the colonel in safety, then scampered back up the slope and considered himself "very lucky to get back without . . . being hit."[26]

The two officers found Steuart on horseback, watching the performance of the Baltimore Light Artillery to his left while prudently sheltering himself "behind a large oak." The "din of musketry and bursting shells was deafening," to such a degree that the general and colonel could not hear each other. Steuart, "in order to be heard, leaned down to reach his ear, only exposing his shoulder, and was immediately struck by a grape shot, and severely wounded." The metal that hit the general probably was a piece of an exploded shell, but four independent primary sources call the round either grape shot or canister. (Despite the almost universal contemporary use of "grape and canister" as interchangeable names for the scattershot artillery round, Civil War field pieces never used grape.) The maximum range for canister was about four hundred yards on level trajectory. Given the elevation at which Steuart was hit, the overwhelming likelihood is that no Federal canister could have reached him at the moment he made his poorly timed lean toward the colonel.[27]

The missile, whatever it was, struck Steuart "in the side of the neck near the shoulder, the ball ranging over the shoulder & lodging in the muscles of the back." There had been some uncertainty about how serious General Elzey's wound would prove to be, but everyone agreed that General Steuart was hard hit. Witnesses agreed that the "ghastly wound" had hurt the general "desperately," or at least "severely." The only major source that did not attribute the wound to canister raised the suspicion that the Yankees must have been using outlawed explosive bullets to cause such a dreadful wound. Captain Bond rounded up a stretcher and some bearers and saw his general off the field.[28] Steuart would be out of service for a year.

The 1st Maryland Infantry fought its first—and last—major engagement from a position near the Baltimore Light Artillery and on a prolongation of Steuart's line. The Marylanders had started that morning near the main road and Mill Creek Church. They became part of Ewell's mass migration toward his left flank, the reaction to the potential for Federal mischief in that quarter. Colonel Bradley T. Johnson led the 1st Maryland to a point farther to the left than any other Confederate infantry reached until well into the afternoon, when the 31st Virginia passed beyond to become the widest protection Ewell would have. With the Baltimore Light Artillery emplaced nearby, the Confederate left became a Maryland enclave.[29]

Artillery fire that swelled into a hellish roar opened the Cross Keys fight for the 1st Maryland just as it did on most of the line. The Baltimore battery acted as a magnet for Federal shells, and its supporting infantry absorbed a share of the unwelcome attention. "We were soon into it hot and heavy," one of the infantrymen wrote in a letter home. "Such a shower of ball and grape it is impossible for you to imagine; protected by small trees we stood this tremendous fire." One particular Union gun "some 800 yards distant" played steadily on the regiment with what Johnson called "grape." Canister could not cover eight hundred yards, but the inexperienced colonel and his soldiers clearly came under heavy fire, nomenclature notwithstanding.[30]

Colonel Johnson sent one of his ten companies down the bluff to act as skirmishers. John Gill, who served in the advance company, recalled being "on the advance line for more than six hours, constantly under fire." The skirmishers each carried 128 rounds of rifle ammunition with them when they went down the hill; when orders finally arrived to fall back at the end of the fight, they "had scarcely a cartridge left." Two of Gill's special friends went down with apparently mortal wounds, but both survived.

John Gill himself escaped by a narrow margin. A "glancing ball" cut what seemed to be only "a slight scratch" on his right cheek, but the blow left his entire face "practically paralyzed for some weeks." The next morning the cheek had turned "perfectly black," and Gill suffered from severe nausea. The private's amateur prognosis was that the aftereffects had been "produced by this nervous shock."[31]

The main body of the 1st Maryland was small enough to resemble a skirmish line even when in full battle array, being fewer than 200 in number on June 8. Fortunately for the Marylanders, their position wound through a wooded portion of the bluff. Johnson did not insist on a geometrically precise alignment, instead allowing the men to take advantage of the valuable cover. "We were on a slope, just below the ridge of the hill," wrote J. W. Thomas in his diary. "On the slope were small oak trees, behind which we were ordered to shelter ourselves when possible instead of keeping line." By contrast, the ground beyond the creek was devoid of cover for the Federals.[32]

Colonel Johnson reported that soon after he put the regiment into position, it "was attacked by a regiment." Washington Hands of the 1st Maryland described the approaching enemy as moving "in beautiful order." Hands thought that they advanced within one hundred yards, which is extremely unlikely. This relatively minor initial probe came from the far right of Milroy's first advance. By the time Milroy uncoiled his column from the sheltering ravine into a battle line near the Mill Creek bottom, it stretched parallel to the Confederate ridge across a rather wide front. Each of Milroy's efforts would have been visible from the Marylanders' aerie, and the last two threatened them directly. Every 1st Maryland account describes multiple assaults—usually three of them—against the regiment. The three were Milroy's tentative early move, then his adjustment toward the Confederate left, and finally his lunge even farther in the same direction. The last of the three focused most directly on Colonel Johnson's ground. Schenck's futile gestures in the vicinity of the 1st Maryland made up an additional feature of the threatening scene that unfolded in the Marylanders' view.[33]

Serious fighting for the soldiers of the 1st Maryland developed as Milroy turned in their direction. When the Yankee right reached into the regiment's zone, the opposing forces opened a hot exchange of fire that continued for some time. Bradley Johnson described the development from his vantage as regimental commander: "another [Union] regiment came up, and got behind a fence some 300 yards from me. This place they obstinately held for an hour. I could not charge them, not having 175 men in ranks, and having to cross a branch, a ravine, and a fence." The branch (Mill Creek), the ravine, and the fences of course constituted every bit as much of an obstacle to Milroy's Federals as to Johnson's Confederates. In fact, given the relative roles of the defense and offense in infantry fighting, all of those impediments to a smooth advance worked very much to Johnson's advantage. Washington Hands, who overestimated the proximity of the first advance against his regiment, agreed with his colonel that the firefight of long duration raged at a range of about three hundred yards.[34]

The random alignment of the Marylanders and the shelter available to them abetted their successful resistance. Being "posted in more or less loose order, behind trees and rocks," the Confederates could aim and fire with some degree of safety. The "skirt of woods," a Marylander wrote, left his regiment "well protected from their fire." Had the unit been holding the bluff from an area devoid of ground cover, and in a straight line devoted to geometric principles, it would have suffered severely. As it was, "so terrible was the enemy's fire that it was almost impossible to expose for an instant any part of the body without being struck."[35] General Steuart would have occasion to attest to that truth during the afternoon.

Both sides used rifled weapons in the action on the Confederate left. Trimble's men had used primarily short-range smoothbores in their fight. Much of Jackson's force was similarly underequipped, and would suffer from that deficiency the next day. Most of the Maryland regiment, however, carried Mississippi rifles. They knew from examining captured weapons that their Federal opponents were using imported Belgian rifles, a common firearm in Northern hands at this stage of the war. The Mississippi rifles reached with deadly effect across the three hundred yards separating the firing lines. Brockenbrough's cannon readily threw canister that far too. There could be no question of Colonel Johnson losing a contest based on firepower when holding ground as strong as that where his men sprawled behind stumps and trees and boulders. The Marylanders' fire "at last drove [the Yankees] out, leaving some dead and quantities of arms, accouterments, and blankets."[36]

The respite was brief. Milroy's final swerve westward put some of his Ohio troops opposite the 1st Maryland's stretch of the hillside. Milroy's move paralleled Mill Creek and the adjacent road and seemed to Colonel Johnson to be made by a "regiment . . . brought up the road, a little to my right." The Marylanders by this time were weary and their weapons had become fouled with black-powder residue. Their .58 caliber Mississippi rifles, acquired with funds raised by home-state supporters, could reach out accurately for five hundred yards and more. One of the Marylanders recalled that "when a man would fall an officer would seize his gun and continue the firing, and the Mississippi rifle told with deadly effect."[37]

J. W. Thomas had picked out a tree about seven inches in diameter as his private fortress, but soon wished that he had found a more substantial shelter. A determined Yankee singled him out with deadly

Cross Keys battlefield in 1994, looking northwest
from behind the crest of Mill Creek ridge. The
steep escarpment dropping to Mill Creek from the
Confederate line atop the ridge begins at the
row of trees across the middle of the view. The
Flory house stood just short of the modern
building at the right edge of the photograph.
Milroy and Schenck approached Mill Creek
using the ravines in the distance.

intent. Thomas could see the smoke from the gun of his personal enemy rising from tall grass behind the fence that sheltered most of the foe, but he could not see the man. The Yankee "plugged the tree several times," Thomas wrote in his diary. "One shot barked the tree and stung my ear. Another touched the side of my shoe and stung my toe." In reflex, Thomas's foot jerked up in a spasm "so energetically that I kicked myself. This caused a roar of laughter and yells that went on down the line." The reaction fit with a peculiar atmosphere that pervaded the regiment. "During the whole fight our men were in a state of hilarious excitement," Thomas recalled. "The slightest thing would cause a roar of laughter and yelling along the line." Thomas's personal adversary never hit him squarely. The Yankee fired seven shots, and Thomas returned each one. His eighth sent into the Northern lines silenced the duelist, whether with fatal results or not the Confederate rifleman could not tell.[38]

Thomas and his mates aimed and fired their Mississippi rifles so often that ammunition began to run short. Sergeant William H. Pope of Company A volunteered to dash to the rear for a resupply. To his mates "it seemed almost certain death to venture for a moment from the shelter of the wood," but Pope's dash succeeded and the Marylanders' rifles maintained their steady, deadly roar.[39]

The final Federal movement did not threaten Colonel Johnson's line directly any more than had the earlier ones. Several Maryland accounts insisted that the regiment's stand repulsed serious threats: "as many as four charges were repelled"; "the enemy making repeated attempts to penetrate our line"; "every assault was repelled with heavy loss to the assailants." No doubt those narrators reported what they believed, novice soldiers that they were. The exchange of fire had indeed been violent and somewhat costly. Washington Hands declared, "we were desperate men, fighting for our lives & liberties." Bradley Johnson recognized that, violence of the fire notwithstanding, the enemy had had no chance of driving him from the bluff by means of a frontal attack. Of the third and final Federal movement he wrote: "my men dispersed them rapidly." J. W. Thomas observed honestly and more sagely than some of his comrades that although "three regiments attacked us," they "did not charge." The Maryland regiment fought long and well under trying circumstances; but it faced no threat of being driven from its hilltop position.[40]

The ammunition supply restored by Sergeant Pope's brave sortie quickly dwindled again. The fire from Colonel Johnson's rifles slowed not only for that reason but also because black-powder residue had left them "so hot and so foul they could no longer be loaded or fired." With his weapons "totally unserviceable," Johnson decided to withdraw the regiment a short distance to the rear. Ewell concurred. There the colonel found a tiny stream where he set the men to work cleaning their weapons in the trickling water.[41]

By the time Johnson pulled out of line, reinforcements had arrived immediately behind the Maryland unit. Several Virginia infantry regiments extended the front on both the right and the left. Furthermore, the Federal effort had slackened and nearly ceased. Even so, Johnson diligently sought ammunition to use in his rifles once the men had sluiced them out at the stream. He also looked for rations for the men, who had not eaten for twenty-four hours. The soldiers in the ranks were content with what they had accomplished and sought no more action. "How anxiously we watched the sun go down that evening," Washington Hands remembered, "for we were well nigh worn out from . . . incessant fighting." J.E.H. Post wrote with palpable relief that "the shades of night began to deepen & we did not return."[42]

The 1st Maryland Infantry had fought its last fight. The dissolution of the volunteer regiment, which had been pending since the expiration of the men's enlistment terms in May, followed soon after the battle. Many of the soldiers continued in service in cavalry units, in the new 2nd Maryland, or in Virginia units containing friends and relatives. At Cross Keys they had stood firmly for hours as Ewell's left anchor. The price of doing that duty was substantial: every sixth man had gone down hit by Federal fire.[43]

The assistance that had rallied to the 1st Maryland as the fight developed included the 31st Virginia on its left, three regiments under Colonel John M. Patton on its right, and two Louisiana regiments of Taylor's Brigade to its rear. The 31st had spent some time with its own brigade, Elzey's, near the artillery cluster at the center. Ewell's concern about his left prompted him to strip his impregnable center in favor of the important flank. Colonel John S. Hoffman led the 31st to the left of the 1st Maryland—and thus to the left of the entire army. There he put the regiment into line "in the edge of a wood on a bluff." One cannon fired from the 31st's left during the afternoon, so evidently the Baltimore Light Artillery split its strength to spread its own impact and dodge enemy return fire.[44]

Once the 31st took up its position out on the last Confederate limb, its experience was similar to that of the neighboring 1st Maryland. The Virginians participated in the firefight against Federals "in the opposite wood and intervening field," to quote Hoffman's report. An officer in the 31st echoed the exaggerated Maryland refrain when he wrote that "the enemy several times attempted to carry our position but were repulsed." The 31st faced no more in the way of a certifiable assault than did the 1st Maryland. Instead it joined in the hot exchange of musketry that occupied the Marylanders and their enemies. An enemy round hit Irish-born Lieutenant Alexander Whitely in the head and killed him. Whitely's men had elevated him to that rank in an election only a few weeks earlier.[45]

Major Joseph H. Chenoweth had won his field-grade rank in the same recent election. Chenoweth wrote a diary entry during mid-afternoon in which he bewailed the fate of "several of our poor men [who] have been wounded. I pity them from the bottom of my heart. . . . Noble soldiers! it tortures me to see them wounded." One of the major's subordinates and friends chatted with him during a lull and found Chenoweth reflective. He expressed strong patriotism, religious fervor, and pride in his troops. Chenoweth also talked of an unshakable premonition of death.[46]

Colonel Hoffman noticed that the Federals facing him in the field (he doubtless saw Schenck more clearly than Milroy) gradually abandoned the open ground and relocated into woods north of the field. Then they fell farther back and ended the action. In a diary entry that he timed at 6:13 P.M., Major Chenoweth noted, "All is now quiet." The 31st was "lying down in line of battle, in full view of the enemy's battery, which [had been] pouring grape into the regiment." The major remained in an introspective mood, probably prompted by the foreshadowing of death that he continued to feel. Refugees such as Chenoweth and his men, whose homes lay in western Virginia regions occupied by enemy forces, faced "a hard life," he thought, having to "fight and suffer without one smile from those we love dearest to cheer us up." The glum major recorded a renewed outburst of musketry as he was writing in his diary, but it ended quickly. The Federal withdrawal and the setting sun marked the end of Joseph Chenoweth's last full day of life.[47]

Sometime after the 31st Virginia joined the left of the 1st Maryland, the 7th and 8th Louisiana of Taylor's Brigade arrived in the vicinity and provided redoubled strength behind the front-line regiments. The men from the Deep South had put in a long day of marching by this time. Taylor's Louisiana troops, after marching and countermarching toward Port Republic, finally returned to a reserve position near Mill Creek Church. Ewell pounced upon this reserve as a handy means of reinforcing his flanks. He sent Taylor and part of the brigade toward the far right in case James A. Walker bumped into serious difficulties. The 7th and 8th Louisiana headed toward the worrisome left flank. When they finally reached that location, Captain William P. Harper of the 7th figured that his regiment had marched about fifteen miles all told. The weary captain probably overestimated the distance, in the process demonstrating just how tiresome a day it had been.[48]

Taylor's men remained in reserve until well after the Federal withdrawal. Few if any of the Louisianians fired a musket all day long. General Taylor reported that his regiments were "not actually in action," but were "much exposed to the enemy's shell." A company clerk in the 8th Louisiana wrote: "we were under fire of Artillery [and] musketry for several hours." The brigade lost only about a dozen casualties. Among them was Captain Conrad Green of the 7th, a thirty-nine-year-old machinist from New Orleans whose wound did not keep him out of service long.[49] Taylor's splendid brigade had proved its mettle in earlier battles, earning Jackson's respect and employment as the army's shock troops of choice.

The final element in the patchwork quilt that Ewell wove to solidify his left was Colonel John M. Patton's Brigade of two regiments and one battalion of Virginia troops. Patton's own regiment, the 21st Virginia, was on detached duty herding thousands of Federal prisoners toward prison camps. Since he was the ranking officer present, the colonel remained with the brigade as its commander rather than accompanying the 21st on its boring detail. Patton and his three units—the 42nd and 48th Virginia and the 1st Virginia Battalion—had spent the night not far from Port Republic. The noise of the sudden Yankee raid into the village prompted the brigade (and everyone else for miles around) to race south toward the emergency. After their hurried trip, the men did nothing but wait in a field near the contested bridge all morning. The roar of battle back toward Cross Keys finally produced orders for the small brigade to head back north. The 48th Virginia led the way up the road, moving rapidly.[50]

John Patton rode ahead of his men to consult with Ewell about their disposition. By the time the 48th's rapid march reached Mill Creek Church, Patton had orders to send it toward Ewell's nervous zone—the far left. The 48th hurried in that direction under Lieutenant Colonel Thomas Stuart Garnett. Garnett was a thirty-seven-year-old physician who had practiced in central Virginia after attending Virginia Military Institute and the University of Virginia. He began the war as a cavalry captain but soon won a field-grade commission in the 48th. Patton told Garnett that a battery on the left (Brockenbrough's) was "strongly threatened with being charged by the enemy." When he reached the assigned point, Garnett found the battery "already badly crippled and strongly threatened by the enemy infantry." He also found a worried Ewell on hand to knit the 48th into the defense under his own direction. Garnett's main line adjoined the right end of the 1st Maryland. On Ewell's orders, all of the men in the 48th carrying "long-range guns" moved in front of the line as skirmishers. Evidently some companies could boast at least a few rifles, while others had only smoothbore muskets.[51]

The small 1st Virginia Battalion, known informally as the "Irish Battalion," moved separately from the two regiments; in fact all of the movements of Patton's Brigade took place in piecemeal fashion. The 42nd Virginia followed the 48th toward Cross Keys before the 1st Battalion moved, but the 42nd did not arrive at its ultimate destination on the left until later because of uncertainty about its role. Captain Benjamin Watkins Leigh, commanding the battalion, met Captain Nelson of Ewell's staff near Mill Creek Church and followed him toward the left. Leigh anchored his right on the left of the 58th Virginia, narrowing the gap between that component of Steuart's Brigade and the 1st Maryland–48th Virginia group farther up the ridge.[52]

Meanwhile the 42nd Virginia had bounced across the battlefield under confusing orders without sticking anywhere. Lieutenant Colonel William Martin, a forty-eight-year-old lawyer from Henry County, led the regiment north from the Port Republic bridge. He departed promptly and marched rapidly. The column met brigade commander Patton at Mill Creek Church. Patton's orders, surprisingly, sent the 42nd east of the road, in the general direction of where Trimble was struggling to drive away Bohlen's infantry and capture his artillery. Ewell obviously hoped to augment the force in that area in order to exploit the advantage that Trimble had won. Martin covered "several hundred yards," then received orders to move back to the road and beyond it to the left. The rest of the brigade had gone in that direction, and it made sense for the 42nd to conform.[53]

Ewell had hoped for something better, however, on the right of the road. Patton later conceived the notion that Ewell was disgusted with him over the matter. In an 1867 letter responding to Patton's query, Ewell reassured his former subordinate that supporting Trimble "was an accessory not a condition" regarding Trimble's degree of success. For Trimble's results—of which Ewell was astonishingly critical—"you were in no way responsible," the general told Patton.[54]

William Martin moved his men in the direction indicated across open ground about a half mile behind the batteries. An unpleasantly heavy rain of shells and small-arms fire kicked up dirt around the marching column. Martin met Captain Nelson when he reached the woods near Mill Creek Church. Nelson led Martin a little farther in the same direction to Ewell in person. The general ordered Martin to put the 42nd Virginia "in position on the brow of the hill to the left of our batteries." For about thirty minutes the regiment clung to the bluff in that vicinity. Fire of all sorts whistled past, and the regiment could do very little in response.[55]

Finally someone, presumably Ewell, concluded that reuniting Patton's scattered brigade made good sense. The general's concern for his left no doubt eased the decision. Patton led Martin and his men three hundred yards farther west. There the 42nd "drew up in line of battle" just to the left of the 1st Virginia Battalion and with the 48th Virginia connected to its own left. Martin threw out two companies of skirmishers under the command of Captain Abner Dobyns and awaited developments.[56]

By the time the 42nd went into the line, few developments remained on the battle agenda. Federal focus had wavered for some time, and the crisis all across the front had passed. The 1st Battalion had been in line long enough to spend some time under fire. Captain Leigh mentioned in his report only that "a number of shells and Minie balls passed near us."[57]

Of Patton's three units, only the 48th saw any serious battle action once in position on the bluff. Garnett's Virginians participated with the 1st Maryland in repulsing Milroy's last advance, and perhaps the penultimate one as well. The regiment's ground did not include the trees that proved so valuable as shelter for the 1st Maryland. Thomas Garnett described in a letter home the result: "this place . . . exposed us terribly without giving us an opportunity to fire except when the infantry would venture sufficiently near." A single Northern shell inflicted the majority of the casualties that the 48th suffered when its fragments hit ten men. Garnett "was on horseback near the spot and was struck in the face by the hat of one of the men knocked off by a fragment of shell."[58]

A mixture of small Confederate cavalry commands roaming the countryside beyond and behind Ewell's left complemented in minor fashion the defensive posture of his infantry line. One squadron (two companies) of the 6th Virginia Cavalry operated in that region. Portions of the 2nd Virginia Cavalry played a similar role out on Trimble's right; some of the 2nd also lounged behind Ewell's center and left. An unaffiliated company of mounted local men commanded by Captain William N. Jordan also operated on Ewell's left. Jordan's home and farm lay "just outside of the line of battle." "The Yankees broke open my corn crib," Jordan recalled ruefully, "and took corn to feed their horses, but did not disturb my family."[59]

As Milroy and Schenck and their legions faded away, Ewell could sigh with relief. His shuttle system had successfully fed enough gray-clad infantry into the threatened left to hold that sensitive spot. Charles Webb was perceptive enough to recognize at once what the Confederate commander had done. He grumbled that on his side of the line, Frémont failed to get "our right wing . . . into action." Meanwhile the Confederate reserve "was kept shifting from wing to wing during the engagement, as occasion demanded."[60]

Aside from Trimble's triumphs, both defensive and offensive, the Battle of Cross Keys from the perspective of Confederate high command consisted of steadily buttressing the left. General Ewell visited that threatened point at least twice, and probably frequently. The general's official report offered typically generous accolades to diligent subordinates, but barely mentioned Steuart as "rendering valuable aid in command of the left." Steuart had been a notable failure earlier in the campaign, but Ewell's sparse mention in this instance likely was the result of the fact that he commanded the left in person, leaving Steuart a lessened role.[61]

Dick Ewell's personal involvement on the left was especially evident during the arrival of his final reinforcements in the form of Patton's little brigade. Ewell actively participated in placing the 48th Virginia in the line. As mentioned earlier, Patton wrote to his former chief after the war to complain a bit about his treatment on June 8. In response, Ewell made light of the matter: "You refer to some temper shown by me in reference to a discussion as to the position of one of your Regts. I forget it & think it more than likely the chief cause was my habitual annoyance during a fight when my attention was called from important points on which it was necessary to act. Having to decide promptly on the most important steps it was impossible for me to discuss coolly unimportant occurrences."

John Patton came away from his battlefield encounter convinced that Ewell had called him a coward. Ewell's later disclaimer attempted to "distinguish between the caution of a commander & more personal fear. I saw in you the first but not" the other sort. "I might have expressed such a difference," Ewell admitted, "but never anything reflecting in the slightest degree on your courage." The general concluded with an assurance that Colonel Patton had done nothing that would have resulted in "forfeiting my respect."[62] The careful letter probably soothed Patton's feelings. It also reveals with some clarity how very concerned Ewell had been five years earlier about his left.

General Ewell responded skillfully to the potential threats to his left, but did not succumb to the common tendency to inflate what actually happened there. While his opponents and some of his subordinates described the infantry fight as a veritable Armageddon, Ewell coolly reported that enemy efforts were "principally directed against General Trimble" on the other end of the field. Captain Brown, for his part, variously described Federal performance on the Confederate left as "several attacks . . . all feeble"; "most weakly pressed"; and "all easily repulsed."[63]

None of that accurate analysis of the Federal potential for victory should detract from what the soldiery went through around Mill Creek, the Flory house, and the opposite ridge. The torrent of fire poured out by both sides, especially by the respective artillery, turned the afternoon into a certifiable ordeal for the men doing the fighting. The inexperience of the vast majority of them made the situation worse. The ground rising from Mill Creek to the Flory house site and on toward the Armentrout house site has yielded far more small-arms relics than any other spot on the battlefield, as well as a tidy harvest of artillery shells and fragments. That Milroy and Schenck could not threaten the capture of Mill Creek Ridge and the rout of its defenders does not mean that the men engaged on both sides faced an insignificant battle experience.[64]

Frémont and Schenck could readily have turned Ewell out of his position without firing a gun. The potential for then wreaking havoc on Jackson at Port Republic was dazzling. As Major Dabney cogently noted, for such a movement "the Keezletown road, proceeding west-ward from Cross Keys, provided . . . facilities." Dabney was himself a military cipher, but he clearly saw that "nothing but the most impotent generalship" could account for missing that golden opportunity.

Ewell's duty to prepare for what his foe should reasonably do prompted him to guard that end of the line rigorously. The history of that afternoon shows how thoroughly he discharged the duty. In the aftermath, Ewell thought back to his days fighting poorly orga-nized levies during the 1840s, remarking "that he felt all day as though he were again fighting the feeble, semi-civilized armies of Mexico."[65] Before many hours had passed, Ewell and his men and their comrades in Jackson's main force would face Federals led with far more skill.

1st New York Light
Artillery, Battery
I (Captain Michael
Wiedrich) at Cross Keys

CHAPTER 13

DUSK AND DARKNESS

AT CROSS KEYS

s the Federal line recoiled all across the front, it peeled rearward, first on the east, then the center, then the west. Confederates followed prudently, after Ewell exorcised some phantom demons said still to be threatening his dangling left flank. As a result, Southern infantry pursued with less than its accustomed zeal. Inevitably, Confederate accounts talk smugly of occupying enemy ground; Federal reports boast of deliberate, unhurried withdrawal.

Trimble's repulse of Stahel and then his attack upon Bohlen had forced back Frémont's left far enough to leave the Union commander eager to realign his whole front. The unhinging of his left had been the only real trauma Frémont suffered. Milroy and Schenck had not dented—could never have dented—Ewell's dominant ridge, to be sure, and Frémont did not have enough imagination to maneuver Ewell off the position. But neither could Ewell descend gracefully from his ridge to chastise Milroy and Schenck, even had he possessed the strength and the inclination to do so.

Frémont's discomfort on his left had not been of alarming proportions, at least not by standards established in the war's major battles. For a nervous novice general, though, in the midst of the confusion of a battlefield, the forced relocation of part of his line must have been daunting. Stahel and Bohlen inevitably came back in some disarray. Stahel's 27th Pennsylvania learned of the final withdrawal only when it found itself all alone. The 27th's soldiers could see Confederates to the rear, apparently isolating them. Colonel Buschbeck extricated the 27th almost unmolested, but the business seemed exciting and desperate at the time. The regiment did pass through one indisputably hot spot: as the Pennsylvanians headed into the amorphous Federal position, they were mistaken for Confederates and were fired upon by an ostensibly friendly battery.[1]

Although Milroy and Schenck shared a common heritage and a common cause, they were by no means of one accord. Milroy described his disgust at finding Schenck's Brigade "standing perfectly idle as spectators of the battle." "Had this Bgd. been thrown forward on my right to have cleared the rebles out of the forest, which they could have done with perfect ease," Milroy opined, "we could have swept the battle field like a tempest and captured the whole of Jackson's army." Milroy pinned the ultimate blame on Frémont, in whom he had "lost confidence . . . tremendiously and so has his whole army here." Milroy is easy to deride because of his bombast and unbalanced behavior, but his analysis of Federal shortcomings here is difficult to dispute.[2]

After giving the handy Union guns time "to peg the rebles well," Milroy sent an aide back to General Frémont to inquire whether he must retire farther. The army commander reiterated his instructions. "I slowly and reluctantly obeyed," Milroy told his wife in a letter, but once he had complied, the brigade commander cornered Frémont in person to complain. "I could have held my position where I was a month," the junior general told his superior. Frémont professed surprise, "and said he was sorry[;] he did not know it." Milroy's disdainful glance around headquarters took in the "whole cloud of aids . . . setting around," whose business it was to know such things.

When he cooled off a bit, Milroy reached the more temperate

conclusion that the rebuff of Stahel and Bohlen gave Frémont reason to worry about his skewed line. Even so, had Frémont "ordered the advance of his whole right wing we could have swept around and captured everything for at that time our forces . . . was holding the bridge at Port Republic." Since by now it was six P.M., Milroy actually had missed the transitory bridge opportunity by about nine hours.[3]

Notwithstanding an overdose of self-importance, General Milroy supplied to Frémont's army a much-needed dash of aggressive spirit. It is interesting to contemplate what might have happened had Milroy been in overall command. He would fail miserably when given the chance in 1863, but not for want of effort. By coincidence, at the same time that Milroy was agitating for aggression from the Federal right his Confederate alter ego, I. R. Trimble, was agitating for similar aggressive behavior against the Federal left. As had been the case at the First Battle of Manassas, the two sides considered simultaneous assaults on opposite ends of the line. The revolving-door results would have been amazing to see, but neither battle actually developed in that fashion.

General Robert Schenck's account of his disengagement might have been ghostwritten by Milroy, so similar is its spirit. Schenck too claimed to be on the verge of a stunning victory when ordered back. "I felt reluctant to obey," he reported, since headquarters could not know of his splendid opportunity. Schenck too held in place long enough to send back a request for release from the requirement, but "the order came back repeated." The brigade fell back easily, covered by artillery fire. During the withdrawal, a messenger from Frémont arrived asking whether Schenck still could hold his forward ground; perhaps this was just after Milroy's opening remarks to Frémont. By then Milroy's retirement had exposed enough of Schenck's left to make reconsideration impossible. The enlisted men of his brigade, Schenck professed to know, were worn and exhausted but "actively and cheerfully eager to meet the rebel forces, and only regretted that it could not be their fortune to encounter them for their share in more obstinate and decisive battle."[4] No doubt this facile summary constituted a bit of whistling in the cemetery by a politician-turned-general; but to a degree hard for modern readers to understand, Schenck probably told the truth about the spirit of an amazing number of his volunteer soldiers.

The most important visitor of the day to Frémont's headquarters rode wearily into camp in the twilight confusion. As officers hurried about logistical tasks "with everything bent towards our immediate renewal of the fight," one of them wrote, up dashed a cavalryman asking for General Frémont. Aides took the "splashed and travel-worn" fellow to the general, where he handed over a dispatch. Colonel Tracy watched while the army commander read it with "a smile not only of satisfaction, but almost of relief." The message came from Shields and bore that morning's date. It boasted of troops and artillery closing in on Jackson's trains near Port Republic. "I hope you will thunder down on his rear," the communiqué said optimistically. "I think Jackson is caught this time."[5]

Did this good news from his ally stir Frémont to action? On the contrary, it somehow supplied him with reassurance that *inaction* was in order! Colonel Tracy, recording the consensus around head-quarters, summarized the aberrant notion that prevailed: "The battle, as it now stands, is not in our favor; but, with the recuperation of a night's rest, the concentration at our front of a force to prevent the escape of the enemy, with the encouragement and strength to be infused by the whole—we will be better able to renew the fight with the morning, than to continue it now. Such was the conclusion at once and intuitively reached by all."[6] This twisted thinking posited that corralling Stonewall Jackson was so important that work on the project ought to be suspended for half a day.

An undercurrent of commentary in the Federal army wondered whether Frémont and Shields failed to cooperate because of jealousy or animosity. Colonel Tracy expressed the conviction that Shields chose not to help Frémont. Some cavalrymen sent from Frémont to Shields came back convinced of the same thing. They reported that Shields read the communication they had carried and then "made some slurring remarks about General Fremont." The cavalry officer narrating the tale concluded: "The jealousy among the higher officers of the army, which was often very apparent, was disgraceful and costly."[7] He was right. Unseemly bickering ran rife in the Federal high command. The lack of Federal coordination on June 8 and 9, how-ever, probably had little connection to such frivolous motives. Events dictated that Shields could not help Frémont. Frémont's inability to help Shields resulted from incompetence rather than unwillingness.

Having reached their intuitive decision to relax, Frémont and his myrmidons formed a tidy line back near the Keezletown Road. Cluseret had reached a point far enough away from danger for the army's leadership to form on him in comfort. "Under a gradual cessation of the heavier firing, the whole was accomplished, a substantial line of pickets thrown out athwart the general front," and the blue-clad host prepared for night. Frémont placed artillery near the intersection of the Harrisonburg and Keezletown roads to guard his left. Many units wound up by reflex precisely where they had started that morning. An artillerist with Milroy's Brigade wrote: "At night we camped on the hill where we took position at the beginning of the fight."[8]

Before Frémont's men could settle down for the night, artillery action interrupted the twilight calm. Two enterprising Confederate gun crews opened suddenly from the western end of the Confederate bluff not far from Union Church. Their first rounds sought out Frémont's headquarters with uncanny accuracy just "as the shades of night were beginning to fall." Correspondent Webb distinctly heard an approaching cannonball that landed about fifty yards from Frémont. The general "immediately called out, 'Leave this hill, gentlemen; they have got the range exactly'; and at once all present dispersed." Tracey could see the muzzle flashes and gushes of smoke in the woods. He noted with gratitude that the Confederate projectiles did not explode. The agrarian South never did master the knack of making ordnance explode with regularity.[9]

Milroy was chatting with Frémont when the excitement began and noted that as "the rebles commenced pitching cannon balls," the first shell threw dirt over the "whole cloud of aids" about Frémont. The second killed a staff officer's horse without touching the rider. Milroy "was amused to see what a hurry he and his staff were in getting back to the rear out of reach of the rebles."[10]

The bold Confederate cannoneers also threw shells into the Federal artillery park near Schenck's position. An officer's horse was the first casualty there too. Northern guns promptly replied in overwhelming strength against their reckless tormentors. "In an instant the heavens were aglare and the hills trembled in the rage of battle" as Union batteries "belched forth defiantly." The impudent Confederate gesture lasted only a few minutes. A Northern observer gloated over the battering of his foe, but speculated prudently that the withdrawing Confederates probably had probed with intent and learned something: that the Yankee withdrawal had ended near the Keezletown Road. By sunset at 7:15 this last test of battle had ceased.[11]

Richard Ewell's defenders climbed down from their dominant ridge to follow Frémont, but not until the general reassured himself yet again about the integrity of his far left. Frémont's precise order of march having reached Ewell during the day, he had a clear under-standing of enemy strength. The captured document showed seven Federal infantry brigades. Ewell knew he could not match those numbers.[12]

Ewell also received an alarming report from his left. The general explained that he "did not push my successes at once, because I had no cavalry, and it was reported, and reaffirmed by Lieutenant [Oscar] Hinrichs, topographical engineer, sent to reconnoiter, that the enemy was moving a large column 2 miles to my left." Here was alarming indication that Frémont was doing precisely what Ewell most feared, and what the Federals should have done as their primary initiative. Whatever confused Hinrichs (there were no Yankees out there) dissi-pated, and Ewell "advanced both my wings, drove in the enemy's skirmishers, and when night closed was in position on the ground previously held by the enemy, ready to attack him at dawn."[13]

On the Confederate center and left the twilight advance was straightforward and not particularly complicated. Patton's small bri-gade did most of the work, aided by the two Louisiana regiments left in the vicinity by General Taylor. John Patton's orders from Ewell were to make "a flank movement on the enemy's right to take posses-sion of a wood which they had occupied all day." Bradley Johnson left his 1st Maryland in the rear but went in person to the front to coordinate the advance under Ewell's orders. Colonel Harry T. Hays of the 7th Louisiana was also a highly competent individual; within a few weeks he would be promoted and then outrank Patton and Johnson for the remainder of the war. Hays also received instructions from Ewell.[14]

Patton's 48th Virginia probably did not participate in the ad-vance. The 42nd Virginia and the 1st Virginia Battalion moved concur-rently to their left toward Union Church, on a prolongation of the line that Ewell had held all day. The two units then turned at right angles to face Mill Creek again, dropped down the bluff ("a consider-able declivity," Captain Leigh of the 1st called it), crossed the stream, and approached the parallel road beyond it in a long line of battle. Skirmishers advancing in front of the main line brushed against Fed-eral pickets and exchanged a few snarling volleys with them.[15]

Captain Abner Dobyns of the 42nd had been in charge of two companies deployed as skirmishers all day. They continued in that role during the advance. As the 42nd approached the road, the 7th Louisiana caught up with it. The Louisianians hurried across the back of the 42nd to reach the Virginians' left and extended the line farther in that direction. A "sharp fire" from the Federal advance guard stopped Dobyns. The remainder of the 42nd closed up, rolled forward to the road, and halted, "which was then about dark."[16]

Because the skirmishers from the 42nd did their job effectively, the 1st Battalion was virtually unengaged and unscathed. Captain Leigh went forward from the road to examine the situation facing his battalion. He spotted an enemy artillery position about five hundred yards to his left front. Around the guns a line of blue-coated infantry lay in support behind another of the convenient Cross Keys fences. Northern skirmishers lurked in a wheat field. More Yankees infested some nearby woods. The Federals visible to Leigh had more than enough troops to hold the Confederates along the road in check; no doubt more hovered in the nearby darkness. Orders reached Colonel Patton "to lie down on our arms" and the men prepared for an uneasy night on debatable ground.[17]

While Patton and his colleagues looped to their left front, the Confederates who had stood to their right on the main ridge did little more than edge forward a bit. The 44th Virginia had been in front of the rest of Steuart's Brigade most of the afternoon. Its colonel, William C. Scott, assumed temporary command of the brigade when General Steuart fell wounded. The 58th Virginia moved toward the stream to support the 44th in the gathering darkness. An exchange of long-range sharpshooter fire developed, but "there was no regular fight," Scott reported. The colonel, out of touch with Ewell and ignorant of the trends to his left, expected an enemy attack that never came.[18]

Back near Mill Creek Church and the main road, Ewell's center had nothing to do with the advance on the wings. The 21st North Carolina held fast to its piece of the bluff "for an hour or two." Then the Tarheels moved back near the church and camped in a little hollow. Most Confederates returned reflexively to their campsites of the night before. As Eli Coble of the 21st prepared for the night, he glanced back toward the hill that he and his mates had defended. Smoke still "hung like a pall over the Field," he recalled. High above the now-quiet artillery knoll Coble "saw a lone Bird in mid air high up. . . . I noticed it Hovering & lingering—the size of a dove—and now and then it would Soar a little higher and hover. . . . I felt Sad."[19]

Fiery Isaac Trimble had spent most of the afternoon pressing forward with marked success. Now he would spend the evening confusing Ewell and fighting with him, then importuning Jackson for permission to launch a private war in southern Rockingham County. We last saw Trimble at victorious high tide, driving Bohlen's artillery away in hurried discomfiture. Not long after he accomplished that, Dick Taylor arrived in the vicinity with half of his strong and skilled brigade. Ewell had responded to the roar on his right front by sending help to that sector.[20]

Trimble's battle-weary troops viewed their reinforcements with a degree of awe. The Louisiana brigade enjoyed an honestly earned reputation for both soldierly virtues and rowdy misbehavior. A captain in the 21st Georgia watched with interest as the legendary men from the Deep South drew near. They did not disappoint him. The column approached with each set of four men "in perfect line, arms at 'right shoulder shift.' " Colonel Isaac G. Seymour of the 6th Louisiana, a fifty-seven-year-old newspaperman and politician with "long, silvery locks," looked especially martial. The alignment of his troops adjusted to obstacles and "perfected without a wobble." On orders, "the rifles of 800 men struck the ground as one man." The Louisianians promptly validated the other side of their reputation when they fell to looting the dead all around them. One of the many Irishmen in Taylor's Brigade chatted with the Georgia captain about the threat from his countryman Shields. The Louisiana soldier was certain that Shields's Irish troops would prove to be far more dangerous foes than had Frémont's "German bounty-men," whom he called "poor creatures."[21]

General Taylor reported simply and in good humor that his arrival constituted a "display of force" that "caused the enemy to retire still farther from the position to which it had been driven by the vigorous charge of Trimble's command." Taylor did no fighting and did not remain long. Trimble predictably did not repay Taylor's compliment. In fact he contradicted Taylor's assertion about the impact of visible reinforcements, declaring grumpily that Taylor departed "not having been engaged or seen by the enemy." By Trimble's account, he as always had known exactly what to do and how to do it; but the dullard Taylor "passed too far to the right, and lost time."[22]

Trimble and Taylor both held commissions as brigadier generals, but Trimble's antedated Taylor's by a few weeks; however, Ewell had sent Taylor to Trimble for the specific purpose of aiding in a fight that now had ended. With Ewell's detail of Taylor to meet a specific need no longer in force, the Louisiana general should revert to Ewell's direct control. Accordingly, Trimble must enlist Taylor's support in his new scheme, rather than command it. The two generals went to "an eminence in view of the enemy, then a mile distant." They could see an enemy battery and some infantry but could not ascertain their strength. Trimble typically proposed to charge directly toward the battery without regard for any larger considerations. The far more prudent and able Taylor agreed with his frenetic colleague "that we could soon wipe out that force if it would do any good." With his more mature perspective, Taylor (who would become a successful lieutenant general later in the war) could find no advantage in a local success that pulled his force so far from alignment with the rest of the army.

Dick Taylor also had to consider his men's preparedness for battle. They had marched far that day and "needed rest and food," Taylor told an unsympathetic Trimble. Taylor's judgment was validated the next morning when his brigade marched long and hard again, but had enough strength left to deliver a desperate attack at the climax of the Battle of Port Republic. Without Taylor's help, Trimble had to spread his three regiments out in the woods and send word to Ewell "that the enemy had been repulsed on our right, and that I awaited orders."[23]

Despite Trimble's unmistakable ardor, Ewell somehow came to believe that Trimble held back at a time when his chief sought to coordinate an attack all across his front. Patton and Hays and Johnson on the left filled a less important role in Ewell's scheme for the dusk advance than did Trimble. The two men certainly were not at odds in principle; the confusion of a far-flung battlefield blocked coordination. Campbell Brown, Ewell's young alter ego, wrote: "by some misunderstanding (Trimble waiting to hear plans before attacking), the attack was delayed for a time, & in the interval orders came from J[ackso]n to be ready to retreat . . . & the attack was suspended." The rest of the night Trimble would be panting to attack, anyone and anywhere; but in the view of Ewell's headquarters, he had retarded the army at the one time that an attack had actually been ordered. Captain Brown, sounding very much like the spoiled son of his general's forceful lady friend (which he was), grumbled that Stonewall Jackson had deprived Ewell of a great opportunity: "when he had Fremont in the hollow of his hand, Jackson made a night march . . . & attacked Shields' comparatively unimportant force."[24]

Trimble's view of the proceedings differed dramatically. Major

James Barbour of Ewell's staff delivered orders to Trimble about thirty minutes after Taylor had departed. Barbour told of the plan to move Patton to the left while Trimble pressed forward on his own front. Under the color of this new directive Trimble longed to dragoon Taylor into his force, but by now he had marched out of reach. So Trimble moved forward with his three regiments to a point about five hundred yards from the Keezletown Road. He was operating, however, under a mistaken notion that foiled the entire operation: either Barbour wrongly told the general to await the sound of Patton's attack, or more likely Trimble inferred that. Patton's diversion was of course not intended to trigger Trimble's effort. The reverse situation was more nearly true. The sloppy staff work that so often afflicted Civil War engagements lay at the root of this problem. Orders almost always went forward in casual oral form, rather than in unmistakable written form, often with damaging results. Civil War armies tried no more than a half-dozen major night attacks during the four years of conflict, and none succeeded notably.

After waiting impatiently for thirty minutes, Trimble sent a courier to ask Ewell about the untoward delay. After another half hour the general sent another courier. On the heels of the second messenger Trimble dispatched Lieutenant John E. Lee of his staff to find Ewell. Lee was "to say that if the attack was made on their [Confederate left] flank, to divert [Federal] attention from my movement, I thought I could overpower the enemy in front, but that it would be injudicious to do so alone." Trimble also instructed Lee to inform Ewell that he could count three Federal batteries and five brigades of infantry. This first note of caution from Trimble may have betrayed an abatement of adrenaline flow and a resultant return of reason, although this mildly altered state would not deter the general from plotting and ranting through much of the night. The cautionary note and associated suggestions probably are what led Campbell Brown to suggest that Trimble was "waiting to hear plans before attacking." Before any among the string of messengers completed their round-trips, however, darkness had fallen.[25]

As twilight faded, Trimble noted with pride that his regiments held a sharp, straight line, "as composed as if they had been on drill." He called up Colonel Walker's force, thereby nearly doubling his strength. Why the hard-fighting Virginia regiments had not advanced with him before is hard to imagine. Perhaps they had been licking their wounds after the fray around the Evers house, but their losses had been no worse than those in Trimble's regiments. Walker and the 13th and 25th remained at the front for about three hours after dark and then went to the rear to camp. In retrospect Trimble contemplated what he had wrought in his operations on the Confederate right. No other officer at Cross Keys had accomplished much, Trimble announced. He believed that he had single-handedly stymied 7,000 Yankees. Trimble professed to know somehow that by "moderate estimate" he had inflicted 1,740 casualties.[26] That display of misplaced concreteness and exponential exaggeration notwithstanding, Trimble was the star of June 8. He had carried the day, immodestly but well.

Now, by his own remarkable admission, Trimble seriously considered attacking toward Frémont's strength entirely on his own hook and without permission. "I was strongly tempted to make the advance alone at night," he boasted. Only "some scruples in regard to a possible failure" deterred him. If he had only had the forethought to demand Taylor's obedience, he wrote regretfully, he could have attacked despite Ewell's opposition: "the result would have been reasonably certain without consulting General Ewell."[27] To express such insubordinate notions in the body of an official report was amazingly bad military protocol. Only General James Longstreet's boastful postwar accounts of his imagined hegemony over Robert E. Lee reach an equally vainglorious level.

While Trimble fretted rebelliously, he watched "the enemy go into camp, light their fires, draw rations, and otherwise dispose themselves for the night, evidently not expecting any further attack." He then dashed off to track down Ewell "to recommend a night attack." Ewell was not at the headquarters near Mill Creek Church. He had ridden to Port Republic to meet with Stonewall Jackson. The night meeting revealed Stonewall's determination to bring Ewell down from Cross Keys to participate in squelching Shields's advance party early the next morning. Before Ewell left Cross Keys, he and Jackson had exchanged status reports by courier. Jackson's reliable aide Sandie Pendleton went to Ewell to convey his chief's worried message: "I will keep Shields back if you can hold Fremont in check." By that hour Ewell was able to answer confidently: "The worst is over now, I can manage him."[28]

Ewell arrived in Port Republic to find Jackson in a more typical mood. With both of the June 8 crises behind the halves of his army, Jackson's mindset had turned—as it almost always did, given the tiniest opening—toward aggressive measures. Most of the content of the generals' session at Port Republic belongs to the next phase of the campaign, and must be narrated in another chapter. For purposes of Trimble and the night of the 8th, it is clear that Jackson's instructions to Ewell contemplated no further engagement at Cross Keys. Trimble nonetheless set upon the unfortunate Ewell when he returned and "urged more than ever the attack, and begged him to go with me and 'see how easy it was.' " Ewell said no. To get rid of the importuning gadfly, he finally passed the buck to Jackson. In Trimble's words, Ewell "could not take the responsibility, and if it was to be done I would have to see General Jackson."[29]

No doubt Ewell did not imagine that his subordinate would ride through the night to beard Stonewall Jackson on such a matter, but Trimble did just that. He made the seven-mile round-trip through the darkness and confusion of two battlefields and saw the commanding general. He probably had to awaken Jackson. Trimble reported the result in an elliptical sentence. "I . . . obtained his consent to have Colonel Patton's battalion co-operate with me and his directions 'to consult General Ewell and be guided by him.' " Despite Trimble's attempt to paint Jackson's response as "consent," he was back where he started: Ewell remained in charge of affairs at Cross Keys, in accord with the simplest of military precepts of rank, authority, and local control.[30]

When Trimble returned to the Cross Keys headquarters with his useless credentials from Jackson, Ewell was predictably unimpressed. Trimble presented what he styled "this permission" with as much vim as he could muster—and that was a great deal—but his superior "declined taking the responsibility which he said thus rested on him, and continued, with General Taylor, to oppose it against my urgent entreaties to be permitted to make the attack alone with my brigade." Ewell dismissed Trimble with a bit of irrefutable logic: "even a partial reverse would interfere with General Jackson's plan for the next day."[31]

Even though Trimble's fulminations about pitching into Frémont could not have resulted in any tactical advantage, and surely represented strategic quicksand, many in the army appreciated his eager spirit. The Lynchburg *Virginian* quoted an unnamed officer as praising Trimble because he "strongly counselled a night attack on Frémont's whole army." An admiring Confederate told the Richmond *Dispatch* that "General Trimble's theory seems to be unexpected and sudden assaults upon the enemy, and desperate fighting only when a great point can be gained."[32]

Even Ewell acknowledged the value of his bumptious subordinate's ardor, according to Colonel Thomas T. Munford. Munford (who was prone to confusion in some of his postwar writings) quoted Ewell as saying on June 9: "old Trimble is a real trump . . . he is as bold as any man, and, in fact, is the hero of yesterday's fight. . . . Trimble won the fight." Sam Buck supplied a cogent analysis from the ranks of the 13th Virginia, where he spent the evening appended to Trimble's forward position. "I have always thought we gained only half a victory at Cross Keys," Buck wrote; but he added thoughtfully, "not until I saw a report of the battle did I know the cause."[33]

Much of the Confederate army rested for the night along a line close to that from which their enemy had fought during the day. Patton's men held up not far beyond the road paralleling Mill Creek, where Schenck had been earlier. There, Patton wrote, "we were ordered to lie down on our arms, in line of battle, in the immediate neighborhood of the enemy. General Ewell . . . desired to hold this vantage ground." Patton carefully "arranged the pickets, and had everything snug for the night, the men being profoundly asleep after their labors." His 42nd Virginia and 1st Virginia Battalion remained at the spot all night, but an hour after dark the 48th Virginia was sent halfway to Port Republic to camp. Whatever fate designated the separate campsites affected the units profoundly: the 48th would fight next day at Port Republic, but the other two did not reach that battlefield in time to participate.[34]

Taylor's Louisianians who had barely escaped Trimble's clutches gathered near Mill Creek Church and made a brief camp there. Their comrades of the 7th and 8th Louisiana remained with Patton's detachment for several hours, then rejoined Taylor. Before daybreak the reunited brigade took the road toward Port Republic. Trimble's three regiments tried to sleep in the far forward position from which their brigadier hoped all night long to launch them in an attack. Tom Hightower of the 21st Georgia wrote that he "slept on the battlefield that night within 3 hundred yards of the Enemy." Confederate cavalrymen spent the night in small clusters in as close contact with the enemy as they could manage. In their commander's words, "the exhausted cavalry were . . . distributed on picket duty over the many roads in front of the two armies, now so near at hand."[35]

Although the two outer Confederate wings spent the night in proximity to the enemy, Trimble's front remained quiet while Patton's experienced some desultory action. The inexperienced soldiers in Trimble's 15th Alabama were amazed at how clearly they could watch their mortal enemies. "All night we lay in line of battle," Captain Oates remembered, "and could see the Yankees around their camp-fires and hear them talking." Patton's troops watched their Northern foes around campfires too, and "could distinctly hear the voices of the skirmishers in the wheat field." Twice during the night their observation developed into militant action.[36]

As though to make up for his daylight lassitude, General Schenck sent out a company of the 73rd Ohio to probe in the dark. Patton's men killed one of the Ohioans and wounded another. Schenck then dispatched a Connecticut cavalry sergeant and four troopers to look for the Southern lines. Virginia infantrymen captured them easily near Union Church. "They were entirely ignorant of the fact that we were there," a captor wrote.[37]

Federal soldiers fared better for food overnight than did the Southerners, both because Frémont's men built blazing fires and could cook over them while the Confederates maintained a dark front for security, and because the Northerners apparently had fewer qualms about stealing food from civilians. A captain at Frémont's headquarters stole a "nice fat lamb," butchered it, and passed pieces around. Colonel Tracy in his journal pronounced the barbecue that resulted "toothsome to the extreme." A few hundred yards away Patton's men remained hungry in their dark bivouac. Officers sent back a detail from each company to find the regimental wagons and cook rations from them. The ravenous troops finally caught up with the detail and the wagons the next morning while en route to Port Republic.[38]

Frémont's army looted in 1862, but officers checked the worst excesses, unlike Sheridan's army two years later. Some of the damage to private property resulted from the need to care for wounded soldiers. Ann Kemper, the seventy-year-old widow of Rodham Kemper, left her house at the Cross Keys intersection during the morning to avoid the shelling. When she came back in the evening, she found "as many as eighty wounded soldiers" in her house. She also found "every thing distroyed and carried off, all the bed clothes of all kinds sheets pillow cases table clothes all the dishes knives and forks, tore up the girls bonnits ... destroyed everything ... even took there under clothes." At the nearby home of Edward S. Yancey, a captain in the 6th Virginia Cavalry, Northern soldiers also "destroyed every thing . . . even got Fan's spoons."[39]

One Cross Keys woman resorted to subterfuge to avoid unwanted attention. The anonymous young mother of three ("Mrs. K.") was beautiful and wealthy, but anxious to appear unattractive and old. To that end, she recalled, "I took from my mouth a set of false teeth, (which I was compelled to have put in before I was 20 years old,) tied a handkerchief around my head, donned my most sloven apparel, and in every way made myself as hideous as possible. . . . I was sullen, morose, sententious. . . . It had the desired effect. The Yankees called me 'old woman.' " Federals filled Mrs. K.'s home with wounded that night, leaving her the use of a single room. She helped nurse the wounded, in response to her "own heart-promptings." But she "did not feel disposed to be compelled to prepare food for those who had driven from me my husband, and afterwards robbed me of all my food and . . . furniture." The Northerners generally ignored her. "I endured all the inconveniences and unhappines of my situation with as much fortitude as I could bring into operation," Mrs. K. declared stoutly, "feeling that my dear husband, at least, was safe from harm." The doughty woman and her babies were destitute when the occupation of their home finally ended, but were content to have survived.[40]

The agonizing ordeal of the hundreds of wounded around Cross Keys brought out the better instincts of soldiers and surgeons on both sides of the lines. Frémont's army had access to fewer than one half of its wounded because of Confederate advances across contested ground. Many of them received care in private homes commandeered for hospitals. The largest number clustered under the ecumenical shelter of Union Church. The sanctuary "was a ruin, and its walls showed many scars of heavy shot and shell." A passing staff officer vividly described the gruesome scene: "the groaning and misery of the crowds brought in . . . and deposited by the banks of the road, or in the church . . . or other of the few buildings about—converted suddenly to hospitals—attested full sadly the destruction wrought both of limb and body."[41]

Frémont's wounded in Confederate hands worried about the quality of care they might expect. Bitter sectional propaganda insisted that Southerners abused wounded captives. A Jacobin committee of radicals in the U.S. Congress had smugly satisfied itself that Confederates had murdered wounded men after the First Battle of Manassas and saved their skulls for souvenirs. Charles Webb of *The New York Times,* who could be as jingoistic as any Yankee, firmly refuted such nonsense by reporting the kindness displayed by Confederates to the wounded of the 8th New York: "I am glad to learn from their lips that they have been kindly treated by the Southern soldiers. Two Germans have just told me how the latter came during the night, covered them over with blankets, brought them water, and in some cases washed their wounds. What I have here witnessed, entirely dispels any faint faith I ever had in what is commonly termed 'rebel barbarity.' . . . These stories [of mistreatment of wounded] are rife on both sides; manufactured by knaves, they are told to fools with the intention of engendering a mutual hate."[42]

Rufus W. Wharton, a thirty-five-year-old major from Beaufort County, North Carolina, described what he found as he walked under a brightly shining moon across the field where so many of the 8th New York had fallen: "the wounded would speak to me. I could not understand what they said. Finally one of them in broken English said they were asking me to have them removed to the hospital. They were all Germans and I learned that some of them had been in America only a few weeks. In a short time the ambulances came up and removed the poor fellows who were paying dearly for the greenbacks, for which only, they were fighting."[43]

General Ewell, normally one of the most chivalrous of men, indulged in a bit of gloating about the Yankee losses as retribution for their misbehavior during the campaign. The casualties, he reported, "were chiefly of Blenker's division, notorious for months on account of their thefts and dastardly insults to women and children in that part of the State under Federal domination." He also reported, however, that he provided for the treatment of as many enemy wounded as possible. Fortunately for those wounded obliged to wait for treatment, the weather was ideal. At nine P.M. a weather station a few score miles to the north reported 59 degrees. At seven A.M. on June 9 the mercury had risen one degree to 60.[44]

Wounded Confederates all were within reach of friendly hands. Trimble's Brigade "got all of our dead and wounded off" before the men lay down to sleep. Ewell reported that he buried the army's dead "and brought off all the wounded except a few, whose mortal agonies would have been uselessly increased by any change of position."[45]

Unfortunately, some wounded Southern boys suffered from medical incompetence as dangerous as enemy projectiles. Harry Lewis of the 16th Mississippi, as mentioned earlier, complained bitterly about the treatment available for his wounded mates by the regiment's surgeons on the battlefield. Surgeon Graves surely "could have saved two poor fellows['] lives had he been at his post at Cross Keys to my certain knowledge." A youngster from Natchez had his leg torn off at the knee by a cannonball. If the soldier "had been properly tended [he] probably would have recovered. As it was however he lay in the [Mill Creek] church for long hours until a Virginia Surgeon dressed his wound in time to die."

An even more pathetic case was that of twenty-two-year-old George Estes of the 16th. A cannonball took off George's foot near the ankle. The mangled soldier cheerfully "told the boys when shot that he was sorry to lose his leg but was grateful his life was spared." An inept doctor amputated the lower leg, "which George stood like a noble boy, as he was, but the wound healing it was found that the bone protruded so our young Surgeon cut it off a second time just below the knee." The physician clumsily failed to secure the arteries adequately; they soon burst "and threatened to bleed George to death, so the wise Dr. concluded to saw the poor boy's leg off a third time above the knee which caused his death" six weeks after the Battle of Cross Keys. Estes had "told the Surgeon after the Second amputation he knew he was bound to die and if his leg had been properly taken off at first he would have lived." Harry Lewis offered a simple, heartfelt tribute to the victim: "Poor George was a good boy and an excellent soldier."[46]

Village of Port Republic in 1994, looking east toward the
confluence of the rivers. Jackson's headquarters knoll
is in the foreground.

CHAPTER 14

THE NIGHT OF THE

BRIDGE BUILDERS

A t Port Republic the most consequential events of the night of June 8–9 were Stonewall Jackson's conferences with his subordinates and the construction of a bridge. Controversy was already rampant in the Northern lines over whether Carroll should have burned the North River bridge. Confederates had that span firmly under control, but faced the need to cross in strength and with trains over the South River.

Federals under Colonel S. Sprigg Carroll and General Erastus B. Tyler spent the night around Lewiston, about two miles northeast of Port Republic. Rather than occupying the obvious defensive position behind the fence-lined sunken lane from Lewiston to the South Fork, the Unionists "took shelter in a strip of woods at the base of the Blue Ridge Mountain . . . and bivouacked." The 1st Virginia (Union) "laid thair all night beside the run."[1]

Carroll's men went to their rest sobered by the fighting they had faced. Sam List's reverie in the 7th Indiana camp was, "What a lesson of the shortness of life has this day taught us." Tyler's men, having missed the shooting, were more daunted by the exertion exacted of them. Wallace Hoyt of the 29th Ohio wrote to his parents that endless marching had destroyed his shoes. With battle imminent and no replacement footgear in prospect, the Ohio soldier had no choice: "I went it bare foot." Hoyt's homely letter used the quaint closing "Adjurned."[2]

General Tyler prepared for the night in uncertain country by prudently throwing "a heavy picket . . . well to the front to observe any movement." At four A.M. Tyler and Carroll jointly rode the outer Federal lines and talked to the forwardmost skirmishers. The Unionist focus remained the much-mooted North River bridge. Pickets reported that no body of troops had crossed it during the night. The two officers could see Confederate pickets on the Union side of the river, but there appeared to be nothing of substance behind them. A Northern private called the Southern advance scouts "a few men in a wheat field."[3]

The reason that Federals had heard nothing at the North River bridge was simple: Jackson already had crossed all of his force but Ewell over that river into the angle above its confluence with South River. Thousands of troops jammed Port Republic and its environs, but Stonewall intended to put them in motion after a short rest and well before daylight.

Most of the Confederate infantrymen who hurried down the left bank of the South Fork that morning spent the entire day in the advanced positions they had reached. The Stonewall Brigade, which went farthest in that direction, marched back to Port Republic "at nightfall." The brigade crossed the now-famous North River bridge, continued through the village and bivouacked beyond town in fields west and north of Madison Hall. The regimental commanders estimated their distance from the edge of the village as one-half mile (5th Virginia) to "about a mile" (2nd Virginia). Under the inexorable rules of marching columns, the 2nd had to move farthest to camp because it arrived last. The 2nd left its position opposite Lewiston last, after full darkness had fallen. Jackson's artillery batteries also moved out the Staunton Road beyond Port and camped soon after dark around the bivouacs of the Stonewall Brigade.[4]

Unfortunately for the brigade's cohesion, one of its five regiments did not come in to bivouac with the rest. Colonel John Neff's 33rd Virginia spent the day near the army's far left, two miles downstream from Port Republic. It joined the dusk relocation toward town, and even crossed the North River. There Neff received orders apparently (a biographer called the result a "misapprehension of orders") directing him to retrace his steps to where he had spent the day. The colonel marched the 33rd in the dark to a point opposite the Lewis Mill and Lynnwood. A brigade staff officer suggested that the 33rd's role was "to watch for a possible advance of the enemy on that side after crossing below." In fulfilling that reasonable function, the regiment was beyond close tactical reach of the rest of the brigade. The next morning the Stonewall Brigade would be split in half, and two of its regiments would fight desperately against huge odds. Adding the absent 33rd to that little handful, augmenting its strength by one half, would have served the brigade—and Jackson's designs—wonderfully well.[5]

General William B. Taliaferro's men had spent the day in Port Republic, or close by, guarding against a repeat of Carroll's raid. They remained in town during the evening as the Stonewall Brigade marched through. Jackson ordered Taliaferro to retain responsibility for the village overnight. A member of the 10th Virginia wrote in his diary next morning: "was on guard last night at the bridge." No enemy was going to approach the precious bridge unbidden, now that the morning raid had pointed out its vulnerability. During the night a few of Ewell's troops marched to the bluffs above North River and camped near where the Stonewall Brigade had spent the night of June 7-8. None of them crossed into the congested village.[6]

Confederates camped cheek by jowl between the rivers faced the night in as many different humors as there were soldiers. McHenry Howard of Winder's staff remembered that his only contact with this village far from his Baltimore home had been a legal document executed in it by a notary public so unsophisticated that he certified himself as a "Note Republic." John Apperson of the 4th Virginia looked apprehensively downstream where Federal campfires remained "in full view of us all night." Private Humphreys of Carpenter's Battery was worried too. "Much speculation . . . soldiers rather distrustful—fearing a second trap," he wrote. Kyd Douglas of Jackson's staff waxed philosophical, at least in retrospect. He reflected on this day's reinforcement of "the wholesome belief of the old soldiers that the side that inaugurated a battle on Sunday, lost it."

Douglas also thought of the proximity of many of the soldiers to their homes: "the moon that shone over the Valley that night threw her rays upon the wounded soldiers and not far off upon their mothers and sisters going to church to pray for them."[7]

Most of Jackson's handful of wounded men, together with those coming in from Cross Keys, received treatment in a field hospital west of Port Republic. Campbell Brown had started toward Port Republic from Cross Keys after suffering his painful wound during the afternoon. On the road Brown was smitten by "the sudden thirst I have often heard of as attacking the wounded . . . and a mouthful of dirty water from a convenient canteen tasted like nectar." As he neared the North River bridge, Keith Boswell met him and gave him his hat to replace the one Brown lost when unhorsed by his wound. When Brown finally reached the hospital beyond Port Republic, a surgeon promised him that his wound would hurt a lot but heal promptly. Early on the 9th, medical staff moved Brown and his fellow sufferers up into Brown's Gap, out of harm's way.[8]

William L. Palmer of Company B, 10th Virginia, had just joined the army in April. His mother still lived in town. William's brother, J. W. Palmer, owned three lots in Port, one opposite Madison Hall and two next to the famous bridge; one of the latter two had a building on it. No doubt young Palmer spent the night there, full of excitement and pride, and perhaps some fear as well. Two months later he would be back to convalesce from a Cedar Mountain wound, but he died in his mother's house after a month of suffering.[9]

Three other boys from Company B of the 10th belonged to Port's prominent Kemper clan. Their first cousin, William Penn Kemper, served beside them. Such local lads must have reveled in the opportunity to spend this emotional night at their homes. Whether they had similar chances again is not certain: all three were killed in action within the next two years.[10] Did Stonewall Jackson assign the brigade that included the 10th to man the village that afternoon and night out of consideration for the local boys? Such sentiment was not in keeping with his usual behavior. When the same brigade remained in town the next morning, while Jackson desperately needed reinforcements, did he leave it there to avoid taking youngsters into mortal danger in sight of their homes? Almost surely not. His motivation in the latter case doubtless was a more pragmatic one: he did not trust brigade commander William B. Taliaferro.

The majority of Jackson's army was not within reach of the comforts of home. Once they had reached their camping locations, the men of each unit set about looking for something to eat. Because the wagon trains "had been sent off to Waynesboro"—a delicate euphemism to describe the morning's panicked flight—commissary officers had no rations to distribute. Some of the strayed wagons returned before the night had worn on far, and the men gratefully drew two days' worth of rations and began to cook their scanty meals. No doubt virtually every man among them followed the usual Confederate pattern of eating the entire allotment immediately.[11]

Ned Moore of the Rockbridge Artillery struggled to cook his flour and bacon in the darkness. The nineteen-year-old cannoneer had only been in service a few weeks and during that time had relied on communal cooking by a mess made up of several soldiers. The exhaustion and confusion of that night had ruptured usual arrangements. With each man scratching to get by on his own, Moore did not know how to turn raw bacon and dry flour into food. A domestic mentor appeared in the person of battery mate Robert E. Lee, Jr. Young Lee—whose father had assumed command around Richmond a week earlier—showed his friend how "to mix flour and water together into a thin batter, then fry the grease out of the bacon." The amateur cook then poured the batter into the grease and "just let her rip awhile over the fire." Moore found the recipe "a good one and expeditious." Lee had introduced Ned Moore to a Confederate staple. Soldiers called this nutritional nightmare "coosh," or "slosh," probably because of the sound that resulted from pouring the batter into sizzling grease.[12]

While the soldiers ate, most of the civilians of Port sorrowfully evacuated their homes. "They took their horses with them and stayed in the hills nearby," a resident reported. The citizens of town were a day late: the June 8 fighting in the streets of Port would not be repeated on June 9.[13]

Inside the Federal lines downstream, civilians coped with the invaders rather than abandoning their homes. The Fletcher and Walton women at Lynnwood soon found their house "filled with Union . . . officers of every grade." At dinner, Colonel Lewis P. Buckley of the 29th Ohio waxed eloquent about the harm his army would do to Southerners in general and to Stonewall Jackson in particular. The cocky colonel blustered that "they had come to destroy everything that would give comfort to the enemy, and would do it if it took ten

**Private Ned Moore of the
Rockbridge Artillery did not
know how to turn raw bacon
and dry flour into edible
food. Robert E. Lee, Jr., showed
his batterymate how to make
batter, pour it into bacon grease,
and "just let her rip awhile
over the fire."**

years." Buckley's concluding boast was, "By sundown tomorrow night we will have sent Jackson and his army to hell!" Sue Fletcher suggested gamely, and with apparent yearning, that Buckley ought not to speak too soon because "he might be the first to get there." His unabashed reply was, "Oh, we have Jackson sewed up in a bag and have only to pull the strings to have him tight." Lynnwood's occupants would watch the next day's battle with special attention focused on Buckley's fate.[14]

While Sue Fletcher stood up for her friends, Stonewall Jackson was laying plans that would puncture Colonel Buckley's confident forecast. The general sent orders to Dick Ewell to ride to Port Republic for a midnight conference. Similar orders reached Colonel T. T. Munford, the ranking cavalry officer, near Mill Creek Church. After a four-mile ride through the darkness, Munford and Ewell found their chief at Henry B. Harnsberger's house, Cherry Grove, across South River from Madison Hall.[15]

The Harnsberger home was a decade old in 1862. The square, brick, two-story house still stands in 1993, a dignified and impressive reminder of Stonewall Jackson's days at Port Republic. Why Jackson selected that location for his several nighttime conferences is not clear. His headquarters remained at Madison Hall, and he apparently returned to Kemper's before dawn on the 9th. Harnsbergers married Kempers and the two families shared both relations and propinquity; perhaps Jackson accepted a dinner invitation based on those connections and then simply stayed on. Or perhaps the general's characteristic secrecy prompted him to move away from the bustle at Madison Hall. Since Stonewall intended to throw his troops across South River soon, relocating his center of gravity in that direction and putting the river behind him might have seemed appropriate.[16]

Jackson's own terse summary of the orders he delivered to Ewell at Cherry Grove required a single phrase: Ewell was "to move from his position at an early hour on the morning of the 9th toward Port Republic." Munford recalled that Jackson said he "intended crossing the river & attacking Shields at *light*." Ewell's confidant Campbell Brown reflected his chief's own asperity over Jackson's expectations when he wrote that Ewell's first instructions were "to cook his rations & retreat across River by 2 A.M.—that is to ride five miles, get his Division withdrawn from the presence of the enemy—within range of their guns—& march them five miles, in two hours at night." Jackson had to back away from that unrealistic timetable, but Ewell obviously left Cherry Grove with firm instructions and the understanding that celerity was demanded of him.[17]

Whatever he thought of Jackson's immediate plans, Dick Ewell's view of Stonewall's abilities had changed completely. Ewell had grumbled openly earlier in the campaign that Jackson was crazy, in his frank, eccentric, somewhat cranky style. That night Ewell said to Tom Munford as they mounted their horses outside the Harnsberger house, "Munford do you remember my conversation with you at Conrads Store, when I called this '*old man an old woman*'? Well, I take *it all back*." Another account had Ewell stating "in his brusque, impetuous manner: 'Well, sir, when he commenced [the campaign] I thought him crazy; before he ended it I thought him inspired.' "[18]

Munford's and Ewell's duties lay in opposite directions. Jackson had complained to Munford that his engineer—Jed Hotchkiss—was sick, so he had to entrust all reconnaissance duties to his cavalry. Jackson instructed Munford: "I desire you to ascertain at once if the road is open to Brown's Gap, and have a heavy picket under a reliable officer placed on the road from Brown's Gap towards Conrad's Store." Once he had found what Jackson wanted, Munford was to return and report "as speedily as possible." If the Brown's Gap Road was impassable, the range of Stonewall's options would narrow dangerously. Munford found it open. He sent Major Cary Breckinridge, a twenty-two-year-old graduate of Virginia Military Institute from Botetourt County, to serve as the "reliable officer" down the road toward Tyler's camps. Munford probably chose the major because Jackson knew him from VMI. Breckinridge and his two companies were dutifully skirmishing when Jackson's infantry reached the battlefield the next morning.[19]

John D. Imboden, later a Confederate brigadier general, wrote an often-quoted account of meeting with Jackson during this night. Unfortunately, Imboden's postwar declarations are almost entirely worthless for historical purposes. By Imboden's account, he received about ten P.M. a note scribbled on a newspaper margin ordering him to move at once with his tiny artillery command to Port Republic. Once Imboden reached headquarters, he claimed, Jackson unveiled his entire plan of battle, referring by fond diminutives to Winder and Taylor in the process and untangling problems that had not yet arisen. If Stonewall Jackson did encounter Imboden, it certainly was not in an intimate setting, nor did their talk include casual byplay.

As one of the general's staff noted in deriding Imboden's fanciful tale, Jackson "spoke to and of *Sandy* Pendleton but to no one else in that way: he did not know how to do it."[20]

General Ewell's conference with Stonewall was not the one that drew the most attention over the years. Colonel John M. Patton's encounter with Jackson spilled much more ink because so many have since misinterpreted its content. Ewell selected Patton to manage the rear guard that would protect his troops as they moved to Port Republic. As soon as Ewell returned to Cross Keys, he called the colonel to his side. Patton left his men asleep on the front lines and reported to Ewell. The general told him "confidentially" that Jackson planned to attack Shields. All of Ewell's force except Patton's small brigade would start back "at daylight." Patton "remonstrated on the grounds of [his] small command," Ewell reminisced after the war, "but did not change my intention." With his 21st Virginia away guarding prisoners, Patton had only 800 men. Furthermore the 48th Virginia had moved toward Port Republic in the dark, leaving the brigade only about the size of a single strong regiment.[21]

Jackson remained at Cherry Grove after Ewell and Munford left, sitting "in a large comfortable chair" rather than retiring to bed. Colonel Patton found him there at two A.M., "actively making his dispositions," full of "animation and pleasure" at the prospects for the morning. The general instructed Patton minutely on how his rear guard was to behave. "I wish you to throw out all your men if necessary, as skirmishers," he ordered, "and to make a great show and parade, so as to make the enemy think the whole army are behind you." Only at the last moment was Patton to retire, then at once he must "take a new position and hold it in the same way, and *'I'll be back to join you in the morning.'* " Patton made so bold as to inquire when he could expect Jackson's return. Jackson "turned his face aside, and a little up, as he sometimes did, and replied, *'By the blessing of Providence, I hope to be back by ten o'clock.'* "[22]

The next morning Patton did not command the rear guard; General Trimble did. Despite that substantial change, writers about the campaign have uncritically accepted Jackson's off-the-cuff response to Patton as his plan for June 9. Ewell ascribed the realignment of the rear guard to Trimble's meddling with Jackson, over the head of his division commander. "Trimble saw Genl Jackson & had his own command left behind in addition," Ewell wrote to Patton in 1867, "but with no result, as I had anticipated, beyond depriving the command of too few to fight Fremont & too many to take from the field of Port Republic."[23]

Jackson of course never let anyone bulldoze him—he had just rejected the more earnest plea for a night attack by Trimble. What must have happened was that he evaluated his situation and quickly saw that he could not fight both near Lewiston and back toward Cross Keys under the circumstances. He therefore needed a much stronger rear guard than Patton alone could provide. Jackson reported that he left Trimble, "with his brigade, supported by Colonel Patton . . . to hold Fremont in check, with instructions, if hard pressed, to retire across the North River and burn the bridge in their rear." Patton noted that at first Trimble's Brigade had been substituted for his own, and only later was Patton reattached to augment it. The rear guard must buy enough time for Jackson to whip Tyler before Frémont could reach the commanding bluffs on the left bank of the South Fork. In the event, the rear guard did exactly that.[24]

The Reverend R. L. Dabney set the tone for later writers who took Patton's account as showing Jackson's inflexible intent for June 9. Dabney wrote, "Here then we have the disclosure of his *real plan,* to which he makes no reference in his own official report. He proposed to . . . *finish Shields,* by ten o'clock." Jackson "adhered to his purpose," by Dabney's reckoning, throughout the night. The general's "bold purpose" was also, significantly, "his *secret* [emphasis added] design." In this instance Jackson's carefully maintained secrecy served to "mislead, mistify, and confuse" Dr. Dabney instead of the enemy. The only "evidence of this startling design" adduced by Dabney was Patton's account.[25] Jackson thus joined any number of others in successfully confusing Dr. Dabney. Most later writers have followed Dabney's lead.

The procession of visitors to Jackson continued through the night. On the heels of Ewell, Munford, Patton, and perhaps Imboden came General William B. Taliaferro, responding to a summons from the army commander. He found Jackson "pacing the floor of a small bedroom." After a brief outline of what he expected from Taliaferro, Jackson offered his subordinate the use of the bed while he himself went out into the garden to walk. Taliaferro presumed that Jackson's "object in seeking the seclusion of the garden was to engage in prayer." A visitor from Scotland heard a story that confirmed what Taliaferro expected. The general's servant, he was told, said "on the morning of Port Republic" that there was "Gwine to be a fight, sartin," because Jackson had "bin a prayin' all night."[26]

Keith Boswell probably was Jackson's last visitor that night. It was four A.M. when Jackson told his bright young staff officer "to proceed immediately" to Mechum's River Station "for the purpose of meeting re-enforcements which were expected at that point." Re-inforcements from Lee at Richmond would not reach Mechum's River for several more days, but Jackson did not know that because of the primitive communications system. The general was methodically searching for every option and weighing every opportunity. He had also spent the whole night awake. Six visitors and a prayer session between midnight and four A.M. left little time for rest.[27]

A fortnight later Jackson would slip into the only extended funk of his brilliant career while attempting to support Lee during the Seven Days Campaign around Richmond. The most convincing expla-nation of the general's atypical performance in late June 1862 is that he had completely worn himself out. The result was a kind of stress fatigue. The rigorous ordeal Jackson underwent during the first week of June while escaping up the Valley, added to a sleepless night on June 8-9, set the stage for the later letdown. It may also have left Stonewall somewhat below par as he started downstream the next morning to chastise Tyler's Yankees.

Many of Jackson's subordinates who did get some sleep that night went to bed with troubled hearts. The series of sessions he had held with ranking officers had not been intended to solicit their advice, but rather to convey the orders he had determined upon independently. Taliaferro's generic description of Stonewall's style nicely fit the crisis before him that night. "Certainly we had some nice shaves," Taliaferro wrote, "which kept us pretty generally in a state of anxiety and suspense. Jackson sought advice and counsel, as far as I know, of none. He ... acted solely on his own responsibility."[28]

Lieutenant H. Kyd Douglas, a strong Jackson loyalist, admitted to anxiety on the staff that night. The clever men who served as Jackson's official family had felt relief when June 8 ended with Carroll and Tyler checked and Frémont repulsed. They had assumed that Jackson would use the night to slip out of the narrowing trap with prisoners and supplies intact. It became obvious that the general had no such intention when he ordered Major Harman to bring wagons back into the village to feed the troops. The instructions astonished the staff. "Pendleton, McGuire, Crutchfield, Boswell, and all present exchanged looks and smiles," Douglas recalled. "Pendleton said, 'crazy again.' We were getting used to this kind of aberration, but this did seem rather an extra bit of temerity."[29]

Ten months later Jackson revealed what went into his decision that night as he considered where to attack. Retreat had hardly crossed his mind, even if it had been high on others' lists. In April 1863 a staff officer was at work on the general's tardy official reports. When the report writer asked Jackson what had "induced him to fight Shields instead of Fremont, at Port Republic," the general offered several reasons: "First I was nearer to him"; second, Shields's command had the smaller enemy force; third, Jackson would be nearer to his own base of supplies; fourth, from Port Republic the Confederates "had a good way of retreat if beaten"; fifth, "Fremont had a good way to retreat if I had beaten him"; and sixth, "Shields had a bad road to go over" if he were routed, as happened. Jackson usually played his hand so close to his vest that students are left to hypothesize, sometimes wildly, without adequate background. The view into his thoughts on the eve of the Battle of Port Republic is unusual, perhaps unique.[30]

None of Jackson's six reasons assumed that he could ignore either enemy force while concentrating on the other. Dabney's notion of a secret plan to fight both Frémont and Tyler in the same morning cannot survive the general's autobiographical summary of his options. Jackson took advantage throughout the campaign of the military precept of interior lines—being able to move across the shorter interior angles of an arc—but Cross Keys and Port Republic were too close together for ideal employment of the principle. As an astute British student of the campaign observed: "The necessity for space in which to make full use of mobility was brought out in these battles." Jackson was "acting on interior lines . . . against his two opponents, but he had too little space between his two battle-fields . . . to be able to disregard the one and use his whole force against the other."[31]

While Stonewall Jackson dealt with his procession of visitors and prayed in the Harnsbergers' garden, a detachment of black pioneers enlisted as an engineer detachment laboriously constructed an ad hoc bridge over South River. Without the bridge, the general's scheming would be for naught. No wagon bridge had ever spanned the usually modest flow of South River; the first one went up in 1889. A series of crude footbridges had spanned the river from time to time for use when the fords had become impassable. None stood in June 1862.[32]

When work on the bridge began, Jackson briefly gave it his personal supervision, then went on about his busy agenda. Dabney insisted that his ubiquitous mentor "collected his pioneers" and then "caused them, under his own eye, to construct a foot-bridge." Other writers have followed Dabney's lead. Why a Jackson admirer should demand personal credit for the general when the construction job caused so much trouble the next morning is hard to imagine. In fact he had nothing to do with the details, nor should he have.[33]

Captain Claiborne R. Mason superintended the job. Mason was a doughty sixty-two-year-old engineer who had handled tough civilian mining and railroading challenges for years. With help from Captain Sandy Garber (who had run into Jackson that morning while scampering through the North River bridge), Mason undertook the chore of bridging the South River. Mason's crew of black workmen, known in the army as his "African Pioneers," labored all through the night. Their first chore was preparing the North River bridge for burning. Then they started on the new bridge.[34]

The pioneers benefited from extra light after the moon rose near midnight. Their raw materials were a half-dozen wagons and some loose boards from a nearby sawmill. Men threw stones into the wagons and then dragged them into the river "by means of a large rope." Straining pioneers muscled the first wagon into the river and nearly to the opposite bank. Then they jostled a second into position some feet behind it. When these makeshift caissons stretched from shore to shore, the laborers gathered boards to run across between the wagons. Unfortunately, the planks were "very long and thin" and there were no adequate means at hand to secure the planks firmly to the beds. Although Garber pronounced the result "a grand success," soldiers crossing the temporary bridge the next day would discover its shortcomings.[35]

At four A.M. the bridge was finished. Mason, "in his characteristic way," devoid of frills, said to Garber: "Sandy, you can go and tell Gen. Jackson that the bridge is done and he can take his folks and things over." Garber tracked down the general "a half mile off," at either Madison Hall or Cherry Grove. He found Jackson asleep—the only one who did all night long—and gave him the good news about the bridge.[36] The Confederates now could get at Tyler's detachment. Jackson at once set them to that task.

**The Lewis family of
Lewiston fled
from what one
Confederate
called a "handsome
villa." By the time
the family returned,
Lewiston was scarred by
shells and by military
occupation.**

CHAPTER 15

MOVING DOWNSTREAM

TO BATTLE

Before Claiborne Mason and his pioneers finished the temporary bridge, the soldiers who would lead Jackson's force across it were stirring in their camps. General Winder scribbled in his diary that morning that he arose at 3:45, an hour before sunrise. Winder had not had orders for June 9 when he retired. It was their arrival at 3:45 that roused him. The directive from Jackson ordered Winder to be at Port Republic at 4:45. Perhaps Jackson chose that hour because his almanac showed him that it was the exact moment of sunrise.[1]

Winder at once issued commands that pulled his regiments out of camp and into motion. Winder had elicited strength returns from each regiment in such detail that he could report his total strength that morning as 1,334 men, rank and file. That number was rather slender for a full brigade at this stage of the war, reflecting hard service. Worse, one full regiment (the 33rd Virginia) was off on picket duty and would be of no use. That left about 1,000 men on hand. Jackson's employment of two of the remaining four regiments on a failed flanking venture early on June 9 would leave Winder holding the hard-pressed center of the Confederate line for a crucial hour with perhaps 500 men.[2]

The morning was a cool but gorgeous one, with temperature in the 50s. Many participants commented on the still, pastoral loveliness of the Valley early on June 9. One of Jackson's biographers aptly declared, "No battle-field boasts a fairer setting than Port Republic." Although both Winder and his aide Lieutenant Howard reported that the head of the brigade met its required deadline, reaching the river "at the hour indicated," the regimental commanders' reports suggest a bit less precision. Everyone concurred that the move began "at an early hour," but Colonel James W. Allen of the 2nd Virginia innocently reported that he received "an order to get under arms at once" only sometime "soon after dawn." Since the 2nd Virginia led the brigade's march, the whole column obviously had not reached town by dawn, if in fact any of it had.[3]

Sandy Garber had reported that Jackson was asleep sometime after four A.M. when he went to headquarters to announce completion of the bridge. Garber probably walked into a quiet building and aroused sleeping staff without actually seeing the general abed (an unlikely encounter under any circumstance), because Boswell had left Jackson awake at four A.M. and Winder met Jackson almost at once when the Stonewall Brigade commander reached the river forty-five minutes later.[4]

Confederates sleepily converging on Claiborne Mason's wagon bridge were glad to discover that it was not quite ready for them to use. The pioneer detachment was working to rectify some problems that had already surfaced. Hungry soldiers used the delay, which lasted for "some time," to make up for their hurried departure from camp. A member of the Danville Artillery recalled: "we had not had our breakfast when the long roll sounded." He and his mates spent the waiting period "munching our crackers and half-cooked bacon, without water or coffee."[5]

Colonel Charles Ronald of the 4th Virginia reported that orders to cross the bridge finally reached him "at 5:30 a.m." A member of the 4th wrote the next day that "about sunrise we crossed." Jackson's official report, written ten months later, insisted that "before 5 in the morning, General Winder's brigade was in Port Republic, and having crossed . . . was moving down the River road." In this as at most dawn and dusk hours in the Valley, the mountains looming on both horizons offered a wider variety of benchmark moments than in flat country. Sunup and sundown came slowly, with light or dark creeping over the mountains by stages. Ronald's estimate seems to fit the evidence.[6]

Jackson's tough, ragged veterans of his old brigade filed through the jammed streets of Port Republic in the growing light toward two bottlenecks at South River. First they had to cross the short slab bridge across the millrace, then move over crowded ground on the island to reach Mason's bridge. The 2nd Virginia led the way, with an artillery battery right behind it. The 4th pushed across the island to the bridge as soon as the 2nd had cleared it. Crossing was a painfully slow business, even for the head of the column; it would grow worse with further use. The delay, one of Winder's officers wrote, resulted from the need to step carefully "on the narrow two or three insecure planks which made the top."[7]

Carpenter's Battery crossed first among Jackson's artillery commands. As the 2nd Virginia moved gingerly across the bridge, the battery drove right into the river and splashed its way across. The Rockbridge Artillery soon followed. Most of the artillerists crossed on the bridge, pushing their way into the column between infantry units. The batteries forded just downstream from the new bridge.[8] Presumably the water was a little deeper there, but it also was calmer because the wagons in the bridge served as a breakwater.

As Colonel James W. Allen and the 2nd Virginia turned left and began to move downstream, they had some foreboding of what they faced. A member of the Stonewall Brigade wrote just after the battle that when "the head of our column turned down the stream . . . then we knew there was bloody work in store for us." The men knew that Ewell had beaten Frémont on the 8th. A whole new Federal force awaited their advance near Lewiston. The Southerners were buoyed by a strong sense of confidence and pride in their general. "Like the great Napoleon," the same man concluded, "General Jackson determined to fight the other column before it could effect a junction with the defeated army."[9]

Jackson's wagon trains meanwhile were fording South River near the upper end of town. Since Munford's reconnaissance had estab-

**Captain William T. Poague
commanded the Rockbridge Artillery as it
splashed through South River en
route to action.**

lished that Brown's Gap was accessible, Jackson could start his trains toward that high, safe lair in the Blue Ridge. Infantry crossing South River and then turning away from Brown's Gap toward the Yankee position could see the "long white train, moving on its serpentine way to the top of the mountain." Major John Harman was prodding the trains toward their goal with his accustomed profanity and impatient energy. A staff colleague was glad to have Harman in command of the trains: "no one was more equal to such a task, although it must be said he possessed as little of Job's special virtue as any man in the army."[10]

Jackson's selection of the Stonewall Brigade as the army's spearhead was an easy decision. By contrast, his use—or rather lack of use—of Taliaferro's Brigade is surprising. Taliaferro's men had spent all of June 8 after Carroll's repulse in Port Republic. They were still there at dawn, the closest Confederates to the new wagon bridge and therefore closest to what would become the battlefield of June 9. Taliaferro did not cross South River first; he did not cross until the battle was decided. At the same time that Jackson ordered the Stonewall Brigade to march to the wagon bridge, he ordered Taliaferro away from it and back across North River to the bluffs on its left bank. The brigade's commission, as reported by its general, was "to co-operate with General Trimble's and Colonel Patton's brigades." Taliaferro stood quietly by while virtually all of Jackson's and Ewell's troops crossed both rivers.[11]

Jackson did need to provide a linchpin to serve as connector between his force moving away from Port Republic and Ewell's moving toward that point. To use an entire brigade, especially the one that started the day closest to the front, made little sense. Any of Ewell's units could have filled the role, or it could have been rotated among regiments moving through the area. The probable explanation was simply that Jackson did not like or trust General Taliaferro.

For a brief period Jackson evidently contemplated the importance of the positions he had held on June 8 on the left bank of the South Fork. The general told Taliaferro to pick a good company to move in that direction. Jackson told the designated company commander, "You take your company . . . and go down the river opposite the enemy, where there is a ford, and hold it at all hazards." The river was booming so high that Jackson's worry was unfounded, and the company did not remain downstream very long.[12]

General Jackson's brief defensive gesture toward the ground

around Bogota removes any doubt about his intentions on the morning of June 9. Clearly he recognized the necessity of beating Tyler *without* counting on subsequently turning back against Frémont. Although Dr. Dabney and later writers assume without exception that Jackson intended to go after Frémont on the 9th until well into the Battle of Port Republic, he unquestionably would have used the bluffs on the left bank of the South Fork to accomplish that. Confederate artillery emplaced opposite Lewiston would have made the line on which Tyler fought on June 9 absolutely and instantaneously untenable. Jackson had recognized, however, that he could not fight both Federal forces on the same day and so chose the best arrangement available: detaining Frémont long enough to beat Tyler. That left him no option for artillery across the South Fork.

The one Southern regiment that remained downstream on the left bank that morning was there through oversight rather than design. Colonel John F. Neff's 33rd Virginia had left that area late on the 8th and marched to Port Republic at dark only to be sent back downstream. The colonel slept so soundly that by the time he awoke "the sun was shining brightly." He concluded that he had been forgotten. Meanwhile Winder had remembered his neglected regiment and sent Lieutenant James M. Garnett to find it. The 33rd marched at once, but Garnett, incredibly, did not know whether the brigade was moving "on the Brown's Gap road or whether it would go down the river." The result was that the 33rd did not reach its brigade in the hour of its extremity.[13]

General Richard S. Ewell's victorious troops at Cross Keys began moving steadily toward Port Republic to assist Jackson at about the same time that the Stonewall Brigade tiptoed across the wagon bridge. Some of Ewell's troops had camped far enough south to be within easy reach of Port Republic. Dick Taylor's Louisianians had returned to Cross Keys late on June 8 and left first on June 9. They camped near Mill Creek Church, so did not have to disengage from a nearby enemy when orders came to head south. A member of the brigade wrote a few days later that his regiment left for Port Republic at two A.M. General Taylor's official report stated that the brigade departed "at daylight."[14]

Taylor's men would prove to be Jackson's salvation on this day, unknotting a dreadful tactical mess into which Stonewall had aggressively hurled his small advance guard. As they covered the rolling countryside leading to Port Republic, the Louisianians luxuriated in the glories of the late spring morning. One of them recalled lyrically: "The limpid waters of the Shenandoah softly murmured along the base of the majestic Blue Ridge. . . . The rich wheat fields waved their nodding plume to the music of the soft sighing winds, that played so gently through them; while the peaks of the Blue Ridge rose in their towering height from the deep blue mist which enveloped them. . . . All nature hushed and still, its peaceful tranquillity shortly to be disturbed by the fierce conflict of arms."[15]

The 48th Virginia marched toward Port Republic close behind Taylor's Brigade. Although it belonged to Patton's small brigade, and Patton had been given rearguard duties, the 48th had camped away from its mates and was ordered at earliest dawn ("that hour when the glow would show," its commander explained) to get on the road south. As the 48th reached "the hills overlooking P. Republic the sun was just clearing the summit of the blue ridge throwing a flood of light and loveliness over the valley beneath." The scene smote Lieutenant Colonel Thomas S. Garnett as forcibly as it had the Louisiana correspondent. In a letter to his father, Garnett waxed eloquent about his feelings: "Every bush and twig was sparkling in the morning diadem: on every hillock the lambs were seen to gambol: the luxuriant clover fields were unfolding their blossoms to the radiant beam . . . filling the air with the sweetest odor—while the chirping birds and beautiful country . . . made this seem to me an enchanted vale." The contrast between nature's setting and man's intentions on June 9 prompted Garnett to reflect: "little did I think that this beautiful secluded valley . . . this spot set apart t'would seem by Heaven for peaceful purposes, should so soon be witness to the carnival of death."[16]

Back at Cross Keys, Dick Ewell set about untangling his division from its lines opposite Frémont in order to head toward Jackson's new battle front. By the time of his departure, day was breaking. Many of the weary victors of Cross Keys faced a march of as much as seven miles having been "without food for twenty-four hours." The hungry but whole men were far better off than Southern boys too badly wounded to be transported from the field. Someone saw Ewell passing among the wounded he must leave behind "and giving the wounded Confederate money out of his own pocket." In a lighter moment, Ewell burst into exuberant profanity when he recognized a courier sent to him as "a young Southerner of large wealth." "Who ever saw such a d——d army," Ewell crowed. "Here I sent for a man to run errands and carry notes and they give me a ——— rascal worth $500,000!''[17]

The brigades that had been Steuart's and Elzey's before both generals went down wounded made up the heart of Ewell's column. Taylor had started ahead, and Patton and Trimble were to be the rear guard. The 25th Virginia was up shortly before four A.M. to prepare for the march to Port Republic. The 13th Virginia, ravenous after a day without food, arose at three A.M. when its wagons finally arrived. The Virginians eagerly rounded up cooking gear and were starting fires when Ewell rode up and said: "Boys, I'm sorry for you, but you must put your utensils back as we have to march at once." The 1st Maryland had its fires burning brightly, not for cooking but to deceive the enemy while its men stealthily abandoned their position.[18]

Despite all of the attention that has been paid to Jackson's meticulous instructions to Colonel Patton about rearguard tenacity, the rear guard neither resisted very ardently nor wound up being led by Patton, Trimble with his stronger brigade having been placed over him. Patton's 48th Virginia was already heading separately toward Port Republic.[19]

John Patton dug his two units out of the woods where they had spent the night in close enough proximity to the enemy to snare some prisoners. The commanders of both the 42nd and the 1st used identical language when they reported officially the time that Patton called them in: "A little before daybreak. . . ." The brigade commander then conducted them to Mill Creek Church, where they awaited Trimble's orders.[20]

Trimble's three forward regiments spent a tense night far to the front, "under arms" instead of resting, while their restless brigadier stormed about looking for permission to attack someone. Near sunup the general finally allowed his weary troops to fall back. Trimble moved his regiments into the familiar woodline from which they had slaughtered the 8th New York a few hours earlier. The Confederate rear guard had no artillery (yet another indication that Jackson long since had abandoned the notion of holding Frémont in place for a second battle on June 9). When Federal artillery shelled the woods, Trimble promptly decamped. Once started, the brigade paid no attention to defensive opportunities. One of Trimble's officers wrote that the march proceeded "in quick time. . . . No brigade ever marched five miles in a shorter space of time." As Trimble passed Mill Creek

Church, he picked up his other regiment, the 21st North Carolina, which had camped just south of that building.[21]

Had Frémont pursued energetically, he could have made a significant difference in the way June 9 developed. The general marched at six A.M. on June 8; now, under the far greater exigencies in effect, he lost several hours of daylight. Had he moved more rapidly, with better scouting and intelligence—had he, simply put, been something other than the mediocrity he was—Frémont could have reached the vicinity of Bogota in time to overlook the battlefield of the 9th. With Frémont and some artillery positioned there, Jackson's options would have been few and unappealing.

A young soldier in Frémont's army excoriated the general for his sloth, in a letter written later in the week. Had the advance been pushed firmly, John Polsley told his wife, "we would have cut Jackson's army in twain. . . . We did not move . . . [until] late . . . and by our delay and timid policy, Jackson was enabled to . . . defeat Shields." Cutting Jackson in half was not likely; harrying him and denying him a notable victory *was* achievable. Federal operations on June 8–9 illustrated eloquently the dangers of divided command and poor communication.[22]

Frémont's first order was for General Schenck to advance with his brigade. Schenck obeyed methodically, rather than with urgency. His orders probably came in that context. The men ate breakfast before they went forward. Lieutenant Colonel Ebenezer H. Swinney of the 32nd Ohio gave his men a pep talk, exhorting the regiment "to do its duty." Schenck's skirmishers glided forward "very cautiously"; they were "fully expecting a renewal" of the previous day's fighting. As the scouts advanced through the June 8 battle zone, a staff officer wrote, "to our great surprise no picket was met, no shot fired, and no enemy in sight." Confederate disengagement had been abetted by a "very dense" fog that "obscured everything."[23]

Despite the disappearance of his opponents, Frémont's advance moved laboriously through the former Confederate position "in battle order, and with its supporting lines" arranged behind the front. There was no reason for this elaborate alignment. It was as though Frémont had only the most rudimentary grasp of tactics. The whole army degenerated into a tangled mess as it attempted to cross Mill Creek and then scale the rough bluffs beyond in full battle array. When finally the ungainly moving mass reached the vicinity of Mill Creek Church, common sense reared its head. The advance re-formed, "closing in . . . our lines, and [arranging] the formation in compact columns, the order was spread to push forward at the maximum of the march." By the time the head of the realigned advance moved about one mile south of the church, stark evidence that it was too late billowed up on the horizon. A column of dense black smoke spiraled up above Port Republic. The North River bridge was on fire. Some officers retained the hope that it had been torched by Federals who had trapped Jackson. Most realized the truth: Ewell had gotten across North River and made sure that Frémont could not follow him.[24]

Federals filing past Mill Creek Church at a slow pace noticed the suffering wounded who jammed the building. As the 55th Ohio reached the vicinity, the men discovered outside an open window "a great pile of arms and legs which the surgeon's knife and saw had helped the shot and shell to take off." Colonel John C. Lee of the 55th discovered that most of the wounded had no rations available, so he asked his troops to share their hardtack, "and they hustled out their crackers at once." The cemetery of Mill Creek Church would grow in size in the next few days. About sixty years later while the sexton was cleaning up in the cemetery, he "dug up some 10 sets of . . . bones of Civil War soldiers." The man gathered the fragmentary remains and reburied them with care and respect in the cemetery.[25]

Charles Webb, correspondent for *The New York Times,* dashed off a memorable description of the Federal dead scattered along the army's route that morning. Perhaps Webb's war-weariness, which is unmistakable in his poignant lines, was among the reasons he emigrated to California soon after this campaign. (Webb became a prominent figure in San Francisco literary circles as an intimate of Bret Harte and Sam Clemens, both of whom he published.)

Monday Morning, June 9, 1862
The glorious sun is looking over the hill-tops, and the smouldering ashes of our camp-fires grow gray in the early light, but the soldiers that slumber around me with their faces turned skyward, know not that the night has passed and day dawned. Nor will they wake to the *reveille,* though bugle and drum play it ever so loudly. Poor pale faces, these, looking upward but seeing no sky, their lips parted as though to reproach the fate that stretched them here, but uttering no complaint. But yester-

day and these men were busy with all the little problems that agitate the camp and the world, what should they eat, where should they sleep, were they well used, did their comrades encroach upon their individual rights and privileges. What care they now, whether rations are short or long, whether the supply train comes up in season or lags behind, until the year has run its round? Their bitterest enemy, from whom yesterday they would not have borne a look, may now pluck them by the beard and no hand will be raised to resent the insult. They are wiser than they were a few hours ago; vaster problems occupy them, for they are now solving the mighty secrets that only the dead can know. The petty marches of a day will vex them no more, for they have gone on that long, eternal march whose end is never reached, and where the soldier carries neither canteen nor knapsack, musket nor blanket,—in this case, not even a winding-sheet.[26]

Soldiers less sensitive than Webb busily looted bodies of the dead of both sides. Others spread in a wide, ugly arc across Frémont's rear and swarmed into homes and barns intent on plunder. Alexander Kyger lost during the day two horses, three colts, three barrels of flour, and fourteen hogs. After the war he was able to establish a claim of Unionist sentiment, and the government reimbursed him $723 for the loss. William Rodehafer, a peaceable Dunkard, had his last horse stolen by an officer of the 4th New York Cavalry. Yankees robbed Joseph Beery of one mare and took two mares together with food supplies from Elias Hudlow, who lived near Good's Mill.[27]

James Smith had lived just south of Mill Creek Church for nineteen years. The fifty-year-old farmer tilled fifty-nine acres and ran a few head of livestock. Federal scavengers settled on Smith's place that morning and cleaned him out. Smith's weary deposition reported the loss of "flour, hogs, hay, & cattle taken—my cow, my calf, and the lard. . . . It was taken in the daytime." Yankees also burned all of his fences. Smith's loss included 29 sides of bacon, 3 barrels of flour, 150 bushels of corn, 9 hogs, and 1 ton of hay.[28]

Andrew J. Baugher of Cross Keys suffered the greatest recorded loss on June 9 among claimants able to establish some credibility as pro-Unionist. (After the war the government casually threw out all claims by civilians who had sons in Confederate service or otherwise had betrayed some discernible Virginian sentiment, so there is no ready means of determining the extent of losses inflicted on that vast majority of the populace.) Looting of Baugher's farm netted Northerners 18 hogs, 15 sheep, 4 cows, 25 bushels of corn, 1 wagon, 1½ barrels of flour, 25 gallons of molasses, 200 pounds of bacon, and 75 pounds of dried beef. Farmer Baugher watched the destruction of his worldly goods from inside his house, where Union officers recommended that he remain for safety from personal harm.[29]

About three miles from Andrew's place, the home of another Baugher was just coming onto center stage on a new battlefield. Stonewall Jackson's advance would soon come opposite Westwood on its left. During much of the Battle of Port Republic, that house would be in the midst of the Confederate line. Westwood was a two-story frame building constructed early in the nineteenth century by William Benjamin Lewis. At the beginning of the war Westwood had been the home of Evaline Baugher, the widow of Scott Baugher. Fortunately, Evaline had closed up her home and was staying with relatives near Weyer's Cave.[30]

A number of women, one of them in an extraordinarily helpless condition, began June 9 in the Federal lines not far downstream from Westwood. The extended Lewis family at Lewiston abandoned breakfast on the table and hurried north toward the river when the first artillery fire exploded from Jackson's advance guard. They left behind what one Confederate called a "handsome villa." By the time the family returned to Lewiston many hours later, it was scarred by shells and by military occupation. They found that one Southern artillery round had crashed through the west wall of the house and exploded inside a china press in the dining room. (Lewis descendants still treasure some of the scarred china pieces that survived the explosion.)[31]

As the Lewises of Lewiston passed Lynnwood en route to the river, they joined forces with their kinfolk from that beautiful estate. Among the refugees from Lynnwood, Maggie Fletcher clutched her newborn baby as servants carried the pair out on a feather bed. Other servants carried necessities for the baby and food for the family gathered up in aprons.[32]

When this unhappy entourage reached the bank of the South Fork, its members gazed in despair at the raging torrent. Fortunately the Lewis Mill at the end of the lane was protected by a dam built in 1856 to control the flow there and to provide a millrace.[33]

Short of remaining at the heart of what was obviously going to be a bloody battle zone, the civilians had no choice but to cross the booming South Fork. Servants from Lewiston and Lynnwood and from Bogota beyond the river ferried the frightened people across in small boats. Maggie and the baby lay on the feather bed while some of the servants held the bed above the gunwales on their shoulders. The journey on the little flat-bottomed rowboat must have been terrifying for the new mother. With their fragile cargo delivered, the boatmen made two more roundtrips to the dock near the mill to ferry over the rest of the civilians. When the families eventually returned home, they found Lynnwood perforated with holes made by cannonballs, including one that had torn through the wall of Maggie's bedroom.[34]

Once beyond the river, the refugees—excepting Maggie and the baby—gathered on the second-floor balcony of Bogota and watched the battle. From this "high portico," as Lucy Fletcher's diary called it, they had a commanding vantage point. Bogota's high portico survives in 1993 and still looks down across the river at the battlefield.[35]

Meanwhile, Confederates had been crossing South River as rapidly as their officers could prod them over the crude wagon bridge. Jackson himself was among the first to cross. By the time the general and his staff reached the far bank, the sun was starting to peep over the Blue Ridge. At first "a little rim of light rose, scintillating, flashing above the green fringe," then the sun's "segment of light grew larger, now larger still, then half round, all round, filling the world with glory." Cursing and straining officers welcomed the light not for poetic reasons but with the hope that it would enable them to increase the flow of troops across the wagon tops.[36]

As the Stonewall Brigade and its artillery supports turned left to move toward the Yankee positions, they at once came across reminders of yesterday's fighting. "Dead and wounded Yankees lay along the road, and the trees and houses were badly torn by the balls," wrote Captain Hugh A. White of the 4th Virginia, the second regiment in the column. White knew that what he could see "was but the ante-chamber. We would soon enter upon more horrible scenes." The most startling of the Yankee corpses was one almost entirely beheaded, with "a few inches of the spinal column projecting above the shoulders."[37]

General Winder had borne in mind the Yankee cannon that escaped from the village the day before and disappeared into the brush. The general sent McHenry Howard of his staff to look for the piece.

Howard searched in vain, but other Confederates soon stumbled across the stranded Yankee gun. They also found and salvaged its limber and the limber for Gildea's gun that the Federals had been forced to abandon in town.[38]

Advancing Southerners ran into some crude obstacles thrust into their path by Unionist rear guards the preceding afternoon. Carroll's pioneer detachment had frantically "guarded the rear by chopping down trees to obstruct the road" against pursuit that never came on the 8th. Since no Confederate account mentions struggling to clear the road, the impediments evidently caused little difficulty. It helped that June 9 was the coolest day of the entire month in the region. As a result, Port Republic was one of the few mid-year battles during the war that did not engender complaints about terrible heat from its fevered participants.[39]

After moving just over a mile, the 2nd Virginia came up behind the cavalry pickets Munford had distributed in the area the night before. Major Cary Breckinridge, who commanded them, rode up to Winder and Jackson and told them that enemy skirmishers lay under cover just ahead. The army commander characteristically ordered Winder to drive in the pickets and attack whatever was beyond them.[40]

Colonel James W. Allen of the 2nd Virginia had prudently thrown out skirmishers to protect his front and flanks. Captain John Quincy Adams Nadenbousch, a thirty-seven-year-old prewar mayor of Martinsburg, commanded the two companies assigned to that duty. In executing Jackson's order to push the Federal pickets aside, Winder merely ascertained that Nadenbousch's troops covered both sides of the road, then unleashed them. Captain Joseph Carpenter's Battery was in the column immediately behind the 2nd and ahead of the 4th Virginia. To make sure that Nadenbousch had his way, Winder ordered two of Carpenter's guns to move to the left of the road and unlimber. (The direction of the road leading toward Lewiston dictated that most Confederate maneuvers during the day began with a left oblique from the road into the fields.) Carpenter's pieces each fired two rounds in the direction of the enemy pickets, doubtless hitting nothing of their elusive target. Return fire sent "Yankee bumblebees over our heads," one of Carpenter's men wrote. In the face of such might, however, the Northern skirmishers quickly disappeared and Nadenbousch's men rolled forward. The time was about seven A.M. The first shots of the Battle of Port Republic had been fired.[41]

This opening clash developed as Jackson pushed past the home

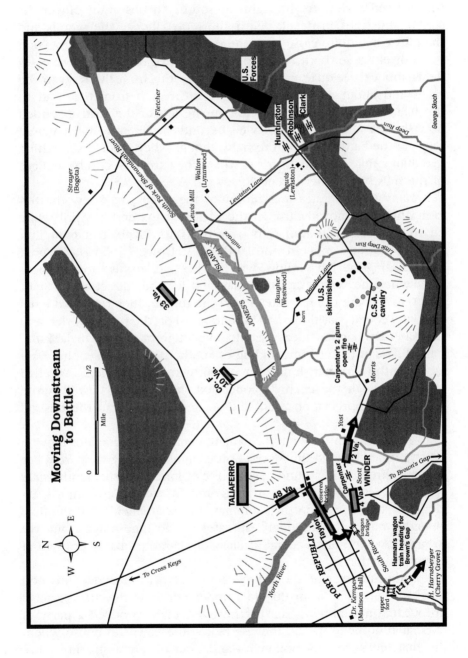

Moving Downstream to Battle

N / E / S / W

To Cross Keys

0   1/2   1 Mile

U.S. Forces

Fletcher

Huntington
Robinson
Clark

George Stoch

Deep Run

South Fork of Shenandoah River

Strayer (Bogota)

Walton (Lynnwood)

Lewis Mill

Lewiston Lane

Lewis (Lewiston)

milltrace

ISLAND

33 Va.

JONES'S

Baugher (Westwood)

barn

Baugher Lane

U.S. skirmishers

C.S.A. cavalry

Little Deep Run

CO. F, 10 Va.

Carpenter's 2 guns open fire

Morris

Yost

2 Va.

WINDER

Carpenter

Scott

4 Va.

To Brown's Gap

TALIAFERRO

48 Va.

covered bridge

PORT REPUBLIC

Taylor

wagon bridge

North River

South River bridge

Harman's wagon train heading for Brown's Gap

Dr. Kemper (Madison Hall)

upper ford

H. Harnsberger (Cherry Grove)

of George Morris. The road at that point emerged into its only stretch that offered a view to the right, or south. An observant officer described the vista in detail: "Near the Morris house the woods and the hills came quite close in to the road to the right . . . but, beyond the Morris house, both to the right and left of the road, were open fields about three-quarters of a mile in breadth from the road to the river, and about a quarter of a mile in breadth from the road to the hills on the right." The fields on the left of the road extended downstream for three miles—well beyond the limits of what would become the battlefield. On the right, though, they "end at something less than a mile beyond Morris's, where they are closed in by a curve of the hills, which here trend in toward the river."[42]

Many Confederates marching into the open area knew the terrain. They had moved through the region at the end of April while en route from Swift Run Gap over the Blue Ridge in a feint that opened Jackson's move to the Battle of McDowell. John H. S. Funk, commanding the 5th Virginia, was harking back to his earlier experience when he wrote that he "marched in [the] direction of Swift Run Gap." If the Confederates knew the terrain, they remained ignorant of Federal positions and intentions. For their part, Tyler and Carroll had no good idea what to expect from Stonewall Jackson. Carroll sought to get some inkling of Southern plans by sending Daniel Keily, the daring Irishman, on a stealthy reconnaissance. "You had to pass through the enemy's concealed skirmishers," Carroll wrote to Keily in appreciation, "but did so and brought me the desired information."[43]

Keily's enterprise went for naught, because Confederates moving into the open beyond the Morris house came into easy view from the Unionist stronghold around Lewiston. Not long after the Southerners appeared, Federal artillery roared vigorously into action from a spectacularly strong position that dominated the battlefield until the final climactic moments. Although estimates of the time range from five to nine A.M., the first Federal artillery discharge probably erupted at about seven-thirty.[44]

Clara Strayer and the refugees from Lewiston and Lynnwood watched nervously from Bogota's upper porch as the first skirmish fire rattled intermittently across the river. Clara "noticed a party of horsemen grouped . . . on the rise below the Lewiston house where the road goes up the mountain—and immediately a stream of fire issued from the cannons' mouth, followed by a report that seemed to shake the very earth." Miss Strayer had witnessed the first round fired from the Unionist aerie at the Coaling. Many Federals around Lewiston heard this close discharge clearly and assumed it was the first artillery round of the day. Artillery chief Philip Daum knew better. "I promptly *replied,*" he reported, to Joe Carpenter's firing at the Union skirmishers.[45]

The shells poured from Federal cannon in their excellent position caused considerable concern and many casualties to Confederates on the plain throughout the battle. This initial flurry continued for about fifteen minutes without any response from Southern guns. The civilians at Bogota watched impatiently through a telescope as the one-sided barrage continued. Later in the day gunsmoke would obscure much of the action, but during the battle's early stages Clara Strayer and her friends could see everything that happened.[46]

Confederates attempting to form line in the impact zone liked the situation even less than did the civilian onlookers. General Winder described the effect as "a rapid fire of shell with great accuracy on the road and vicinity." A Southern artillerist admitted that the "long cannonade" that opened the battle was delivered "chiefly by the enemy." Even that modest account was too optimistic as a description for the opening rounds. Joe Carpenter had received orders to limber up and move to the right, so he could not respond at all.[47]

The Rockbridge Artillery, the second battery in Jackson's column, could not get into action for some time. As the gunners slogged doggedly toward the front, enemy shells were "tearing by us with a most venomous whistle." Cannoneer Ned Moore had a memorable encounter during the advance. Among the infantrymen on the roadside was a stern teacher who had terrorized Moore's youth, Alfonso Smith of Company H, 27th Virginia. "I had many times quailed under his fierce eye and writhed under his birch rod," Moore recalled. The stern ogre of the classroom, who also had edited the Lexington *Gazette* before the war, was now only another frightened soldier. Moore could see in Smith's countenance that "the strain to which he was subjected under these circumstances was doubly trying, waiting inactive for his first baptism of fire." As Ned followed his gun past Smith's roadside resting point, he saw that the older man's "eye was restless . . . perhaps he had a presentiment." Before the morning was over, Alfonso Smith would receive his death wound.[48]

Most Northern regiments were "up at daylight" or "aroused

early," as would be expected under the uneasy circumstances. The men of the 29th Ohio "had scarcely got our breakfast out of the way" by the time the artillery opened. Colonel Lewis P. Buckley attempted to fire them up with a jingoistic address that concluded, "Aim low, men, and at every shot let a traitor fall!" The 7th Indiana choked down some hardtack and coffee and then fell into line. To the Hoosiers it appeared that the Confederates who first became distant targets for Northern cannon were cavalrymen. The 5th Ohio's soldiers could vaguely see Southerners across the river moving toward and through Port Republic. For the moment, though, Federal infantry had nothing to do with the developing hostilities.[49]

That the Federal force remained near Lewiston, neither advancing nor retreating, provoked second-guessing in both directions. The fiery Colonel Philip Daum, whose brashness rubbed Tyler (and others) the wrong way, had been eager for an attack toward the North River bridge late on the 8th. He was promoting that same incredible and impractical notion early on June 9. A heavy fog that hugged the ground until shortly after sunrise gave Daum the idea that Tyler's outnumbered force could somehow slip up on Jackson in secrecy. Carroll, who knew the ground from his recent adventures across it, rode forward with Tyler in the early morning hours and showed him "the impracticability of such a proceeding." Carroll urged instead that the Federal force should retreat.[50]

From his vantage point well down the Valley, and enlightened by hindsight, General Shields declared that Tyler should have retreated overnight. With a typical mixture of ill-informed quibbling and reckless pronouncements, Shields blamed everything on Tyler and Carroll. "My surprise and disappointment may be imagined when I learned . . . that they were still posted within 2 miles" of Port Republic, Shields wrote. Somehow he professed to know that "the locality" where Tyler was forming to fight "was not defensible, being liable to be turned on both flanks." Shields's entire force in the wretched position near Lewiston, he ignorantly insisted, could only "have protracted the struggle . . . but could not have maintained the field."[51]

Actually, the Lewiston position he derided was one of the strongest held by a defensive force during the war. Tyler's relative handful held it long and well and from it nearly defeated Jackson's stronger army. The position was not "liable to be turned" on *either* flank in normal circumstances, not to say "on both flanks." Tyler's right beyond Lynnwood could not have been turned, given the swollen state of the river, without a pontoon train of twentieth-century sophistication.

The Federal problem in fact was not of a tactical nature, but rather a strategic one. Shields's after-the-fact solution of combining his force in the rear would of course have saved him from defeat. An even better combination of force would have been to push reinforcements down to Tyler in his strong position. Frémont's arrival across the river would have won a battle that lasted any longer than Port Republic actually did. Shields's immediate superior, General Irvin McDowell, aptly highlighted the problem in a cogent dispatch written early on June 9, but too late to do any good. Lincoln wanted Shields back for the move to Richmond, McDowell acknowledged; but the high command would love to punish the irksome Jackson for "his late dash [up] the Valley." Strong prospects for that happy result could supersede other considerations. It sounded to McDowell, though, like the Federal force down near Port Republic was too small. "If this is so," McDowell said accurately to Shields, "the general thinks you have forgotten your instructions not to move your force so that the several parts should not be in supporting distance of each other."[52]

Tyler's formidable position drew its strength from a knoll beautifully situated for artillery service. Baron Antoine-Henri de Jomini, the much-quoted (then and now) European military theorist, declared in 1838: "There is in every battlefield a decisive point the possession of which, more than any other, helps to secure victory by enabling its holder to make a proper application of the principles of war." That decisive point at Port Republic was the elevated knob, mentioned earlier, known as the Coaling, from which the first Federal artillery fire of the morning had belched forth. Many hundreds of rounds would follow the path of that initial shot.[53]

The Coaling, a place whose name deserves the status of a proper noun because of the location's prominence, was so called because of a domestic operation of Lewiston farm carried out there. "Charcoal was needed by the Lewises in the blacksmith shop, in stoves . . . since there was no coal nearby," a family member wrote, so the Lewises made charcoal at the Coaling. Controversy about the precise location of the Coaling continues to this day: was it atop the ridge that ends abruptly above Lewiston, or partway down its side; were the guns at the top, midway down the hill, or even at its foot? That is the knottiest single question about Port Republic. A twentieth-century Lewis descendant wrote that the "Coaling" name "doubtless refers to the little hill on the side of the Mapleton hill which you reach as soon as you enter the gateway leading to Mapleton [Mapleton is the pretty postwar house that still stands at the crest of the ridge]. It was always called the Coal Pit Hill, & during the War the Federal Battery was *there* & they made charcoal there."[54]

Two knowledgeable Southern participants described the origins of the Coaling accurately. Jed Hotchkiss called it "a hearth leveled for burning charcoal." Colonel Henry B. Kelly, who led the climactic attack on the Coaling, called the place "an old coal hearth." Most Confederates never understood the name. Two literate soldiers who took part in Kelly's charge referred to it as "Cole Mountain," as though called after a local family.[55]

Federal sources offer a wide range of options for how high up the ridge the Coaling and the guns were located. A Union officer's map (which is accurate otherwise) shows the battery behind three distinct sets of hachures, at the very highest point above the ravine. A Federal infantryman called the site "on [not near] a knoll." Captain James F. Huntington, who commanded half of the artillery that fought there, wrote that his guns were "placed on the low ridge near where it began to descend," with pieces running from that high ground down to the road. He described the Coaling thus: "At the mouth of the ravine on our side was an excavation made for burning charcoal."[56]

Captain Joseph C. Clark, who commanded most of the guns other than Huntington's, described their location as "a rather contracted position, which, however, commanded the enemy's guns." Clark hinted at the highest ground but leaves some doubts: "In my rear and on the left flank woods approached within a few yards of my guns. Close to the flank was also a ravine, beyond which the ground rose rapidly, giving a plunging fire upon our guns if occupied by the enemy." Artillery "close to . . . a ravine" must be on high ground above the draw. Enemy on the opposite side of the ravine with "plunging fire," however, would have to be above the guns. The western knoll does rise higher—about thirty feet higher—than the Coaling, but it does so more gradually.[57]

Artillery chief Daum fueled the controversy when he contradicted both battery commanders, reporting that Clark was "in the road" and Huntington was entirely to Clark's right. His implication that the farthest south any of the guns reached was "in the road" at

Lewiston contradicts every other primary account.[58] Daum spent most of the fight quarreling with Tyler about infantry matters and evidently lost track of his artillery.

Confederates under hot fire from the Coaling gave clear evidence that some Federal guns were on the highest ground above the ravine. Jackson described the enemy line with a statement obvious to everyone but the absent Shields: "The enemy had judiciously selected his position for defense." About the Coaling he wrote: "Upon a rising ground, near the Lewis house . . . six guns . . . commanded the road . . . and swept the plateau for a considerable distance in front." Jackson's topographer placed the Coaling "on the slope of the terrace overlooking the stream valley . . . across a ravine." In Colonel Kelly's language, it "was sufficiently elevated to enable artillery . . . to command the approaches [and] sweep the fields."[59]

One of the Louisianians who called the ridge "Cole Mountain" added that Federal guns there were "admirably posted." The other wrote that the enemy guns were "*on* [emphases in this paragraph are added] a small hill . . . commanding the whole position." Other Confederates used these descriptions: "*on* a cleared plateau"; "a little way up the side of the spur"; "*on* the ridges of the mountains"; "on the *point* of a low ridge"; and on "a little spur jutting out from the . . . Blue Ridge, the *top* of which was crowned with . . . guns." A local historian steeped in local lore wrote about 1900 that the Federal guns were "on the old coal hearth and the bank back of the mission house." The "mission house" stands on a shoulder of the ravine, opposite the 1880s chapel.[60]

The Coaling guns included six pieces from three batteries. Joseph Clark had two Parrott rifles on the far Federal left, in the Coaling proper. To his right a single twelve-pounder howitzer from Robinson's Battery stood between the Coaling and the road. Huntington's three pieces, at least two of them rifled, were around the road just below the Coaling. The elevation advantage Clark enjoyed in shooting at Confederates on the river plain was substantial. Most of the farmland on which the infantry maneuvered is about 1,060 feet above sea level (Port Republic's elevation is 1,063 feet). The road through the ravine below the Coaling is at about 1,080 feet. The top of the Coaling directly above the ravine is 70 feet higher at 1,150 feet. The high ground preferred in military doctrine rarely rises as suddenly as does the Coaling hill above the Port Republic battlefield.[61]

Evidence about the location of the Federal guns leaves some

question about how high up the hill the uppermost were situated. Did Clark fire from the geographical crest, or the slightly lower military crest, or from a shelf halfway down toward the ravine? Much of the uncertainty can be resolved by recognizing that the six guns covered a great deal of ground. Clark was much higher than Huntington, it is evident from primary sources, and he must have been all the way atop the hill. Six cannon and their crews and limber chests and caissons take up a great deal of room; hub-to-hub positioning is for novels and Hollywood. The Federal cluster at the Coaling, which became the cynosure of attention, sprawled up and down the ridge, some guns firing from a point fifty or more feet above others.

Federals looking down from the Coaling and Confederates looking up at it all recognized the obvious value of that commanding knoll. Most of them, however, would fight and die on the rolling, relatively level farm fields stretching northwest from the Coaling. A 7th Ohio soldier described the heart of the battlefield as "a beautiful, level farm one and a half miles long, and one half a mile wide, enclosed by the Shenandoah . . . and a ridge of high hills on the south-east side." A comrade in the 5th Ohio wrote of the battlefield as "flat farming land, mostly in wheat." One of the Louisiana troops destined to play a prominent role remembered that the predominant crop was a healthy, "heavy crop of wheat." What Jackson's Virginians saw as they marched into the battle arena—in addition to the forbidding Coaling and its guns—was a scene so pastoral as to be disarming: "No more beautiful spot could have been selected in all . . . Virginia, for a decisive struggle. The sun . . . lit up the fields of golden wheat, the shining river, and the forests, echoing with the songs of birds. Those who died that day were to fix their last looks on a sky of cloudless blue."[62]

Both of the Confederate leaders at the front knew the field from operations in the area a few weeks before. Winder had spent most of two days steering his brigade through the mud around Port Republic on April 30 and May 1. The road down which Winder was advancing on June 9 had become so disgustingly familiar on May 1 that the general had called it "a terrible road" in his diary: "Never saw one so bad." When Winder climbed through Brown's Gap on May 3, he found that road (which is impassable in the 1990s) a vast improvement over the ones down near the river. On June 9 the same corridors had to serve as arteries for attack, rather than merely as logistical quagmires.[63]

Stonewall Jackson had accompanied Winder during that earlier march, lashing him and his troops through the mud to the railroad at Mechum's River. Jackson had become well acquainted with Lewiston because he had spent the night in the building on May 1. The Southern legend was not a perfect guest, having "slept in bed with his muddy boots on, making it difficult to get the sheets clean after he left."[64]

Although Jackson's attention remained focused to his front, where deadly battle was about to erupt, an important problem affecting the destiny of his army was developing out of sight behind him: the wagon bridge over South River began breaking up. The jury-rigged line of wagon parts and crude lumber connections had caused its first users some trepidation. Each succeeding unit had more reason for concern, and accordingly crossed ever more carefully. Colonel Munford thought that the problem began because troops marching "under cadence step" caused the bridge "to waver . . . up and down."[65]

A local historian believed it more likely that the breakdown of the bridge came from misalignment of two wagons. One high-wheeled wagon adjoined a low-wheeled wagon, "making a drop of somewhere between eighteen inches and two feet, so that instead of four men walking abreast, it became single file and a slow one at that." Dr. Dabney, who was impotently attempting to control traffic around the bridge, agreed. The uneven wagon match came at the worst possible spot, "at the deepest and angriest part of the stream." The ends of all the boards away from the treacherous spot were "unsupported at their ends, and elastic, but one." Several soldiers "were thrown into the water by this treacherous and yielding platform, until, at length, growing skittish of it, they refused to trust themselves to any except the one solid plank; and thus the column was converted . . . into a single file."[66]

Major Dabney recognized that the prudent reaction to this deadly bottleneck would be to halt the column and effect a repair, or to push the troops through the water, ignoring the discomfort involved. The best idea would be to do both—fixing the bridge while hurrying troops through South River in the meanwhile. Dabney was so ineffectual, however, that he could not induce any of the infantry officers to listen to his proposals. The chief of staff to all-powerful Stonewall Jackson could not impose his will on a single regimental commander. "Thus three ill-adjusted boards cost the Confederates a

... bloody battle," Dabney fumed. Unfortunately for Jackson, Claiborne Mason's pioneer detachment had left the bridge site as soon as they pronounced it fit to use. Mason's second-in-command later wrote in blissful ignorance of the problems that the wagon bridge "was a grand success." Had Jackson had the forethought to order the builders to stand by their handiwork in case of difficulties, Mason doubtless could have halted the column and fixed the problem. Infantry officers almost certainly would have respected the engineer's professional judgment as readily as they rejected suggestions from the pathetically unmilitary Dabney.[67]

Dick Taylor's fine Louisiana troops reached the bridge after it had lost most of its capacity. His 8th Louisiana led the way through the jammed streets of the village to the north end of the wagon bridge. Before he pushed the 8th across, Colonel Henry B. Kelly met with General Taylor to receive instructions. The colonel soon discovered the bridge's inadequacy. It was "narrow and unsteady," Kelly wrote, "and could be crossed only in single file, man after man." Another Louisianian called the span "a frail structure, built on wagon wheels, and . . . only capable of allowing the troops to make the passage in single file."[68]

By the time Kelly and the 8th crossed and moved downstream far enough to re-form the brigade, the Stonewall Brigade had long since disappeared. The regiments behind Kelly continued the tedious process of tiptoeing past the midstream danger point. Taylor's Brigade had arrived in town "about sunrise," according to one of his captains. Another soldier in the column wrote that he reached the village just as the sun peeped over the Blue Ridge—which was also the moment that Jackson and his staff left the southern end of the bridge. The soldier who arrived as the sun cleared the mountains provided a good gauge of the effect of the bottleneck on Taylor's progress: after complaining of the delay, he added that "the morning was well advanced" before all five units had crawled across South River.[69]

Dick Taylor finally rebelled at the frustrating pace of the crossing and forced some of the companies near the end of his column "to take the water by wading." With the bothersome river finally behind him, General Taylor determined to give his troops a chance to rest and eat (and in some cases, to dry out). The brigade's train was headed into Brown's Gap and in any case there was no time to cook, but the soldiers could eat whatever they had in their haversacks.

They broke ranks, stacked arms, and prepared to eat what they could find. The general's good intentions, however, went for naught. The banging of artillery and popping of muskets downstream where Jackson's handful of men had approached Tyler were swelling steadily into a deadly roar. One of Jackson's staff officers galloped back from the front and ordered Colonel Kelly "to advance at once and report to the general commanding in the fight." Down the road, the other Louisiana regiments "sprang into ranks, formed column, and marched," following Kelly's lead toward the sound of the guns without receiving direct orders.[70]

Stonewall Jackson's favorite shock troops were coming to his aid, but before they could arrive, the Stonewall Brigade and its artillery supports faced a painful battering.

The Coaling about
1890

CHAPTER 16

Opportunity in the Woods, Trouble in the Fields

T he outnumbered Stonewall Jackson's position was problematical. He had to win quickly, before Frémont could reach the commanding bluffs across the river. Looming above all other considerations was the Coaling. Jackson could not prevail so long as Northern guns bellowed from that knoll. Taking it by frontal assault would probably be far too costly. Therefore he must capture the Coaling from its wooded mountain flank—as quickly as possible, to avoid Frémont's intervention; and he must assign some of the modest force that had arrived at the front to the painful duty of standing on the river plain against heavy odds. Jackson fought the battle on those unavoidable premises.

For his opening move, Jackson had available just four infantry regiments of the Stonewall Brigade and two batteries to support them. The scattering of cavalrymen who had been picketing in his front became useless once battle was joined. Jackson first ordered Winder "to send a regiment through the woods to endeavor to turn their battery, also a battery to get a position above them." Winder turned the mission over to Colonel Allen and his 2nd Virginia, "he being in advance and near the wood." Apparently on his own initiative, Winder expanded Jackson's one-regiment order by adding the 4th Virginia to the flanking party. Joe Carpenter and his battery were to accompany the infantry.[1]

Confederates looking downstream could see at a glance that the enemy position was formidable. It also looked as though a column ought to be able to climb the wooded mountainside and successfully flank the Coaling. Jackson cherished the fond notion that the flanking regiments and battery could "creep through the labyrinths, avoiding all disturbance of the enemy, until he had passed clear beyond his left . . . to control the narrow road which offered the only [Federal] line of retreat."[2]

Unfortunately, the plan was based on wishful thinking rather than solid information. Jackson was sending troops into totally unreconnoitered ground. The familiarity of leaders and men with the river plain from their early May visit did not extend to the densely wooded shoulders of the Blue Ridge. Sending an important maneuver element into unknown country constituted disregard of basic military principles. A. P. Hill would win lasting calumny for doing the same thing at Bristoe Station in October 1863. Jackson, however, had no other choice. Nothing else would win the day. If he failed, much of the fruits of the months-long campaign in the Valley would be spoiled.

The 2nd Virginia moved south across the open field on the right of the road. Allen carried only 224 officers and men on his crucial mission. His orders from Winder, the colonel reported simply, were "to advance under cover of the woods to the right and take the battery which commanded the road." Colonel Ronald's 4th Virginia briefly conformed to the movements of the rest of the brigade, but Winder soon sent it to reinforce the 2nd. Federals peering down the road from the Coaling could see the Virginians "marching towards our left" until they "disappeared behind the trees." Someone quickly carried the news to General Tyler, who of course ordered that the Confederates be brought under fire. Union pieces on the highest ground—Clark's and Robinson's—"opened . . . upon them with effect," Tyler reported, and Huntington's guns "were soon doing the same good work.'' The 2nd Virginia did not complain of this fire, but the 4th, trailing behind, had to hurry through the shell bursts. The regiment reached the woods without losing a man.[3]

The trees actually were a haven against enemy artillery fire, and they provided necessary secrecy; but the undergrowth grew so densely that the woods seemed like an archenemy. Carpenter's Battery made no progress at all and quickly had to abandon the effort. Jackson's visionary notion of Carpenter finding ''a position above'' the Coaling died in its infancy. The infantry could slip through the brush, but not in good order. Allen and Ronald formed a long, ragged line, with the 4th on the right of the 2nd and skirmishers in front, ''and advanced through a very dense wood and laurel thicket.'' Captain White of the 4th wrote: ''We climbed back and forth over ridges and through the thick tangled brush, till we were worn out.''[4]

After much labor and uncertainty, the 2nd Virginia reached the bluff across the ravine from the Coaling. Colonel Allen glimpsed more infantry supports (understandably exaggerating their number to three regiments) around the enemy guns than he had expected to find. He was not behind the Coaling, but directly in front of it. Even so, the 2nd lay within reach of the key to the battlefield. Allen sent word to Winder of his situation and prepared to bring the Coaling under fire. Most of the 2nd's line ran uphill beyond the Coaling. Beyond that Colonel Ronald and the 4th Virginia had reached the western rest of the ravine. Ronald, who was easily bewildered in combat situations, did not know where he was. The colonel forthrightly described his confusion in his report, writing that the 4th had reached ''a point on a hill, that I afterward learned was very near the enemy's battery.''[5]

Before the 2nd and 4th Virginia reached the lip of the ravine opposite the Coaling, their mates in the 5th and 27th Virginia and the Rockbridge Artillery had begun fighting hard. As soon as Jackson and Winder sent infantry to their right toward the Coaling, they hurried some artillery into the fields to the left of the road to answer the Federal barrage. Carpenter's Battery was supposed to be going with the 2nd and 4th. That left Poague's Rockbridge Artillery, on the road. Four of Poague's six cannon were smoothbores of range so short that they could not hope to reach the Coaling, so he kept them out of action and under cover. Jackson placed Poague's two Parrott rifles ''in position on the left of the road to engage, and if possible dislodge, the Federal battery,'' the general wrote. The dislodgment for which Jackson hoped was completely impossible. Two Confederate guns were no match for six Yankee counterparts. Given the inequality of the ground, two dozen Southern cannon would have been required to smother the Coaling. Winder had his orders, however, and bravely set out to execute them. He personally directed the two Parrotts into position.[6]

Poague's two rifles rolled left off the road into the field of wheat, short of the Baugher lane, unlimbered, and opened fire. Jackson said that the Rockbridge rifles went into operation "promptly," and his artillery chief Crutchfield described their response as coming "at once." The Southern gunners knew where to shoot, because the Coaling presented an unmistakable target. They could not actually see their counterparts, however, because black-powder smoke had already boiled up in enough volume to obscure the view.[7]

Winder and Poague did not have much luck with their counter-battery fire. Captain Huntington, who was participating from the Federal end of the exchange, nicely summarized the situation. The one-sided duel was "greatly to our advantage," he wrote, because "our guns were on higher ground [and] most of the enemy's shot passed over us, while our shells exploded among them with deadly effect." From the other end of the duel, McHenry Howard of Winder's staff described the unhappy result: "We were now under a severe shelling."[8]

Ned Moore helped to serve one of the Parrotts in the wheat. The soft, rain-soaked ground away from the road complicated his duties. When the cannon recoiled at each shot, it dug its trail into the mire and bucked out of position. "The ground on which we stood was level and very soft," Moore recalled, "and, having no hand-spike, we had to move the trail of the gun by main force. The enemy very soon got our range, and more accurate shooting I was never subjected to."[9]

Since Carpenter's Battery had been unable to follow the two regiments scrambling toward the Coaling, one of its two sections went out to the left of the road to add its fire to Poague's. Carpenter's pieces remained closer to the main road than the Rockbridge pair. They made little impact on the uneven exchange. Jackson was forced to admit in his report that "the artillery fire was well sustained by our batteries, but found unequal to that of the enemy."[10]

Winder's two regiments of infantry soon followed Poague and Carpenter into the wheat field to support them. The 5th and 27th

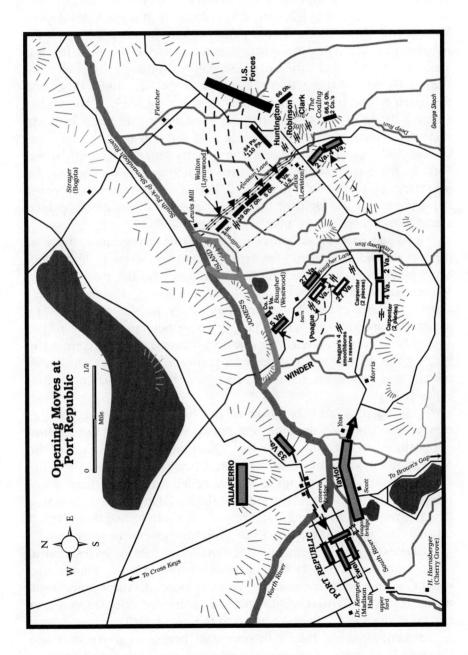

Opening Moves at Port Republic

N W E S

0 1/2 Mile

To Cross Keys

To Brown's Gap

U.S. Forces

Fletcher

Strayer (Bogota)

South Fork of Shenandoah River

Lewis Mill

Walton (Lynnwood)

84 Pa. +110 Pa.

Lewiston Lane

Huntington 66 Oh.
Robinson Clark 66.5 Oh.
The Coaling 2 Co.'s

George Sketch

Deep Run

2 Va. 2 Va.

U.S.
Lewis (Lewiston)

5 Oh. 29 Oh. 7 Oh.

millbrace

27 Va.

Baugher Lane

2 Va.

2 Va.

Deep Run

ISLAND

JONES'S

Co. L 5 Va.
5 Va.
Baugher (Westwood)

barn

5 Va.
Poague

27 Va.

Carpenter (2 pieces)

4 Va.

Carpenter (2 pieces)

Poague's 4 smoothbores in reserve

WINDER

Morris

Yost

33 Va.

TALIAFERRO

covered bridge

Taylor

Scott

PORT REPUBLIC EWELL

lower bridge

North River

South River

upper ford

Dr. Kemper (Madison Hall)

H. Harnsberger (Cherry Grove)

Virginia could have supported the artillery as well from under cover near the road, dashing leftward if any threat to the guns developed. Moving into the wheat near the guns, which served as a magnet for incoming artillery, put the infantry at risk. Colonel Funk of the 5th Virginia reported that "the enemy shelled us furiously." Colonel Andrew J. Grigsby of the 27th Virginia, just to the 5th's right, described the artillery thrown at him as "a heavy fire of shell." After what Grigsby thought was "over an hour" and Funk estimated as thirty minutes, Winder decided that he had to do something to improve the situation. To split the target, the general separated Poague's two Parrotts from one another. The 5th Virginia went with the one he sent farthest to the left, and the 27th relocated behind the other Parrott, well to the right of the 5th. Carpenter's two pieces played a part somewhere in the mix.[11]

Poague's four smoothbores had no better opportunity to fire in this broadened alignment, but trailed along to be ready if needed. They found shelter in a ravine forty yards behind the rifle that Ned Moore was serving. "We were hotly engaged," Moore recalled, "shells bursting close around and pelting us with soft dirt as they struck the ground." Robert E. Lee, Jr., who belonged to one of the smoothbore crews, crawled up toward his friend and yelled from the edge of the ravine over the noise of battle, in humorous allusion to his cooking lesson the night before, "Ned, that isn't making batter-cakes is it?"[12]

This opening artillery phase of the battle lasted for as long as two hours, Captain Poague judged, during which he had been "shifting position occasionally to the left." That movement put part of the 5th Virginia next to the South Fork. An Ohio colonel wrote that "the enemy's battery" was opposite the far Federal right. Northern shells thrown in that direction smashed into the Baugher house. When Mrs. Baugher returned from exile, she traced the route of one that crashed through the roof and attic and out the chimney on the west end.[13]

The extension of Winder's line northward inevitably resulted in similar movement by Tyler's Federals opposite him. Winder also sought to find better ground for his guns closer to the enemy. Lieutenant James M. Garnett went forward in search of "a position nearer and more desirable." Poague joined in the quest. Neither found what he wanted, because Tyler's infantry had begun to move into line opposite Lewiston and the purely artillery aspect of the clash faded as infantry combat loomed near. Clara Strayer and the civilians watching anxiously from Bogota's porch thought that "perhaps an hour" of artillery fire had elapsed "before we heard any response of small arms."[14]

Federal preparation for battle did not include an early rush into the strong infantry positions available to them. Tyler calmly kept his soldiers in the woods parallel to the road. Poague's shells worried them there, but did little harm. An Ohio soldier wrote to a friend that "the shells soon came flying through the are with their shrill scream and we knew the Ball was opened." Around one Ohio regiment's campfire, where the men had coffee warming, the first Confederate shell startled the colonel into action. He hurried to the fire and kicked it apart, in the irrational fear that it was drawing Confederate attention, and ordered the men to fall into line.[15]

Colonel Carroll thought that the arrival of Confederates opposite Lewiston meant certain defeat, he claimed in retrospect. As soon as Poague's guns opened, Carroll "again urged upon General Tyler the necessity of immediately organizing for an orderly retreat." Rather than giving in to such defeatist notions, Tyler displayed admirable poise in delaying the deployment of his infantry. The regiments spread along the main road could simply pivot on their left when Tyler was ready to put them into line. By moving across the meadows through an arc of ninety degrees until their right anchored on the river, Tyler's regiments would stand squarely athwart Stonewall Jackson's way.[16]

The position Tyler would occupy when he made that move was a truly formidable one. James Shields, who had not seen the battlefield, asserted with customary guile that the position was "utterly indefensible." Tyler and his men knew better and proved it, though Shields was immune to factual evidence. The dominant Coaling anchored the position's left; the impassable South Fork protected its right. Military science could hardly have imagined two more solid flank protectors. The heart of the position, connecting the flanking features in a straight line, was the lane from Lewiston to the river. This was "a narrow road at right angle to the main road," topographer Hotchkiss wrote. A "heavy rail fence" enclosed the road on both sides, offering additional protection to its defenders. In some places, particularly on the end of the lane near Lewiston, banks of earth on its west side offered further defensive shelter.[17]

Confederates approaching the lane would have to wade through "an extensive field of standing wheat just ready for the harvest." Lewiston and its substantial barns, stables, and orchards would be a mixed blessing to Tyler's defense. Those features provided useful cover—but they also could shelter attackers who pushed far enough forward to reach them.[18]

Several other features affected operations. The Baugher lane would serve Confederates as a benchmark and rally point just as the Lewiston lane became the focus of Yankee maneuvers. The two lanes were parallel to one another and about three quarters of a mile apart. Most of the battle would be fought within the rectangle of which the lanes constituted two sides. Parallel to the two lanes and bisecting the rectangle was a "division rail fence" of the zigzag variety called "worm fence" in Virginia. This division fence, two thirds of the way from the Baugher lane to the Lewiston lane, served both sides as a landmark and defensive line during the battle.[19]

Three streambeds that cut through the battle rectangle affected tactical events, but not as much as might have been expected because they were, astonishingly, almost dry. Two intermittent streams rambled diagonally across the fields close to Lewiston, and the more regular Little Deep Run flowed north toward the river not far east of the Baugher lane. "Notwithstanding the recent rains they were dry, or nearly so," Colonel Kelly of the 8th Louisiana wrote. He attributed that remarkable fact to their character: "the waters of a rainfall being poured very rapidly into the main streams by these mountain 'runs.' " Had any of the streambeds been full, the battle would probably have developed in different fashion.[20]

Winder shifted to his left more in hopes of lessening fire against his hard-pressed artillery than as an aggressive measure. Tyler reacted to the movement as though it were a threat to advance along the riverbank, finally moving his infantry in that direction. The 7th Indiana went first and farthest, moving nearly to the river in support of Federal guns pushed out to that vicinity. Tyler's report suggests that he sent the Hoosiers to the river's edge to counter a Southern threat, and followed up with artillery. The men who made the move reverse that order, depicting the 7th Indiana as hurrying to support Union guns already sent to that sector. In either case, Northern infantry and artillery arrived on their far right, near the northern end of the Lewiston lane. Tyler sent Colonel Carroll out to command operations on the right.[21]

Tyler's guns near the river found no dominant Coaling, but they did locate "other elevations from which artillery could sweep these fields." The knolls that they chose hardly impress the casual visitor today, but upon examination a series of useful slopes can be discerned that offered Union gunners protection and a vantage point from which to fire. Most were in the wheat field over the fence in the direction of the Confederates. The 7th Indiana's first action was to send out one company as skirmishers. These "had fired but a few shots" when one of them fell wounded and Confederate pressure began to mount. The 29th Ohio came up to tie in with the 7th's left flank as Tyler's line took shape.[22]

Confederates watching from near the Baugher lane could see the Union line unfolding. One Virginian wrote: "The Yankee regiments are moving into line, the old 'Stars and Stripes' can be distinctly seen." Another was impressed by the sight: "It was an army with banners; clean and bright was the array. The long line of bayonets glittered in the sunlight."[23]

Five Union regiments took up positions along and in front of the Lewiston lane. The final alignment leftward from the 7th Indiana descended in order through the regimental numbers: 29th Ohio, 7th Ohio, 5th Ohio, and 1st Virginia (Union). That neat configuration did not develop smoothly or immediately. For a time the 5th and 7th Ohio remained in a second line, randomly overlapping the regiments in their front, and the 66th Ohio stood about two hundred yards behind the 5th and 7th. By the time the battle raged in earnest, however, the line had formed in the order described. The 66th never participated as part of the main line. Its primary role was on the left near the Coaling, but the 66th spent much time in a ceaseless—and useless—shuttle between the left and center.[24]

The 29th Ohio hurried out of the woods to join the left of the 7th Indiana "on the double quick," shedding knapsacks and other equipment as it moved. The Ohioans supported two guns that quickly went into action. They could see what looked like three Confederate regiments threatening them from the wheat. The 29th climbed the fence at the west edge of the Lewiston lane and took position in the field. By then "a heavy fire of musketry" was coming in from the Southerners in the wheat. The 7th Ohio followed by the 5th Ohio also moved "on double-quick," and also seemed most intent on supporting the artillery already in place, the 7th with Clark's guns and the 5th with Huntington's.[25]

The last Federal regiment knitted into the front line along the Lewiston lane was the 1st Virginia (Union). Tyler did not send the 1st out of the woods until later than the others, after the Ohio troops had been in action for some time. When the regiment at last left the woods, it "enter[ed] the open field with a loud shout." With that, Tyler reported, "my entire force was now in position."[26]

According to the historian of the 1st Virginia (Union), his regiment's right tied into the left of the 5th Ohio. Captain Huntington, an astute observer with much at stake, reported instead that an ominous gap remained between Federals on the right and those near the Coaling. The line, "so far as we had one," Huntington wrote, "was formed in two distinct and unconnected parts: on the right, the infantry and five guns; then a vacant space; the remaining guns were on the extreme left, and really held the key of the position." In that disjointed manner Tyler awaited Jackson with about 3,000 troops, unaware that fewer than 600 Confederates faced him on the plain.[27]

Tyler's left, the unmistakable "key of the position," ought to have been impregnable if protected by a moderate infantry force. Detractors later assailed the general for providing an inadequate force for the purpose. The contentious Colonel Daum claimed that he pled for infantry behind the left of the Coaling, "fearing a flank movement." Carroll made a similar claim, but admitted that Tyler sent the 84th and 110th Pennsylvania up into the woods, together with one company each from the 5th and 66th Ohio. That should have been enough to protect the Coaling, but the Pennsylvania regiments were not of maximum efficiency. When Tyler heard skirmish fire near the Coaling (occasioned by the arrival of the 2nd and 4th Virginia on the opposite crest), he ordered the rest of the 66th Ohio to the area.[28]

Three regiments should have held the Coaling against almost any force. Unfortunately for Tyler the swaying fortunes of battle all across his front prompted him to shuffle units away from the Coaling and back again. In responding to what seemed to be crises farther to his right, Tyler would lose his best chance to win the battle. Confederates on the plain actually posed no threat to the Federals; they were hanging on for dear life. Once Tyler pushed the 66th Ohio up behind the Coaling, it stayed there, fifty yards behind the guns. About 100 skirmishers, mostly from the 5th Ohio, deployed in the woods to the left of the Coaling, up the ridge finger. The 84th and 110th Pennsylvania became Tyler's shuttle elements, always on the move and never at the right place. The tactical result was not to Tyler's advantage; another result is that we have difficulty being certain who was at the Coaling at any given moment.[29]

What seemed to Tyler and his men like a Confederate infantry threat was actually Winder's effort to find good positions for his artillery and then protect it with infantry. The general's orders from Jackson were "to attack in front," one of Winder's aides wrote. The intent was not the impossible one of driving Tyler away using only two regiments, but rather "to amuse the enemy meantime," while the flanking party conquered the Coaling. As one his soldiers wrote in retrospect, "Jackson could not delay for fear that Fremont would come up behind him. Already the morning breeze brought to his ears sounds which told him that the [rear guard] was being pressed." An aggressive stance on the plain was essential.[30]

Stonewall Jackson must have reflected on the extremities to which he was being driven on June 8-9. His entire brilliant campaign in the Valley had been built upon calculated risks. Those risks almost never involved disadvantages in numbers or position. They were, in fact, usually taken for the purpose of gaining advantages in both of those areas. A British analyst has aptly noted that "owing to his insight, resource, and rapidity," Jackson "was never in close contact with more than 10,000 of his enemy at any of his Valley battles." June 8 was the only time that he faced as many as 10,000 Yankees, although many times that number had been chasing him. Cross Keys was Jackson's only Valley battle against a larger enemy force.[31] Now on June 9 he faced the campaign's only major disadvantage of ground. There was no helping it. Tyler must be driven and driven promptly.

The 5th and 27th Virginia were the only infantry on the plain, so they became the victims of Jackson's immutable needs. Winder intended to put his other regiment, the 33rd Virginia, on their right if it came up in time; it did not, because of the bottleneck in the village and at the bridge. The two lone regiments suffered from the heavy artillery fire as they dutifully supported Poague's and Carpenter's guns. During the artillery exchange the 5th was nearer the river as well as a bit to the rear of the 27th. For about an hour the infantry served as nothing more than a target for Federal shells. Then Tyler's line took shape opposite Lewiston, and inexorably the infantry of both sides were drawn into the battle.[32]

The Virginia colonels involved in the opening infantry exchanges never considered their actions to be an attack in force. They were simply supporting the batteries as ordered when contact burgeoned into musketry, especially around the 5th Virginia. Colonel Funk had thrown forward his Company L, under Captain Thomas J. Burke, as skirmishers. Burke and his men ran into a swarm of Yankees on similar duty and drove them back about one hundred yards. Winder witnessed this minor advance and ordered the entire regiment forward to support Burke. Funk obeyed by moving to the bank of the river, as far left as the Confederate line could possibly go, and moving ahead.[33]

This almost casual advance of about three hundred yards—catching up with the skirmishers and then covering the one hundred yards farther that they had driven the enemy—was the only opening infantry initiative that Winder dared to display. Federals uneasy about their strategic situation reacted as though to a thunderous onslaught. Some Confederate descriptions were almost as fevered. Once the Virginians had formed "along the Baugher road . . . in the open field," wrote the usually judicious Colonel Kelly, "the battle was joined at once." Another Louisianian wrote colorfully of how "artillery boomed, musketry crashed . . . sheets of flame leaped over the wheat . . . and a cloud of smoke covered all. For twenty-five minutes there was fighting to kill." A Virginian writer proudly described "the *Sic Semper* banner of Virginia . . . bending forward, rippling as it moved; the rattle of musketry resounded; cheers echoed from the mountain side."[34]

Civilians watching from Bogota had reason to be excited, concerned as they were about their home places and their friends fighting to defend them. The citizen gallery saw "the proud Confederates march down . . . the field of wheat, golden in the early sunshine, with their bayonets glittering and colors flying [while] Union pickets retreat in the face of the advancing Confederates." Puffs of smoke "from coal pit hill" and "the thunder of heavy artillery" soon showed the Lewises and Fletchers and Strayers what the Virginia soldiers already knew all too well: "the Confederates . . . were too far away to reply with their muskets. Unceasingly, and all too accurately for the Confederates, the cannon fire continued. Man after man went down."[35]

The 5th and 27th Virginia neither expected as much from the skirmishers' advance nor suffered as severely in the process as the civilians and other onlookers supposed. They were doing their duty while awaiting a decisive stroke from the 2nd and 4th Virginia around the Coaling. Federals responding to the perceived Rebel threat understandably considered stalling its progress a laudable feat. General Tyler's newly forming line of five regiments, buttressed by a dozen guns at the Coaling and elsewhere, included at least 3,000 men. It could hardly be threatened by the offensive capacity of two regiments and four guns. From his perch near the Coaling, Captain Huntington enjoyed a splendid vantage point from which to scan the field. He reported that Federal cannon ignored the Confederate artillery, just as they should, and instead "kept up a steady fire on his infantry." The captain could see that Southern soldiers advancing from near the village "were constantly increasing in number, but so far as we could see failed to display their customary vigor."[36]

General Tyler did not share Huntington's casual optimism, or at least did not admit to it in his report. "Two rebel regiments under cover of the river bank" faced the 7th Indiana, Tyler said. The Rebels brought enough fire to bear on the 7th "from their masked position" that the regiment had to "retire a short distance . . . in admirable order." The "masked position" of the Confederates meant that the Federals generally could not see their enemies—in no small part because there were not many Virginians in the wheat to be seen.[37]

Colonel Carroll, who commanded the right on Tyler's behalf, reported that after the 7th Indiana fell back, canister checked the Southern infantry. Colonel Daum, Tyler's restless chief of artillery, had gravitated to the right as well. Daum believed that Confederate activity in the wheat field constituted an attempted flank movement down the riverbank. He too credited the artillery with halting this threat, doing "excellent execution, as they drove the enemy back" without much Northern infantry support. By the time the three Ohio regiments pulled into position down the lane to the Hoosiers' left, Tyler reported, "regiment after regiment of the enemy moved upon the right, and the engagement became very warm." Between their screen of skirmishers and their main bodies, the 5th and 27th Virginia had made a big impact on the Federals.[38]

The view from the Lewiston lane and its environs, where soldiers from Indiana and Ohio faced the beginnings of battle, was that things were plenty warm even at this stage. Because the advance of the 5th Virginia behind its skirmishers near the river was the most visible Confederate action, Northerners considered the early phases of the battle as focused on their right. The fact that the 7th Indiana arrived first on the far right, and the line then built up from the Indiana regiment leftward, served to confirm Federal notions that the right near the river was where the battle concentrated what little opening fury it had.

Company K of the 7th Indiana moved forward into the wheat as skirmishers. It was that group that the skirmishers of Funk's 5th

Virginia clashed with at the initial contact. Billy Davis of the 7th thought that he spied Confederate cavalry advancing "across the wheat in our immediate front." Billy claimed that the 7th Indiana "formed a hollow square," the traditional reaction by infantry to a cavalry charge in the smoothbore era. Whatever horses Davis saw— and they surely were not cavalry—soon "passed to the rear and a heavy infantry line" appeared in their stead. Another observer described the modest Confederate advance approaching "stealthily through a wheat field until within about two hundred yards," at which distance three full regiments "sprang up and started with a yell upon us." The Hoosiers "poured volley after volley into them, which was returned."[39]

John Hadley of the 7th Indiana also described the Confederate advance as a noisy and deliberate affair. He did not suggest any attempt at stealth. "We heard a tremendeous yell arise in our fron[t]," Hadley wrote. "Following it [we] saw rais up over a hill a rebel brigade & with flying colors & prancing steeds they came steadily up. Within 200 yds of us they poured a volley into our ranks when we without delay returned the compliment which brought them to a halt." Samuel List of the 7th believed that the Southerners who made the "dash on us" had "the intention of turning our right."[40]

A few yards to the left of the Hoosiers, the 29th Ohio suffered from Confederate artillery, which none of the Indiana troops even mentioned. N. L. Parmeter complained that a Southern battery "forced its deadly messengers among us while advancing and all through the fight." The ordeal of Private George W. Eastlick of the 29th serves as a microcosm of the suffering endured by hundreds of Port Republic wounded. A Confederate rifled bullet fired from very long range struck the thirty-year-old Eastlick on the left side of his head and fractured his skull. It knocked him unconscious for a long period, during which he lay insensible to the battle raging around him. Eastlick regained consciousness in time to stagger to a Union hospital, where the bullet was removed from his skull.[41]

Six days after the battle, Private Eastlick was in a Washington hospital suffering from "considerable mental confusion, loss of memory, marked deficiency in the strength and sensibility of the right arm, [and] slight but persistent and daily increasing contraction of the fingers." The wound itself looked healthy and seemed to be healing. Eastlick's symptoms worsened steadily until on June 23, under an ether anesthetic, a surgeon opened his skull and removed pieces of bone that had been pushed into the brain. Within thirty minutes after the operation, the patient's arm and fingers had returned to normal. Thereafter Eastlick's condition improved rapidly, and he was discharged on August 5. As of September 1867 he was rated as having a permanent two thirds disability, based on impaired vision in his left eye and intolerance of light on that side.[42]

Federals of the 7th Ohio, 5th Ohio, and 1st Virginia (Union) lined up to the left of Eastlick's 29th Ohio and watched the firing toward the river without taking much part in it. A member of the 7th boasted that his unit "arrived just in time to save them [Federal guns] from a brigade of the enemy who were charging with fixed bayonets." James Clarke of the 5th wrote, "we saw a large force of secesh coming toward us along the flats supported by two guns." The historian of the 1st Virginia (Union), farthest from the action and last to arrive in position, inflated the Confederates to a "strong force" that attacked "three and four deep" and must have constituted "a whole division apparently."[43]

The battle's first climactic moment was at hand. The 2nd and 4th Virginia were poised to assail the Coaling; the 5th and 27th Virginia had advanced as far as they could against a far larger Federal force in a strong position; and the Northern line had taken the shape that it would maintain throughout the battle. However this initial climax broke, Jackson badly needed more troops at the front to bolster his thin line or to exploit any advantage that the 2nd and 4th Virginia might win.

Ample reinforcements awaited Jackson's orders within two miles, but they were jammed into the village and stymied by the flimsy wagon bridge. When the general sent Colonel Crutchfield back to hurry reinforcements forward, the aide found Taylor across South River and set about pushing artillery to the front. Infantry behind Taylor trickled across "the crazy bridge," as a local man called it. As the midstream wagons and the clumsily affixed boards across them slipped farther out of alignment, more men fell into the river. The spectacle caused the thin line to pause, laugh, and then slow down to avoid the same fate.[44]

Major Dabney, who was operating under "a strict injunction" from Jackson to "expedite the crossing," raged impotently about his inability to enforce his will on anyone. Everything became "mingled in almost inextricable confusion," the staff officer grumbled, "amidst much wrong-headedness of little Q.M.'s swollen with a mite of brief authority." No better epitaph for Dabney's own failed efforts could be imagined than his description of the officers who blithely ignored him.[45]

If one Confederate around Port Republic was even more frustrated than Dr. Dabney, it was Colonel Neff of the urgently needed 33rd Virginia. Neff started on the wrong side of the congested village at daybreak. Winder's belated order, carried by Lieutenant Garnett, put Neff into motion too late for smooth progress. "I had scarcely collected my regiment and started for the bridge when our artillery opened," he reported.[46]

When the 33rd reached the North River, the bridge there was packed with Ewell's troops and with a tangled mass of "wagons, ambulances, artillery, and infantry." It was only "with great difficulty and considerable loss of time" that Neff finally managed to wedge the 33rd into the moving column and cross into town. That achievement proved to be only a preliminary to the greater difficulty of advancing snail-like through the village to the pesky wagon bridge. Neff reported wearily that he "encountered almost every obstacle in crossing the temporary [bridge] across the smaller stream."[47]

His Company I no doubt relished the delay, because the men were near their homes. The "Rockingham Confederates," as the company had named itself, was made up of men from the region, including those Sons of Temperance William Lewis and Levi Sipe of Company I. (Sipe must have been a backslider, because his name was lined through on the rolls of the SOT.) Soldiers from Port could not, however, help to find a way through their home hamlet: every street was clogged and impassable. Neff was hardly culpable for the delay, but he felt and expressed, during the two months of life left to him, guilt about not being at the front with the rest of his brigade.[48]

General Ewell described the South River mess succinctly in his official report: "The difficulty in effecting the crossing . . . occasioned a delay, which separated the forces in my command." The 31st and 52nd Virginia crossed the wagon bridge right after Taylor's Louisianians. Major Joe Chenoweth of the 31st, whose intermittent diary entries on June 8 had brimmed with patriotic ardor, Christian sentiments, and longings for homefolks, tried to write in his journal on horseback at eight A.M. "The ball is open again and we are from what I can see and hear to have another hot day. . . . I may not see the result." The major reiterated to Lieutenant Joseph F. Harding his "presentiments of his coming death," then crossed the bridge when his turn came and rode downstream toward the firing.[49]

John Robson inched toward the wagon bridge in the ranks of the 52nd Virginia. He and his comrades had been able to see across to the battlefield from above the North River bridge; now they could hear the roar of battle echoing up the Valley. "We were hurrying as fast as we could to their assistance," Robson recalled, "when a plank in our wagon bridge slipped out, almost breaking up our means of crossing, and did delay us considerably." The 58th Virginia crossed after the 52nd. Its men were stuffing ammunition into their cartridge boxes from ordnance wagons they had run across when a colonel shouted: "Hurry up, boys, those troops will get in ahead of us." One pragmatic soldier who understood the consequences of the rising roar from the front retorted, "I wish they would all get in before me." The 13th Virginia crossed still later. Joe Kern of the 13th remembered that "now and then a plank would tilt and somebody would get a bath."[50]

In that desultory fashion Jackson's reinforcements oozed through the bottleneck: all of Mighty Stonewall's methodical preparations and diligent striving during almost three months nearly went for naught as a consequence of a half-dozen wagons and several dozen boards.

Winder's
Confederates
were forced to fall
back to
reorganize near the
lane that led to
the Baugher house,
"Westwood."

CHAPTER 17

FIASCO IN THE WOODS,

MORE TROUBLE IN

THE FIELDS

The first turning point in the Battle of Port Republic unfolded in the woods near the Coaling with a whimper rather than a bang. Colonel James W. Allen's 2nd Virginia Infantry had completed its laborious approach to the Coaling while Winder's other troops provided distraction down on the river plain. Allen immediately sent a report of his situation back to General Winder. He then ordered his two left companies, which had the best head-on shot at the Coaling, "to take deliberate aim and fire at the gunners." Those few men—about 45 of them—could hardly drive away the Federals with musketry. They could, however, force the Federal gunners away from their cannon and give the Confederates on the plain some relief from the incessant shelling issuing from the Coaling.[1]

With hindsight it is clear that Allen's plan to throw surprise fire against the Federal crews was inadequate. Loosening the Yankees' grip on the Coaling would require a great deal more than simply shooting at it. The colonel never had an opportunity to test his plan, however, because before the two companies could open fire, two ill-disciplined Confederate soldiers fired prematurely and gave away Allen's hopes of employing stealth. Although Allen manfully implied in his report that the misdeeds were done by his own regiment, Colonel Ronald of the 4th Virginia admitted that his men were at fault. A hurried and poorly aimed volley from the 2nd Virginia that followed the premature discharges did succeed in driving off the Federal gunners momentarily. Northern infantry around the Coaling promptly returned the fire, however, and under its cover the cannoneers put their pieces back into operation. They hurled canister across the ravine in such volume that the 2nd Virginia scrambled away and could not be re-formed for quite some time.[2]

The 4th Virginia, meanwhile, had accomplished even less than the 2nd. The 4th was farther up the shoulder of the Blue Ridge on the right, where it could not even bring fire to bear on the Coaling. The two impatient members of Colonel Ronald's regiment who ruined the Confederate surprise probably were beyond the angle of fire for the Federal guns, but they did bring down infantry fire on their own heads. This "considerable volley from the enemy, who were concealed in the brush," Ronald reported, did "no damage . . . the enemy overshooting." Such of the 4th as the Coaling guns could reach faced canister fired "for a short time with great violence." The few casualties that Ronald suffered came from those volleys.[3]

Colonel Allen, who fortunately outranked Ronald, ordered the 4th Virginia to retire a short distance while he re-formed the 2nd. Soon thereafter he took both regiments farther back to "a more eligible position." From there Allen "reported to General Jackson . . . my position and utter inability to carry the battery without assistance." The two regiments remained impotent in the dense thickets as Taylor's Brigade of Louisianians moved past them sometime later. Ronald never noticed Taylor's advance, or at least did not mention it.[4]

Hugh White of the 4th Virginia wrote in a letter what many others in the regiment must have been discussing: "we were once very close to the enemy's cannon on the mountain side, and thought our duty was to charge it. But no, we must march back," even when others took up the assault in a later phase of the battle. Ronald probably had heard such mutterings and been stung by them. In a phrase unlike most found in official reports, the colonel saw fit to suggest that his soldiers would have done well if given a chance. "While not actively engaged with the enemy," Ronald wrote, "yet the conduct of all was such as to justify me in saying that the Fourth Regiment *would have been* equal to any emergency."[5]

The 2nd Virginia's brief ordeal under the muzzles of the Coaling's guns had surprisingly cost only one man killed, but another 24 men had been wounded, for an almost instantaneous loss of about 11 percent of the regiment's strength. The dead man was Lieutenant Robert M. English, a thirty-seven-year-old farmer from near Winchester. The larger 4th Virginia had suffered but little during its ineffectual display of premature fire. It lost only four men wounded all day long. The four wounded Virginians were typical of the composition of the Stonewall Brigade. Privates Joshua B. Major and Samuel J. Cox and Corporals John D. Cox and Edwin C. Haller were each either nineteen or twenty years old when they enlisted. Their prewar occupations were farmer, cooper, carpenter, and student. All four young men recovered from their wounds. Haller and Major soon followed the popular reenlistment route to cavalry service. The Cox boys stayed with the 4th. John survived the war, but Sam was mortally wounded in 1863.[6]

The brief, ill-fated Confederate attempt opposite the Coaling had an exaggerated effect on the Federals there. The artillerists felt vulnerable. Captain Huntington was no alarmist, but he had noticed with some concern the heavily brushed slopes across the ravine from the otherwise-impregnable Coaling. This "dense growth extending to the road would conceal the approach of the enemy to within pistol-shot of the coal-pit," he wrote with hindsight. What Huntington described as "a tremendous volley of musketry at close range" had seemed to Allen and Ronald to be a disappointing spattering of early shots and an ill-aimed volley. Huntington and his men and the other batteries reacted instinctively: "In return we gave them canister in allopathic doses, and repulsed the attack without the aid of a musket."[7]

Captain Joseph Clark's two guns stood on the highest Coaling ground, and farthest to the Federal left, so they were closest to the point of Confederate impact. While Clark's attention was focused on shooting at Poague's and Carpenter's Confederate guns on the plain, suddenly Southern "riflemen appeared in the woods . . . and opened a sharp fire at short range." With help from the one gun of Robinson's Battery on his right, Clark scoured the opposite knoll with canister "with such destructive effect as to drive them immediately from the position." From his high vantage point, Clark could see what Huntington could not, that Federal "infantry skirmishers in the woods [to his left] assisted in this repulse."[8]

General Tyler's nerves must have suffered a major jolt when musketry erupted from the vicinity of the Coaling. To his great relief, Tyler reported, the "sharp fire was kept up in the woods for a few moments only, when the enemy retired." The general imagined that he could see the attackers come back out into the open near the Confederate line shortly thereafter. He must have been confused by new Southern units arriving from the rear. That confusion may have contributed to the unwarranted nonchalance that Tyler subsequently displayed about protecting the Coaling with infantry.[9]

The same set of circumstances prompted artillery chief Philip Daum to an opposite reaction. Colonel Daum worried about a renewal of the Confederate threat through the woods near the Coaling, or so he claimed in retrospect. The colonel had been on the Federal right when the 2nd and 4th Virginia were repulsed, but he returned to the Coaling and found evidence of the small-arms fire brought against it. Daum "earnestly entreated General Tyler," he claimed, "to throw infantry into the woods, to clear them of the enemy." Such action would have accomplished nothing more against the retreating Virginians. A Federal infantry force emplaced across the ravine opposite the Coaling might, however, have won the battle for Tyler during its later stages.[10]

With the total repulse of the 2nd and 4th Virginia, the prospects for Jackson's troops under Winder on the plain worsened significantly. The Coaling would continue to smother Jackson's few guns and harass Winder's infantry with well-directed artillery fire. The Southern situation would have been improved by the availability of more and longer-range guns.

In truth, Jackson's outmoded notions about artillery organization hampered his army, and his poor choice of an artillery chief exacerbated the problem. The general had written to A. R. Boteler, his mentor in the Confederate Congress, one month earlier damning the concept of artillery battalions, insisting that "the Batteries shall not be united into a battalion, as the best arty organization . . . is that of separate batteries and only one field officer for all, and that officer should be one of preeminent [stature]." In the same letter he ardently urged the promotion of Stapleton Crutchfield to be his chief of artillery, apparently unaware that Crutchfield was not of a "preeminent" stripe. The battalion system actually worked far better than Jackson's preferred mode. Grouping guns of particular types simplified ammunition supply and made available long-range guns of the sort needed against the Coaling.[11]

During the early stages of the battle, Colonel Crutchfield was in the rear trying "to order up the rifled guns from our different batteries." Many of them were, he found, short of ammunition from the fighting on June 8 and ignorant of "the exact locality of our ordnance train. To supply them took some time, and they could only go into action in succession." A battalion organization would have removed the necessity of sorting through various batteries to pull out the long-range rifles. Even without that system, it is hard to imagine why Crutchfield waited until mid-battle to see to refilling empty ordnance chests. He had complained of similar problems during June 8 without learning anything from the experience. Now Confederates suffering under a storm of fire at the front would suffer further as a result of Crutchfield's sloth.[12]

The Parrott rifles of Poague's Rockbridge Artillery continued to contend valiantly if vainly against the Coaling's batteries. Muddy terrain "made it necessary to move several times to more solid ground." Three times enemy shells "passed between the wheels and under the axle of our gun, bursting at the trail," Ned Moore wrote. One of them blew up under the foot of a gunner. Another artilleryman dodged out the way of a shell and into the path of a gun wheel as it recoiled, knocking him out of action. Some artillerists found shelter under the abrupt bank of the river. The crew felt that they were sacrificial lambs awaiting relief from flankers headed for the Coaling. The ordeal seemed to Moore to last "for two or three hours."[13]

Poague's Battery came out of the ordeal below the Coaling badly mangled. In the aftermath, Winder approved and Jackson endorsed a request allowing the battery time to refit and heal at Staunton. Tom Wade described the battered state of the unit in a letter dated June 17: "Out of 150 men we have 70 on duty, & of six guns .. only one of them fit for service. The horses are nearly all killed up. The men are pretty well broken down also."[14]

The only guns firing from the plain with Poague's two rifles belonged to Carpenter's Battery. A two-gun section under Lieutenant George McKendree went to the far left. Winder personally positioned

McKendree's pieces and directed their fire. The rest of the battery also opened fire on the right for a time, but without much effect. William Humphreys, who was with the right section, wrote: "we ceased firing, our section was inactive—having no position to attain under the circumstances." Other short-range guns near the front could accomplish nothing. They remained under cover while the whole army awaited Colonel Crutchfield's tardy completion of his efforts to send forward more long-range guns.[15]

The 5th and 27th Virginia were in for an even harder time than Poague's guns. Their modest advance quickly came to a halt once it had prompted Tyler to spread his five regiments along the Lewiston lane. Grigsby's report of the 27th's actions did not even acknowledge an advance at this stage. The 5th Virginia on his left, facing stronger Federal reaction, fell back as much as a half mile. A veteran of the Stonewall Brigade described "the rattle of musketry" as being "sharp, especially on our left." In a typical Southern reaction, he credited the strong Federal showing to their Midwestern origins; disdain for Northeastern Yankees did not extend so uniformly to what were then called "Northwestern men."[16]

In the face of the Federal strength and the incessant pounding from the Coaling, Winder was forced to fall back to reorganize near the Baugher lane. The temporary repulse "was only from overwhelming numbers," he reported. Winder applauded, as well he should have done, the "courage, gallantry, fortitude, and good conduct" of his troops. "They fought gallantly and desperately, as our holy cause urged them to do," the brigade commander declared. Winder expressed astonishment that, despite the enemy's "withering fire, the killed are few in number, a kind Providence having guarded many from the great dangers." Providence in fact had missed guarding quite a number of Winder's men, and in the next hours would fail to protect many more. Some of the brigade's less devout men were trusting instead to Jackson's expedients. A sympathetic observer suggested: "In the face of that fire, the bravest veterans were unwilling to move forward. 'Why do so?' they may have said; 'Jackson is coming; the day is before us; he will find some way to stop that fire.' "[17]

The Federals most prominent in driving the 5th Virginia and Winder back to the Baugher lane belonged to the 7th Indiana, which had advanced into position first and farthest to the Federal right. In company with most defenders on both sides throughout the war, the Indiana men believed themselves outnumbered by "a vastly superior

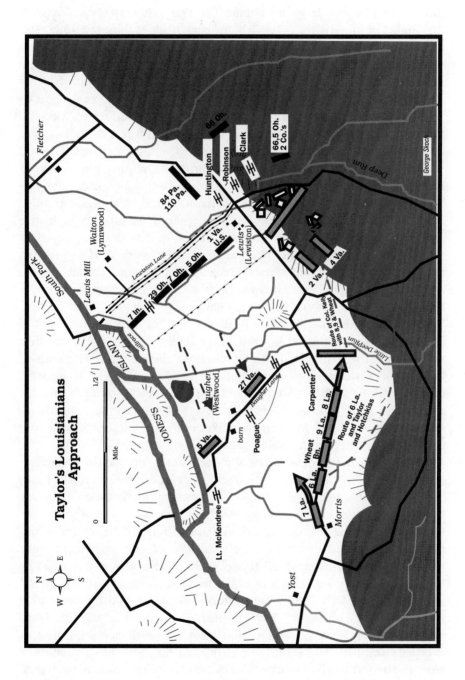

Taylor's Louisianians Approach

N
W · E
S

0   1/2   Mile

Fletcher

South Fork

Walton (Lynnwood)

Lewis Mill

84 Pa.
110 Pa.

Huntington

86 Oh.

Robinson

Clark

66,5 Oh.
2 Co.'s

Deep Run

George Stock

1 Va. U.S.

Lewiston Lane

29 Oh. 7 Oh. 5 Oh.

Lewis (Lewiston)

2 Va.

4 Va.

7 In.

millrace

ISLAND

Route of Col. Kelly with 8,9 & Wheat

Little Deep Run

JONES'S

augher (Westwood)

barn

Poague

Baugher Lane

27 Va.

5 Va.

Lt. McKendree

Carpenter

Wheat Bn.

9 La.

8 La.

Route of 6 La. and Taylor and Hotchkiss

6 La.

7 La.

Morris

Yost

force," despite the large advantage the Federals actually enjoyed at this stage of the battle. The 7th Indiana itself numbered only 300 men, having left about 500 soldiers sick and disabled along the road since starting the campaign. The regiment would lose almost exactly one half of its numbers at Port Republic.[18]

Students of the Civil War sometimes forget that early battles were fought primarily with smoothbore muskets, effective for only about one tenth the distance rifled muskets could reach. By mid-war every Federal carried a rifle, while some Confederates still labored with antiquated smoothbores. That enormous inequity affected later battles, but at Port Republic most men on both sides used smoothbores. The historian of the 7th Indiana admitted of the first repulse of the Confederates that "our regiment [had a] small part in it, the distance being too great for its smooth-bore guns."[19]

Other veterans of the 7th Indiana's fight were not so modest. Similarly equipped Confederates had closed to smoothbore range, and the volleys that ensued from both sides were accordingly effective. Billy Davis described the exchange as "a galling fire" before "we repulsed them." Elliott Winscott wrote of "volley after volley into our ranks," returned in kind. John Hadley boasted that the first volley from the 7th halted the attackers in their tracks. The soul of the Hoosiers' defense was the regiment's colonel, James Gavin, who calmly ignored balls whistling through the air and "jokingly told his men they were enough for Jackson's entire command in themselves."[20] So long as Jackson's entire command included only two regiments, Gavin was on solid ground.

Most Northern accounts of Winder's early repulse do not differentiate between it and the subsequent heavier Southern attack. From ground level in the wheat field, the swaying fortunes of a distant enemy were not clearly distinguishable. The historian of the 29th Ohio, next to the left of the 7th Indiana, spoke of heavy incoming fire and concluded that "the rebels in front of our right wing were behind a strong post and rail fence"—the mid-field fence parallel to both lanes. There he left them until the next Confederate advance.[21]

One of the 7th Ohio's men referred to its smoothbores as "our old Queen Ann muskets." Two published histories of the 7th Ohio suggest a more active participation than the 29th accomplished in Winder's repulse. The difference may well lie more in the accounts than in the event. Theodore Wilder claimed, with obvious exaggeration, that the Confederates actually charged "with fixed bayonets" until heavy volleys of Ohio musketry pushed them back to the rail fence.[22]

In its position midway down the lane, the 7th Ohio was close enough to the Coaling to witness the repulse of the 2nd and 4th Virginia. George Wood, historian of the 7th, provides the important information that the Confederate fiasco near the Coaling unfolded before Winder's repulse on the plain. Winder had held up his end of Jackson's hurried plan. Captain Wood described his regiment's role in repulsing Winder with an excess of drama and with unmistakable exaggeration: the 7th "reserved its fire until the rebel column approached within easy range, when . . . the regiment, which had hitherto been concealed by the tall spires of wheat, rose to its feet, and delivered its fire. This shower of lead made a fearful gap in the lines of the advancing column. It staggered, and finally halted." The 7th Ohio actually "plunged into the midst of the foe, when an awful scene of carnage followed," by Wood's breathless account. Then the 7th, flanked by the 5th and 29th Ohio, "exultant victors" all, pushed the Rebels for a half-mile before re-forming and falling back to near the Lewiston lane.[23]

Men fighting with the 5th Ohio reported more modestly on Winder's repulse. Frederick Fairfax had been out in the lane, but his company pulled back near the Coaling in answer to the brief threat there. Fairfax never mentioned a Confederate infantry onset on the plain at all. James Clarke of the 5th styled his unit's advance as being "to give them a show." The 5th Ohio delivered a volley when its officers thought it had drawn within range. "At last their left broke and run and soon they all gave way," Clarke concluded.[24]

Winder's tentative advance, made to protect his artillery and to buy time for the move against the Coaling, inevitably had foundered in the face of brutal artillery fire and numerous infantry. The advance achieved its purpose of allowing the 2nd and 4th Virginia to achieve their vital assigned goal. When the 2nd and 4th failed miserably, there remained no reason for Winder to push his little force forward. The 5th and 27th Virginia back near the Baugher lane, supported by the few Southern cannon that had arrived, could hold on for a time. If Jackson was to accomplish anything further, however, he must have more troops. Fortunately for Stonewall, reinforcements were approaching the field.

**Louisianian General
Richard Taylor
was witty, cultured,
ambitious, egotistical,
brilliant, devoted to
duty, and moody
because of
rheumatism,
headaches, and
intermittent
paralysis of his right
side.**

CHAPTER 18

TAYLOR'S LOUISIANA

BRIGADE MOVES

FORWARD

After an hour of infantry fighting, Jackson had gained neither an inch of ground nor any advantage over his foe. The towering tactical imperatives remained unchanged: he must take the Coaling from its flank; and he must do so promptly. Troops arriving from the rear must repeat the march of the 2nd and 4th Virginia toward the Coaling, this time under better control and with more determination. The repulse of the first attempt made a renewed effort even more important.[1]

The approaching troops of Dick Taylor's fierce Louisiana brigade grasped the battlefield's simple verities. One of them wrote: "Unless that park of artillery on the Federal left could be taken Jackson was defeated." Henry B. Kelly, who commanded the first regiment in the reinforcing column, nicely summarized what Jackson recognized—that the disadvantage of committing troops piecemeal must be borne under the circumstances. Because of delays at South River, new arrivals went into battle "by battalions, successively, as they came forward," Kelly recalled.

> Time is always an element of prime importance in battle movements, and by no officer, in either service, was its value more keenly appreciated than by Gen. Jackson, whose style of strategy was pre-eminently and distinctively of the most rapid and aggressive character. At this particular juncture, especially, was time of vital consequence, as it was essential that the battle on the right bank of the river should be fought and won before Fremont could come up with his army to the heights.[2]

Stonewall Jackson did not need Winder's pleas for help to tell him that Confederate fortunes on the river plain were deteriorating. Any other commander almost certainly would have plugged the freshly arriving troops into Winder's line with a sigh of relief. Jackson instead went for the Federal jugular at the Coaling. Winder must bear further suffering in his role as sacrificial lamb. The Confederates could not lose the battle if Taylor's regiments went to Winder's aid on the plain, but neither could they win it there. Only by seizing the Coaling could Jackson cap his two days of battle, and his three months of campaigning, with a sweeping victory.

Jackson not only determined to make the Coaling his primary target, he deliberately dispatched the Louisiana column on a wider arc, hoping that Taylor's men might sneak all the way to the Federal rear. Circumstances elsewhere on the battlefield would deny the flankers that opportunity, but the intention is a gauge of Stonewall Jackson's daring. As the march developed, the Louisiana troops did swing far enough up the shoulder of the Blue Ridge to pass above the withdrawn 2nd and 4th Virginia.[3]

Dabney grumbled in later years that the march to the rear should have been prosecuted to completion. In doing so he ignored the exigencies of battle that deflected the Louisianians into an emergency attack on the Coaling. Dabney's complaint is without merit, but the information that he stumbled upon raises a fascinating prospect. A few days after the battle, Jackson's aide met a cavalry courier at headquarters who lived on the Fletcher farm, just below Lewiston.

The "genteel, intelligent" private had hunted game on the surrounding hillsides since his youth. Dabney asked if a column including artillery could have gotten around the Coaling into the Federal rear. "Yes, I know of wagon tracks in the woods," the quondam rabbit hunter replied. "I could have done it the easiest in the world."[4] With careful reconnaissance, taking advantage of the hundreds of men in his army who knew the ground, Jackson might have crafted a dazzling stroke that would have crushed Tyler. As it was, he could not reconnoiter. Time and the enemy pressed too urgently.

As the Louisiana troops pushed down the road, the battlefield came into view before them. General Taylor, who was far behind the head of his brigade's column, recorded the impressive scene:

> From the mountain, clothed to its base with undergrowth and timber, a level—clear, open, and smooth—extended to the river. This plain was some thousand yards in width. Half a mile north, a gorge, through which flowed a small stream, cut the mountain at a right angle. The northern shoulder of this gorge projected farther into the plain than the southern, and on an elevated plateau of the shoulder were placed six guns, sweeping every inch of the plain to the south. Federal lines, their right touching the river, were advancing steadily, with banners flying and arms gleaming in the sun. A gallant show, they came on. Winder's . . . brigade, with a battery, opposed them. This small force was suffering cruelly, and its skirmishers were driven in on their thin supporting line.[5]

Stonewall Jackson had come to rely on Dick Taylor and his brave troops. They had won the Battle of Winchester for him just two weeks earlier with an irresistible frontal assault. In most ways, the aristocratic Taylor was as unlike Jackson as any man could be. The Louisianian was witty, cultured, ambitious, egotistical, brilliant, devoted to duty, and moody because of a mixture of rheumatism, headaches, and "a stroke of paralysis when young that permanently affected his right side." When his suffering became intense, Taylor's staff avoided his "ugly" temperament. At such times, however, "the excitement of battle seemed to soothe him, and he would become pleasant and playful as a kitten." The morning of June 9 would offer ample cause for Taylor to be soothed.[6]

Although Jackson and Taylor had forged a relationship based on mutual respect, the junior officer initially had fought hard to avoid being placed under Stonewall's command. Jackson's well-won reputation for crustiness had not then been offset by any display of military prowess, and Taylor was "uneasy . . . under Jackson's command. . . . Dick Taylor didn't like it." In hopes of escaping from Jackson, or having him supplanted by someone else, Taylor went to Richmond with Dick Ewell's blessing to see President Jefferson Davis—who happened to be Taylor's brother-in-law. When he returned from his seditious mission, Taylor told a staff officer: "We won't be under this damned old crazy fool long." He had assurances that James Longstreet would take over the Valley from Jackson. Fortunately for the Confederates, Taylor's machinations failed.[7]

Before Taylor met Jackson on the battlefield of Port Republic, most of his brigade had already begun its march through the woods toward the Coaling under orders given to the head of the column. General Taylor's accounts of his experiences during the battle are understandably focused on what he saw and did. He exaggerated his participation and its importance to a degree; but at least some of the differences in emphasis between Taylor's accounts and those of subordinates can be traced to the egocentrism inherent in all first-person narratives.

Henry Kelly and his 8th Louisiana had been at the front of the brigade's column all morning long. As Kelly wrote a few years later, the 8th moved "rapidly down the road to some distance beyond the Morris house" before coming in view of the 5th and 27th Virginia. The reinforcements saw "sharp fire . . . from the enemy's battery" striking among the Virginians. Another Louisianian remembered that the guns at the Coaling "could be plainly observed" as they fired at the "small force" of Confederates on the plain. Northern gunners could of course see the approaching Confederate column and promptly switched some of their unwanted attentions to it.[8]

Kelly's advance came under artillery fire about one-half mile beyond the Morris house. Fortunately the Coaling's shells passed "low along and just above the ranks" as they spiraled down the long axis of the column. Colonel Kelly hastily ordered the 8th off the road and into the field to its right before the Federals could lower the range with fatal effect. There he moved them through an arc of ninety degrees, out of column and into line. In that formation the best-aimed shell could hit only two men rather than many. The 8th advanced obliquely to its right front to the shelter of the edge of the woods, halting where Little Deep Run marked the boundary of the field.[9]

As Henry Kelly held his regiment on the verge of the woods, he met a few of the Virginians who had failed in the first attempt to capture the Coaling. Soon Colonel Leroy A. Stafford and the 9th Louisiana came up behind the 8th, having imitated Kelly's route and formations. Kelly placed Stafford in charge of the two regiments and went looking for Stonewall Jackson to request orders. Kelly soon came across the brigade's third unit, Wheat's rowdy battalion of Louisiana Tigers. Major Chatham Roberdeau Wheat had just seen Jackson, who had ordered that the Louisianians should advance. Kelly appended Rob Wheat's unit to the other two at the edge of the field and then headed into the woods toward the Coaling. Kelly, Stafford, and Wheat disappeared into the thickets with three fifths of Taylor's Brigade, leaving Taylor to his own devices with the tail of the column.[10]

Taylor colorfully reported his encounter with Stonewall Jackson as he reached the battlefield. Jackson of course never wrote anything about such episodes:

> Jackson was on the road, a little in advance of his line, where the fire was hottest, with reins on his horse's neck, seemingly in prayer. Attracted by my approach, he said, in his usual voice, "Delightful excitement." I replied that it was pleasant to learn he was enjoying himself, but thought he might have an indigestion of such fun if the six-gun battery was not silenced. He summoned a young officer from his staff, and pointed up the mountain.[11]

Jefferson Davis, perhaps on the basis of conversations with his brother-in-law Taylor, embellished Jackson's setting with a bit more danger and a bit more piety. "Shot and shell were hissing and bursting around him," the president declared in a postwar speech, "and there he sat motionless on his old campaigner, a horse as steady under fire as his master . . . and Jackson was wrapt in prayer. He had done all which human foresight could devise, and now was confiding himself, his compatriots and his cause, to the God of the righteous."[12]

Popular contemporary lore in the army insisted that Jackson and Taylor engaged in a stirring colloquy about capturing the Coaling. Captain Daniel A. Wilson of the 7th Louisiana, the regiment just behind Taylor and the 6th, reported in a contemporary account that attacking seemed "rash and even desperate." By Wilson's account, Jackson

> looked for a while thoughtfully on the scene, and then turning to Taylor, inquired, "Can you take that battery? It must be taken or the day be lost." Taylor replied, "We can," and pointing his sword to the battery, called out to his men, "Louisianians, can you take that battery?" With one universal shout that made the mountains to echo, they declared they could; whereupon, he gave the order.

Colonel T. T. Munford embellished the exchange to "Yes sir, I think I can, and I will try and turn their flank. . . . Or a thousand true hearts will be cold on the ground."[13]

Some subordinate officers insisted that Dick Taylor did not even encounter Jackson in person. Taylor's official report, written two days later and addressed to Jackson himself, declares that the brigadier "received orders from" the commanding general. That implies that the two men met, although the receipt of orders might have been from a staff officer. However he got them, Taylor's report described the orders as directing him "to leave one regiment near the position then occupied by [Jackson], and with the main body to make a detour to the right for the purpose of checking a formidable battery planted in that locality."[14]

Taylor's postwar memoir is probably only slightly embellished in describing his personal encounter with a prayerful but exuberant commanding general. On the other hand, a more substantial demonstration of the memoir's impeachable nature is Taylor's account of his astonishment when he subsequently learned that his last regiment had been pulled out of line by Jackson. As quoted above, Taylor's own contemporary report cited orders "to leave one regiment." The careful Hotchkiss concluded that Taylor's memoir contained "more fiction than fact" in describing Port Republic. "His subordinate officers have denounced its statements in no measured terms," Hotchkiss declared years later.[15]

Jed Hotchkiss and Taylor reached Jackson at about the same time. Hotchkiss's chief, Keith Boswell, wrote in his official report to Jackson that Hotchkiss guided Taylor's Brigade, "by your order, through the wood, so as to flank the enemy's battery." Jed's own description of his orders from Jackson were that he must "lead that command around through the forest, turn the Federal left and capture the battery on the coal hearth." Taylor was "just then coming up." Hotchkiss believed that Taylor never did reach Jackson's position, "because I turned back and led him across the field into the woods some little distance back from where Gen. Jackson was." Despite Hotchkiss's certainty, Taylor and Jackson probably did have a brief encounter. Perhaps it came after Hotchkiss had plunged into the dense thickets at the head of the 6th Louisiana.[16]

Whatever orders Taylor received from Jackson, and wherever Hotchkiss was at the time, the majority of the Louisiana brigade had already begun to claw its way through the hillside thickets. The first sensation the men felt when they plunged into the tangle was relief at getting under cover for protection from enemy artillery fire. Relief soon gave way to frustration as the soldiers grappled with an "extremely difficult dense growth of mountain laurel." A Confederate who followed the same route a short while later declared that "in many places the men had to crawl on their hands and knees." One Louisianian described the ground cover as an "impenetrable wood."[17]

Colonel Kelly felt bewildered by the task facing him. Jackson was in the process of detailing the capable Hotchkiss to direct Taylor's march, but Kelly's larger advance group had no guide at all. The colonel and his subordinates were "altogether ignorant of the local topography." The best he could do was guide on the steady roar emanating from the Coaling. Henry Kelly insisted that he managed to move through the underbrush not in column but in line, "up the face of the hills in front, covered with a growth of forest trees and thickets of mountain laurel." Upon reaching an intermediate crest, Kelly halted for the purpose of "rectifying the alignment as well as practicable on such ground" and to throw forward two companies on skirmish duty.[18]

Federals atop the Coaling and along Tyler's line had seen the fresh Confederates deflecting into the woods to threaten them. To counter that threat, now invisible but clearly in mind, a portion of the Northern artillery cluster unleashed "a tornado of shot and shell in the supposed direction of the advancing column, but the random and ineffective fire did not impede their progress," according to a Louisianian. The shelling, even though randomly aimed, doubtless spurred Kelly's men forward. "It is a run . . . with guns at a trail—a dash up the mountain side—a rush through the undergrowth," an eyewitness declared.[19]

Dodging enemy shells and running with guns at a trail combined with the tangled nature of the ground to keep Kelly's ranks in constant disarray. To deal with that, "frequent halts were made to maintain a compact front and correct the alignment." The colonel's insistence on proper arrangement of his line was not just slavish devotion to the linear tactics of the era. "Though difficult to do so over such ground," Kelly explained, "the advance was made in line of battle, for the reason that it was to be expected that a Federal infantry force would be found in the woods to the left of their batteries as their support, and it could not be known at what point we might come upon them."[20]

Although Kelly's tortuous advance covered only slightly less than one mile, it took a long time. He knew it was nearing its target when indications of the Federal infantry's nearness began to appear. "The musical whistle of the minie bullet, those deadly messengers, as they now and then coursed on their way through the thick foliage overhead," told the Louisianians that enemy soldiers were not far ahead. Henry Kelly and the thousand or so men with him awaited specific orders or further developments. As stragglers closed toward the front, Kelly spotted Dick Taylor approaching from the right rear.[21]

General Taylor and the 6th Louisiana had marched to the vicinity of the Coaling by a longer but somewhat easier route. Jed Hotchkiss made the difference. Hotchkiss, as was his charge, knew the terrain well enough to accomplish his guide duties successfully. He led the 6th directly south across the field to the right of the main road and put it on a tiny woods road. Taylor called it "a path running parallel with the river." Secondary feeder paths made by wood-cutting expeditions from the Coaling also twisted through the tangled forest.[22]

The main path swerved away from the intended line of advance short of the ravine in front of the Coaling. There Hotchkiss plunged into the rough woods to his right front, "bearing well to the right, to be sure of completely turning the Federal left." Away from the path, which had allowed for rapid movement in column, the 6th Louisiana (probably on a suggestion from Hotchkiss rather than orders from Taylor) spread out into line of battle, with skirmishers in front, and continued the advance more cautiously. Despite the broad front that both Kelly and Taylor used while groping through the thickets, they managed to miss the 2nd Virginia waiting impotently in the woods. Colonel Allen of the 2nd reported that Taylor "passed around my right"; but Kelly's larger detachment more than likely had thrashed its way through the laurel to Allen's left. The Louisiana troops apparently straddled Allen without the Virginians knowing it. The episode demonstrates vividly the inevitable confusion of battle, compounded here by rough ground and dense vegetation.[23]

Taylor's approach from Kelly's right avoided the scattered rounds that bothered the latter's men as they neared the ravine. The general spotted Federal soldiers across the ravine, but on his line of march, "our approach, masked by timber, was unexpected." Dabney insisted in his account of the battle that Taylor—meaning the Louisiana detachments under both Taylor and Kelly—came into the Coaling area in confusion. "By a slight mistake of their direction in these pathless coverts," Dabney wrote, "they approached the left front, rather than the flank of the dangerous battery." The Louisiana troops in fact faced the Coaling head on, with the 6th Louisiana out on the flank. Their final movement to action came not as the result of a mistake, slight or otherwise, but rather at the behest of General Winder. The Virginian had sent an aide to beg for a diversion to relieve the unbearable pressure he faced on the river plain.[24]

Kelly's laborious advance and Taylor's trek through the woods to catch up had taken time to execute. The story of the dramatic attack the Louisianians made on the Coaling as the climax of their exertions must be delayed long enough to examine what had been happening behind them and to their left. On the open fields below the Coaling stretching to the river, Winder's men, with help from the last regiment in Taylor's column, had made a brave but futile attack.

General Charles S.
Winder faced the
stern responsibility of
deciding what to
do with his heavily
outnumbered
force. He bravely
decided to attack
with the limited
means at his disposal.

CHAPTER 19

WINDER'S DARING

ATTACK

W hen Stonewall Jackson bade Dick Taylor fare-
well, he knew that his best hope for winning
the battle rode with the troops disappearing
into the hillside woods. The poise with which Jackson resisted the
urge to splice his bleeding line with the Louisiana troops did not
blind the general to Winder's desperate need for help. Accordingly,
he ordered Taylor to detach his last regiment for that purpose. Taylor
had forgotten those orders after the war and professed astonishment
to have found one regiment missing. On June 11, 1862, however, he
reported the detachment as a planned arrangement with Jackson.[1]

Colonel Harry T. Hays and his 7th Louisiana drew the emergency
assignment as a plug in Winder's line. The colonel was one of a
strong cadre of leaders in the brigade. Five men rose from the ranks

of the brigade's four regiments to the rank of general. Neither the most famous man in the brigade, Major Rob Wheat, nor the author of the best book on Port Republic, Colonel Henry Kelly, was among the five. Upon his promotion six weeks after Port Republic, Harry Hays would prove to be a solid brigadier, leading Taylor's old command for nearly three years. Hays was well fitted for the role he faced on the morning of June 9 as he and the 7th headed into deadly combat. He later described what happened to General Taylor: "Old Jack told us to stop the rush—we stopped it!"[2]

Winder quickly slid the 7th Louisiana into the middle of his reeling line. That left the 5th Virginia on the far left near the river, with the 7th Louisiana on its right and the 27th Virginia on the right of the 7th.[3]

Confederate artillery filtered to the front as Taylor approached and began his swing into the thickets. Captain Edmund F. Bowyer's Virginia battery appeared on a table of organization as part of Taylor's Brigade; a Louisiana officer reported that it "nobly participated in the fight," but nothing more is known of its role. Captain John J. Rivera's Louisiana battery also had been with Taylor throughout the Valley campaign. Its six-pounder smoothbores, however, were of no use in the long-range duel with the Coaling.[4]

R. P. Chew's horse artillery also reached the front close behind Taylor's men. It had stocked up with 150 rounds of ammunition per gun while encamped overnight above Port Republic. By the time the battery took to the road, artillery fire already echoed from the surrounding peaks. Chew somehow managed to push his unit to the front ahead of many others, probably because artillery waded South River and therefore avoided the bridge bottleneck. One of Chew's men described the "roar of battle" that "grew fiercer and louder" as they neared the front, "the musketry being fearfully terrific." A stream of wounded passed the guns, "limping, bleeding and groaning. Some of them greeted us to the field with the unpleasing and discouraging expression of 'Hurry up; they are cutting us all to pieces.' "[5]

Captain Chew's horse artillerists faced a disheartening scene, one of them wrote, when they passed a farmhouse "converted into an operating field hospital; dissecting room would be a more appropriate name, for as we passed the house I saw a subject on the kitchen table, on whom the surgeons were practicing their skillful severing operations. They tossed a man's foot out of the window just as we passed." As Chew's Battery headed warily forward, a staff officer galloped out of the billowing gunsmoke and asked the captain whether he had plenty of ammunition. When Chew responded that he did, the officer ordered: "Hurry to the front, captain." Chew continued at a double quick, unlimbered the guns under fire, and went into action.[6]

The last unit Winder stitched into his makeshift line at this crucial point was the 48th Virginia, which had moved just behind Taylor from near Cross Keys. Its Lieutenant Colonel Thomas S. Garnett was operating independently; the rest of the 48th's brigade was far away with the rear guard. Garnett's terse official report declares simply: "I was ordered to take position with General Winder's brigade, and acted in conjunction with his and the Louisiana brigade." Because of the inadequate report, historians have assumed that the 48th accomplished nothing.[7]

A letter from Garnett to his father reveals more about the regiment's participation: "As we hurried on to take our assigned position we passed the dead and the dying amid the whiz of bullets, the bursting of shells and all the melee of battle which to be appreciated must be witnessed." Garnett estimated that he spent five hours amidst "the tide of battle." That duration is much exaggerated, but demonstrates that the 48th arrived well before the end of the fight, as its marching position immediately behind Taylor suggests. The colonel wrote: "the tide of battle, with varying success, swept the verdant fields. . . . I was greatly exposed but God be praised, escaped without injury."[8] The 48th certainly played a part, but further details are wanting. Since the regiment suffered only moderate casualties, it probably served as a reserve line and rally point for Winder.

Once Winder had aligned the support within his reach, he faced the stern responsibility of deciding what to do with it. His regiments constituted a force only half as large as that facing him along the Lewiston lane. The number of artillery pieces available approximately matched those of the enemy, but their weight and range were far smaller and the dominant Coaling multiplied the effect of every Northern round. Winder might have been able to resist a Federal attack by remaining passive, especially if he had rounded up the missing 2nd and 4th Virginia from where they huddled after failing to flank the Coaling. In any event, he needed to cover Taylor's crucial march toward the Coaling. To do that, he bravely decided to attack with the limited means at his disposal.

Winder entrusted the attack to Colonel Harry Hays, adding Winder's two regiments to his command. Hays was "to move forward, drive the enemy from his position, and carry his battery at the point of the bayonet," Winder reported matter-of-factly. The general remained behind to push artillery forward and seek further help. No three regiments could have accomplished such a goal on that ground, against the Federal force assembled there, and Winder must have known it. He was gambling desperately on Taylor's prompt success around the Coaling.[9]

The order to attack came from Winder, not Jackson, who said that Winder, "seeing no mode of silencing the Federal battery or escaping its destructive missiles but by a rapid charge and capture of it, advanced with great boldness." The army commander evidently was spurring reinforcements forward at the time, and away from the tactical command zone. At some point during the morning, staff officers W. L. Jackson and Abner Smead began "quarreling in the midst of the fighting." Their disagreement may have been over interfering with Winder's attack in their roles as extension of General Jackson's authority. Enlisted men in the ranks faced no uncertainty about their prospects as they gazed across the fields. Private George M. Mooney of the 5th Virginia spoke for most when he wrote simply: "I was badly scared."[10]

As the advance under Hays developed, it became an en echelon movement—with the regiments offset from one another like stair steps. The 5th Virginia on the left advanced first. To its right the 7th Louisiana moved a bit behind the front of the 5th. The 27th Virginia on the far right advanced last. Attacks made en echelon by design sometimes suited a general's purposes. (The best-known example was Lee's plan to attack in that fashion along the Emmitsburg Road near Gettysburg on July 2, 1863.) Winder and Hays did not intend such a maneuver at Port Republic; the battle just developed that way.

The attackers left their cover near the Baugher orchard and moved forward "in gallant style with a cheer," Winder reported. The cheer was soon stifled by enemy fire that smothered the Confederate line with lead and iron. Colonel Funk of the 5th Virginia had thrown skirmishers fifty yards to his front by the time the 7th Louisiana came up on his right. The advance of the 5th's 450 men took them out of the orchard into a wheat field east of Baugher's barn. The regiment soon came to the mouth of Little Deep Run. High water in the South Fork had backed up to form a sizable estuary. Undaunted, Funk and

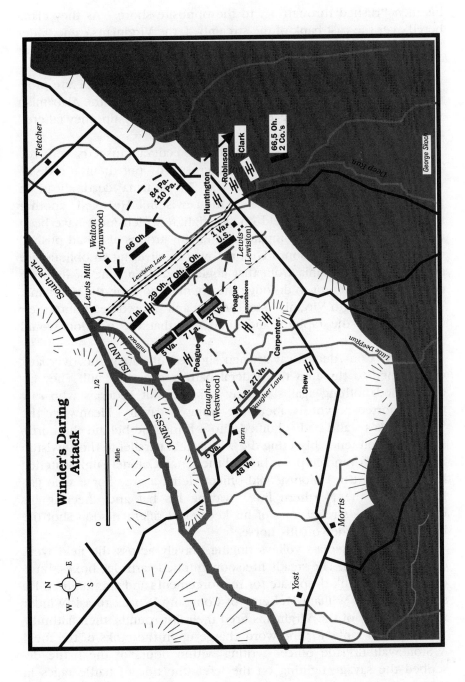

Winder's Daring Attack

N
W — E
S

0   Mile   1/2

South Fork

Fletcher

Lewis Mill

84 Pa.
110 Pa.

Walton
(Lynnwood)

66 Oh.

Lewiston Lane

7 In.   29 Oh. 7 Oh. 5 Oh.

ISLAND

millrace

JONES'S

5 Va.   7 La.
Poague

27 Va.
Poague

Huntington

Robinson

Clark

66,5 Oh.
2 Co.'s

1 Va.
U.S.

Lewis
(Lewiston)

Poague
smoothbores

Carpenter.

Baugher
(Westwood)

barn

5 Va.

7 La. 27 Va.
Baugher Lane

48 Va.

Chew

Morris

Yost

Deep Run

Little Deep Run

George Skoc.

his men "rushed through . . . to the opposite shore." As they clambered over the east bank of the streambed, the Virginians came under "a terrific fire" from the enemy to their front. An Alabama soldier with the rear guard far across the river probably saw the 5th's advance as he looked toward the battlefield to gauge Confederate progress. "We saw one line of our men charge the enemy," the Alabamian wrote, "but [they] were received with such a galling fire they faltered and lay down on the grass."[11]

Colonel Funk's soldiers countered the Federal musketry with volleys of their own, but "a murderous cross-fire" put them at a disadvantage. The colonel could see the 7th Indiana dead ahead in positions around the buildings near the Lewis Mill. He spied "another regiment . . . in a wheat field on our right," which must have been the 29th Ohio. Several companies of enemy troops also had pushed down the edge of the South Fork and were delivering an oblique fire against the 5th Virginia from that angle. Funk sent one of his own companies to attempt to dislodge the enemy troops on the riverbank. The rest of the 5th Virginia "stood firmly and poured death into their ranks with all the rapidity and good will that the position would admit."[12]

A few Confederate cavalrymen showed up along the riverbank and seemed to threaten the Federal battery near the mill. They accomplished nothing against enemy infantry, but Federals who saw them reported nervously about the ominous cavalry. Meanwhile the 5th Virginia's stand had solidified into a firing line behind the north-south wooden fence bisecting the wheat field parallel to the Lewiston lane. From his vantage point behind the fence Colonel Funk watched his counterpart, a Unionist field officer riding a gray horse who galloped along the Northern line "waving his hat and cheering his men." To Funk's relief, one of his keen-eyed riflemen soon shot the brave enemy leader off his horse.[13]

The 5th Virginia's volleys ringing bravely across the field were doing some good. The steady fire soon emptied cartridge boxes, however, and left Funk desperate for reinforcements and ammunition. He sent Lieutenant William McKemy of Company D back to ask Winder for help. Many of the Virginians fired their last rounds, then faithfully "remained in ranks for the word charge upon the ranks of the foe." A Stonewall Brigade officer writing within hours of the battle described the savage fighting on the left: "the tide of battle rages in the bottom next the river, for there the fighting is desperate. Nothing is now heard save the roar of artillery and the rattle of musketry."[14]

John Funk had ample reason to be proud of his men, who "behaved more gallantly than I ever witnessed them before," he wrote. They "held their position in face of superior numbers under the murderous fire." Major Hazael J. Williams, a thirty-two-year-old farmer from Augusta County who would survive the war by nearly a half century, earned Funk's special praise for behaving "honorably, cheering and encouraging the men by example to the work which was so well executed." The colonel also singled out for mention Lieutenant Arthur J. Arnold, "a noble young officer" mortally wounded at the head of his company. The dead lieutenant was twenty-three years old and had been a schoolteacher. Color Sergeant Robert H. Fisher "bravely bore the colors" of the 5th "amid the showers of shell and bullets" until he fell wounded. Corporal Walter Monteiro picked up the precious fallen flag and carried it "manfully through the engagement."[15]

Private George Mooney fought with the 5th behind the fence. He had been in the regiment since before Kernstown, but had been armed for only the last two weeks; before that he had waited to inherit a musket from a wounded comrade or get a captured enemy weapon. As he headed for his first experience with combat, Mooney tried to encourage a friend who was burdened with a certain premonition of death. This worried comrade had been to the rough California goldfields, so he was hardly a shrinking violet. The unshakable conviction that he would die prompted the former '49er to entrust his gold watch and purse to Lieutenant Thomas Killeen. The man moved resolutely forward in the charge and was instantly killed, leaving Killeen with the painful chore of writing to his widow. The former prospector had plenty of company on the regiment's casualty return: the 5th Virginia lost more than one fourth of its strength.[16]

The 7th Louisiana advanced on the right of the 5th Virginia not long after Funk moved forward. Colonel Hays and his men "moved forward steadily in line from the Baugher road over the open field" for several hundred yards to the mid-field fence. Some crossed it temporarily. Every step of the way the 7th's ranks were torn by "a fierce fusillade" from the Federal infantry. Even more daunting was the artillery fire from both the Coaling and the guns spread along the Lewiston lane. Captain Daniel Wilson described the fire from the

Coaling: "From this battery was belched forth one incessant storm of . . . canister and shell, literally covering the Valley, so that the work of attack on our part seemed almost hopeless." The Louisianians pressed forward still. As the range shortened, the Coaling loomed even more ominously. "From its mouth now, with renewed violence, poured streams of shell and shot, mowing down our men like grass. The earth seemed covered with the dead and wounded."[17]

While the 5th Virginia breasted the worst infantry fire, being closest to the river and the Federals lurking on its banks, the 7th Louisiana was closer to the deadly Coaling. An onlooker heard the "wild cheers" of the 7th Louisiana rising "above the sullen boom of cannon." A Virginian marveled at the prowess of the Louisianians when he heard the same battle cry. "A shout comes up from the centre," he wrote. " 'Tis the 7th Louisiana charging one of the enemy's batteries. They take it, but are soon driven back by three regiments and canister from three other pieces." The admiring Virginian exaggerated the 7th's success, but accurately reflected the army's appreciation of the bravery of the Louisianians.[18]

The cost to the 7th Louisiana was predictably high. It carried fewer than 400 men into action (Captain Wilson said that only 308 "effective men" participated) and lost nearly one half of them in the battle. The regiment's leaders went down during the advance, reducing the 7th's efficiency and cohesion. "In the very vortex of this storm of lead and iron—in the centre of the open field[—] . . . Hays . . . was borne dangerously wounded from the field; and here, too, fell mortally hurt its lieutenant-colonel, the *preux-chevalier*, De-Choiseul." A bullet hit Colonel Hays near the shoulder, leaving him "badly wounded" and unable to continue in command. Hays had recovered enough to return to duty, with a promotion to brigadier general, by July 26.[19]

The forty-three-year-old Lieutenant Colonel Charles DeChoiseul came from an aristocratic French family that had fled Europe in 1794 during the Terror. He had experienced considerable difficulty in commanding the wildly rebellious men in the ranks of the 7th Louisiana— men valorous in combat, but uncontrollable when away from the battlefront. A Virginia woman who met DeChoiseul in Winchester during the Valley campaign called him "particularly pleasant," a trait ill-suited for dealing with his rowdy troops. As the lieutenant colonel strode along his line near the fence, "again and again endeavoring to hold his place on the field," a bullet tore through his chest and hit both lungs. By the time friendly hands bore DeChoiseul to the rear, he had become "almost insensible." He survived for ten days but died on June 19.[20]

While the 5th Virginia fought to the fence and stood behind it, and the 7th Louisiana did the same a short while later, Colonel A. J. Grigsby's 27th Virginia aimed for the same goal from a position on Winder's right. The 27th had been closer to the road than the 5th since the battle had opened, and generally farther to the rear. Under Winder's orders, the 27th "promptly" closed in on the right of the 7th Louisiana as soon as the latter regiment reached the front. Then the 27th jumped off in the attack. At once shells from the Coaling and canister from closer guns swept the regiment's front, "by which my ranks were considerably thinned," Grigsby reported sorrowfully.[21]

When the 27th reached the fence to the right of the 7th Louisiana, it kept going "some distance farther." The enemy infantry pressure focused on the Confederates on Winder's left did not affect Grigsby. General Winder scribbled in his diary that night: "had a terrible fight[;] the left repulsed and enemy in strong force." The general's specific mention of special trouble on his left, as opposed to all along his front, explains why the 27th was able to advance as far as it did.[22]

Grigsby and his infantrymen could not accomplish much in their lunge beyond the fence. The 27th had fewer companies than most regiments and brought only 150 men to battle on June 9, making it the smallest regiment in Jackson's force. A few of the 27th's soldiers filtered into the outbuildings of Lewiston, where they would play a role later in the battle. Grigsby soon ordered the rest "to drop back on a line with" the 7th Louisiana at the fence. There they settled down for an exchange of musketry that kept them "under a perfect shower of balls" for what seemed to the colonel like "near an hour," but must have been a far shorter period. Grigsby praised his subordinates lavishly "for the gallant manner in which they bore themselves throughout the entire action, braving every danger coolly and deliberately" and "obeying all orders cheerfully." The colonel clearly behaved with similar distinction; he was so exposed to fire that his horse was shot twice and he had to abandon it.[23]

Much of the lead hurtling into the ranks of the 27th Virginia was fired by men who had been friends and neighbors a few months before. In one of those episodes that made the Civil War literally strife between brothers, the 27th was facing the 1st Virginia (Union), which was positioned near the southern end of Lewiston lane. Five of the Unionist regiment's ten companies were from the vicinity of Wheeling, Virginia. So too was Company G of the Confederate 27th Virginia. The two regiments had faced one another at the Battle of Kernstown near the beginning of Jackson's Valley Campaign. In that battle a young Confederate in the 27th, with two brothers in the Yankee 1st (and two more brothers in other Federal units), had been mortally wounded.[24]

Among the casualties was Major Daniel McElleran Shriver of the 27th Virginia. The twenty-six-year-old son of a Wheeling businessman fell with bullets in both shoulders. The wounds, together with election to the Virginia Senate, prompted Shriver to resign in 1863. They may eventually have killed him, for Shriver died in 1865 at the age of twenty-nine. During its advance and the fight at the fence the 27th Virginia lost two lieutenants killed and total casualties of almost precisely one third of its strength.[25]

While the three regiments advanced boldly toward the Yankees, then stood behind the mid-field fence, Winder did his best to push artillery up in support. Two guns of Carpenter's Battery followed rapidly behind the 27th Virginia and unlimbered behind "a small ridge" about thirty yards in rear of the regiment. The southern half of Lewiston's field includes a number of terrain fingers that hide the western half from the eastern half. Those gentle swells in the ground made the lot of the 27th Virginia easier; their absence on the northern portion of the field contributed to the troubles of the 5th Virginia.

William Humphreys, who fought with Carpenter, described the advance in a fashion that makes clear its tiered, en echelon, nature: "a daring charge on the left was made by a fragment of the Stonewall [Brigade] upon a Yankee Battery, [then] the centre closed in, followed rapidly by our section." Humphreys and his mates unlimbered their two pieces under "a terrible fire of small arms" and opened fire with shell, concentrating on the Federal artillery. Because of the width of the Confederate line, Captain Carpenter reported, his guns on the far right combined with pieces in the direction of the river to "get a cross-fire upon the enemy." The converging fire could not, however, seriously shake the Federal line. Carpenter's pieces helped to solidify that end of the line, of course, but "owing to overwhelming numbers against us," Humphreys concluded, the Confederate infantry could not make headway.[26]

Winder also welcomed the arrival of two guns from Raine's Virginia Battery. One of them had no cannoneers present, but Winder gratefully spliced the manned piece into his line. The largest Southern artillery complement on the plain remained, as it had been from the start, Poague's Rockbridge Artillery. Winder sent Captain Poague in person with one of his rifles to the right front "within short range of the enemy's batteries." In that dangerous location (near the 27th Virginia and Carpenter's two guns), Poague kept up "a rapid fire . . . partly on their batteries and partly on their infantry, with canister." Back on the left the action had come to such close quarters that Winder ordered up the four short-range pieces of the Rockbridge Artillery. They did not fight long. By the time Poague returned to the left, the four pieces had fallen back whence they had come.[27]

Randolph Fairfax, who served with Poague's guns on the left, described the fighting there as "a hard struggle" against "almost the whole force of the enemy." The Confederate artillery on the right, however, suffered far more difficult circumstances. Because of the Coaling looming above the Confederate right at point-blank range, the Southern right was artillery hell while the left was infantry hell.[28]

Ned Moore's piece accomplished its mission under intense fire by diverting the Coaling's attention from Confederate infantry. The cannon had a good new gunner, William Graham Montgomery. "He could not be hurried, and every time the smoke puffed from our gun their cannoneers slid right and left from the coal-hearth, then returning to their guns loaded and gave us a volley." Montgomery and others like him helped Winder to hold on while waiting anxiously for signs of Taylor's attack on the Coaling itself. The enlisted men bearing the brunt of the ordeal fretted over the delay. Moore recalled, "As usual in such cases, our flanking party was longer . . . than expected."[29]

Chew's Battery contributed its shells against the Coaling from farther to the rear. Despite being a greater distance from the enemy guns, George Neese also recalled the Coaling with awe. "The fire of that battery was terrible for a while," he wrote; it had "perfect command of the field we were in." Chew proceeded "with the utmost endeavor to give the enemy the best work we had in the shop. . . . The air trembled with a continual roll of musketry and the thunder of the artillery shook the ground."[30]

The continuous musketry and thunderous artillery were more than Winder's small force could handle. Jackson's official report used this language to describe the result: "Winder . . . advanced with great boldness for some distance, but encountered such a heavy fire of artillery and small-arms as greatly to disorganize his command." McHenry Howard of Winder's staff said simply: "a most destructive fire of musketry as well as artillery . . . checked our inadequate force."[31]

Colonel Kelly, then floundering through the thickets, described the situation on the plain based on what he later learned from the 7th Louisiana. "There, in the narrow quadrangle of three-quarters of a mile square, between the hills and the river and the Mill Road and the Baugher road," Kelly wrote, "the battle was fought with a courage and pertinacity on both sides not surpassed on any field of the war, and with the most disastrous results to the Confederate arms in that quarter."[32]

Their momentum exhausted, the three regiments held on at the fence as long as they could. Jefferson Davis had said of Taylor's troops, "This brigade would, if ordered, have formed line to stop a herd of elephants." The 7th Louisiana lived up to the high reputation of its parent brigade as it held tenaciously to the fence. Winder found the three regiments there after he had exhausted all of his options for placing artillery. Despite the "heavy fire" they faced, the men in the Confederate line "stood it boldly for some time and fought gallantly—many until all their cartridges were gone," Winder reported.[33]

Henry Kelly's subsequent tribute to his brigade mates in the 7th also mentioned dwindling ammunition supplies: "The advanced ground . . . was held with unyielding tenacity until many of the men had fired their last cartridge; when at last, shattered and torn by direct and cross-fires of shot, shell, canister, and musketry, the gray line gave way and fell back." Some infantry officers at the fence thought they held there for an hour. Joe Carpenter reported that the Southern withdrawal came "very soon." The stand cannot have lasted more than thirty minutes, if that long.[34]

Winder's regiments did not leave unmolested. Federals who watched the attack with some trepidation, then resisted it stoutly, sensed the dwindling fire from their front and seized the opportunity to counterattack. The 7th Indiana on the Unionist right fought first and longest against Winder's attack. One of them estimated that the contest lasted for half an hour, "our ranks being thinned by every fire from the enemy." Fortunately for the 5th Virginia, the Hoosiers' primary opposition, the Federals also had smoothbore muskets. The historian of the 7th admitted that his unit was hampered by the inadequate armament. So was the 5th Virginia. As a result, the ratio of men wounded to killed in the 7th Indiana was fifteen to one—three times higher than usual. The big, slow-moving, short-ranged smoothbore balls inflicted many wounds "of an insignificant character," an Indiana soldier wrote, "fully two-thirds of them shot in the extremities—arms or legs." A correspondent a few days later described the 7th's injuries as "mostly flesh wounds in the arms and legs."[35]

Despite the low mortality in the 7th relative to total losses, casualties thinned the regiment's ranks drastically. John Hadley heard a ball strike his friend Alvah Montgomery, who turned and said, "Here goes." Montgomery then "laid gently down—rested his head on his left arm—laid his gun by his right side & without speaking a word or moving a limb he shut his eyes & died." Captain Solomon Waterman was another fatal casualty. In a letter home Hadley described the field in front of Lewiston lane as "the place to try mens soulds. We were in an open field without a stump or even a bush to shelter us. . . . We stood & fired 80 rounds." Billy Davis recalled that Confederate fire forced the Hoosiers to fall back "a short distance to an open corn field near the bank of the river."[36]

Colonel James Gavin performed gallantly in holding the 7th Indiana to its dangerous duty. A witness reported that the colonel "rode coolly up and down the lines, giving the word of command, and cheering up the men, who [were] inspired by the gallant daring of their leader." After five bullets hit Gavin's horse he strode about on foot animating the defense. Confederate fire also killed Major Alexander B. Patterson's horse and Colonel Carroll's when the latter officer rode to the right to superintend the defense there. Surgeon J. L. Worden of the 7th won praise for his bravery and diligence in retrieving and treating the regiment's wounded.[37]

The most distinguished Federal leader near the riverbank was the officer on a gray horse cited by Colonel Funk of the 5th Virginia. The brave fellow rode along the Union line "waving his hat and cheering the men," Funk reported, until a Southern soldier shot him off his mount. The conspicuous Northerner may have been Gavin, who escaped wounds but whose horse went down. A more likely candidate was Captain Daniel J. Keily, the young Irishman newly arrived in the country and attached to Shields's staff. The captain had distinguished himself on the 8th, and on the morning of the 9th was shot through the face and his horse fatally wounded as he galloped across the front.[38]

Inspired by such examples (and even more reassured by the ample support on their left), the men of the 7th Indiana easily resisted Funk's small force. By the time the episode ended, however, nearly 150 of the Indianans had been hit. John Hadley had never before been near such a bloodbath and it sickened him, he told his sweetheart in a letter. Battle required a soldier to "learn to look upon a man floundering in his blood, with no more feelings of remorse than if he were a beheaded dog & hear the groans of suffering humanity with as much indifference as if it were the groans of a dying hyena," Hadley wrote. In mortal combat "a man may & will become so infuriated by the din & dangers of a bloody fight" that his heart will be "turned to stone & his evry de sire [be] for blood."[39]

The 29th Ohio, just to the left of the 7th Indiana, shared in the repulse of the 5th Virginia, as well as facing some of the fire from the 7th Louisiana. Hoosier Sam List noted the strong support farther down Lewiston lane. "The contest on our left was fierce," List wrote in his diary, and "brave men were falling around us." The 29th's regimental historian described dramatically how his unit repulsed the Confederate onslaught. "When in close range the rebels charged," he wrote. "Reserving our fire until they were almost upon us, the order was given, and with a yell the entire line poured its leaden hail into the gray clad columns . . . producing fearful slaughter."[40]

Writing that night, Ohioan N. L. Parmeter was far less boastful than the 29th's postwar historian. The Ohio diarist admitted that Southern artillery annoyed his unit tremendously and that the 29th was "in easy range of the enemy musketry." Parmeter's regiment probably was the one complimented from afar by a Confederate staff officer who wrote: "For the only time in my life I saw a regiment, from Ohio I believe, change front to rear on first company, under fire, and with admirable precision." The Southerner "knew then, that it would be no easy matter to defeat an army of such troops"—and such proved to be the case, as Jackson was finding out.[41]

Next south in line from the 29th Ohio, the 7th Ohio faced the right of the 7th Louisiana and the left of the 27th Virginia. Confederate pressure on the far Federal right prompted the 7th Ohio to swing its front in that direction. Then the Confederate center arrived a bit later, and the 7th Ohio had its hands full looking directly across the wheat field to its front. When the Southerners settled in behind the fence, they kept up "a severe fire" that lasted about a half hour, one Ohioan estimated. An artillery round exploding above Company C killed R. J. Kingsburg and mangled the thigh of a comrade. Two other men of the company went down mortally wounded. The company's historian insisted that "no less than twenty pieces of artillery, standing in the form of a semicircle," focused on the 7th Ohio's part of the line. In fact about one third that many were shooting at the entire Federal position. Regardless of where the incoming fire was generated, the 7th Ohio took plenty. "The hissing of bullets and shrieking of shells were frightful," Theodore Wilder wrote.[42]

A few Confederates shooting at the 7th Ohio carried rifles rather than smoothbore muskets. William Rogers of Company G, a twenty-three-year-old private, went down when a conoidal rifle bullet hit him one inch above his right eye. The bullet knocked out Rogers "for a few moments," but he regained consciousness and walked to the rear under his own power. Although the bullet had penetrated into his skull, the wound looked healthy when Rogers reached a Washington hospital six days after the battle. On June 17 the wounded man complained of worsening pain, so a surgeon enlarged the wound and pulled bone splinters from it with forceps; he could not locate the bullet. Bill Rogers felt better on June 18, but by the 20th the wound was festering and suppurating. He never became delirious and spoke intelligibly until the evening of June 28, when Rogers slipped beyond the reach of the surgeons. An autopsy located the bullet in his brain, where a cyst had formed around it.[43]

The 5th Ohio stood opposite the 27th Virginia, just to the Federal left of the 7th Ohio. Its position was a bit behind the Lewiston lane, at least at the outset. Furthermore, Confederate pressure on that end of the line was not nearly as great as on the Federal right, where the 7th Indiana and 29th Ohio fought long and hard. As a result, Tyler's casualties were progressively lighter for each regiment along his line, from highest in the 7th Indiana to lowest in the 5th Ohio and 1st Virginia (Union). Even so, the 5th Ohio lost at least eleven men dead, including regimental adjutant Charles Smith and Lieutenant Robert Graham. Five dozen more were wounded.[44]

Tyler's last front-line regiment along Lewiston lane was the 1st Virginia (Union), which had remained in the woods behind the Coaling until after Winder's attack began. Colonel Carroll, who was coordinating the defense along the lane, sent an officer to Tyler asking for help to meet the threat that Winder posed. Tyler sent the Virginia

Unionists. They moved into the field behind the lane for some distance before returning to the left and going into position right behind the Lewiston orchard, where they faced little pressure. The regiment's historian contented himself with touting the bravery of the 5th Ohio on its right, rather than recounting what little role his own unit played.[45]

Three other Northern regiments jockeyed across the plain during Winder's attack and repulse and played brief, indistinct parts in the fighting. The 66th Ohio had two companies above the Coaling on the shoulder of the Blue Ridge as skirmishers, while the rest of the regiment supported the guns from "directly in the rear." At some point during the fighting on the plain the main body of the 66th reached far enough north to support the 29th Ohio before being called back to the Federal left.[46]

The 84th and 110th Pennsylvania played even less effectual parts. Tyler also had those two units stacked up behind the Coaling "well up into the woods" at the outset. He responded to Winder's advance by ordering the 84th and 110th onto the plain to help block the Confederates. In Tyler's words, however, "before they reached the position assigned them the enemy was in full retreat . . . and I at once ordered them across into the woods again." A contemporary Union map shows the two regiments barely out of the woods. Perhaps this employment of the Pennsylvania regiments as a deep reserve was intentional, because both had suffered very heavily at Jackson's hands at Kernstown in March. Whatever the intention, the result was that they contributed almost nothing at Port Republic. Between them, the two regiments lost two men killed.[47] Tyler's equivocal dispositions ensured that an important part of his force pivoted from left to right and back again just in time to miss helping in either place.

Winder's attack had stalled, but it did achieve one lasting tactical coup. As mentioned earlier, some hardy Confederate infantry, mostly from the 27th Virginia, wormed their way into the Lewiston outbuildings and clung stubbornly to a foothold there. Captain Huntington had observed from his Coaling aerie that the "numerous out-buildings" would form "a strong point of vantage if occupied by our opponents." When that happened, Huntington received orders to send a piece down to the yard to blast out the pesky Confederates, who had begun "seriously annoying our infantry." The Southern riflemen of course turned their attention to the artillery piece and "made it so hot for the gunners," Huntington wrote, that the commander of the piece "found it best to withdraw while he was still able to do so." "To shell good troops out of good cover," Huntington observed, "is about as futile a task as can be undertaken by artillery."[48]

The handful of Confederates fighting tenaciously from Lewiston's outbuildings could continue their minor role indefinitely. The rest of Winder's troops, however, had exhausted their momentum and had no alternative but to retreat. The Yankees, of course, were eager to help them on their way with volleys of musketry, and to pursue them across the wheat fields.

Major Joseph Hart Chenoweth, who had been a student under Jackson at V.M.I., strode behind the line toward its left flank, then turned right and moved up the front of the regiment. Sheets of fire swarmed around the major's unprotected head and eventually, inevitably, struck him down. "He fell without a groan with his sword still in his grasp pointed toward the enemy."

CHAPTER 20

WINDER'S ROUT

T he 5th Virginia, 7th Louisiana, and 27th Virginia clung to their advanced positions behind the midfield fence for a half hour before the line began to fall apart. The trickle of beaten men skulking rearward gradually became a stream, then the entire front collapsed. Winder's en echelon advance had thrown his left forward ahead of the right. The retirement that turned into a rout did not unfold in the same sequence, left to right, or even with enough order to describe the movements with precision. The Confederate center manned by the 7th Louisiana apparently broke first. The best way to unravel the confused story of Winder's disaster, however, is to follow the units in geographical order in the same sequence as they advanced.

John Funk's 5th Virginia Infantry had been so tightly locked in a deadly struggle with the 7th Indiana that neither regiment noticed much south of its front. A nettlesome fire came against the Virginians from the riverbank to their left rear. A millrace skirting the river's edge there and "a skirt of woods with undergrowth" between the two watercourses provided cover for adventuresome Yankees who crawled to a vantage point dangerous to Funk's men. The 5th Virginia learned of the danger only when, "suddenly, their line was enfiladed by a scathing fire opened upon them at short range by a body of infantry from behind the mill-race." An eyewitness wrote that "the tide of battle rages in the bottom next the river, for there the fighting is desperate." Funk learned that his men were low on, or out of, ammunition. The enfilading fire, the dwindling supply of cartridges, and the obviously superior Federal numbers convinced the colonel that his regiment was in danger. "In the mean time," he reported, "the center of our line [the 7th Louisiana] gave way, exposing my regiment . . . and I deemed it prudent to fall back." Funk declared that he retired only "when completely overpowered." A member of the 5th wrote that Funk fell back only on the second orders and did so walking backward to face the foe.[1]

The soldiers of the 5th Virginia who abandoned the mid-field fence had reason to be proud of themselves. Private James E. Beard told his diary, "our regiment fought on the river bank against great odds, [and] we had to give back at one time." Beard left behind two friends "killed dead on the ground." Another member of the 5th had just been refused a badly needed furlough, but "went cheerfully into the battle" anyway. A friend passed this "fine soldier . . . as we fell back from the charge . . . he was gripping his leg [which had been torn by a shell] & said George I will get a furlough now." Private Samuel F. Wagener of Company C, who raced rearward through the hellish wheat field on one of his company's worst days, would have been amazed to know that he would farm the battlefield for years after the war.[2]

John Funk managed to rally a sizable body of 5th Virginia survivors east of the Baugher place. At that uncertain moment, the 7th Louisiana, itself newly re-formed, "was scattered by a raking fire and rushed through my line scattering my men," Funk wrote disgustedly. The colonel reassembled his disorganized regiment behind the Baugher barn with help from Major H. J. Williams and Winder, who "asked them to go no farther." Colonel Funk was proud to be able to report that his men were "rallied by the *words* of their commanders."[3]

The 5th Virginia probably benefited from its position near the South Fork. As bothersome as the few Federals around the millrace were, the 5th Virginia faced no concentrated oblique fire from both front angles as had the 7th Louisiana, in the center of Winder's line. The Louisianians' left probably took a little fire from the 7th Indiana. It certainly suffered from both direct and oblique fire delivered by the 29th Ohio and 7th Ohio, and no doubt rounds from the far right front angle fired by the 5th Ohio and 1st Virginia (Union). The impression of a contemporary writer that the 7th was "driven back by three regiments" is readily understandable.[4]

The price exacted of the 7th Louisiana during its advance and retreat was "fearful," General Taylor wrote. His report asserted with sad pride that the "heavy loss" of "50 per cent. of the number carried into action" demonstrated the valor of the regiment. A contemporary list named 162 casualties in the 7th Louisiana, as many losses as those suffered by the other four fifths of the brigade combined. Taylor and Kelly would fight under the brightest spotlight on the Port Republic stage. In the process they won far more renown than the orphaned 7th Louisiana, isolated from its mates out on the bloody plain, but the cost they paid would be much less.[5]

One reason that the 7th Louisiana retired first from the mid-field fence was the loss of its command structure. With Colonel Hays badly wounded and Lieutenant Colonel DeChoiseul mortally hurt, the regiment's two top leaders were out of action. Captain Conrad Green and Lieutenant William C. Driver of Company E also were down wounded, as were Lieutenant Lawrence Pendergrast of Company A and Lieutenant James Brooks of Company H. Brooks's company took 32 men into the battle and lost 14 of them.[6]

Another officer of the 7th who fell at Port Republic was a Virginian. Both Captain Daniel A. Wilson of Company I and Lieutenant John C. Didlake of Company D were from Lynchburg. They had been in Louisiana in 1861 and joined the different companies independently. Early on June 9 they came across some cavalrymen from Lynchburg and joined them for a reunion breakfast before moving into battle. Wilson survived the day (and the war), but an enemy bullet killed Lieutenant Didlake in the wheat field.[7]

Private Frederick "Fritz" Reid, a twenty-two-year-old German native, could not escape when his mates in the 7th retired. His gun having been damaged by a bullet, he picked up a wounded friend's to fire. The other soldier had not seated his cartridge properly before being hit, so when Reid fired the weapon, the kick knocked him senseless. When he came to, a strapping Hoosier was standing over Fritz and made him a prisoner.[8]

The final 7th Louisiana casualty traceable to the battle did not reach his fate for nearly eighteen months. The soldier "at the battle of Port Republic . . . had deserted to the enemy," according to a Confederate officer. The deserter went north "and plied the vocation of a bounty jumper, enlisting in one regiment and then another, getting the bounty, spending it in debauchery and then enlisting again and repeating the operation." When Confederates captured the disloyal Louisianian, a court-martial sentenced him to be executed. A firing squad of a dozen men carried out the sentence during a lull in the Mine Run Campaign at the end of November 1863. The executioners shot the deserter at noon beside an open pit, threw dirt on top of him, and returned to the ranks. Snow soon covered the grave.[9]

Colonel Grigsby's 27th Virginia on Winder's right reached the mid-field fence last and were last to abandon it, although a handful of 27th soldiers ensconced in the Lewiston outbuildings stood fast. "My command, though small, boldly maintained its position until two regiments of the enemy [5th and 7th Ohio] came within 20 paces of their line," Grigsby reported with obvious pride. The colonel ordered his men back "amid a perfect shower of balls." Grigsby's horse was dead and his sword belt had been shot away, and Major Shriver was out of the fight by the time the 27th limped rearward. Fortunately for the regiment, the Federal thrust gained most momentum in the center, beyond its left. Some Confederates thought the Yankees who "pierced the centre of Jackson's feeble line" intended "to throw back the fugitives against the river . . . and thus to cut them off from retreat." Difficult though that made things for the 5th Virginia and 7th Louisiana, it lightened pressure on the 27th Virginia.[10]

Federals looking at the Confederate retreat from the other end of the field were convinced that they had been far outnumbered by Winder's handful of attackers. Sam List of the 7th Indiana wrote of standing firm for what seemed like hours against "a force vastly superior." Elliott Winscott of the 7th also cited the "vast superior numbers" of the Confederates. Another Hoosier insisted that his regiment

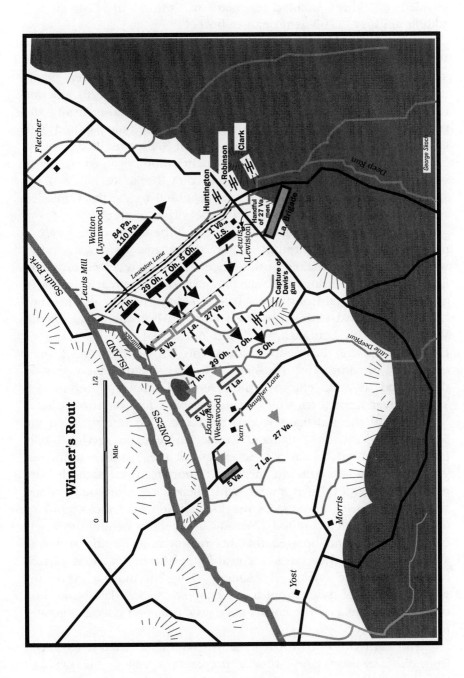

unaided put "three vaunted regiments of Cottondom . . . to flight," adding uneasily, "This is no empty boast."[11]

Some 7th Indiana soldiers had fired eighty rounds by the time Winder's desperate attack flickered out. The regiment started the action with 323 men in its ranks. Before the day was over, nearly one half of them had become casualties. Those still able to function responded readily when Colonel James Gavin "dashed in front" and yelled, "Load, charge bayonets, and at them." The men "started with an unearthly yell on the double quick," John Hadley recalled proudly. "It was too much for the guilty rebels. Their line began to stagger & when within about 40 yards of them they broke & ran with all speed." Hadley admitted that he was delighted to see the Confederates leave, "for . . . I dont like to try the virtue of steel."[12]

The mid-field fence that had halted and then protected Winder's men did the same two things to the 7th Indiana. Its rapid advance with fixed bayonets halted at the fence. The men received orders to lie down without firing while details hurried to the rear in quest of ammunition. Several Hoosiers managed to identify the regiments they had fought against with surprising accuracy. All of them had the 5th Virginia and 7th Louisiana right, but one listed in error the 10th Louisiana. Another erroneously added the 7th Georgia, and a third erred on a phantom 16th Louisiana. Billy Davis settled accurately on the 5th and 7th and went no further. He recalled having faced the 5th Virginia over Kernstown's famous stone wall a few months earlier.[13]

Some of the Indianans lauded their foe. One report called the 5th Virginia "the best regiment in the Confederate service." Billy Davis commented on the visible effects of the "canister from our guns and from the ball and three buckshot from our smooth bore muskets; the ground was strewn with their dead and wounded and with guns, cartridge boxes, knapsacks, clothing haversacks and canteens." John Hadley counted 27 dead Confederates behind the newly captured fence and boasted that his regiment drove the survivors away in panic—"They ran like coward[s]." Another account gloated over "driving the enemy like sheep." The 7th Indiana eventually would run out of momentum too, of course. As Sam List wrote in a brief diary summary, "the enemy gave way, but soon rallied in greater force than ever."[14]

The 29th Ohio drove back the 7th Louisiana when it advanced from the Lewiston lane. After a preparatory volley, the Ohioans launched a charge that hurried the Louisiana regiment away from its protective fence. The 29th pulled up at the fence. While some elements of the regiment went over it, part of the 29th did not advance farther in any organized thrust. During the fight with the 7th Louisiana, Allen Mason of the 29th Ohio captured the Confederate regiment's flag and Lieutenant Hamblin Gregory with part of his Company F claimed to have captured two dozen prisoners.[15]

Farther left the 7th Ohio had ample Southerners in sight between the 7th Louisiana to its right front and the 27th Virginia to its left front. Fortunately for their targets, the Ohioans were very poorly armed. Nine days later, Company B of the 7th Ohio received a few rifled muskets and forty "Springfield Muskets Smooth Bore Cal 69" in "worn" condition. When he saw those dreadfully outmoded weapons, the 7th's colonel rejoiced, noting that they constituted an upgrade over the bad muskets issued to him fourteen months before and now in bad condition![16]

Theodore Wilder of the 7th Ohio described how his unit and the adjacent 5th Ohio charged "with deafening shouts." When they reached the mid-field fence, the Ohioans saw "a long line of dead, dying and wounded men. One was getting a bullet out of his foot, another was rubbing his shin, a third was rolling and groaning, and thus scores were passing their time." Chaplain D. C. Wright of the 7th described the heavy damage done to the Confederates and was surprised to have survived after hearing "the bullets whistle, & shells whiz, in uncomfortable proximity to my head."[17]

John Burton found special inspiration in the exhortations of artillery chief Philip Daum, who was with some of his guns near the 7th Ohio's position. Just as Daum shouted for the infantry to launch its pursuit of Winder, a bullet hit young Burton (he had celebrated his nineteenth birthday four days earlier) in the mouth. The blow injured his jaw and loosened several teeth. "I was not going to give up at that," he insisted, "and having loaded my gun sank down on my knees to fire once more when a piece of a shell which burst by my side, hit me in the shoulder disabling me." Burton made his way to the rear while his mates chased Winder's men across the bloodstained wheat.[18]

Part of the 7th Ohio swung out as though on a hinge and wheeled toward the river. That convinced Confederates that the Federals planned to trap them against the bank of the South Fork. The historian of the 7th credited the Southerners opposite them (primarily the 27th Virginia) with stout resistance and even with a brief renewal of the attack. He also applauded the valor of the 5th Ohio. That sister regiment, fighting just to the left of the 7th Ohio, played a bolder role in the counterattack than it had during the defensive phase in the lane. John Paver described the 5th's charge as "fierce and hot . . . a hard day's work." The 5th Ohio eventually would slice past the frayed edges of the 27th Virginia, penetrate the farthest of any Federal regiment, and capture the one Confederate gun that would be lost at Port Republic.[19]

The 1st Virginia (Union) made an advance from the Lewiston lane, even though the regiment never cleaned out Confederates lurking in the farm's outbuildings. Leaving those pesky foemen behind them, the Virginian Yankees took advantage of the success of the 5th Ohio by following along on its left rear. The 1st Virginia historian claimed that his unit drove back the Confederate right "for nearly half a mile across and beyond a ravine [Little Deep Run], when the enemy was heavily reinforced by cavalry and artillery." That cannot stand scrutiny, because no Confederates were there to be driven. The three Ohio regiments and the 7th Indiana did the driving, while the 1st Virginia watched.[20]

This victorious interval for Tyler's forces affected the peripatetic 84th and 110th Pennsylvania the same way every other battle development did: they marched from one end of the line to the other, never reaching the critical zone in time. Tyler had sent them to Carroll just before Winder broke. Carroll sent them back unused when he found that he was succeeding without them.[21]

Men were falling steadily on both sides, but neither Winder nor Tyler suffered as heavily during this fluid phase as they had while slugging it out with massed musketry around the mid-field fence and the Lewiston lane. Even so, casualties mounted as Yankees fired at retreating Confederates who paused to shoot back. Tyler, with pardonable exaggeration, declared that his artillery and small arms "mowed them down like grass before a well-served scythe . . . they suffered severely." A Confederate officer heard from eyewitnesses that Winder's few regiments had been "pretty thoroughly whipped," and the Yankees had pursued "in beautiful order." From his vantage point at the Coaling, Captain Huntington could see the cost Federal infantry paid for their beautifully executed pursuit. They "seemed to be gaining ground," he wrote, "keeping up a heavy fire and a vociferous cheering, though the prostrate forms behind them, and the stream of wounded hobbling to the rear, showed they were suffering some loss."[22]

Fortunately for Jackson's hard-pressed army, six more regiments approached the field at this critical juncture. The 44th, 52nd, and 58th Virginia of Steuart's Brigade (now commanded by Colonel W. C. Scott) arrived under Dick Ewell's personal direction. Colonel James Walker, who had distinguished himself so markedly at Cross Keys, brought the 13th, 25th, and 31st Virginia of Elzey's Brigade toward the front. Three of the regiments would supply emergency aid to Winder's line in the plain; the other three headed for the woods.

The 52nd Virginia reached the action first of the newcomers, after the usual delay at South River. As a consequence, one soldier wrote, "by the time we got over, formed our line and commenced our advance . . . we met Gen. Winder's troops retiring in confusion." Jackson spied the head of the badly needed regiment from a point near the Baugher lane. The army commander hurried off his chief quartermaster, John A. Harman, to tell the colonel of the reinforcing unit "to take it into the fight." The 52nd's leader asked the quarter-master "how, or where, he was to take them in." Harman, whose skills did not extend to tactical matters, could only respond, "The Gen. says take them in"; and, in the words of an admiring onlooker, the colonel "took them."[23]

The officer receiving Harman's confusing directive was Lieutenant Colonel James H. Skinner, a thirty-six-year-old lawyer from nearby Staunton, newly promoted from captain. Colonel Scott meanwhile followed Ewell into the woods on the right with the 44th and 58th Virginia. So chaotic was the ensuing fighting that a lieutenant in the 52nd thought his comrades in the rest of the brigade never got into action.[24]

Skinner and his men angled across the plain behind Winder's reeling line and neared action not far from the river. John Robson recalled the unsettling sensation of bullets flying about his ears. As the 52nd approached the front "through a fine field of wheat border-ing on the river bottom, chin high . . . the minnie [sic] balls clipped the grain worse than reapers," Robson wrote. "It was a very bad job of harvesting[;] . . . a harvest of death it proved." Colonel Skinner also noticed Federal bullets "cutting off the heads of the wheat." The whistling balls spread casualties unevenly through the 52nd. Lieutenant Benton Coiner estimated that the regiment lost 100 men, but his own company had only two wounded. On Coiner's part of the line the soldiers were able to "protect themselves behind a bank of a small branch in front of them."[25]

Most of the 52nd found the banks of Little Deep Run less accommodating. Yankees infesting the thicket near the mouth of the run promptly drove them back as part of the flood tide of Confederates retreating across the run toward the Baugher lane. Skinner's regiment flowed back into the orchard around Baugher's barn and joined the tangle of Southern units re-forming to stem the Federal advance. It reported the loss of a dozen killed, including Captain Benjamin T. Walton, and 72 other casualties.[26]

While the 52nd strove to help near the river and the rest of Scott's Brigade pushed into the woods, the three regiments under James A. Walker arrived and also split into two chunks. Two of Walker's regiments went out onto the plain and one headed for the woods, reversing the relative distribution of Scott's Brigade. Jim Walker met Stonewall Jackson as the brigade neared the front. The general at once ordered Walker to send one regiment and Raine's Battery to Winder's aid. The 31st Virginia drew the unenviable assignment of helping Winder. Colonel Walker then led his old command, the 13th Virginia, into the woods to reinforce Taylor's vital flanking effort. The 25th Virginia, at the rear of the column, he also earmarked for the woods, but it wound up on the fire-swept plain without Walker knowing its fate.[27]

Walker and the 13th accomplished nothing. The regiment floundered through the same thickets recently penetrated by Taylor's men but arrived at the front too late to have any impact. Joe Kern of the 13th did not regret missing the bitter contest that he and his mates could see unfolding. In all of his battle experience Port Republic was "the hardest fought & hottest—& I believe the most stubborn I saw fought." The Coaling awed Kern with its wicked dominance of the battle zone. The enemy guns, Kern marveled, were "planted on a little knoll or foot hill of the Blue Ridge, and commanded the whole field. The guns were wonderfully handled & had a good support."[28]

The 25th Virginia marched at the end of Walker's Brigade. Captain Wilson Harper of Company K had been born in Port Republic in 1833. He had left a teaching career, which included posts in western Virginia and Kansas, to defend his home state—and now his very birthplace. What Harper and the 25th Virginia did on the plain remains obscure. A member of Ewell's staff reported that the regiment fought next to the Stonewall Brigade in the river bottoms. Captain William T. Gammon and three lieutenants were among the 25th's casualties. Captain Harper survived to win promotion to major and to live for many years in the vicinity. He died in 1914 near Port Republic.[29]

Edward D. Camden was one of the wounded lieutenants. As Camden plunged into the muddy bottom, a bullet crashed through his upper shoulder and out his back, taking "one knuckle and part of my back bone off." The impact felt to Camden "just like a person had some big weight hit him to knock him out of breath and down." Clayborn Hosey tried to help Camden to the rear, but the lieutenant sent him back into the fight, pulled himself out of the mud, and staggered unaided to a field hospital a half mile to the rear and eventually groped his way to the churchyard in Port Republic. Lieutenant Camden had the good fortune to stumble upon an acquaintance there, Dr. William J. Bland, the forty-five-year-old surgeon of the 31st Virginia and a graduate of Jefferson Medical College in Philadelphia. The physician deftly removed six thicknesses of oilcloth and blanket that had been forced into Camden's neck and left him on his back with the injunction, "don't move a particle until I come back, which will be about two hours." When Bland returned, he observed cheerfully, "Ed, you are not dead yet," and admitted that it surprised him. The bullet that tore off part of Camden's spine also had nicked his jugular vein, which "was almost cut through," the surgeon reported, "and the clotted blood in the wound is the only thing that saved you." Before the summer was over Ed Camden rejoined his company and he survived the wound by sixty years.[30]

Colonel John S. Hoffman led his 31st Virginia onto the plain before the 25th arrived, the last support that reached there during the battle. Not far from the main road Hoffman found a good position, from which he fought stoutly to anchor Winder's right. Winder's initial intention had been to relieve the reeling 7th Louisiana with Hoffman's fresh troops. Remarkably, Winder actually considered sending the 7th Louisiana off to rejoin Taylor's movement once the 31st had taken over its place in the line. "This change it was impossible to effect . . . as the infantry line began to waver," Winder reported in restatement of the obvious. Instead, Winder hurried his artillery to the rear, directed Hoffman to support it, and endeavored to rally the retreating front line on this knot of strength.[31]

Winder was fortunate to have the 31st Virginia as promptly as he did. Just before Walker's Brigade reached the South River bridge, someone finally rigged up a more workable alternative to the shifting planks. Lieutenant William Lyman of the 31st recalled "planks laid upon wagons," as did so many others. Lyman, however, added that his unit crossed "rapidly." The cluster of reinforcements that arrived in quick succession to help Winder benefited from long-overdue adjustments to the temporary bridge. McHenry Howard of Winder's staff dragooned Colonel Hoffman as soon as he saw the head of the 31st come into view.[32]

When the 31st followed Howard toward the Baugher lane, Stonewall Jackson's entire force to be employed in the primary fighting at Port Republic had arrived. The Stonewall Brigade was strewn across the plain and in the woods. Most of Taylor's Brigade was catching its breath near the Coaling. Scott's and Walker's new brigades were wedged into frayed segments of the patchwork Confederate line. Clara Strayer and her friends trying to penetrate the gunsmoke haze to discern the battle's progress could see little. The roar of musketry had reached a crescendo that it never exceeded, though, so Clara knew that "the fight [had] become general." It had been about an hour, she thought, since the first volleys from small arms had broken out.[33]

The 31st Virginia suffered from the same enemy fire that had broken Winder as it headed toward the Baugher lane and crossed the fence on its east shoulder into the wheat field. Despite the storm swarming around them, the men of the 31st could tell that the far left was even more hotly engaged. Artillery fire was drawn as though by a magnet to the Rockbridge guns not far in front of the 31st. The advance breasted a "murderous hail of bullets [flying] through [the] wheat field." One man thought that "ardor carried us too far"—a common problem with Confederate infantry at this stage of the war.[34]

Sergeant William F. Gordon strode into the wheat with the 31st. He had heard that all three of the brigade's regiments were to participate and felt lonely when he found his unit alone. "We crawled up . . . on our bellies," he recalled, "rising to shoot, dropping again to load and advance. And every time we rose some comrades dropped to rise no more." Five soldiers carrying the 31st's flag went down in succession. Gordon jumped out to take the colors after the fifth casualty, but Lieutenant William Pope Cooper stopped him: "Better let that d——d thing alone, Bill," growled Lieutenant Cooper. "Use both hands with your bayonet next rise."

Cooper, age thirty-six, had returned to Virginia from Pennsylvania at the outbreak of the war to enlist, and would win promotion to major in 1863. When he and Bill Gordon reached safety that afternoon, Cooper asked: " 'What were you looking up and down the line in there for, Bill?' ... 'I was looking for a chance to run.' 'By G——d, so was I!' gruffly retorted the quondam man of valor; 'but d——d if every fellow in the regiment wasn't looking right at me.' " From such ties and pressures grew bravery in battle.[35]

The advance of the 31st Virginia beyond the lane did not progress far before it stalled. Colonel Hoffman ordered the men to lie down in the wheat. Federals surged toward them in "dense columns," an officer wrote, "and we were subjected to a most deadly and destructive front and enfilading fire." The strongest enemy attacks were to the left of the 31st. Bullets from two directions flew over, and all too often hit, the prone soldiers. William Lyman recalled sprawling on the ground "in the ripening wheat and the sensation caused by the cutting of minie balls through the ripe grain was novel and not altogether pleasant."[36]

An unidentified member of Company D of the 31st recalled vividly the regiment's experience "in line of battle across [the] open wheat field," which he called "the hottest [place] I ever was in." The wheat "was beginning to turn yellow [and] each minnie ball seemed to cut its little swath, and the cannon balls a big one. We fought most of the time lying flat on the ground." Charles W. H. Goff, a twenty-three-year-old sergeant in Company D, died as "a hero. ... He had often said he wanted to die at his post of duty and so it was granted." The memoirist concluded that by the time the fighting in the wheat ended, "not much was left for the owner to reap that was not shot or tramped by us or the enemy."[37]

Major Joseph Chenoweth was an exemplar of the iron spirit that held the 31st to its duty in the wheat. As noted earlier, the brilliant young man (he had just turned twenty-five) was well acquainted with Stonewall Jackson from the Virginia Military Institute, where Chenoweth graduated first in the Class of 1859 and then taught. He was from near Beverly and had known Professor Jackson's sister there. In a January 1858 letter home from the institute, Chenoweth identified Jackson to his father as "Mrs. Arnold's brother." Cadet Chenoweth earned a first by a wide margin in natural philosophy—taught by Major Jackson. Now he stood firm at a crucial hinge in Major General Jackson's battle line.[38]

When the 31st Virginia crossed the fence next to the Baugher lane, Chenoweth had been forced to dismount. He took a position just behind the left center of the regiment when it lay down in the wheat. As the battle progressed, Chenoweth strode behind the line toward its left flank, then turned right and moved up the front of the regiment, encouraging the men (and interrupting their field of fire as he passed in front). The sheets of fire that forced the regiment to lie down swarmed around the major's unprotected head and eventually, inevitably, struck him down. A bullet hit Joe Chenoweth behind his left ear and passed entirely through his head. "He fell without a groan," Lieutenant Joseph Harding reported, "with his sword still in his grasp pointed toward the enemy." The major had served at that rank for thirty-nine days.[39]

Chenoweth's body still lies somewhere on the battlefield where he fell, as do the remains of many of his men. In 1866 Joe's father, Lemuel, wrote to VMI to ask that his son's alma mater move the corpse to Lexington. An uncle had buried the body "near one mile east of Port republick in a feild under a large Oak tree. his grave was pailed in & head board put up." Superintendent Francis H. Smith promised the grieving father, "Your son's remains will be brought here as soon as we can make the arrangements to do so, & will be deposited in our vault." Nineteen years later nothing had been done. Joe's sister wrote sadly that the family "will never be so merry again because our dear brother is gone from us." In 1890 the Chenoweths were still petitioning VMI on the matter. At that late date Superintendent Scott Shipp told the family that he had approval to bury the body in the institute cemetery, but during a recent visit Joe's brother had "seemed in doubt as to whether the remains of your brother . . . could be identified." There the matter ended. Somewhere in the fertile river bottom near where he died, the remains of Joe Chenoweth have blended with detritus from "a large Oak tree," no doubt itself now long dead.[40]

Thirty-one other members of the 31st Virginia died at Port Republic, including Captain Robert H. Bradshaw and Lieutenant Alexander Whitely, the latter, like Chenoweth, shot through the head. Three lieutenants were wounded. About 220 men went into battle with the 31st; slightly more than one half of them became casualties during

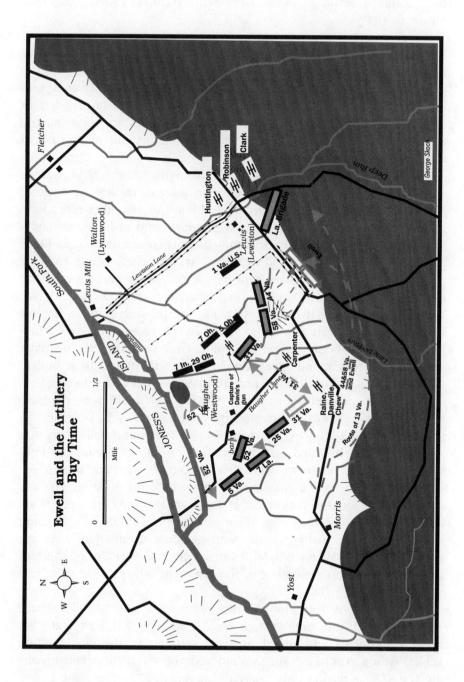

Ewell and the Artillery Buy Time

the sacrificial stand in what Lieutenant Harding called "the fatal wheat field."[41]

Lieutenant William Lyman of the 31st was philosophical about the sacrificial role assigned to his regiment. In "almost any great battle of the world," Lyman declared, "the consummation of the general result aimed at" required "at one point or another an apparent sacrifice of men." At Port Republic, "the troops on the left of our line were that day the 'food for gun-powder' put there mainly to draw the enemy in and on to apparent victory but really to final discomfiture and defeat."[42]

The retreat of the 31st Virginia from the wheat field was as dangerous as had been the regiment's advance or its defensive stand. As the men dashed back toward and beyond the Baugher lane, Jeremiah Church came across a badly wounded friend and prewar neighbor, James M. Steuart. Church slung the hurt soldier over a shoulder "and was making fairly good headway, when bullets began to whiz past him. When one nipped him in the right side and slivered the rib, he felt compelled to drop his human load and flee to safety." Church suggested that they both would be prisoners unless he laid his burden down. Steuart agreed. As Church raced away unencumbered, Yankees shouted at him to halt. "They shot at him repeatedly and pursued him at full speed but he outran them and their bullets too." Steuart's wounds killed him after twelve days of suffering.[43]

Another member of the 31st survived in a different manner. "A half witted little man" named Billy, of Company B, became "so thoroughly frightened by the whistling of the minie balls thro' the wheat" that he huddled on the ground behind the regiment's line. "He laid still and when we were driven from the field and the enemy came on," Lieutenant Lyman wrote, Billy "held his position. He was a cadaverous looking little man at best, and, closing his eyes, Billy let the enemy roll him over and turn his pockets inside out, feigning death among the many actually warm bodies around him." At the end of the day, "when Billy showed up he was boastful of the fact that he was the only member of the regiment who had actually held the field, and he was."[44]

The stand by the 31st Virginia, with help from the 52nd and 25th, bought a little time at high cost. It allowed Winder to rally his broken regiments and added precious minutes to the clock tolling Dick Taylor's crucial advance. Winder summarized the stand involving the 31st as having only "partially succeeded" because the Federals "thinned our ranks so terribly." A Louisiana observer watching "the trampled and bloody wheat field" saw the advancing blue line meet "three fresh regiments, and yet they were not checked." Clara Strayer from the Bogota porch could tell despite the gunsmoke that things were going badly: "you may be sure it was an anxious moment for us," Clara wrote in her diary. Federals pouring forward in the seemingly irresistible wave did not view the pressure from Confederate reinforcements very seriously. A member of the 7th Ohio, which was applying some of the enfilade pressure on the left of the 31st Virginia, estimated that his unit had advanced about 450 yards after passing the mid-field fence before meeting "another rebel brigade. . . . These were soon put to flight."[45]

**General Richard S.
Ewell recognized
that his flank position
offered a chance
to do some harm. With
the roadside fences
leveled, Ewell
was able to do what his
temperament always
suggested—attack!**

CHAPTER 21

EWELL AND THE

ARTILLERY BUY

TIME

Fortunately for Jackson, Dick Ewell and two Virginia regiments were lurking in the woods south of the main road and east of the Baugher lane, ready to provide a diversion at this desperate moment. The 44th and 58th Virginia had filled their cartridge boxes from ordnance wagons in the streets of Port Republic before hurrying across the South River bridge. The advancing troops were disheartened by Confederates along the roadside who had been killed by cannon fire. They saw the source of the fatal artillery rounds when they came in view of the Coaling. To avoid them, Ewell decided to swing right "and take to the mountain, still however, moving to the front."[1]

The third regiment in Scott's Brigade, the 52nd Virginia, dropped out of the column and went onto the plain to help Winder as the

44th and 58th swerved into the woods. Colonel Scott reported that his orders (presumably from Jackson) were to be "in the rear of" and "to support General Taylor." The best way to do that would be to delay the Federal tidal wave on the plain.[2]

Once under the protection of the woods, Ewell and Scott veered up the mountainside before dropping back toward the road again. When they reached "the edge of the thicket," the road was right in front of them. In the fields beyond it the battle was running strongly against their friends. The front of the Yankees giving Winder and his reinforcements so much trouble was perpendicular to Ewell's line.[3]

Scott and Ewell and the several hundred Virginians with them had, wrote Adjutant C. C. Wight of the 58th, "a perfectly fair view of the fighting then going on in the open valley." Wight described the plain as "covered with wheat & the rest [nearest him] with Luxuriant clover." The bloody fighting staining the crops at first confused him; "we did not know what to think of it," the adjutant wrote. He soon realized that the strong double line stretching across the plain was made up of Federals "advancing steadily and in fine order, driving our men before them—ours however disputed the ground taking advantage of the high staked fences which enclosed the fields." By the time Wight found his vantage point, the fence being defended was that along the Baugher lane; the mid-field fence had been abandoned well before the 58th reached the woodline. A Louisianian described the sight dramatically: "Like a great wall of fire [the Federal] lines swept on through the wheat. . . . Jackson was being driven!"[4]

Dick Ewell had no difficulty evaluating the scene on the river plain. His soon-to-be stepson, Campbell Brown, explained what a mess faced "Old Bald Head" and his handful of men. Each regiment all morning had been fed into the fight at once, "without being allowed time to form or to collect a large body & make a strong simultaneous attack." The inevitable consequence was that when Ewell arrived, "three or four Brigades having been successively sent up against a force of Yankees just strong enough to whip them, our whole force previously engaged was in full retreat from the field, having suffered heavily."[5]

While Ewell watched, Yankees chasing Winder on the plain "came opposite" the two Virginia regiments in the woods. Adjutant Wight shared Ewell's dismay, but had no idea the uneven struggle on the plain would affect him personally. "At length," Wight recalled, "the enemy in his advance was directly abreast of our two regiments as we stood by a high fence watching the combat. We privately thought that a diversion by so small a body [as ours] would not do at all." The Coaling's fire swept harshly at short range across the ground in front of the 44th and 58th.[6]

Wight's comfortable tactical notions did not influence General Ewell, who recognized that his flank position relative to the Yankee advance offered a chance to do some harm, weak though he was. The general called in his shrill voice for volunteers to pull down the fences bordering both sides of the main road. With them out of the way he could launch a desperate assault bound to distract the victorious Federal lines; troops simply did not stand for attacks from the flank or rear. Brave men from the 44th and 58th dashed out under fire and hurriedly knocked down the fences. Ewell later expressed regret that "the rapid course of events made it impossible to record their names." The general ordered that a third fence, farther into the field and higher than the two enclosing the road, be saved. He was "intending the two Regts to take post behind it."[7]

With the roadside fences leveled, Ewell was able to do what his temperament always suggested—attack! Federals closest to the river had advanced beyond the front of the 44th and 58th, and the van of the enemy nearest to him had slipped past as well, by the time Ewell told Scott to send the two regiments forward "diagonally across the field." Scott led the way in person, but the diagonal intention never bore fruit. Charles Wight and his mates were astonished when Scott "sung out the startling command . . . 'we will make a charge.' We were amazed at the audacity of the thing, but could not demur of course." The several hundred Virginians burst from the woods, trampled the remnants of the fences, and flowed into the field, "yelling more to keep our courage up than to frighten the enemy," Wight admitted, though Ewell and Scott thought that the "loud cheers" daunted the enemy.[8]

Northern guns at the Coaling turned their muzzles toward this new and nearer target. When they took the 44th and 58th under fire, a Confederate wrote, "the dirt and clover was thrown all over us, and many of our men fell." The Virginians trotted forward through the shell bursts until they reached the high fence behind which Ewell intended to shelter them. Perhaps as a result of the momentum they had generated, and in part because the fence ran the wrong direction to provide shelter from the Coaling, the 44th and 58th scrambled over the fence and kept right on going. No doubt few of the men had any idea that Ewell wanted them to stop there anyway.[9]

Once beyond the last fence, the two regiments posed an imminent threat to the flank and rear of the Yankee line, but at first the enemy paid them little heed. "That portion of the enemy's line nearest to us," Adjutant Wight wrote, referring to troops that must have been from the 5th and 7th Ohio, "paus[ed] at our approach, but seeming to notice the fewness of our numbers they again moved on." The 44th and 58th caught their attention by halting in the clover, loading their muskets, and pouring in a volley "at short range." The result was favorable. "For the first time that day," Ewell reported proudly, "the enemy was then driven back in disorder for some hundreds of yards."[10]

The high fence that the two regiments vaulted had not slowed them down much, but it had succeeded in "breaking their array," Ewell complained. The loss of alignment broke down tactical cohesion and doomed the advance to disintegrate. Ewell's first-draft report grumbled about the fence crossing as "contrary to my intention," intimating that the two regiments, if behind the fence and in good order, might have accomplished more. That is unlikely, although the 44th and 58th might have achieved nearly as much by serving as a noisy threat from behind the fence. They assuredly would have suffered less severely there.[11]

When momentum ran out in the face of "overwhelming fire," the 44th and 58th "halted in the field and sat down." Lieutenant Noah D. Walker of the 44th particularly distinguished himself at this juncture. Colonel Scott's official report described how the twenty-eight-year-old son of a prominent Baltimore family stood erect when everyone else sprawled in the clover and stalked down the line encouraging the men "to advance still nearer the enemy." No one budged, but Noah Walker's example held them steady for a time. The lieutenant was as modest as he was courageous. In a letter to his mother the next week, he calmly lied about the danger he had faced, saying "Our Regt did not get into this fight, arrived just as it was over." Walker survived this brave display, but was killed at Chancellorsville before his next birthday.[12]

Dick Ewell made a courtly gesture toward the enemy at this point that provoked Stonewall Jackson's wrath in an episode often cited as typical of both men. A Federal officer "riding a snow white horse was very conspicuous for his gallantry."

> He frequently exposed himself to the fire of our men in the most reckless way. So splendid was this man's courage that General Ewell, one of the most chivalrous gentlemen I ever knew, at some risk to his own life, rode down our line and called his men not to shoot the man on the white horse. After a little while, however, the officer and his white horse went down. A day or so after, when General Jackson learned of the incident, he sent for General Ewell and told him not to do such a thing again; that this was no ordinary war and the brave and gallant Federal officers were the very kind that must be killed.

In the same vein, Jackson later shuddered at the horrors of a battle-field, but answered a query about what Southerners could do in reaction to invasion, looting, and insulted women: " 'Do?' he answered, and his voice was ringing, 'Do? why shoot them!' "[13]

After the Yankee officer and his white horse went down, and the two regiments proved unwilling to follow Lieutenant Walker, Ewell's forlorn hope held on for a little longer. Awesome enfilade fire from the Coaling and musketry sleeting in from in front were "almost too much for us," Charles Wight wrote. "Our loss here is very heavy and after a short stand we begin to retire to the cover of the fence we have climbed." The men fell back without orders, as far as Wight could tell, "at least I heard none given." The father of Ben Jones of the 44th was among the civilians watching the battle and saw this crucial action. When he learned after the battle that his son's regiment had been in that "desperate charge," Ben later wrote, "he felt so certain that I had fallen, he was wondering how he would get my body home."[14]

The rally at the high fence accomplished some good, but it did not last long. The two regiments, by now almost completely without tactical organization, "poured a sharp fire into the still advancing ranks of the Federals," every man loading and pulling trigger at will. The men fighting from behind the fence soon found it "untenable," so they scampered back into the woods as fast as they could. Ewell and Jackson used identical language: "driven back to the woods with severe loss." Ewell met the 58th Virginia at "the edge of the thicket" where they had started and encouraged them, saying "We had done nobly."[15]

Ewell's encouragement worked. The two regiments rallied more rapidly than expected, depleted as they were, and were able to help when needed a few minutes later. The 44th Virginia had lost nearly one half of its slender strength, including Lieutenant W. T. Robertson killed. Two other of the 44th's lieutenants and two captains were wounded; one of the latter was Thomas Buckner, who had distinguished himself at Cross Keys the day before. Lieutenant George W. Teaford of the 58th (age twenty-two) had been killed and two other lieutenants and a captain were wounded.[16]

What had the two regiments accomplished at such cost? They had bought the last few minutes that Dick Taylor needed to prepare to smash the Coaling. "They had checked the enemy's advance with great loss," Ewell wrote. Stonewall Jackson complimented the 44th and 58th in his official report: "The enemy's advance was checked by a spirited attack upon their flank directed by General Ewell and led by Colonel Scott."[17]

An important feature of Winder's defense was of course his artillery. Most Confederate cannon concentrated their fire on enemy infantry because counterbattery fire against the Coaling was impractical. Because the Rockbridge Artillery had the most guns in action and suffered most heavily, its experiences are better known. Captain Charles I. Raine's Battery arrived late (just before the 31st Infantry went in), but it lost two men killed, seven wounded, and eighteen horses. The nine casualties constituted a loss of 15 percent, considerable for an artillery unit, especially one in action so briefly.[18]

The Danville Artillery also fired in support of Winder. The Danville cannoneers bolted half-cooked breakfasts and began the difficult advance across South River and then downstream. One of them later wrote that "for three hours . . . we were in heated action." It is impossible to determine precisely where the Danville battery was positioned.[19]

Part of R. P. Chew's Battery of horse artillery had been firing for some time by the time the crisis arrived. When Tyler threw back Winder and his supporters on the plain, the intermingled infantry lines denied Chew (and doubtless other artillery) a clear target. The gunners then turned their attention on "a Federal battery . . . on an eminence near the Lewis house"—the Coaling. Chew's pieces "promptly got the range of this battery and poured upon it a terrific enfilading fire, crippling the enemy's guns." The unit historian who wrote those words had succumbed to exaggeration. The Coaling guns were neither crippled nor silenced. George Neese, who served with one of Chew's guns, recalled: "The musketry right in front of us raged fearfully, far, far beyond the powers of description that my poor pencil can delineate. The shell from the . . . coaling was ripping the ground open all around us, and the air was full of screaming fragments of exploding shell, and I thought I was a goner." Neese was not "a goner," of course, because he survived to describe the ordeal; in fact, he survived until 1921. His minutes (thirty of them, he estimated) at the mercy of the Coaling, however, remained one of his most frightening experiences.[20]

Carpenter's Alleghany Artillery did more, over a longer period, than any other Confederate battery except the Rockbridge Artillery. Two of its four guns wasted time trying to plow through the underbrush during the first advance aimed at the Coaling. They later fired from Winder's right, near the road, while the others fought farther left. Joe Carpenter positioned himself with the left pair, and his brother, Lieutenant John Carpenter, managed the right one. The Confederate right was particularly hellish for artillery because it lay closer to the Coaling. Clarence Fonerden declared that the right section was "nearly demolished" by guns "located in an elevated charcoal pit."[21]

John Carpenter's section fired from about "30 steps" behind the 27th Virginia until ordered to the rear. The guns had been screened by the sizable north-south terrain finger that reached northward from the road near the mid-field fence. As the 27th "began a slow and dogged retreat," Carpenter's guns galloped back 150 yards and unlimbered. From this new location near the Baugher lane, the cannoneers could see the entire field; but, William Humphreys noted, they also faced "the dangers from small arms equal to the infantry, something quite rare [for artillerists], & inpolitic [sic]." Impolitic or not, Carpenter's men had to fire at infantry ranges to defend themselves.[22]

As Federals drew closer, Joe Carpenter (who had arrived to help his brother) "ordered a round or two of canister, which staggered them." The good results prompted the Carpenter boys to use canister "in abundance." William Humphreys observed with relief that the clusters of hissing balls "mow[ed] the ranks of infantry as it has seldom done before in this war." The guns fired so fast and long that they exhausted their stock of canister—nearly every Confederate piece on the field did. Bereft of that valuable round, and "in consequence of . . . the close proximity of the enemy," Joe Carpenter ordered his brother and the two guns to the rear. When the artillery pieces galloped off, "it had *an appearance* that we were whipped," Humphreys admitted, before adding gamely, "But not so."[23]

Clarence Fonerden wrote dolefully of the ordeal borne by Carpenter's Battery, but losses for both sections combined amounted to only 5 men wounded among the 44 men engaged, and 5 horses lost. The battery's limbers and caissons "were wofully [*sic*] besmattered with shells and the fateful minie balls," Fonerden reported. He conjectured that the unit's loss "would undoubtedly have been doubly as great as it was, in a very little longer continuance of that deadly fire." Thomas M. Jordan's head wound was considered mortal, and Samuel S. Carpenter (a brother of the two officers) was hit "severely." In fact Jordan was alive in Rhode Island in 1895, Carpenter lived until 1909, and the other three casualties died in 1888, after 1911, and in 1929. Aside from making a case for lead as a tonic, their fates demonstrate afresh the relative safety of Civil War artillery service, as compared to infantry, in even the hottest battlefield corner.[24]

The two Parrott rifles from the Rockbridge Artillery had been fighting since early morning. The rifle near the road fired so steadily that it ran out of ammunition before the crisis and went to the rear. The rifle on the left also missed the climax. As a consequence of their hard usage, both Parrotts were sent to Richmond three days after the battle to be "bushed," or relined. Meanwhile Poague's four shorter-ranged, smoothbore guns had gone into action on Winder's direct orders.[25]

The Rockbridge smoothbores did good service under difficult circumstances. "We could see and hear the balls cutting through the wheat on every side," one of the gunners wrote. "Nothing but the mercy of God kept us from suffering severely." The Rockbridge men cut some wheat of their own with roaring discharges of canister. When "the whole Federal line charged," one of them boasted, "their ranks rapidly thinned, some hesitating to advance, while others were shot down in full view. Still they drove us back."[26]

Captain Poague was near the road when the Confederate collapse near the river gathered momentum. By the time he reached the left, three of his smoothbores had fallen back well behind the front. Lieutenant Archibald Graham had ordered a partial retirement and then lost control of the movement. Graham was afoot, his horse having been killed; the three messengers he had dispatched to halt the guns in Baugher's orchard all missed connecting. Men from the two rifles and the three departed smoothbores had reason to believe, one of them wrote, that "the day was lost." One of Jackson's staff came across Holmes Boyd of the battery, who reported disconsolately that "they had had a severe time and pointed to a poor fellow, lying in a fence corner with his brains scattered about as a sickening sight."[27]

The Rockbridge Artillery's sixth piece, a bronze six-pounder commanded by Lieutenant James Cole Davis, had an even more difficult time than the rest of the battery. Technology had rendered the little smoothbore obsolete, but Confederates were loading rounds into anything that would shoot. Cole Davis and his outmoded gun were retreating as part of the heavy rearward tide when Winder dashed up and ordered him "to halt and fire on [the Yankees'] advancing column." Ewell, who just at that moment launched the 44th and 58th on their desperate assault, saw Lieutenant Davis's crew execute the order and admired the "great quickness and decision in the officer commanding it." An aide called Davis "an officer who, when retreating at a gallop, stopped the very second he perceived the effect of [Ewell's] charge, stopped his pieces & commenced firing on the enemy, checking them effectually."[28]

When Ewell first drafted his official report, he waxed warmly enthusiastic. Subsequently he rewrote the section, deleting all but the brief compliment quoted in the preceding paragraph. The general's first-draft description of Davis's courageous stand is worth quoting at length:

> No act of a subordinate that I have seen during the Valley campaign has so excited my admiration for its coolness, judgement & bravery. I have tried in vain to find this Officer's name. His mind might well have been occupied in extricating his battery, in imminent danger & in retreat—but the attack [by Ewell] and its effect, as unexpected to him as to the enemy, was instantly at coup d'oeil turned by him to profit. This is the fire referred to by Gen. Taylor in his report as so important, although out of sight of his part of the field.[29]

Cole Davis suffered for his bravery. He was "severely wounded in the side" and left on the field. The lieutenant's hurts seemed mortal. Frank Singleton was also badly wounded and taken prisoner. Several other men received minor wounds. The casualties further reduced the short-handed crew and made serving the piece more difficult. The Yankee lead sleeting through the position also knocked down two or more horses, one of which fell across the limber pole, immobilizing the gun. When the enemy advance swept within pistol range of the stranded piece the surviving crew abandoned it and dashed for safety.[30]

The Federals swarming toward Davis's cannon belonged to the 5th Ohio, which had rolled forward largely unchecked. John Gray of the 5th, known as Scotty to his friends, won the race for the prize. Gray made sure of his trophy by mounting a team of unwounded horses and dragging the six-pounder to the rear, leaving its limber behind. The 5th Ohio promptly faced pressure to its left, first from the 44th and 58th Virginia and then from the attack on the Coaling. Scotty Gray kept right on going with his captured cannon, even though Federal artillerists surely would have disdained it as an obsolete relic. Poague noticed that "the enemy seemed to prize this gun highly, for in their disorderly retreat . . . they managed to get the gun away."[31]

Efforts to stabilize the dangerous situation on the plain drew strength from Lieutenant Davis's sacrifice and the charge of the 44th and 58th. Colonel Stapleton Crutchfield reported that Ewell's attack "soon checked" the Yankees and enabled Confederate batteries to resume firing. The renewed artillery support helped Winder, but the general never did rally his infantry to his satisfaction. Winder's diary entry that night was terse and disappointed: "tried to rally my men but failed. the musketry was tremendous. loss great. My horse shot three times. obliged to dismount. thanks to our Heavenly Father I escaped unhurt."[32]

Despite Winder's discouragement over the results, Lieutenant Howard of his staff thought that the general's performance at Port Republic "shows . . . conduct on a battle field at its best." Howard boasted of his chief's "tenacity in resistance," and thought that Winder's "persistence under adverse circumstances, contributed not a little to the success of the final attack. . . . The way he handled his artillery . . . is particularly noticeable. No one can read his report without forming a high opinion of his ability." Winder praised Howard, Garnett, and O'Brien of his staff and several line officers for helping him during the ordeal.[33]

The tenacity that Howard touted enabled Winder to fashion a new, slender line of resistance made up of the 7th Louisiana and the 5th Virginia. Major Davidson B. Penn, a native Virginian who emigrated to Louisiana and later became that state's lieutenant governor, managed to hold together the 7th Louisiana as its third commander of the day. The 27th Virginia never rallied in any numbers. In what seems to be a remarkable oversight, Winder never used the 2nd and 4th Virginia after their early failure near the Coaling. A captain in the 4th wrote in mystification, "We marched to the rear and were left there." Winder credited both regiments with participating in the ultimate attack on the Coaling; in fact, they had given up on that goal hours earlier.[34]

Stonewall Jackson's personal role at this desperate moment cannot be determined with precision. The general reported bluntly how Winder had been battered so badly "as greatly to disorganize his command, which fell back in disorder." James A. Walker, who did not arrive until the crisis was already breaking, remembered that he saw Jackson looking "like a farmer riding over his estate." Stonewall obviously maintained his accustomed stoic calm through these worried moments. The army commander probably was near the Baugher lane, because he reported that two of Poague's smoothbores back in operation from that vicinity "again opened fire on the enemy, he having halted in his advance."[35]

The Federal advance thus halted would never resume. All of the sacrifice on the plain—by Winder's long-suffering brigade, the reinforcing 7th Louisiana, the late-arriving Virginia regiments, and several artillery units—at last would receive its reward. The Louisiana brigade finally had completed its struggle through the wilderness and launched its might against the Yankee stronghold at the Coaling.

The Coaling
(upper right) **in 1908**

The Coaling
(upper right) in 1908

CHAPTER 22

THE COALING

"HELL-SPOT"

Confederates struggling on the bloody plain, no matter how stout their spirits, shared the pessimism later expressed by Randolph Fairfax of the Rockbridge Artillery: "I thought the day was lost." John Apperson of the 4th Virginia, peering out from the hillside thickets, felt exactly the same way: "I was afraid the day was lost." In the words of John Robson of the 52nd Virginia, "the time dragged slowly enough until it did seem that Shields was fully a match" for Jackson. To the surprised delight of the men on the plain, however, at the darkest moment "a loud and prolonged shout now burst on the ear." The "mighty shout on the mountain side" came from Taylor's Brigade as it erupted from the thickets and swarmed toward the Coaling.[1]

Southerners in danger would have agreed with artillerist Bill

Humphreys, who growled of the Louisianians, "they were rather late in this movement." The timing of the attack on the Coaling actually was not delayed far beyond the moment when Federals broke Winder's last line near the Baugher lane. Artillerist George Neese estimated the time as "about thirty minutes" after the Federal counterattack began, and therefore just at its high tide. An infantryman wrote the next day that the Louisiana brigade struck "soon after" Winder's left was broken, and an artillerist also timed it "soon" after the darkest moment. A member of the 7th Indiana, who experienced an understandably different reaction, reported that it came "*just* as [the breakthrough] was accomplished." Even Clara Strayer, watching with anticipation that must have exaggerated her concerns, admitted that the suspense was of short duration.[2]

Despite the relief of Confederates at the time, some postwar historical thinking insisted that Taylor should not have attacked where he did. A well-balanced account written in 1875, based on information from participants, concluded: "The Louisianians being misled failed to strike the flank of the Yankee left, and came out of the thicket immediately in front of that part of the line." The chief proponent of this notion was R. L. Dabney, who convinced himself that swinging farther around beyond the Coaling was not only a better plan (it was) but also that it was practicable under the circumstances (it was not!). Writing in an environment far from the smoking battlefield, and remote from its emergencies and exigencies, Dabney expressed "regret that the expedient was not adopted which would have saved the lives of so many brave men and made our victory so much more complete."[3]

Colonel Kelly and General Taylor found the decision to attack the Coaling head-on easy to make. Kelly's three units had arrived "within a few paces of the crest of the hill overlooking the Deep Run ravine." He began to align them while peering through the thickets at the Coaling. Most of the men could not see the mighty enemy battery but could hear its steady roar from startlingly close range. The colonel was more concerned by the "sounds of the yells and shouts of the combatants and of the rattling fire of musketry, now heard far to our left and rear." He could tell "the battle was going disastrously against us in the lowlands." At this point Taylor arrived with the 6th Louisiana, completing its more circuitous route.[4]

Dick Taylor listened with Kelly as "the sounds of battle to our rear appeared to recede." Soon "a loud Federal cheer was heard. . . .

It was rather an anxious moment,'' Taylor recalled, ''demanding instant action.'' Had any doubt remained about the emergency, a messenger from Winder came crashing through the thickets with a plea for help, ''urging [Taylor] to precipitate a front attack upon the batteries in the old coaling hearths.'' Jed Hotchkiss, who was serving as Taylor's guide, recalled the inevitable response to this call for assistance: ''After a consultation, it was agreed, in view of the present emergency, that the flank movement should be abandoned and an immediate attack, obliquing to the left, should be made upon the Federal position and the battery across the ravine.''[5]

The veteran Louisianians who held the outcome of the battle in their hands numbered 1,700 men. The Deep Run ravine separating them from the Coaling was open, with neither buildings nor fences to interrupt their charge and lure soldiers from the line into shelter.[6] Taylor's men outnumbered the Coaling's defenders by a wide margin, but they faced concentrated artillery fire at point-blank range and high ground that must be assaulted frontally. Taylor and his regiments stood alone at center stage.

Henry Kelly's quick reconnaissance had found that the only Federal infantry in evidence were a few skirmishers. These ''infantry supports of the Federal batteries were found to be posted beyond the ravine of Deep Run, in the woods to the left of the guns.'' While Confederate companies and regiments struggled to achieve some sort of tactical formation, some of the 9th Louisiana on the far right bumped into the enemy skirmishers up the mountainside. The ''sudden . . . encounter'' soon produced a ''lively racket of small arms.'' To that martial accompaniment Kelly and Taylor hurriedly sought to prepare their attack.[7]

The 6th Louisiana's approach as directed by Hotchkiss and Taylor had been well to the right of the rest of the brigade, but as it reached the front, the 6th had to edge down the steep mountain slope. In order to find a position, the 6th was obliged to march clear across the rear of the other regiments, then extend the brigade line down toward open ground on the left. In that location it enjoyed the least cover and faced the heaviest combat risks. The fortunes of war, compounded by geography, threw the 6th Louisiana onto ground where it would lose almost as many killed as the other three units combined.[8]

Rob Wheat's little battalion of roughnecks joined the right of the 6th, then came the 9th, and finally the 8th Louisiana on the far right. One company of the 8th formed into column, rather than line, to cover the bothersome right flank. All across the front "a strong skirmish line covered the advance." The difficult deployment in the dense woods was made even more complex by the terrain on their side of the ravine. On the Confederate side, the shoulder of the ravine not only stopped short of the road, it also angled obliquely away from the Federal side. The Louisianians' line necessarily conformed to its ridge, so it was not parallel to the enemy ridge, "but at an angle with it, conforming to the direction of the crest of the hill." The 8th therefore was closer to the opposite crest than the other Louisiana units. Taylor's troops faced almost due north; the Federal line opposite them faced more nearly west than south.[9]

A Louisianian described the final moments before the attack:

> The formation of the line had scarcely been completed when loud and prolonged cheers[,] rendered . . . in that measured term peculiar only to the enemy, were heard on the left, announcing his success, while the hoarse thunder of artillery, mingled with the sharp rattle of musketry, heralded the bloody work being there enacted. [The Louisiana men] waited with breathless anxiety: not a man in the line but understood the import of that measured cheer . . . they stood transfixed, hoping to hear in reply the defiant yell of the Confederates, but the only sound that greeted them was the renewed cheer of the enemy. Even the cannoniers working the enemy's guns . . . took up the shout and tauntingly re-echoed it. . . . It was evident to all that the left of the Confederate line had been repulsed. The time for action had arrived . . . they relieved themselves of everything likely to encumber them in their movements. . . . The order was rapidly passed along the line, "prepare for the charge. . . ." It is a necessity that will not permit a doubt—*the battery must be carried* or the day irretrievably lost. . . . The suspense of those few moments was terrible.[10]

Taylor could not afford to wait. The brigade's deployment "was not completed," Taylor reported, and it suffered from "some disorder." Even so, "without delay," Taylor shouted in what one Louisianian called "that sonorous voice, 'Forward, charge the battery and take it.' " The men responded eagerly by doing what they did best: attacking with savage determination.

The Louisianians dashed forward; the wild spirit of the men found vent in one loud, prolonged yell, which ran along the entire line as an electric current. Who that has ever heard that unearthly yell, will forget it; the preface to a charge, it was always the certain index of success; the spontaneous outburst of the soul, filled with wild enthusiasm; it was utterly incapable of being rendered by dictation.

One of Jackson's staff called the screams that echoed down the valley "the regular old 'Tiger yell.' " An Alabamian with Trimble's rear guard watched with awe as the Louisianians dashed out of the woods shrieking "the Rebel yell."[11]

Stunned Federals across the ravine recovered quickly and began hurling everything in their reach at the charging Southerners. The few Unionists among the trees up the slope from the Coaling fired their rifles frantically. Taylor called their fire "most destructive." Colonel Kelly, whose 8th Louisiana was closest to this threat, wrote that the surprise bought almost no time, the Federals opening fire "at once" against him. The awesome power of the cannon at the Coaling took little longer to react to the threat. Turned "full in the . . . faces" of the Louisiana infantry, the deadly artillery pieces unleashed "a storm of shot and shell . . . full upon their front, tearing great gaps in their ranks, strewing the [slope] behind them with the wounded and dying." An admiring Virginian who saw the attack, but was unaware of the decision to defy the odds, concluded that Taylor's men inadvertently "came out of the woods a little too soon and found themselves almost in front of the battery, which instantly began to shower [canister] upon them."[12]

Writing later in calm retrospect, Dick Taylor described the assault simply: "With a rush and shout the gorge was passed and we were in the battery. Surprise had aided us." Louisiana's designated Confederate historian paraphrased Taylor's language: "his brigade, with a rush and shout, swept through the gorge." Even Colonel Kelly, whose account is the single most reliable piece of primary writing on the battle, summarized those frantic minutes as telescoped in time: "With *one* volley in reply, and a Confederate yell heard far over the field, the Louisianians rushed down the rough declivity and across the ravine, and carried the batteries *like a flash*."[13]

Colonel Kelly's situation on the right of the angled line left him with the shortest distance to cross, which contributed to his sense

of brief moments dedicated to the attack. His wide command responsibilities doubtless also helped to shape Kelly's shrunken time frame.
By contrast, time seemed to stand still to men wielding muskets as
they plunged "down the rough declivity" and up the other side. The
steep slopes on both sides of the ravine must have saved hundreds
of men from being shot, because the steadily changing elevations
made them difficult targets. Civil War troops often shot high, and
the vertical dimension has always been more difficult than the horizontal for men using shoulder arms. A Lewis family account describes
the down-and-up sequence, providing further evidence about how
high up the hill the guns stood: "Taylor's exhausted men had penetrated the thicket to the south top of a ravine, on the opposite
heights of which was the battery. Down into the ravine went Taylor's
Louisianans, and up to the other side."[14]

Henry Kelly dashed ahead of the 8th Louisiana on foot and
reached the guns first. Colonel Leroy A. Stafford led the 9th forward
just to Kelly's left, but he went at least part of the way astride his
striking black stallion Harry Hays, named in honor of Stafford's friend
commanding the 7th Louisiana (who had been wounded a few minutes
earlier on the river plain). After laboriously leading their horses through
the thickets, most of the 9th's officers had to leave the animals behind
when a high stone wall interdicted their route of attack. Stafford turned
Harry Hays back a few feet, then put spurs to the strongly muscled crea-
ture and vaulted over the wall without difficulty.[15]

Major Rob Wheat advanced ahead of his battalion on horseback.
The major was not only one of the most colorful figures in the army,
but also among the largest. A traditional story declares that Stonewall
Jackson followed the course of the attack by tracking Wheat's towering figure as it moved toward the Coaling summit. Somewhere the
bulky battalion commander had acquired a horse sturdy enough to
carry him into battle, even up a slope such as the one facing him
on this violent morning. A board of officers had evaluated the animal
as worth $500, still a substantial sum for horseflesh in 1862. Rob
Wheat and his straining mount pushed through the Yankee lead and
iron to within twenty yards of the enemy guns before the horse
went down with a bullet in its head. Wheat regained his balance and
continued on foot, cheering the Louisianians forward.[16]

A Virginian cannoneer not far to the rear wrote of the dreadful
Yankee artillery fire pouring into the woods from which Taylor's
men were debouching. The brigade "suffered very severely . . . from

a continuous, raking fire of . . . canister," Clarence Fonerden recalled, "which tore and roared through that body of undergrowth like a cyclone, or the racket of the fiercest thunder devasting a forest of timber." Another gunner marveled at the Louisianians advancing "like a wave crested with shining steel . . . toward the fatal coaling . . . with fixed bayonets, giving the Rebel yell like mad demons. The crest of the coaling was one sheet of fire as the Federal batteries poured round after round of canister into the[ir] faces." Despite the fire, a third Virginian wrote, "those glorious soldiers halted not a second. Closing up their ranks, on and on [they went], hidden by the over-hanging clouds of smoke." Even an Indiana witness near the river wrote with respect of his enemies who "rushed over the low ground and up the hill in the face of ball and flame."[17]

Southern infantry on the plain well knew just what the Louisiana brigade was facing. One of them was amazed at their "irresistible impetuosity." Another wrote, "They are splendid in a charge!" Yet another observed, "Volumes on volumes of shot continue to salute their advance—but they do advance." A Virginia historian writing in 1867 concluded histrionically:

It is the best charge of the war. There will be only one more as desperate—that of Pickett's Virginians on the last day of Get-tysburg. [The Louisianians'] ranks are torn asunder, and where a line but now advanced, are seen only bodies, without legs, without arms, without heads, with breast[s] torn open—the whole lying still, or weltering in pools of blood.[18]

The dramatic charge was among the most notable achievements by Louisiana troops in a war they filled with desperate valor. As one of them wrote:

On the Louisianians dashed, regardless of the terrific fire of can-ister poured into their ranks by the battery. . . . its only effect is to accelerate the speed of the men in their impetuous charge. The nearer they approached the given point, of which the bat-tery was the centre, the less regard seemed paid to the preserva-tion of the line, until finally the regiments became so intermingled as to present a disorganized, but formidable mass. Still they press on, over fences, through the grounds adjoining the Lewis House, up hill and down dale . . . they vie with each

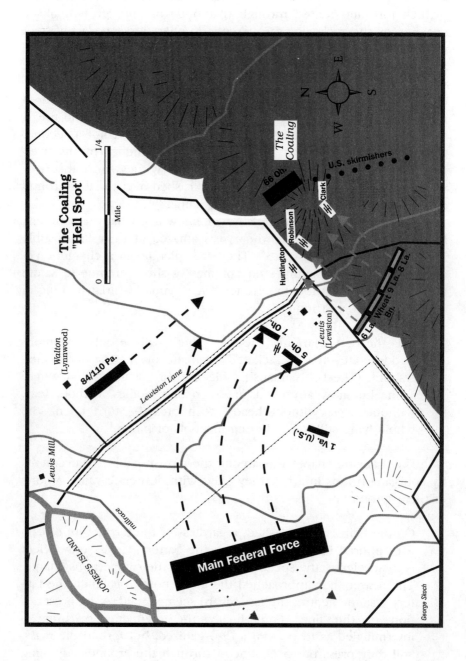

The Coaling
"Hell Spot"

The Coaling

U.S. skirmishers

66 Oh.

Clark

Robinson

Huntington

6 La. Wheat 9 La. 8 La.
Bn.

Walton
(Lynnwood)

84/110 Pa.

Lewiston Lane

7 Oh.

5 Oh.

Lewis
(Lewiston)

1 Va. (U.S.)

Lewis Mill

millrace

JONES'S ISLAND

Main Federal Force

George Skoch

other in their eagerness to reach the guns. . . . Words no matter how carefully selected, or highly wrought, fail to convey the sublimity of such a scene—attempt it, ransack the lexicon you only discover that to reveal the picture in its true color, words are totally inadequate.[19]

The screaming, helter-skelter mass of Confederates spread into the plain beyond the mouth of the ravine and up the mountainside and swarmed about the Federal artillery position. Brief, ugly, hand-to-hand combat ensued. A Confederate artillerist looking on anxiously described the onslaught as "a mighty billow of glittering steel [that] closed in on the belching batteries and their infantry supports with the bayonet." Colonel Kelly's 8th Louisiana arrived first, "followed immediately by the commands to the left of us." Rob Wheat was foremost among those other commands; his proponents would claim that he was "the first field officer" among the guns. In Kelly's words, "all formation was lost, and officers and men were all thrown into one unorganized mass around the . . . guns."[20]

Staunch Federal gunners delivered a last burst of canister into the forms looming in the gunsmoke "at the very muzzles of the guns," then the struggle degenerated into a powderless fight. No one had time to load a weapon. Even a proud Louisiana account praised the Northern cannoneers, who "fought their pieces to the last; no words can do justice to their heroism." Yankees who had loads in their muskets exchanged a final volley with those few Louisianians who had carried loaded weapons this long, or had stopped to reload them. Then the opposing infantry was at arm's length in the smoky melee.[21]

At such close quarters swords and bayonets came into play. Modern writers reviewing Civil War accounts often reject contemporary reports of the use of edged weapons, dismissing them as hyperbole for popular consumption. Virtually every witness of the bloody encounter at the Coaling recorded bayonet fighting. In General Taylor's words, "many fell from bayonet wounds." One of Taylor's subordinates wrote that the brave Federal gunners resisted until "thrust with the bayonet, and hacked to pieces with sword and sabre." Two Virginia gunners on the plain described bayonet encounters: "Bayonets gleamed in the morning sunshine one moment and the next they were plunged into living human flesh and dripping with reeking blood."[22]

In mortal combat at that range, men grabbed and swung anything with the potential to inflict harm. The artillerists' long-staffed ramrods became defensive utensils, their iron-tipped extractors making one end like a medieval lance. They "used their rammers in a way not laid down in the Manual," Dick Taylor recalled. Combatants snatched up musical instruments and flailed about with them. Others on both sides simply used their fists.[23]

Taylor's men overlapped the Federal guns on both sides and clearly could not be driven back unless Northern reinforcements arrived. Unionists around the Coaling stubbornly refused to give up. Southerners attested to the "obstinate resistance" and "bulldog tenacity" of their foe, who continued "fighting like fiends." The result was "a whirlwind of blood and death sweeping round and round the guns for five minutes" that "raged frightfully, resembling more the onslaught of maddened savages than the fighting of civilized men." Ed Stephens of the 9th Louisiana told his parents a few days later that this was "the bloodiest fighting of all," during which his gun "was shot half in t[w]o."[24]

A Louisiana account summarizes the fighting:

> Men ceased to be men. They cheered and screamed like lunatics—they fought like demons—they died like fanatics. . . . It was not war on that spot. It was a pandemonium of cheers, shouts, shrieks, and groans, lighted by the flames from cannon and muskets—blotched by fragments of men thrown high into trees by bursting shells. To lose the guns was to lose the battle. To capture them was to win it. In every great battle of the war there was a hell-spot. At Port Republic it was on the mountain side.[25]

From time to time amidst the maelstrom could be seen the figures of two gigantic Confederate officers, Major Rob Wheat and Lieutenant Colonel William R. Peck, "both bellowing like bulls." The three-hundred-pound Peck eventually would become a brigadier general. Wheat was one of the army's great characters. A staff officer described the major aptly as "big, blackguard, good-natured Major Wheat . . . a strange compound of some good & a great many bad qualities, all of them equally open & on the surface." The men who followed him were perfectly suited for the brawl at the Coaling—so long as Wheat controlled them. "Such a motley herd of humanity was probably never got together before, and may never be again," according to an officer who knew them well. Some were dressed "in the Zouave fashion—red fez caps and jackets, with striped baggy trousers." "They were very conspicuous," the officer added in dramatic understatement."[26]

Bill Trahern, a comrade from the 6th Louisiana, declared bluntly, "a greater lot of thieves and cut-throats never trod this hemisphere." That reputation, combined with "gorgeous uniforms and fairly good drilling," had persuaded many soldiers and civilians to think that Wheat's Tigers were "men of great courage and bravery"; but in fact "they possessed neither of these qualities," Trahern noted. Those familiar with Wheat's men at first hand knew them to be "Cowards and Wharf rats," drawn from "the low down population of every human race known." Only Rob Wheat could control them. Trahern more than once heard the major announce, "whilst standing up straight in his stirrups, 'if you don't get to your places, and behave as soldiers should, I will cut your hands off with this sword.' " With Wheat and his sword to encourage them, the wharf rats stormed through the Coaling bent on officially sanctioned mugging.[27]

These rowdy troops inexorably overcame Federal resistance around the Coaling, and "one long, loud yell announced the capture of the battery." This "grateful sound re-echoed along the base of the Blue Ridge," carrying the glad tidings to worn-out Confederates all across the battlefield. A Virginia cavalryman well behind the front lines remembered hearing "high above the thunder and roar of battle that long ringing Confederate yell which told us that the guns were taken." The Louisianians had turned the tide. In Dick Taylor's proud—and entirely accurate—assessment, "nobly did the sons of Louisiana sustain the reputation of their State." A captain in the brigade echoed Taylor's sentiment: "This was one of the most glorious battles of this war, and one of the bloodiest."[28]

Dozens of horses died at the Coaling. Some had fallen victim to the ordnance flying through the air, but most were killed by Louisianians worried that if Federals retook the ground they would use the horses to drag away the cannon. Rob Wheat, whose own horse lay dead just down the slope, saw the necessity of this cruel step and went to work shooting the poor creatures. After he had emptied his pistol loads, Wheat began cutting their throats with his knife. An onlooker saw the major looking "as bloody as a butcher." Big Lieutenant Colonel Peck also helped arrange the necessary slaughter.[29]

Some Federal horses had been killed by their own masters before the Confederates reached the Coaling. The excitement caused by Taylor's sudden appearance and the attackers' shrill yells stampeded the horses. The frenzied animals "ran over the [Northern] men to such an extent as to interfere with the defense of the guns that . . . the colonel [of the 66th Ohio] ordered his men to shoot the horses." An Indiana soldier heard that two of the batteries lost a total of 68 horses killed. Soldiers and civilians who visited the Coaling after the battle marveled more about the mounds of dead horses than about the human corpses.[30]

Accounts by the defenders of the Coaling manfully admit that they had been surprised. General Tyler called the attack "sudden and unexpected." Captain Joseph Clark, whose guns were on the highest ground, reported that about an hour after the easy repulse of the 2nd and 4th Virginia, "the enemy suddenly charged through the ravine. . . . The thick undergrowth prevented our seeing them until they were quite near us."[31]

Captain James Huntington did not profess to see Taylor marshaling for the attack, or claim foreknowledge that it was coming. He did, however, worry (aided by hindsight) that if Confederates had managed to come as close undetected as the 2nd and 4th Virginia had, others might follow. Was it not prudent "to suppose that . . . another [attack] would soon be made in stronger force?" It seemed to Huntington that the location of Clark's guns "was awkward in the extreme . . . jammed into the coal-pit so that it would be impossible to extricate them if the left was turned." On the other hand, the elevation that Clark enjoyed in the Coaling was a key feature in giving that position its mighty influence on the battle.[32]

Captain Huntington prepared for an infantry threat by piling canister on the ground "near the muzzles of the pieces ready for instant use." He also fired random bursts of case shot into the opposite woods. Despite such preparations, Huntington was looking in the wrong direction when Taylor burst upon him. As the captain examined Confederate artillery reinforcements through a telescope, "from the woods on our left rushed forth the Tigers, taking the line in reverse and swarming among Clark's guns."[33]

The three pieces of Huntington's Battery (H, 1st Ohio Light Artillery) at once swung their muzzles and began belching the convenient canister. They could hit the 6th Louisiana and Wheat's men, but no one farther up the ravine. To Huntington's left the single gun of Robinson's Battery (L, 1st Ohio Light Artillery) joined in. Clark's two pieces of Battery E, 4th U.S. Artillery, had almost no field of fire, because the Louisianians hurtling toward them were in defilade in the ravine. Clark's muzzles could not be depressed enough to hit the soldiers threatening his guns. Colonel Daum's official account declared that the Confederate approach came "from the left flank through a ravine on which Captain Clark's guns could not bear." Clark suggested unconvincingly that he might eventually have been able to shoot downhill when he reported: "it being impossible to bring the guns to bear upon the ravine *in time*."[34]

Federal guns that had Confederate targets made the most of their opportunity. The historian of the nearest Union regiment on the plain noted that Huntington and his friends fired canister, "chains, and even the rat-tail files supplied to each battery for spiking guns." Another Northern infantryman wrote admiringly that "the gunners . . . fought like tigers when the enemy were close on them. They put in armfulls of . . . canister, stones, chains and every thing they could put into their [cannon], and at every shot mowed down heaps of the enemy."[35]

Unfortunately for Tyler, he had withdrawn many of the artillery's infantry defenders assigned to the Coaling at just the wrong time. The 66th Ohio crouched in the woods behind the Coaling as the primary supporting regiment. Two infantry companies extended up the mountainside above the artillery cluster. An ample infantry force, the 84th and 110th Pennsylvania, had been waiting near the road behind the Coaling as reinforcements. Tyler, however, had been unable to resist calling on the Pennsylvania regiments to support the thrust on his right near the river. They did not reach position there in time to do any good, and when Taylor struck, they were en route back to the Coaling—having accomplished nothing in either place.[36]

Colonel Philip Daum, Tyler's fractious chief of artillery, complained bitterly in his official report about this misuse of the reserve infantry. He claimed (after the fact, of course) that he had from the outset of the battle been begging Tyler to support the guns on the left with infantry. After the repulse of the 2nd and 4th Virginia, Daum wrote angrily, "I now demanded of General Tyler to increase and push forward some more infantry into the woods to the left of the guns, whereupon he rebuked me for asking or suggesting to him."[37]

The language of Tyler's official report probably betrays some discomfort about his use of the 84th and 110th. "So rapid was this movement [by Taylor's men] that they passed the line on which [the 84th and 110th] were ordered unobserved, making a dash upon the battery." In other words, Taylor attacked the point to which the Pennsylvania regiments were returning before they could get there.[38] Daum was exactly right in his criticism. The artillerist was so quarrelsome and self-righteous, though, that his testimony about when the revelation reached him must be viewed with suspicion. Daum was shouldered out of field service soon after the battle—not because of his embarrassingly acute judgments, but rather to be rid of his obnoxious demeanor.

An adjustment even more damaging to Federal operations was the transfer of some of the slender infantry support that had been uphill to the Federal left of the Coaling. Company C of the 5th Ohio was one of the two companies situated there. When the 84th and 110th moved away, the importance of the companies' roles increased substantially. According to Frederick Fairfax of Company C, however, they "were ordered to fall back as the 2 Regiments who were to support us had been withdrawn." The removal of one company probably did not come to Tyler's personal attention. Whoever was at fault, it made the task of the attacking Louisianians far easier. Fairfax and his comrades hurried back up to their original position when the excitement erupted, but they were too late. As they neared the lip of the ravine, he wrote, "we discovered the enemy passing up the hill in a double quick between us and our artillery. We gave them what we had in our guns and then it was every man for himself."[39]

With the Pennsylvania regiments marching fruitlessly behind the Federal line, and at least one of the companies on the left out of reach, the 66th Ohio stood as the Coaling's only close infantry support. Upon Colonel Charles Candy and his men, General Tyler admitted, "depended everything at this critical moment. . . . Had they given way the command must have been lost." Unfortunately for the Federals, the 66th was not aligned parallel to the ravine, but rather almost perpendicular to it. Much of its front faced toward the river. Therefore, in Tyler's words, only "the left wing . . . was . . . close in the rear of the battery."[40]

A Confederate soldier who examined the ground after the battle remarked upon the strength of the Union infantry's location "on the hill, in the brush . . . and just in rear of his artillery [in] a low depression. . . . This made a very strong position." Its defensive virtues notwithstanding, the reverse slope behind the Coaling was almost useless as a point from which to defend against an attack in front. Captain Huntington remarked aptly, "in an emergency where seconds counted, they were practically out of the game." Tyler described the participation of the 66th Ohio with phrases such as "commendable bravery," "great coolness," and "well and gallantly executed." The 66th Ohio earned those laudatory mentions, but not by firing on Taylor's men as they charged through the ravine: that action most of them could not even see.[41]

For the Coaling gunners, the outcome could only be disastrous. Clark's men on the highest ground had the worst time because they could not shoot at the assailants climbing the steep slope toward them. "Nearly all the horses and part of the men were immediately shot down," Captain Clark reported. Huntington described events above his left with praise for Clark's men: "His cannoneers made a stout but short resistance, as pistols and sponge staffs do not count for much against muskets and bayonets. His guns were taken, so was [Robinson's] howitzer."[42]

One of the Coaling guns loaded in a frenzy by its crew had a charge seated and ready to fire when the Confederates boiled over the lip of the ravine. A big Louisianian loomed out of the smoke at the gun's muzzle, waved his bayonet at the gunner holding the lanyard, and bellowed, "You damned Yankee, give up! This is my gun." The damned Yankee jerked the lanyard and the bold Rebel disappeared, but there were hundreds more to take his place.[43]

A member of Jackson's staff who visited the Coaling not long after the battle recorded what he saw with obvious admiration for the Northern gunners who had stood to their guns so stoutly:

> They were nearly all killed in position—men and horses. One bright boy, with a brave smile on his fair Northern face . . . lay, shot through the heart, with his left arm over the muzzle of his gun, his knees on the ground and his right hand on the shell he was about to place in the piece, and behind it, was the gunner, his body lying over the sight, one eye open, shot in his tracks, and near him one with a broken rammer in his hand, the other part having snapped off in the piece as he was ramming the charge home.[44]

When Taylor's men swept the Coaling clean of Federals, they did not end the battle, but they effectively determined its ultimate result. The moment Colonel Carroll saw Confederates astride the Coaling position, he wrote in his report, "I then told General Tyler that we must organize for a retreat."[45] A great deal of deadly fighting lay ahead, but none of it would reverse the tide that 1,700 Louisiana Tigers had set in motion.

**The 5th Ohio had
difficulty passing
Lewiston because the
barn and other
outbuildings were full
of Confederates
plying their rifles
with deadly
effect.**

CHAPTER 23

THE STRUGGLE TO

HOLD THE COALING

The capture of the Coaling turned the tactical tide at Port Republic, but it by no means ended the battle. Confederate control of the Coaling was not ensured until four more surges had swept over the bitterly contested position. The moment of triumph seemed to Taylor in retrospect to have lasted only "a short time." In a postwar memoir he rhetorically described the first Federal rally as coming "in a moment," and another Louisianian wrote with some exaggeration that "a minute hardly passed" before fresh trouble loomed near.[1]

Clearing the Coaling had shattered the tactical formations and cohesion of the victorious Southern units. A Louisianian described the chaotic scene: "The groans of the dying mingled discordantly with the shouts of the victors, who, carried away by the excitement of the moment, were huddled promiscuously around the guns, totally oblivious of the storm about to burst upon them. . . . Disregarding the possibility of further resistance, [they] never attempted to re-form their shattered ranks." The Confederates could see frantic activity among Union troops all across the plain below them, most of it "rapid movement to the rear . . . and the belief gained ground that the enemy were in full retreat." Delighted Louisiana infantrymen gave another yell at the sight, and the officers had to hold their men back from charging down into the midst of the apparently beaten Federals.[2]

The focal point of the Northern masses, however, was not the retreat route below the Coaling—but rather the Coaling itself! The Louisiana troops were isolated from help on their newly won position. Not even Southern cannoneers could offer support. The moment Taylor's men burst out of the woods in their attack, Confederate artillery had been obliged to shift fire away from that point for fear of hitting friends. What had looked like a retreat "was merely the gathering cloud that precedes the storm. The Louisianians, excited by their success, were not a little surprised when . . . the enemy . . . turned to the right about, and commenced steadily to advance." Confederate officers who had failed to restore order soon after their triumph discovered that, predictably, "all efforts to re-form the disorderly mass under the fire which now raged were unavailing."[3]

Federal masses resolved into regimental lines a few hundred yards from the Coaling and prepared to retake it. Colonel Kelly of the 8th Louisiana described the abrupt change in outlook: "While this exultant crowd were rejoicing and shouting over their victory, suddenly a scathing fire of canister was poured into them by a section of Clark's Battery, which had been rapidly brought over from the Federal right to within two hundred yards of the position of the captured guns." Federal resurrection on short notice in the face of disaster showed considerable grit. Stonewall Jackson gave his enemy full credit, calling this thrust "a vigorous and well-conducted attack, accompanied by a galling fire of canister from a piece suddenly brought into position."[4]

Confederates could see a brave Federal officer, one of several observed across the lines this day, inspiring his troops to attack. The "conspicuous figure" on a gray horse directing the Federal advance prompted a Confederate witness to write, "there is not a Confederate survivor of that fierce fight who would not be proud to salute him."[5]

Resurgent Federals quickly—and surprisingly, so soon after a major repulse—gathered momentum and swept toward the Coaling "with a rush" and in a "solid front" that proved irresistible. Dick Taylor called the enemy move "a determined and well-conducted advance upon us." Unable to re-form into units in the midst of this new crisis, individual Louisianians "generally chose their own position, and fought on their individual responsibility." Despite their best efforts, the Confederates were obliged to abandon the Coaling. One Louisiana source described their retirement as "a slow but stubborn retreat," but another admitted having been sent "whirling over the corpses—across the valley." Jackson's official report simply announced: "Taylor fell back to the skirt of the wood near which the captured battery was stationed."[6]

The Federal rally that impressed the Confederates as a seamless whole actually was made up of pieces welded together from the 66th Ohio near the Coaling and the 5th and 7th Ohio, drawn from their pursuit of Winder on the plain. At the moment the Louisianians erupted over the Coaling, the 1st Virginia (Union) was closer to the emergency than any other of Tyler's troops on the plain; but it seems to have done nothing. From their positions farther north, and also farther west because of their pursuit of Winder, the two Ohio regiments executed a remarkable maneuver under pressure. The colonel of the 8th Louisiana watched with surprise from atop the Coaling as the enemy successfully "changed front to their left and rear" and managed to re-form facing in an entirely new direction. Having accomplished that delicate maneuver, the two regiments advanced steadily toward their goal. James Clarke of the 5th Ohio calmly summarized an undertaking anything but placid: "We had to reform and go there. . . . We went up . . . and took the guns."[7]

Colonel Dunning of the 5th Ohio had difficulty passing Lewiston because the house, orchard, and outbuildings were full of Confederates plying their rifles with deadly effect. Some of Taylor's men had sought cover in the buildings, and a portion of the 27th Virginia still hung on there too. The Ohio colonel pushed his regiment past "on a full run" and occupied some of the buildings, but a pesky knot of Southerners remained in the complex to the last. Dunning's attention to Lewiston establishes something nowhere else documented, that the 5th Ohio's counterattack toward the Coaling was to the right of the 7th Ohio as both regiments faced in that new direction.[8]

The 7th Ohio had been winning its battle against Winder as the middle regiment in Tyler's line on the plain. From that considerable distance, however, Tyler successfully disengaged the 7th and in short order had it beside the 5th Ohio and charging toward the Coaling. To reach the left of the 5th, the 7th had to loop well to the rear of the point from which it had launched its attack against Winder. Once behind the Lewiston lane and facing roughly south, the 7th "dashed up the hill and over the guns." In the process, the regimental historian lamented, "five color-bearers [were] shot down, while advancing as many rods." A lieutenant seized the colors and carried them into the Coaling. One of the Ohioans complained that the "constant shifting" had by this time thoroughly "wearied the troops." The exhausted counterattackers had accomplished a considerable feat.[9]

A pair of Federal guns drawn near the Coaling on the plain provided the nexus upon which the 5th and 7th Ohio marshaled their effort. They came from the section of Clark's Battery that had been fighting near the river. Artillery chief Philip Daum put them into action and egocentrically saw their role as pivotal. In his view, the guns "and the musketry of some infantry near by was too much for the enemy." Daum never even mentioned the infantry counterattack. Tyler's more balanced report applauded the artillerists' role, but he credited the successful assault to the 5th and 7th as well as the 66th Ohio.[10]

The 66th had been positioned closest to the Coaling when Taylor struck. After falling back in the face of the surprise, the 600 men of the 66th prepared to attack after "a few stirring words" from their officers. One Buckeye recalled candidly that "matters certainly looked critical . . . buglers were held in readiness to sound the retreat for the whole Union army." With fixed bayonets the 66th moved out, yelling vigorously. "Imagine this terrific collision," one of them wrote histrionically, "then imagine the volleys of . . . many muskets, the clashing and plunging of . . . bayonets. Mingle with these sounds and sights, the yells, hurrahs, screams, and dying groans and gasps of fierce, bleeding, victorious and dying combatants, and [you] will have a mental picture of the fight." The 66th failed at first. "Though making a noble effort," the regiment was "thrown back as a clenched fist might be thrown back from a wall of India rubber, against which it has been dashed." The 66th suffered the highest total of men killed in the Federal army. The advance by the 5th and 7th Ohio probably could not have succeeded without the effort of the 66th to pave the way.[11]

The three Ohio regiments received some support, though less than they hoped for, from the 84th and 110th Pennsylvania. Those two peripatetic units had been moving from point to point without ever reaching any crucial action. An account of the 84th's participation boasted that, with the Ohio troops, "we had them between two fires"; but in fact the Pennsylvanians' contributions had primarily nuisance value. Colonel Kelly of the 8th Louisiana wrote that his men "were assailed at the same time by numbers from other regiments . . . who, in falling back, swarmed like so many hornets about the Confederates."[12]

Captain Huntington grasped the opportunity afforded by the Federal rebound to try to save his pieces on the lower ground just north of Clark's and Robinson's guns. The cannon farthest to the Union right got away, leaving behind its caisson and limber. It would drop trail and fire again when a Federal renaissance reclaimed the Coaling. That was the extent of Huntington's good fortune. The next team that approached had two drivers shot from the saddle. The remaining driver could not handle the frightened horses, and they dashed off with the limber. Huntington's gun farthest to the left was squarely in the road. The captain hurriedly ordered the sergeant in charge, twenty-four-year-old Edward Allen ("a splendid soldier"), to limber up. "Cool as if on parade, the sergeant turned to obey," Huntington recalled, "when he fell almost at my feet, shot through the heart, and died without uttering a sound." The battery also lost killed Privates Philip Isnaugh and John McGill, both aged thirty-three. Huntington ran back to round up the team in person, but could not convince its drivers to leave the relative safety they enjoyed.[13]

On the higher ground above Huntington, Unionists who had recaptured the Coaling put Clark's and Robinson's guns back into service and fired briefly toward the confused melee on the plain. Other Federals corralled a few of the tough Louisianians who had not managed to get away. A correspondent who saw some of them a few days later wrote what many observers thought: "They are a hard looking set." One Confederate claimed that the Yankees perpetrated atrocities on Louisiana captives in their power. Captain Eustace Surget of General Taylor's staff declared just after the battle that "the Yankees bayonetted our wounded & struck them in the head with the butts of their muskets when temporarily in possession of part of the battle field." In consequence, Surget predicted, "Jackson's army will . . . take few prisoners in the future."[14]

It did not take Taylor's troops long to revenge any misdeeds their comrades suffered. They had made good use of the interval since being driven away by peppering the area with a scalding fire that kept the Federals from consolidating their renewed grip on the Coaling. Winder's situation on the plain had at once smoothed out when every Federal eye turned back toward the struggle around the ravine. That allowed Winder to open artillery fire against the Unionists fighting Taylor.[15]

Once they grudgingly yielded the Coaling to the enemy, Taylor's men looked for the best positions from which to neutralize it. "To sweep the ground occupied by the battery," one of them wrote, "it was necessary that positions in its immediate vicinity should be selected and maintained." Colonel Henry Kelly recognized the Lewiston house and outbuildings as a good vantage point for such duty. He led a number of Louisiana infantry into the "substantial brick edifice, from the doors and windows of which a musketry fire could be kept up at short range upon the [Coaling] and the approaches to it." Others of Taylor's men ("most of the command," according to a witness) repaired to the thickets whence they had launched the attack.[16]

Colonel Kelly and most of his supporters were forced out of Lewiston after firing from its cover for a time. The colonel fell in with Captain Surget, and the two men scrambled into the thickets beyond the ravine looking for Taylor. They found him on the hillside above the main road, surrounded by a gaggle of troops "without formation, except a short line with the colors of the 6th Louisiana." The soldiers, "dispersed in irregular bodies on the hillsides along the road, and on both sides of the ravine," resolutely poured "an irregular but persistent" fire toward the Coaling. This musketry was holding Federals across the ravine at bay, but to the surprise of the Louisianians "it did not create disorder": the Federals kept shooting back.[17]

For a time Taylor apparently believed that bringing fire against the Coaling could fulfill his purpose. A Louisianian described the firefight that dragged on for some time:

> The Louisianians defiant and resolved, their ranks torn, mutilated, and greatly reduced[,] . . . maintained with Spartan courage the unequal strife. For well they knew that the success of the day rested with them. . . . The conflict increased and swelled with renewed vigor into the full roar and fury of determined battle. . . . the deadly fire of . . . small arms . . . could not be with veteran troops other than of the most vital and effective character.

Henry Kelly proudly described his men's valor: "disorganized as they were, they held their ground with unyielding tenacity until . . . enabled to again go forward."[18]

Getting the disorganized men to go forward again was not easy. The general's subordinates did yeoman work to accomplish that goal. Taylor reported that the energetic Captain Surget "distinguished himself greatly, and rendered the most important service." Lieutenant James Hamilton earned special plaudits by "rallying and reforming the men when driven back to the edge of the wood." Lieutenant John Killmartin of the 7th Louisiana, a temporary aide, seconded Hamilton's efforts. Somehow they nerved the troops for another assault.[19]

As Taylor's men tumbled out of the thickets to retrace their steps to the Coaling, they came under particularly irksome fire from up the slope on their right. Federal riflemen up the shoulder "worried us no little," Taylor wrote. He sent two companies of the 9th Louisiana "up the gorge" to get above the pesky Yankees. The detachment sent on that mission accomplished the dislodging "cleverly," putting a permanent end to interference from that quarter.[20]

A Pennsylvanian who saw the renewed assault said it boasted "such numbers as to make a resistance out of the question." Others of sterner stuff resisted anyway. The few Unionist artillerists back at their guns "fought like tigers," persisting "till their ammunition was out and the loads of their revolvers exhausted; and then they took stones . . . and threw them at the advance of the enemy." Taylor's infantry responded in kind:

> They re-form under a terrific fire and rush with an impetus which even the hand of death cannot stop. They reach the guns again, and again men shoot, stab, cut, hack—aye! they grapple and roll under the wheels of cannon so hot that they would almost blister. . . . It is a grapple to the death. For the second time the Federals are pressed back.

As Dick Taylor walked over the bloody ground after the battle, he found members of each regiment in the charge distributed evenly "under the guns of the captured battery."[21]

Henry Kelly became the leading authority on the battle by expanding his firsthand knowledge through careful study of other sources. Kelly concluded, of course, that the Coaling "was the key of the enemy's whole position." He added: *From the instant the batteries were first taken by the Louisiana infantry the battle was lost, irretrievably, to the Federal forces.*[22] Kelly may have been too sanguine about that initial impact. Had the Louisiana troops not spurred themselves through the ravine and up the slope once more, resolute Federals might have retrieved the day. The Louisianians, however, did not give them that chance.

The second charge on the Coaling probably cost Taylor's regiments as dearly as the first. Throughout, Wheat's rowdy battalion lost 30 of 95 enlisted men as casualties, and 6 of its 9 officers. The much larger 9th Louisiana lost only one more man than Wheat's unit; chasing the Yankee sharpshooters from the upper slopes obviously was a less dangerous business than bulling straight through the ravine. The 46 casualties in the 8th Louisiana put it midway down the brigade's loss column. In Taylor's four units engaged at the Coaling, a captain and three lieutenants were killed. Another fourteen lieutenants fell wounded. The attrition among Taylor's company officers destroyed much of the brigade's capacity to react to opportunities and to obey commands.[23]

The dead captain was Isaac A. Smith of the 6th Louisiana. The dead in that regiment offer a chance to analyze the truism (fostered by Taylor himself) that the brigade was predominantly made up of Irishmen. As with the 8th New York at Cross Keys, the truism survives under scrutiny. The 6th had eighteen men killed; places of birth are available for twelve. Nine of them were born in Europe and two others outside the Confederacy. The native Irishmen were Thomas Kane, Michael Murray, James Noonan, Daniel Mullen, James Gallagher, John Smith, Daniel Fitzpatrick, and Delon Foley. Michael Martin was born in the German state of Baden, John McCormick in New York, and Thomas Windsor in Ohio. The sole native-born Confederate was Daniel A. Fitch, a son of Louisiana.[24]

Some of the Louisiana survivors again turned the coveted cannon toward the Yankees, "and for the second time the guns speak under Confederate hands." "Will it end here?" a contemporary asked rhetorically, and answered his own question in the negative. The tenacious Federals were putting together yet another drive to capture the Coaling once more. Federals from all across the plain slid south toward the Coaling and eastward—toward the beckoning retreat route. The sturdiest of them gathered around the threatened point, some in the woods behind the Coaling, others on the plain below it.[25]

The 66th Ohio had been an integral part of the first recapture, before being thrown rudely back. Private Calvin C. Irwin of Company I of the 66th helped to rally the regiment. "Stand to your colors, boys!" Irwin shouted. "Give them another dash! Another one, boys

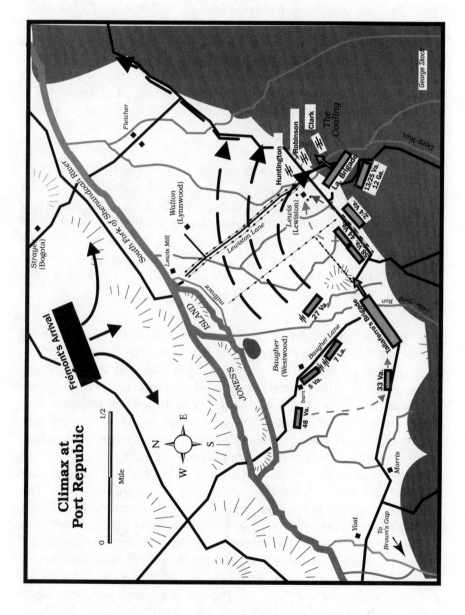

Climax at
Port Republic

Frémont's Arrival

South Fork of Shenandoah River

Strayer
(Bogota)

Fletcher

Walton
(Lynwood)

Lewis Mill

millrace

Lewiston Lane

Lewis
(Lewiston)

Huntington

Robinson

Clark

The
Coaling

La. Brigade

13/25 Va.
12 Ga.

Deep Run

George Stott

21 Va.

58 Va.–44 Va.

27 Va.

Taliaferro's Brigade

Little Deep Run

Baugher Lane

7 La.

5 Va.

barn

48 Va.

33 Va.

Baugher
(Westwood)

Morris

ISLAND

JONES'S

Yost

To
Broun's Gap

N
W   E
S

Mile

0   1/2

and they'll break." Such efforts slowed, then halted, the fleeing refugees. Many re-formed into line, then the order echoed across the front, "Column, steady, forward, double-quick, charge!" An Ohioan described the result of this new counterattack: "There was the same terrible collision, the same volleys, the same clashing and plunging of bayonets; there were more shouts, and hurrahs and screams, and dying groans and gasps. . . . Every man kept grimly to his dreadful work, foot to foot, face to face, weapon to weapon[,] . . . rough and tumble."[26]

A Louisianian painted the same scene from the opposite perspective:

> Panting like dogs—faces begrimed—nine-tenths of them bareheaded [hats were important to Civil War soldiery; and their absence indicated discomposure]—the Federal wave rolls back on the guns, and now there is a grapple such as *no other battle ever furnished*. Men beat each other's brains out with muskets which they have no time to load. Those who go down to die think only of revenge, and they clutch the nearest foe with a grasp which renders death stronger.[27]

The new Federal thrust had enough power to drive the Confederate from the Coaling yet again. Captain Joe Clark hurried back to the high ground where his two rifles again were in Federal hands. He found thirty of his horses dead around the guns and therefore could not salvage anything; the bloody slaughter of the animals by Rob Wheat and others paid off. Colonel Daum, a hard man to please in every way, applauded Clark's valor. He also damned Captain Huntington simply because he could not see him from his personal vantage point.[28]

For a quarter hour a relative lull settled around the Coaling. Each side had exhausted its available momentum. A third assault by Taylor's men clearly could secure the vital ground permanently, but they did not have the numbers or the energy to launch one. "Anxiously awaiting the result of the struggle at the battery," a Louisianian wrote, "hostilities in other parts of the field had now almost subsided." When orders came forward to take the Coaling again, "a murmur ran down the line" at the daunting prospect and "eyes swept up that fatal slope, now gray with southern dead." The word from the rear was, "General Jackson says he must have those guns— he must have them!" A "lank and ragged private" sparked laughter in the midst of the grim scene when he drawled loudly, "Say, boys, let's we-all-1-1 chip in an' buy them air guns for Ole Jack!"[29]

Yankees meanwhile moved back toward the Coaling in strength. Taylor described his unease: "[The enemy] had countermarched, and, with left near the river, came into full view of our situation. Wheeling to the right, with colors advanced, like a solid wall he marched straight upon us. There seemed nothing left but to set our backs to the mountain and die hard."[30]

At this worrisome juncture ("at that instant," Taylor declared gratefully), Dick Ewell arrived on the scene "like a healthy breeze, to be welcomed with cheers." Reinforcements following him soon came into view. Ewell crashed through the underbrush, on foot with his cap in his hand, and at once invigorated the stalled Confederates. Pointing toward the Coaling, Ewell cried, "Men, you all know me. We must go back to that battery." The Louisianians gave "one loud, prolonged yell." Ewell's troops hastening to their aid took it up "and in encouraging tones reechoed it back to its authors." The spirited shout announced the doom of the Federal position.[31]

Ewell's arrival gave the weary Louisianians the spark they needed for one last push. Colonel Kelly "went forward again with the officers and men immediately about me," without any pretense of commanding his regiment or even its fragments. "The men rose to their feet," another Louisiana source reported, and "a shout—the death knell of the enemy—burst spontaneous[ly] from the line, and without further orders they again dashed forward to the battery, over the ground already strewn with their fallen comrades." This "desperate rally," as Taylor called it, "in which . . . the drummer-boys shared," looked to Yankees on the receiving end like "an overwhelming force."[32]

Most Virginians hurrying to Taylor's support arrived just too late to be of help. One of them wrote that the Louisiana troops in the third attack on the Coaling looked "like a hawk on a chicken." The 13th Virginia had been scrambling through the brushy woods intent on providing support. They arrived at the Coaling "on a little knoll" to find "the La boys in charge—one Irishman astraddle of one of the Guns." Sam Buck of the 13th described what he saw: "It was a sickening sight; men in grey and those in blue piled up in front of and around the guns and with the horses dying and the blood of men and beasts flowing almost in a stream." A Marylander who reached the Coaling soon thereafter found the dead "just as they had fallen, the blue and the gray intermixed. In all my experience, I never saw dead men and dead horses lying so thick. Every horse in the battery had been killed, and men were lying among and on them."[33]

The Federal last stand at the Coaling did not have as much staying power as their earlier efforts. Some Confederates faced little fire and found the enemy "in the act of withdrawing . . . as we advanced." Others, primarily on the Confederate left, "met . . . a terrific fire" before they succeeded in driving off the Unionists. A Louisianian thought that if the Yankees "had had two more regiments in reserve behind the guns they could not have been taken. When the Federals were driven for the third time they were not disheartened, but wiped out."[34]

Clark's guns atop the knoll had no chance; because of their circumscribed position, they had been doomed since the first attack. Robinson's single gun to Clark's right also could not be extracted. Corporal Sam Cochran fought that gun's last stand virtually alone. He single-handedly fired the final three rounds from the piece, then knocked down an attacker with a stone and somehow made his escape. In addition to the gun, Robinson lost all of his wheeled vehicles and twenty-four horses.[35]

Once again Huntington's three guns near the road faced the heaviest fighting, primarily because they had the best chance for escape. One of his pieces had escaped between Southern surges, but it now joined in the final desperate defense. Huntington recalled how a portion of the last Confederate assault, "yelling like demons, came pouring up the road" straight at his position. The loader stood firmly to his duty and rammed down two canister rounds, but the man on the other side of the muzzle went down. The crewman responsible for firing the piece stuck the primer into the vent, but then panicked and dashed off. Someone else seized the lanyard and jerked it, firing the canister, which "opened a lane and checked the onset of that particular lot of Tigers for an instant." Grasping the moment, the gunners limbered up and clung to the caisson and gun carriage as it careened away—the only Coaling piece that escaped. James Huntington did not get away with the crew and for a moment contemplated surrender. "But having a wholesome dread of Southern hospitality as dispensed at that period," he wrote, "I concluded to take the chances, and was lucky enough to slip out between the bullets."[36]

Three times the Louisiana troops had thundered through the ravine and into the Coaling. Twice the Federals had mustered the courage and determination to expel them. The charmed third time closed the door on Yankee efforts and sealed a narrowly won victory for Stonewall Jackson. In its aftermath, word tardily reached Taylor from Jackson "to fall back, that we were repulsed in the center and on the left." The victory had been won in the meantime.[37]

The Richmond *Whig,* normally prone to trumpeting the exploits of Virginia troops, stated categorically that Taylor's men "virtually won the battle at Lewiston. . . . The world produces no better fighters than the Louisianians—few, very few, so good. . . . There is a little touch of the very devil in the Louisianians."[38]

Louisiana sources glowed with deserved pride, tempered by sorrow at the loses. "As the saviors of the day," one man wrote, "the Louisianians covered themselves with glory"; but the victory was "sealed with the best blood of the brigade . . . at the sacrifice of many a heroic life." Another of Taylor's soldiers boasted, with the same mixture of sorrow: "The Brigade have immortalized themselves, and Jackson credits them with having turned the tide. . . . They are terribly cut up, and I have lost many an old friend." George Ring, commanding a company in the 6th Louisiana, hastened to reassure his wife of his safety—and of the valor of his unit, which lost half its strength in the battle. "So you see darling I dont command a lot of cowards," Ring wrote. "Only one man in the crowd has as yet shown the white feather and we are going to give him one more trial[;] if he fails again he will be drummed out of the service."[39]

Almost every Confederate who passed the Coaling and wrote anything of the battle boasted about the "splendid battery" captured there, usually calling them brass guns and reporting their number as from five to seven. There were in fact five of them: Clark's two, Robinson's one, and two of Huntington's three. The reports using larger numbers included the two trophies from the June 8 fight. Dick Taylor dispensed the captures, as was the prerogative of the captor, to Confederate batteries that had impressed him. Two brass pieces went to the Baltimore battery that had fought near Taylor at Cross Keys. The rest he gave to the Louisiana Guard Artillery, which lost them in Jubal Early's debacle at Fisher's Hill in 1864. Twelve years later there was talk in the North of returning them to the Louisiana veterans as part of an early postwar sectional rapprochement.[40]

Stonewall Jackson quickly grasped the greater, though less tangible, prize that the Louisiana Brigade had won—the momentum necessary to build into an overwhelming victory. No one knew better than Stonewall what to do with an edge over an enemy.

**View from the
Coaling about
1900, looking toward
the South Fork of the
Shenandoah River**

CHAPTER 24

THE CLIMAX ON THE PLAIN: "HUNGRY TIGERS TURNED LOOSE"

N o Federal could now contemplate a farther advance on the river plain with armed and dangerous Confederates far to the left rear. What happened to Winder and Ewell and their supports while Taylor fought at the Coaling remains to be told.

General Ewell summarized the effect of Taylor's advent in the Federals' midst: "As soon as his fire was heard in rear and flank the whole force of the enemy turned to meet this new foe." An officer of the Stonewall Brigade, which was harder pressed than Ewell's force, enthused about his comrades from Louisiana: "They are splendid in a charge! The enemy feel the loss of their guns and their line wavers.—Cheer after cheer bursts from our lines." Soldiers of both armies who had been fighting for their lives before Taylor's eruption paused to watch and listen. The sounds of combat that reached them attested to the ferocity reigning at the Coaling:

> Down where the Federal right is pushing Jackson they hear this pandemonium of shrieks and screams on the mountain-side, and they halt. It is a sound ten times more horrible than the whistle of grape or the hiss of canister. Men cease firing to look up. They can see nothing for the smoke, but what they hear is a sound like that of hungry tigers turned loose to tear each other to death.[1]

The stunned pause on the plain did not last long. Federals at once recognized that retrenchment was in order, and the stouter of the Confederate foemen they had been driving sought to harass them as much as possible. General Winder recognized that the reprieve did not inspire all of his retreating troops. He wrote frankly in his diary that night that only "some men rallied on the left." Enough soldiers of the 5th Virginia responded to knit together a new line. Major Penn of the 7th Louisiana took over from the regiment's wounded colonel and dying lieutenant colonel and joined Winder's re-forming line. Some artillery joined the knot of determined Southerners using the Baugher lane as a rallying point. Fragments of other Confederate regiments adhered to this cluster as well.[2]

Farther to the Confederate right, Colonel Grigsby and the 27th Virginia also halted and regrouped when the pressure on them abated. The 27th's troops had been facing what they called "portions of the . . . 1st Bogus Va."—a Union regiment raised in what the next year would become West Virginia. The Confederate Virginians opposite them captured four dozen prisoners. A member of the Stonewall Brigade gloated: "We took prisoners claiming to be of Virginia Regiments—a mean, low thing in the federal government to form regiments of foreigners and call them Virginia Regiments." The 27th Virginia probably had not retired quite as far as others and accordingly moved forward from the most advanced Confederate position on the plain.[3]

The artillery played an important part in the rally, just as it had in delaying disaster a few minutes earlier. As soon as Winder noticed Taylor's plight under the first enemy counterattack, he turned a Parrott rifle on the enemy with good effect. Federals who reoriented themselves toward the Coaling simultaneously exposed a flank, and sometimes their rear, to Winder's guns. Confederates who had suffered so much under artillery fire all morning now turned the tables gleefully.[4]

One of Captain Poague's Rockbridge guns had fallen into enemy hands, and two others had been driven from the field. At the climax, however, three of his pieces had enough ammunition and élan left to join the renewed barrage against the Yankees. Joe Shaner told his diary "we had a hot time of it" before "we whiped them out." Some of Shaner's mates had by this time been wiped out physically and emotionally. Ned Moore collapsed: "I found myself utterly exhausted, my woolen clothes wet with perspiration. Having been too tired to get out of the way when the gun fired, my eardrums kept up the vibrations for hours." Moore fell into a drugged sleep just behind the line while, as he recalled, "the battle reverberated in my head." His respite lasted only a few minutes, before someone shook him awake to participate in pursuit of the beaten foe.[5]

Confederate artillery continued to arrive. Colonel Crutchfield had at last rounded up the artillery ammunition he should have restocked the night before, and rifled pieces belonging to Chew, Brockenbrough, Raine, Courtney, and Lusk joined in the bombardment. Winder moved the guns forward to what he described as "a far better position"—in fact a series of better positions. "I continued to advance them as rapidly as possible," he reported, "pouring in a heavy and well-directed fire." The men and guns that were so desperately needed moments before now arrived in profusion. With so many at hand, Winder and Crutchfield were able to divide their fire between Federal artillery and infantry. The contested buildings and grounds of Lewiston took a battering, no doubt some of it hard on friends clinging to cover there unbeknownst to the Confederate gunners. Unionists could not count on shelter at Lewiston when the main house and "buildings, orchards and fences . . . were scourged by a pitiless storm of cannon-shot."[6]

The Confederates closest to the Coaling, other than the Louisianians, were Dick Ewell's two regiments, the 44th and 58th Virginia. Their headlong assault out of the woods into the flank of Yankees chasing Winder had played an important part in winning time for Taylor. Taylor's eruption onto the Coaling in turn saved the 44th and 58th from paying a dear price for their audacity; once Taylor attacked, all other Southerners became secondary concerns to Federals.

Freed from concern for his own front, Ewell stoutly began to realign his survivors in order to make them useful in Taylor's further work. He managed to reorganize them despite the losses they had suffered, the confusion that reigned, and artillery fire striking in their midst. The general paid this proud tribute to the men of the two regiments: "It would be difficult to find another instance of volunteer troops after a severe check rallying and again attacking the enemy."[7]

In his draft official report, Ewell bluntly recounted his personal role: "I led them to the assistance of . . . Taylor . . . [who] was heard engaging the enemy far to the rear." In a typical burst of modesty, Ewell then deleted the mention of his own performance. His men well knew the credit the general deserved. Captain Henry W. Wingfield of the 58th Virginia called Ewell "a gallant officer" in describing Port Republic:

> I could but notice his coolness in leading us in a charge against the batteries. A shell exploding under his horse he did not even look to see the effect but with his eye fixed steadily on the piece before him moved steadily on. The men are willing to follow him. . . . He mounted a wagon horse with a blind bridle and followed the retreating enemy.[8]

As recounted in the preceding chapter, Ewell and his brave remnant arrived near the Coaling just in time to play a vital part in the third and final capture of that key point. Campbell Brown grumbled that his chief's achievements were ignored in accounts of the battle. "So far from appreciating the true circumstances of the battle," Brown wrote to his doting mamma on June 17, some in the army accused Ewell's detachment of "having behaved very badly!" Brown's complaints were ill founded, or at least premature. Comments about Dick Ewell's behavior and that of his troops, including Stonewall Jackson's official report, are all positive.[9]

Numerous Louisiana accounts cite Ewell's arrival in person to lead the third capture of the Coaling. In the smoky confusion, most of them did not recognize the troops who accompanied him, but the 44th and 58th contributed to the final success. The 44th Virginia joined in the assault, probably around Lewiston, where the 58th was situated. Charles Wight of the latter regiment wrote: "We were placed on their [Taylor's] left & we all moved forward again . . . directly against the battery. . . . We could not see it for the thicket around us but it was not long before we saw some of the guns stationed on a knowl near the road." The Virginians helped to over-whelm all resistance in short order.[10]

Private George Ailstock of the 58th particularly distinguished himself in the attack. The twenty-four-year-old laborer from Rockbridge County, who was renowned in the regiment for his courage and strength, outran his comrades. By the time a handful of friends caught up with him, Ailstock had corralled a Yankee lieutenant and 28 enlisted men as prisoners. When an astonished regimental officer asked how he managed to capture so many, George replied, "I just surrendered 'em, Major."[11]

Five other Confederate regiments floundering in the thickets southwest of the Coaling did not lend a hand. Winder spotted the 2nd and 4th Virginia "lying quietly on their arms to the right under the woods" and sent an aide to prod them forward. The colonel of the 2nd admitted that the fighting had ended "before we came up." The colonel of the 4th concurred. When the Federals broke for the last time, the 4th "rent the air with a shout of victory," but contributed little else.[12]

Colonel James A. Walker had the other three regiments still in the woods—the 13th and 25th Virginia and 12th Georgia—attempting to follow Taylor's confusing route. Despite the colonel's best efforts, his units became twisted and snarled in the underbrush and finally fetched up against a completely impassable precipice. He laboriously turned the troops around and guided them toward what seemed like the sound of the guns echoing through the woods. Walker plunged forward in person and found Ewell, who ordered him to fall in behind the 44th and 58th. The three regiments obeyed Ewell's instructions, but arrived just in time to witness the triumph without participating in it. "Though we had had a hard time we did not fire a shot," Walker admitted.[13]

While Confederates rallied toward the Coaling, Federals all across the plain streamed in the same direction. Their motives were mixed: helping their friends on one hand, reaching the retreat route on the other. Unionists closest to the river were farthest from immediate danger—and at the same time farthest from the only avenue to safety in the rear. Two members of the 7th Indiana on the far right claimed that they withdrew for the mundane reason that their ammunition was exhausted. Other Hoosiers admitted more honestly that the "heavy firing at the timber on our extreme left" triggered the reaction; that Confederates "came pouring out of the woods . . . in numbers almost innumerable ... and we had to give way"; and, quaintly, that Southerners "began to come against us by acres." A spurious report typical of the war's early battles spread through the ranks that enemy cavalry were sneaking down the riverbank toward the 7th Indiana's flank. The rumor lent wings to the heels of a retreat that quickly gathered momentum.[14]

Wallace Hoyt of the 29th Ohio admitted that after "a Desperate fight ... we were whiped. ... the 29th is all cut to pieces." N. L. Parmeter of the same regiment acknowledged that at the end "they were too strong for us," and only regretted that the 29th was squeezed away from the retreat point until most of the rest of the army had passed. A brief stand with the rear guard cost the 29th heavily when Confederates turned the Coaling guns toward the regiment and "did fearful execution."[15]

Charles Bard of the 7th Ohio blamed the developing debacle not on Taylor's Louisianians, but on a coincidental shortage of ammunition: "we were soon all without ammunition and dispair was written upon evry face as came the order for retreat." The regimental historian attributed the retreat to worry over Confederate reinforcements visible far to the rear. Another chronicler of the 7th Ohio laughably insisted that "the eager enthusiasm of the men," rather than any Confederate achievements, disordered the line. John H. Burton knew better. "They were outflanking us on the left," he wrote bluntly and honestly, "and thus gained an advantage which decided the battle in their favor."[16]

Colonel Dunning of the 5th Ohio had moved toward the Coaling almost as soon as Taylor exploded out of the woods. It was his regiment that cleared most of the Confederates from the Lewiston buildings. Dunning professed "astonishment" when orders came to retire and criticized the undisciplined rout that ensued. In the melee the 5th's colors became separated from the main body of the regiment. The color guard ignored Southern orders to surrender, raced toward the river, and escaped on a raft with the precious flags tucked inside their clothing.[17]

The 1st Virginia (Union) held the far Federal left just below the Coaling. It accomplished less than any other Northern unit on the plain both during the Federal advance and—despite its close proximity to the Confederate threat—during the attempt to resist Taylor. An unsophisticated youngster in the regiment described the battle in his diary with two words: "Hard fiting." In a subsequent letter the same soldier wrote: "thay got in the mountain and cum in behint us on our canans. we had to fall back . . . we lost a good menne min." The regimental historian dishonestly described the 1st as at the vortex of a veritable firestorm, in which it lost "at least one-half" of those engaged. Official casualty returns show that in fact the Virginia Yankees suffered relatively lightly (one killed). The regimental history reveals the unit's war record with stark clarity when it declares that Port Republic, with its minuscule casualties, was "as hard and stubborn a contest as the regiment was ever engaged in."[18]

Without full knowledge of the circumstances, Federals in Shields's army bitterly condemned the 84th and 110th Pennsylvania and the 66th Ohio for losing the Coaling. "The stampede occurred in the 66th Ohio," wrote a soldier whose unit had not quite reached the battlefield. He added even more pointedly, "It is an insult to soldiers to call the 110th Pennsylvania by any other name than that of a mob."[19] The aspersions cast on the 66th Ohio are at least in part countered by available evidence, but criticism of the other two regiments is so widespread and recurrent as to suggest that it has some validity.

Among the fewer than two dozen Pennsylvanians wounded was eighteen-year-old Private Warren Post of Company G, 84th Pennsylvania. A bullet hit Post in the abdomen, shattered several ribs, and penetrated his colon before passing out his back. Confederates sweeping the field captured him, and he spent the next three months in Southern hospitals before being repatriated to Fort Delaware. After six weeks in the Union hospital there he transferred to a Philadelphia facility for more care.

Post's wounds had bled heavily at once, and blood also poured from his mouth and anus. "Small pieces of paper and cloth . . . driven into the wound . . . were also discharged" during the first three weeks. Post's lower extremities became paralyzed on June 14 and did not return to normal for seven weeks. A surgeon who marveled at the wounded boy's difficult case recorded that when "attempting to evacuate the bowels, faeces and wind passed from both [entry and exit] wounds. . . . The seeds of fruit he had eaten were also discharged from both wounds." In testament to the human body's remarkable restorative powers, the examining surgeon at his discharge six months later declared that Post "was enjoying good health."[20]

By the time Post went down, the Federal line had collapsed.

Tyler "at once" had rallied to his left when Taylor struck. The Union commander directed Colonel Carroll to superintend preparations for the retreat. Carroll designated the 5th Ohio as his rear guard, but the sturdiest souls from all regiments no doubt clustered about the 5th to lend a hand. Putting the best possible face on the matter, Tyler denied being driven from the field in his report, declaring instead that Confederates crossing South River far upstream looked like they eventually would be too many to handle.[21]

No Federal on the field could ever be deceived by Tyler's published posturing: they knew at first hand that they had been driven hard. Captain Dan Keily of Shields's staff stormed through the melee insensible to danger until a Confederate finally shot him down. The daring Irishman was part of the "desperate struggle to rescue some . . . artillery" when he was hit. Carroll recalled, in a letter to Keily, "when yourself and horse were shot, you had to pass under a cross fire that a mounted man could hardly expect to live through, but made the attempt." Two months later a surgeon described Keily's wound as "a severe gun shot wound of the face, fracturing the upper jaw, & doing much injury to the soft parts." The captain had not healed enough to return to duty by the end of the year. Port Republic probably was the high point of Keily's adventuresome career, which included some uneven spots—such as a stint at carpetbagging in Louisiana—before his death in October 1867.[22]

The Union forces did a reasonably good job of delaying the ultimate collapse, according to an admiring Louisianian. At a stage in the fighting at which defeated armies tended to unravel in short order, Tyler "shortened his lines and for half an hour held Jackson with a fire of musketry. . . . Foot by foot he lost ground." Only "when there was no longer any hope" did the last Federal stand dissolve. Any attempt to unsnarl the troop dispositions at this stage would be pointless. As British general Sir A. P. Wavell aptly reminded some junior officers after World War I, "Remember that war is always a far worse muddle than anything you can produce in peace." The battlefield chaos reduced by historians (including the author of this book and its neat maps) to good order is unimaginable. Creating artificial good order is essential to understanding—but the reader must remember to reimpose a layer of confusion atop the events under discussion.[23]

With Stonewall Jackson's battle won, the troops he had been so desperately needing began to reach the field in numbers, their movement aided by the repaired wagon bridge. Taliaferro's Brigade had been in town all during the battle. Any need to garrison the village was by now long gone, with thousands of other Confederates converging on the place. Jackson must have ignored Taliaferro's men because he so loathed Taliaferro himself. One month earlier Jackson had written to his favorite congressman damning Taliaferro's promotion in terms atypically bitter for such an organization man. "When will political appointments cease?" Jackson inquired rhetorically. "The great interests of the country are being sacrificed by appointing incompetent officers. . . . The times demand that we should for the moment make professional merit the basis of promotion." In a remarkably sassy summary Jackson declared: "I wish that if such appointments are continued, that the President would come in the field and command them, and not throw the responsibility upon me of defending this District when he throws such obstacles in my way."[24]

Jackson's need for support became so great at the nadir of Winder's fight on the plain that he finally, reluctantly, called Taliaferro forward. Although the brigade advanced with what its commander called "wonderful celerity," it arrived only in time to find Taylor's men atop "the hills on the right of the road" around the captured battery. Jackson charitably reported that "Taliaferro came up in time to discharge an effective volley into the ranks of the wavering and retreating enemy." The men of Taliaferro's 10th Virginia, unencumbered by any need to be politic, admitted that they arrived just in time to see the Yankee flight. Joe F. Kauffman wrote in his diary, "our Regiment did not get into the fight at all." The 23rd Virginia of Taliaferro's Brigade got close enough for its fifty-three-year-old Colonel Alexander Galt Taliaferro—the general's uncle—to take a painful bullet wound in the shoulder.[25]

The unlucky 33rd Virginia and its unhappy Colonel John Neff also showed up too late to be of any use. In a report far too long for its contents, betraying his discomfort by special pleading, Neff detailed the woes that had delayed him. Once clear of the river and its glut of trains, which he energetically bypassed, Neff still did not know where to go. He had the misfortune to meet a 2nd Virginia ambulance driver who knew that that regiment, also of Neff's brigade, had gone into the woods on the right. Neff eagerly turned in that direction and promptly got as lost as several other unit commanders had earlier. He contemplated joining Colonel Jim Walker's command in the woods, but meanwhile received orders ("in abundance," Neff reported) to move back to the road and advance down it.[26]

Poor John Neff—the son of a pacifist family and a fine officer—reported with evident disgust: "My situation on the 9th was a perplexing and unpleasant one. I used my best efforts to reach my brigade in time . . . [but] was unable to do so." Two months later the frustrated colonel wrote to his parents of rumors libeling him over Port Republic, spread by the family's neighbor, Parson Rude: "I understand that it was reported I got lost with my Reg't. at Port Republic. . . . some trifling scoundrel who left the Regt. when the fight commenced and ran off home brought the report. Men instead of listening to their lies and wonderful stories ought to arrest them and send them back to the army." Neff protested that he did not care what such creatures thought, but in fact he obviously did. At the date of his worried letter, Neff was in more unjustified trouble, having been arrested by Winder for not doing things that he could not do because of contrary orders from Stonewall Jackson. His role as a pawn in that struggle between generals was short-lived: five days after Neff mailed the letter, Winder was dead, and less than three weeks later Neff followed the general to an early grave.[27]

Jackson and Winder, their mutual grievances forgotten for the moment, collaborated side-by-side to orchestrate the final push. They met Colonel Garnett of the 48th Virginia, having moved over from its uncertain role on the left, and hurried him down the road. William Allan found Jackson on the right of the road near the front and watched him dispatch officers and units in several directions. Another witness reported that as the tide turned, "Jackson at once rode to the front and ordered the whole line to charge." The battle's momentum by this time was flowing in just one direction—downstream. Confederates "pouring upon the long blue lines, now staggering and reeling, they were driven like leaves before the blasts of a hurricane back again over the valley." A Virginian of Carpenter's Battery who had borne much danger during the morning described the stirring scene when the Yankees pulled back, "followed by [our] entire force in line . . . with the firing on the left, cross firing on the right & bayonets glistening of 5 regiments in the centre who know how to use them."[28]

The retreating Unionists had no choice but to elbow their way onto the single narrow road leading away from the battlefield. One of Taliaferro's arriving men wrote that "the Federals becoming confused and thrown together in compact bodies . . . artillery and small arms did greatest execution." Another account used similar language: "The destruction was immense, for crowded as they were, every shot told with marked effect, and such was the panic that seized them, hundreds scattered over the hills."[29]

Perhaps the most relieved of all Southerners observing the collapse of the Federal position were the civilians clustered on Bogota's upper porch. The women and children watching anxiously from that vantage point had friends and loved ones on the battlefield, fighting to protect them, while they could only watch impotently. With vast relief Clara Strayer and her companions "heard the shout of *victory* which none know how to give better than our own brave Confederates."[30]

General John C. Frémont's fire on a
cold battlefield covered with
wounded men must be condemned. Jed
Hotchkiss called it "the safe but
shameful business of shelling the
ambulances and the relief parties
looking after the wounded of both
armies."

CHAPTER 25

THE BRIDGE AFIRE

AND FRÉMONT'S IRE

General I. R. Trimble's rear guard fell back almost at leisure during the morning while Jackson fought for his army's life. At daybreak the front-line Confederates near Cross Keys had assembled near Mill Creek Church to begin their measured retirement. It was about eight A.M. when the 21st North Carolina moved south from that vicinity. The Tarheels could hear the sound of battle echoing across the landscape from Port Republic. About a half hour later, the 42nd Virginia and 1st Virginia Battalion took to the road, bringing up the rear of the column.[1]

The rearguard exercise turned into a cakewalk for Trimble's men because Frémont displayed no ardor whatsoever in pressing them. The Yankees only pushed Trimble "slowly back," in the words of a contemporary. Frémont later claimed to have been "stubbornly resisted," but Trimble never found it necessary to fight hard. The Southerner who insisted that "not a shot was exchanged during the withdrawal," exaggerated a bit, but the morning unfolded quietly. Frémont's report boasted irrelevantly that his troops maintained "admirable steadiness and exactness," as though his mission was a parade rather than a pursuit.[2]

So tepid was Frémont's demeanor that some rearguard units found the leisure to halt and eat breakfast. Trimble's weary officers were the only Confederates in the column who had a difficult morning. They had been busy all day on the 8th and then had ridden and watched all night long. One of them wrote to his wife the next morning: "When I staggered out of my saddle last night, I had been in it for thirty-six hours, including the whole of the night previous. I slept not a wink [and] only dismounted twice during the period . . . for short periods."[3]

Frémont had little effect on Trimble's march, but Jackson found cause to speed it up. At some point Stonewall sent orders to Trimble to hurry because, Jackson admitted, he had found "the resistance more obstinate than I anticipated." The aide carrying the message to Trimble had moved at top speed. He reached the rear guard "with his horse foaming," Colonel Patton recalled, "and ordered us to break up our positions . . . and hurry up to the battle-field double quick." Another messenger from Jackson soon arrived. Jackson must not have made his call until Winder's battle was fully joined, since the rear guard did not arrive until the fighting was over. He was not abandoning a fantastic two-battle scheme (that notion was long gone, if it had ever existed), but rather simply tightening up his army's rear.[4]

As the rear guard pulled onto the high ground above Port Republic, much of the battlefield came into view downstream. One of Trimble's Alabamians commented of the human drama below, "Jackson's division was charging . . . and driving everything before them." A Tarheel in the column noted that as "the road made a winding descent . . . a beautiful valley lay beyond and then the great blue ridge mts. reaching far off. . . . what a magnificent scene." He could see his comrades on the distant battlefield "in line & perfect order . . . Stretching from the river about to the Mountain."[5]

It was just past ten A.M. when Trimble's infantry rear guard approached North River. Two responsible sources inexplicably reported that the last Confederate had crossed "by daylight" and "before day," estimates some five hours awry! The commanders of the 42nd Virginia and the 1st Virginia Battalion, both of whom reported times carefully all day long, said that they were across by ten-fifteen. The matter is not of great importance, but it highlights the imprecision of clock chronologies during the Civil War. Jackson timed the last infantry crossing at "soon after 10 o'clock."[6]

The fire that burned the North River bridge was a spectacular sight, and a number of Confederates reported taking part in setting it off. Most of them agreed that the tinder for the big fire was hay or straw. Harrison Bateman's barn, conveniently located near the east end of the bridge, supplied two wagonloads of hay that were parked just short of the bridge on either side of the road. Men of the 21st North Carolina and its attached sharpshooter battalion each grabbed as much hay as could be carried under one arm and bore it to the bridge. Over their shoulders as they hurried forward they "could see the Glittering Bayonets of Fremont's Army coming up"—or imagined they could.[7]

George Hulvey, an eighteen-year-old member of the 10th Virginia, was a local boy charged with dragging the hay onto the bridge, and he always claimed proudly that it was he who applied the torch. The excitement of the moment prompted the soldiers to leave the hay in the wagons inside the bridge, rather than unloading them. That complicated the passage of the last of the rear guard, particularly the mounted cavalrymen. Someone had taken the precaution of having the interior boards of the bridge's superstructure "split and splintered" to aid the spread of the flames. A few unexploded shells stacked inside the bridge ensured a volatile result.[8]

Most of the rearguard cavalry crossed the bridge last. A detachment of the 2nd Virginia Cavalry had orders to herd over the final friendly soldiers and then ignite the hay. Craig McDonald of the 11th Virginia Cavalry also claimed the honor of starting the fire "for which he was promoted to a captaincy," according to his brother (who later was major of the 11th). Perhaps each claimant scratched a match, because a watching infantryman recalled that "as the last foot left it, the bridge was fired in many places, and having been filled with combustable material, was almost instantly enveloped in . . . lurid flames and dense black smoke."[9]

A company of the 6th Virginia Cavalry pounded down the slope toward the burning bridge too late to cross it, so the men put their horses into the water and swam the rapid stream without incident. Three cavalrymen from the 2nd Virginia attempted to follow, but with less success. The hundreds of excited Southern infantrymen watching the bridge burn looked on in horror as one of the three was swept under by the raging current. The unfortunate fellow was Lieutenant Thomas Macon Waller from Amherst County, commanding a mounted detachment covering the rear. A few confused Confederates on the far shore had begun shooting at him, thinking the horsemen were Frémont's advance. Waller could not swim, but his horse could, and he boldly spurred the animal toward the river.[10]

The bank of the river just below the bridge was very steep and high, with brush growing densely up the slope from the water. The cavalrymen plunged through the undergrowth as far as they dared and then urged their mounts to leap for the water. A North Carolinian watching recalled: "The poor beasts in making the terrible leap seemed to squat almost to the [ground] & leaped well into the river below—the water must [have] been very deep [to allow such a plunge]." The sabers and carbines of the riders tangled during the dive and posed a hazard when riders and animals both sank below the surface. Only Lieutenant Waller could not recover from the dangerous plunge. He "seemed to be confused" when he came to the surface separated from his horse, according to a fellow lieutenant. The horse floated away downstream and disappeared while Lieutenant Waller drowned.[11]

Two years later a Yankee suffered the same fate in the same spot. Northerners burned some buildings in town as a diversion while awaiting installation of a pontoon bridge. An impatient cavalryman attempted to cross, only to be unhorsed and drowned. Local civilians were not surprised at either drowning, though the one during the 1864 arson season probably delighted them. A village historian compiled a lengthy roster of victims; residents agitating for a bridge asserted that "the fords along the river are very dangerous and often cannot be crossed at all."[12]

Unionists followed Frémont's placid lead and apparently absorbed their leader's lack of zeal. Thomas Evans of the 25th Ohio noted that the Federals advanced "in line of battle," rather than in column, which was a poor way to make rapid progress. Evans expressed surprise that no enemy stood in their way—"all was . . . still." The sluggish Federal movement required no Confederate resistance. Then "all of a sudden a huge black smoke ascended, as if issuing from a great smokestack." The column of smoke went up in a "great black mass . . . diffusing at last at its top . . . as it were in a sort of somber path." Mounted men dashed ahead of Frémont's behe-

THE BRIDGE AFIRE AND FRÉMONT'S IRE

moth and returned to report the bridge afire. When Yankee infantry came in view of the river, they found the bridge "falling to pieces in the flames." A 73rd Ohio soldier boasted bravely about "heavy fighting at the bridge," but in fact there was none. The Confederates dashing on through Port Republic did draw some scattering fire before they crossed South River and got beyond effective range.[13]

Federal officers put the best possible light on their leisurely approach. The biographer of Colonel Krzyzanowski of the 58th New York—the "Polish Legion," the colonel affectedly called it—reported "a brief skirmish at the Port Republic ford." The few volleys, he claimed lamely, "helped to relieve the frustrations of the previous day." Colonel Tracy of Frémont's staff convinced himself that the army had moved with "vigor and determination . . . putting every nerve to the strain." Milroy found solace in "the long lines of reble baggage wagons and their cavelry filing away for miles in the distance on the other side," even though those Confederates were retiring victorious. Another Federal account carefully concentrated on the capture of "rebel wounded" along Frémont's route.[14]

Frémont grotesquely fumbled his opportunity on the morning of June 9. Once the Confederate rear guard began to fold away from his front, Frémont had nothing to lose and everything to gain by pressing with all of his considerable might. An English historian has stated aptly, "Frémont had an opportunity of co-operating with Shields by following [Trimble's men] up vigorously and preventing them from being used. Instead Frémont moved very slowly and only occupied the hills west of the South Fork after Tyler had been driven back."[15] Any considerable Unionist force on the bluffs near Bogota would have made Tyler's position along the Lewiston lane virtually impregnable.

The Confederates marching through town beyond the burning bridge could sense their pursuers' lack of purpose. When Frémont appeared on the bluffs, he did not press forward to the mouth of the disintegrating bridge. There would have been no point in doing so. Eli Coble of the 21st North Carolina thought he discerned contentment in the Federal movements: "we don't believe that Fremont's men were very sorry that it was a water haul." A Mississippian expressed a similar perception when he wrote in his diary that Frémont's forces, "seeming glad of the obstacle, made no attempt to cross." Colonel Patton imagined the Yankees "doubtless gnashing their teeth in impotent rage." The colonel was cocky about the prospects for any further fighting involving Stonewall. Frémont's men, Patton wrote, "might well feel grateful . . . that the burning of the bridge rendered them secure against the wonderful resources of our chief."[16]

When the last of the Confederate rear guard cleared the village and hurried across the South River wagon bridge, Sandy Garber and his black pioneers broke up that temporary span. One of the black drivers, Garber recalled, performed "as brave an act as we witnessed during the war." Federal riflemen had crawled down to the riverbank near the confluence and begun shooting at the Confederates. "Just as [the driver] was ready to pull out, his saddle horse was killed under him, but he coolly snatched the harness off, mounted the off wheeler and drove out whistling a march, being a regular fifer on a whistle." Sandie Pendleton, who had dashed back from his post with Jackson to check on the rear guard, showed up at this juncture, and Garber asked him what to do next. Pendleton responded succinctly, "Run like the devil, you fools." Garber and his pioneers did just that: "we stood not upon the order of our going, but *went*." They left 19 dead horses and mules behind them.[17]

The rear guard arrived at the battle front too late to be of any use in the pursuit. Fiery Isaac Trimble, with apparent disappointment, admitted that he "reached the field after the contest had been decided." Officers of the 1st Maryland, 42nd Virginia, and 1st Virginia Battalion reported the same experience.[18]

They were in time to see Frémont's tardy arrival. At a few minutes before noon, as the sound of Jackson's pursuit faded in the distance, "large bodies of the enemy's infantry, cavalry, and artillery commenced to appear on the heights of the left bank of the river, and rapidly deployed in long lines." Confederates still on the battlefield they had won were impressed by Frémont's display of force, "marshaled in battle array. . . . Their long regular lines, as they moved down with measured step to the river, the sun sparkling along the glistening rows of bayonets, seemed a waving mass of splendor." An officer of the 52nd Virginia who was looking around the Coaling turned and saw the Federals arriving. They "made a fine Show," he admitted, then added gratefully, "but they were too late." Ned Moore of the Rockbridge Artillery reveled in the spectacle, which he "exultingly enjoyed": "On the ground where we stood lay the dead and wounded . . . with much of their artillery and many prisoners in our possession, while crowning the hills in full view and with no means of crossing an intervening river, even should they venture to do so, stood another army—Frémont's—with flags flying."[19]

Confederate glee at Frémont's impotence turned to amazement and disgust when the Yankee general opened artillery fire on the now-quiet battlefield. "As if infuriated that Jackson had outgeneraled him and whipped both armies by detail," a Virginian wrote, Frémont "commenced firing upon the Hospital." Stonewall Jackson had left the pursuit to subordinates and was riding slowly over the field. He commented, "I never saw so many dead in such a small space in all my life before." Just then "a roar came suddenly from the opposite bank of the river. Then shell began to whistle and . . . burst right in the midst of the ambulances full of wounded." When Frémont "opened his batteries upon the ambulance and burial parties," a Marylander observed, he "killed many of his own wounded people, and compelled us to leave the balance on the field uncared for, and his dead unburied."[20]

Federal gunners seemed to pay special attention to Lynnwood, despite the conspicuous display there of "the yellow flag, the sacred badge of suffering." The building was full of wounded soldiers in both uniforms among whom the exploding shells "produced some excitement." A Confederate cavalry lieutenant ran through the building looking for men wounded slightly enough to be carried out of harm's way on horseback, but surgeons in charge of the hospital discouraged further exposure of their patients. One of Taylor's Irishmen who had been shot through both thighs pleaded for the chance to get away. The man had two brothers fighting with Frémont and he was afraid they might cross the river, capture him, and "give him Hell."[21]

Civil War artillery fire was less devastating than it was awe-inspiring. Few if any men in Lynnwood were further hurt by Frémont's spiteful shelling. Out in the fields, though, ambulances and stretcher teams bringing succor to wounded men stood defenseless. A cavalryman observed that "many a poor fellow who had escaped with his life from the storm and tempest of the morning's battle was thus murdered ere the close of the day." A staff officer thought that Frémont ended up "hurting his Union friends about as much as he did us." Others noted that since Confederates had cared for their own first, Frémont's behavior harmed his friends disproportionately. The tall wheat and tangled thickets hid many suffering soldiers of both sides. The artillery fire, a Marylander wrote, had the result of "forcing us to forego our merciful ministrations and to retire out of range." Local tradition had it that one of Frémont's shells exploded in a wagon carrying one man from each side, killing the Yankee but missing the Confederate.[22]

A bare minimum of Frémont's fire accomplished legitimate military ends. Captain Frank Bond and Colonel Bradley T. Johnson were riding "very deliberately" side by side across the field, headed for a gap in one of the fences, when the first shell landed. The two officers were about twenty yards from the gap when the round struck squarely in it. "It made a tremendous havoc of earth and fence rails," Bond recalled. He and Johnson "contemplated what would have happened" had they been a few moments quicker and "decided we would try to reach camp by a route that was less objectionable to [Frémont]."[23]

Two members of the 37th Virginia found Frémont's shelling an obstacle to their military missions. William H. Ropp was scavenging for Federal weapons (two companies of the 37th would be armed with Belgian rifles salvaged at Port Republic). Ropp upgraded his own armament to an English Enfield that amazed him with its range and accuracy. George C. Pile of the 37th had chased the Yankees downstream a bit and then came back to find Frémont's fire interdicting the main road. As a result, Pile complained, "we were unable to reclaim our cast off blankets and other trappings that we intended to get on our return."[24]

Those few legitimate targets notwithstanding, Frémont's fire on a cold battlefield covered with wounded men must be condemned. A Maryland officer wrote of "the brutal Fremont, wild with disappointment." Jed Hotchkiss called Frémont's misdeed "the safe but shameful business of shelling the ambulances and the relief parties . . . looking after the wounded of both armies." Dabney predicted that for his "malice" and "inhumanity," Frémont "will be execrated until his name sinks into its merited oblivion." Gunner George Neese seethed at the thought of "an act in itself so atrocious that it would make even a barbarous vandal blush with shame . . . and consider it an infamy of the first water."[25]

Several Confederates involved in burial rites abandoned their soulful task under the fire. Chaplain Stephen J. Cameron of the 1st Maryland was reading the burial service over a grave when "a cannon ball tore through the group, and the bearers dropped the dead." Sandy Garber and his black pioneers stuck to their burial duty near the Coaling, beyond the easy reach of Frémont's fire. "We buried them where they fell, sadly and sorrowfully, as well as we could," the captain recalled, "under Fremont's cowardly fire from the opposite side of the River, where he safely vented his wrath at defeat, on both wounded and dead, friend and foe." Another black detachment, this one of stretcher-bearers for the wounded, also persevered under fire. Chaplain Richard McIlwaine of the 44th Virginia was superintending the removal of a wounded soldier from his regiment when Frémont opened. "Not one of the negroes flinched," McIlwaine reported proudly, "and in a few moments by quick-step we were hidden from the malicious and cowardly scoundrels by the woods." McIlwaine stumbled upon the man thus saved—Robert S. Campbell, by then the sheriff of Fluvanna County—in 1906.[26]

Stonewall Jackson's official report included stern language condemning Frémont for having "opened his artillery upon our ambulances and parties engaged in the humane labors of attending to our dead and wounded and the dead and wounded of the enemy." In a subsequent exchange of messages with Shields, Jackson complained to his counterpart of "the unsoldierly conduct of General Frémont's command." Dabney of Jackson's staff posited, conceivably on the basis of something Jackson said, that Frémont had fired on the battlefield as part of a political stratagem: "The design of this outrage was obvious; it was supposed that the humanity of General Jackson, would prompt him to demand by flag of truce, an unmolested opportunity to tend the wounded; and on that request, the Federal General designed to found a pretext for claiming . . . the command of the field and the victory; which he knew belonged to Jackson."[27]

Even at the points that Frémont's shells could not reach, the battlefield contained enough horrors and human suffering to astonish Southerners wandering over it. Tom Munford told his sister that "dead Yankees lay thick in every direction with their bodies terribly mangled, and the groans of the dying resounded on every side." Another cavalryman said later, "that grain field presented the most ghastly appearance of any he saw during the war—the growing crop smooth mown, and the bodies . . . strewn over the ground almost literally covering it." General Taylor wrote a similar estimate: "I have never seen so many dead and wounded in the same limited space."[28]

John Fravel, an eighteen-year-old infantryman from nearby Shenandoah County, lived for fifty years after the battle, but he never forgot a Pennsylvanian who lay dying on the field. A cannonball had torn away the Northerner's entire breast bone, leaving his heart and lungs exposed. The poor fellow gave his money and watch to Fravel's lieutenant, telling him to keep the money and send the watch to his father in the North. Nearby Fravel saw a headless corpse with six or eight other dead men surrounding it. Grieving friends of Major

Chenoweth of the 31st Virginia buried him where he fell, one of them wrote, "with no pillow save his soldier's knapsack and no shroud but his soldier's blanket & yet . . . shrouded in the glory of his own noble deeds." Jackson's staffers William Allan and John A. Harman found the latter's nephew, Lieutenant Lewis Harman of the 52nd Virginia, down with a bullet in his arm but "in fine spirits." Allan put the young officer up behind him on his horse and carried him about seven miles toward Staunton to a hospital house.[29]

Other Confederates continued the war in desultory fashion, picketing along the river and firing across it at Frémont's pickets. Robert Stratton of Munford's cavalry saw enough activity and confusion on the opposite bank to convince him that Federal engineers were attempting to bridge the river. As Stratton looked on from shelter, he saw six men creeping toward him on the Confederate side of the river. Just as he was about to shoot their leader—who was urging his comrades to shoot Stratton—the dismounted cavalryman identified a Mississippi insignia on his target. His intended victims had thought Stratton a Yankee because of the informal blue cap he was wearing in typical catch-as-catch-can Confederate style.[30]

Members of the 1st Maryland near the river spotted an important-looking officer on a white horse far inside enemy lines. Colonel Johnson asked Wellington Blakiston, renowned for his marksmanship, to shoot the officer. Blakiston consulted with his comrades about the distance. When they agreed that it must be just about one mile, the Marylander set the sight on his Enfield rifle at 1,700 yards, took painstaking aim, and pulled the trigger. The officer fell, whether because he was hit or his horse had been it was impossible to say.[31]

The perspective of Frémont's men on their futile arrival and the shelling of ambulance parties is predictably less bitter than Confederate testimony, but their accounts betray some discomfort—and occasional disgust—about the proceeding. Jacob Frank of the 41st New York simply recorded the shelling without specifying a target. One of Frémont's staff saw "a lengthened line of men in . . . blue, guarded . . . under conduct of the force in gray," but said nothing of shooting at either party. Milroy boasted of having "dispersed their cavelry and stoped a few of their wagons by knocking their teams to pieces," ignoring the humanitarian purposes of the wagons. Robert Bromley of the 55th Ohio saw a burial party under the fire, and reported that it sent over "a 'white rag' requesting permission to bury their dead."[32]

Carl Schurz, the iconoclastic German general, heard a few days later from a staff officer that when Frémont "beheld the burnt bridge and groups of Federal prisoners and wounded in the plain beyond, he ordered his artillery to fire upon the retreating foe, killing several Federal prisoners, who had hoisted signals of distress." One Federal with ample reason to rue Frémont's behavior was Smith J. Shaffer of the 66th Ohio, a "wild harum scarum chap from Delaware County." A bullet had shattered Shaffer's right thigh above the knee. He lay on the battlefield for two days before Confederate surgeons returned and amputated the leg. Infection forced a second amputation in Richmond. Despite it all, Shaffer survived the war.[33]

The Strayers and their guests at Bogota had no difficulty deciding what they thought of Frémont. Clara Strayer was shocked to see fire directed at "the hearse-like ambulances" across the river, and at Lynnwood despite its yellow hospital flag. Early rounds at long range whistled past Bogota. One of them plunged through the roof of a cabin in the orchard and landed within two feet of a slave sheltered there. The man "yelled lustily, being more scared than hurt," since fortunately the shell did not explode. Federal cavalry soon swept into the yard and carried off the family's nine horses. Slaves persuaded them to leave two old animals that were beloved pets.

Yankees swarmed over Bogota, breaking into every closet and looting at will. Clara attempted to repulse some from her bedroom by announcing: "This is a lady's chamber and as such will be respected by *gentlemen*." The girl's sturdy stand did no good. "The leader, a big bluffy Dutchman," she recalled, responded, "Yah, yah! if dere be any Dutch gentlemen! Come boys, let's go to town!" When the looters mistreated her father, who was sixty-nine years old and ailing, Clara found a Federal captain willing to drive the miscreants from the house. They then emptied the smokehouse and dairy, but to the family's intense delight "were completely routed" by thousands of bees protecting their hives in the yard. That afternoon the assembled slaves of the Strayers and the Lewiston and Lynnwood refugees tired of the attention they were getting from the Northerners and fled to nearby woods for protection.[34]

If the civilians were helpless against Frémont's scavengers, Frémont was equally helpless to do anything to support Tyler's flying Federals on the other side of the river. While Clara Strayer defended her bedroom, Stonewall Jackson's victorious army was chasing another set of Yankees full tilt toward Conrad's Store.

Port Republic battlefield in 1994, looking north down Lewiston Lane. The Coaling looms in the immediate foreground, the heavily contested ravine dropping off to its left. The large farm in the center is on the site of Lewiston. The South Fork runs through the trees across the top of the picture.

CHAPTER 26

DOWN THE RIVER AND

UP THE MOUNTAIN

Stonewall Jackson's triumph reached its climax at about ten-thirty A.M., when Tyler's Federals broke for the rear.[1] As with most retreats, the withdrawal began with some restraint but quickly broke into disorder. General Taliaferro, who was just reaching the front, saw the enemy "slowly retreating down the flat." When his men delivered volleys into the mass of fugitives, the Federals "became demoralized, broke, and precipitately retreated." A private in Taliaferro's command wrote that the enemy "started back in a wild, uncontrollable, panic-stricken mob, without staying long enough to fasten the lid on the pepper box." A Stonewall Brigade officer, on the other hand, gave the enemy credit for poise: "Some of them break and run, but others retreat in tolerably good order."[2]

Dick Ewell did his part to hurry the retreat, serving as a gunner on the captured Coaling pieces turned against their recent owners. Stonewall Jackson also rode into the Coaling "with intense light in his eyes" and mixed with the victorious Louisianians there. "I thought the men would go mad with cheering," General Taylor wrote. "A huge fellow, with one eye closed and half his whiskers burned by powder, was riding cock-horse on a gun, and, catching my attention, yelled out, 'We told you to bet on your boys.' " Jackson soon reverted to more typical behavior. An officer saw him riding slowly across the battlefield shortly thereafter, his head bowed and a gauntleted hand pointing toward heaven. The general "seemed oblivious to all around him and presented the appearance of being in supplication or rendering thanks." Stonewall was still in the area when Frémont arrived to shell the ambulances, but then he rode rapidly downstream to join the pursuit of Tyler.[3]

With Federal infantry teetering on the brink of panic, Confederate cavalry had a golden opportunity to drive the final wedge between Tyler and control of his army. Some of Ashby's old command went forward in what a Virginia infantryman called "one of the grandest charges I saw during the war. They . . . came up in solid line." Another witness thought the cavalry charge "down the bottoms" made "the very ground quake and the Yankees tremble." A Fletcher youngster was among the mounted men chasing enemy soldiers off his home place. "That was on my mother's farm," he told one of Jackson's staff, "and that charge was made across our back field and into our back woods."[4]

The Southern cavalry under Colonel Munford had been with the rear guard all morning and did not arrive in time to help break the enemy. That left them fresher to pick up the pursuit, which they did with "a Confederate yell[;] wild with delight the tattered old command went whooping as they hurried forward, clearing the field," Munford wrote. As the mounted pursuit thundered down the narrow road, the cavalrymen quickly found their opportunities constricted by the ground. "The bushes," one of them wrote, were "so thick the cavalry could not manoeuvre." Munford described the terrain as "a piney country, with a single wagon road." His men could only ride two abreast.[5]

The Confederate riders eventually broke up into detachments, abandoning all semblance of formation, and gathered in prisoners by the scores from roadside thickets. Munford claimed for his force the capture of 150 prisoners, 800 muskets, and a half-dozen wagonloads of plunder. The captives quickly became a burden. One lieutenant found his troops' effectiveness destroyed by the disarmed prisoners each man had dragged up to ride behind. Most of the Southern cavalry had a field day chasing the rout, but their excursion was not without cost. Captain Thomas B. Massie of the 12th Virginia Cavalry went down wounded. Captain Edward H. McDonald of the 11th met his brother Craig Woodrow McDonald and was horrified to see that "Wood" was covered with blood. The wound on the side of C.W.'s head actually was more unsightly than serious—"not even a furlough," the wounded man complained. Ed McDonald rode on in relief, but he never saw his brother again; Wood was killed in front of Richmond a few weeks later.[6]

When Confederate infantry gave up the pursuit several miles downstream, the cavalry forged ahead "much farther." Jackson's report declared that Munford continued about three miles beyond the farthest infantry advance, but some in the army grumbled about a perceived inadequacy in the cavalry effort. Campbell Brown of Ewell's staff complained that "our Cavalry . . . halted with exemplary prudence, 'that rascally virtue,' as soon as a single Regt of the enemy showed any signs of standing." Brown recounted the cavalry's numerous other shortcomings during the campaign and dismissed the effort at Port Republic as "showing pusillanimity, or at least pursuing very timidly." Dick Taylor offered a defense: that Munford and the best of the cavalry had been facing Frémont and "could not get over till late." Since Brown's complaint did not specify timing, but rather lack of energy, Taylor's comment hardly answers the issue.[7]

The infantry that pressed downstream deteriorated into a disorganized mob as promptly as had the cavalry preceding it. Some of Taylor's Louisianians scrambled off the Coaling in high glee to follow up on the victory they had ensured. The Louisiana troops quickly found that the exertions of the morning left them unable to keep up with the fresher pursuers. Most quit after covering about a mile and sat down to watch the booty come in. Lieutenant Ring of the 6th Louisiana figured that he saw 800 prisoners straggle past him to the rear. He was guessing too high, but had every right to enjoy the process.[8]

Walker's Brigade had worn itself out trying to reach the Coaling, but when Ewell ordered it, the men still had enough left "to follow the retiring foe," Walker reported, "which we did until ordered back." As Walker led his troops "past Battery Hill [the Coaling] they could see streams of blood running down it, making it too slippery to walk up." Some of Patton's Brigade also joined the pursuit. The 42nd Virginia pursued for "2 or 3 miles," and the 48th gobbled up 60 prisoners. Ewell's other troops generally stayed behind. The 58th Virginia, for instance, "stopped for the rest we so much needed."[9]

Stonewall Jackson credited the brigades of Taliaferro and Winder with carrying the infantry pursuit. Jackson's distaste for Taliaferro and affinity for his old Stonewall Brigade probably prompted him to give the two equal billing, but in fact Taliaferro did most of the work. His 37th Virginia led the way, just as it had the morning before at the North River bridge. "In pursuing . . . we cast off everything that retarded our movements, even to our haversacks," George Pile of the 37th remembered. Taliaferro spread plaudits through his report for the commanders of his other regiments, but acknowledged that the 37th captured "most of the prisoners." The captives taken by Taliaferro numbered "between 300 and 400," he thought, exclusive of what other commands accomplished.[10]

Winder's battered brigade could not play an important role in the pursuit after what it had been through. Colonel Grigsby averred that "a part" of the 27th Virginia joined in. Ronald of the 4th reported "I followed," and Allen of the 2nd specified that his regiment "followed on in rear." That left poor Colonel Neff, still itching for action to erase the frustration of two confused days. He pushed his 33rd Virginia forward "vigorously," but of course could not overtake Taliaferro's leading troops on the congested road.[11]

To Jackson's delight, and to some degree under his personal supervision, Confederates of his favorite arm—the artillery—took an energetic part in the pursuit. Just as the Federal flight began, Carpenter's Battery used its last rounds and lapsed into silence. Chew's Battery had arrived later and still had ammunition on hand. Captain Chew pushed his guns to a spot next to Lewiston and fired down the road at the Yankees, "producing great havoc amongst them." The Baltimore Light Artillery under Captain Brockenbrough, which had borne a heavy burden well at Cross Keys, arrived fresh "just as the retreat commenced." Winder directed the battery's fire against the road and the woods crowding its shoulders, "and the enemy scattered in every direction."[12]

Captain W. T. Poague had one half (three pieces) of the strength of his Rockbridge Artillery still serviceable when the rout began. He led that hardy remnant down the road for two miles before halting. One of Poague's goals was to find the brass piece that the enemy had captured from Lieutenant Davis's section. It did not turn up, but another old friend did when the battery "overtook one of our battery horses which we had captured from Banks two weeks before. [Tyler's] men then captured him from us, and we again from them. He had been wounded four times, but was still fit for service." Poague had stopped a mile too soon. Other Confederates found the brass gun abandoned three miles from the battlefield, its carriage disabled and the piece "nicely spiked with a horseshoe nail." The enemy had run the gun into "a big sink hole, filled with water," near the road.[13]

After their brief salvage venture, the Rockbridge boys returned to Lewiston. Ned Moore, who had been wakened from his peculiar, intense mid-battle nap to go with the pursuit, examined the Coaling with the fascination of an artillerist bedeviled by it all morning:

> I ... had the satisfaction of seeing the five cannon that had played on our gun standing silent on the coal-hearth, in our hands. There being no room in their rear, their caissons and limbers stood off to their right on a flat piece of heavily wooded ground. This was almost covered with dead horses. I think there must have been eighty or ninety on less than an acre; one I noticed standing almost upright, perfectly lifeless, supported by a fallen tree.

Other battlefield tourists would comment on the lifelike standing corpse during the next two days.[14]

Wooding's and Caskie's batteries pressed farthest and hardest during the pursuit. When Jackson caught up with Winder near the head of the column four or five miles below the battlefield, he ordered the infantry halted. Stonewall continued forward in person with the batteries, and two pieces from Chew's Battery which had also reached the front. The artillery galloped far beyond its infantry support under Jackson's direction, firing with "great spirit and serious effect." Wooding's Battery had been "rendering most effective service, and the effect of his shot was remarkable." Two of Wooding's pieces spurred on "for many miles beyond the infantry ... under the eye of the commanding general," Taliaferro reported. Their technique was to dash forward from knoll to knoll, "pouring grape into their ranks from every eminence."[15]

The unraveling of the battle lines on both sides created a fluid situation that offered wide opportunities for personal endeavor. The results were sometimes dramatic or gallant, sometimes humorous, and sometimes pathetic. The 5th Virginia triumphantly gathered in the colors—the greatest treasure on Civil War battlefields—of the 5th Ohio, which had been fighting across from the regiment all morning. Sergeant Sam Gray of the 37th Virginia captured a Federal captain and eleven of his men. All of the Yankees were armed and some fired at Gray, but he dashed up to the captain, seized his sword, and made the enemy soldiers throw down their weapons.[16]

William S. Lacy took advantage of his position with Wooding's guns near the front of the column to make a capture at least as gratifying as Sergeant Gray's. Lacy started in the pursuit on a military high and ended it as a hungry boy:

> It was at Port Republic that I felt [most] the *gaudia certaminis*—the glory of the warrior. . . . When the enemy gave back, his retreat became a rout, and we chase as boys run rabbits, with dog and yell. That was the first, last and only time I ate any real candy. We overtook a sutler's wagon, boxes all tumbled out in the flight, and I saw the brown paper package, which I first supposed contained pencils, then cigars, and, oh! joy, I found to be peppermint candy. Oh! how good it was to us hungry boys, and oh! how thirsty we were afterwards.[17]

Captain E. H. McDonald had orders to parole a number of captured enemy wounded. Any of them unwilling to accept parole were to be transported to the rear by ambulance. One dreadfully wounded youngster had "a bullet just buried in his forehead," but refused to be paroled. The Unionist lad had signed on to stamp out the foul rebellion and would not hear of treating with the enemy. Knowing that the wagon ride would almost certainly kill the stubborn boy, McDonald ignored his orders and left him where he was, unparoled.[18]

Abram D. Warwick of the 2nd Virginia Cavalry was returning with his detachment toward the battlefield when a Confederate trooper came out of a narrow path with word that an entire company of Yankees was around a spring just a few yards into the woods, armed with muskets but talking of surrender. Friendly soldiers were scattered in all directions, "from the top to the foot of the Mountain side," but without cohesion or leadership. Warwick could not see the enemy, nor could he charge them through the dense thickets. He called the Yankee commander out to the road and told him truthfully that he was surrounded, without dwelling on the state of the besiegers. Warwick embellished his tale by saying that it was Turner Ashby's cavalry lurking on all sides, Ashby being "a *name* to conjure with!"

The Federal agreed to have his men stack their arms and march out to the road. Abram Warwick counted 84 of them, mostly from the 66th Ohio. Thirteen Louisianians the Buckeyes had captured around the Coaling were repatriated at the same time. To Warwick's relief, Confederate reinforcements gradually arrived in enough strength to escort the large body of Yankees to the rear. Other Southerners helped Warwick's men deliver the immense pile of stacked guns to the yard at Lewiston.[19]

Cavalry herded prisoners by the hundreds back past Lewiston and eventually to Staunton. One officer sent a Northern prisoner back in care of a servant, with orders "to see him shut up safe, and the key turned on him." The servant hauled his charge clear to Staunton and attempted to turn him over to Major Michael G. Harman, quartermaster of the post there. Harman suggested that the one-man guard should finish the chore by herding the captive on to the city jail, which he did proudly.[20]

Dick Ewell had pressed energetically forward, accompanied by a company of cavalry from the "Comanches." The horsemen "had very warm and exciting work" keeping up with the energetic general, capturing a company of Ohio infantry in the process. Captain Frank Myers of the Comanches stayed close to Stonewall Jackson for much of the distance, prompting a rebuke from the crotchety Ewell, who scolded Myers "that he was no courier for Gen. Jackson, and that his business was to keep his (Ewell's) Division supplied with couriers, and to obey his orders and nobody else's."[21]

During the pursuit, Jackson ran across several "diabolical explosive rifle-balls" allegedly used by the Federals in contravention of the rules of warfare. According to Dr. Dabney, the illegal projectiles were made up of two pieces of lead with a cavity inside "filled with fulminating powder, which was intended to explode by percussion, upon the impact of the ball against the bone of the penetrated body." Allegations about the use of such improper ammunition recurred regularly on both sides. The chances are that most, if not all, of the instances involved anomalies or disfigured rounds. Dabney's level assertion about the matter makes it likely that Jackson believed what he saw near Port Republic to be diabolical and illicit devices.[22]

The most excited Confederate involved in the battle's pursuit phase may have been Lieutenant Ned Willis of Jackson's staff. Willis had been a prisoner for twenty-eight hours by the time he began to see signs of Federal deterioration around the house of the widow Ergenbright, where he was being held. The lieutenant exploited his genuine illness for all it was worth. He "played sick—very ill," according to a colleague's account. When a Yankee examined Willis, he groaned terribly. His captors announced their determination to carry the lieutenant away as a trophy, even if it killed him; but approaching artillery fire frightened the guards away. Willis grasped the opportunity to escape and soon turned up among friends mounted on a captured horse with his Federal soldier-nurse sitting quietly behind him.[23]

A young neighbor of the widow Ergenbright, George E. Sipe, aged eleven, had listened to the thunder upstream since early in the morning. A lull in the "terrific" roar had nervous listeners on tenterhooks until a Yankee courier dashed past, "his horse literally belathered with sweat." An onlooker yelled out, "What news?" The flying messenger responded, "They have captured all of our artillery." Young George was ecstatic at the announcement of victory for his home people. "Soon the road was full of groups of men in scattered disorder, wagon trains, litters and ambulances."

One ambulance driver crashed to a halt at the Sipe gate, grabbed a leather bucket from his wagon, and hurriedly filled it at the pump in the yard. When the attendant pulled back the gate of the ambulance, George saw "in full face, the pale, stark features of the first dead soldier I had ever seen." He would see a great many more, but that first impression "was so horrible," he wrote long afterward, "I have never been able to get rid of it." The driver threw his water in the road, saying "He don't want any water," and raced away.

A Yankee officer rode up to the fence and encouraged George's dad to take his family into the hills to avoid the Confederate artillery fire that was drawing nigh. The Sipes dashed across their farm to the top of the highest pasture and sat there, in company with a convalescent Stonewall Brigade soldier they had been sheltering for six weeks, to watch the unfolding drama. From their lookout they saw Northern reinforcements in the distance, coming from Conrad's Store. Southern cavalry then swarmed through the fields and artillery fired over their heads toward the enemy.

After the crisis had passed, George and his family returned to their home and found a surgeon probing the wounds of a Confederate officer "over a tub of water that looked more like a tubful of blood than water." In the Sipes' eastern fields, wounded horses "were plunging in helpless agony, till soldiers came and with army revolvers close to their heads put them out of their misery." Later, Unionist stragglers came sheepishly out of the surrounding woods to surrender. Two of the fugitives approached the Sipes' maid as she was milking, grabbed the bucket, and each drank copiously from it. One handed the woman a five-dollar bill before hurrying off. The incident ended the most memorable day of George E. Sipe's life. He had cause to remember the incident fondly at the end of the war, when the five dollars constituted the family's total assets.[24]

F. M. Hay and John M. Johnson of the 7th Indiana had reason to be grateful to two young women in the same neighborhood. They had chatted with the girls during the Federal advance two days earlier. The two "were bitter rebels," Billy Davis of the 7th recalled, who "said they hoped their army would whip our army and that we would every one be killed." As they tumbled rearward, Hay and Johnson hoped to slip unseen past the two jingoistic Southern girls. The Hoosiers were astonished to find them at the gate with a bucket of spring water doling it out to passing soldiers. The girls had decided to treat the enemy the way they hoped their brother in Jackson's army would be treated in like circumstances. "If brother was in the battle and was wounded," they explained, "or is as tired as all these men are, wouldn't it be nice if some Union folks would give him water to drink?"[25]

The Confederate pursuit beyond Lewiston covered a considerable distance before it ran out of steam. Weary Southerners turned back in ever larger numbers, then Shields's reinforcements began to supply some starch to Tyler's routed column. The Battle of Port Republic ended as the pursuers and the pursued drew gradually apart. Stonewall Jackson, who had been near the forefront during much of the chase, estimated his deepest infantry penetration as five miles beyond the battlefield. Cavalry and some artillery went "about 3 miles beyond the other troops," the general thought. Two Confederates claimed pursuing as far as twelve miles, but the consensus conforms to Jackson's figures.[26]

The view from the other side showed about the same thing the Confederates saw: a withdrawal that turned into a rout. Tyler brazenly declared in his official report that the retreat, organized at his direction by Colonel Carroll, "was made in perfect order, and . . . the retreat was quite as orderly as the advance." An Ohio regiment's historian, paraphrasing Tyler's report, picked up the refrain and even insisted that the escape was "marvellous." No one else thought so, including Colonel Carroll. In his report he admitted that the captured guns firing from the Coaling "threw the rear of our column in great disorder, causing them to take to the woods, and making it . . . apparently a rout." Southern cavalry then charged, Carroll reported, "increasing the confusion."[27]

Virtually every Federal unit on the field claimed the role of primary rear guard for Tyler's retreating column. Colonel Carroll did not rule on the subject, simply reporting, "I did all I could to organize the rear." Because of its position near the river, the 7th Indiana probably was last to reach the road. The 7th's historian made the usual claim of having protected the column's tail. Billy Davis wrote of forming line to repulse Southern cavalry, then falling back past the 1st Virginia (Union) in a leapfrog pattern that the units repeated. The 1st's historian agreed that his regiment was at the rear ("a heavy duty to the small band remaining"), but did not mention the 7th.[28]

The 29th Ohio's historian wrote that his unit left the field only after "all our troops had passed . . . and we were nearly surrounded." A sober diarist in the 29th concurred. The 5th Ohio also felt that it came out last; it too was "nearly surrounded before we could get out." Colonel Dunning of the 5th presented the most convincing case for making the final stand, then admitted heading into the forested hillsides with his men to escape capture. A portion of the 5th clung to the road, and Shields specifically mentioned that regiment as bringing up the rear when the two Federal forces merged miles down the Valley.[29]

Unionists dashing toward the rear generally made no attempt to disguise the nature of the flight. Carroll reported that his efforts to organize the rear guard were hampered because "the front was led with such speed that it was impossible to do so under 2 or 2½ miles." A member of the 29th Ohio complained especially of the

"strong force of Cavalry which cut through our ranks taking many
. . . prisoners. To avoid the cavalry the men took to the woods and
went into the mountains." The historian of the 7th Indiana agreed
that they had been "smartly annoyed" by Southern riders. Artillerist
James Huntington grumbled about the Federal cavalry. The primary
instance of "unmanly panic" that came under Huntington's eye was
a cavalry captain who galloped past, roweling his horse mercilessly
and screaming, "The enemy are upon us!" To Huntington's intense
disgust, a bullet fired at the fellow by "an indignant officer" missed
its target.[30]

When Dunning had to abandon the road, he rode his horse as
far as it could go into the tangled thickets, then sent the men on
ahead toward the top of the Blue Ridge. Behind him Dunning could
hear Southern cavalry shouting at his men to surrender. The remnant
of the 5th Ohio that remained on the road turned back mounted
charges with what James Clarke called "little trouble." Clarke joined
Huntington in damning friendly troops for engendering panic. When
Unionist cavalry and artillery thundered "pell-mell" through the infantry columns, their horses and vehicles cutting a wide swath, many
infantryman bolted. The frightened fugitives discarded their guns and
equipment and, in Clarke's words, "made some splendid double-
quick practice."[31]

Soldiers advancing with Shields to Tyler's aid described the disorganized mass they met. "We met hundreds of our soldiers coming
back," David Been of the 14th Indiana wrote, "and soon the whole
of the two brigades came back in the wildest disorder; completely
demoralized." Augustus Van Dyke saw comrades pouring past without guns, barefoot, and missing uniform pieces. Some limber chests
were missing their cannon and other cannon had no limber chests;
some horses raced in without riders and some cavalrymen trudged
past without horses. It was, Van Dyke wrote simply, "a most dreadful
rout and defeat."[32]

Billy Davis noticed that Confederate artillery fire inevitably flew
too high; the falling branches sheared off by the flying metal posed
a far milder threat than would have well-aimed rounds. Four members
of the 7th Indiana, finding themselves trapped against the river, swam
through the turbulent water and scurried west toward the Valley
Turnpike. Two of them reached Front Royal six days later, the other
two the next day.[33]

One weary Hoosier faced his direst moment at the hands of a

putative friend. The soldier's shoes had worn through, and he was waiting beside the road for a wagon to mount when General Tyler spotted him. The general snapped an order for the barefoot boy to move on, even after he saw his condition. Tyler, who was experiencing the worst day of his life, drew his pistol and took aim at the recalcitrant soldier. Joe Beetem of the 7th saw Tyler's intentions, leveled his musket, and shouted, "Drop that!" The general discreetly recognized the better part of valor and raced away "as rapidly as his horse's legs could carry him."[34]

Colonel Lewis P. Buckley of the 29th Ohio rallied his men at a crisis by waving his sword rather than threatening with his pistol. Confederates threatened to surge around the colonel and a knot of his men, who "fought with the desperation born of despair." The sword-wielding Buckley, afoot after having two horses shot beneath him, led a small detachment through the Southerners and up onto the wooded mountainside. Several dozen soldiers camped with him in splendid isolation that night.[35]

Two enlisted men were especially distinguished as heroes in the 7th Ohio. Charles King and Henry H. Rhodes applied extraordinary effort attempting to extricate the captured Confederate bronze gun from the miry sinkhole where it had foundered. Rhodes, who was barefooted, and King, who had been shot through the face, each grasped a cannon wheel and strained to help the begrimed horses. King's exertion was so tremendous "as to force the blood out of the openings in his cheeks [from his bullet wound] in distinct spurting streams." The next morning King's face was swollen beyond recognition.[36]

Fred Fairfax of the 5th Ohio, a twenty-three-year-old lieutenant, found himself stranded near the Coaling when friendly lines collapsed. Fairfax obliqued toward the road but was again "surrounded by Secesh." They ignored the lieutenant, so he scrambled back into the woods. Fairfax eventually caught up with his unit after a frantic hour of effort. Colonel Dunning impressed his men by his stout spirit. Confederates "all the time" were shouting at Dunning to surrender; "as many times [he] told them to go to hell." Inspired Ohioans would then "pour in a few 2 ouncers" and buy a bit more time. James Clarke spied the chaplain of the 66th Ohio, "dividing his time between shooting secesh cavalry and comforting the wounded." The cleric cursed at the runaways, "which he was very effective in doing."[37]

Accusations flew back and forth over the conduct of the confused retreat. Colonel Daum damned Captain Huntington for carelessness and sloth over the abandoned gun. Shields picked out the 1st Virginian (Union) for special calumny, reporting that it "was nowhere to be seen." The 1st's historian, of course, drew a contrasting picture of valor and skill.[38] The two Pennsylvania regiments and the 1st Virginia probably did not perform to standard, but by and large Tyler's Federal force behaved well. Running briskly downstream made good sense, both personally and tactically, once the Lewiston line collapsed.

Once the routed Federals reached Shields and his reinforcements, their vanished ardor gradually returned. An Ohioan wrote: "At last we met Jimmy himself alone in the road, speaking to every man that passed him . . . telling them that they were only repulsed and not whipped." Fresh troops who had come forward with Shields emplaced artillery on high ground and prepared to fight, but the Confederates had reached the end of their tether farther up the road, and no action ensued. Shields later claimed that his brave stand caused the Southerners to recoil in horror from so sturdy an opponent as himself. Charles Bard of the 7th Ohio reflected Shields's ludicrous posturing. Having been routed and chased for miles ("22 miles," Bard thought), the 7th Ohio now was feisty again and disdainful of the foe: "the cowards dare not come."[39]

The Federal denouement was prompt and final. By his own immodest account, Shields had skillfully crafted a new plan guaranteed to ensure Jackson's slaughter. A courier hurried to Frémont to inform him of the brilliant concept. Unfortunately, Shields received at that juncture "positive orders to return to Luray immediately." Irvin McDowell, his immediate superior, later wrote that the recall order of which Shields complained "was given by me from the War Department by direction of the President, who at the same moment wrote a similar order to General Frémont, it being not considered expedient to continue the chase [a peculiar word, considering the events of June 9!] . . . it being greatly the desire of the President and myself that the forces under my command should as speedily as possible return to Fredericksburg to move on Richmond."[40] Another direct result was that Jackson was also put in position to move on Richmond.

The Confederates meanwhile slogged back toward Port Republic on leaden legs. It was nearly sunset by the time the leading pursuers returned to Lewiston. Frémont's guns menacing them from beyond the river compelled Jackson's men to turn off and climb toward their destination at Brown's Gap on roads through the woods. Most of them used the road running through the Coaling ravine for that purpose. That led them into the main road—such as it was—to Brown's Gap at Mount Vernon Furnace. An artillerist grateful to find the covered route wrote that the use of that "old mountain road . . . was the key to our whole success." Otherwise, he opined, "we would have been shelled to pieces."[41]

As so often happened in Jackson's maneuvers, Jed Hotchkiss provided the guidance, leading the army in person. Battle maps make the route look like a regular road, but a local historian described it as a set of "old coal roads, following near the route of [an] Indian path." A soldier who trudged up the slope thought Jackson had cut part of the route, but he probably noticed minor improvements on existing traces. An officer described the road as so obscure that "the mouth . . . cannot be noticed from the main road. . . . Until we entered this road I thought we were gone," because of Frémont's artillery. In the woods the Confederates were able to unwind and move "deliberately," a great blessing because they were unutterably weary.[42]

Stonewall Jackson's preparation for the day of battle had included sending his wagon trains up into Brown's Gap starting in the morning. Before the first infantry neared the gap, the wagons had reached the top of the mountain. Some dropped down the other side of the crest to make room for the army. The "amphitheatral basin" within the shoulders of the gap provided some room, but Jackson's army soon would jam the area to overflowing. The trains had crossed South River above the congested town. They approached the furnace from the southwest over another "miry road," rather than from west and northwest, as did the rest of the army. Ordnance officer William Allan established headquarters for his portion of the trains on the roadside between the furnace and owner John F. Lewis's house.[43]

The head of the immensely long gray-clad army that snaked its way up Brown's Gap in the tracks of the wagons was made up of troops that had been the rear guard that day. When Trimble's men crossed South River and destroyed the ersatz bridge, there remained little to be done downstream where the battle had been decided. This tail of Jackson's column became the head of the reversed column. The 42nd Virginia and 1st Virginia Battalion started toward the gap early in the afternoon. They moved so leisurely that it was evening before they went into bivouac on the eastern slope beyond Brown's Gap. The 10th Virginia, relieved from duty in Port Republic, also climbed the Blue Ridge among the lead units and finally made camp three miles beyond the crest.[44]

Confederates farther back in the column had more to contend with. Most of them had suffered considerably during the day. As they headed for much-needed rest, the skies opened on them. What had started as a gorgeous spring day ended with a "cold rain" falling, sometimes at a "tremendous" rate. What one Virginia artillerist called "quite a brisk shower" turned into a steady irritating rain that lasted all night and half of June 10.[45]

Darkness caught most of Jackson's army still tiredly pressing upward through the woods. When the sun set at 7:15, many Confederates faced four or more hours of marching. Their tedious movement on what Marylander Frank Bond remembered as "a rough and very crooked road" was complicated by congestion and darkness. "Everything," Bond wrote, "cavalry, artillery, infantry and baggage crowded in, completely filling the road for its entire length, and often several wagons abreast."[46]

The wounded of course faced worse travails. Lieutenant James Cole Davis of the Rockbridge Artillery had been shot through the body when his gun was captured. He was "suffering dreadfully, able to move only in an upright position." Enlisted men in the battery had heard that their officer was mortally wounded and presumed him dead. As they moved slowly up the hillside, however, the cannoneers saw someone riding gingerly up the column. It was Davis, a man on either side of his horse to hold him erect, but with a plume still waving in his hat. The brave lieutenant's anguished ride finally carried him to a rude field hospital, from which he went on to a surprisingly full recovery. Cole Davis served with distinction later in the war, became an Arkansas congressman, and died in 1886.[47]

Hunger compounded bone-deep weariness. General Taylor had snacked on food taken from the haversack of a dead Federal, but he could tell that his troops were thoroughly "tired and famished." Colonel Munford reported that by the end of the march his command had been "without rations for either man or horse for twenty-four hours," and now they had to go to sleep again without anything to eat. The infantrymen of the 13th Virginia had been rousted out that morning by Ewell without a chance to cook, and so had gone two entire days and nights without food. During that time, Walker complained with understandable exaggeration, "we had fought two battles and marched thirty miles."[48]

Those few famished Confederates who found a bite to eat grumbled over the quality despite their hunger. Captain Poague of the Rockbridge Artillery ate only some "tough flap jacks, the toughest I ever tackled." Bill Lacy, who had consumed a pound of peppermint candy during the day, found somewhere an issue of flour with a little fat bacon. Lacy mixed rainwater with the flour to make dough and attempted to cook it over a campfire of green, wet wood. When that experiment failed miserably, he added the fat bacon to his stomach full of candy and went to a very uneasy rest.[49]

Hundreds—perhaps thousands—of Confederates never reached their units' loosely arranged bivouacs. Colonel Funk admitted that "many" men of the 5th Virginia simply "fell at the road-side, worn-out and exhausted from the hard labors of the day." He had the good sense to leave them where they lay. Colonel Garnett treated his men of the 48th Virginia the same way: "I allowed them to lie down and sleep till morning." General Winder's stern spirit might have rebelled at so casual an arrangement, but the general himself was "greatly exhausted" and succumbed to an enervated slumber. In the words of a local historian, "many tired, hungry and wounded men . . . fell on the grass when orders came to cease pursuit; and, forgetful of all else, slept until the next morning . . . when the haversack was overhauled once more, and farm houses sought."[50]

One pair of Virginians halted informally to avoid continuing in place behind a macabre headless corpse being removed from the field. They spread their rubber ponchos on a steep hillside just off the trail and braced their feet against a big tree to keep from slipping back into the valley. The two men's stupor held them asleep in the rain until morning, by which time they had slid into an indiscriminate heap sprawled athwart the tree.[51]

Tired men marching in the wet darkness were as testy as might be expected under the circumstances. General Dick Taylor's temper, always frayed under trying conditions (and exacerbated by rheumatism in wet weather), exploded twice during the march. As the general spurred his horse up the trail, he came across Walter Packard, a Virginia artillerist not under his command, riding on a caisson, contrary to standing orders. Taylor ordered Packard to get down.

Walter, however, was "a droll fellow, rather given to arguing, and had a way of enraging his adversary while he kept cool, and, when it suited, could put on great dignity." The sassy private glanced back when he heard Taylor's curt order and, "looking coolly at him, said, with his usual sang-froid, 'Who are you, and what the devil have you to do with my riding on a caisson?' " After a stunned moment, Taylor "opened on poor Walter with a volley of oaths that our champion swearer, Irish Emmett, would have envied." Packard's time afoot doubtless lasted precisely as long as it took the general to ride out of sight.[52]

Taylor's temper suffered a further jolt when he reached the area designated as his brigade's bivouac. In a fit of regional paranoia he blamed Stonewall's Virginian staffers for partiality in assigning bivouac space, because the Louisiana men had wound up on the steeply sloping roadside. The assumption was false—Virginians spilled over the top and down the equally steep far side for miles—but nonetheless irritating for that. In response to the uncomfortable situation, Dick Taylor "made things 'blue' around him." His companions wearily did the best they could amid the "steepness and darkness, mud and rain; but our General only got the madder and 'cussed' the louder."

Taylor finally sought rest beneath a wagon. Sometime later the camp was roused by "Taylor's deep voice, calling loudly above the storm." The general had slid partway down the mountain, bed and all, and decided to take it out on the "kindly and beloved" Quartermaster Captain T. R. Heard, who was responsible for logistical arrangements. The more Heard protested, the louder Taylor swore. The entire brigade listened with amusement, adding their "ludicrous remarks and laughter" to the bizarre rain-swept performance. So ended the day of battle for the men who had won the Coaling.[53]

The 13th Virginia chuckled over an exchange nearly as laughable. A Frenchman in the 13th cherished an inexplicable enthusiasm for Confederate general John B. Magruder, who had commanded far away on Virginia's Peninsula. In the aftermath of the victory at Port Republic, someone asked the Magruder booster if this latest exploit by Jackson had not won him over. The weary Frenchman answered angrily, and with some accuracy, "Magruder no march man up a tree!"[54]

Not every Confederate had the opportunity to find even the uncertain ease of a muddy bed. Jackson fretted over the possibility that useful ordnance might have been left on the field. A company of the 8th Louisiana had dragged the captured Coaling guns to safety, but the Rockbridge piece remained mired in the sinkhole below the battlefield. Stonewall sent a detachment of bone-weary ordnance men and pioneers into the inky, rainy darkness after it. William Allan's brother John went along, and so did Sandy Garber. They returned at daybreak after "a fearful night, with but little to pay for the exposure."[55]

Jackson did not hesitate to order General Taliaferro to bring in a single "unserviceable caisson" that had been left behind for want of horses. The stern army commander responded to a complaint about the weather and other difficulties with the admonition that "if it took every horse in the command, that caisson must be brought up before daylight." The officer detailed by Taliaferro to retrace those steep miles in the darkness "was very much of the opinion" that the command ought to "take up a subscription to pay for the thing, and let it be." He did not offer the suggestion to Stonewall Jackson, of course, and the caisson came in before the deadline.[56]

Two Confederate cavalrymen blundering through the bushes beyond the battlefield stumbled across three dozen Union stragglers guarding a few Rebel prisoners and cooking supper. The two Southerners succeeded in routing the Federals by shouting back and forth to create the illusion of strength. The freed prisoners picked up arms and managed to round up 36 enemy soldiers and escort them back toward Port Republic.[57]

Chaplain Richard McIlwaine's midnight duty was of a more somber nature. Having been driven from burial efforts by Frémont's ill-tempered fire that afternoon, the chaplain led a squad back to finish the job by night. He read the burial service over 14 Confederate bodies in shallow graves, using subdued tones "lest the enemy . . . should open fire on us." McIlwaine regretted the absence of the usual "beating of drums [and] the firing of guns"; he offered instead an "earnest invocation of the merciful kindness of our God."[58]

Stonewall Jackson and General Ewell remained close to the Valley floor that night, ready to respond to any exigency. The headquarters entourage set up, as mentioned above, around John Lewis's house near the furnace, but the generals were "at the foot of the mountain, and near the enemy." The 1st Maryland stayed behind to cover the withdrawal for hours, but finally marched up the ridge. The 21st North Carolina never did move up the slope, remaining "in Gun shot" of the South River all night, and in fact for several days thereafter.[59]

The 21st North Carolina faced no real threat. The Federal armies beaten on the two days just past contemplated making some movement toward Jackson's new lair, but never did anything about putting thought into action. Frémont made tentative gestures toward bridging the South Fork of the Shenandoah, but soon abandoned the effort. During the night Frémont beat the long roll, rousting his troops from their blankets to meet a phantom threat. They soon went back to bed and "Slept soundly until morning." Far downstream Shields managed to contrive a ferry crossing of the South Fork in the opposite direction, to reach Frémont's bank, but he never connected with his counterpart.[60]

By midnight most of the Confederate infantry and cavalry had collapsed for the night. Some troops who had not fought on the 9th and headed up the mountain early went into bivouac soon after dark. Most accounts named the convenient midnight hour as the estimated time of arrival. The colonel of the 48th Virginia timed his encampment at two A.M. Those artillerymen who remained with their pieces—an earnest minority, at most—had a hellish night picking their way around muddy soldiers sleeping in the road. Winder's batteries did not reach the end of their ordeal until daylight on the 10th. When the cannoneers unlimbered, unhitched, and collapsed, the Battle of Port Republic had finally reached its conclusion.[61]

Stonewall Jackson
proclaimed June
14 a day for religious
observances. "It
was a very
impressive
celebration of the
Lord's Supper, amid the
din of camps hushed
for a brief
period." The humbly
devout Jackson received
the sacred emblems
from a regimental
chaplain.

CHAPTER 27

"NEVER TAKE

COUNSEL OF YOUR

FEARS"

The morning of June 10 dawned grudgingly through a steady drizzle. The rain spit intermittently all day, and temperatures never reached 60. A staff officer who rode down the mountain to the furnace to meet Stonewall Jackson had difficulty finding his way. "It was raining hard," he remembered, "and the fog was thick; I could hardly see." The aide heard fiddling and tracked down its source—a private in the 9th Louisiana seated on an ammunition box, "fiddling away for dear life, all to himself, and the smile on his face told how he enjoyed it."[1]

Federal behavior that morning provided ample cause for Confederate glee. Both Shields and Frémont gave signs of retreating. Frémont abandoned his half-hearted bridging gesture by eight A.M. He broke up the beginnings he had made and disappeared from the neighborhood. Frémont's disgruntled soldiers trudged through the steady rain toward Harrisonburg, reaching there late in the afternoon thoroughly drenched. Most units camped on the same ground they had occupied just two days earlier.[2]

The physical and spiritual state of Frémont's column left it in what one of the men called "a sad predicament." Another admitted frankly that the movement "resembled a rout more than anything else." General Carl Schurz met the army in Harrisonburg and was shocked by its "rather loose order." Schurz could see that the men were "ragged, tired, and dejected." He heard a good deal of "hard swearing in the ranks in various tongues, English, German, and Hungarian—signs of a sorry state of mind." Attempting to sleep in wet clothes under a continuing rain did nothing to improve Federal morale. Numbers of them took the opportunity to desert, or at least to surrender and claim the more comfortable status of willing deserters.[3]

As Frémont's men streamed back past the Cross Keys battlefield, an Ohioan noted the desolation that war had wreaked. "The ground trees &c was pretty well torn up by our artillery," he wrote. Civilians suffered another round of losses as the enemy swept through their homes once more. According to widely circulated local lore, Federal casualties also suffered at the hands of Frémont's army. Several contemporaries reported the purposeful burning by retreating Yankees of an old building just north of Cross Keys that had been a hospital. A Southern cavalryman wrote of passing a building "that they had burnt containing large numbers of their killed." Mary Yancey of Harrisonburg identified the house in a June 20 letter and reported that she had seen the charred bones of enemy dead consumed in the fire. A local newspaperman estimated the number of corpses cremated in the blaze at 500. Soon after the war another journalist declared that the burned Northerners included not only dead but also "wounded and dying soldiers." Neighbors "heard the shrieks and the groans of the wounded Yankee soldiers as they were roasted alive in the burning building."[4] The prevalence of the tale makes it certain that some such episode actually transpired, probably involving a few (far fewer then 500) Federal corpses.

John Frémont's pride must be added to any listing of Northern casualties. His cronies in the army put the best possible face on the results in accounts written on June 10 and soon thereafter. Krzyzanowski insisted that "Frémont performed miracles" in the campaign.

Others launched a campaign of special pleading mixed with dark hints of a conspiracy against the heroic explorer. Staff officer Albert Tracy attributed the unhappy results to others: "Is it treachery, is it persecution, or possibly, a simple indifference, which, from the first, has been deaf to our appeals for the means; which . . . has left us to ourselves . . . at moments when everything depended upon a close and vigorous unity?" The adjutant of a Federal regiment could readily see the more accurate source of Frémont's trouble—Stonewall Jackson. "General Jackson is a sharp fellow," Adjutant John Polsley told his wife ten days later, "and has a well drilled and disciplined army and he knows how to handle it." Even at that late date Polsley nurtured a healthy fear that Jackson might appear on Frémont's flank yet again."[5]

Stonewall Jackson's situation on June 10 was diametrically opposite to that of his opponents. Confederate morale stood at a fever pitch, and his army was nicely concentrated either to renew the offensive or to march toward Richmond. Jackson's headquarters remained all day at the Lewis house near the furnace. Directives poured out of headquarters ordering completion of tasks great and small. The general sent orders to each brigade to ascertain whether all of its dead had been buried; if not, a detail with shovels was to report to headquarters at three-thirty P.M. to go down and complete that chore. Jackson also issued minutely detailed orders about how a cavalry detail was to escort the hundreds of fresh Federal prisoners (more stragglers were coming in steadily) to North Carolina by way of Lynchburg and Danville. He may also have arranged for construction of some crude earthworks to strengthen the natural defensive features of Brown's Gap.[6]

The general's attention also fastened on quartermaster and commissary details. Major John Harman crossed the mountain toward Mechum's River Station with orders to be ready to provision the army from the eastern side of the Blue Ridge. Harman and the army commander also had one of their sporadic spats. The major, who had supervised the gathering of arms from the battlefield, incautiously responded to Jackson's questioning by admitting that "a good many of them look like our own arms." That set the army commander into "a towering passion." Jackson raged at Harman that he did not want to hear such nonsense. Harman stalked off, offended by being abused for telling the simple truth, and sent in one of the several resignations he submitted during 1862. Stonewall then called him in, apologized on the grounds that he had been "much annoyed at that time, and many others had fretted him" and disapproved the resignation.[7]

The same day, Stonewall Jackson wrote to his beloved wife to announce his stunning victories: "God has been our shield, and to his name be all the glory.... How I do wish for peace, but only upon the condition of our national independence!" Another happy bit of correspondence on this date went from Jackson's desk to Adjutant General Samuel Cooper, applauding in gaudy terms the performance of Dick Taylor and urging his prompt promotion. "The success with which he has managed his Brigade in Camp, on the March, and when engaged with the enemy . . . make it my duty as well as a pleasure to recommend his promotion," Jackson enthused.[8]

The subject of Stonewall's lavish praise arose on June 10 in a mood as sweet as that of the preceding night had been sour. He was, an aide wrote, "as gentle as a lamb . . . all the more pleasant and agreeable to everyone, as was his custom after explosions of temper." Despite the continuing rain, Taylor moved his brigade three miles up and over the top of the mountain.[9]

Some Confederates pressed even farther east. The 1st Maryland Infantry continued all the way to the foot of the Blue Ridge and found a bivouac strategically situated in the midst of ripe cherries and wild strawberries. The Stonewall Brigade remained "on the very summit of the Blue Ridge." Up on the cloud-shrouded crest, it rained "very hard" on the Stonewall Brigade. Men inured to hardships by following Jackson through months of sturdy endeavor were not likely to be daunted by a bit of rain. One Confederate noted stoically, "Our toilet was soon completed by a yawn and a stretch of our limbs." Winder's diary entry reported rain all day. A series of officers called on the weary general, but he found opportunity for a much-needed nap.[10]

Winder's subordinates undertook a variety of tasks associated with policing the Port Republic battlefield. A detachment from the Rockbridge Artillery went out to salvage a gun that had careened off the steep road in the darkness. They found the piece at the bottom of a forty-foot escarpment, two horses of the team on their backs but still hitched to the limber. The artillerymen managed to recover the gun after some effort, and the horses too; somehow the animals had survived their ordeal. The two drivers responsible for the accident had jumped off barely in time to escape. To the amusement of their mates, the two men quarreled for months about the blame.[11]

Civilians all across the battle zone were more active on June 10 than was the average Confederate soldier. Some of them coped with the final incursions of retreating Federals; others helped tend the wounded; and residents driven from battlefield homes returned to assess the damage and pick up their lives.

Harrison Bateman had a brief encounter with General Frémont on the road toward Cross Keys. Frémont inquired if the elderly civilian knew where Jackson had gone. When Bateman responded that he had no idea, the general flared up and called him a liar. "God knows whether I lie or not, sir," Bateman answered. Frémont calmed down, playfully pulled Bateman's whiskers, and said, "You are an old gray-headed philosopher." Civilians farther north, near Good's Mill, hid their silver in a cradle under a newborn baby just before Northerners burst in upon them. The ravenous enemy ate everything in sight, including raw eggs and uncooked flour, but never thought to look under the baby.[12]

Northeast of Port Republic, Federal stragglers fumbled through the wooded hillsides all day on June 10. Charles Bonfanti and John Randleman of the 14th Indiana, which was among Shields's reinforcing regiments, wandered into a mountain shack and either persuaded or forced a woman to cook for them. The two Hoosiers were lounging on her bed awaiting dinner when Confederate scouts dashed up. Bonfanti managed to escape, but his comrade wound up a prisoner.[13]

Civilians in Luray rejoiced at the sight of Federals streaming back in defeat. "The female portion of the community," an Ohio soldier reported, "seemed to enjoy our defeat—hugely! You could see them skipping from door to door happy as larks over the defeat of Shields' men." The women of Harrisonburg of course were just as happy. One of them wrote, "to our joy . . . the wagons came pouring in by dozens, And in a short time hear they all came Skadaddeling to use there own word." Frémont spoke sternly to the mayor of Harrisonburg about caring for Federal wounded to be left in town, then prepared to move farther north.[14]

Frémont need not have worried about the treatment of his wounded. Civilians surrounded by Northern casualties generally treated them as suffering humans rather than as enemies. A soldier from New York who spent June 10 helping tend "a whole barnfull of our wounded soldiers" found them in universal agreement "that they had been very kindly treated by most of the enemy among whom they fell . . . with tender and delicate humanity." The New Yorker admitted that this news made him feel warm toward Confederates. He wished "that we could join hands and be friends once more." The reflective Northerner also shuddered at the mistreatment of Southern civilians, imagining how he would feel if his homefolks had been similarly mishandled.[15]

Southerners returning fearfully to their battlefield homes faced scenes beyond their worst imaginings. At Cross Keys civilians found that enemy "dead and the dying thickly strewed the field in every direction, and days afterwards it was spotted all over with pools of human gore, making it look like a field of blood sure enough." When widowed Evaline Baugher reached Westwood, she found shell damage to the house. All of her sheets, towels, and other linens had been torn up and used as bandages. Along her entrance lane Mrs. Baugher discovered that many bodies had been buried in a mass grave crudely made by filling the roadside ditch.[16]

The Lynnwood civilians walked into "a terrible scene of desolation" as they entered their yard. The family first saw "a dead Yankee propped up against a tree with some of the family silver spoons sticking out of his pocket." Inside the main house they found dozens of wounded soldiers "lying on the floor amidst pools of blood." The Federal nurse left to care for the wounded men treated them so callously that Richard Fletcher sent him away, took over as head nurse and undertaker, and did his best to alleviate the suffering. For weeks and even months in some cases, Fletcher tended wounded who lingered on. One poor fellow "had become a maniac from a wound in his head," requiring special efforts from the volunteer nurse. The family's women returned to Bogota to live, visiting Lynnwood daily to cook and to help Richard.

Compassion for suffering foemen did not preclude disgust for Federals who had so savagely ravaged Lynnwood property. Northerners had destroyed everything they could not remove—"cut the throats of sheep, ruined farm utensils, clothing, and even carried off ladies' dresses." The angry Lynnwood women took consolation in the notion that Colonel Buckley, who had been so chauvinistic and rude to them before the battle, had been shot dead from his horse in their view. They found confirmation of that happy denouement in a New York newspaper. In fact, Buckley had escaped, but the

Fletcher and Walton women enjoyed their revenge in blissful ignorance for the rest of their lives.

Postwar attempts to secure reimbursement for losses and for
expenditures on behalf of Northern wounded were routinely rejected
because the Lynnwood civilians were wanting in political purity.
Meanwhile, late in the war Anne Lewis Walton had to sell Lynnwood
and move to Georgia. Her cousin John F. Lewis bought it for $80,000
in Confederate bonds, which promptly became worthless. The oppor-
tunistic Yankee sympathizer, who parlayed that pose into immense
postwar gains, had hedged his bets by holding a cache of Southern
war bonds. The loss of her "beloved Lynnwood," Anne maintained,
"was the tragedy of her life."[17]

The heel of war fell as heavily on Lewiston as on Lynnwood,
but not as irrevocably, because John F. Lewis of Lewiston, unlike the
denizens of Lynnwood, maintained the correct political hedges. The
Lewises met the same startling scenes of blood and horror as their
Lynnwood cousins, and also began tending wounded in their house.
John Lewis's successful postwar claim for reimbursement cited special care supplied to a soldier named Grace from Michigan, even
though no Michigan troops fought at Port Republic! Lewis supplied
a statement from a former slave named Abram James, who deposed
that Lewis "could not have been more attentive to [Federals] if they
had all been his own children. The Union soldiers considered &
treated him as a Union man, they talked to me about him, and said
they had always heard he was a Union man." John Lewis held on to
Lewiston, acquired Lynnwood as well, and received Federal money
for his trouble.[18]

Civilians from beyond the outer limits of the fighting wandered
over the battlefields on June 10 to see the historic ground. Eleven-
year-old George Sipe and a black youngster joined with Sipe's father
and a neighbor named David Gilmore to visit Port Republic battlefield
that afternoon. They gravitated to the Coaling, the obvious focus of
the fighting. There they found "over twenty horses . . . dead almost
in touch of each other." Young George was transfixed by the sight
of a beautiful bay that had been killed by a bullet in the brain but
remained aright, propped up by a tree. The dead animal had "his
right foreleg reaching forward above the ground as if about to spring
forward, arched stiff neck and head up, his wide open eyes seemed
to gaze with awful composure, vacant and sphinx-like, across the
bloody field." Years later Sipe remembered how "the posture of the

poor animal, so suggestive of action and vigor, and the contrasting death stare of the eyes, produced a strange impression of awe and terror on every beholder."

David Gilmore came across the end of an episode that had begun in his yard early on June 9. Gilmore's wife had surprised a Northerner ransacking her beehive. The fellow brashly called to her, "Old woman, don't you want some honey? You look damned hungry." When filled to capacity with the sweet treat, the Yankee broke off some of Mrs. Gilmore's phlox, stuck it in his cap, and went forward down the road. Now as Gilmore and his friends made their way north from the Coaling along the Federal line near Lewis Run, Gilmore suddenly exclaimed, "Look there at that cap. Do you see the phlox?" It was on the corpse of a Unionist, his leg torn off by a cannonball.[19]

During June 11 and 12 the strategic situation resolved into a clear picture of Confederate triumph as Jackson consolidated his position and his enemies moved out of the arena. Federals who had scampered into the wooded mountains to escape capture at Port Republic filtered back into friendly lines. On the 11th, the colonel and adjutant of the 29th Ohio reappeared. So did 100 of their subordinates, doubling the regiment's numbers present. A few more Ohioans straggled in on the 12th, but soon thereafter the knapsacks of men still missing were piled up and burned. Frémont's troops also plodded northward in the separate valley beyond Massanutten Mountain. They reached New Market late on June 11 and moved on to Mount Jackson the next morning.[20]

General Shields boasted in official correspondence on June 12 about his soldiers' prowess, declaring that they "fought like devils." That accurate assessment was only a preface for Shields's familiar refrain. Carroll should have burned the bridge but "wanted the good sense." Tyler "took up an indefensible position . . . instead of a defensible one." With an insistence more pathetic than tenacious, Shields maintained his confidence that "the plan for Jackson's destruction was perfect."[21] None of this made any more sense on the 12th than it had on the 9th, or than it would in endless future reprises.

Jubilant Confederates could not be certain on June 11 that the campaign was over. Major John Harman, long a Jackson detractor, now declared that Stonewall "could clean the Valley sure" with a few reinforcements. Harman remained certain on the 11th, however, that Frémont would head to Staunton and pose a new threat—at a time when Frémont's destination was in the opposite direction. Jackson's weary men were not certain they could respond if renewed action broke out. A Georgian wrote home that he was "broke down. . . . Iv been so worn out that I hardly had time to think. . . . I am worn out, tired, want rest but cant get it."[22]

General Jackson's concern for the comfort of his frazzled men was at its usual level—low to nonexistent. Although no further combat developed, Stonewall kept his troops moving. On the 11th he ordered them to prepare one day's rations, after which the wagons were to move to the foot of the Blue Ridge. There they must park in an alignment carefully contrived to allow rapid movement in either direction. The meticulous Jackson added an injunction about "avoiding a jam or collision." When Jed Hotchkiss found the South River fords still impassable for caissons, Jackson detailed some infantry at his suggestion to pile stones in the fords of the still high stream.[23]

One June 12 Jackson took advantage of the augmented fords to move his army off the mountain, over South River, through Port Republic, then upstream. Hotchkiss employed his new-found technique with rocks and fords to ease passage of the trains at Patterson's Mill, using some men detailed from the 16th Mississippi as laborers. That night army headquarters were pitched in a wooded road corner near Weyer's Cave.[24]

Stonewall Jackson kept his cavalry busy extending the army's horizons. He ordered Colonel Tom Munford back into the Valley on the 11th. Munford's mounted column reached Mount Crawford that day and picked up a few prisoners. The next morning the cavalry reoccupied Harrisonburg and captured 200 wounded Federals. That evening pickets pushed past New Market to the edge of Mount Jackson. Other cavalry detachments faced the distasteful duty of burying dead at Cross Keys, which was beyond easy reach of infantry details.[25]

Jackson wasted not a moment resting on his newly won laurels. Hours after winning at Port Republic the general was in ardent quest of more troops. He wrote to his friend and Lexington neighbor, Governor John Letcher, exhorting the state's chief executive to enforce the new draft law aggressively: "no time should be lost in bringing the conscripts into the field," Jackson wrote earnestly.[26]

Had Jackson been inclined toward resting on them, laurels were headed his way. Robert E. Lee, ten days into command of the Army of Northern Virginia, wrote warmly: "Your recent successes have been the cause of the liveliest joy in this army as well as in the country. The admiration excited by your skill and boldness has been constantly mingled with solicitude for your situation. The practicability of re-enforcing you has been the subject of earnest consideration." Lee announced that he was dispatching fourteen strong regiments to the Valley in a feint. Jackson's enlarged army was then to sweep across the mountains to raise havoc in the Federal rear and help lift the siege of Richmond. The stakes for which Stonewall Jackson was playing would be appreciably elevated.[27]

The five days beginning with June 13 proved to be among the most pleasant that Jackson's troops ever spent, but their retreating foemen faced a very different set of circumstances. Despite their plight, an astonishing number of Federals making their way northward from Luray and Mount Jackson convinced themselves that they had whipped Stonewall Jackson! General Schenck wrote to his daughter with an apparently straight face that his troops marched to Mount Jackson "after . . . chasing Jackson out of the valley." A member of the 29th Ohio indulged the same fantasy when he declared that Frémont had "Attacked them & whiped them sevearly & took 5000 prisoners & 15 pieces of Artilery." Another Ohioan calmly reported on June 13, "Suffice it to say, that Jackson is driven out of the Valley burning the bridges behind him, and we are all safe."[28]

Many Northerners who did not claim resounding victory at least insisted that their withdrawal was made in good order and resulted from mature military wisdom rather than Confederate initiatives. The cavalrymen chasing them, a member of the 73rd Ohio admitted, were "scouring the country in every direction." Shields's men, who had had the harder approach march, were "destitute of clothing." Many were barefoot, with no prospect for replacement foot gear.[29]

Hundreds of wounded Union soldiers were dropping out of the transportation system at points all along the route back to Washington. On the night of June 15, ten railroad cars carrying 209 wounded Federals reached the capital. A bureaucratic snarl resulted in no one to greet them. The rectors of two churches near the train station threw open their doors, and local civilians came laden with food and tended them until hospital authorities arrived tardily.[30]

Another train delivered 50 Confederate prisoners to Washington the same day. All of them were full of ardor to return and fight, they assured a newspaperman. The capital's newsmen were already eager to blame Carroll for not burning the North River bridge, and fished for comments from the prisoners about how badly a burned bridge would have hurt their cause. An onlooker described the captive Southerners as "a very ordinary-looking lot of men," clad mostly in civilian clothes without even military buttons: "every man appeared to be arrayed in such garments he could first find or best suited his individual fancy." It seemed hard to believe that such casual ragamuffins could so often trounce the fancily outfitted Federalists. Local women brought edibles for the prisoners, just as they had for Union wounded; but guards refused to allow them to deliver the food, to the righteous delight of the politically active reporter. The guards even arrested civilians who expressed sympathy with the prisoners' plight.[31]

Northern soldiery filled their mid-June missives with venomous commentary on the officers who had led them. Ill-founded criticism of Carroll already echoed widely. An intelligent member of the 7th Ohio, believing Carroll had disobeyed orders to burn the bridge, noted that the colonel had "won for himself the execration of the whole army." A Hoosier damned the entire army establishment, writing: "but for the want of sound judgment, all this sad casuality [*sic*] to life and the cause we are defending, might have been avoided." Another Indiana soldier blamed the reverses on "too much *rivalry,* too great a desire to gain a name . . . among our Gen's at the present time."[32]

Some Federals chose to blame Irvin McDowell, who had been a popular scapegoat before. The 55th Ohio relished the rumor that McDowell had been hurled into irons at "Ft. Layfoette; if so, good." The tide of criticism ran strongest against James Shields. The historian of the 7th Ohio concluded that, "to make himself a name, [Shields] came near sacrificing his command." He noted that the order relieving Shields "received the approbation of both officers and men." The chaplain of the 7th called Shields a traitor and "one of the most unprincipled men who ever disgraced an American uniform." A soldier in the 13th Indiana described Shields's conduct as "outrageous" and sarcastically added, "I further hope there will be no more traps set to bag Jackson." Augustus Van Dyke of the 14th Indiana echoed the sentiment when he wrote the week after the battle, "I wish that Old Paddy Shields was in the lowest pit of Hell. . . . He is cursed by all and should be sent into private life." Van Dyke humorously summarized the impact of the campaign on a foot soldier when he concluded with wry humor: "The next time I go for a soldier I am going to enlist as a Brigadier General. I would not give a farthing to be anything else."[33]

Several Federals, including some officers of rank, expressed chagrin over the mistreatment of Southern civilians. Adjutant (later Colonel) John J. Polsley thought of resigning over the outrages. "Never was a country more foully ravaged than this beautiful valley," he told his wife. "I much fear that this people can never be conciliated. Already do they treat us as if we . . . were foreign invaders." A New York correspondent recorded the origins of a neologism. "When an article is missed under suspicious circumstances," he wrote, "it is said to be 'Blenkered.' " Frémont's whole army, he admitted, not just Blenker's troops, were pillaging riotously in every direction—"a sad fact that cannot be disputed." Even General Milroy, who within a year would be the chief tormenter of Valley civilians, thought "the misery—anguish and distress depicted in the countenances and appearance of the women and children is painful to behold." Warming to the task before him, however, Milroy quickly backpedaled: ". . . but they have brought it on themselves—let them enjoy it."[34]

By June 17 most civilians had returned to reckon their losses and to help one another start anew. Among their ugly chores was burying or reburying Yankee dead, most of whom had been interred right next to dwelling houses for convenience. Others had to be fished from wells, where they had been unceremoniously dumped. As late as a week after the battle, Cross Keys remained blanketed by an "almost insufferable" stench of death. A cavalryman riding through saw infantry details assisting civilians in moving Federal dead away from the wells, springs, and front doors.[35]

In Harrisonburg, Mary Yancey patiently set about cleaning "Yankey dirt" from every object in her home, noting, "I cant tel you half there meanness." She expressed gratitude for Jackson's prompt whipping of Frémont's army. Otherwise, she knew, "they would have done a great deal worse." One of Jackson's staff summarized Federal behavior as "very brutal to the women. . . . [They] stole everything they could get hold of." The same officer quoted General Ewell as gloating over the military punishment the brigands received: "they came up spoiling for a fight and a good many of them spoiled after the fight."[36]

A Virginia journalist who traveled the road past Cross Keys to Port Republic recorded individual losses in detail. The locals he interviewed reported "that they could perceive but little difference between officers and privates; they seemed all to be upon a regularly organized plundering expedition in the name of the government." At Philip Cole's home, an officer enforced his demands by calling Mrs. Cole "a damned secesh bitch" and threatening to shoot her if she did not obey him. Federals did shoot several times at Joseph Good without hitting him. German immigrant Daniel Wine, a "harmless old gentleman . . . nearly 80 years old, declared he had no idea there were 'such bad beepels in the world' " as the Yankees who descended upon his home. John Yount, who lived near Mill Creek Church, lost property worth $5,200, but was so pious that he bore the damage with "christian resignation and without murmuring."

Between Union Church and Port Republic, before entering the village or going beyond to the battlefield, the journalist visited forty-nine households. Twenty had suffered damage in excess of $1,000; all had lost every earthly asset. Among the hundreds of items enumerated were bedding, clothing, molasses, vinegar, books (repeatedly), food of every sort, cash, scales, musical instruments, spectacles, trinkets, medicines, furniture, crops, tools, bees (almost every home kept bees), family heirlooms, watches, and outbuildings burned or torn down for fun.[37]

Confederate soldiers helped civilians as they could, but mostly they relaxed. With weeks of hard marching on short rations behind them, and no near prospect of renewed fighting, Stonewall Jackson's army reveled in the beauty and bounty of late spring in the Valley. For several days the weather remained cool as the Southern men recovered from the campaign. The Louisiana Brigade named its bivouac "Camp Ashby" in honor of the fallen cavalry leader. Carpenter's Battery spread out in a "beautiful" campsite, "well shaded and convenient to excellent water," close to the celebrated spectacle of Weyer's Cave. Bill Humphreys wrote his mother a letter so long that he apologized, suggesting that she had not "bargained for a newspaper." After Bill died at Gettysburg, his mom no doubt cherished her boy's long account of his experiences. Other Virginians camped on the riverbanks. V. W. Southall wrote home: "I took a nice wash in the Shenadore. Our Soldiers are strewed on the banks of this river, catching fish & bathing." A Georgian described one day's activities prosaically: "Rested & Washed up there close & selves & so past the Day."[38]

The renowned cave provided thousands of soldiers with a nearby touring option. Marylander J. W. Thomas admired the sights, even though "seen under disadvantageous circumstances." The stalactites were muddy because of the recent rains, and Thomas was with a large crowd and a poor guide. McHenry Howard overcame "a strong disinclination for underground exploration" to accompany Colonel Bradley Johnson's touring party. "The entrance . . . is very small—like an enlarged fox's hole," Howard reported, "and it goes down steeply and has several narrow passages through which one can hardly squeeze; but further in there are rooms and a large long, wide and high chamber . . . [and] stalactites and stalagmites, a bridal veil, etc."[39]

Army bureaucracy did not deliver goods equally to all of the farflung encampments. A cavalryman in Brown's Gap for three days complained of having no rations for men or animals. That led to "much suffering" and the death, he claimed, of huge numbers of horses who had only bushes to eat. The cavalryman remained uncertain whether " 'Old Jack' as he was familiarly called, was not crazy." Several men of the 44th Virginia, one of the units stranded around Brown's Gap, faded away down the east side of the mountain to their homes in adjacent counties. The loss of twenty or more men by the regiment in three days constituted the heaviest desertion in its history. The colonel of the 52nd Virginia had to offer amnesty in a plea to the numerous deserters from his regiment to return to duty.[40]

Confederates among the well-fed, relaxing majority enjoyed the applause of their peers and the nation, which by June 17 was reaching them in waves. James Dinwiddie of the Charlottesville Artillery boasted to his wife that because of the stand by his guns, "we have become quite famous." Thomas Hightower of the 21st Georgia told his homefolks that the army now "goes by the name of the Flying Infantry." Jed Hotchkiss's pious letters to his wife included some exultant, almost cocky musings.[41]

The Louisianians of Taylor's Brigade consigned the guns taken as trophies at the Coaling to Bowyer's Virginia Battery. Teenager Ben Hubert of the 6th Louisiana wrote to his sweetheart Letitia in Charlottesville asking that she make the 6th a new battle flag. The government-issue flags of thin silk "blow into shreds and tatters in a week," Ben said, urging Letitia to use something strong, "say bunting." Hubert assured his girl that no Yankee hands would ever pollute the flag. Best of all, General Taylor had promised him a furlough to go pick it up! The Louisianians soon joined the rest of the army—

and the rest of the South—in singing a new song about Stonewall Jackson. The lilting air "Stonewall Jackson's Way," which became one of the best-known tunes rising from the war, first came into circulation just after Port Republic. "Here first we heard the ringing notes of 'Stonewall Jackson's Way," a staff officer wrote, "found, it is said, upon the body of a soldier of his Brigade, killed in the last charge at Lewis House."[42]

Southern medical facilities spent the middle days of June tending the wounded of both sides (Valley hospitals suffered the unhappy distinction just after Port Republic of having the first reported cases of gangrene in Virginia's war). The well-documented convalescence of Lieutenant William C. Driver of Company E, 7th Louisiana, can serve as an example of what many hundreds experienced. Driver had been hit in the eye by a spent bullet near the Coaling and fell into enemy hands during one of the Confederate reversals. Driver's adopted son, Arthur Waugh, a boy of nineteen, accepted capture to wait on his injured parent. The two wound up as prisoners in the home of a family named Ashby in Front Royal, where the thirty-six-year-old lieutenant required constant assistance. "He suffered greatly," an Ashby youngster recalled, "and aroused much sympathy by his patient, gentle manners and almost helpless condition." Federals eventually carried Lieutenant Driver off to Washington. He recovered to some extent, was exchanged, and died in 1873.[43]

Confederate care for wounded enemies continued to astonish Northern observers. A black cook employed by the 7th Indiana, who originally had escaped from slavery near Staunton, fell into Rebel hands again on June 9. He soon was turned loose and returned to his Hoosier friends. The cook told John Hadley that Federal prisoners were "well fed & kindly treated. . . . our dead all buried & wounded all kindly cared for." A Northern surgeon left behind with wounded at Harrisonburg reported that ladies supplied food and even delicacies for wounded Federals in his charge. "The Union prisoners," he declared, "met all the humanity that could be expected by prisoners of war."[44]

On the other hand, Mary Gibbons Yancey, who was a widow and who had suffered extensively at the hands of the invaders, said: "wounded Yankeys . . . I have no sympathey for any of them." An injured enemy soldier brought to her house died within hours. "I tel you," Mary wrote, "[I] was glad we got rid of him so soon." On June 13 a Unionist major and surgeon approached under a flag of

General Robert E. Lee sent a
dispatch to Jackson on June
16 in which he reasoned that the
Valley Army could not both
fight again soon and then reach
Richmond in time. Lee
therefore told Jackson, "the
sooner you unite with this
army the better."

truce with twenty-eight ambulances, wanting to take away Federal wounded. Jackson refused through a cavalry officer "for military reasons," no doubt the need to maintain secrecy about strength and positions. Stonewall pointed out that an adequate number of Northern surgeons had remained behind with the wounded. The general already had made specific arrangements for feeding and caring for suffering Yankees around Harrisonburg.[45]

General Jackson resisted the urge to visit Weyer's Cave on a sentimental journey—he had once gone there with his wife. The recollection moved him in a domestic aside to write to her, "Wouldn't you like to get home again?" The ever diligent Stonewall issued orders that the men must use the rivers to wash themselves and their gear. Captured weapons superior to the army's own were distributed among the units. Jackson methodically feinted down the Valley every day, sending a detail to Port Republic to pretend to build a bridge. He followed the pseudo-bridging detachment with infantry, which lounged wearily on the roadsides.[46]

Jackson paid more attention to his disorganized cavalry than to any other matter except his plans to head for Richmond. A dispatch to Colonel Munford on June 13, ordering him beyond Harrisonburg, stands as a primer on Jackson's notions about cavalry. "The only true rule for cavalry is to follow as long as the enemy retreats," the general admonished Munford. His other advice included these premises: "It is important to cut off all communications between us and the enemy." "Press our lines forward as far as practicable." "It is very desirable that . . . no information should pass to the enemy."[47]

Religious considerations, never far from the forefront of Jackson's consciousness, manifested themselves in public thanks to God for the army's success. Stonewall proclaimed Saturday, June 14, a day for religious observances. A "season of thanksgiving by a suspension of all military exercises, and by holding divine service in the several regiments" was to begin at three P.M. Jackson's religious mentor, Robert L. Dabney, tireless when it came to spreading the gospel (and infinitely better at it than at military duties), had warmed up by preaching on Friday evening in the camp of the Stonewall Brigade. An earnest young cannoneer pronounced Dabney's sermons "delightful," and said in a letter what "a comfort and a great cause for thanksgiving" it was "to have such a Christian as Jackson for our General."[48]

Saturday's exercises in no way reduced Jackson's enthusiasm for the usual Sunday services. That portion of the army that had not observed the sacrament of the Lord's Supper on Saturday evening did so the next day. Jackson attended the ceremony staged for Taliaferro's Brigade in a large grove of trees beside the road leading to Port Republic. Dabney preached yet again at this convocation in "nature's own great temple." Hotchkiss, who was in the audience, wrote: "It was a very impressive celebration of the Lord's Supper, in the woods, amid the din of camps hushed for a brief period." As always, Jackson was "humbly devout." The general received the sacred emblems from a regimental chaplain. Other units had their own services. George B. Taylor preached from the 124th Psalm to the 13th and 25th Virginia. Later Taylor circulated among soldiers lounging on the riverbanks and distributed religious tracts.[49]

By the time the religious weekend ended, the period of rest and recuperation had nearly expired. Within forty-eight hours Stonewall Jackson would be moving his command toward new battles. Robert E. Lee sent a dispatch to Jackson on the 16th in which he reasoned that the Valley Army could not both fight again soon and then reach Richmond in time. Since Frémont and Shields were falling back in disarray, Lee concluded, "the sooner you unite with this army the better." General Lee enjoined Jackson to beware of spies and to deceive the enemy about his intentions. Both injunctions were unnecessary, although Lee did not yet know his subordinate well enough to recognize that fact.[50]

Jackson set about fooling his staff and subordinates in the apparent conviction that if he could confuse *them,* the Yankees were bound to remain in the dark. On the 17th he ordered Munford to picket with his cavalry all the way to the mountains west of Harrisonburg, and to correspond with Winder at Weyer's Cave—making no mention of the movement about to begin. Jackson directed Munford to meet him in secret at Staunton at five A.M. on the 18th, then changed the rendezvous to ten P.M. on the 17th at Mount Sidney. An hour before the appointed time, Jackson sent Hotchkiss in his place to meet Munford. The cavalryman did not show up, having moved meanwhile toward Port Republic only to find the army gone. Munford would finally reattach his command to Jackson's near Richmond.[51]

General W. H. Chase Whiting also suffered under Jackson's fetish for secrecy, and did not like the experience. Chase Whiting had been one of Jackson's mentors at West Point; now he found himself chasing phantoms on the orders of the once-awkward boy from western Virginia. General Whiting had been sick for several days (curing himself with vinegar and salt). In a weakened state he rode forty miles on June 17 to report to Jackson as ordered, but, he wrote disgustedly to his wife, "when I got there I found there was no occasion." Whiting grumbled about his most recent week of war: "So I have marched up the hill, to turn around & march down again. . . . it seems to me a singular move."[52]

Jackson left for Staunton at ten P.M. on the 17th in company with W. L. Jackson of his staff. The general clumsily tried to fool Jed Hotchkiss by ordering him to return to camp after his mission to Mount Sidney, even though the army obviously was preparing to leave. Hotchkiss obeyed wearily. After returning to the abandoned campsite, the aide went on to Waynesboro to await the general, who arrived there at five P.M. on June 18 and started up the west slope of the Blue Ridge. The mountainside was blanketed with Confederate camps marked by sparkling camp fires. "It was," Hotchkiss thought, "a very fine sight."

The headquarters entourage met a querulous Chase Whiting at the foot of the mountain. Hotchkiss rode ahead and found General Winder atop Rockfish Gap, but could not locate the wagons of the headquarters camp. He rode back to General Jackson and confessed, "General, I fear we will not find our wagons tonight." Stonewall responded with his usual earnestness—more than the occasion apparently required: "Never take counsel of your fears."[53] That sentiment, applied to a vast panoply of battles and campaigns, stood Stonewall Jackson in good stead when he crossed the summit the next morning and launched himself on eleven months of warfare that would cement his place in America's pantheon of military heroes.

USAMHI

Cross Keys battlefield
about 1890

CHAPTER 28

THE IMPACT OF CROSS

KEYS AND

PORT REPUBLIC

Stonewall Jackson hurt the enemy armies that stood in his path at Cross Keys and Port Republic. He captured valuable stores from them. By the end of June 10 it was obvious that the Confederate general had driven his foe away. None of those desirable results, however, constituted the most important impact of the battles. Colonel Kelly of the 8th Louisiana aptly described one of the larger consequences of the double fight on June 8 and 9: "Its importance is not to be measured by the immediate results of the field; but rather by its relation to, and effect upon, the grand strategy of the war in Virginia."[1]

Beginning on June 10, Stonewall was drawn steadily into the other military focal point in Virginia—the siege of Richmond. For months he had contributed substantially, if indirectly, in that arena by detaining Northern forces that otherwise would have joined McClellan near Richmond. Now Jackson was free to join Robert E. Lee for a decisive battle in defense of the Confederate capital. A contemporary Virginia writer summarized the result with a bit of hindsight:

> Port Republic decided [Gaines' Mill]. When Jackson crushed the Federal column operating in the Valley, General Lee could concentrate the entire force in Virginia, in front of McClellan, and that concentration . . . meant victory. . . . It was . . . one of those peculiar contests which act upon events around them, as the keystone acts upon the arch. With Jackson beaten here, Richmond, humanly speaking, was lost, and with it Virginia. With Jackson victorious, Richmond and Virginia were saved.[2]

A second important impact of Cross Keys and Port Republic was the bounty of captured matériel that Jackson harvested. The proud report by the general's quartermaster enumerated weapons and military gear—among it 212 shovels, 29 bundles of telegraph wire, 134 tents, 303½ pounds of rope—but it also listed such ephemeral supplies as 3,425 envelopes, 6 handkerchiefs, 7 pairs of suspenders, and 33 neckties. Jackson's hard-earned reputation as a scavenger received another boost.[3]

More significant than spoils was the produce of the Shenandoah Valley ripening in the fields. Stonewall Jackson's campaign ensured the survival of the Valley as the granary of the Confederacy. It would be two years before the next serious threat to Southern predominance in the Valley. Despite Jackson's apparent disdain for the diet and other comforts of his men, he knew well the truth of Napoleon's famous mot, "An army travels on its stomach." His troops insisted the general had no thought at all for their rations. A contemporary jape declared that Jackson was a far greater man than Moses: instead of using forty years and a manna diet to clear the wilderness, " 'old Jack' would have double-quicked through it on half rations in three days."[4]

Confederates in the ranks swore that their famous leader ignored their basic wants—then admitted that his system was a resounding success. An Alabama boy grumbled, "it takes a person with an iron Constitution" to put up with marching "day and night without a thing to eat." He acknowledged, ironically, "I have had better Health since I have been under Jackson than I ever had before" and added significantly, "If all of our Generals was like Jackson this war would not last long." A Tarheel wrote on June 13 in the same vein: "I believe that General Jackson is one of the keenest Generals in the South . . . but he is horrible hard on his men." A Georgian suggested that Jackson would move north again as soon as the routed Yankees "get in a pretty good supply of sugar, coffee and army stores."[5] All of the grumbling about tactical marches aside, Jackson was keenly aware of war's logistical requirements. He must have relished the tremendous accomplishment of holding the Valley as a Confederate larder.

A third distinct consequence of Cross Keys and Port Republic was the deadly impact on Federal morale. Two months later a Virginian suggested that Northern veterans "have not, nor ever will, cease to remember with terror the awful days at Port Republic & Cross Keys [when] a part of their army beheld Jackson slaughtering the other [and] held their breaths as the ragged rebels charged & slew." An English historian thought that one of Jackson's greatest achievements was "shaking the morale of the Federal President and his commanders." Federal participants murmured and muttered. An Indiana sergeant sarcastically concluded that Jackson must have read the military textbooks written by leading Union officers but misunderstood them completely. An artillery captain concluded bluntly, "Our failure was due to the military skill and boundless audacity of the Confederate leaders"—mixed with Federal incompetence. A Yankee surgeon wrote of Jackson, "This great leader outgeneralled all our commanders." A New York gunner called Stonewall "this prince of bushwhackers . . . a man of decided genius" by comparison with Northern commanders. And a Unionist general described the fallen hero Frémont as " 'played out' and down forever," and called him "intellectually a poor thing."[6]

Confederate morale skyrocketed. Postwar memoirists often found meanings and turning points writ large even when contemporary participants did not notice such crossroads. The end of Jackson's Valley battles, however, echoes in similar tones from primary sources of every date. A Virginia cavalryman wrote enthusiastically after the war about Port Republic, "Was there ever a deed in all the annals of human achievement that could compare with this!" A Louisiana officer recalled that the two battles served to "cement the confidence of his troops in Jackson, and after those fights his men were ready to follow him blind-folded. [Jackson] gained the greatest victory of his career in crystalizing the belief on the part of his troops that he was invincible." A colonel who had known Stonewall before the war and had worried about his ability now "had undoubted confidence in all his movements." A horse artillerist colorfully characterized the decisive element at Port Republic as the "lightning that flashed from [Jackson's] little faded cap."[7]

Contemporary encomiums for Jackson were at least as ardent as the postwar reviews. A Stonewall Brigade captain wrote on June 14 that the men had "implicit confidence" in Jackson, whose "recent success has greatly increased our admiration for him." An enlisted man in the same brigade proclaimed of Stonewall's achievement at Port Republic, "there is none more brilliant connected with the war." A commissary officer estimated that with reinforcements, Jackson could find a cozy spot near Philadelphia and "go to ditching [entrenching]"; the more enemy who approached the better, "the better Effectually to stampede the whole concern." A literate artillery officer looked on Jackson's maneuverings with good humor, writing that "it was amusing . . . to see how Old Jack euchred Fremont and Shields."[8]

Harry Lewis of the 16th Mississippi wrote to his mother attesting to "the utmost confidence" the regiment had in Jackson's skill. George Ring of the 6th Louisiana told his wife in a June 14 letter of an attitude that boded well for the army's future: "it will be something to boast of hereafter, that I was one of Stonewall Jackson's Army. . . . I had rather be a private in such an army than a field officer in any other army. Jackson is perfectly idolized by this army." Captain (later Colonel) James Cooper Nisbet of Georgia called Jackson "our glorious leader" in a June letter. "We all feel that what he does is all right," Nisbet reported proudly. "His soldiers all love the old fighting cock." Sidney Richardson, the twenty-one-year-old son of an illiterate Georgia farmer, supplied an unaffected view from the ranks: "he was one time cut off intilery, but he cut his way out by his wise movements, and bravery, he prayed . . . and it rally looks to me his prays was answered." Richardson wrote angrily that Yankees had begun "disstorying all the property they can," but promised that under Jackson's guidance, "we will kill the last one of them if they dont leave this state."[9]

Whether or not Jackson truly had achieved invincibility (he was making a good case), his soldiers had developed unbounded confidence in him, which would serve Stonewall well in the difficult campaigns ahead. Jackson's dramatic accomplishments in the Valley had the same salutary effect on civilian morale throughout a nation bowed by a steady diet of dire news all spring. "No one who has not been present under similar circumstances," wrote an observer in Richmond, "can imagine the thirst for information that raged under the fever of apprehension." Day and night the public crowded telegraph offices. When at last good news arrived from the Valley: " 'Port Republic! Staunton?' exclaimed the wondering crowd. 'Why, we thought Jackson was at Winchester.' . . . There was something in the brilliancy of his exploits which dazzled the imagination."[10]

A woman diarist wrote of Jackson on June 21, "Oh! Noble, brave and victorious warrior, I hope every engagement may prove a victory for you until this terrible strife is ended." A Richmond matron quoted Jackson's victorious telegram with relief, then added thoughts about the painful butcher's bill still unseen. "Each telegram that is brought . . . makes me blind with apprehension," she admitted, "until it passes me, and other countenances denote the same anxiety."[11]

The relief from intense pressure, long endured, produced humorous gibes about Jackson in the public press. The Richmond *Whig* published in mid-June a pseudo-reward circular headed STRAYED in an elaborate joke at the expense of Jackson and his foes. The prank, signed by SUPERINTENDENT OF THE LUNATIC ASYLUM AT STAUNTON, offered a liberal reward

> for the apprehension of a confirmed lunatic, named Old Stonewall, who escaped from the Asylum . . . in the Spring. . . . He endeavors to avoid detection by calling himself T. J. Jackson. . . . When last heard from he was offering personal indignity to an aged and feeble Ex Senator [Frémont] of the United States. . . . He is reported to have misdirected an imbecile cobbler from Massachusetts [Banks], who was making his way peaceably towards Staunton . . . molesting and sometimes even maiming other good and loyal citizens of the United States. It is thought that he is attempting to make his way to Washington, near which city he was caught lurking a week or two since. He is marked by an excessive irrascibility, a propensity to steal wagons and munitions of war, and an indisposition to sit down quietly and behave himself.[12]

Whatever Jackson thought of that drollery, he must have found immense satisfaction in a motion submitted to the Confederate Congress a few weeks later by his friend, Congressman A. R. Boteler.

> *Resolved,* by the Congress of the Confederate States of America, That . . . Congress has learned with lively satisfaction, of the brilliant successes achieved by the Army of the Valley District . . . under the command of Major-General Thomas J. Jackson. *Resolved,* That the thanks of the people of the Confederate States are justly due, and through their Representatives . . . are hereby cordially tendered to Major-General Thomas J. Jackson and to the gallant officers and men of his command, for the signal exhibition of valour, skill, enterprise and endurance displayed by them in the . . . triumphant conflict with Fremont at Cross Keys; in the utter route of Shields on the following day at Port Republic. . . . *Resolved,* That a copy of these resolutions be transmitted by the Secretary of War to Major-General Thomas J. Jackson, with a request that he communicate the same to the invincible army of the Valley District.[13]

In winning the thanks of a grateful Congress and nation, Jackson had crafted a campaign marked by astounding marches, skillful use of terrain, and cunning employment of interior lines. Stonewall Jackson had created a legend of epic proportions by the time his columns trudged up the Blue Ridge and then eastward into Piedmont Virginia. The general left behind a Valley that would always be synonymous with his name and fame. Jackson would pass through the Valley again, briefly and farther north, but he would fight no more battles within its grandeur. Beyond the Blue Ridge there lurked puzzlement and near failure for Stonewall during the Seven Days; astonishing success at Second Manassas; collaboration with Robert E. Lee in the most famous military tandem in American history; and eventually a hero's grave after Chancellorsville.

None can ever know for certain, but it seems likely that the river of Jackson's delirium, as on the verge of death he muttered "Let us cross over the river and rest under the shade of the trees," must have been the Shenandoah. Perhaps his fevered imagination had carried the dying general back to the river's confluence beside the Port Republic bridge, where he had experienced his most exciting morning of the war. One of Jackson's soldiers who lived in Port

Republic supplied a moving epitaph for his mates from the village who died fighting for the Confederacy. "All these years have come and gone since we crossed over the old wood bridge at 'Port' to meet the foe," he wrote feelingly, "but your names and deeds will ever live on memory's page." The aging veteran wished that an elegant stone monument marked the riverside battle site, but he concluded, "so long as . . . the river rolls where Jackson fought, there will never need be a song of everlasting praise to the deeds of immortal honor once enacted upon her shores." The sentiment applies to the general too. The Valley and the River remain a perpetual memorial for Stonewall Jackson.[14]

ACKNOWLEDGMENTS

he village of Port Republic is blessed not only with a stunningly beautiful and richly historic setting, but also with an earnest and active preservation group in its midst. The Society of Port Republic Preservationists, especially Anita Cummins and Barbara Moore, proved wonderfully helpful during the research for this book. So did Mr. M. Ellsworth Kyger, Mrs. Faye Witters, and Miss Maxine Early of the Harrisonburg-Rockingham Historical Society. Lewis F. Fisher of San Antonio, Texas, graciously supplied me with important information and photographs about his ancestors, the Lewises of Lewiston and Lynnwood; he is not, needless to say, responsible for my conclusions about the perfidy of one of them.

Several professional historians and archivists provided important research leads and other assistance. The late and much-lamented Waverly K. Winfree of the Virginia Historical Society served as an invaluable liaison at that admirable repository on this and many others of my research projects: *requiescat in pace.* J. Michael Miller, USMC archivist, shared with me the research he is amassing for a book on the entire campaign. Counselor Robert G. Tanner of Atlanta did the same from the raw material he is using to revise his standard 1976 study. T. Michael Parrish of Austin, Texas, was kind enough to provide me with a tattered but treasured copy of H. B. Kelly's essential tract. Wilbur E. Meneray, custodian of the archival riches of Tulane University, helped me use the critical materials there. Robert E. L. Krick, a splendid historian in ultimate proof of Mendel's work with garden peas, uncovered dozens of sources for this work over many years.

Brian C. Pohanka of Alexandria and Richard S. Skidmore of Greencastle, Indiana, added greatly to my comfortably meager understanding of Yankee officers and units. Dr. Richard J. Sommers of the U.S. Army Military History Institute, nonpareil archivist and roué, contributed important guidance as he has on every serious Civil War study in recent decades. George F. Skoch of Cleveland Heights, Ohio, deftly turned my grotesquely sketched maps into the polished finals that appear in the book. Stephen M. Rowe of Raleigh, North Carolina, helped tremendously by making available copies of the apposite sections of the Samuel J. C. Moore papers while they were still in private hands.

Shenandoah Valley farmers living on the battlefields maintained the region's high reputation for hospitality. I particularly owe thanks to John Lewis Kaylor, Jr., who farms Lewiston, and to his mother, Wilda Sandy Kaylor, matriarch of the clan; Mr. and Mrs. Billy Wonderly, who own the Baugher site; Mrs. Mary Catherine Jarrels, who lives in the Widow Pence's house; Lawrence D. Good, who owns the Flory farm; and William B. Kyger, who is the Rockingham County supervisor for the district as well as an enthusiastic local historian. Regional help also came from Gordon W. Miller, Information Services Librarian, James Madison University, and Nick Whitmer, Rockingham Public Library.

Prominent among the small army of historical people who deserve thanks are Wayne L. Wiltfang of Morocco, Indiana, who supplied contemporary letters; Ray Fuerschbach of Tonawanda, New York, the ranking authority on Wiedrich's Battery; Valley oracles Robert J. Driver of Brownsburg and Richard L. Armstrong of Millboro; Diane Jacob and Keith Gibson of the Virginia Military Institute; Lewis Leigh of Fairfax, John J. Hennessy of Frederick, Maryland, and Lee A. Wallace, Jr., of Falls Church, for good primary accounts; Dave Roth of *Blue and Gray* magazine, for loan of fine photographs; Ben Ritter of Winchester; John R. M. Bass of Spring Hope and Las Vegas, for leads to the Snakenberg and Blacknall sources; Dr. Linda A. McCurdy, William R. Erwin, Jr., and Patricia S. Webb, at the incomparably helpful and useful Duke University manuscript room (than which no Civil War archive is more fruitful and accommodating); Arnold Blumberg of Baltimore, for *National Tribune* leads; Lowell Reidenbaugh of St. Louis; Michael P. Musick of the National Archives (only a battle subject, on which the Archives is relatively barren, keeps Mike from his usual billing atop a Civil War acknowledgments page); and Keith S.

ACKNOWLEDGMENTS

Bohannon, Francis A. O'Reilly, Peter S. Carmichael, Noel G. Harrison, and Mac Wyckoff of the National Park Service.

Thanks too to David M. Sherman, U.S. Forest Service; Aloha South, Treasury Department Branch, National Archives; LeRoy S. Strohl, Rebecca E. Elswick, and Jack Bales of the Mary Washington College Library; Marilyn J. Snyder, Annandale, Virginia; Robert F. Schwent, St. Louis; Conley Edwards and Minor Weisiger, Virginia State Archives; Barbara Pratt Willis, Judy Webster, Sue Willis, Vikki Dembowski, and Carmela Witzke of the Central Rappahannock Regional Library; Suzanne Christoff, U.S. Military Academy; Harold E. Howard of Lynchburg; Marilyn Bell Hughes, Tennessee State Library and Archives; Tim McKinney, who is stuck in West Virginia; Glenn L. McMullen, Special Collections, Iowa State University; Sandra R. Kenney, Silver Spring, Maryland; A. Thomas Wallace, Annapolis; Dr. David W. Scott III, Fredericksburg; Dallas and Anna Hemp, Augusta County, Virginia; Walter Moore, Oronoco, Minnesota; Sarah Taliaferro Rohrer, Orange, Virginia; and David Q. Updike, Staunton.

Other institutions that helped with the research included Antietam National Battlefield; J. Y. Joyner Library, East Carolina University; Robert W. Woodruff Library, Emory University; Georgia Department of Archives and History; Historic New Orleans Collection; Historical Society of Pennsylvania; Indiana Historical Society; Indiana State Library; Library of Congress; Maryland Historical Society; Huntington Library; Miami University Library, Oxford, Ohio; Museum of the Confederacy; Mississippi Department of Archives and History; National Weather Records Center, Asheville, North Carolina; Ohio Historical Society; Potter County (Pennsylvania) Historical Society; Northwestern State University of Louisiana; Bentley Historical Library, University of Michigan; Stonewall Jackson House, Lexington, Virginia; University of Virginia; Barker Texas History Center, University of Texas; Southern Historical Collection, University of North Carolina; West Virginia University; and Western Reserve Historical Society.

Appendix A:

ORGANIZATION AND CASUALTIES AT THE BATTLES OF CROSS KEYS AND PORT REPUBLIC, JUNE 8–9, 1862

STONEWALL JACKSON'S ARMY

	Killed or MWA	Wounded	Missing	Total
JACKSON'S DIVISION				
CHARLES S. WINDER'S BRIGADE				
2ND VIRGINIA[1]	1	25		26
4TH VIRGINIA		4		4
5TH VIRGNIA[2]	8	85	20	113
27TH VIRGINIA[3]	8	28	11	47
33RD VIRGINIA[4]			2	2
Brigade Total	17	142	33	192
JOHN M. PATTON'S BRIGADE				
21ST VIRGINIA				—
42ND VIRGINIA	1	3		4
48TH VIRGINIA[5]	3	14	1	18
1ST VIRGINIA BATTALION				—
Brigade Total	4	17	1	22
WILLIAM B. TALIAFERRO'S BRIGADE				
10TH VIRGINIA				—
23RD VIRGINIA[6]		1		1
37TH VIRGINIA				—
Brigade Total		1		1+
DIVISION ARTILLERY				
ALLEGHANY ARTY. (CARPENTER)[7]		5		5
HAMPDEN ARTY. (CASKIE)		1		1
CHARLOTTESVILLE ARTY. (CARRINGTON)[8]		1	1	2
JACKSON ARTY. (CUTSHAW)[9]		6		6

	Killed or MWA	Wounded	Missing	Total
ROCKBRIDGE ARTY. (POAGUE)[10]		6	1	7
DANVILLE ARTY. (WOODING)				—
Artillery Total		19	2	21
Division Total	21	179	36	236
EWELL'S DIVISION[11]				
DIVISION STAFF		1		1
GEORGE H. STEUART'S BRIGADE[12]				
BRIGADE STAFF		1		1
1ST MARYLAND[13]	9	37		46
44TH VIRGINIA[14]	20	33		53
52ND VIRGINIA[15]	25	106	7	138
58TH VIRGINIA[16]	22	55	3	80
Brigade Total	76	232	10	318
ARNOLD ELZEY'S BRIGADE[17]				
BRIGADE STAFF[18]	1	1		2
12TH GEORGIA	2	12		14
13TH VIRGINIA	2	14	1	17
25TH VIRGINIA[19]	10	20		30
31ST VIRGINIA[20]	34	83	8	125
Brigade Total	49	130	9	188
ISAAC R. TRIMBLE'S BRIGADE				
15TH ALABAMA[21]	13	33	5	51
21ST GEORGIA	4	23	1	28
16TH MISSISSIPPI	6	28		34
21ST NORTH CAROLINA[22]	2	11		13
Brigade Total[23]	25	95	6	126
RICHARD TAYLOR'S BRIGADE				
BRIGADE STAFF[24]		2		2
6TH LOUISIANA[25]	15	51	2	68
7TH LOUISIANA	11	137	24	172
8TH LOUISIANA	11	35	1	47
9TH LOUISIANA	14	26		40

	Killed or MWA	Wounded	Missing	Total
WHEAT'S BATTALION	2	19		21
Brigade Total	53	270	27	350
DIVISION ARTILLERY				
BALTIMORE ARTY. (BROCKENBROUGH)	2			2
COURTNEY'S BATTERY[26]	4	8		12
2ND ROCKBRIDGE ARTY. (LUSK)[27]	4	2		6
LEE BATTERY (RAINE)	2	7	8	17
NEW MARKET ARTY. (RICE)				—
BEDFORD ARTY. (BOWYER)[28]				0
Artillery Total	12	15	8	35
Division Total	215	743	60	1,018
CAVALRY				
CAVALRY STAFF	1			1
2ND VIRGINIA				—
6TH VIRGINIA		1		1
7TH VIRGINIA[29]		3		3
11TH VIRGINIA	1			1
12TH VIRGINIA	1	2		3
CHEW'S HORSE ARTILLERY[30]				0
Cavalry Total	3	6		9
CONFEDERATE TOTAL[31]	239	928	96	1,263

Appendix A

Shields's and Frémont's Armies

	Killed or MWA	Wounded	Missing	Total
Shields's Army				
Army Staff		1		1
S. S. Carroll's Brigade				
7th Indiana[32]	18	123	32	173
84th Pennsylvania[33]	1	10	30	41
110th Pennsylvania[34]	1	10	23	34
1st Virginia (Union)[35]	4	18	48	70
1st Virginia Cavalry (Union)[36]	1	4	3	8
1st Ohio Light Artillery, Battery L (Robinson)[37]	2	4	6	12
Brigade Total	27	169	142	338
E. B. Tyler's Brigade				
5th Ohio[38]	11	61	197	269
7th Ohio[39]	15	51	10	76
29th Ohio[40]	17	41	136	194
66th Ohio	20	75	110	205
1st Ohio Light artillery, Battery H (Huntington)[41]	3	4	5	12
4th U.S. Artillery, Battery E (Clark)	1	5	3	9
Brigade Total	67	237	461	765
Shields's Army Total[42]	94	406	603	1,103
Frémont's Army				
Headquarters Cavalry				
3rd Virginia (Union)				—
6th Ohio				—
advance Brigade (G. P. Cluseret)				
Brigade Staff		1		1
8th Virginia (Union)[43]	3	8	3	14
60th Ohio	3	4		7
Brigade Total	6	13	3	22

	Killed or MWA	Wounded	Missing	Total
LOUIS BLENKER'S DIVISION				
DIVISION STAFF	1	1		2
STAHEL'S BRIGADE				
8TH NEW YORK[44]	80	107	50	237
39TH NEW YORK[45]	10	28	12	50
41ST NEW YORK[46]	2	7	11	20
45TH NEW YORK[47]	4	5	10	19
27TH PENNSYLVANIA[48]	17	74	14	105
PENNSYLVANIA RIFLES (BUCKTAILS)[49]	1	8	1	10
NEW YORK LIGHT ARTILLERY,				
2ND BATTERY (SCHIRMER)[50]	2			2
VIRGINIA (UNION) BATTERY C (BUELL)		2		2
HOWITZER BATTERY (DILGER)				—
Brigade Total	116	231	98	445
J. A. KOLTES'S BRIGADE				
29TH NEW YORK		2	6	8
68TH NEW YORK	2			2
73RD PENNSYLVANIA				—
NEW YORK LIGHT ARTILLERY,				
13TH BATTERY (DIECKMANN)				0
Brigade Total	2	2	6	10
HENRY BOHLEN'S BRIGADE				
54TH NEW YORK	3	3		6
58TH NEW YORK	11	14	4	29
74TH PENNSYLVANIA	3	11	1	15
75TH PENNSYLVANIA	2	16	3	21
1ST NEW YORK LIGHT ARTILLERY,				
BATTERY I (WIEDRICH)[51]	1	1	2	4
Brigade Total	20	45	10	75
4TH NEW YORK CAVALRY[52]	1	1	10	12
Division Total	140	280	124	544

	Killed or MWA	Wounded	Missing	Total
ROBERT H. MILROY'S BRIGADE				
2ND VIRGINIA (UNION)	3	19	2	24
3RD VIRGINIA (UNION)	4	23		27
5TH VIRGINIA (UNION)[53]	9	38	4	51
25TH OHIO[54]	6	54	5	65
1ST VIRGINIA CAVALRY (DETACHMENT)			7	7
VIRGINIA LIGHT ARTILLERY,				
BATTERY G (EWING)		1		1
1ST OHIO LIGHT ARTILLERY,				
BATTERY I (HYMAN)	1	1		2
OHIO LIGHT ARTILLERY,				
12TH BATTERY (JOHNSON)[55]	1	4		5
Brigade Total[56]	**24**	**140**	**18**	**182**
ROBERT C. SCHENCK'S BRIGADE				
32ND OHIO		1		1
55TH OHIO				—
73RD OHIO[57]	4	5	2	11
75TH OHIO				—
82ND OHIO		2	1	3
1ST CONNECTICUT CAVALRY BATTALION			4	4
1ST OHIO LIGHT ARTILLERY,				
BATTERY K (DEBECK)				—
RIGBY'S BATTERY (INDIANA)		1		1
Brigade Total	**4**	**9**	**7**	**20**
GEORGE D. BAYARD'S BRIGADE				
1ST NEW JERSEY CAVALRY	4	1	27	32
1ST PENNSYLVANIA CAVALRY				—
MAINE LIGHT ARTILLERY,				
2ND BATTERY (B)				—
Brigade Total	**4**	**1**	**27**	**32**
FRÉMONT'S ARMY TOTAL	**178**	**443**	**179**	**800**
FEDERAL TOTAL[58]	**272**	**849**	**782**	**1,903**

Appendix B:

DISTANCES BY AIR BETWEEN KEY POINTS

Kemper house to North River bridge: 1,175 yards

Lewiston to North River bridge: 4,000 yards

Baugher barn to Lewiston: 1,700 yards

Coaling to river: 1,275 yards

Lewiston lane to Deep Run: 1,000 yards

Bogota to Coaling: 2,000 yards

Yost's Hill to northeast end of North River bridge: 800 yards

Union Church to Confederate ridge at road crossing: 2,500 yards

Confederate ridge near Mill Creek Church to Port Republic bridge: 5,700 yards

CROSS KEYS AND PORT REPUBLIC, 1862 TO 1993

Rockingham County's long-suffering civilians patiently knit their lives back together after the armies moved away. Memories of the days of deadly battle would remain with them forever. Among the tangible reminders were military projectiles strewn in every direction. An adolescent boy wandering in his family's woods near Port Republic battlefield during the fall of 1862 noticed a tree broken off peculiarly. Upon investigation he found a live artillery round buried in the wood. The boy and a friend put the explosive in a pile of brush scheduled for burning. The youngsters were gratified by the resulting noisy explosion of what apparently was the final round of the Battle of Port Republic.[1]

When war let the county alone for a time, other disasters took their turns. In November 1863, fire swept through one of the Flory houses near Cross Keys, destroying everything the family owned. War resumed its role as leveler of the Valley in 1864. Port Republic had rapidly returned to its vibrant commercial posture after the battle. The ledger books of the William S. Downs tannery show that he was busy during the war's middle years. Many days showed dozens of transactions. Few had direct military overtones and the majority were in the $4 to $8 range, but some ran into three figures. Then, suddenly, entries ceased after September 23, 1864: Yankee raiders had reached that latitude and destroyed nearly everything that would burn.[2]

Wounded Confederates received strong support from the community. At a public meeting near Cross Keys on February 21, 1864, citizens raised $1,700 to buy artificial limbs for maimed soldiers. A similar affair on November 28 raised $894.66 for the same purpose; that meeting was held in the Methodist Church at Port Republic, where Hunter McGuire had cursed and Stonewall Jackson had admonished, and blood had stained the floors in June 1862. In 1865 Harrisonburg residents formed a society "for the relief of widows and orphans of Rockingham soldiers." Citizens of nearby Bridgewater did the same thing the next year.[3]

Many Confederate dead remained beneath the soil where they fell for decades; some remain there today, such as Major Joseph H. Chenoweth of the 31st Virginia. In 1886, when the Lewis family built Mapleton squarely atop the Coaling hill, excavations for its footings uncovered several skeletons, which were reinterred under the steps of the postwar chapel in the ravine below.[4]

At least two attempts were made to identify Confederate dead and move them to a central location. In the summer of 1866, the Rockingham Memorial Association was organized in Harrisonburg. From that beginning grew the Ladies Memorial Association. Strayer women from the family that had seen the battle at close range were prominent in the effort. By 1876 they had moved many Southern dead to Harrisonburg and completed a monument to them. A contemporary described the association's ceremonies:

The bodies of the Confederate soldiers who had died or were buried in this Rockingham County were removed to a lot adjoining Woodbine Cemetery, and every year since the war the ladies have designated a day, and with processions, dirges, muffled drums, and tolling bells laid spring flowers and ever greens above the dust of the dead soldiers.[5]

Although Harrisonburg was the closest town to Cross Keys and Port Republic, some of the dead were moved to Staunton. The Augusta (County) Memorial Association formed in that city in June 1870 with Colonel James H. Skinner of the 52nd Virginia—which had been engaged at Port Republic—at its head. In 1888 the association erected a monument to the Confederate dead it had gathered in Thornrose Cemetery. The soldiers buried there included 870 identified by name and unit and another 700 "not recorded by name from the fields of Alleghany, McDowell, Cross Keys, Port Republic, Piedmont, etc."[6]

Most Federal dead eventually reached the Staunton National Cemetery, courtesy of a victorious (and wealthy) Union government. Confederate detachments had buried the majority of their slain foe at Cross Keys and Port Republic in 1862. Some mortally wounded Northerners died at relatively distant locations and were buried elsewhere. Robert Spellman of the 5th Ohio, for instance, was treated for a foot wound at Weyer's Cave, died in a Lynchburg hospital, and was reburied in a government cemetery in far-distant Norfolk. Staunton National Cemetery was established after the war and filled with 749 bodies from Valley sites. Only 230 of the 749 are in identified graves. Ten of them were killed in June 1862; another 36 burials without names or units specify deaths during that month (primarily on June 9). Since the ratio of unknown to known burials is about nine to four, the 46 bodies at Staunton with evident Cross Keys or Port Republic origins suggest about 150 total burials from those battlefields. That number is more than one half of the Federals killed and mortally wounded.[7]

The most notable inanimate casualty of June 1862 was the famous covered bridge over North River at Port Republic. A new bridge was high on the list of postwar needs. The village was incorporated on January 26, 1866, and John Harper became mayor two months later after the first election. Before the year was out the villagers had spent about $3,000—a huge sum in Reconstruction Virginia—for a new span. Captain John Harris, who lived in town, superintended the job. In September 1870, when an immense flood swept the Valley, Harris happened to be at Harpers Ferry and saw a span of the bridge he had built float past that point, more than 100 miles downstream from Port Republic. Another bridge built in 1874 was swept away by an 1877 freshet, despite strong stone piers. The next effort, part of iron and part of wood, lasted from 1885 until 1898, when a Roanoke firm built an all-iron structure. The road from Port Republic to Harrisonburg retained much of its nineteenth-century character until a major improvement project straightened it out in 1972.[8]

The Baugher house, Westwood, stood until about 1945, the scars from Union shells still readily discernible on its surface. Lewiston was twice destroyed and twice rebuilt after the war. John F. Lewis is buried in the family cemetery on the battlefield. Lynnwood still stands in an impressive setting near the Shenandoah. Soldier initials carved in the floor are visible today, and faded bloodstains remain from the dreadful days of 1862. The Strayers of Bogota fled to Harrisonburg to avoid the war, only to find themselves in the path of savage pillaging by Federals under Hunter, then Sheridan, in 1864. They moved back to Bogota in 1876, and the handsome old building still looks across the river at Port Republic battlefield.[9]

Citizens of the historic area took pride in its Civil War heritage. A journalist who visited Cross Keys in 1873 noted that local residents "are still gratified to talk about the battle at this point." They especially loved to tell Stonewall Jackson anecdotes. By then the countryside had recovered, and was "groaning with plenty, crowned with peace, and stretching itself actively and vigorously." Throughout the region, the reporter declared, "the dreadful scars made by the war are all effaced, and nothing now remains but the memory of the eventful struggle." Veterans returning to the scenes of their youthful battles passed along traditional accounts. The children of the fertile Lewis clan walked over the battlefield with survivors, who especially appreciated the excellent view from atop the Coaling hill.[10]

Infantry captain Sam Moore enjoyed a long, eventful life after his moment of glory repulsing the Yankee raiders from the Kemper yard. As he lay dying in the fall of 1908, a lifelong friend rang the doorbell. Moore's son told the visitor that his father was unconscious and it would do no good to visit him. The man replied, "I was one of the 23 men with him at Port Republic. I should like to see him once more before he dies." The veteran stood beside his unconscious captain, "looking at him," Moore's son wrote. "After a moment or two of silence, my father's friend turned to me with his eyes full of tears and, shaking his head, walked out of the room. We went down the stairs together and stood on the porch. The next day my father died."[11]

Officers of later eras have been drawn to the Valley ever since Jackson's maneuvers made it famous in the annals of military history. An English military writer grumbled: "To be able to enumerate the blades of grass in the Shenandoah Valley . . . is not an adequate foundation for leadership." A pervasive tradition insists that German general Erwin Rommel traced Jackson's campaigns during the 1930s. The story rose in the confused fashion of legend out of visits by a prewar German attaché, Friedrich von Boetticher. Even without Rommel, foreign students of military matters have been and continue to be fascinated by Jackson's campaign that climaxed at Cross Keys and Port Republic.[12]

Preservation efforts on the two battlefields began in the 1920s, when the United Daughters of the Confederacy erected a large bronze plaque on the north edge of the road opposite the site of the Flory house, just below Ewell's stoutly defended bluffs. The marker was moved northeast a half mile in 1959, and then a few yards away to a third location in 1976. The Stonewall Jackson Memorial, Inc., a brainchild of businessman and history student Jay W. Johns, acquired the Coaling at Port Republic in 1959 and also purchased nearly one hundred acres at Cross Keys. The Cross

Keys tract includes the site where Trimble slaughtered the 8th New York. For about fifteen years Johns's group operated museums at the two places. Both tracts remain in the hands of private preservation organizations in 1993.[13]

Port Republic lies almost as quietly beautiful today as it did in 1862. Occasional incursions by insensitive government bodies foist such incongruities as a noisy boat ramp on the pastoral calm, but local preservation interests protect most of the setting of Port. A regional history published in 1976 criticized the village bitterly for not being full of industry, complaining that it "should have become the leading town between Roanoke and Harpers Ferry had it not been for the narrow ideas of those who preceded us . . . men with limited visions, lacking in energy." In consequence of such thoughtless sloth, denizens of Port must drive several miles to the outskirts of booming Harrisonburg to find a tanning salon or a fast-food biscuit.[14]

New generations of Valley youngsters still harvest relics from the battlefields. A boy named Good, of the Cross Keys family name familiar to 1862 residents, was uncovering "bullets, shot, fragments of cannon balls and shells and other pieces of metal" early in 1992. Young Good spoke wistfully of the stories told by his father and grandfather, who said that "the bullets would shine in the fields after a good rain. . . . they picked up some of the metal and melted the pieces into fishing weights."[15]

The ultimate fate of Cross Keys and Port Republic battlefields is bound up in legislation introduced into both houses of the United States Congress in early 1993. The two bills, somewhat different in details, propose creation of a National Military Park in the Valley, to preserve for all time key portions of the battlefields from the 1862, 1863, and 1864 Shenandoah Valley campaigns.

NOTES

Abbreviations

CSR   Compiled Service Records, National Archives. Washington, D.C.
FNMP   Fredericksburg and Spotsylvania County Battlefields Memorial National Military Park. Fredericksburg, Virginia.
GDAH   Georgia Department of Archives and History. Atlanta, Georgia.
HL   Huntington Library. San Marino, California
HRHS   Harrisonburg-Rockingham Historical Society. Dayton, Virginia.
HSP   Historical Society of Pennsylvania. Philadelphia, Pennsylvania.
IHS   Indiana Historical Society. Indianapolis, Indiana.
ISL   Indiana State Library. Indianapolis, Indiana.
JMU   Carrier Library, James Madison University. Harrisonburg, Virginia.
LC   Library of Congress. Washington, D.C.
MDAH   Mississippi Department of Archives and History. Jackson, Mississippi.
MHS   Maryland Historical Society. Baltimore, Maryland.
NA   National Archives. Washington, D.C.
NCDAH   North Carolina Department of Archives and History. Raleigh, North Carolina.
NWRC   National Weather Records Center. Asheville, North Carolina.
OHS   Ohio Historical Society. Columbus, Ohio.
OR   U.S. War Department. *The War of the Rebellion: A Compilation of the Official Records of the Union and Confederate Armies.* 128 vols. Washington, D.C., 1880-1901. All references are to volume XII, part 1, unless otherwise stated.
SHSP   *Southern Historical Society Papers.*
SPRP   Society of Port Republic Preservationists. Port Republic, Virginia.
TSLA   Tennessee State Library and Archives. Nashville, Tennessee.
UNC   Southern Historical Collection, University of North Carolina. Chapel Hill, North Carolina.
USAMHI   United States Army Military History Institute. Carlisle Barracks, Pennsylvania.
UT   University of Texas. Austin, Texas.
VHS   Virginia Historical Society. Richmond, Virginia.
ViRC   Museum of the Confederacy. Richmond, Virginia.
VMI   Virginia Military Institute. Lexington, Virginia.
VPI   Virginia Polytechnic Institute and State University. Blacksburg, Virginia.
VSA   Virginia State Archives. Richmond, Virginia.
WRHS   Western Reserve Historical Society. Cleveland, Ohio.
WVU   West Virginia University. Morgantown, West Virginia.

Chapter 1: The Valley Campaign

1. Fisk, *Anti-Rebel,* 250. Fisk's wry comment is in a letter dated August 1864.

2. Henderson, *Stonewall Jackson,* I, 304.

3. An interesting example of Jackson's delicate dealings with Ewell in early May is Herst, "Unrecorded," in which Stonewall was coaxing his counterpart: "All that I desire you to do is to keep near enough to Banks to let him know that if he goes down the Valley you will follow him and that you are all the time in striking distance of him."

4. An obscure communication from Joseph E. Johnston to Jackson, dated May 27, is in Johnston, "The Purpose of It." In that document, Johnston atypically (if in qualified terms) urged Jackson to be aggressive, "threatening Washington and Baltimore, unless the enemy . . . make it rash to attempt it." He added a nice compliment: "You compel me to publish orders announcing your success so often that you must expect repetition of expressions."

5. Snakenberg memoir, p. 15, Private Collection of John R. M. Bass; Mobile *Register and Advertiser,* December 31, 1862. Snakenberg's description is from July 1862. The Mobile correspondent summarized Jackson's battlefield metamorphosis: "the awkward, calculating pedagogue, becomes a hero—calm and self-possessed, it is true—but full of fire and energy, quick as lightning, and terrible as the thunderbolt."

6. Ms. marginalia by H. K. Douglas in his personal copy of M. A. Jackson, *Life and Letters* (1892), Antietam N.B.

7. Bond reminiscence, 59-60, ViRC.

8. Keily file, Private Collection of Brian C. Pohanka.

9. Schurz, *Reminiscences,* II, 344.

10. Ewell, *Making of a Soldier,* 108; J. A. Harman letter of May 9, Hotchkiss Papers, LC; Winder diary, June 5, MHS.

11. Ashby to Boteler from Conrad's Store, April 25, 1862, HSP.

12. Harman letters of April 26 and 27 (two on the 27th), Hotchkiss Papers, LC. Revised estimates from Harman and Ewell appear in later chapters.

13. John Apperson letters of May 2 and June 10, Black Papers, VPI; White, *Sketches,* 88.

14. Douglas, *I Rode,* 84; Mathis, *Land of the Living,* 43.

15. John Esten Cooke, "Humors of the Camp," in King and Derby, *Camp-fire Sketches,* 556.

16. Wayland, *Virginia Valley Records,* 288; Becker and Thomas, *Hearth and Knapsack,* 35. The Wayland account insists, in a denouement too delicious to trust, that the optimistic drummer got his comeuppance when hurrying back through town several days later.

17. Blacknall memoir, NCDAH; "Weather Journal . . . Georgetown," NWRC. The 1901 comment about rainfall came from farmers just below the Virginia-Carolina line. Average Virginia rainfall in June is 3.64 inches. Georgetown reported 1.93 on June 4 alone. Temperatures were recorded at 7 A.M., 2 P.M., and 9 P.M., so they do not reflect absolute highs or lows. Valley temperatures normally are several degrees cooler than in Georgetown.

18. Parmeter diary, June 4-6, OHS; Paulus, *Papers of . . . Milroy,* 43-44.

19. William Allan memoir, UNC.

20. Houghton, *Two Boys,* 28; George P. Ring to wife, June 14, Tulane; Fogelman diary, FNMP (emphasis added); Thomas M. Wade letter, June 17, Private Collection of Lewis Leigh. Ring's plaintive letter includes an ironic admission that when he weighed himself after the ordeal, his toughened body was heavier than when he enlisted in 1861.

21. Moore, "Through the Shadow," 14. Thomas Wade's letter cited in the previous note also includes comments about the dire need for resupply of drawers and trousers.

22. Circular dated May 13, 1862, John Q. A. Nadenbousch Papers, Duke. Nadenbousch was on provost duty in the Valley; presumably this copy was his enforcement guide.

23. Thomas M. Wade letter, June 14, Private Collection of Lewis Leigh; Irby G. Scott letter, June 12, 1862, Emory U.

24. Bassford, *Evolution of Harrisonburg;* Randolph, *Gleanings,* 29-30; *OR,* 783. A vivid account of Yankee depredations during this early phase of the campaign, not used in this narrative, is in the Lucy Muse (Walton) Fletcher diary, Duke.

25. Paulus, *Papers of . . . Milroy,* 49-50; "The Battle of Cross Keys"; Becker and Thomas, *Hearth and Knapsack,* 35-36; Culp, *25th Ohio,* 45. Ladley (*Hearth*) repeated the rumor that near Woodstock "there was two women killed or nearly so . . . by Jacksons men." Nothing confirms such an incident.

26. C. Benton Coiner to J.R. Anderson, March 3, 1913, in Coiner's file at VMI. As for embellished memories,

Hess, *Heartland,* 336, is an inaccurate civilian account claiming that Jackson addressed his troops "just before they marched into battle" at Cross Keys, from a surviving porch well behind *Federal* lines.

Chapter 2: The Approach to Port Republic

1. Munford to Hotchkiss, August 23, 1896, Reel 49, Hotchkiss Papers, LC.
2. Sandie Pendleton to mother, June 4, 1862, in Bean, "The Valley," 363; Wayland, *Virginia Valley Records,* 288; Hotchkiss, *Make Me a Map,* 51.
3. Hotchkiss, *Make Me a Map,* 51-52; *OR,* 719.
4. *OR,* 718-19; William Allan memoir, 134, UNC; Hotchkiss, *Make Me a Map,* 52. The North River ferry was on the Harrisonburg-Staunton route, not southeastward toward Port Republic.
5. Harman letters of June 5-6, Hotchkiss Papers, LC.
6. *OR,* vol. XII, pt. 3, pp. 905-6.
7. Sandie Pendleton letter, June 4, in Bean, "The Valley," 363; "Battery I," Barnett Papers, WRHS.
8. Merchant, *Eighty-Fourth ... Penna.,* 42; Samuel V. List to "Dear Parents," June 6, 1862, IHS; John C. Henderson diary, Private Collection of Walter Moore; Davis, "7th Indiana," ISL; N. L. Parmeter diary, OHS; Evans, ed., *Confederate Military History,* III, 257; Wood, *Seventh Regiment,* 115.
9. Hotchkiss, *Make Me a Map,* 52.
10. Hess, *Heartland,* 340-41, 344; May, "Early Days," 119-20. Port's early history is somewhat hazed over because Unionist arson burned the county records in 1864.
11. Hess, *Heartland,* 345-47; Martin, *Gazetteer of Virginia,* 432. Cross Keys never had a population of more than a widely scattered handful. Port Republic boasted 160 souls in 1835 and no doubt climbed to several times that number during its heyday. Census records make precise populations hard to determine.
12. Baldwin, *Gazetteer of the United States,* 1000; Hess, *Heartland,* 67; Martin, *Gazetteer of Virginia,* 432; Kennedy, *Eighth Census,* 288. The wheat, corn, and oats crop in 1850 totaled an amazing 1,221,911 bushels. The Valley generally was not tobacco country, but that fragrant weed was growing at Lewiston (the main battle site on June 9) in August 1844, and in 1888, Harrisonburg manufactured more cigars than any other Virginia town except Richmond. By 1910, only three acres of tobacco were growing in Rockingham. The 1860 census reveals that the county's male-female ratio was precisely even.
13. Fannie Kemper letters, February 21, June 24, 1862, Fannie V. Kemper Papers, Duke U.; Sons of Temperance ... Worth Division, No. 44, Ledger and Account Book, 1853-1856, Duke U. (with comparisons to Confederate unit muster rolls); May, "Port Republic," 74-75, JMU; Tenth Virginia "Reminiscences," SPRP. May's careful compilation numbers 68 names, including families whose homes would be landmarks in the battles—5 Kempers, 3 Lewises, 2 Harnsbergers, 2 Batemans, a Yost, a Maupin, etc.
14. Waddell, "Cross Keys," HRHS; May, "Register of Deaths, Rockingham County, 1862-1870," Reel 46 of Rockingham Records, VSA; Murphy, *10th Virginia,* 160. Layman was executed by musketry on August 19 near Gordonsville. His death is in the Rockingham records only because some relative reported it there on a whim.
15. May, "Port Republic," 171-75, JMU.
16. CSR of Benjamin H. Greene (filed as Green) of Ewell's staff, M331, NA. Greene used infantrymen from the 7th Louisiana under Lieutenant John Killmartin as boatwrights. One month later the same men would play a crucial role on the plain next to the Shenandoah.
17. Jackson to A. R. Boteler, May 6, 1862, Boteler Papers, Duke U. The two of whom Jackson complained were W. B. Taliaferro and John Echols. Ashby's commission as a general was dated May 23.
18. Yancey, "Civil War Letter," 35; Bradley T. Johnson in Jones, *American Heroism,* 495.
19. The unnamed Cincinnatian's letter of June 2 appeared under the title "The 'Ashby Boys,' " New York *Tribune,* June 12, 1862.
20. Webb, "Overtaking the Enemy"; Yancey, "Civil War Letter," 35; Heneberger, *Diary of a Citizen,* June 6; Frederick A. Wildman to wife, June 13, Wildman Papers, OHS; Brunk, *Hartman,* 62. Wildman wrote that his 55th Ohio reached Harrisonburg about three-thirty P.M.
21. Neese, *Three Years,* 67-68.
22. John Esten Cooke, "Humors of the Camp," in King and Derby, *Camp-fire Sketches,* 559; Bilby, "Rashly Led Forward," 17-19; Miers, ed., *Ride to War,* xiii-xvii, 268; Foster, *New Jersey,* 415. The "military dandy" quote is from Cooke.
23. Foster, *New Jersey,* 415; Webb, "Overtaking the Enemy"; Paulus, *Papers of ... Milroy,* 44; Bilby, "Rashly Led Forward," 19. The modern road net from Harrisonburg to Port Republic, while winding and of old engineering patterns, dates from 1868. The 1868 route was supposed to have carved twelve miles off the distance (Hess, *Heartland,* 345). Even discounting some exaggeration in that estimate, the postwar change is enough to make precise location of the Wyndham-Ashby encounter difficult to pin down. Even the 1885 county atlas shows a wiggly set of roads and intersections, relative to the twentieth-century configuration.

24. Caffey, *Battle-Fields,* 289-90; Abram D. Warwick, "Last Battle of General Turner Ashby," Box 24, Daniel Papers, U. Va.; Krick, *Lee's Colonels,* 167; *OR,* 732.

25. For the controversy, which was entirely typical of veteran affairs, see: Crisman, "Gave Yell" and "Crisman Claims It"; Crawford, "Took Him Prisoner"; Dorsey, "Percy Captured?"; and McDonald, "Wyndham Was Not Captured."

26. Buck, *Old Confeds,* 35; Lightsey, *Veteran's Story,* 15; unidentified old clipping in Ammen compilation, USAMHI; Neese, *Three Years,* 71. Wyndham's postwar escapades mirrored his earlier life. He went back to the Italian Army; established an oil refining business in America; published a newspaper in Calcutta and ran an opera; speculated in Burmese timber with money from a rich widow he married; and died in an 1879 balloon accident in Rangoon. The London *Times* observed that "the unfortunate aeronaut fell into the Royal Lake, whence he was extricated quite dead. . . . His characteristic death closed a career more chequered than falls the lot of many in this common-place age." (Miers, *Ride to War,* xiii–xvii, 268; Bilby, "Rashly Led Forward," 62; and "Wyndham," London *Times.*)

27. Arehart, "Diary," 117; Switzer, *Descendants, passim* (pages are poorly numbered and collated); Hess, *Heartland,* 341–42. May, "Port Republic Writer," provides thorough refutation of the silly notion that Jackson had his headquarters in another Kemper house in the middle of the village. The current building on the site of Madison Hall dates from 1916. W. M. Kemper was killed at Chancellorsville and G. B. Kemper at the Wilderness. George's death came one day after birth of a new half-brother on May 4, 1864. Adelaide's birthday was March 3, 1862.

28. Hotchkiss, *Make Me a Map,* 52; *OR,* vol. XII, pt. 3, 579, 906-7.

29. Webb, "Overtaking the Enemy"; A. M. Crapsey to "Kind Friend," June 14, Potter Co. Histl. Soc.; Brunk, *Hartman,* 62. Crapsey's letter describes attachment of the Bucktails to "Byards" cavalry brigade.

30. *OR,* 732; T. T. Munford ms. account in Munford-Ellis Papers, Duke U. Sources report two or three guns. The smaller number is more likely accurate.

31. Neese, *Three Years,* 68; May, "Port Republic," 76, JMU; Bradley T. Johnson in Jones, *American Heroism,* 496; A. M. Crapsey to "Kind Friend," June 14, Potter Co. Histl. Soc.

32. Wingfield, *Two Confederate Items,* 12; Neese, *Three Years,* 69; Johnson in Jones, *American Heroism,* 496.

33. Johnson in Jones, *American Heroism,* 496; J.E.H. Post letter, June 17, MHS; Neese, *Three Years,* 70; A. M. Crapsey to "Kind Friend," June 14, Potter Co. Histl. Soc.; Gill, *Reminiscences,* 58-59. A glowing tribute to Johnson from Ewell for his role in this charge is in Johnson's CSR, M331, Roll 141, NA.

34. Abram D. Warwick, "Last Battle of General Turner Ashby," Box 24, Daniel Papers, U.Va.; *OR,* 732.

35. Booth, *Personal Reminiscences,* 42; Neese, *Three Years,* 69-70; Caffey, *Battle-Fields,* 290; Johnson in Jones, *American Heroism,* 496. Errant rumors about the circumstances of Ashby's death found instant circulation. Even the careful Jed Hotchkiss (*Make Me a Map,* 53) reported that Ashby was shot by one of his own men while reconnoitering. Thomas G. Penn to "Dear Brother," June 8, Penn Papers, Duke U., declared that Ashby was killed by the Marylanders firing at his cavalry. The direction of the fatal side-through-breast bullet was reported as right-to-left by Penn and left-to-right by Caffey. The well-connected Colonel W. L. Jackson (June 8 letter in Roy Bird Cook Papers, WVU) wrote that the deadly shot hit "in the breast going first through his arm."

36. O'Ferrall, *Forty Years,* 41; Thomas G. Penn to "Dear Brother," June 8, Penn Papers, Duke U.; Wayland, *Virginia Valley Records,* 289; Moore, *June 1862,* unnumbered lvs.

37. Munford, "Reminiscences," 529; William L. Jackson letter, June 8, Cook Papers, WVU.

38. P. C. Kaylor to G. E. May, December 6, 1929, SPRP; May, "Port Republic," 76-77, JMU; Hotchkiss, *Make Me a Map,* 53. Kaylor identified the militiaman as Wesley Levell. The inquisitive lad was Wilson C. Harper, according to May.

39. T. T. Munford ms. account in Munford-Ellis Papers, Duke U.; G. Campbell Brown reminiscence, Brown-Ewell Papers, TSLA; Hotchkiss, *Make Me a Map,* 53; Wayland, *Virginia Valley Records,* 289; Booty, "Jackson's Battle," 31; Hess, *Heartland,* 349.

40. May, "Port Republic," 77, JMU; "Location of Madison Hall," Rockingham Co. Publ. Lib.; Hess, *Heartland,* 349; William Allan memoir, 134, UNC; Thomas S. Garnett to father, July 2, FNMP; H. Kyd Douglas to "My Dear Cousin Tippie," July 24, 1862, Duke U. Garnett dated the display "in the Chapel of P. Republic" (no one else deviates from the traditional location of Frank Kemper's house) on June 7, and—obviously erroneously—the march to Charlottesville on the 8th. Allan described the funeral cortege of this "glorious day" as "making an impression I can never forget." See also Allan, *History of the Campaign,* 144.

41. J. W. Thomas diary, Private Collection of A. T. Wallace; Washington Hands notebook, MHS; Abram D. Warwick, "Last Battle of General Turner Ashby," 8, 18, Box 24, Daniel Papers, U.Va.; *OR,* 732; G. Campbell Brown reminiscence, Brown-Ewell Papers, TSLA; T. T. Munford ms. account in Munford-Ellis Papers, Duke U. Since there is now no trace of this burial, it is worth noting that Thomas specified the site as "a little to the right of the gate, 8 paces from the rear rank."

42. Howard, *Recollections,* 120-21; Wingfield, *Two Confederate Items,* 12; Kirkpatrick diary, U. of Texas; Webb, "Overtaking the Enemy."

43. Kearsey, *Shenandoah Valley*, 32; Moore, "Jackson at Port Republic"; James Dinwiddie to wife, June 7, VSA; Humphreys letter, Private Collection of David Q. Updike.

44. George P. Ring to wife, June 7, Tulane; Dabney, "Stonewall Jackson," 145-58; "The Squarest Battle of the War."

45. Paulus, *Papers of ... Milroy*, 44; Robert Bromley diary, OHS; Frederick A. Wildman diary, OHS; *OR*, 781; Kaylor, "Cross Keys Battlefield," HRHS. Bromley gives the timing for Milroy's departure and return.

46. Kirkpatrick diary, U. of Texas; G. Campbell Brown reminiscence, TSLA; Oates, *The War*, 102; Neese, *Three Years*, 71-72; Eli S. Coble reminiscence, NCDAH.

47. *OR*, 686, 695; Wood, *Seventh Regiment*, 115; Ray, "Journal," 59-60; SeCheverell, *Twenty-ninth Ohio*, 45-46; Parmeter diary, OHS; Fairfax diary, Chicago Historical Society; Rawling, *First ... Virginia*, 90-91. Distances and times of departure and arrival vary in the sources cited (understandably, given the length of the column as well as the vagaries of evidence) from thirteen to sixteen miles; from eight A.M. to noon; and from "early evening" through six P.M. to midnight.

48. Davis, "7th Indiana," ISL; Samuel V. List diary, IHS; Merchant, *Eighty-Fourth ... Penna.*, 42; Huntington, "Operations," 326; "Battery H," Barnett Papers, WRHS. An endearing tale about Colonel Carroll's stop at Conrad's Store is in Cartmell, *Shenandoah*, 344. A Unionist accosted his overnight host, a Mrs. Miller, and announced that he was confiscating her Rebel house. The frightened woman informed Carroll, who gave her his pistol and suggested that she shoot the fellow. She tried but did no better than two near misses.

49. Fravel, "Valley Campaign," 419; Howard, *Recollections*, 121; A. J. Barrow diary, USAMHI; Booty, "Jackson's Battle," 31; W. F. Davis memoir, 49, U.Va.; Whitehead, "An Historic Scene."

50. Hotchkiss, *Make Me a Map*, 53; Neese, *Three Years*, 72; A. S. Pendleton to mother, June 7, in Bean, "The Valley"; May, "Port Republic Writer."

51. *OR*, vol. XI, pt. 3, pp. 580, 907.

52. Myers, *Comanches*, 64; *OR*, 712; Wayland, *Rockingham County*, 142.

53. Willis, "Letter," 161; Arehart, "Diary," 117. Willis says the party, which he accompanied despite a high fever, stayed out "late"; but the evidently reliable Arehart reported leaving with a dispatch for Ewell at nine and returning by eleven. Since Daylight Saving Time did not yet exist, nine P.M. was reasonably late by Willis's fevered standards.

Chapter 3: Stonewall Jackson Betrayed by Indolent Cavalry

1. The rankings of Carroll and Fitz Lee are from *Official Register ... U.S. Military Academy*, 8, 19. Deportment standings, which were arranged institution-wide rather than by class, were 174th for Carroll and 177th for Lee out of 207 cadets. George May, local postwar oracle on the battle, declared that the 8th "dawned with unqualled splendor" ("Port Republic," 77, JMU).

2. Wilson, *Itinerary of the Seventh Ohio*, 161, quoting F. M. Cunningham of the 1st Virginia (Union) Cavalry; Rawling, *First ... Virginia*, 91-92. Cunningham thought his detachment numbered about 75; Carroll in *OR*, 698, said 150. His contemporary, authoritative account must be held the more believable; commanders minimize rather than exaggerate their own strength. The James Gildea memoir, Barnett Papers, WRHS, 14, estimated cavalry strength at 115. Kephart and Conner, "Shenandoah Valley," says 150. The table of organization in Appendix A shows alignments as I have deduced them. The *OR* table (p. 690) for some reason does not attempt to provide that basic information.

3. Dixie, "Letter from the 7th."

4. Thomson, *Seventh Indiana*, 98-99; Wilson, *Itinerary of the Seventh Ohio*, 161. Thomson put the start of the march at ten P.M., but timing of all the night's events varies widely between sources. Carroll can hardly have left much later than ten and probably marched much sooner.

5. "Letter from the Army of the Shenandoah"; Rawling, *First ... Virginia*, 91; Davis, "7th Indiana," ISL.

6. Hotchkiss in Evans, *Confederate Military History*, III, 258; Moore, *Rebellion Record*, V, 113.

7. Winters, *Civil War Letters*, 37; Rawling, *First ... Virginia*, 91; Winscott, "From the 7th"; Davis, "7th Indiana," ISL; Samuel V. List diary, IHS. The timing of the march of course is widely and variously reported. Winters and Rawling both use 1 A.M. Davis reports a 2 A.M. wakeup and 4 A.M. march. Winscott says 3 A.M. wakeup and march. List says "Started at 4 oclock." The 7th Indiana was in front, and each of the last three sources were contemporary and by Indiana soldiers, so I have accepted the later starting time.

8. Pohanka, "Keogh"; Keily file, Private Collection of Brian C. Pohanka.

9. Winscott, "From the 7th"; Thomson, *Seventh Indiana*, 99; *OR*, 698; Davis, "7th Indiana," ISL; James Gildea memoir, 14, Barnett Papers, WRHS. Both Davis and Carroll (*OR*) use six A.M. for time of arrival. Several other sources use vaguer schedules, such as "about sunrise."

10. Hadley, "Indiana Soldier," 212; Davis, "7th Indiana," ISL; Winters, *Civil War Letters*, 37.

11. Wilson, *Itinerary of the Seventh Ohio*, 161.

12. *OR,* 698; James Gildea to Thomas J. Burke, ca. 1896, Hotchkiss Papers, LC; James Gildea memoir, 14, Barnett Papers, WRHS.

13. Gildea's memoir is an anonymous portion of the ms. "History of Bat. 'L' 1st Ohio Lt. Artly" in the Barnett Papers, WRHS. The author's identity is firmly established by internal evidence in the document compared with Ohio Roster Commission, *Official Roster,* X, 430. Furthermore, Gildea's 1896 letter cited in other notes to this chapter uses identical phrasing in describing some events at Port Republic. This important source will be cited hereafter as Gildea memoir, Barnett Papers, WRHS, without further reference to its connection with the ms. battery history.

14. James Gildea memoir, Barnett Papers, WRHS.

15. May, "Battle of Port Republic," 96. George E. May, a local resident who made a lifelong study of the battle, is an invaluable authority for regional names, usages, and lore.

16. *OR,* 698; Skidmore, *Billy Davis,* 142-43.

17. List diary, IHS; Thomson, *Seventh Indiana,* 99; Rawling, *First . . . Virginia,* 92-93.

18. *OR,* 698; James Gildea memoir, 14-15, Barnett Papers, WRHS; Gildea to Thomas J. Burke, ca. 1896, Hotchkiss Papers, LC.

19. Humphreys letter, Private Collection of David Q. Updike; Fonerden, *Carpenter's Battery,* 25.

20. The relative position of Taliaferro and Winder near the bridge is obvious from the sequence of reaction to Carroll's raid. Patton's location is fixed by a letter of T. G. Penn to "Dear Brother," June 8, Penn Papers, Duke U. Obviously writing before the morning's excitement, Penn said of his 42nd Virginia, "We are now in a mile of Port Republic." The same letter is the source for "bound to have another fight." Taylor's movement toward Port Republic, described elsewhere in connection with Cross Keys, shows that the Louisiana troops were much farther away than Patton. The William P. Harper diary, Folder 6, Box 19, Collection 55-B, LHAC, Tulane U., demonstrates that Taylor was more than three miles from Port Republic.

21. Winder diary, MHS; Howard, *Recollections,* 122.

22. Murphy, *10th Virginia Infantry,* passim.

23. Fravel, "Valley Campaign," 419; Joseph F. Kauffman diary, UNC.

24. M. A. Jackson, *Memoirs,* 515-16; Wood, *The War,* 58; Orr recollections, VSA.

25. *OR,* 745; Krick, *Lee's Colonels,* 32.

26. Moore, "General Jackson at Port Republic." For details on Cleon Moore, see Frye, *2nd Virginia,* 119.

27. Untitled S.J.C. Moore memoir, UNC; John R. Nunn to Moore, ca. 1891, Moore Correspondence, HL. Moore's "Stonewall Jackson's escape at Port Republic," a manuscript dated Sept. 1, 1891, in Moore Correspondence, HL, calculates the detachment at 27 men, including one extra private and one extra sergeant. The rest of Moore's several recollections, all of them carefully crafted, count 25 men, as used in this narrative.

28. May, "Port Republic," 77, JMU; May, "Battle of Port Republic," 95-96; McGuire to Hotchkiss, May 28, 1896, Roll 34, Hotchkiss Papers, LC.

29. Mauzy, *Descendants,* 36-38; Cooke, *Stonewall Jackson,* 22.

30. "Location of Madison Hall," Rockingham Library; May, "Port Republic," 78, JMU. Sue became Mrs. Sue B. Craig of Warrenton, and was alive in 1931.

31. *OR,* 732; William Allan memoir, 135, UNC; James M. Carrington account in his file at VMI. Temperatures at Georgetown, D.C., about 100 miles away, were 64 at 7 A.M., 72 at 2 P.M., and 59 at 9 P.M. ("Weather Journal," NWRC). Weather patterns in the region move from the southwest, so Port Republic would have been a bit ahead of Georgetown's sequence; but the next day's readings in D.C. were only slightly lower.

32. Moore, *Charlottesville . . . Artillery,* 5.

33. Herndon memoir, Private Collection of Robert H. Moore; Whitehead, "An Historic Scene"; Dinwiddie to wife, June 12, VSA; Davis memoir, U.Va.

34. Douglas, *I Rode,* 85; Willis, "Letter," 161.

35. Hotchkiss, *Make Me a Map,* 54; Hotchkiss to S.J.C. Moore, August 3, 1891, Moore Papers, UNC.

36. Two statements from Dabney to Hotchkiss, one dated May 1896 and the other undated but clearly during 1896, both in Hotchkiss Papers, LC. The preacher used slightly different wording in describing the conversation in Dabney, "Stonewall Jackson," 146.

37. *OR,* 712; Willis, "Letter," 161; Hotchkiss to S.J.C. Moore, August 3, 1891, in Moore Papers, UNC. Based on what he could tell from his sickbed, Willis erroneously believed that Jackson and his party had left when the Yankees struck. The group had not departed, but it was about ready to do so.

38. The three times are from the Herndon memoir, Private Collection of Robert H. Moore; Hotchkiss, *Make Me a Map,* 53; and Winder diary, MHS. Sunrise was about 4:45 (*Confederate States Almanac*). Other sources offer these times: "at daylight," untitled S.J.C. Moore memoir, Moore Papers, UNC; 8 A.M., *OR,* 768, Watkins Kearns diary at VSA, and Humphreys letter, Private Collection of David Q. Updike; 8:30 A.M., *OR,* 769; "between 8 and 9 o'clock," Howard, *Recollections,* 122; 9 A.M., *OR,* 727; between 7 and 8, Douglas, *I Rode,* 85; and "about seven o'clock," Jackson in M. A. Jackson, *Memoirs,* 283.

39. *OR,* 733; T. T. Munford letter of June 10, quoted by sister in letter of Lizzie E. Ewell to her mother, June 13, Munford-Ellis Papers, Duke U. Munford was overly sanguine about his own lot, suggesting that his family "would not be surprised to hear . . . that he had been appointed Brig. General"—something that never happened, then or later. He also declared that both Jackson and Ewell "are warm friends . . . and very kind."

40. Douglas, *I Rode,* 84-85; May, "Port Republic," 77, JMU. That Sipe's company was the one close to town also seems apparent from later events as described in the narrative.

41. Moore, "General Jackson at Port Republic."

42. *OR,* vol. XII, pt. 3, 907-8; May, "Port Republic," 77-78, JMU.

43. Harman letter of June 8, Hotchkiss Papers, LC; Hotchkiss to S.J.C. Moore, August 3, 1891, Moore Papers, UNC; *OR,* 713, 732; Gen. Ord. No. 60 in Box 1, Hotchkiss Papers, LC.

44. Cartmell, *Shenandoah,* 344.

45. James Gildea memoir, 15, Barnett Papers, WRHS; Gildea to Thomas J. Burke, undated ca. 1896, Hotchkiss Papers, LC.

46. Davis, "7th Indiana," ISL. Davis believed that the Yost's Hill guns did not fire until Carroll had reached the streets of the village with mounted men, but that obviously was not true. He is convincing enough, however, to make it clear that Gildea's half of the battery must have opened first.

47. Kaylor, "Port Republic Battle," HRHS; Hess, *Heartland,* 349; James Gildea memoir, 15, Barnett Papers, WRHS.

48. *OR,* 698, 700. In addition to sources cited earlier that mentioned Keogh, a Confederate prisoner in Washington heard by June 10 that "Captain Keogh charged with a body of cavalry" ([West], *Experience,* 20).

49. Wilson, *Itinerary of the Seventh Ohio,* 161-62; Cunningham, "Port Republic."

50. May, "Battle of Port Republic," 96; May, "Port Republic," 79, JMU; Wilson, *Itinerary of the Seventh Ohio,* 163.

51. James Gildea memoir, 15, Barnett Papers, WRHS.

52. Wilson, *Itinerary of the Seventh Ohio,* 162; James Gildea memoir, 15, Barnett Papers, WRHS; *OR,* 698; May, "Battle of Port Republic," 96; May, "Port Republic," 80, JMU.

53. Wilson, *Itinerary of the Seventh Ohio,* 162; Cunningham, "Port Republic."

54. *OR,* 698, 683; Thomson, *Seventh Indiana,* 99.

55. Wilson, *Itinerary of the Seventh Ohio,* 162. Two Confederate accounts (Washington Hands notebook, MHS, and Goldsborough, *Maryland Line* [1869]) mention Federal prisoners near the bridge being released by Carroll; Union accounts made no such claim.

56. James Gildea memoir, 15-16, Barnett Papers, WRHS; Gildea to Thomas J. Burke, undated ca. 1896, Hotchkiss Papers, LC.

57. May, "Port Republic," 106, JMU; Hess, *Heartland,* 348; "Some Historic Soil," SPRP; Washington Hands notebook, MHS; Wayland, "The Battle"; Eli S. Coble reminiscence, NCDAH. Several other sources make unmistakably clear the covered aspect of the bridge.

58. *OR,* vol. XII, pt. 3, 335; James Gildea memoir, 14, Barnett Papers, WRHS.

59. "Jackson's Latest Victories"; Henry W. Barrow letter, June 15, Pfohl Papers, UNC.

60. Thomson, *Seventh Indiana,* 99; Winscott, "From the 7th"; Rawling, *First . . . Virginia,* 93; Burton letter in Private Collection of Sandra R. Kenney.

61. *OR,* vol. LI, pt. 1, 95.

62. R. L. Dabney account to Jedediah Hotchkiss, May 1896, Hotchkiss Papers, LC.

63. Chas. H. Bard (Co. F, 7th Ohio) to "My Friend Sade," July 17, 1862, J. T. Woods Papers, Duke U. For more commentary on the bridge burning, see Ray, "Unburned Bridge," Max, "Port Republic," and Brown, "The Mistake That Was Made."

64. Thomson, *Seventh Indiana,* 96-97; Burton letter in Private Collection of Sandra R. Kenney.

65. Thomson, *Seventh Indiana,* 103; "Battle at Port Republic," New York *Tribune,* June 18, 1862.

66. "Fight at Port Republic," *Ontario Repository & Messenger,* June 18, 1862; [West], *Experience,* 20.

67. "From Front Royal." Moore, *Rebellion Record,* V, 112-13, nicely applies the perspective of hindsight.

Chapter 4: A Village Full of Yankees

1. Douglas, *I Rode,* 85. The Washington Hands notebook, MHS, reports that some captured Federals also warned of the raid, but no one corroborates that story.

2. S.J.C. Moore, "Stonewall Jackson's Escape at Port Republic," HL; Moore, "Through the Shadow," 15; untitled S.J.C. Moore memoir in Moore Papers, UNC; Frye, *2nd Virginia,* 111; Musick, *6th Virginia,* 130; Moore, "Clarke County Men at Port Republic," 6-7, ts., Moore Papers, UNC.

3. Whitehead, "Historic Scene"; Moore, *Charlottesville . . . Arty.,* 5-6.

4. G. Campbell Brown memorandum, TSLA; Wayland, "The Battle"; William Allan memoir, 135, UNC; William Allan to J. M. Carrington, Roll 59, Frame 227, Hotchkiss Papers, LC.

5. Hotchkiss, *Make Me a Map,* 53; Hotchkiss to S.J.C. Moore, August 3, 1891, Moore Papers, UNC.

6. Douglas, *I Rode,* 85; Douglas ms. notes in Mrs. Jackson's 1892 book about her husband, margin of p. 173 with references to pp. 345 and 360, Antietam N.B. Douglas's tendency toward exaggeration and egocentricity dilutes the value of his writings. In this instance, however, I have accepted his account because (*a*) he was the only close-up eyewitness who reported on the event; (*b*) the affair does not reflect special credit or behavior to him; and (*c*) the format is marginalia in books from his own library, where no one else would see it.

7. Douglas ms. notes in Mrs. Jackson's 1892 book, p. 275; Douglas ms. notes in G.F.R. Henderson biography of Jackson, I, p. 454. Both books are at Antietam N.B.

8. "Location of Madison Hall," Rockingham Library; May, "Port Republic," 78, JMU; Whitehead, "An Historic Scene"; Dabney, "Stonewall Jackson," 146.

9. McNeer, *Methodist Church,* passim.

10. McGuire to Hotchkiss, June 12, 1896, Hotchkiss Papers, LC; May, "Port Republic," 84, JMU.

11. McGuire to Hotchkiss, May 28 and June 12, 1896, Hotchkiss Papers, LC.

12. McGuire to Hotchkiss, May 18, 1896, Hotchkiss Papers, LC; May, "Port Republic Writer"; "Location of Madison Hall," Rockingham Library. The last two sources contain Harper's story. One reports his age as twelve, the other as fourteen; I split the difference.

13. McGuire to Hotchkiss, May 28, 1896, Hotchkiss Papers, LC; Booty, "Jackson's Battle," 33. May, "Port Republic Writer," using the W. C. Harper account, phrases Jackson's request as: "He asked Dr. McGuire if he could not do as well without so much profanity." S.J.C. Moore, in his untitled manuscript memoir, Moore Papers, UNC, has Jackson saying: "Doctor, can't you get along as well without swearing?"

14. McGuire to Hotchkiss, May 28 and June 12, 1896, Hotchkiss Papers, LC; untitled ms. memoir of S.J.C. Moore, Moore Papers, UNC. The timing in the narrative shows the sequence of events that allowed Jackson to escape despite his brief halt at the church. The only participant who tried to mesh the timing was Moore in his "Clarke County Men at Port Republic," p. 7, Moore Papers, UNC. He thought that the enemy cavalry became scattered in chasing Southern pickets, "but having gotten ahead of the rest of the command, they halted for the column to close up, thus giving time to Gen'l Jackson to cross the bridge." Moore did not recognize that Federal artillery fire preceded the cavalry by some time. Even the reliable William Allan (*Jackson's Valley Campaign* [1878], 24) erroneously thought that the Federal cavalry drove Confederate horsemen "pell-mell into Port Republic" and immediately "dashed across South river after them."

15. *OR,* 719; Moore, "General Jackson at Port Republic."

16. Whitehead, "Stonewall Jackson's Escape"; Hotchkiss to S.J.C. Moore, August 3, 1891, Moore Papers, UNC; Dabney, "Stonewall Jackson," 146.

17. Moore, "General Jackson at Port Republic"; Garber, *John A. Harman,* 19.

18. Hotchkiss, *Make Me a Map,* 53-54; *OR,* 719.

19. John S. Apperson letter to "Dear Friends," June 10, Black Papers, VPI. A typical contemporary newspaper version of the myth is "Coolness of Jackson." For one of many postwar repetitions in similar vein, see LaTourette, "War Time Incident."

20. Hotchkiss, *Make Me a Map,* 53. Hotchkiss specified Pendleton, W. L. Jackson, and Boswell as escaping, ignoring Douglas (whom he did not like, and whose staff role was minor).

21. Douglas to "My Dear Cousin Tippie," July 24, 1862, Duke U.; Douglas, *I Rode,* 85; *OR,* 719; Douglas ms. notes in Mrs. Jackson's 1892 book, p. 275, and in G.F.R. Henderson's biography, I, pp. 454-55, Antietam N.B.

22. Dabney to Hotchkiss, undated but during 1896, and May 1896 statement to Hotchkiss, Hotchkiss Papers, LC.

23. Hotchkiss to S.J.C. Moore, August 3, 1891, Moore Papers, UNC; Hotchkiss, *Make Me a Map,* 54. In his 1891 letter to a colleague, Hotchkiss implied that he returned to the village but too late for the action; in his contemporary version, he acknowledged remaining at Weyer's Cave.

24. Ts. Harman letters, Hotchkiss Papers, LC; Garber, *John A. Harman,* 19.

25. William Allan memoir, 135-36, UNC; Allan to J. M. Carrington, Roll 59, Frame 227, Hotchkiss Papers, LC.

26. McGuire to Hotchkiss, May 28, 1896, Hotchkiss Papers, LC. For the account of a sick Louisianian who did not get away with the ambulances, see Fortson, "Stonewall Jackson."

27. Willis, "Letter," 161-62.

28. Crutchfield account to Hotchkiss, May 1896, Hotchkiss Papers, LC; Crutchfield comments to S.J.C. Moore in "Clarke County Men at Port Republic," 6, ts. in Moore Papers, UNC.

29. Hotchkiss, *Make Me a Map,* 53.

30. Krick, *Lee's Colonels,* 357-58; Moore, "General Jackson at Port Republic."

31. Moore, "General Jackson at Port Republic"; Wallace, *Virginia Military Organizations,* 89, 146.

32. Moore, "General Jackson at Port Republic." Moore's excellent account identifies one hopeful prisoner as a son of the "noted traveler and writer" Bayard Taylor. Taylor, however, was born in 1825 and first married in 1850.

33. "Location of Madison Hall," Rockingham Library.

34. May, "Port Republic," 77, 84-85, JMU.

35. May, "Port Republic," 84, JMU.

36. The Downs-Maupin episode is from the reliable May, "Port Republic," 171-75, JMU. Mrs. Laura V. Lamb, who narrated the tale, called her brother "Harry Maupin"—obviously William Henry Harrison Maupin (Musick, *6th Virginia,* 135). Sheets's adventure is from an unlabeled ms. note in the SPRP files.

37. Dinwiddie to wife, June 12, 1862, VSA.

38. May, "Port Republic," 79, JMU.

39. Moore, "Stonewall Jackson's Escape," HL; Moore, "Clarke County Men at Port Republic," 3, Moore Papers, UNC; untitled Moore memoir, Moore Papers, UNC.

40. Moore, "Clarke County Men at Port Republic," 3, Moore Papers, UNC; untitled Moore memoir, Moore Papers, UNC. For Lieutenant O'Bannon (a twenty-two-year-old printer), see Moore, "General Jackson at Port Republic," and Frye, *2nd Virginia,* 122.

41. Moore, "Through the Shadow," 14-15; May, "Port Republic," 80, JMU; Moore, "Stonewall Jackson's Escape," HL.

42. Moore, "Clarke County Men at Port Republic," 3-4, Moore Papers, UNC; untitled Moore memoir, Moore Papers, UNC. The original quotation reads "the time ha*d* come." I changed the tense.

43. Dabney to Hotchkiss, undated 1896, and Dabney statement to Hotchkiss, May 1896, Hotchkiss Papers, LC. In the first, Dabney admitted that the infantryman he encountered might have been an underling. As his ardent but maladroit attempts at a controversy with Moore escalated, Dabney insisted in the second account that he had talked to Moore in person. Moore denied that convincingly. In his later version, Dabney set the tone by erring egregiously in describing vividly how he bravely pushed forward despite being waved back by Hunter McGuire as the doctor went "flying fast towards Staunton" ("I said to myself, they are non combatants, but it is my duty to stay."). McGuire, of course, actually was a Federal prisoner. Moore to Hotchkiss, June 3, 1896, Hotchkiss Papers, LC, seethes at the "utter groundlessness of Dr. Dabney's absurd pretensions."

44. J. M. Carrington account, Roll 59, Frame 227, Hotchkiss Papers, LC.

45. Whitehead, "Historic Scene."

46. Carrington account, Roll 59, Frame 227, Hotchkiss Papers, LC; L. W. Cox to Hotchkiss, August 17, 1896, Hotchkiss Papers, LC.

47. Herndon "Infantry and Cavalry Service"; L. W. Cox to Hotchkiss, August 17, 1896, Hotchkiss Papers, LC; Dinwiddie to wife, June 12, 1862, VSA.

48. Carrington account, Roll 59, Frame 227, Hotchkiss Papers, LC; Moore, *Charlottesville ... Arty.,* 7; W.F. Davis memoir, 49-51, U.Va.

49. Carrington account in his file, VMI; Dabney statements to Hotchkiss, undated 1896 and May 1896, Hotchkiss Papers, LC.

50. Whitehead, "Historic Scene"; Moore, *Charlottesville ... Arty.,* 6-7. Carrington in Roll 59, Frame 227, Hotchkiss Papers, LC, credited an officer unknown to him (not Dabney, whom he mentioned later) with "the presence of mind to ride by me and in a loud voice halloo, 'Bring up the artillery.' " Only Carrington's inexperience can explain his needing prompting under such circumstances! Dinwiddie (in Whitehead) provides a very precise map that admirably supports his narrative. The map is not unimpeachable, but it constitutes an essential source for unsnarling the mare's nest of conflicting reports. Dinwiddie places Dabney at the northeast corner during preparations around the fence, but that seems impossible. Dabney never claimed to have been at that point then, though he placed himself many other spots, some of them obviously in error. Dinwiddie was confused with the fence opposite the southeast corner of the yard, where he and Dabney soon would swing into action.

51. Whitehead, "Historic Scene"; Whitehead, "Stonewall Jackson's Escape." Timberlake died in 1881, having narrated his account to Whitehead (the second article cited) years before the latter published it. That leaves more room for confusion than in Dinwiddie's account ("An Historic Scene"), published while the narrator still lived.

52. Clement, "With Jackson in the Valley," 38; Musick, *6th Virginia,* 38. The captain was Thomas S. Flournoy, promoted to colonel six weeks prematurely in Clement's account.

53. Poague, *Gunner,* 26; J. F. Minor memoir, U.Va.

54. Slaughter, *Randolph Fairfax,* 26; Fonerden, *Carpenter's Battery,* 25; Humphreys letter, Private Collection of David Q. Updike; Moore, *Cannoneer,* 68; Poague, *Gunner,* 26.

55. James Dinwiddie to wife, June 12, VSA; M. A. Jackson, *Memoirs,* 515-16. Dinwiddie had the story about Taliaferro's shirt directly from the general, whose own account is in Mrs. Jackson's book. It does not seem fully reliable, as is often the case with General Taliaferro's utterances.

56. Fravel, "Valley Campaign," 419; Kauffman diary, UNC; Wood, *The War,* 58-59.

57. Howard, *Recollections,* 122.

58. John S. Apperson to "Dear Friends," June 10, Black Papers, VPI; Howard, *Recollections,* 122; *OR,* 739.

59. *OR,* 768-69. Most units of course began preparing for action on their own when the guns opened (see *OR,* 739).

60. Douglas, *I Rode,* 85; Hotchkiss, *Make Me a Map,* 54; Allan, *History of the Campaign,* 150n. Boswell's report in *OR,* 719, offers a straightforward account of these confusing minutes. The reliable aide saw Jackson ordering up the 37th Virginia then riding "down to the bank of the river." Boswell did not mention Jackson's personal foray into the camps, but a multitude of sources document that rapid side trip.

61. *OR,* 727; Moore, *Cannoneer,* 68-69; Gildea to S.J.C. Moore in "Clarke County Men at Port Republic," 8, Moore Papers, UNC.

62. Gildea to Hotchkiss, August 18, 1894, Hotchkiss Papers, LC; Gildea to Thomas J. Burke, undated ca. 1896, Hotchkiss Papers, LC; Gildea to S.J.C. Moore in "Clarke County Men at Port Republic," 8, Moore Papers, UNC; James Gildea memoir, 16, Barnett Papers, WRHS.

63. James Gildea memoir, Barnett Papers, WRHS; Gildea to T. J. Burke, undated ca. 1896, Hotchkiss Papers, LC.

64. Douglas, *I Rode,* 86; Hotchkiss, *Make Me a Map,* 54; May, "Battle of Port Republic," 97; Slaughter, *Randolph Fairfax,* 26. Douglas, in a ms. note in his copy of Henderson's 1898 biography of Jackson, I, 454, tacitly validated Henderson's version of the affair and affirmed that Douglas "was present when Jackson ordered the gun over &c." The volume is at Antietam N.B.

65. Moore, *Cannoneer,* 69; Poague letter in Allan, *History of the Campaign,* 150n.

66. James Gildea to T. J. Burke, ca. 1896, Hotchkiss Papers, LC; James Gildea memoir, Barnett Papers, WRHS. Claims that an unexpected round from Gildea taught Jackson the Ohioans' identity are in Douglas, *I Rode,* 86; Hotchkiss, *Make Me a Map,* 54; Slaughter, *Randolph Fairfax,* 26; and May "Port Republic," 97. Moore, *Cannoneer,* 69, says the Federals pointed the gun through the bridge (which they in fact did a bit later) in response.

Chapter 5: Routing the Raiders

1. Nunn to S.J.C. Moore, 1891, Moore Correspondence, HL.

2. Moore, "Clarke County Men at Port Republic," 4, and untitled Moore memoir, both in Moore Papers, UNC; Moore, "Stonewall Jackson's Escape," Moore Correspondence, HL.

3. Moore, "Clarke County Men at Port Republic," 4, Moore Papers, UNC; Moore, "Stonewall Jackson's Escape," Moore Correspondence, HL; Moore, "Through the Shadow," 16. Moore, "General Jackson at Port Republic," gives the viewpoint of an interested observer at some distance.

4. Nunn to Moore, undated 1891, and Moore, "Stonewall Jackson's Escape," HL; Havron, "Stonewall," 204; untitled Moore memoir, Moore Papers, UNC; Carrington in Roll 59, Frame 227, Hotchkiss Papers, LC.

5. L. W. Cox to Hotchkiss, August 17, 1896, Hotchkiss Papers, LC.

6. Crutchfield to Dabney, May 1896, Hotchkiss Papers, LC; Crutchfield in Moore, "Clarke County Men at Port Republic," 6, Moore Papers, UNC.

7. Willis, "Letter," 162; McGuire to Hotchkiss, May 28, June 12, 1896, Hotchkiss Papers, LC; McGuire to S.J.C. Moore in "Clarke County Men at Port Republic," 6, Moore Papers, UNC.

8. William Allan memoir, 136, UNC; Moore, "Stonewall Jackson's Escape," Moore Correspondence, HL; Moore, "Clarke County Men at Port Republic," 4, Moore Papers, UNC. In two of Moore's several accounts, he suggested firing a second organized volley from this first position. Firing at will after the initial volley fits far better with demonstrable facts. Soon after the two cannon joined Moore at his first position, he advanced across the Kemper yard to support a second artillery cluster in the southeastern corner of the yard. That movement will be described shortly. In one account, but not the others, Moore confusedly reported this advance as before the first artillery salvo, rather than after it but before the second artillery grouping began its fire straight down Main Street.

9. Moore, "Stonewall Jackson's Escape," Moore Correspondence, HL; untitled Moore memoir, Moore Papers, UNC; Nunn to S.J.C. Moore, undated 1891, Moore Correspondence, HL. The source first cited graciously and carefully acknowledges the accuracy of accounts by O'Bannon, Whitehead, and Dinwiddie. Moore of course did not extend his imprimatur to Dabney's confused claims.

10. Dinwiddie to wife, June 12, VSA; Whitehead, "Historic Scene."

11. L. W. Cox to Hotchkiss, August 17, 1896, Hotchkiss Papers, LC. Julius S. Goodin supplied an affidavit to accompany Cox's account that attested to its accuracy.

12. L. W. Cox to Hotchkiss, August 17, 1896, Hotchkiss Papers, LC; Whitehead, "Historic Scene"; Moore, "Through the Shadow," 16; Moore, "Stonewall Jackson's Escape," Moore Correspondence, HL.

13. Crutchfield to Dabney, May 1896, Hotchkiss Papers, LC; Crutchfield in Moore, "Clarke County Men at Port Republic," 6, Moore Papers, UNC; Havron, "Stonewall," 204.

14. L. W. Cox to Hotchkiss, August 17, 1896, Hotchkiss Papers, LC.

15. Nunn to Moore, undated 1891, and Moore "Stonewall Jackson's Escape," both in Moore Correspondence, HL; Moore, "Clarke County Men at Port Republic," 5, Moore Papers, UNC.

16. W. F. Davis memoir, U.Va.; Dabney to Hotchkiss, May 1896, Hotchkiss Papers, LC. Carrington's account, Roll 59, Frame 227, Hotchkiss Papers, LC, makes it clear he was not involved in firing his two guns from Moore's knoll.

17. Whitehead, "Historic Scene"; Moore, *Charlottesville ... Arty.,* 8; Carrington in Roll 59, Frame 227, Hotchkiss Papers, LC. Despite some intimations that the guns stayed west of the house, the Herndon memoir (Private Collection of R. H. Moore) reports being "in front of Dr. Kemper's lawn." The two unengaged guns doubtless did remain farther west. Herndon was Kemper's great-nephew and therefore an impeccable witness about location in a familiar yard.

18. Dabney to Hotchkiss, May 1896, Hotchkiss Papers, LC; Carrington account in his file at VMI; untitled Moore memoir, Moore Papers, UNC; Moore, "Clarke County Men at Port Republic," 4, Moore Papers, UNC; Moore, "Stonewall Jackson's Escape," Moore Correspondence, HL. Some of Moore's accounts include two small anomalies for this phase. He once stated an erroneous impression that the two guns from the first corner followed him down to the hollow at the end of Main Street. In another he implied that the second cavalry advance came against the second position, not the first. Other evidence and his own better versions rule out those notions. For instance, L. W. Cox to Hotchkiss, August 17, 1896, demonstrates that Cox and his mates did not move.

19. Whitehead, "Historic Scene"; Dabney to Hotchkiss, May 1896, Hotchkiss Papers, LC.

20. Untitled Moore memoir, Moore Papers, UNC.

21. Johnson, *Robert Lewis Dabney,* 265-66; cf., Dabney, *Life,* 412.

22. W. F. Davis memoir, 50-51, U.Va.; Dabney to Hotchkiss, May 1896 and undated 1896, Hotchkiss Papers, LC; Moore, *Charlottesville ... Arty.,* 8. Dinwiddie in Whitehead, "Historic Scene," said that all four guns arrived; by all other accounts only two fit into the position and fired.

23. Crutchfield to Dabney, May 1896, and Dabney to Hotchkiss, May 1896, Hotchkiss Papers, LC; Carrington account in his file, VMI; Moore, *Charlottesville ... Arty.,* 8.

24. W. F. Davis memoir, 50-52, U.Va.; P. C. Kaylor to G. E. May, Dec. 6, 1929, SPRP; Moore, *Charlottesville ... Arty.,* 9, 69; Dabney to Hotchkiss, May 1896, Hotchkiss Papers, LC.

25. Herndon, "Infantry and Cavalry Service"; Herndon memoir, Private Collection of Robert H. Moore; Carrington account, Roll 59, Frame 227, Hotchkiss Papers, LC; Whitehead, "Historic Scene."

26. Dabney to Hotchkiss, May 1896, Hotchkiss Papers, LC; W. F. Davis memoir, 52-53, U.Va.; Moore, *Charlottesville ... Arty.,* 61-62.

27. Moore, "Stonewall Jackson's Escape," Moore Correspondence, HL; Moore, "Clarke County Men at Port Republic," Moore Papers, UNC; Crutchfield to Dabney, May 1896, Hotchkiss Papers, LC.

28. Whitehead, "Historic Scene"; untitled Moore memoir, Moore Papers, UNC.

29. Moore, "Stonewall Jackson's Escape," Moore Correspondence, HL; untitled Moore memoir, 4, Moore Papers, UNC; Moore, "Clarke County Men at Port Republic," 4-5, Moore Papers, UNC; Whitehead, "Historic Scene"; Dabney to Hotchkiss, May 1896, Hotchkiss Papers, LC.

30. *OR,* 713, 762; Moore, *Cannoneer,* 68-69. Moore remembered firing toward Yost's Hill initially. This Edward A. "Ned" Moore is the third unrelated Moore to crop up within a short space. Avoid confusing him with S.J.C. and Cleon.

31. Douglas, *I Rode,* 86; *OR,* 773; M. A. Jackson, *Memoirs,* 516; Humphreys letter, Private Collection of David Q. Updike.

32. Frye, *Recollections,* 171; Krick, *Lee's Colonels,* 146; Douglas, *I Rode,* 57; Green, "Letter and Cover," 34-35.

33. Moore, *Cannoneer,* 69; *OR,* 772; Howard, *Recollections,* 122; Wood, *The War,* 59. Wood reported two killed and others wounded by artillery. Dabney, *Life,* 412, had the 37th approach at "a double-quick," but Dabney was not present or as reliable as Moore.

34. Wood, *The War,* 59-60; LaTourette, "War Time Incident"; Orr recollections, VSA; *OR,* 773.

35. May, "Port Republic," 82, JMU; Dabney, *Life,* 412-13. Confederate descriptions of Gildea's gun "in the south end of the bridge" and being moved "directly into the mouth of the Bridge" are in *OR,* 719, and G. Campbell Brown memorandum, TSLA.

36. The seven paragraphs describing Gildea's ordeal are based on the detailed accounts in James Gildea memoir, 17-20, Barnett Papers, WRHS; and Gildea to T. J. Burke, undated 1896, Hotchkiss Papers, LC. The only other source used is Moore, "Clarke County Men at Port Republic," 7, Moore Papers, UNC. Moore quoted Gildea's explanation of the tangential shot cited first in the final paragraph. A contemporary Confederate account describing Gildea's lone stand is "Near View of the Yankees."

37. M. A. Jackson, *Memoirs,* 516; May, "Port Republic," 82, JMU; *OR,* 773.

38. James Gildea memoir, 19, Barnett Papers, WRHS; John S. Apperson letter, June 10, Black Papers, VPI; Walker, *Memorial* 221; *OR,* 773, 713. Walker claims that Fulkerson led from "not less than fifty yards in advance of his men," which is hardly credible.

39. Walker, *Memorial,* 221; *OR,* 719; M. A. Jackson, *Memoirs,* 516; Orr recollections, VSA; Dabney, *Life,* 413; Wood, *The War,* 60. Taliaferro's suggestion (in M. A. Jackson) that Gildea never fired seems at odds with his official report (*OR,* 773), which said the men "were exposed to considerable fire from the enemy's guns" as they went down the hillside. That, however, might refer to longer-range rounds from Yost's Hill. Moore (*Cannoneer,* 69) thought that the 37th's front rank had been killed.

40. Havron, "Stonewall," 204; May, "Port Republic," 82, JMU; May, "Battle of Port Republic," 97–98; LaTourette, "War Time Incident."

41. Moore, *Cannoneer,* 69–70.

42. Dabney, *Life,* 413; Havron, "Stonewall," 204.

43. *OR,* 713; May, "Port Republic," 82, JMU; Huffman, *Ups and Downs,* 49; Kauffman diary, UNC; Fravel, "Valley Campaign," 419; Yeary, *Reminiscences,* 669. Fravel reported one man in the 10th killed by artillery on the slope above the bridge. Sam Moore twice reported having heard that the 10th crossed before the 37th but that is clearly in error (Moore, "Clarke County Men at Port Republic," 7, Moore Papers, UNC; Moore, "Stonewall Jackson's Escape," Moore Correspondence, HL).

44. *OR,* 773–74; Rankin, *37th Virginia,* 109. Crutchfield (*OR,* 728) specified that the bridge gun was a six-pounder.

45. Orr recollections, VSA; untitled Moore memoir, Moore Papers, UNC.

46. P. C. Kaylor to G. E. May, Dec. 6, 1929, SPRP; Orr recollections, VSA.

47. Wilson, *Itinerary of the Seventh Ohio,* 162; *OR,* 698, 683.

48. *OR,* 699; May, "Port Republic," 83, JMU; James Gildea memoir, 23, Barnett Papers, WRHS.

49. James Gildea memoir, 23, Barnett Papers, WRHS; May, "Battle of Port Republic," 98; *OR,* 699.

50. May, "Battle of Port Republic," 97–98; May, "Port Republic," 60, JMU.

51. James Gildea memoir, 20, 24, Barnett Papers, WRHS; Buck, *Old Confeds,* 37.

52. Jim Gildea's perilous escape, which serves as prototype for many another Federal experience that morning, is reconstructed from pages 20–24 of his memoir, Barnett Papers, WRHS. A briefer parallel version is in Gildea to T. J. Burke, undated during 1896, Hotchkiss Papers, LC.

53. Crutchfield to Dabney, May 1896, Hotchkiss Papers, LC.

54. May, "Port Republic," 84, JMU; McGuire to Hotchkiss, May 28, 1896, Hotchkiss Papers, LC; P. C. Kaylor to G. E. May, Dec. 6, 1929, SPRP.

55. Willis, "Letter," 162–63.

56. William Allan memoir, 136, UNC; James Gildea memoir, 19, Barnett Papers, WRHS; Wilson, *Itinerary of the Seventh Ohio,* 162; Moore, *Rebellion Record,* V, 113.

57. *OR,* 699; Ohio Roster Commission, *Official Roster,* X, 430–35.

58. L. W. Cox to Hotchkiss, August 17, 1895, Hotchkiss Papers, LC; Moore, *Charlottesville ... Arty.,* 9; Carrington in Roll 59, Frame 227, Hotchkiss Papers, LC. Colonel Thomas S. Garnett, whose regiment was encamped above North River, wrote that captures in this affair included "27 prisoners and 17 horses" (Garnett to father, July 2, 1862, at FNMP). Garnett may have included Northern infantry prisoners.

59. The Hotchkiss quotation did not survive editing for the version later printed. It is in the contemporary ms. journal in Box 1, Hotchkiss Papers, LC.

60. Moore, "Stonewall Jackson's Escape," Moore correspondence, HL; Moore, "Clarke County Men at Port Republic," Moore Papers, UNC.

61. Taliaferro, "How History Is Written"; Harman letters, Hotchkiss Papers, LC; Hotchkiss to S.J.C. Moore, Nov. 23, 1891, Moore Papers, UNC.

62. John Apperson letter, June 10, Black Papers, VPI; *OR,* 728.

Chapter 6: The Power of High Ground and Artillery

1. Winscott, "From the 7th"; List diary, IHS; Rawling, *First ... Virginia,* 93; Thomson, *Seventh Indiana,* 99–100.

2. Winscott, "From the 7th"; Davis, "7th Indiana," ISL; Skidmore, *Billy Davis,* 143; Hadley, "Indiana Soldier," 212; *OR,* 699.

3. Rawling, *First ... Virginia,* 93; Bates, *Pennsylvania Volunteers,* II, 1308; Winscott, "From the 7th."

4. *OR,* 728; List diary, IHS; O. T., "Battle at Port Republic."

5. Hadley, "Indiana Soldier," 212; "Letter ... [7th Indiana]."

6. Skidmore, *Billy Davis,* 143; Davis, "7th Indiana," ISL; Winscott, "From the 7th."

7. Rawling, *First ... Virginia,* 93; Winscott, "From the 7th"; *OR,* 699.

Notes

8. Davis, "7th Indiana," ISL; *OR*, 699; Winscott, "From the 7th."

9. Waddell, "Cross Keys," HRHS. This local man (1985) called the knoll above the bridge "Fisher's Hill and the bluffs overlooking New Haven."

10. *OR*, 739, 762.

11. *OR*, 727-28, 774; Fravel, "Valley Campaign," 419.

12. Howard, *Recollections*, 122-23; *OR*, 759, 739-40; Humphreys letter, Private Collection of David Q. Updike.

13. *OR*, 740, 749-51. The 27th Virginia remained with Carpenter's Battery all day (*OR*, 752; Kearns diary, VHS).

14. Humphreys letter, Private Collection of David Q. Updike; Hotchkiss, *Make Me a Map*, 54. Jackson (*OR*, 713) did not attempt to estimate a precise time to match Humphreys's five minutes: he wrote "In a short time the infantry followed the cavalry."

15. Moore, "General Jackson at Port Republic"; Apperson letter, June 10, Black Papers, VPI; Evans, *Confederate Military History*, III, 259; Cartmell, *Shenandoah*, 344; J. F. Minor memoir, U.Va.

16. *OR*, 740.

17. Howard, *Recollections*, 123.

18. *OR*, 759, 740, 713, 728; Winder diary, MHS; Humphreys letter, Private Collection of David Q. Updike. Examination of the ground shows that Jackson, Winder, and Crutchfield reported the one-mile distance accurately. Humphreys's quote about four miles must refer to the entire Federal withdrawal, from the bridge to their final resting point.

19. Dabney, *Life*, 413-14; Slaughter, *Randolph Fairfax*, 26; Kearns diary, VHS; White, *Sketches*, 89.

20. *OR*, 728, 731; Evans, *Confederate Military History*, III, 259; anonymous Union map, NA. Hotchkiss's assertion in Evans that Confederates took up positions "opposite Lewiston" is borne out by the Union map, which shows "enemies Battery" nearly that far east. The map is crude and depicts June 9 action, but the Southern battery shown must refer to June 8, since none of Jackson's guns were near there on the 9th.

21. *OR*, 762, 769-70. The rest of the brigade to which the 1st Battalion belonged, which was commanded by Col. John M. Patton, remained near New Haven in general reserve. It preceded the 1st Battalion in the move to Cross Keys (*OR*, 766, 768).

22. *OR*, 740, 744-45, 747.

23. *OR*, 740, 756-57; J. S. Apperson letter, June 10, Black Papers, VPI; Walker, *Memorial*, 402.

24. The salvage effort details come from these sources: Davis, "7th Indiana," ISL; Skidmore, *Billy Davis*, 143; *OR*, 691, 699; Keily file, Private Collection of Brian C. Pohanka; Thomson, *Seventh Indiana*, 102.

25. Orr recollections, VSA; *OR*, 774; Fravel, "Vailey Campaign," 419; May, "Port Republic," 82, JMU; Kauffman diary, UNC.

26. Neese, *Three Years*, 72; Williams diary, VHS; *OR*, 719; Lathrop, *Atlas*, 39; Hotchkiss, *Make Me a Map*, 54; Hotchkiss to S.J.C. Moore, August 3, 1892, Moore Papers, UNC. General Taliaferro reported (*OR*, 774) that he ordered Carrington's Battery to take position on the hill in Port Republic—which it of course did—held stoutly without advice from him during the recent crisis.

27. T. T. Munford to Hotchkiss, August 23, 1896, Hotchkiss Papers, LC; McDonald reminiscence, UNC; Dabney, *Life*, 415.

28. William Allan memoir, 136-37, UNC; John A. Harman letters, Hotchkiss Papers, LC.

29. *OR*, 695; Wood, *Seventh Regiment*, 115.

30. Ray, "Journal," 60; Clarke, "Some One Has Blundered"; *OR*, 695; Durkee diary and Parmeter diary, OHS; SeCheverell, *Twenty-ninth Ohio*, 45. Accounts agree on the 4 A.M. departure, but the breakfast halt varies from 6:30 (SeCheverell) to 8 A.M. (Durkee). Parmeter estimated the distance to Port Republic as seven miles rather than Tyler's six.

31. *OR*, 691, 695; Davis, "7th Indiana," ISL; Huntington, "Operations," 328. Unlike most matters involving clock time, Tyler's arrival at about 2 P.M. is attested unanimously.

32. Durkee diary and Parmeter diary, OHS; SeCheverell, *Twenty-ninth Ohio*, 45; Col. S. H. Dunning letter in Moore, *Rebellion Record*, V, 112; Fairfax diary, Chicago Historical Society.

33. Parmeter diary, OHS; *OR*, 691.

34. Dunning letter in Moore, *Rebellion Record*, V, 112; Fairfax diary, Chicago Historical Society; Ray, "Journal," 60.

35. Clarke, "Some One Has Blundered."

36. Thomson, *Seventh Indiana*, 100; Davis, "7th Indiana," ISL; James Gildea memoir, Barnett Papers, WRHS.

37. *OR*, 691, 695; Wood, *Seventh Regiment*, 116.

38. Huntington, "Operations," 329.

39. *OR*, 695-96, 683; Davis, "7th Indiana," ISL.

40. Fisher, *Family of John Lewis*, 87-88.

41. John F. Lewis claim on behalf of his father, Southern Claims Commission Case Files, NA; "Port Republic and the Lewises," iv, 3, Private Collection of Lewis F. Fisher.

42. Depositions of Abram James and John F. Lewis and other documents in the John F. Lewis claim, Southern Claims Commission Case Files, NA. For pungent local comment on Lewis's wartime iron manufacturing compared to his postwar pro-Northern behavior, see G. E. May, "Port Republic," JMU.

43. Baugher's file in Confederate Papers Relating to Citizens or Business Firms, M346, NA; "Port Republic and the Lewises," 6, Private Collection of Lewis F. Fisher. Strenuous efforts by the United States to prove misbehavior—such as Baugher's accepting money for corn taken from him—in order to avoid paying claims on that basis led to arranging hundreds of thousands of documents. That work is of tremendous importance to historians of the war diligent enough to use the documents.

44. Sipe recollections, HRHS.

45. "Port Republic and the Lewises," 3, 9-10, Private Collection of Lewis F. Fisher.

46. 1860 Rockingham Co. census, 609. The house name is pronounced *buh-GO-tuh*, rather than like the name of the Colombian capital.

47. Clara V. Strayer diary, HRHS.

48. "Register of Deaths, Rockingham County, 1862-1870," Roll 46, Rockingham Co. Records, VSA; Empsweller's CSR, M324, Roll 75, NA; Armstrong, *7th Virginia,* 141, 247. Military records show Empsweller's death on the 8th and 9th, but the civilian record from his mother verifies June 8 as correct. The surname is spelled several different ways; the family's illiteracy makes the correct one debatable. It is *Empsweller* in the county register.

49. Orr recollections, VSA.

50. McGuire to Hotchkiss, June 12, 1896, and Dabney to Hotchkiss, May 1896, Hotchkiss Papers, LC.

51. Moore, "Through the Shadow," 16; Whitehead, "Historic Scene."

52. Cooke, *Wearing of the Gray,* 38.

53. G. Campbell Brown memorandum, TSLA; *OR,* 801-2; Taylor, *Destruction,* 72-73.

54. Howard, *Recollections,* 123-24.

55. Howard, *Recollections,* 124. Confederates around Port Republic wrote of listening with mixed expectations to the roar from Cross Keys. Chaplain A. C. Hopkins of the 4th Virginia wrote in his diary (VHS) of Ewell's "hard fought battle of about five hours." Jackson could hear the noise less well than most.

56. Dabney, "Stonewall Jackson," 148-49; Dabney, *Life,* 414-15.

57. *OR,* vol. XI, pt. 3, 582-83, and vol. XII, pt. 3, 908.

58. G. Campbell Brown memorandum, TSLA.

Chapter 7: Frémont Lumbers into Action

1. *OR,* 785. Sunrise in Richmond came at 4:44 A.M., according to *Richardson's Almanac.* Westward in the Valley, sunrise would be some minutes later.

2. *OR,* 785.

3. Gardner diary, USAMHI; Bromley diary, OHS; Wildman diary, OHS; *OR,* 669, 785.

4. Wheeler, *In Memoriam,* 335.

5. Tracy, "Frémont's Pursuit," 332; Thomson and Rauch, *Bucktails,* 162-63.

6. T. T. Munford to Hotchkiss, August 23, 1896, Hotchkiss Papers, LC; Krick, *Lee's Colonels,* 166; Thomas Evans diary, OHS; *OR,* 669.

7. Tracy, "Frémont's Pursuit," 332-33; Polsley letter, June 10, LC; C. V. Harrison letter, June 17, Hess Collection, U. of Mich.; Reader memoir, USAMHI; Reader, *Second Virginia Infantry,* 169; Bisel diary, East Carolina U.; G. Campbell Brown reminiscence, TSLA; T. T. Munford account, Munford-Ellis Papers, Duke; "A Visit to the Country."

8. Hess, *Heartland,* 325-26; Yancey, "Civil War Letter," 36; "Some Historic Soil," SPRP.

9. Confederate Papers Relating to Citizens or Business Firms, NA; Southern Claims Commission Case Files, NA.

10. Lossing, *Pictorial History,* II, 396; Fontaine, *My Life,* 110. (Lamar Fontaine, the cavalryman who rode up to the church, proved at times to be a less-than-reliable source.) The building standing in 1995 has been converted into a community center and clearly postdates the mid-nineteenth century. The local tradition that the building contains the shell of the original church is contradicted by the typescript "Some Historic Soil" (SPRP), which dates from about 1900.

11. Imboden, "Stonewall Jackson," 291. One lone account puts the 1st Maryland with the 15th Alabama at the church—an unidentified (evidently nineteenth-century) newspaper clipping in the Ammen compilation, USAMHI; it certainly is in error.

12. McClendon, *Recollections,* 64-65; Oates, *The War,* 102; *OR,* 795; Krick, *Lee's Colonels,* 375.

13. McClendon, *Recollections*, 65; Oates, *The War*, 102.

14. Oates, *The War*, 102; Yeary, *Reminiscences of the Boys*, 463.

15. McClendon, *Recollections*, 65; Culpepper, "15th Alabama"; Oates, *The War*, 102.

16. *OR*, 795; Oates, *The War*, 102.

17. *OR*, 781.

18. McClendon, *Recollections*, 65; *OR*, 795; Oates, *The War*, 102.

19. Culpepper, "15th Alabama"; McClendon, *Recollections*, 65; Oates, *The War*, 102, 745.

20. Yeary, *Reminiscences of the Boys*, 463; Oates, *The War*, 102, 632-33, 673; McClendon, *Recollections*, 65; *OR*, 795.

21. *OR*, 795, 784; Oates, *The War*, 102, 632, 745.

22. Yeary, *Reminiscences of the Boys*, 463; Mathis, *Land of the Living*, 45.

23. Culpepper, "15th Alabama"; Oates, *The War*, 102, 756-67; McClendon, *Recollections*, 65-66.

24. G. Campbell Brown memorandum, TSLA; *OR*, 781; Webb, "Gen. Fremont's Command."

25. Hess, *The Heartland*, 338. Hess uses a photo of a small wooden church "built in 1887, and used until 1920." Local lore says that the second church incorporated elements of the Civil War structure. The modern stone-and-brick building is entirely new. The pastor of the church was churlish and uncommunicative about its history as I did research for this book—the only such response I met with in dealing with many dozens of Valley people.

26. Evans, *Confederate Military History*, III, 255; "Squarest Battle."

27. Robson, *One-Legged Rebel*, 42; *SHSP*, IX, 280; Taylor, *Southern Baptists*, 30; Armstrong, *25th Virginia*, 33; Jones, *Christ in the Camp*, 228, 251. The 44th Virginia also was assembled for church (McIlwaine, *Memories*, 193). "Musketry" was (and still is) used to describe Civil War infantry fire, even when later in the war most of it came from rifles (often termed "rifled muskets").

28. Clark, "Jackson at Cross Keys."

29. *OR*, 781; G. Campbell Brown memorandum and reminiscence, both at TSLA.

30. *OR*, 781; Webb, "Battle of Cross Keys"; Dabney, *Life*, 416.

31. *OR*, 782, 795; "Visit to the Country."

32. *OR*, 795; G. Campbell Brown memorandum and reminiscence, both at TSLA.

33. Coble reminiscence, NCDAH; Krick, *Lee's Colonels*, 230; Wallace letter, March 31, 1863, WVU; G. Campbell Brown reminiscence, TSLA. Captain Alfred R. Courtney was present with the army and may actually have commanded the guns, but everyone spoke of Latimer's conspicuous presence.

34. Evans, *Confederate Military History*, II, 80.

35. *OR*, 795.

36. *OR*, 732.

37. Myers, *Comanches*, 65.

38. Washington Hands Notebook, MHS.

39. G. Campbell Brown to mother, 17th day of an illegible month (likely June) in 1862, Polk-Brown-Ewell Papers, UNC.

40. "Battery I," Barnett Papers, WRHS; Evans memoir, LC.

41. A nice summary of the situation facing Frémont in this regard is in Waddell, "Cross Keys," HRHS.

42. Tracy, "Fremont's Pursuit," 333.

43. Hotchkiss in Evans, *Confederate Military History*, III, 256; Tracy, "Fremont's Pursuit," 334.

44. Kearsey, *Shenandoah Valley Campaign*, 34.

Chapter 8: The Roar of Artillery

1. *OR*, 781; Taylor, *Destruction*, 72.

2. Paulus, *Papers of . . . Milroy*, 45.

3. Tracy, "Fremont's Pursuit," 333-34.

4. Thomas, *Doles-Cook Brigade*, 206; Evans, *Confederate Military History*, III, 256.

5. *OR*, 789-90; Krick, *Lee's Colonels*, 74, 94. The 1860 census (Prince Edward Co., 888) showed hotel-keeper Cobb's net worth as $25,400—a substantial sum in that year.

6. Neese, *Three Years*, 73; Thomas, *Doles-Cook*, 206; G. Campbell Brown reminiscence, TSLA: *OR*, 728, 781; Wheeler, *In Memoriam*, 335; Dabney, *Life*, 416; Tracy, "Fremont's Pursuit," 334; Paulus, *Papers of . . . Milroy*, 48.

7. Dabney, *Life*, 416; G. Campbell Brown memorandum and reminiscence, both at TSLA.

8. *OR*, 782; Walker, *Memorial, VMI*, 332.

9. Eli S. Coble reminiscence, NCDAH.

10. Lightsey, *Veteran's Story*, 14.

11. Brunk, *Hartman*, 62.

12. Tracy, "Fremont's Pursuit," 334; Moore, *June 1862*, unnumbered leaves.

13. Wheeler, *In Memoriam*, 335. Residents on the field in 1991 had no recollection of any old building near the Armentrout site. The house apparently stood a bit north and west of the extant school building, which has for years been a residence but still looks like a turn-of-the-century schoolhouse. Mr. Lawrence D. Good, who owned the ground, told me March 6, 1991, that the school was built between about 1900 and 1910. Good said that far more military relics have come out of the hillside sloping from the school-house toward the Flory house site and the creek than from the rest of the battlefield combined. The finds in the area have included a great many solid shot—the least effective form of artillery round.

14. Paulus, *Papers of . . . Milroy*, 45; "Battery I," Barnett Papers, WRHS; Evans memoir, LC.

15. Webb, "Gen. Fremont's Command."

16. *OR*, 795; Myers, *Comanches*, 65.

17. Clark, *N.C. Regiments*, II, 147-48, and IV, 225-30.

18. Clark, *N.C. Regiments*, IV, 232; Nisbet, *Four Years*, 93.

19. Fontaine, *My Life*, 110-11; Hewes, "Turner Ashby's Courage." Fontaine's accounts of his war experiences are not always entirely reliable, but this episode matches the known facts and rings true.

20. Culpepper, "15th Alabama."

21. Hess, *Heartland*, 338-39.

22. "Fremont's Army in Rockingham." Mrs. Mary Catherine Jarrels has lived in Mrs. Pence's house since 1921. The western two thirds of the building is original.

23. Clark, *N.C. Regiments*, IV, 232.

24. Nisbet, *Four Years*, 93; Culpepper, "15th Alabama"; *OR*, 795.

25. McClendon, *Recollections*, 66; "Sixteenth Mississippi Regiment."

26. *OR*, 781, 791.

27. *OR*, 791; Krick, *Lee's Colonels*, 124. For the sources on Walker's quarrel with Jackson, see Krick, *Cedar Mountain*, 58, 406. The transcript of Walker's court-martial at VMI, in which he evidently received a raw deal, is in the files there. Jackson's support for Walker's promotion is in a May 9, 1863, letter by A. P. Hill in Walker's CSR, M331, NA.

28. G. Campbell Brown memorandum and reminiscence, both at TSLA.

29. *OR*, 669-71.

Chapter 9: The Slaughter of the 8th New York

1. Webb, "Battle of Cross Keys" ("an open wheat field"); Oates, *The War*, 103 ("a field of buckwheat 150 yards wide"); G. Campbell Brown reminiscence, TSLA ("about 150 yards wide"); Nachtigall, *75th Regiment*, 16 ("a gradually ascending field of clover"); Nisbet, *Four Years*, 93 ("a clover-field"); "16th Mississippi," 11, Tulane ("a wheat field"); Clark, *N.C. Regiments*, IV, 232 ("in wheat just headed out"); McClendon, *Recollections*, 66 ("about two hundred yards"). Hotchkiss's Cross Keys maps are especially credible because six days after the battle, he and J. Keith Boswell rode over the site and "sketched the battle field for a map" (Hotchkiss, *Make Me a Map*, 56). Published versions of the map are far less detailed than the original, which is published as an illustration herein. All versions show the slight slant in the line.

2. Culpepper, "15th Alabama"; *OR*, 795; Oates, *The War*, 103; "Squarest Battle of the War" ("an hour before noon"); *Quitman Guards*, 22 (about 2 P.M.); G. Campbell Brown reminiscence, TSLA ("about noon or a little after"). Buschbeck, "Official Report," implies that it was 2 P.M. or later when Confederates, having repulsed the 8th New York, attacked toward the Federal batteries (see the next chapter). Busch-beck time for the 8th's attack then would be about 1 P.M.

3. Lee, "Battle of Cross Keys," 490. Stahel reported no casualties for the 39th, 41st, or 45th New York, but they suffered at least 83, as is demonstrated in Appendix A, based on New York records. A few days earlier, the strength of the 45th New York had been 29 officers and 484 men (RG 94, NA, Office of Adj. Genl., New York [45th Inf.]). That number offers a reasonable estimate for the 45th's unfortunate sister regiment. The ethnic makeup of the 8th will be documented later in this chapter.

4. "Battle Near Port Republic"; *OR*, 798. The first is a contemporary letter by a Confederate officer that is accurate on casualties, so the strength figure probably is good too.

5. *OR*, 796; Clark, *N.C. Regiments*, IV, 232; Webb, "Battle of Cross Keys." Webb of *The New York Times* viewed the advance of the 8th as being "in pursuit."

6. Clark, *N.C. Regiments*, IV, 232, and II, 147; Nisbet, *Four Years*, 93.

7. Crapsey to "Kind Friend," June 14, Potter County Histl. Soc.

8. *Quitman Guards,* 22; Clark *N.C. Regiments,* IV, 232; *OR,* 796; McClendon, *Recollections,* 66.

9. Clark, *N.C. Regiments,* II, 147–48; Hamilton, "21st Georgia."

10. Waddell, "Cross Keys," HRHS; Clark, *N.C. Regiments,* II, 148. Waddell cites a turn-of-the-century visit to the field by a veteran of the 5th Virginia who lived nearby and recounted an army tradition about the leaves as camouflage.

11. Nisbet, *Four Years,* 93; "16th Mississippi," 10, Tulane; McClendon, *Recollections,* 66.

12. Clark, *N.C. Regiments,* II, 148; McClendon, *Recollections,* 66.

13. Yeary, *Reminiscences of the Boys,* 463.

14. Oates, *The War,* 103; *OR,* 798; Clark, *N.C. Regiments,* II, 148.

15. Oates, *The War,* 103; Clark, *N.C. Regiments,* II, 148; Krick, *Lee's Colonels,* 270.

16. McGuire, *Confederate Cause and Conduct,* 197.

17. "16th Mississippi," 11, Tulane ("about thirty steps"); Clark, *N.C. Regiments,* IV, 232 ("within sixty or seventy yards") and II, 148 ("not more than forty yards"); McClendon, *Recollections,* 66 ("within seventy-five or one hundred yards"); "Visit to the Country" ("40 yards"); Culpepper, "15th Alabama" ("50 or 60 yards"); Nisbet, *Four Years,* 93 ("forty yards"); *OR,* 796 ("within fifty steps"). Trimble himself said "about sixty paces" (Allan, *History of the Campaign,* 154n.).

18. Kaylor, "Cross Keys Battlefield" HRHS; unidentified contemporary clipping in Ammen compilation, USAMHI; Clark, *N.C. Regiments,* II, 147–48; "From Stonewall Jackson." G. Campbell Brown memorandum, TSLA, shows that Ewell and the army recognized the preeminent role of the 21st Georgia, which "bore the brunt of the fight, & its fire was peculiarly deadly."

19. *Quitman Guards,* 22; Kirkpatrick diary, UT; Wilson letter, June 15, MDAH.

20. McClendon, *Recollections,* 66; Yeary, *Boys in Gray,* 463.

21. Oates, *The War,* 103; Culpepper, "15th Alabama."

22. "Visit to the Country"; *OR,* 796, 799.

23. McClendon, *Recollections,* 67; Nisbet, *Four Years,* 93; Hamilton, "21st Georgia"; Lightsey, *Veteran's Story,* 15; Wight memoir, VHS.

24. Nachtigall, *75th Regiment,* 16; Webb, "Battle of Cross Keys."

25. Nisbet, *Four Years,* 93; Hamilton, "21st Georgia"; "16th Mississippi," 11, Tulane; Clark, *N.C. Regiments,* IV, 232; Lightsey, *Veteran's Story,* 15; Yeary, *Boys in Gray,* 463; Thomas, *Doles-Cooks,* 350.

26. *OR,* 795–96, 782; G. Campbell Brown memorandum, TSLA; Clark, *N.C. Regiments,* IV, 232; Dabney, *Life,* 417; Hamilton, "Private Dispatch."

27. Richardson letter, June 14, GDAH; Nisbet, *Four Years,* 93.

28. Webb, "The Battle of Cross Keys."

29. *OR,* 782, 798–99.

30. *OR,* 664; N.Y. Adjutant General, *Registers,* XVIII, 439–64.

31. "From Stonewall Jackson"; Lightsey, *Veteran's Story,* 15.

32. "The Battle of Cross Keys." For a German-speaking woman damning the German invaders as they neared action, see Svenson, "Backyard Battlefield," 16.

33. "Battle Near Port Republic."

34. Webb, "Gen. Fremont's Command"; "16th Mississippi," 12, Tulane.

35. *OR,* 784.

36. Wilson letter, June 15, MDAH; Lightsey, *Veteran's Story,* 15–16; Kirkpatrick diary, UT; Sparkman obituary in *Confederate Veteran,* XXI (1913), 452.

37. *OR,* 783, 798; Waddell, "Cross Keys," HRHS.

Chapter 10: Trimble's Attack

1. *OR,* 796; Trimble in Allan, *History of the Campaign,* 154n.; Clark, *N.C. Regiments,* IV, 232.

2. *OR,* 796. Ewell's emissary to Trimble was Thomas T. Turner (G. Campbell Brown reminiscence, TSLA).

3. Ewell to John M. Patton, May 12, 1867, Box 1, Folder 19, Polk-Brown-Ewell Papers, UNC. Ewell's comments may have referred to his attempts to coordinate a wide advance later in the afternoon, but that is not certain.

4. *OR,* 796; Havron, "Stonewall," 205.

5. Oates, *The War,* 103; Allan, *History of the Campaign,* 155n.

6. Lee, "Battle of Cross Keys," 490, puts the 41st New York on the right with the 27th. Given subsequent events, it must have been to the right *of* the 27th. Thomson and Rauch, *Bucktails,* 163-64, provides the best Northern analysis of unit alignments. Crapsey to "Kind Friend," June 14, Potter County Histl. Soc., identified Buell's guns as "4 rifled Cannon."

7. Bates, *Pennsylvania Volunteers*, I, 385.

8. Crapsey letter, June 14, Potter County Histl. Soc.; Thomson and Rauch, *Bucktails*, 163–64.

9. *OR*, 796; Thomson and Rauch, *Bucktails*, 164.

10. Crapsey letter, June 14, Potter County Histl. Soc.; Oates, *The War*, 103, 691–92.

11. Mathis, *Land of the Living*, 45; Houghton, *Two Boys*, 29; Oates, *The War*, 739, 684.

12. Oates, *The War*, 622; "Casper W. Boyd," 296–98.

13. Oates, *The War*, 103, 692–93.

14. *OR*, 796; Oates, *The War*, 103.

15. *Quitman Guards*, 22; *OR*, 796; "16th Mississippi," 11, Tulane.

16. *OR*, 796, 799.

17. *Quitman Guards*, 22; "16th Mississippi," 11–12, Tulane; Richmond *Dispatch*, June 19, 1862. Captain Nisbet of the 21st Georgia (*Four Years*, 94) also called Posey "badly wounded."

18. *OR*, 799.

19. Harry Lewis to "Dear Mother," July 30, Harry Lewis Papers, UNC. Groves's identity and full name come from M232, Roll 16, NA.

20. Buschbeck, "Official Report"; Thomson and Rauch, *Bucktails*, 164, 165n. Buschbeck said Buell had eight guns, but there were probably only four (see the Crapsey letter in note 6, this chapter); he probably counted Schirmer or even Dilger.

21. Nisbet, *Four Years*, 93–94.

22. Nisbet, *Four Years*, 94; Oates, *The War*, 103–104; *Quitman Guards*, 22; "16th Mississippi," 11, Tulane.

23. Hightower letter, June 13, GDAH; Hamilton, "21st Georgia"; Richardson letter, June 14, GDAH.

24. Nisbet, *Four Years*, 94; Hamilton, "21st Georgia"; Hightower letter, June 13, GDAH.

25. Oates, *The War*, 104.

26. *OR*, 796, 783.

27. *OR*, 799; Tracy, "Fremont's Pursuit," 339. Tracy said that Dunka fell "with two bullets through his breast," so Private Long had some help. The captured order is in *OR*, 785. Long's war ended when he surrendered in Maryland in Sept. 1864 (Henderson, *Soldiers of Georgia*, II, 855).

28. Davis, "Death of Lieut. Mack."

29. Nisbet, *Four Years*, 52; Henderson, *Soldiers of Georgia*, II, 915.

30. Nisbet, *Four Years*, 95–96; Henderson, *Soldiers of Georgia*, II, 927, 933.

31. Lee, "Battle of Cross Keys," 490–91; Thomson and Rauch, *Bucktails*, 165; Webb, "Battle of Cross Keys."

32. Tracy, "Fremont's Pursuit," 335; Paulus, *Papers of . . . Milroy*, 48–49.

33. Webb, "Battle of Cross Keys"; Thomson and Rauch, *Bucktails*, 165.

34. "16th Mississippi," 11, Tulane; *Quitman Guards*, 23.

35. Frank diary, LC; *OR*, 664; Phisterer, *New York*, III, 2189, 2238, 2306. The *OR* casualties in the 27th total 92, but Bates, *Penna. Volunteers*, I, 385, reports 115. The account in the text of the Federals' fight around Buell's Battery focuses on the 27th and the Bucktails because they carried most of the fight, as is evident from both sides' accounts and from casualties, and because it is impossible to determine what the less-engaged units to the Federal right were doing. The hour of Stahel's final withdrawal is as difficult to fix as all other movements on this day. It probably came about 2:30 P.M. Buschbeck of the 27th, in "Official Report," spoke of being within cannon range "for more than six hours," starting at 8 A.M. That matches a 2:30 estimate.

36. Lee, "Battle of Cross Keys," 490; *OR*, 664, 669.

37. *OR*, 669, 672–73; Pula, *Liberty and Justice*, 31.

38. Pula, *Liberty and Justice*, 29, 31.

39. *OR*, 669.

40. *OR*, 669, 673–74

41. *OR*, 674

42. *OR*, 674; Nachtigall, *75th Regiment*, 16–17.

43. *OR*, 671–72.

44. 1860 Rockingham Co. census, 462, NA.

45. *OR*, 791–92; Armstrong, *25th Virginia*, 33–34.

46. Oates, *The War*, 103.

47. *OR*, 796, 792.

48. *OR*, 792; Buck, *Old Confeds*, 35; Armstrong, *25th Virginia*, 34.

49. Buck, *Old Confeds*, 35–36; *OR*, 796, 792.

50. *OR*, 792, 796.

51. Buck, *Old Confeds*, 36; *OR*, 671; Pula, *Liberty and Justice*, 31.

52. *OR,* 792; Buck, *Old Confeds,* 36. Relative alignment of the 25th and 13th is from the ms. map by Hotchkiss in his papers, LC.

53. Buck, "Walker," 35; *OR,* 792, 798.

54. *OR,* 792; Armstrong, *25th Virginia,* 34; Buck, *Old Confeds,* 36-37.

55. *OR,* 670-72; Lee, "Battle of Cross Keys," 490-91. The far left position of the 54th New York is confirmed by the Schluembach manuscript map at FNMP.

56. *OR,* 674; Barnes, *Medical and Surgical,* IV (collation 7), 238.

57. *OR,* 674-75; Bates, *Pennsylvania Volunteers,* II, 917.

58. *OR,* 675, 670, 672-73; Pula, *Liberty and Justice,* 31.

59. *OR,* 792, 796; Armstrong, *25th Virginia,* 34.

60. Hotchkiss, *Make Me a Map,* 56; "James A. Walker," VHS.

61. *OR,* 792, 800; Hotchkiss in Evans, ed., *Confederate Military History,* III, 256; Ewell to A&IG, January 26, 1863, in Walker's CSR, M331, NA.

62. Buck, *Old Confeds,* 36; *OR,* 796.

63. *OR,* 798, 796.

64. Buck, *Old Confeds,* 36. Buck thought the fortunate regiment might have been the 44th Virginia, which was more than a mile away. He obviously had seen the 15th Alabama.

65. *OR,* 670-71.

66. *OR,* 675, 674, 670; Lee, "Battle of Cross Keys," 491. Hamm claimed his retirement covered only 20 yards, a distance of no tactical consequence. A fence 20 yards behind the firing line would have been the place from which to fight in the first place. Bohlen said that the 74th's initial retirement covered 100 yards.

67. *OR,* 672, 670, 664, 673; Krzyzanowski, *Memoirs,* 45; Pula, *For Liberty and Justice,* 31-32. The 58th New York actually lost at least 11 dead (Phisterer, *New York in the War,* 2503).

68. *OR,* 797; Oates, *The War,* 104.

69. *OR,* 673, 670; Webb, "Gen. Fremont's Command"; Pula, *For Liberty and Justice.*

70. Schluembach marginalia, FNMP.

71. *OR,* 664; Wheeler, *In Memoriam,* 336; Phisterer, *New York in the War,* 2063, 2674.

72. Munford to Hotchkiss, August 23, 1896, Reel 49, Hotchkiss Papers, LC; Myers, *Comanches,* 66.

73. *OR,* 781.

Chapter 11: The Fire-Swept Confederate Center

1. *OR,* 728.

2. Coble reminiscence, NCDAH.

3. *OR,* 799.

4. *OR,* 728, 718.

5. *OR,* 717; Barrow diary, USAMHI.

6. Wise, *Long Arm of Lee,* I, 174.

7. Boyd, *Reminiscences,* 14.

8. *OR,* 728, 799.

9. G. Campbell Brown reminiscence, TSLA.

10. *OR,* 728.

11. "Battery I," Barnett Papers, WRHS; Paulus, *Papers of . . . Milroy,* 45; Webb, "Battle of Cross Keys."

12. "Battery I," Barnett Papers, WRHS.

13. "Battery I," Barnett Papers, WRHS; Gardner diary, USAMHI; Frank Bisel diary, East Carolina U.

14. Paulus, *Papers of . . . Milroy,* 48; Webb, "Battle of Cross Keys."

15. *OR,* 665; Paulus, *Papers of . . . Milroy,* 45; Reader, *Second Virginia Infantry,* 170.

16. Webb, "Gen. Fremont's Command."

17. Paulus, *Papers of . . . Milroy,* 45.

18. Evans diary, OHS; Evans memoir, LC; Reader, *Second Virginia Infantry,* 170. Evans's two accounts are virtually identical.

19. Webb, "Battle of Cross Keys"; Paulus, *Papers of . . . Milroy,* 45-46.

20. Evans memoir, LC; Evans diary, OHS.

21. Tracy, "Fremont's Pursuit," 335; Reader, *Second Virginia Infantry,* 170.

22. Paulus, *Papers of . . . Milroy,* 46; Evans diary, OHS.

23. Paulus, *Papers of . . . Milroy,* 46; Barnes, *Medical and Surgical,* V (collation 9), 80; Ohio Roster Comm., *Official Roster,* III, 167–68. The roster entry shows Charlesworth promoted to major in May 1862 and to lieutenant colonel later that year. Since the medical records refer to him as captain, the majority arrived after Cross Keys, with rank from May.

24. Paulus, *Papers of . . . Milroy,* 46; Reader, *Second Virginia Infantry,* 170–71.

25. Webb, "Battle of Cross Keys"; *The Soldier of Indiana,* 463.

26. Paulus, *Papers of . . . Milroy,* 46.

27. G. Campbell Brown reminiscence, TSLA.

28. Scott letter, June 12, Emory U. The usually reliable Hotchkiss showed on his ms. map the 52nd, the 44th, and the 31st Virginia from right to left, right next to the road. That is an obvious error. The first two belonged to Steuart, who was left of Elzey. As the next paragraph (and the next chapter in more detail) in the text shows, the 31st moved during the afternoon to Steuart's left. Hotchkiss's alignment therefore is correct within the regiments, but much too far to the southeast.

29. Chenoweth diary, VHS; James E. Hall, *Diary,* 60; Hoffman report, WVU.

30. James E. Hall, *Diary,* 60.

31. Chenoweth diary, VHS.

32. *OR,* 799; Coble reminiscence, NCDAH.

33. Coble reminiscence, NCDAH.

34. Scott letter, June 12, Emory U.; Henderson, *Soldiers of Georgia,* II, 219.

35. Cook, *Baldwin County,* 338; Clark, "Jackson at Cross Keys"; Scott letter, June 12, Emory U.; 1860 Putnam Co. Census, 378, NA.

36. Clark, "Jackson at Cross Keys."

37. Scott letter, June 12, Emory U.; Griffin diary, Emory U.

38. *OR,* 799; Clewell letter, June 13, 1862, NCDAH.

39. Coble reminiscence, NCDAH.

40. *OR,* 782; G. Campbell Brown memorandum and reminiscence, both at TSLA; Randolph, *Jackson,* 168.

41. G. Campbell Brown reminiscence, TSLA.

42. *OR,* 782.

43. *OR,* 728, 782; Goldsborough, *Maryland Line* (1869), 75; Hands notebook, MHS; T. T. Munford address on Elzey, Munford-Ellis Papers, Duke U. (Miscellany, Box 3); unident. clipping in Ammen compilation, USAMHI; G. Campbell Brown memorandum, TSLA. Ewell (*OR,* 782) said a "rifle-ball" hit Elzey, but the reliable Brown said "a piece of shell." The severity of the wound is unclear. Ewell said it made him leave the field; Munford agreed and used the adjective "seriously"; Brown deprecated the severity ("[he] was well again in a week"). All but one of the sources agree that Elzey's leg was hit. The Ammen clipping put the wound "in the face" and insisted that Elzey was observing one of the left batteries at the time, which does not mesh with other accounts. Perhaps Elzey also suffered a scratch on the face at some point.

44. G. Campbell Brown reminiscence, TSLA.

45. McKim, *Recollections,* 111–15.

46. For kind words about Barbour, see Myers, *Comanches,* 39, and French, *Centennial Tales,* 25–26. The conflict with Early is documented in Barbour's CSR, M331, NA. Jones's drinking problem (Freeman hinted at it in *Lee's Lieutenants* and *OR* contains veiled remarks) is documented later in this book. For Nelson, see Johnson, *University Memorial.* Turner's file at VMI is the best source on him.

47. *OR,* 782; Conner, *Letters,* 115. Conner's fascinating and important book unfortunately is among the rarest of all Confederate memoirs.

48. G. Campbell Brown reminiscence, TSLA; Brown to mother, June 17, 1862, Polk-Brown-Ewell Papers, UNC.

49. G. Campbell Brown reminiscence, TSLA; William Allan memoir, UNC, 137.

50. Dabney, *Life,* 418; Havron, "Stonewall," 205; G. Campbell Brown reminiscence, TSLA. That Jackson "calmly surveyed the progress of the struggle" is from Havron, who is of uncertain provenance and authority. The Hewes memoir, 80, MHS, describes seeing Ewell and Jackson together at a distance, mounted, but that may be confusing an earlier instance.

51. Jackson reported that Ewell held command on the field while he (Jackson) remained at Port Republic "the principal part of the 8th." Boswell of Jackson's staff, however, shuttled steadily back and forth between the generals (*OR,* 714, 799).

52. Taylor, *Destruction,* 73. For Ewell's visit or visits to his left, see the next chapter. Whether Jackson sought his subordinate in person remains conjectural.

53. *OR,* 781; Dabney, *Life,* 418; Havron, "Stonewall," 205.

54. 1860 Rockingham Co. census, 399; "Some Historic Soil," SPRP; letter to the author from Lowell Reidenbaugh of St. Louis, March 18, 1991; author's interview with Lawrence D. Good, March 6, 1991. The

Florys were Germans whose family moved south from Pennsylvania early in the 1800s. Reidenbaugh's great-great-grandmother was a Flory. The family still holds annual reunions around Harrisonburg. Good lives across the road from the Flory site. He believes the house burned a year or two after 1915.

55. "Fremont's Army in Rockingham"; Flory claim in Southern Claims Commission Case Files, NA.

56. "Fremont's Army in Rockingham"; Caffey, *Battle-Fields*, 292.

57. Smith, "Virginia Schoolmistress," 40–41. The diarist is unidentified.

Chapter 12: Confusion and Victory on Ewell's Left

1. *OR*, 666, 668.

2. *OR*, 666.

3. *OR*, 666; Wildman letter to wife, June 13, OHS; Keesy, *War*, 34; Osborn, *Trials*, 44–45; Lee, "Battle of Cross Keys," 491. Lee, who was with Schenck's column, noted "several casualties"; but Schenck (*OR*, 666) said that he made the move "without loss."

4. Wildman to wife, June 13, OHS; Keesy, *War*, 34; Bromley diary, OHS.

5. Osborn, *Trials*, 44–45; Bromley diary, OHS; Keesy, *War*, 34.

6. 32nd Ohio Roll Book, Pinnock Papers, WVU; *OR*, 666-67.

7. *OR*, 667.

8. *OR*, 667; Hurst, *Seventy-Third Ohio*, 24; Campbell diary, OHS; Tracy, "Fremont's Pursuit," 335.

9. 32nd Ohio Roll Book, WVU; Hays, *Thirty-Second . . . Ohio*, 27; Bromley diary and Wildman diary, OHS; anon. diary by member of Battery K, 1st Ohio Light Artillery, Barnett Papers, WRHS.

10. *OR*, 667.

11. Lee, "Battle of Cross Keys," 491; Wildman letter to wife, June 13, OHS; Osborn, *Trials*, 45.

12. Tracy, "Fremont's Pursuit," 335; Mesnard memoir, USAMHI.

13. Krick, *Lee's Colonels*, 69; *OR*, 818; Bond reminiscence, ViRC; Brumley diary, OHS; Mesnard memoir, USAMHI; McKim, *Recollections*, 114.

14. Goldsborough, *Maryland Line* (1900), 277.

15. McKim, *Recollections*, 113-14.

16. Goldsborough, *Maryland Line* (1900), 56; *OR*, 728.

17. Johnson's report went to division headquarters without reference to any brigade affiliation (*OR*, 817-18). The Bond reminiscence, ViRC, affirms Johnson's perceived independence. Casualty returns in *OR* (717, 783–84), however, put the Marylanders in Steuart's Brigade. So does the table in the reliable Allan, *History of the Campaign*, 153n. Steuart's wounding (described shortly) no doubt contributed to Johnson's independence.

18. Bond reminiscence, ViRC; *OR*, 789. Hotchkiss was a nearly unimpeachable witness. His ms. map shows the 52nd, 44th, and 31st Va. (right to left) next to the road adjacent to the main artillery cluster. It is certain that the alignment became 52nd, 44th, 58th, at a point far to the left. Perhaps Hotchkiss was depicting the alignment before Steuart went to his main battle position farther left. As other evidence shows (see the preceding chapter, and narrative below in this chapter), the 31st spent some time near the center, but then fought far out on the left, beyond even the Baltimore Artillery.

19. C. C. Wight memoir, VHS; *OR*, 784.

20. McKim, *Recollections*, 112; Krick, *Lee's Colonels*, 327.

21. McKim, *Recollections*, 113.

22. Robson, *One-Legged*, 42; Driver, *52nd Virginia*, 126.

23. Robson, *One-Legged*, 43; [Fifty-Second Virginia], *Notice;* C. B. Coiner to J. R. Anderson, March 3, 1913, Coiner's file, VMI.

24. *OR*, 789-90.

25. *OR*, 789-90; Jones, "Brief Sketch," Private Collection of R. K. Krick; Bond reminiscence, ViRC, 56.

26. Bond reminiscence, ViRC, 56; *OR*, 818.

27. Unident. contemp. clipping in Ammen compilation, USAMHI; Hands notebook, MHS; Bond reminiscence, ViRC, 56; G. Campbell Brown memorandum, TSLA. Ammen and Brown describe the projectile as canister; Hands and Bond as grape.

28. This paragraph is from the same four sources cited in the last note; *OR*, 818; and Goldsborough, *Maryland Line* (1900), 56.

29. *OR*, 818.

30. Post letter, June 17, MHS; *OR*, 818.

31. Gill, *Reminiscences*, 59-60.

32. Thomas diary, Private Collection of A. T. Wallace; Goldsborough, *Maryland Line* (1900), 56; Goldsborough, *Maryland Line* (1869), 73.

33. Hands notebook, MHS; *OR*, 818. Johnson's description of the assaults is in the *OR* citation. He claimed that the opening threat came from his left, which must have been a vague effort by Schenck. Milroy's initial advance was visible, and must be that referred to as the first threat in most other Maryland accounts; but that move cannot have seemed to be from Johnson's left.

34. *OR*, 818; Hands notebook, MHS; Goldsborough, *Maryland Line* (1869), 73; unident. old clipping in Ammen compilation, USAMHI. The Maryland accounts provide differing insights on some aspects of the fight, but most of later dates betray familiarity with earlier reports, and even pirate from them directly.

35. Unident. old clipping in Ammen compilation, USAMHI; Hands notebook, MHS; Goldsborough, *Maryland Line* (1869), 73; Post letter, June 17, MHS.

36. Unident. old clipping in Ammen compilation, USAMHI; Hands notebook, MHS; Goldsborough, *Maryland Line* (1869), 73; *OR*, 818.

37. *OR*, 818; Goldsborough, *Maryland Line* (1900), 56.

38. Thomas diary, Private Collection of A. T. Wallace.

39. Goldsborough, *Maryland Line* (1900), 56.

40. Unident. old clipping in Ammen compilation, USAMHI; Goldsborough, *Maryland Line* (1869), 74; Hands notebook, MHS; *OR*, 818, 782; Thomas diary, Private Collection of A. T. Wallace.

41. Evans, *Confederate Military History*, II, 80; Goldsborough, *Maryland Line* (1900), 56; Post letter, June 17, MHS; *OR*, 818.

42. Evans, *Confederate Military History*, II, 80; Goldsborough, *Maryland Line* (1869), 74; Hands notebook and Post letter, June 17, MHS.

43. Gill, *Reminiscences*, 61; *OR*, 784, 818; Goldsborough, *Maryland Line* (1900), 56. Loss figures vary, as usual; about 30 out of 175 men were hit. Designation of the Maryland unit that replaced the 1st varied widely enough to leave confusion. The 2nd Maryland came to be the most common late-war and postwar name.

44. Hoffman report, WVU; Chenoweth diary, VHS; Harding, "Chenoweth," VHS.

45. Hoffman report, WVU; Harding, "Chenoweth," VHS; Ashcraft, *31st Virginia*, 162.

46. Chenoweth diary, VHS; Harding, "Chenoweth," VHS.

47. Hoffman report, WVU; Chenoweth diary, VHS.

48. Harper diary, Tulane U.; *OR*, 802.

49. Taylor, *Destruction*, 73; *OR*, 802; "Opelousas Guards," Tulane U.; Booth, *Louisiana Confederate Soldiers*, III, 90.

50. *OR*, 766, 768.

51. *OR*, 768; Krick, *Lee's Colonels*, 151; Garnett letter, July 2, 1862, FNMP.

52. *OR*, 770. For a harsh comment on the 1st Battalion, see Jackson to Lee, October 25, 1862, MC3, Folder 198, ViRC.

53. Krick, *Lee's Colonels*, 265; *OR*, 766; Chapla, *42nd Virginia*, 14.

54. Ewell to Patton, May 12, 1867, Box 1, Folder 19, Polk-Brown-Ewell Papers, UNC. Ewell's intentions remain as confusing today as they were to Patton in 1862 I have not been able to find Patton's inquiry to Ewell, which would be extremely useful.

55. *OR*, 766.

56. *OR*, 766, 770; Chapla, *42nd Virginia*, 14.

57. *OR*, 770.

58. Garnett letter, July 2, 1862, FNMP; *OR*, 768, 784.

59. T. T. Munford to Hotchkiss, August 23, 1896, Hotchkiss Papers, Roll 49, LC; Munford account in Munford-Ellis Papers, Duke U.; Wayland, *Rockingham County*, 148.

60. Webb, "Battle of Cross Keys."

61. G. Campbell Brown reminiscence, TSLA; *OR*, 782, 768. The two documented instances of Ewell's presence on the left were when he placed the 48th in position and when Brown had to ride there to find him. Most mentions of the general's actions do not have geographical precision, so the chances are he spent a great deal of time near Steuart and the Marylanders.

62. *OR*, 781; Ewell to Patton, May 12, 1867, Box 1, Folder 19, Polk-Brown-Ewell Papers, UNC.

63. *OR*, 782; G. Campbell Brown reminiscence and memorandum, both at TSLA; Dabney, *Life*, 418.

64. Information about relics comes from an interview with Lawrence D. Good on March 6, 1991. Good owns the Flory and Armentrout sites. He is emphatic about the relic harvest, having watched it for many decades. Good insists that Jay Johns, the preservationist who years ago acquired the site of Trimble's slaughter of the 8th New York, was misled by historian John Wayland into buying the wrong site. Based on the relics, Good says with a laugh, Johns "missed the battlefield." Artillery projectiles unearthed include a big preponderance of smoothbore rounds. Federal rounds fired into the opposite hillside in heavy volume are much harder to recover because of dense ground cover.

65. Dabney, *Life*, 417.

Chapter 13: Dusk and Darkness at Cross Keys

1. Bates, *Pennsylvania Volunteers,* I, 385.
2. Paulus, *Papers of . . . Milroy,* 46–47.
3. Paulus, *Papers of . . . Milroy,* 47–48. Schenck (*OR,* 667) agreed with Milroy's timing (if nothing else), saying he got out at five-thirty or six.
4. *OR,* 667-68.
5. Tracy, "Fremont's Pursuit," 335–36.
6. Tracy, "Fremont's Pursuit," 336.
7. Roberts, *Reminiscences,* 16. Tracy's thoughts about Shields recur throughout "Fremont's Pursuit." The Roberts account is garbled; it includes an impossible punch line about Shields refusing to burn the famous bridge. There is, however, no reason to reject the gist of the tale.
8. Tracy, "Fremont's Pursuit," 336-37; Wheeler, *In Memoriam,* 336; "Battery I," Barnett papers, WRHS.
9. Osborn, *Trials,* 45; Webb, "Gen. Fremont's Command"; Tracy, "Fremont's Pursuit," 338-39. The guns may have been Brockenbrough's.
10. Paulus, *Papers of . . . Milroy,* 47–48.
11. Keesy, *War,* 34-35; Osborn, *Trials,* 45; Paulus, *Papers of . . . Milroy,* 48; *OR,* 668; Tracy, "Fremont's Pursuit," 338-39. Sunset at Richmond was at 7:16. (*Richardson's Almanac*) or 7:14 (*Confederate States Almanac*). The latitude westward from there to Rockingham County pushed the sunset time back a bit.
12. *OR,* 783.
13. *OR,* 781-82.
14. Patton, "Reminiscences of Jackson," Cook Papers, WVU; *OR,* 818. G. Campbell Brown memorandum, TSLA, says Ewell "sent orders to . . . Hays (7th La.) on the left, to advance and attack."
15. *OR,* 770.
16. *OR,* 766; Chapla, *42nd Virginia,* 14.
17. *OR,* 770-71; Patton, "Reminiscences of Jackson," Cook Papers, WVU.
18. *OR,* 790.
19. Coble reminiscence, NCDAH.
20. *OR,* 797, 802.
21. Nisbet, *Four Years,* 94–95; Krick, *Lee's Colonels,* 339.
22. *OR,* 802, 797; Taylor, *Destruction,* 73.
23. *OR,* 797.
24. Ewell to Patton, May 12, 1867, Polk-Brown-Ewell Papers, UNC; G. Campbell Brown memorandum, TSLA; Brown to mother, June 17, 1862, in Polk-Brown-Ewell Papers, UNC. It is possible that Ewell's displeasure with Trimble expressed in the first source cited dated from earlier in the day.
25. *OR,* 797.
26. *OR,* 798, 792, 799.
27. *OR,* 797-98.
28. *OR,* 797; Hotchkiss, *Make Me a Map,* 131.
29. *OR,* 798.
30. *OR,* 798. A late account of Trimble and Jackson at Port Republic is Hewes, "Turner Ashby's Courage." Hewes's tale does not deserve outright rejection, but it contains discernible flaws. Ewell's letter to Patton (May 12, 1867, Polk-Brown-Ewell Papers, UNC) includes Ewell's complaint that Trimble went over his head to Jackson to secure command of the rear guard at Cross Keys, no doubt during this visit as well, although the rear guard and Trimble's offensive fantasies were not related. Jackson's plans for the rear guard and its eventual performance are covered in future chapters.
31. *OR,* 798. Unfortunately Taylor's lively memoir is silent on the events of that night.
32. Lynchburg *Virginian,* June 20, 1862; "Battle Near Port Republic."
33. Munford, "Reminiscences," 530; Buck, *Old Confeds,* 37. Munford represented Ewell as saying "I believe now if I had followed his views we would have destroyed Fremont's army." That clearly is a late-life embellishment.
34. Dabney, *Life,* 418; Patton, "Reminiscences of Jackson," Cook Papers WVU; *OR,* 766, 768.
35. *OR,* 802; Hightower letter, June 13, GDAH; Munford's ms. history of the 2nd Virginia Cavalry, Munford-Ellis Papers, Duke U. The *OR* reference is Taylor's report. In his 1879 *Destruction* (73), Taylor recalled, "In the evening we moved to the river and camped." His contemporary version of course takes precedence. That the two Louisiana regiments remained with Patton for part of the night is shown by a June 14 letter by a participant in an unidentified clipping in Dora Shute's scrapbook, Tulane.

36. Oates, *The War*, 104; June 14 letter in Dora Shute scrapbook, Tulane; *OR*, 766, 770; *Quitman Guards*, 23.

37. *OR*, 668, 766, 770.

38. Tracy, "Fremont's Pursuit," 339-40; *OR*, 770-71.

39. Yancey, "Civil War Letter," 36-37; Wayland, "Wayside Taverns."

40. Underwood, *Women*, 212-13.

41. Lossing, *Pictorial History*, II, 396; Tracy, "Fremont's Pursuit," 339.

42. Webb, "Battle of Cross Keys." A vivid example of Federal choler is a completely fabricated Senate committee report about Manassas atrocities printed on April 30, 1862, and run in a second fifty-thousand-copy issue the next month.

43. Krick, *Lee's Colonels*, 391; Clark, *N.C. Regiments*, IV, 232-33.

44. *OR*, 783; "Weather Journal," June 8-9, 1862, NWRC.

45. Hightower letter, June 13, 1862, GDAH; *OR*, 782-83.

46. Harry Lewis to "Dear Mother," July 30, 1862, UNC; Estes's CSR, M269, Roll 241, NA.

Chapter 14: The Night of the Bridge Builders

1. SeCheverell, *Twenty-ninth Ohio*, 45; Winters, *Civil War Letters*, 37.

2. List diary, IHS; Hoyt letter to "Dear Parents," June 12, OHS.

3. *OR*, 696; Winscott, "From the 7th."

4. Howard, *Recollections*, 125; *OR*, 740, 745, 747, 750, 762; May, "Battle of Port Republic," 98; Kearns diary, VHS; Barrow diary, USAMHI; Humphreys letter, Private Collection of David Q. Updike. These sources show that Poague's, Cutshaw's, and Carpenter's batteries camped beyond town. Presumably the rest did too.

5. *OR*, 740, 757; Kelly, *Port Republic*, 6; Walker, *Memorial*, 402; Howard, *Recollections*, 125-26.

6. May, "Battle of Port Republic," 98; Kelly, *Port Republic*, 6; *OR*, 774; Kauffman diary, UNC; B. A. Jones memoir, USAMHI. Kelly wrote that part of Taliaferro's Brigade was beyond North River, which is unlikely. Jones, a member of the 44th Virginia (Elzey's Brigade), wrote: "That night we proceeded to Port Republic, went into camp on the North side of the Shenandoah River."

7. Howard, *Recollections*, 126; John Apperson letter, June 10, 1862, Black Papers, VPI; Humphreys letter, Private Collection of David Q. Updike; Douglas, *I Rode*, 88.

8. G. Campbell Brown reminiscence, Brown-Ewell Papers, TSLA.

9. *Hardesty's ... Encyclopedia*, Rockingham County ed.; Lathrop, *Atlas*.

10. Tenth Virginia "Reminiscences," SPRP; Murphy, *10th Virginia*, 158.

11. Kearns diary, VHS; *OR*, 750; Humphreys letter, Private Collection of David Q. Updike; Kauffman diary, UNC.

12. Moore, *Cannoneer*, 72. Carlton McCarthy, in *Detailed Minutiae of Soldier Life*, described this greasy mess in detail and named it.

13. Booty, "Jackson's Battle," 32.

14. Fisher, "Port Republic and the Lewises," 10, Private Collection of L. F. Fisher.

15. G. Campbell Brown memorandum, Brown-Ewell Papers, TSLA; Munford, "Reminiscences," 529; Munford account in Munford-Ellis Papers, Duke.

16. Hotchkiss, *Make Me a Map*, 55, pinpoints headquarters "at Dr. Kemper's." The judicious G. E. May placed Jackson's conferences with Ewell and Patton (to be described below) at Cherry Grove ("Battle of Port Republic," 99; "Port Republic Writer"; and "Port Republic," 89, JMU). The son of Henry B. Harnsberger, who married a daughter of G. W. Kemper, Jr., was too young to remember the night's events, but he told May of his father's and uncle's recollections. SPRP files include details on the construction and history of Cherry Grove. P. C. Kaylor, May's rival as local historian and a perpetual gadfly on such matters, argued bitterly that Jackson's main headquarters was not even at Madison Hall. When May documented the temporary use of Cherry Grove, Kaylor leaped on the opportunity to damn him for suggesting that Jackson stayed past the time of the conferences ("You are in error again"). Even Kaylor had "no doubt" that Jackson met with his officers "at Captain Henry Harnsberger's by appointment." (Kaylor to May, Dec. 6, 1929, SPRP.)

17. *OR*, 714; Munford account, Munford-Ellis Papers, Duke; G. Campbell Brown memorandum, TSLA. Munford thought the conference ended at eleven P.M., but Brown's more contemporary account timed its start at midnight. The meeting did not last long; Stonewall Jackson was nothing if not succinct.

18. Munford account, Munford-Ellis Papers, Duke; M. A. Jackson, *Memoirs*, 287.

19. Munford's history of the 2nd Va. Cav., 32, and his account of the campaign, both in Munford-Ellis Papers, Duke; Munford, "Reminiscences," 529; Krick, *Lee's Colonels*, 68; *OR*, 732.

20. Imboden, "Stonewall Jackson," 291-92; H. K. Douglas marginalia, Antietam N. B. Douglas's lengthy

derisive review of Imboden's claims incorrectly uses "Sandy" instead of "Sandie" for Pendleton's nickname.

21. Patton, "Reminiscences of Jackson," Cook Papers, WVU; Ewell to Patton, May 12, 1867, Polk-Brown-Ewell Papers, UNC.

22. May "Port Republic Writer"; Patton, "Reminiscences of Jackson," Cook Papers, WVU; Dabney, "Stonewall Jackson," 149.

23. Ewell to Patton, May 12, 1867, Polk-Brown-Ewell Papers, UNC.

24. *OR,* 714; Patton, "Reminiscences of Jackson," Cook Papers, WVU.

25. Dabney, "Stonewall Jackson," 149; Dabney, *Life,* 419-21.

26. Taliaferro in M. A. Jackson, *Memoirs,* 517; Macrae, *The Americans,* 194.

27. *OR,* 719. Boswell's report reads "Mechanic's River Depot," but that is a mistranscription for Mechum's.

28. Taliaferro in M. A. Jackson, *Memoirs,* 514.

29. Douglas, *I Rode,* 89.

30. Hotchkiss, *Make Me a Map,* 126.

31. Kearsey, *Shenandoah Valley,* 33, 60. Kearsey's fine book has been almost completely ignored.

32. May, "Port Republic," 110, JMU.

33. Munford, "Reminiscences," 529; Dabney, *Life,* 419; Garber, *Harman,* 20; Kaylor, "Port Republic Battle," HRHS. One source claiming that Jackson supervised is Havron, "Stonewall," 319. Munford's account unconvincingly mixes him into the project.

34. Allan memoir, 137, UNC; Evans, *Confederate Military History,* II, 239-42 (West Va. collation, expanded ed.); Garber, *Harman,* 19-20. Mason died in 1885.

35. May, "Port Republic," 89, JMU; Dabney, *Life,* 419; Bond reminiscence, 57, ViRC; Munford, "Reminiscences," 529; Munford's history of the 2nd Va. Cav., 32, Munford-Ellis Papers, Duke; Garber, *Harman,* 20. Bond's valuable memoir supplies details on the wagons, their maneuvering, and the ballast. He calls the wagons army issue; most others speak of farm wagons. Kaylor ("Port Republic Battle," HRHS) in 1938 recounted in detail a system of farm wagon running gear with a span of 58.5 inches from a wheel on one wagon to a wheel of the next. Kaylor probably based this on wagons he examined, rather than on any historical record.

36. Garber, *Harman,* 20.

Chapter 15: Moving Downstream to Battle

1. Winder diary, MHS; *OR,* 740; *Richardson's Almanac.* Sunrise in Richmond was at 4:44, the same as on the 8th. Howard, *Recollections,* 126, says that the brigade had orders to reach the bridge "by dawn"; Winder reported the time rather than the event.

2. *OR,* 740.

3. "Weather Journal," NWRC; Henderson, *Stonewall Jackson,* I, 366; Howard, *Recollections,* 126; *OR,* 740, 745, 750; Hopkins diary, VHS; "Jackson's Latest Victories." The reading at Georgetown at 7 A.M. was 60 degrees (after 59 at 9 P.M. on the 8th). Two hours earlier in the cooler Valley, it must have been a bit lower.

4. *OR,* 740; Imboden, "Stonewall Jackson," 293-95.

5. Howard, *Recollections,* 126; W. S. Lacy, *Memorial,* 49.

6. *OR,* 714, 747; John Apperson letter, June 10, 1862, Black Papers, VPI.

7. Humphreys letter, Private Collection of David Q. Updike; *OR,* 745; Howard, *Recollections,* 126. The temporary bridge must certainly have been started from the island to narrow the gap.

8. Humphreys letter, Private Collection of David Q. Updike; Moore, *Cannoneer,* 72; Howard, *Recollections,* 126.

9. "Jackson's Latest Victories."

10. William Allan memoir, UNC; Douglas, *I Rode,* 89.

11. *OR,* 774; Evans, *Confederate Military History,* III, 260.

12. Fravel, "Valley Campaign," 419. The company was F, 10th Va.

13. Walker, *Memorial,* 402; *OR,* 740, 757. George Buswell's diary (Private Collection of Wiltfangs) described the mess: "Our regt. escaped the fight by being forgotten and left on picket too long by Gen. Winder."

14. June 14 letter by unidentified 7th La. man, Dora Shute scrapbook, LHAC, Tulane; *OR,* 802. Taylor (*Destruction,* 73) forgetfully declared that he camped near the river overnight.

15. "Taylor's Louisiana Brigade."

16. *OR,* 768; Garnett to father, July 2, 1862, FNMP.

17. *OR,* 785; J. E. Cook, "Humors of the Camp," in King, *Camp-fire Sketches,* 565. The dashes are typical Victorian ellipses to hint at profane speech.

18. Armstrong, *25th Virginia,* 34; "James A. Walker," VHS; Hands notebook, MHS; Goldsborough, *Maryland Line* (1869), 75.

19. Patton, "Reminiscences of Jackson," Cook Papers, WVU.

20. *OR,* 766, 770-71.

21. *OR,* 798; Oates, *The War,* 104; Coble reminiscence, NCDAH. Oates said the march began at dawn, but it must have been later. Trimble, with characteristic exaggeration, insisted that he held fast at Cross Keys until nine A.M. Oates said the brigade was marching by the time firing began around Port Republic.

22. Polsley to wife, June 15, WVU; Kearsey, *Shenandoah Valley,* 34.

23. Lee, "Battles of Port Republic," 590; Hays, *Thirty-Second . . . Ohio,* 27; Hurst, *Seventy-Third Ohio,* 24.

24. Lee, "Battles of Port Republic," 590; Brumley diary, OHS; Tracy, "Fremont's Pursuit," 340.

25. Osborn, *Trials,* 45-46; Waddell, "Cross Keys," HRHS. The cemetery's first burial (says Waddell) had been an Edward Pence in 1861. The custodian who dug up the bones about 1930 was a Henry Shifflett.

26. Malone, *American Biography,* XIX, 572-73; Webb, "Battle of Cross Keys."

27. Claims of Alexander Kyger, Elias Hudlow, Joseph Beery, and William Rodehafer in Southern Claims Commission Case Files, NA.

28. James Smith Claim, Southern Claims Commission Case Files, NA.

29. A. J. Baugher Claim, Southern Claims Commission Case Files, NA.

30. Fisher, *John Lewis,* 311, 316; Krick interview with Billy Wonderly, owner of the Westwood site, March 7, 1991. The name is pronounced *BAWK-er,* according to local residents and Lowell Reidenbaugh, whose wife is descended from the clan. According to Fisher, Westwood had been sold by 1830, so was older than that. Mr. Wonderly recalls that the original building was torn down about 1937. The adjacent barn, a highly useful landmark for modern visitors to the battlefield, was built in 1898, he says. The dilapidated house near the barn in 1993 may include foundation and building material from the old house, Wonderly thinks, but its location does not match historic maps.

31. Havron, "Stonewall," 319; Lewis, *Brief Narrative,* 61. In an interview on March 7, 1991, John Kaylor and his mother, who farm Lewiston, said that the large house standing on the Lewiston site today was built in 1917. Before then a girls' school that stood there burned. The original Lewiston predated the girls' school.

32. Hess, *Heartland,* 342-43; Lewis, *Brief Narrative,* 61; Fletcher diary, Private Collection of Lewis F. Fisher; Strayer diary, HRHS. Thomas Dilworth, who owns Lynnwood in 1993, is a descendant of Charles Lewis, who built it in 1812. The age given for the baby varies. Lewis, *Brief Narrative,* gives a birth date of June 1. The Fletcher diary says it was one day old. Strayer's diary says only "a new baby."

33. "Old Mill at Lynnwood"; C. E. Baker of Knox Crutchfield, Inc., to Lewis F. Fisher, March 20, 1959, Private Collection of Fisher.

34. Lewis, *Brief Narrative,* 61; Fletcher diary, and letter of Anne M. Miller to Lewis F. Fisher, February 16, 1959, Private Collection of Fisher; Strayer diary, HRHS.

35. Hess, *Heartland,* 342; Fletcher diary, Private Collection of Lewis F. Fisher; Lewis, *Brief Narrative,* 61.

36. W. F. Randolph reminiscence, VHS.

37. Howard, *Recollections,* 126; Humphreys letter, Private Collection of David Q. Updike; White, *Sketches,* 90-91. Howard saw the first Federal dead within "only a few hundred yards" of the wagon bridge, evidence of the Confederate fire on the 8th.

38. *OR,* 740, 762; Howard, *Recollections,* 126-27.

39. *OR,* LI, pt. 1, 95; "Weather Journal," NWRC. The temperatures at Georgetown at 7 A.M., 2 P.M., and 9 P.M. on June 9 were 60, 60, and 56 degrees; on the 10th, 57, 56, and 56. Weather in the region moves from the southwest, and is normally a half day behind Washington in the Valley, so the June 10 readings at Georgetown bear most closely on the battle time at Port Republic. These low temperatures were much the coldest for that month in 1862. The two 56-degree readings were the lowest for the entire month. The next lowest 2 P.M. reading was 68 on the 16th.

40. *OR,* 732, 740. In his diary (MHS) Winder wrote: "in two miles encountered enemy's pickets." He must have estimated the total distance from bivouac to bridge and beyond. In his report (*OR,* 740), Winder described the march from the bridge to contact as about one mile. Funk of the 5th Va. (*OR,* 750) put the march at "some 2 miles," again presumably from the bivouac site. Grigsby of the 27th Va. (*OR,* 753) estimated a mile and a half. The true airline distance from the wagon bridge to first contact was just more than one mile; marching routes were longer.

41. *Or,* 728, 740, 745, 759; Krick, *Lee's Colonels,* 286; Humphreys letter, Private Collection of David Q. Updike. Carpenter said the pieces fired "one or two rounds"; Humphreys specified two each. Crutchfield (*OR,* 728) reported the seven A.M. timing, which seems accurate. The subsequent Federal fire from the famous Coaling shows up in many reports as the opening artillery rounds of the morning. Carpenter's brief show of force against the skirmishers, however, clearly preceded the first Unionist round. Skidmore, *Billy Davis,* 245, is one Northern account that noted the proper sequence. Colonel Daum (*OR,* 691-92) is another.

42. Kelly, *Port Republic,* 4-5.

43. *OR,* 750; Carroll to Keily, December 1862, M650, NA, copy in Keily file, Private Collection of Brian C. Pohanka.

44. At least fourteen sources offer times for the opening Union round. Jackson himself (M. A. Jackson, *Memoirs,* 283) wrote that the battle lasted "from near six to ten and a half A.M.," perhaps timing the start at the beginning of his march. O.T., "Battle at Port Republic," said "at 5 o'clock the enemy opened fire." Ray, "Journal," 60, wrote that "at 6 a.m. our Batteries opened fire." The hour cited most often was 8 A.M., by Durkee diary, OHS; Caffey, *Battle-Fields,* 293-94; Kauffman diary, UNC; and Hadley, "Indiana Soldier," 213. Winters, *Letters,* 37, said, "canonaiding commenced erlee in the morning. the muskits at 7½."

45. Strayer diary, HRHS; *OR,* 691-92. List of the 7th Ind. (IHS) wrote simply: "Our Artillery opened . . . first." The emphasis is added to Daum's quote.

46. Strayer diary, HRHS.

47. *OR,* 740, 759; Slaughter, *Randolph Fairfax,* 27.

48. Moore, *Cannoneer,* 73.

49. Parmeter diary, OHS; SeCheverell, *Twenty-ninth Ohio,* 47; Davis, "7th Indiana," ISL; Winscott, "From the 7th"; Clarke, "Some One Has Blundered."

50. *OR,* 691, 699.

51. *OR,* 687.

52. *OR,* 690.

53. Heinl, *Dictionary,* 324; Clarke, "Some One Has Blundered."

54. "Port Republic and the Lewises," 16, and letter of Sue Lewis Durkee to Lewis F. Fisher, December 10, 1958, Private Collection of Fisher.

55. Hotchkiss in Evans, *Confederate Military History,* III, 261; Kelly, *Port Republic,* 5; Wilson, "Port Republic"; "Squarest Battle of the War."

56. Anonymous Union Map, NA; Wilder, *History of Company C,* 28; Huntington, "Operations," 330.

57. *OR,* 693.

58. *OR,* 692.

59. *OR,* 714; Evans, *Confederate Military History,* III, 261; Kelly, *Port Republic,* 5.

60. "Squarest Battle of the War"; Wilson, "Port Republic"; Bond reminiscence, 57, ViRC; Neese, *Three Years,* 73; "Jackson's Latest Victories"; contemp. Confederate account in Strayer scrapbook, SPRP; Randolph reminiscence, VHS; Kaylor, "Port Republic Battle," HRHS. Dabney (*Life,* 422) placed the Coaling "upon a hillock just at the edge of the thickets."

61. *OR,* 692-93, 728; Huntington, "Operations," 331; USGS topographic quad for Grottoes.

62. Wilder, *History of Company C,* 28; Clarke, "Some One Has Blundered"; Wilson, "Port Republic"; Cooke, "Battle of Port Republic."

63. Winder diary, April 30 and May 1-3, 1862, MHS.

64. Lewis F. Fisher to Krick, March 11, 1992.

65. Munford, "Reminiscences," 529-30; Munford ms. history of the 2nd Va. Cav., Ellis-Munford Papers, Duke.

66. Kaylor, "Port Republic Battle," HRHS; Dabney, *Life,* 419-20.

67. Dabney, *Life,* 421; Garber, *Harman,* 20. As shown below, "Taylor did send some of his infantry through the water. Taylor's hold on his subordinates was a very different thing from the influence of the ineffectual Dabney.

68. Kelly, *Port Republic,* 4, 15-16; "Taylor's Louisiana Brigade."

69. Kelly, *Port Republic,* 15; Wilson, "Port Republic"; "Taylor's Louisiana Brigade." Taylor declared (*Destruction,* 73) that the sun appeared over the Blue Ridge during the halt, but other Louisiana accounts place it much earlier.

70. Munford ms. history of the 2nd Va. Cav., 32, Munford-Ellis Papers, Duke; Kelly, *Port Republic,* 4, 16; Taylor, *Destruction,* 73-74. Munford is the source for Taylor having "forced a part of his Brigade to take the water by wading." Kelly said "the South River was too deep to be forded on foot, though still fordable for wagons." Kelly and his regiment crossed first. Taylor probably grew restive after long delay and ordered the end of the column to ford. Kelly and Taylor do not conform about the call to battle. Kelly's orders from staff (he said Dabney, probably in error; Dabney himself reported on river-crossing problems) no doubt came at the head of the column; Taylor, at the rear, assumed the movement responded to the sound of firing ahead.

Chapter 16: Opportunity in the Woods, Trouble in the Fields

1. *OR,* 740, 759.

2. Howard, *Recollections,* 127; Dabney, "Stonewall Jackson," 150.

3. *OR*, 745, 745n., 695, 747; Huntington, "Operations," 332; Howard, *Recollections,* 127.

4. *OR*, 759-60, 747; White, *Sketches,* 91. The Humphreys letter (Carpenter's Battery), Private Collection of David Q. Updike, says that unit followed the 2nd Virginia "as far as possible." Carpenter's report in *OR* says that was only to the near edge of the woods.

5. *OR*, 745, 747.

6. *OR*, 714, 763; Howard, *Recollections,* 127.

7. *OR*, 714, 728, 740.

8. Huntington, "Operations," 331; Howard, *Recollections,* 127.

9. Moore, *Cannoneer,* 73.

10. Humphreys letter, Private Collection of David Q. Updike; *OR*, 714. The Kearns diary, VHS, states that the 27th Virginia "was to support Carpenter's Battery." Since the 27th stayed right of the 5th Virginia all during the battle, Carpenter's two guns were right of Poague's.

11. *OR*, 741, 750, 753.

12. Moore, *Cannoneer,* 73-74.

13. *OR*, 763; Humphreys letter, Private Collection of David Q. Updike; Colonel Dunning (5th Ohio) in Moore, *Rebellion Record,* V, 112; Fisher, *John Lewis,* 318.

14. *OR*, 741; Strayer diary, HRHS.

15. Charles H. Bard (7th Ohio) to "My Friend Sade," July 17, 1862, Woods Papers, Duke; Kaylor, "Port Republic Battle," HRHS.

16. *OR*, 699; Evans, *Confederate Military History,* III, 260.

17. *OR*, 684; Evans, *Confederate Military History,* III, 261; Wayland, "The Battle"; May, "Battle of Port Republic," 99.

18. Dabney, *Life,* 422; Evans, *Confederate Military History,* III, 261.

19. Kelly, *Port Republic,* 5; Dabney, *Life,* 422.

20. Kelly, *Port Republic,* 5.

21. *OR*, 696, 699; Huntington, "Operations," 331-32. Sources stating that the 7th went to sustain artillery, rather than vice versa, include O.T., "Battle at Port Republic"; Skidmore, *Billy Davis,* 145; and Davis, "7th Indiana," ISL.

22. Kelly, *Port Republic,* 5; Winscott, "From the 7th"; Skidmore, *Billy Davis,* 145. Davis put the 7th's first position at "the wheatfield fence," presumably the one between the lane and the wheat field rather than the worm division fence closer to the Confederates. The anonymous Union map (NA) shows the Hoosiers and artillery in the field west of the lane, but far short of the division fence.

23. "Jackson's Latest Victories"; Randolph reminiscence, VHS.

24. *OR*, 696; May, "Battle of Port Republic," 99. Colonel Dunning (*Rebellion Record,* V, 11) described the three-tiered initial alignment. The Parmeter diary (29th Ohio), OHS, also mentions the 66th as part of the line on the right for a time.

25. SeCheverell, *Twenty-ninth Ohio,* 46; Parmeter diary, OHS; Wilder, *History of Company C,* 28; *OR*, 696.

26. *OR*, 696.

27. Rawling, *First ... Virginia,* 94; Huntington, "Operations," 332.

28. *OR*, 692, 699, 696. Tyler said he ordered two regiments toward the Coaling when skirmish fire broke out; apparently only the 66th Ohio went.

29. May, "Battle of Port Republic," 99-100; Hadley, "Indiana Soldier," 213; Huntington, "Operations," 332.

30. Howard, *Recollections,* 127; Dabney, "Stonewall Jackson," 150; "Squarest Battle of the War."

31. Kearsey, *Shenandoah Valley,* 53.

32. *OR*, 740-41, 750; "Jackson's Latest Victories." Strayer diary, HRHS, times the period from the opening artillery round from the Coaling until infantry fighting began as one hour (fifteen minutes until Confederate artillery answered, then forty-five minutes of purely artillery action). Strayer thought the ensuing infantry struggle lasted an hour before "the fight became general" (presumably the massive Federal counterattack and Taylor's triumph).

33. *OR*, 750.

34. Kelly, *Port Republic,* 6; "Squarest Battle of the War"; Cooke, "Battle of Port Republic."

35. Fisher, "Port Republic and the Lewises," 18, Private Collection of Fisher.

36. Kaylor "Port Republic Battle," HRHS; Huntington, "Operations," 332. Kaylor's account says: "Tyler told Samuel H. Lewis, in the morning before the battle, that he did not have but 3900 men with him." This probably is a typographical error for 3,000. Tyler was prone to minimizing his numbers.

37. *OR*, 696.

38. *OR*, 699, 692, 696.

39. Winscott, "From the 7th"; Skidmore, *Billy Davis,* 145; O.T., "Battle at Port Republic."

40. Hadley, "Indiana Soldier," 213; List diary, IHS.

41. Parmeter diary, OHS; Barnes, *Medical and Surgical,* IV (Collation 7), 231. Eastlick's wounding belongs

in this early phase of the battle because he remained unconscious a long time (overstated as four hours in Barnes), but reached the Federal rear in time to avoid capture. The conoidal ball removed from his skull had to have come from a rifle. Since it crushed the parietal bone but did not kill Eastlick, its velocity must have been spent after traveling a long distance.

42. Barnes, *Medical and Surgical,* IV (Collation 7), 231.

43. Wilder, *History of Company C,* 28; Clarke, "Some One Has Blundered"; Rawling, *First . . . Virginia,* 94.

44. *OR,* 728; Wayland, "The Battle"; Kaylor "Port Republic Battle," HRHS; Munford, "Reminiscences," 530.

45. Dabney, "Stonewall Jackson," 151.

46. *OR,* 740-41, 757.

47. *OR,* 757.

48. Sons of Temperance collection, Duke; Neff letter to parents, August 4, USAMHI.

49. *OR,* 786; Chenoweth diary, VHS; Harding, "Chenoweth," VHS.

50. Robson, *One-Legged,* 45; Wight memoir, 70-71, VHS; Kern reminiscence, NCDAH.

Chapter 17: Fiasco in the Woods, More Trouble in the Fields

1. *OR,* 745.

2. *OR,* 745, 747.

3. *OR,* 747.

4. *OR,* 745, 747. Allen and Ronald were both full colonels, but Allen's commission was dated fully a year earlier than Ronald's.

5. White, *Sketches,* 91; *OR,* 747. The emphasis is added.

6. *OR,* 745, 747; Confederate . . . Casualties, Roll 7, M836, NA. Ronald's report in M836 is nearly the same as that in *OR,* but it includes the names of men wounded.

7. Huntington, "Operations," 330-32. Huntington is using "allopathic" as the antonym for "homeopathic." Homeopathy was a quackery popular in the mid-nineteenth century that suggested employing tiny doses of medicine.

8. *OR,* 693.

9. *OR,* 696.

10. *OR,* 692.

11. Jackson to Boteler, May 6, Boteler Papers, Duke. The last page of this important letter has been stolen. The last surviving word is "preeminent." For contemporary disdain about Crutchfield's abilities, see Krick, *Cedar Mountain,* passim.

12. *OR,* 728.

13. Moore. *Cannoneer,* 74; *OR,* 763; Minor memoir, U.Va. Poague (*OR*) estimated two hours.

14. Wade letter, June 17, 1862, Stonewall Jackson House.

15. *OR,* 760; Humphreys letter, Private Collection of David Q. Updike. What happened to some of Poague's short-range guns has been described in the last chapter. J. D. Imboden's fanciful tale of his adventures with a mule-drawn battery, including repartee with Jackson himself, is in Imboden, "Stonewall Jackson," 295.

16. *OR,* 741, 753; May, "Battle of Port Republic," 100; "Jackson's Latest Victories."

17. *OR,* 742; Cooke, "Battle of Port Republic."

18. "Battle at Port Republic"; *OR,* 690.

19. Thomson, *Seventh Indiana,* 100.

20. Skidmore, *Billy Davis,* 145;. Davis, "7th Indiana," ISL; Winscott, "From the 7th"; Hadley, "Indiana Soldier," 213; "About the Fight at Front Royal."

21. SeCheverell, *Twenty-ninth Ohio,* 46.

22. Molyneaux speech, Duke; Wilder, *History of Company C,* 28.

23. Wood, *Seventh Regiment,* 117.

24. Fairfax diary, Chicago Historical Society; Clarke, "Some One Has Blundered."

Chapter 18: Taylor's Louisiana Brigade Moves Forward

1. Patton, "Reminiscences of Jackson," Cook Papers, WVU, claims that after "the untoward result of his first charge on the Yankee battery," Jackson hurried an aide to Trimble's rear guard to call it forward. The aide "reached us with his horse foaming . . and ordered us to . . . hurry up to the battle-field double quick." The rear guard's orders had always been to disengage steadily. The bottleneck around the South

River made Trimble's rate of march nearly irrelevant. Dabney and his followers have swallowed Patton's interpretation whole.

2. "Squarest Battle of the War"; Kelly, *Port Republic*, 16.

3. *OR*, 745; Dabney to Hotchkiss, August 2, 1897, Hotchkiss Papers, LC. Dabney is responding to a letter (which seems to be lost) in which Hotchkiss reported Taylor's original intention to move far more widely than he finally had to do.

4. Dabney to Hotchkiss, August 2, 1897, Hotchkiss Papers, LC.

5. Taylor, *Destruction*, 74.

6. Boyd, *Reminiscences*, 13.

7. Boyd, *Reminiscences*, 7-10.

8. Kelly, *Port Republic*, 16; "Taylor's Louisiana Brigade."

9. Kelly, *Port Republic*, 16-17.

10. Kelly, *Port Republic*, 17; Kelly's official report, M331, NA.

11. Taylor, *Destruction*, 74.

12. *SHSP*, IX, 218.

13. Wilson, "Port Republic"; Munford's history of the 2nd Va. Cav., 32-33, Munford-Ellis Papers, Duke.

14. *OR*, 802.

15. Hotchkiss to Dabney, August 4, 1897, Hotchkiss Papers, LC.

16. *OR*, 719; Hotchkiss in Evans, *Confederate Military History*, III, 262; Hotchkiss to Dabney, August 4, 1897, Hotchkiss Papers, LC; Hotchkiss, *Make Me a Map*, 55. Taylor's memoir generally is uneven. Kelly's *Port Republic* is much more reliable. William R. Lyman in his "Cross Keys and Port Republic," Tulane, agrees emphatically with that judgment.

17. "James A. Walker," VHS; "Taylor's Louisiana Brigade."

18. Kelly, *Port Republic*, 17.

19. "Taylor's Louisiana Brigade"; "Squarest Battle of the War."

20. "Taylor's Louisiana Brigade"; Kelly, *Port Republic*, 17.

21. Kelly, *Port Republic*, 17-18; "Taylor's Louisiana Brigade."

22. Taylor, *Destruction*, 74, 77; Kelly, *Port Republic*, 18. Taylor identified his guide as Lieutenant English, from near Harpers Ferry. Robert M. English was the officer killed at the head of the 2nd Virginia near the Coaling during the first abortive assault. Hotchkiss unquestionably guided Taylor, even if not adequately introduced under the stress of the moment. Taylor probably ran across mention of English's death at the forefront of the effort to reach the Coaling and made a mistaken assumption.

23. Evans, *Confederate Military History*, III, 262; Hotchkiss, *Make Me a Map*, 55; *OR*, 745.

24. Taylor, *Destruction*, 74-75; Dabney, *Life*, 422; Evans, *Confederate Military History*, III, 262.

Chapter 19: Winder's Daring Attack

1. Taylor, *Destruction*, 74-77; *OR*, 802.

2. Evans, *Confederate Military History*, X, 218. "Battle of Port Republic" put the strength of the 7th La. at 308.

3. *OR*, 741; Howard, *Recollections*, 127-28.

4. Morning Report, Taylor's Brigade, HL; Wilson, "Port Republic"; Manning, "Historical Memorandum," Tulane. Rivera's Battery was turned into infantry (a company in the 6th La.) two months later.

5. Neese, *Three Years*, 73.

6. Neese, *Three Years*, 73, 76. A lieutenant in Chew's Battery, far less wordy than Neese, recorded Port Republic in seven words: "Our Battery in the fight. loss none." (Williams diary, VHS.)

7. *OR*, 768.

8. Garnett to father, July 2, 1862, FNMP.

9. *OR*, 741.

10. *OR*, 714; Hotchkiss, *Make Me a Map*, 131; Mooney memoir, VHS. Whether Smead and W. L. Jackson quarreled over Winder's attack is speculation. There is no firm evidence that General Jackson had no part in the decision to attack. Winder's language implies that and there is no indication of Jackson's presence or influence. He doubtless would have agreed in any event. Language in Jackson's report (*OR*, 714) suggests that Winder was responsible.

11. *OR*, 741, 750-51; Wallace, *5th Virginia*, 31; Houghton, *Two Boys*, 29.

12. *OR*, 750.

13. Myers, *Comanches*, 68; *OR*, 750. Myers wrote that Jackson sent him in person to order Munford to

charge a battery. Federal accounts of Southern horsemen near the river pin down where they went. The mission aborted before it made any real impact.

14. *OR,* 750; Wallace, *5th Virginia,* 31; "Jackson's Latest Victories."

15. *OR,* 751; Krick, *Lee's Colonels,* 399; Wallace, *5th Virginia,* 91, 116, 145.

16. Mooney memoir, VHS; *OR,* 751. Funk reported loss of 113 out of 447 engaged, or 25 percent. Mooney named the prescient soldier as Bill Via, who has no direct match on the 5th's roster, so I used the story without citing the victim's name.

17. Kelly, *Port Republic,* 13; Wilson, "Port Republic."

18. "Jackson's Latest Victories"; "Squarest Battle of the War."

19. Kelly, *Port Republic,* 14; Wilson, "Port Republic"; Morning Report, Taylor's Brigade, HL; June 14 letter and an unrelated clipping, both in Dora Shute scrapbook, Tulane; *OR,* XI, pt. 3, 655. Wilson claimed a loss of 158 killed and wounded among 308 "effective men." The June 14 letter reported fewer than 400 men present and estimated a loss of 200. The other Shute clipping lists losses of 162 (10 killed, 5 mortally wounded, 133 wounded, and 14 missing). The June 11 morning report showed the 7th with 335 men present, excluding those present sick and one in arrest.

20. Krick, *Lee's Colonels,* 116; Wilson, "Port Republic"; Lee, "An Extract," 392; June 14 letter in unident. clipping, Dora Shute scrapbook, Tulane. DeChoiseul's papers, which include a striking photograph of him in uniform, are in the Walton-Glenny Papers, Historic New Orleans Collection. He was buried in Flat Rock, N.C.

21. *OR,* 753.

22. *OR,* 753; Winder diary, MHS.

23. *OR,* 753.

24. Rawling, *First . . . Virginia,* 19-20, 68; Wallace, *Virginia Military Organizations,* 111.

25. Krick, *Lee's Colonels,* 343; *OR,* 753.

26. Humphreys letter, Private Collection of David Q. Updike; *OR,* 760.

27. *OR,* 741, 763.

28. Slaughter, *Randolph Fairfax,* 27; Moore, *Cannoneer,* 74.

29. Moore, *Cannoneer,* 74-75.

30. Neese, *Three Years,* 74.

31. *OR,* 714; Howard, *Recollections,* 128.

32. Kelly, *Port Republic,* 6.

33. *SHSP,* IX, 218; *OR,* 741. Robson, *One-Legged,* 47, quotes a prisoner on Southern accuracy: "You fired over our heads at Winchester, but you fired under them here."

34. Kelly, *Port Republic,* 13; *OR,* 753, 760.

35. O.T., "Battle at Port Republic"; Thomson, *Seventh Indiana,* 100; "Letter . . . [7th Indiana]"; "About the Fight at Front Royal." *OR,* 690, lists the 7th Indiana's killed as 9 out of 145 total casualties. "Letter . . ." says 9 of 141.

36. Hadley, "Indiana Soldier," 213-14; Skidmore, *Billy Davis,* 145; Davis, "7th Indiana," ISL.

37. O.T., "Battle at Port Republic"; Skidmore, *Billy Davis,* 145; *OR,* 700.

38. *OR,* 750; letter from B. C. Pohanka to the author, October 9, 1991, based on Keily file in Pohanka's private collection.

39. Davis, "7th Indiana," ISL; Hadley, "Indiana Soldier," 214.

40. Samuel List diary, IHS; SeCheverell, *Twenty-ninth Ohio,* 46-47.

41. Parmeter diary, OHS; Douglas, *I Rode,* 89-90.

42. Wood, *The Seventh Regiment,* 117-18; Wilder, *Company C,* 28.

43. Barnes, *Medical and Surgical,* IV (Collation 8), 302.

44. Anon. Map, NA, shows the 5th Ohio behind the lane and the 7th Indiana well to the lane's front. Casualties for the 5th Ohio were reported in *OR,* 690, as 4 killed, 63 wounded, and 197 missing. The huge number of missing came during the retreat after the battle. Ohio Roster Comm., *Official Roster,* II, 123-70, includes 9 killed outright, however, and at least 2 more who died of wounds. Smith was twenty-seven when he died and Graham was thirty-five.

45. Rawling, *First . . . Virginia,* 94; *OR,* 699-700; Anon. Union Map, NA.

46. *OR,* 696; Parmeter diary, OHS.

47. *OR,* 696-97; Anon. Union Map, NA. The casualty returns for the 84th and 110th in *OR,* 690, seem impossibly low, but Bates, *Pennsylvania Volunteers,* shows no more killed (that source is of little use for wounded).

48. Huntington, "Operations," 330-33.

Chapter 20: Winder's Rout

1. Kelly, *Port Republic*, 14; "Jackson's Latest Victories"; *OR*, 750-51; "Near View of the Yankees." Federal claims that Southern cavalry operated next to the river may have been the result of seeing their own troops creeping through the millrace and nearby woods. Anon. Union Map, NA, shows a cavalry symbol next to the 5th Virginia and parallel to the millrace. Hadley, "Indiana Soldier," 213, says that from his perspective it also seemed that the Confederate center gave way first.

2. Beard diary, Private Collection of Hemps; Mooney memoir, VHS; Wallace, *5th Virginia*, 167. Wagener died at Port in 1880.

3. *OR*, 750-51; Wallace, *5th Virginia*, 31.

4. "Jackson's Latest Victories."

5. Taylor, *Destruction*, 76; *OR*, 802-3; unident. clipping in Dora Shute scrapbook, Tulane.

6. Evans, *Confederate Military History*, X, 219; Harper diary, Tulane.

7. Abram D. Warwick, "Last Battle of General Turner Ashby," 20, Box 24, Daniel Papers, U.Va.

8. Dyer and Moore, *Tennessee . . . Questionnaires*, V, 1817-20.

9. J. W. Daniel, "The Deserter," Box 22, folder "1904-1908," Daniel Papers, U.Va.

10. *OR*, 753; Kearns diary, VHS; "He Served His Country Well," *Confederate Veteran*, IV, 69; "Twenty-Seventh Virginia"; Dabney, *Life*, 423. Winscott, "From the 7th," thought the Federal attack was "driving them [Confederates] back to the river," *not* parallel to it and upstream.

11. List to parents, June 17, IHS; Winscott, "From the 7th"; O.T., "Battle at Port Republic."

12. O.T., "Battle at Port Republic"; List letter, June 17, IHS; Hadley, "Indiana Soldier," 213.

13. Thomson, *Seventh Indiana*, 100-101; Davis, "7th Indiana," ISL; Skidmore, *Billy Davis*, 145; O.T., "Battle at Port Republic"; Hadley, "Indiana Soldier," 214; W.C.F., "Letter." Civil War opponents rarely identified units opposite them accurately. The precision of four separate members of the 7th Indiana in this instance is amazing, perhaps unique.

14. W.C.F., "Letter"; Hadley, "Indiana Soldier," 213-14; "Battle at Port Republic"; Skidmore, *Billy Davis*, 145; List diary, IHS.

15. SeCheverell, *Twenty-ninth Ohio*, 47; Parmeter diary, OHS. Mason was twenty-one; he died of wounds in November 1864. Gregory, who was forty-three in 1862, resigned in January 1863. Ohio Roster Comm., *Official Roster*, III, 364, 374. Gregory's prisoners probably escaped when the tide turned soon thereafter.

16. Ordnance receipts for Company B dated June 18 in Container 20, Barnett Papers, WRHS.

17. Wilder, *Company C*, 29; Wright to mother, June 16, U. of Michigan; Chas. H. Bard to "My Friend Sade," June 17, Woods Papers, Duke U.

18. Burton letter, Private Collection of Sandra R. Kenney.

19. Wood, *Seventh Regiment*, 118; Paver, *What I Saw*, 81-82; Clarke, "Some One Has Blundered"; S. H. Dunning in Moore, *Rebellion Record*, V, 112.

20. Rawling, *First . . . Virginia*, 94.

21. *OR*, 697; Bates, *Pennsylvania Volunteers*, III, 980.

22. *OR*, 698; G. Campbell Brown memorandum, TSLA; Huntington, "Operations," 333.

23. Robson, *One-Legged*, 45; Hotchkiss, *Make Me a Map*, 129-30.

24. *OR*, 786, 789-91; Krick, *Lee's Colonels*, 347; C. Benton Coiner to J. R. Anderson, March 3, 1913, Coiner's file, VMI. For some reason the 1st Maryland of this brigade did not fight on the 9th.

25. Robson, *One-Legged*, 46; Hotchkiss conversation with Skinner, July 13, 1865, Hotchkiss Mossy Creek marginalia, U.Va.; Coiner to J. R. Anderson, March 3, 1913, Coiner's file, VMI. The official return (*OR*, 717) of 52nd losses totals 101. Coiner's company should have lost about 10 as a proportionate share. W. R. Lyman of Company B, 31st Virginia, in his memoir (Tulane), 11, places the 52nd Virginia between the 31st and 27th, but that is an error.

26. Kelly, *Port Republic*, 14; *OR*, 787, 791. Four lieutenants were among the 52nd's wounded.

27. *OR*, 792.

28. Kern reminiscence, NCDAH.

29. Krick, *Lee's Colonels*, 182; G. Campbell Brown memorandum, Brown-Ewell Papers, TSLA; *OR*, 787. Ewell (*OR*, 786) reported sending one regiment to the left from Scott's Brigade; in his draft report (Brown-Ewell Papers, TSLA), he specified the 31st Virginia, which was not from Scott. In neither place did Ewell refer to the role of the 25th Virginia.

30. Camden memoir, Private Collection of Armstrong; Armstrong, *25th Virginia*, 141. Armstrong's reliable roster calls Camden "Edwin," but the heading of the autobiographical memoir uses "Edward." George Kemper Young, a sergeant in the 31st Virginia and a relative of the local Kempers, also tended wounded

despite his combat role. He later became a surgeon in military hospitals (F. L. Kemper to Mrs. G. K. Pruitt, May 3, 1915, "Widow's Application for a Pension," Texas State Archives, Austin).

31. *OR,* 741.

32. Lyman, "Cross Keys and Port Republic," Tulane; Howard, *Recollections,* 128.

33. Strayer diary, HRHS.

34. Lyman memoir, 11, Tulane; unidentified 31st Virginia memoir in the regiment's file, WVU.

35. Gordon, "Under Sentence," 589; Krick, *Lee's Colonels,* 99; Ashcraft, *31st Virginia,* 128. Ashcraft's CSR-based roster suggests that Gordon actually did go missing for a time.

36. Harding, "Chenoweth," VHS; unidentified 31st Virginia memoir in 31st file, WVU; Lyman memoir, 11, Tulane.

37. Unidentified 31st Virginia memoir, 31st Virginia file, WVU.

38. Chenoweth Collection (#107), VMI.

39. Harding, "Chenoweth," VHS.

40. Chenoweth Collection, VMI. Lemuel Chenoweth was a famous bridge builder near Beverly.

41. Harding, "Chenoweth," VHS; Lyman memoir, 12, Tulane; *OR,* 787; Ashcraft, *31st Virginia,* 31. Gordon ("Under Sentence," 589) reported the regiment's strength as 214. Harding says 226. Ashcraft's casualties, based on a thorough roster, total 114.

42. Lyman memoir, 10, Tulane.

43. Church memoir, WVU.

44. Lyman memoir, 12-13, Tulane.

45. *OR,* 741; "Squarest Battle of the War"; Strayer diary, HRHS; Wilder, *Company C,* 29.

Chapter 21: Ewell and the Artillery Buy Time

1. Wight memoir, 71, VHS.

2. *OR,* 790-91.

3. G. Campbell Brown memorandum, Brown-Ewell Papers, TSLA; *OR,* 786; Wight memoir, 71-72, VHS; May, "Battle of Port Republic," 101.

4. Wight memoir, 72-73, VHS; "Squarest Battle of the War."

5. Campbell Brown to mother, June 17, Polk-Brown-Ewell Papers, UNC.

6. Campbell Brown memorandum, Brown-Ewell Papers, TSLA; Wight memoir, 73, VHS.

7. Ewell draft report, Brown-Ewell Papers, TSLA. The draft is much fuller than the published version on this phase. Without it, untangling the sequence of events would be far more difficult.

8. *OR,* 786, 791; Wight memoir, 73-74, VHS.

9. Wight memoir, 74, VHS.

10. *OR,* 786; Wight memoir, 74, VHS. Ewell's amanuensis and alter ego Campbell Brown (memorandum, Brown-Ewell Papers, TSLA) thought the enemy withdrawal covered "several hundred yards."

11. Ewell's draft report, Brown-Ewell Papers, TSLA.

12. Ewell's draft report, Brown-Ewell Papers, TSLA; *OR,* 789-90; Beirne, "Three War Letters," 294.

13. The Ewell story is as told by Hunter H. McGuire in Couper, *One Hundred Years,* IV, 77. McGuire was a thoroughly reliable source and present with Jackson at Port Republic. He almost certainly did not witness Ewell's action, but may well have heard Jackson's exchange with Ewell or at least heard of it at once. The account is often derived from the memoirs of Robert Stiles, who was nowhere near the affair and was prone to exaggeration, so it is better cited from McGuire.

14. Wight memoir, 75, VHS; Jones, "Brief Sketch," Private Collection of R. K. Krick.

15. Wight memoir, 75, VHS; *OR,* 715, 786.

16. Wight memoir, 76, VHS; *OR,* 787, 791; Krick, *Lee's Colonels,* 74. Buckner is not on the *OR* list for some reason. The 44th's casualties of about 50 men compare to a strength on June 8 (before Cross Keys) of only 120 or 130.

17. Ewell's draft report, Brown-Ewell Papers, TSLA; *OR,* 714-15.

18. *OR,* 793.

19. W. S. Lacy, *Memorial,* 49.

20. McDonald, *Laurel Brigade,* 71; Neese, *Three Years,* 74.

21. *OR,* 760; Fonerden, *Carpenter's Battery,* 26.

22. Humphreys letter, Private Collection of Updike; *OR,* 760.

23. *OR,* 760; Humphreys letter, Private Collection of Updike. The emphasis on *"an appearance"* is in Humphreys's original.

24. Fonerden, *Carpenter's Battery,* 26; *OR,* 760; Bohannon, *Giles,* 103, 107-8; "Confederate . . . Casualties"

(M836), NA. Carpenter had 70 men on duty on June 8, but for some reason reported only 55 on the 9th, 11 of them unengaged.

25. *OR*, 763; Fishburne, "Historical Sketch," 138.

26. Slaughter, *Randolph Fairfax*, 27; Moore, *Cannoneer*, 75.

27. *OR*, 763; Slaughter, *Randolph Fairfax*, 27; Allan memoir, UNC.

28. *OR*, 741, 786; Brown memorandum, Brown-Ewell Papers, TSLA.

29. Ewell's draft report, Brown-Ewell Papers, TSLA.

30. Moore, *Cannoneer*, 75; *OR*, 760, 763; Driver, *Rockbridge Artillery*, 64, 78; "Confederate . . . Casualties" (M836), NA. Davis recovered and lived until 1886. Singleton survived, went west, and raised a company in Kentucky. Carpenter's four-gun battery had 70 men present, while Poague had only 71 to service six pieces.

31. Dunning in Moore, *Rebellion Record*, V, 112; Clarke, "Some One Has Blundered"; *OR*, 763; Poague, *Gunner*, 27.

32. *OR*, 729; Winder diary, MHS.

33. Howard, *Recollections*, 129-30; *OR*, 741.

34. *OR*, 741; White, *Sketches*, 91.

35. *OR*, 714, 741; James A. Walker to John F. and M. Botts Lewis, on a postwar visit to the battlefield, Fisher, "Port Republic and the Lewises," 20, Private Collection of Fisher.

Chapter 22: The Coaling "Hell-Spot"

1. Slaughter, *Randolph Fairfax*, 27; Apperson letter, June 10, Black Papers, VPI; Robson, *One-Legged*, 46; "Jackson's Latest Victories"; Neese, *Three Years*, 74.

2. Humphreys letter, Private Collection of Updike; Howard, *Recollections*, 128; Neese, *Three Years*, 74; Apperson letter, June 10, Black Papers, VPI; Slaughter, *Randolph Fairfax*, 27; O.T., "Battle at Port Republic" (emphasis added); Strayer diary, HRHS.

3. Paris, "Soldier's History," 403; Dabney to Hotchkiss, August 2, 1897, Hotchkiss Papers, LC. Paris, a chaplain in the 5th N.C. who was not present, probably simply echoed the Dabney line in his otherwise solid narrative.

4. Kelly, *Port Republic*, 18; Kelly's official report, M331, NA; "Taylor's Louisiana Brigade."

5. Taylor, *Destruction*, 75; Dabney to Hotchkiss, August 2, 1897, Hotchkiss Papers, LC; Evans, *Confederate Military History*, III, 262.

6. Morning Report, Taylor's Brigade, June 11, 1862, HL. The strengths therein for the 6th, 8th, 9th, and Wheat's Bn. are 439 + 558 + 473 + 127, a total of 1,597. Casualties of 166 (138 of them wounded) in unident. clipping, Dora Shute Scrapbook, Tulane, must be added for a June 9 strength. If one half of the wounded were on hand on June 11, the four units had had 1,700 men near the Coaling. The old chapel now standing in the ravine was built in 1884 (Hess, *Heartland*, 352). Some men killed in the bloody horror nearby in 1862 were later buried around the building.

7. Kelly, *Port Republic*, 18; "Taylor's Louisiana Brigade."

8. *OR*, 803; unident. clipping in Dora Shute scrapbook, Tulane.

9. *OR*, 803; "Taylor's Louisiana Brigade"; Kelly, *Port Republic*, 18.

10. "Taylor's Louisiana Brigade."

11. Kelly, *Port Republic*, 19; Wilson, "Port Republic"; Taylor, *Destruction*, 75; "Taylor's Louisiana Brigade" (whence the long quotation); Garber, *Harman*, 20; Houghton, *Two Boys*, 29.

12. *OR*, 802; Kelly, *Port Republic*, 19; Randolph reminiscence, VHS; unident. Confederate account in Strayer scrapbook, SPRP.

13. Taylor, *Destruction*, 75; Evans, *Confederate Military History*, X, 217; Kelly, *Port Republic*, 19. Both of the emphases in the Kelly quotation are added.

14. Fisher, "Port Republic and the Lewises," 24, Private Collection of Fisher.

15. Kelly, *Port Republic*, 19; Kelly's official report, M331, NA; Stafford, *General Stafford*, 42.

16. Moore, *Louisiana Tigers*, 67; "Wheat's Battalion"; CSR of S. H. Early, Roll 83, M331, NA. The valuation for Wheat's horse is in Early's CSR because Early's horse had been evaluated concurrently (and then killed, elsewhere). Within two years, Confederate horses were often valued at $2,500.

17. Fonerden, *Carpenter's Battery*, 27; Neese, *Three Years*, 74; Randolph reminiscence, VHS; *Indiana Soldier*, 467.

18. Unident. Confederate account, Strayer scrapbook, SPRP; "Jackson's Latest Victories"; Wilson, "Port Republic"; Cooke, "Battle of Port Republic."

19. "Taylor's Louisiana Brigade."

20. Neese, *Three Years*, 74-75; "Wheat's Battalion"; Kelly, *Port Republic*, 19.

21. "Taylor's Louisiana Brigade"; Neese, *Three Years*, 75.

22. Taylor, *Destruction*, 75; "Squarest Battle of the War"; Wilson, "Port Republic"; Humphreys letter, Private Collection of Updike; Neese, *Three Years*, 75; Cooke, "Battle of Port Republic." The text does not quote all of these accounts of bayonet fighting.

23. Taylor, *Destruction*, 75; Moore, *Louisiana Tigers*, 66.

24. *OR*, 802; Neese, *Three Years*, 75; "Squarest Battle of the War"; Edmund Lewis Stephens to parents, June 14, Stephens Collection, Northwestern State University. Ed Stephens died in front of Richmond in 1864.

25. "Squarest Battle of the War."

26. Moore, *Louisiana Tigers*, 66-67; G. Campbell Brown to mother, June 17, Polk-Brown-Ewell Papers, UNC; Boyd, "Major Bob Wheat."

27. Trahern memoir, VHS. Trahern did not specify whether his analysis encompassed the earth's northern or western hemisphere.

28. "Taylor's Louisiana Brigade"; Randolph reminiscence, VHS; *OR*, 803; Wilson, "Port Republic."

29. Kern reminiscence, NCDAH; Buck, *Old Confeds*, 38; Abram D. Warwick, "Last Battle of General Turner Ashby," 10, Box 24, Daniel Papers, U.Va.; Kelly, *Port Republic*, 20.

30. Kaylor, "Port Republic Battle," HRHS; Hadley, "Indiana Soldier," 213. One astonished postbattle visitor to the Coaling was C. C. Wight (memoir, 77-78, VHS). Other accounts will be cited in a later chapter.

31. *OR*, 697, 693.

32. Huntington, "Operations," 333.

33. Huntington, "Operations," 334.

34. May, "Battle of Port Republic," 99; *OR*, 692-93. The emphasis is added.

35. Rawling, *First ... Virginia*, 96-97; Clarke, "Some One Has Blundered."

36. Anonymous Union map, NA; Bates, *Pennsylvania Volunteers*, II, 1308-9 and III, 980.

37. *OR*, 692.

38. *OR*, 697.

39. Fairfax diary, Chicago Histl. Soc. The other Federal company apparently remained on the upper slope, since Confederates spoke of fire coming from that sector.

40. *OR*, 696.

41. Huffman, *Ups and Downs*, 50; Huntington, "Operations," 333; *OR*, 696-97.

42. *OR*, 693; Huntington, "Operations," 334.

43. Clarke, "Some One Has Blundered"; Rawling, *First ... Virginia*, 96-97.

44. Garber, *Harman*, 20-21.

45. *OR*, 700.

Chapter 23: The Struggle to Hold the Coaling

1. *OR*, 715, 802; Taylor, *Destruction*, 75; "Squarest Battle of the War." Hotchkiss in Evans, *Confederate Military History*, III, 262, wrote that enemy reaction came "soon."

2. "Taylor's Louisiana Brigade."

3. Neese, *Three Years*, 75; "Taylor's Louisiana Brigade."

4. Kelly, *Port Republic*, 19; *OR*, 715.

5. Kelly, *Port Republic*, 19. The distinguished Yankee may have been Captain Keily again, depending on when he was hit, but I have placed that story in the next chapter.

6. "Taylor's Louisiana Brigade"; "Squarest Battle of the War"; *OR*, 715, 802.

7. Kelly, *Port Republic*, 19-20; Clarke, "Some One Has Blundered."

8. Dunning in Moore, *Rebellion Record*, V, 112. Because of their alignments in the attack on Winder, in the counterattack the 5th probably was on the Federal right. Dunning's remarks about Lewiston confirm that.

9. Wood, *Seventh Regiment*, 118-19; Wilson, *Itinerary*, 169. Wood's account divides the 7th Ohio's attack into stages, the second being a further attack against a second Confederate ridge. He must have meant crossing the hollow behind the Coaling. No Federals pursued across the main ravine of Deep Run.

10. *OR*, 692, 697.

11. *Soldier's Casket*, vol. I, no. 3 (March 1865); *OR*, 690.

12. Bates, *Penn. Volunteers*, II, 1308-9; Kelly, *Port Republic*, 20.

13. Huntington, "Operations," 334; *OR*, 715, 802; Ohio Roster Comm., *Official Roster*, X, 409-14.

14. "Squarest Battle of the War"; "From Front Royal"; G. M. Morgan (quoting Surget) to unidentified correspondent, June 18, 1862, Dawson Papers, Duke. Surget was from New Orleans, where "Beast"

Butler's goons had looted his house and gleefully published a will they found leaving $1,000,000 to the Confederate government.

15. *OR,* 741, 802.

16. "Taylor's Louisiana Brigade"; Kelly, *Port Republic,* 20.

17. Kelly, *Port Republic,* 20; "Taylor's Louisiana Brigade." These two little-known accounts are far the best for the swirling fight around the Coaling.

18. "Taylor's Louisiana Brigade"; Kelly, *Port Republic,* 21. Taylor's official report and his postwar memoir both speak vividly of the fighting at the Coaling but ignore the combat between his brigade's three overt attacks.

19. *OR,* 803. Surget became a lieutenant colonel on Taylor's staff. Killmartin was captured at Spotsylvania but survived the war.

20. Taylor, *Destruction,* 75; Evans, *Confed. Military History,* X, 218.

21. Bates, *Pennsylvania Volunteers,* II, 1309; "Latest from Front Royal"; "Squarest Battle of the War"; *OR,* 803. In some sources (see Evans, *Confed. Military History,* X, 218) Taylor is said to be still wondering what had happened to the 7th La. His confused postwar pronouncements led to the error. He knew at the time that Jackson had preempted the 7th for use on the plain.

22. Kelly, *Port Republic,* 21.

23. "Wheat's Battalion"; unident. clipping in Dora Shute scrapbook, Tulane; "Historical . . . Opelousas Guards," Bound Volume 6, "Record Roll, Eighth Regiment, Louisiana Volunteers," Tulane; *OR,* 787, 803; Evans, *Confederate Military History,* X, 219.

24. "Record Roll, Sixth Regiment," Tulane; "Port Republic Killed," Tulane; Booth, *Louisiana Confederate Soldiers,* passim.

25. "Squarest Battle of the War"; Parmeter diary, OHS; Dabney, *Life,* 424.

26. *The Soldier's Casket,* vol. I, no. 3, March 1865.

27. "Squarest Battle of the War." The emphasis is added.

28. *OR,* 692-94.

29. "Taylor's Louisiana Brigade"; Kelly, *Port Republic,* 21-22; "Humor in Battle." The quote's "them air guns" is an awkward rendering for "them there guns" in dialect.

30. Taylor, *Destruction,* 75.

31. Taylor, *Destruction,* 75-76; Evans, *Confederate Military History,* X, 218; Kelly, *Port Republic,* 22; Wingfield, *Two Confederate Items,* 12; *OR,* 802; "Taylor's Louisiana Brigade." Taylor described Ewell crashing through the underbrush on horseback, but the far more reliable Kelly put Ewell afoot, hat in hand. Accounts of Ewell's attempts to inspirit troops around him make it obvious Taylor was not nearby. Wingfield explained that Ewell's horse had just been killed. Kelly's deprecation of Taylor's role might be chalked up to intrabrigade jealousies, but the detailed and judicious "Taylor's Louisiana Brigade," without criticizing Taylor once, also fails to mention any personal participation by the general.

32. Kelly, *Port Republic,* 22; "Taylor's Louisiana Brigade"; Taylor, *Destruction,* 75; *OR,* 692.

33. Huffman, *Ups and Downs,* 50; Kern reminiscence, NCDAH; Buck, *Old Confeds,* 38; Bond reminiscence, ViRC.

34. Kelly, *Port Republic,* 22; "Taylor's Louisiana Brigade"; "Squarest Battle of the War."

35. *OR,* 700; "Most Brilliant Action"; Ohio Roster Comm., *Official Roster,* X, 430-35. Cochran became a sergeant in 1863, was wounded at Mine Run, and was discharged in October 1864.

36. Huntington, "Operations," 334-35.

37. The chaotic events near the Coaling of course did not fit into three neat sequences visible to everyone on the field. Some accounts ignore the repeated surges; a few mention only two. The majority, however, including the highest-quality sources, saw three distinct Confederate assaults and two successful Northern counterattacks. A dozen sources used in the last two chapters confirm the three-surge scenario, these among them: *Indiana Soldier,* 467; *OR,* 715 (Jackson) and 803 (Taylor); Wayland, "Battle"; Huffman, *Ups and Downs,* 50; Boyd, "Bob Wheat"; Hotchkiss, *Make Me a Map,* 55 ("several times"); and Hotchkiss in Evans, *Confederate Military History,* III, 262 ("for some time"). The startling news of Jackson's withdrawal order is in Kelly's report, M331, NA.

38. "The Louisiana Brigade."

39. "Taylor's Louisiana Brigade"; Morgan to unident. correspondent, June 18, Dawson Papers, Duke; Ring to wife, June 14, 1862, Tulane.

40. Post letter, MHS; Ring diary, Tulane; "Extract of a Letter" ("seven pieces"); E. L. Stephens letter, June 14, Stephens Coll., Northwestern State U. ("five pieces"); *OR,* 802; Manning, "Histl. Memorandum," Tulane (five); unident. old clipping, Ammen comp., USAMHI; Garber, *Harman,* 21. Another gun, presumably from the June 8 captures, went to Wooding's Battery (*OR,* 729).

Chapter 24: The Climax on the Plain

1. *OR,* 786; "Jackson's Latest Victories"; "Squarest Battle of the War."
2. Winder diary, MHS; *OR,* 715, 750; Kelly, *Port Republic,* 21.
3. *OR,* 753; Kearns diary, VHS; John Apperson letter, June 10, 1862, Black Papers, VPI; Kelly, *Port Republic,* 21.
4. *OR,* 741; Kelly, *Port Republic,* 21.
5. *OR,* 763; Shaner diary, Private Collection of Dr. David Scott; Moore, *Cannoneer,* 75.
6. *OR,* 715, 728-29, 742; Neese, *Three Years,* 75; Dabney, *Life,* 424.
7. Dabney, *Life,* 424; Ewell's draft report, TSLA; *OR,* 786.
8. Ewell's draft report, TSLA; Wingfield, *Two Confed. Items,* 12.
9. G. Campbell Brown memorandum and Brown letter to his mother, June 17, 1862, Brown-Ewell Papers, TSLA; *OR,* 786, 715.
10. Statement by Lieutenant James M. O. Hillsman, Company H, 44th Virginia, in Roll of Honor, ViRC; Wight memoir, 76-77, VHS.
11. Driver, *58th Virginia,* 24, 88.
12. *OR,* 742, 745, 747; John Apperson letter, June 10, Black Papers, VPI. Dabney, *Life,* 424, insists in error that the 2nd Va. participated in the final attack.
13. *OR,* 792-93; Ewell's draft report, TSLA (the only source for his meeting with Walker); "James A. Walker," VHS; Buck, "Walker," 35; Buck, *Old Confeds,* 38. The 1st Md. "was not under fire on the 9th," although Joshua Simpson of its Company D was wounded when he hooked up with the 52nd Va. to get into the fight (*OR,* 818).
14. List diary, IHS; O.T., "Battle at Port Republic"; Davis, "7th Indiana," ISL; Winscott, "From the 7th"; Hadley, "Indiana Soldier," 213; Thomson, *Seventh Indiana,* 101.
15. Hoyt letter to "Dear Parents," June 12, 1862, OHS; Parmeter diary, OHS; SeCheverell, *Twenty-ninth Ohio,* 47.
16. C. H. Bard to "My Friend Sade," June 17, Woods Papers, Duke; Wood, *The Seventh Regiment,* 119; Wilder, *History of Company C,* 29; Burton letter, Private Collection of Sandra R. Kenney.
17. S. H. Dunning in Moore, ed., *Rebellion Record,* V, 112; Clarke, "Some One Has Blundered."
18. Winters, *Civil War Letters,* 37-38; Rawling, *First . . . Virginia,* 94-95.
19. W.C.F., "Letter." This letter by a 13th Indiana soldier was written within two weeks after the battle.
20. Barnes, *Medical and Surgical,* vol. V, collation 9, page 88.
21. Huntington, "Operations," 335; *OR,* 697, 700.
22. Keily reference file, Private Collection of Brian C. Pohanka. The contemporary correspondence is in M650, NA. In August 1862, Shields called Keily the "noblest soldier on that field . . . a glory to his country and race" (this to the archbishop of New York, which accounts for the ethnic strutting).
23. "Squarest Battle of the War." The "muddle" quote from Wavell is dated February 1933 (Heinl, *Dictionary,* 64).
24. Jackson to A. R. Boteler, May 6, 1862, Boteler Papers, Duke.
25. *OR,* 774, 715; Fravel, "Valley Campaign," 419; Kauffman diary, UNC; Krick, *Lee's Colonels,* 365-66; Taliaferro memoir, Private Collection of Sarah T. Rohrer; *CV,* XXIX, 127. Hotchkiss, *Make Me a Map,* 55, credits Taliaferro's Brigade with delivering "a volley or two by a flank fire."
26. *OR,* 757-58, 742; Walker, *Memorial,* 402.
27. *OR,* 758; Walker, *Memorial,* 403; Neff letter to "Dear Parents," August 4, 1862, USAMHI.
28. *OR,* 742; Allan memoir, 138, UNC; Randolph reminiscence, VHS; Humphreys letter, Private Collection of David Q. Updike. John Apperson's letter of June 10 (Black Papers, VPI) recounts caring for the desperately wounded William Frederick Goodman of the 48th Va. Like Private Post of the 84th Pa., Goodman survived his grievous wound and was still alive in 1904 (Chapla, *48th Virginia,* 125). Despite Goodman's personal ordeal, the 48th saw little action.
29. Wood, *The War,* 64; Caffey, *Battle-Fields,* 294.
30. Strayer diary, HRHS. The emphasis is hers.

Chapter 25: The Bridge Afire and Frémont's Ire

1. Coble reminiscence, NCDAH; *OR,* 766, 771.
2. Evans, *Confederate Military History,* III, 263; Cartmell, *Shenandoah,* 345; *OR,* 22.

3. Evans, *Confederate Military History*, II, 81; Thomas diary, Private Collection of A. T. Wallace; *OR*, 769, 771; "Extracts of a Letter." The officer-author probably was Colonel Patton.

4. *OR*, 715, 798; Evans, *Confederate Military History*, III, 263; John M. Patton, "Reminiscences of Jackson," Cook Papers, WVU. In explaining his expectations of the rear guard, Jackson gave no hint of the double-battle strategy so often attributed to him. Taliaferro's Brigade near Port Republic had no offensive intent. To the absolute contrary, some of it remained on the left bank of North River "for the purpose of co-operating, if necessary, with General Trimble and preventing his being cut off" (*OR*, 715).

5. Culpepper, "15th Alabama"; Coble reminiscence, NCDAH.

6. Dabney, *Life*, 421, 424-25; Hotchkiss, *Make Me a Map*, 55; Goldsborough, *Maryland Line* (1869), 75; *OR*, 766, 771, 715. Dabney specifically put the *dispatch* of orders to Trimble to hurry at ten A.M., which obviously is too late. Hotchkiss and Goldsborough are the badly mistaken daybreak sources. F. A. Wildman of the 55th Ohio (letter to his wife, June 13, OHS) wrote that he saw the smoke from the burning bridge "about 10 oclock."

7. May, "Harrison Bateman," SPRP; Oates, *The War*, 104-5; Clark, *North Carolina Regiments*, IV, 233; Coble reminiscence, NCDAH.

8. Wayland, *Rockingham County*, 144; Murphy, *10th Virginia Infantry*, 156; Armstrong, *11th Virginia Cavalry*, 153; Hess, *Heartland*, 348; May, "Port Republic," 107, JMU; Walker, *Memorial*, 526-27. Hulvey was born at Cross Keys, later served in the 11th Va. Cav., became Rockingham's superintendent of schools, and lived until 1920. His claim to center stage in the burning cannot be certified on other word than his own. The careful George E. May phrased Hulvey's claim with apparent caution: "Hulvey . . . said at different times, that he had charge of the squad."

9. Stratton, *Heroes in Gray*, 84; Abram D. Warwick, "The Last Battle of General Turner Ashby," 8, Box 24, Daniel Papers, U.Va.; McDonald reminiscence, UNC; Hands notebook, MHS; Hess, *Heartland*, 349. Port kept losing its bridges, even after Jackson was no longer around to burn them. A flood carried away the replacement bridge in September 1870. The next edition, built in 1874 with stone piers, succumbed to an 1877 flood. Then the town went eight years without a bridge over North River. The current bridge dates from 1955. It is farther upstream than the 1862 span and crosses the river at a different angle.

10. Myers, *Comanches*, 67; Walker, *Memorial*, 527-28; *OR*, 732.

11. Coble reminiscence, NCDAH; Abram D. Warwick, "Last Battle of General Turner Ashby," 8-10, Box 24, Daniel Papers, U.Va; Lynchburg *Virginian*, June 18, 1862, p. 3.

12. Strother, *Virginia Yankee*, 242; May, "Port Republic," 104, JMU; Rockingham *Register*, February 6, 1879.

13. Evans memoir, LC; Tracy, "Fremont's Pursuit," 341; Polsley letter to "My Dear Nellie," June 10, LC; Reader, *Second Virginia Infantry*, 171; Osborn, *Trials*, 46; Campbell diary, OHS.

14. Pula, *For Liberty*, 32; Tracy, "Fremont's Pursuit," 341; Paulus, *Papers of . . . Milroy*, 48; "From Gen. Fremont's Army."

15. Kearsey, *Shenandoah Valley*, 61.

16. Coble reminiscence, NCDAH; Kirkpatrick diary, UT; Patton, "Reminiscences of Jackson," Cook Papers, WVU.

17. Garber, *Harman*, 20. J. M. Kern of the rear guard (diary, UNC), spoke with apparent derision of the "Stonewall Jackson pontoon bridge." Some idea of the logistical bottleneck around the two bridges, of which Garber's brave driver was the last element, comes from Colonel T. S. Garnett's estimate that it included "at least 700 wagons" (Garnett to father, July 2, 1862, FNMP).

18. Oates, *The War*, 105; *OR*, 798, 766, 771; Bond reminiscence, 57, ViRC.

19. *OR*, 771; John Apperson letter, June 10, Black Papers, VPI; Hopkins diary, VHS; "Taylor's Louisiana Brigade"; letter of "J.J.H.," a 52nd Va. commissary officer, to his wife, June 23, Leigh Collection, USAMHI; Moore, *Cannoneer*, 76.

20. Wingfield, *Two Confederate Items*, 12; Cooke, "Battle of Port Republic"; Goldsborough, *Maryland Line* (1869), 76.

21. Dabney, *Life*, 426; Abram D. Warwick, "The Last Battle of General Turner Ashby," 17-19, Box 24, Daniel Papers, U.Va.

22. May, "Battle of Port Republic," 101; Randolph, *Jackson*, 172-73; Boyd, *Reminiscences*, 14; Booth, *Personal Reminiscences*, 43; Davis, *Shenandoah*, 206.

23. Bond reminiscence, 58, ViRC.

24. Ropp to father, June 14, VSA; Pile, "The War Story."

25. Goldsborough, *Maryland Line* (1869), 76; Evans, *Confederate Military History*, III, 263; Dabney, *Life*, 425; Neese, *Three Years*, 76.

26. Cooke, "Battle of Port Republic"; Garber, *Harman*, 21; Ruffner, *44th Virginia*, 78; McIlwaine, *Memories*, 194-95. Camper and Kirkley, *Historical Record*, 71, said some Federal wounded who lay untended overnight were bothered by hogs loose on the field.

27. *OR*, 716; Douglas, *I Rode*, 91; Dabney, *Life*, 426. The unreliable Imboden, in his "Stonewall Jackson," 296, recounted a fanciful tale about Jackson reacting to Frémont's fire by forbidding further attention to Yankee wounded.

28. Munford quoted indirectly by Lizzie E. Munford to mother, June 13 (citing his letter of June 10), Munford-Ellis Papers, Duke; Thomson, *Seventh Indiana,* 102-3; Taylor, *Destruction,* 76.

29. Fravel, "Valley Campaign," 419; Harding, "Chenoweth," VHS; Allan memoir, 138, UNC.

30. Stratton, *Heroes in Gray,* 84.

31. Thomas diary, Private Collection of A. T. Wallace.

32. Frank diary, LC; Tracy, "Fremont's Pursuit," 341; Paulus, *Papers of . . . Milroy,* 48; Brumley diary, OHS.

33. Cartmell, *Shenandoah,* 345; 66th Ohio memoir, USAMHI; Ohio Roster Comm., *Official Roster,* V, 539. Shaffer was twenty years old when he enlisted in October 1861. Without Frémont's shelling, he doubtless would have been treated much more promptly.

34. Strayer diary, HRHS.

Chapter 26: Down the River and Up the Mountain

1. Estimates of the time the battle ended range from 8 A.M., to 3 P.M., as is typical of Civil War chronology. The careful timing of events in the reports of the 1st Va. Bn. and 42nd Va., cited in the last chapter, conform to a 10:30 conclusion. Jackson estimated that the fight lasted "to ten and a half A.M." (M. A. Jackson, *Memoirs,* 283). Wilder, *Company C,* 29, also uses 10:30. Myers, *Comanches,* 68, and McClendon, *Recollections,* 67, both say "by 10 o'clock." Strayer diary, HRHS, says "about 10 o'clock." Sources suggesting the battle lasted until noon are Kephart, "Shenandoah Valley" (110th Pa.) and Caffey, *Battle-Fields,* 294.

2. *OR,* 774; Huffman, *Ups and Downs,* 50; "Jackson's Latest Victories."

3. Taylor, *Destruction,* 76; Wood, *The War,* 63-64. Jackson at the time of Frémont's firing is described in the preceding chapter.

4. Fravel, "Valley Campaign," 419; "Jackson's Latest Victories"; Dabney to Hotchkiss, August 2, 1897, Hotchkiss Papers. LC.

5. *OR,* 732; Munford's history of the 2nd Va. Cav., 33, Munford-Ellis Papers, Duke; Coles, "War Reminiscences," 28; Munford, "Reminiscences," 530.

6. Krick, *Lee's Colonels,* 266; McDonald reminiscence, UNC.

7. "Jackson's Latest Victories"; *OR,* 715; G. Campbell Brown memorandum, Brown-Ewell Papers, TSLA; Taylor, *Destruction,* 76.

8. Kelly, *Port Republic,* 22; Ring diary, Tulane.

9. *OR,* 766-68, 786, 793; Fisher, "Port Republic and the Lewises," 30, Private Collection of Lewis F. Fisher; Wight memoir, 78, VHS. Post's letter (MHS) shows that the 1st Md. did not go with Walker.

10. *OR,* 715, 774-75; Pile, "War Story." Taliaferro also lauded his staff officers, including his commissary, who can hardly have been a pivotal figure in the pursuit.

11. *OR,* 745, 747, 753, 758; Walker, *Memorial,* 403.

12. Carpenter to father, June 16, Private Collection of Bohannon; McDonald, *Laurel Brigade,* 71; *OR,* 742.

13. *OR,* 763; Moore, *Cannoneer,* 75-76; Neese, *Three Years,* 76; Kaylor, "Port Republic Battle," HRHS. The sinkhole remained a familiar landmark in the twentieth century. Colonel Crutchfield (*OR,* 729) also reported the recovery of "the only gun" lost on the field, so Poague must have learned of it soon. Crutchfield's report was dated seven weeks after Poague's, which no doubt accounts for Poague's statement.

14. Moore, *Cannoneer,* 75.

15. *OR,* 715, 729, 742, 744; Walker, *Memorial,* 244. Chew's Battery was scattered, and Jackson used a fragment of the unit near the front. Neese (*Three Years,* 75) guessed that he pursued for five miles; the history of the unit with which Chew served (McDonald, *Laurel Brigade,* 71) reported that the battery covered "about two miles"; and Lieutenant Williams's diary (VHS) claimed pursuit for ten miles ("got some blankets" was the high point for him).

16. *OR,* 750, 774.

17. Lacy, *Memorial,* 49.

18. McDonald reminiscence, UNC.

19. A. D. Warwick, "Last Battle of Turner Ashby," 11-17, Box 24, Daniel Papers, U.Va.

20. Hopley, *"Stonewall,"* 86-87.

21. Myers, *Comanches,* 68-69.

22. Dabney, *Life,* 427. In addition to viewing alleged explosive bullets, Jackson also marveled at Federal body armor found on the field. The VMI museum owns a set recovered at Port Republic.

23. Douglas marginalia in 1892 edition of Mrs. Jackson's memoir, 275, Antietam N.B.; Willis, "Letter," 164-65; Douglas, *I Rode,* 87. The usually reliable H. H. McGuire, in a May 28, 1896, letter (Roll 34,

Hotchkiss Papers, LC), garbled Willis's escape, timing it overnight on June 8-9 rather than during the retreat.

24. Sipe recollections, HRHS.

25. Skidmore, *Billy Davis*, 146-47.

26. Jackson's estimate is in *OR,* 715. Other sources (often reporting on individual advances) offer these distances: "some 4 miles" (Winder diary, MHS); "4 miles" (Funk, *OR,* 750); "about five" (Neese, *Three Years,* 75); "about six" ("Jackson's Latest Victories," a Stonewall Brigade officer); "7 miles" (Taliaferro in *OR,* 774); "about 8" (Munford, *OR,* 732, and Parmeter diary, OHS); "some 8 or 9 miles below Port Republic" (Winder, *OR,* 742, not necessarily in deviation from his diary entry, because he cited the town not the battlefield, and on 742 noted that his infantry halted at four miles); "about nine miles" (Kauffman diary, UNC, by a member of the 10th Va.); "nine mile pursuit" (Myers, *Comanches,* 68); 8 or 10 miles (Apperson letter, Black Papers, VPI); 10 miles (Williams diary, VHS, of Chew's Battery); "chased 10 or 12 miles" (Hopkins diary, VHS, chaplain in the 4th Va.); and "some 12 miles" (Hotchkiss, *Make Me a Map.* 55).

27. *OR,* 697, 700; Wood, *Seventh Regiment,* 119-21. Shields's fatuous claims about the calmly marching army that he met are reported later in this chapter.

28. *OR,* 700; Thomson, *Seventh Indiana,* 101; Davis, "7th Indiana," ISL; Rawling, *First ... Virginia,* 95.

29. SeCheverell, *Twenty-ninth Ohio,* 47; Parmeter diary, OHS; Clarke, "Some One Has Blundered"; Dunning in Moore, *Rebellion Record,* V, 112; *OR,* 687.

30. *OR,* 700; Parmeter diary, OHS; Wilder, *Company C,* 29; Thomson, *Seventh Indiana,* 101; Huntington, "Operations," 335-36. Some sources insisted that Southern cavalry was readily repulsed (see Ray, "Journal," 60, and Bates, *Pennsylvania Volunteers,* II, 1309). The indignant officer likely was Huntington himself.

31. Dunning in Moore, *Rebellion Record,* V, 112; Clarke, "Some One Has Blundered."

32. Been to wife, June 11, and Van Dyke to "Dear Brother," June 12, both at IHS.

33. Skidmore, *Billy Davis,* 145-46; List to parents, June 17, IHS.

34. Thomson, *Seventh Indiana,* 103-4. Beetem was killed in June 1864 in front of Petersburg (Indiana Adj. Gen., *Report,* IV, 102).

35. SeCheverell, *Twenty-ninth Ohio,* 47-48.

36. Wilson, *Itinerary of the Seventh,* 170-71.

37. Fairfax diary, Chicago Hist. Soc.; Clarke, "Some One Has Blundered." Fairfax was killed at Chancellorsville (Ohio Roster Comm., *Official Roster,* II, 135).

38. *OR,* 687-88, 692; Rawling, *First ... Virginia,* 95.

39. Clarke, "Some One Has Blundered"; Been to wife, June 11, IHS; *OR,* 688; C. H. Bard to "Sade," July 17, Woods Papers, Duke.

40. *OR,* 688-89, which includes the text of the withdrawal message.

41. Howard, *Recollections,* 129; Slaughter, *Randolph Fairfax,* 27.

42. Hotchkiss, *Make Me a Map,* 55; Kaylor, "Port Republic Battle," HRHS; Pile, "War Story"; "Extract of a Letter"; Hopkins diary, VHS.

43. John Apperson letter, June 10, Black Papers, VPI; Evans, *Confederate Military History,* III, 263; Allan memoir, 138, UNC.

44. *OR,* 767, 771; Kauffman diary, UNC.

45. Taylor, *Destruction,* 77; Hotchkiss, *Make Me a Map,* 55; Barrow diary, USAMHI; Harper diary, Tulane. Georgetown, D.C., just more than one hundred air miles away, reported "drizzle & rain" all night and all of the 10th ("Weather Journal," NWRC). Port Republic's location meant earlier arrival and departure for weather fronts than in Georgetown.

46. *Richardson's Almanac* (sunset at 7:16 in Richmond); Ring diary, Tulane; Bond reminiscence, 58-59, ViRC. McDonald's reminiscence (UNC) describes the congestion in words nearly identical to Bond's.

47. Moore, *Cannoneer,* 77-78; Driver, *Rockbridge Artillery,* 64; Poague, *Gunner,* 27.

48. Taylor, *Destruction,* 77; *OR,* 732; McDonald reminiscence, UNC; "James A. Walker," VHS.

49. Poague, *Gunner,* 27; Lacy, *Memorial,* 50.

50. *OR,* 750-51; Garnett to father, July 2, 1862, FNMP; Winder diary, MHS; Cartmell, *Shenandoah,* 346.

51. Moore, *Cannoneer,* 78; Buck, *Old Confeds,* 39.

52. Moore, *Cannoneer,* 77.

53. Boyd, *Reminiscences,* 15-16.

54. "James A. Walker," VHS.

55. Kelly, *Port Republic,* 27; Allan memoir, 138, UNC.

56. M. A. Jackson, *Memoirs,* 514-15.

57. Fontaine, *My Life,* 111-13.

58. McIlwaine, *Memories,* 195.

59. Hotchkiss, *Make Me a Map,* 55; Allan memoir, 138, UNC; Boyd, *Reminiscences,* 14; Thomas diary, Private Collection of A. T. Wallace; Coble reminiscence, NCDAH.

60. Paulus, *Papers of... Milroy,* 48; Brumley diary, OHS; *OR,* 685.

61. *OR,* 732, 742, 750-51, 768, 771; McDonald reminiscence, UNC; Shaner diary, Private Collection of Dr. Scott. Colonel Garnett of the 48th, in a letter to his father (FNMP), put his arrival in camp at one A.M.; his official report said two A.M. Munford's account of his bivouac includes another version of Ewell's recanting earlier criticisms of Jackson (Munford, "Reminiscences," 530), but they fit far better on the preceding night, as used in an earlier chapter. This version includes some other historical errors; furthermore, Ewell evidently was farther downhill than Munford.

Chapter 27: "Never Take Counsel of Your Fears"

1. Hotchkiss, *Make Me a Map,* 55; "Weather Journal," NWRC; Kauffman diary, UNC; Boyd, *Reminiscences,* 16-17.

2. Dabney, *Life,* 427; Brumley diary, OHS; Webb, "Gen. Fremont's Command"; Wildman diary, OHS.

3. Evans memoir, LC; Polsley letter, June 15, WVU; Schurz, *Reminiscences,* II, 343; "Battle Near Port Republic."

4. Brumley diary, OHS; Woods letter, June 15, U. Va.; Yancey, "Civil War Letter," 36; "Fremont's Army in Rockingham"; "Visit to the Country"; Hotchkiss, *Make Me a Map,* 56. Ewell mentioned the episode in his official report (*OR,* 783). His men also buried 101 Federals at one location. Ewell gloated over the opportunity because the dead men "were chiefly of Blenker's division, notorious for months on account of their thefts and dastardly insults to women and children." An account of W. N. Jordan's burial party is in Hess, *Heartland,* 325-26.

5. Krzyzanowski, *Memoirs,* 45; Tracy, "Fremont's Pursuit," 343; Polsley to wife, June 17, WVU.

6. Evans, *Confederate Military History,* III, 263; Hotchkiss, *Make Me a Map,* 55; *OR,* XII, pt. 3, 908-9; *OR,* 732. The Civil War breastworks in Brown's Gap probably date from 1864, but it is possible that Jackson began them in primitive style during this period. Moon, *Brown's Gap,* 7-8, discusses the works.

7. Harman letters, Hotchkiss Papers, LC; Hotchkiss, *Make Me a Map,* 129; Apperson letter, June 10, Black Papers, VPI.

8. M. A. Jackson, *Memoirs,* 283; Jackson to Cooper, June 10, in Taylor's CSR, M331, Roll 243, NA.

9. Boyd, *Reminiscences,* 16-17; Harper diary, Tulane.

10. Thomas diary, Private Collection of A. T. Wallace; Apperson letter, June 10, Black Papers, VPI; McIlwaine, *Memories,* 195; Winder diary, MHS.

11. Moore, *Cannoneer,* 79.

12. G. E. May, "Harrison Bateman," SPRP; Svenson, "Backyard," 15-16.

13. Been to wife, June 11, IHS; Indiana Adj. Gen., *Report,* IV, 285-86.

14. Anon. 66th Ohio memoir, USAMHI; Yancey, "Civil War Letter," 35; Webb, "Gen. Fremont's Command."

15. Wheeler, *In Memoriam,* 337.

16. "Visit to the Country"; Fisher, *John Lewis, Pioneer,* 317.

17. "Port Republic and the Lewises," 27, 31-33, Private Collection of Lewis F. Fisher.

18. "Port Republic and the Lewises," 34, and Sue Lewis Durkee to Lewis F. Fisher, December 10, 1958, both in Private Collection of Fisher; John F. Lewis claim, Southern Claims Commission Case Files, NA. Durkee's letter reports the inevitable family recollection that blood stains marred Lewiston's floor for the half century until the house burned.

19. Sipe recollection, HRHS.

20. Parmeter diary and Brumley diary, OHS; Wood, *Seventh Regiment,* 119; Been to wife, June 12, IHS. Been reported reaching Luray about two P.M. on the 11th.

21. *OR,* 683-84.

22. Harman letters, Hotchkiss Papers, LC; Pryor, *Post of Honor,* 198-99.

23. *OR,* XII, pt. 3, 909; Hotchkiss, *Make Me a Map,* 55-56; Harman letters, Hotchkiss Papers, LC.

24. Hotchkiss, *Make Me a Map,* 56.

25. *OR,* 732-33; Wayland, *Rockingham County,* 148. Wayland uses an account by local cavalryman W. N. Jordan, who buried 102 Federals. Jordan also told the story about Northern bodies purposely burned in a large house, adding that some live wounded were in the pyre.

26. Jackson to Letcher in CSR of J. R. Braithwaite, M331, NA.

27. *OR,* XII, pt. 3, 910. The same message is in *OR,* XI, pt. 3, 589-90, accompanied by Lee's supporting communications with other officials. One is a disingenuous suggestion to the Secretary of War that secrecy be maintained, which if thoroughly done would have canceled much of the effect of the feint.

28. Schenck to "Sally," June 12, Miami University; Hoyt to parents, June 12, OHS; Wildman to wife, June

13, OHS. Schenck five days later retreated to the more comfortable ground of politics, discerning a plot to get him out of the U.S. House of Representatives race by running him for the Senate! (Schenck eventually won election to the lower house.)

29. Hurst, *Seventy-Third*, 24-25; "Latest from Front Royal."

30. "Arrival of Sick and Wounded Soldiers."

31. "More Secesh Prisoners."

32. Burton letter, Private Collection of Sandra R. Kenney; Winscott, "From the 7th"; List to parents, June 17, IHS.

33. Abner Royce to parents, June 9-13 (written in increments), WRHS; Wood, *Seventh Regiment*, 120-21; Wright to mother, June 16, U. Michigan; W.C.F., "Letter"; Van Dyke to brother, June 12, and letter without salutation dated June 13, IHS.

34. Polsley to wife, June 15, WVU; "Jackson Believed to be Reinforced"; Paulus, *Papers of . . . Milroy*, 55.

35. Strayer diary, HRHS; Hotchkiss, *Make Me a Map*, 56; unident. ms. note reporting experiences of Surgeon Johnson of the 1st Md., B. T. Johnson Papers, Duke; Micajah Woods letter, June 15, U.Va.

36. Yancey, "Civil War Letter," 36-37; Hotchkiss to wife, June 15, Roll 4, Hotchkiss Papers, LC.

37. "Fremont's Army in Rockingham." This enormously long article provides a detailed look at early war depredations by an invading army. Among the households mentioned elsewhere in this narrative were Jacob Strayer's Bogota, which lost $1,600 worth of goods, including all of Jacob's clothing, leaving him without a change of "linen"; and Mrs. Ann Kemper at Cross Keys, whose loss came to $7,295, including "every article usually found in a well furnished house" and a variety of farm animals, implements, and accessories.

38. Hotchkiss, *Make Me a Map*, 57; Ring to wife, June 14, Tulane; Humphreys letter, Private Collection of Updike; Southall to mother, June 14, USAMHI; Griffin diary, Emory U. Confederate soldiers teased local civilians, as was their habit, poking fun at big hats and other peculiarities (Lightsey, *Veteran's Story*, 16).

39. Thomas diary, Private Collection of A. T. Wallace; Howard, *Recollections*, 129-30.

40. Bond reminiscence, 59, ViRC; Ruffner, "Civil War Desertion," 89; [Fifty-second Virginia], *Notice*.

41. Dinwiddie to wife, June 12, VSA; Hightower letter, June 13, GDAH; Hotchkiss to wife, June 10 and 15, Roll 4, Hotchkiss Papers, LC.

42. Wilson, "Port Republic"; Hubert to "Letitia," June 13, Duke; Garber, *Harman*, 22. "Stonewall Jackson's Way" sometimes is said to date from Winchester in May, but Sandy Garber firmly puts it in the aftermath of Port Republic. Wharton, *War Songs*, 47, says only a Valley battle. Hubert was born in Texas, and lived in New Orleans when he enlisted at age eighteen (Booth, *La. Soldiers*, II, 372).

43. Cunningham, *Doctors*, 239; Ashby, *Valley Campaigns*, 141-42. For Driver and Waugh, see Booth, *La. Soldiers*, II, 684; III, pt. 2, 1012.

44. Hadley, "Indiana Soldier," 215; Moore, *June 1862*, unn. lvs.

45. Yancey, "Civil War Letter," 35-36; *OR*, 732; *OR*, vol. XII, pt. 3, 911-12.

46. M. A. Jackson, *Memoirs*, 283-84; Hotchkiss, *Make Me a Map*, 56; Armstrong, *25th Virginia*, 35; Ropp to father, June 14, VSA; Myers, *Comanches*, 69; June 14 letter by Louisiana soldier in unident. n.p., Shute scrapbook, Tulane. The rearming of the 25th Va. with "Infield Rifles" is recounted in Armstrong. Ropp's letter reports that two companies of the 37th Va. had received "the Belgum Rifle which shoots 1,000 yards"; Ropp picked up an Enfield.

47. *OR*, 716; *OR*, XII, pt. 3, 912.

48. M. A. Jackson, *Memoirs*, 282-83; Hotchkiss, *Make Me a Map*, 56; Slaughter, *Randolph Fairfax*, 28.

49. Hotchkiss, *Make Me a Map*, 56-57; M. A. Jackson, *Memoirs*, 282-83; Taylor, *George Boardman Taylor*, 70-72.

50. *OR*, XII, pt. 3, 913.

51. *Ibid.*, 914; *OR*, 733; Hotchkiss, *Make Me a Map*, 57.

52. Whiting to wife, June 18, NCDAH.

53. Hotchkiss, *Make Me a Map*, 57.

Chapter 28: The Impact of Cross Keys and Port Republic

1. Kelly, *Port Republic*, 3.

2. Kearsey, *Shenandoah Valley*, 61; Cooke, "Battle of Port Republic."

3. *OR*, 723-24. One of the general's several nicknames was "Wagon Hunter," based on his ardor for taking and protecting spoils.

4. M. A. Jackson, *Memoirs*, 285. Mrs. Jackson (284) wrote of this period that "his men said he always marched at 'early dawn,' except when he started the night before."

5. Burnett, "Letters," 365; Clewell letter, June 13, NCDAH; "From Stonewall Jackson." Gunner Joe Carpen-

ter wrote a similar refrain on June 16 (Private Collection of Bohannon) that Jackson "will ruin his old brigade unless he allows them to recruit a little now."

6. Chamberlayne, *Chamberlayne*, 87; Kearsey, *Shenandoah Valley*, 53; Crose, "Letter"; Huntington, "Operations," 337; Moore, *June 1862*, unnumbered lvs.; Wheeler, *In Memoriam*, 335; Paulus, *Papers*, 54.

7. Randolph reminiscence, VHS; Lyman, "Cross Keys and . . . ," Tulane; Carson memoir, VHS; Kelly, *Port Republic*, 4; Neese, *Three Years*, 77. A report about unease over Jackson's style is in Howard, *Recollections*, 130–31. Howard reports a discussion among four brigadiers (Winder and Trimble were two; Taliaferro and Taylor may have been the others) in mid-June: "all were of the opinion that Jackson could not continue to take such risks without at some time meeting with a great disaster." A contemporary anti-Ewell sentiment is in Woods's letter, June 15, U. Va.: "General Ewell is thought by the soldiers generally, to be a humbug. He supplies his deficiency in sense by loud sounding words."

8. White, *Sketches*, 93; Apperson letter, June 10, Black Papers, VPI; J.J.H. of 52nd Virginia to wife, June 23, USAMHI; Carpenter to father, June 16, Private Collection of Bohannon. Another letter full of Jackson plaudits (not quoted in the text) by a Virginian is that by Humphreys, Private Collection of Updike.

9. Lewis to mother, July 30, [1862], UNC; Ring to wife, June 14, Tulane; Nisbet, "From Stonewall"; Richardson letter, June 14, GDAH.

10. Hopley, *Stonewall*, 70–71.

11. Edmonds, *Journals*, 100; McGuire, *Southern Refugee*, 120.

12. Cooke, "Southern Generals"; Richmond *Whig*, June 13, 1862.

13. *SHSP*, XLV, 198. The thanks of Congress prompted an amusing counterpoint from General Joseph E. Johnston. With impotent jealousy, Johnston wrote disdainfully (unident. clipping Aug. 16, 1885, Scrapbook 33, LHAC, Tulane) of Jackson's June battles as "really a defeat," and of his maneuvers as "scarcely strategy. . . . Yet Jackson for this received the thanks of Congress." Johnston's matchless talents at ex post facto analysis, which bore no resemblance to the difficulties he invariably encountered when campaigning himself, also helped him identify glaring shortcomings in Lee and other successful Confederate officers.

14. Anonymous Tenth Virginia "Reminiscences," SPRP.

APPENDIX A: Organization and Casualties

1. Frye, *2nd Virginia*, 29.

2. Wallace, *5th Virginia*, 75, identifies eight dead, which requires juggling the *OR* statistics without altering the total.

3. "Twenty-Seventh Virginia" includes a nominal list of 8 killed, 28 wounded, and admits omitting 4 or 5 slightly wounded. The regiment began the day only 140 strong. The nominal list in "Army Casualties" (M836), NA, shows the same killed and wounded, plus 11 missing.

4. Reidenbaugh, *33rd Virginia*, 102.

5. Chapla, *42nd Virginia*, 26, lists one killed, six wounded, and one missing. Hospital Steward Apperson claimed in a June 10 letter (Black Papers, VPI) that the 48th had nine killed.

6. The absence of reports of course does not mean no losses, although this brigade was virtually unengaged. The 37th, for instance, lost several men storming the brigade on June 8. Colonel Taliaferro's own wound (Taliaferro memoir, Private Collection of Rohrer) is the one cited here.

7. Both "Army Casualties" (M836), NA, and Fonerden, 26, show five wounded rather than the four in *OR*, 717.

8. Moore, *Charlottesville Artillery*, 9.

9. Bohannon, *Giles . . . Artillery*, 16.

10. Driver, *Rockbridge Artillery*, 140.

11. All casualties for Ewell's division combine the June 8-9 losses from *OR*, 784, 787, and 791, and are amended by further sources cited in these notes.

12. May 1 figures on present in the brigade survive in Roll 52, Hotchkiss Papers, LC: 52nd, 625; 44th, 338; 58th, 413; Miller, 92; Wooding, 95.

13. The 29 wounded of *OR*, 784 and 787, included some (perhaps 3?) who died. The Thomas diary, Private Collection of Wallace, says "some fatally" wounded; and the Hands notebook, MHS, reports that "several . . . afterwards died."

14. *OR*, 784, 787, 791; Ruffner, *44th Virginia*, 25; "Army Casualties" (M836), NA.

15. *OR*, 791; Driver, *52nd Virginia*, 18–19; [Fifty-Second Virginia], *Notice*.

16. Letter to author from Robert J. Driver, February 21, 1990.

17. A May 6 morning report in Roll 52, Hotchkiss Papers, LC, shows strengths of the following: 12th, 562; 31st, 538; 25th, 478; Lee Battery, 68.

18. "Army Casualties" (M836), NA.

19. Armstrong, *25th Virginia*, 34-35.
20. Harding, "Chenoweth," VHS; Ashcraft, *31st Virginia*, 30-31; Hoffman ms. report, June 12, WVU.
21. A nominal list in "15th Alabama," shows 13 killed.
22. These figures include the 1st N.C. Bn., organized just a few weeks earlier out of the 21st N.C., but not yet shown independently on the table of organization. Clark, *N.C. Regiments*, 4: 225, 227, 230.
23. Trimble typically lied about his losses (54, he claimed) in *OR*, 800. A contemporary account by a brigade officer, "Battle Near Port Republic," accurately reported 124 casualties.
24. "Army Casualties" (M836), NA.
25. Casualties for this brigade are the best composite from "8th Louisiana Brigade" (which provides full nominal lists); unident. contemporary clipping in Dora Shute's scrapbook, Tulane (also nominal lists); and Morning Report, Taylor's Brigade, June 11, HL. "Wheat's Battalion" lists 5 wounded officers by name and adds that 30 of 95 enlisted men present were wounded.
26. Burrus to wife, June 8 and 13 (Box 160-187a, Folder 164, ViRC), reports four men killed. No doubt two of the *OR* wounded died later.
27. Driver, *Rockbridge Artillery*, 141.
28. Bowyer's Battery is not on the *OR* table of organization, but it was present with Taylor's Brigade. A Louisiana officer (Wilson, "Port Republic") wrote that it "had nobly participated in the fight," and the battery received from Taylor the captured Coaling guns. See also Morning Report, Taylor's Brigade, June 11, HL.
29. These cavalry regiments had not been formed from Ashby's disorganized fragments, but their losses are reported here in accordance with the company alignments that soon made up regiments. Numbers are from a letter to the author by Richard L. Armstrong, March 30, 1992.
30. Williams diary, VHS, specified that the battery suffered no loss.
31. Federal sources report 58 Confederate prisoners at Front Royal on June 13 ("From Front Royal") and 67 delivered to Luray (*OR*, 697), which fits well with Confederate totals. Lower net casualties appear in Barnes, *Medical and Surgical*, vol. 4 (Coll. 7), Table XLVII.
32. O.T., "Battle at Port Republic," reported 323 men engaged in the 7th Indiana. Losses are calculated from that source and: "Letter . . . [7th Indiana]"; Winscott, "From the 7th"; and *Indiana Soldier*, 467. Company losses in Hadley, "Indiana Soldier," 213 (1 killed, 13 wounded), and Davis, "7th Indiana," ISL (1 killed, 13 wounded, 9 missing) extrapolate nicely to the regimental totals.
33. *Pennsylvania at Gettysburg* 1:452; "Most Brilliant Action."
34. Bates, *Penna. Volunteers* 3:980, reports loss "considerable in killed and wounded, and especially so in prisoners," so these figures doubtless are low. "Most Brilliant Action" supplies the statistic for men missing.
35. "Battle at Port Republic." W. Va. Adj. General, *Annual Report*, 45-76, names four members of the regiment killed.
36. The names are on a nominal list in "Most Brilliant Action."
37. Ohio Roster Comm., *Official Roster* 10:430-35.
38. Ohio Roster Comm., *Official Roster* 2:123-70, names nine killed and two mortally wounded, but is useless for wounded.
39. Wood, *Seventh Regiment*, 121-22, shows nine killed, six mortally wounded, and 51 wounded.
40. "Most Brilliant Action."
41. Ohio Roster Comm., *Official Roster* 10:409-14.
42. Jackson reported (*OR*, 715) capturing "about 450 prisoners" and paroling "some 275 wounded . . . near Port Republic." That fits well with the wounded-captured mix in this table. Many men of course fit both categories.
43. "Battle of Cross Keys"; Polsley to "Nellie," June 10, LC.
44. N.Y. Adj. General, *Registers* 18:439-64; Phisterer, *New York*, 1815.
45. "Battle of Cross Keys"; Phisterer, *New York*, 2189.
46. *Ibid.*, 2238.
47. *Ibid.*, 2306.
48. Bates, *Penna. Volunteers* 1:385.
49. Thomson and Rauch, *Bucktails*, 166n. This loss excludes the very heavy casualties on June 6.
50. Phisterer, *New York*, 1563.
51. Records of Adj. General of N.Y., 1st Light Artillery, Box 2654, RG 94, NA. The names on the return were traced and refined for me by Ray Fuerschbach of New York, the leading authority on Wiedrich's Battery.
52. Phisterer, *New York*, 804.
53. "Battle of Cross Keys."
54. Culp, *25th Ohio*, 46; "Battle of Cross Keys"; C. V. Harrison to brother, June 17, Hess Collection, U. of Michigan (6 killed, 59 wounded); Evans diary, OHS (63 net loss).

55. Bisel diary, East Carolina U. ("one man killed and several wounded").
56. Milroy estimated the army's losses accurately, but he downplayed his own brigade's by one half to 115 (Paulus, *Papers,* 49).
57. Hunt, *Seventy-Third,* 24; Campbell diary, OHS; "Battle of Cross Keys."
58. Jackson reported (*OR,* 716) capturing "about 975" Yankees, wounded and unwounded, between June 6 and 12. The casual listing in Barnes, *Medical and Surgical,* vol. IV (Coll. 7), Table XLVII, gives total Federal casualties as 1,692.

Appendix C: Cross Keys and Port Republic, 1862 to 1993

1. Sipe recollection, HRHS. For descriptions of both fields in the fall of 1862, see Hotchkiss, *Make Me a Map,* 89, 96.
2. "Destructive Fire"; Downs tannery daybook in Kemper Daybooks, Duke. An immense collection of Port Republic commercial and other civilian documents survives at Duke. The tannery ledger (in the collection numbered 2977) picks up again on January 24, 1865, Downs having put together some semblance of routine life by then.
3. Wayland, *Rockingham County,* 312.
4. Sue Lewis Durkee to Lewis F. Fisher, December 10, 1958, and "Port Republic and the Lewises," 39, Private Collection of Fisher. Mapleton still stands atop the Coaling, affording a beautiful view of the battlefield. The story of Chenoweth's body has been told above in connection with his death. His grave-stone in Beverly city cemetery evidently is only a memorial marker.
5. Wayland, *Rockingham County,* 159, 169-70, 312.
6. *Beautiful Thornrose,* 14th unnmbd. leaf. The monument in Thornrose also declares that bodies from Cross Keys and Port Republic are included.
7. Wayland, *Rockingham County,* 148; Spellman family notes, SPRP; *Roll of Honor,* XV, 257-75. Most Federal prisoners went first to Lynchburg. Several were there by June 13 (Camper and Kirkly, *Historical Record,* 54-55).
8. May, "Port Republic," 109-10, JMU; Wayland, *Rockingham County,* 196; Waddell, "Cross Keys," HRHS.
9. Kaylor, "Port Republic Battle," HRHS; "Port Republic and the Lewises," 36-37, 39-40, Private Collection of Fisher; Strayer diary, HRHS.
10. "Visit to the Country"; "Port Republic and the Lewises," 40, Private Collection of Fisher. In aftermath of the organized violence that swept its streets, Port became notorious after the war "for its fights—personal encounters" (Wayland, *Rockingham County,* 196).
11. Moore, "Through the Shadow," 16-17.
12. Liddell Hart, *Remaking of Modern Armies,* 170-71. An amusing story about English fetishism on the Valley, involving Cross Keys, is in Fuller, *Army in My Time,* 53-54. Definitive debunking of the hoary Rommel tale is in the Johnston Papers, VHS (Mss 1J6445b). Rommel's widow said her husband never came to North America at all, nor ever spoke of Jackson or the Civil War. General Hindenburg, however, was interested—but from afar.
13. "Battlefield Memorials"; Waddell, "Cross Keys," HRHS. Plat of Cross Keys Battlefield property, Lee-Jackson Foundation, Charlottesville.
14. Hess, *Heartland,* 350.
15. Mellott, "Heavy Metal."

BIBLIOGRAPHY

Manuscript Sources

Antietam National Battlefield. Sharpsburg, Maryland.
  Henry Kyd Douglas manuscript marginalia in books from his personal library.
Chicago Historical Society. Chicago, Illinois.
  Frederick Fairfax Diary.
Duke University. William R. Perkins Library, Manuscript Department. Durham, North Carolina.
  Alexander R. Boteler Papers.
  Francis W. Dawson Papers (George M. Morgan letter).
  Henry Kyd Douglas Papers.
  Lucy Muse (Walton) Fletcher Diary.
  Benjamin Hubert Letters.
  Bradley T. Johnson Papers.
  Benjamin F. Kemper and Brothers Daybook and Inventory.
  J. B. Molyneaux Papers.
  Munford-Ellis Family Papers.
  John Q. A. Nadenbousch Papers.
  Green W. Penn Papers.
  Irby G. Scott Papers.
  M. J. Solomons Scrapbook.
  Sons of Temperance of North America . . . Worth Division No. 44, Ledger and Account Book.
  Joseph T. Woods Papers.
East Carolina University, J. Y. Joyner Library.
  Frank Bisel Diary.
Emory University. Robert W. Woodruff Library, Special Collections Department. Atlanta, Georgia.
  John Levi Griffin Diary.
  Irby G. Scott Letters.
Fredericksburg and Spotsylvania National Military Park. Fredericksburg, Virginia.
  Isiah Fogleman Diary.
  Thomas S. Garnett Letter.
  Friederich von Schluembach Marginalia in prayer book.

Georgia Department of Archives and History. Atlanta, Georgia.
   Thomas M. Hightower Letters.
   Sidney Jackson Richardson Papers.
Harrisonburg-Rockingham Historical Society. Dayton, Virginia.
   "Battle of Port Republic," by G. E. May.
   "Cross Keys, An Interdiction," by W. R. Waddell, Jr.
   "Cross Keys Battlefield," by P. C. Kaylor.
   "Port Republic Battle," by P. C. Kaylor.
   George Edgar Sipe Recollections.
   Clara V. Strayer Diary.
Historic New Orleans Collection. New Orleans, Louisiana.
   Walton-Glenny Family Papers.
Historical Society of Pennsylvania. Philadelphia, Pennsylvania.
   Turner Ashby Letter to A. R. Boteler, Simon Gratz Collection.
Huntington Library. San Marino, California.
   Samuel J. C. Moore Correspondence.
   Morning Report, Taylor's Brigade, June 11, 1862.
Indiana Historical Society. Indianapolis, Indiana.
   David Enoch Been Papers.
   Augustus Van Dyke Papers.
   Samuel V. List Collection.
Indiana State Library. Indianapolis, Indiana.
   William Davis, "Record of . . . Seventh Indiana Infantry."
James Madison University. Carrier Library. Harrisonburg, Virginia.
   Margaret B. Burruss Collection.
   George E. May, "History of Port Republic."
Library of Congress. Washington, D.C.
   Thomas Evans Memoir.
   Jacob J. Frank Diary.
   Jedediah Hotchkiss Papers.
   John J. Polsley Letters.
Maryland Historical Society. Baltimore, Maryland.
   Washington Hands Notebook.
   John Eager Howard Post Letter.
   Charles S. Winder Diary.
Miami University Library. Oxford, Ohio.
   Robert C. Schenck Papers.
Mississippi Department of Archives and History. Jackson, Mississippi.
   J. J. Wilson Letters.
Museum of the Confederacy. Richmond, Virginia.
   Frank A. Bond Reminiscence.
   William B. Burruss Letter.
   James M. O. Hillsman statement in "The Roll of Honor."
National Archives. Washington, D.C.
   Compiled Service Records of Confederate Soldiers Who Served in Organizations from the
      State of Virginia (M324).
   Compiled Service Records of Confederate General and Staff Officers (M331).
   Confederate Papers Relating to Citizens or Business Firms (M346).
   Confederate States Army Casualties: Lists and Narrative Reports (M836).
   Eighth Census of the United States, 1860, for Rockingham County, Virginia (M653).

Hotchkiss semi-final manuscript map of Cross Keys, filed with *Official Records* atlas plates, cartograhic branch.

Henry B. Kelly's unpublished official report of Port Republic, January 11, 1863, M331, Roll 146.

Record of Events, 58th New York, May–June 1862.

Records of Office of Adjutant General of New York. Record Group 94.

Southern Claims Commission Case Files. Record Group 217.

Trimble Map of Cross Keys. File VA-13, Record Group 109.

Union Map (anonymous) of Port Republic Battlefield. Record Group 94. Union Battle Reports, Volume 12, Box 12.

National Weather Records Center. Asheville, North Carolina.

"Weather Journal Recording Observations at . . . Georgetown, D.C., June 1858–May 1866."

North Carolina Department of Archives and History. Raleigh, North Carolina.

Charles Christopher Blacknall Memoir.

Augustus A. Clewell Letters.

Eli S. Coble Papers.

Joseph M. Kern Reminiscence.

William H. C. Whiting Papers.

Northwestern State University of Louisiana. Cammie G. Henry Research Center, Watson Library. Natchitoches, Louisiana.

Judge Paul Stephens Collection.

Ohio Historical Society. Columbus, Ohio.

Robert Bromley Diary.

Alexander A. Campbell Diary.

Albert Durkee Diary.

Thomas Evans Diary.

Frederick Fairfax Diary.

Wallace B. Hoyt Letters.

Nathaniel L. Parmeter Papers.

Wildman Family Papers.

Potter County Historical Society. Coudersport, Pennsylvania.

Angelo M. Crapsey Letter.

Private Collections

Richard L. Armstrong. Millboro, Virginia.

Edward D. Camden Memoir.

John R. M. Bass. Spring Hope, North Carolina.

Typescript memoir of W. P. Snakenberg.

Keith S. Bohannon. Smyrna, Georgia.

Joseph Carpenter Letter.

Lewis F. Fisher. San Antonio, Texas.

Lucy Walton Fletcher Diary.

Miscellaneous Correspondence and Clippings.

"Port Republic and the Lewises—1862."

Dallas and Anna Hemp. Augusta County, Virginia.

James E. Beard Diary.

Sandra R. Kenney. Glenelg, Maryland.

John Howes Burton Letter.

Anne Baxter Knutson. Afton, Minnesota.

William Henry Baxter Diary.

Robert K. Krick. Fredericksburg, Virginia.

Benjamin Anderson Jones, "A Brief Sketch of My Relation to the War Between the States."

Lewis Leigh. Fairfax, Virginia.
  Thomas M. Wade Letters.
Robert H. Moore. Havelock, North Carolina.
  John G. Herndon Memoir.
Walter Moore. Oronoco, Minnesota.
  John Calvin Henderson Diary.
Chuck Norville. Alexandria, Virginia.
  John William Fravel Memoir.
August Payne. Chicago, Illinois.
  "Lieut-Colonel A. S. Pendleton," attributed to B. T. Lacy
Brian C. Pohanka. Alexandria, Virginia.
  Daniel J. Keily Reference File.
Sarah Taliaferro Rohrer. Orange, Virginia.
  Alexander Galt Taliaferro Memoir.
Dr. David Scott III. Fredericksburg, Virginia.
  Joseph F. Shaner Diary.
Marilyn J. Snyder. Annandale, Virginia.
  Thomas Clark Letters.
David Q. Updike. Staunton, Virginia.
  William H. Humphreys Letter, June 14, 1862.
A. Thomas Wallace. Annapolis, Maryland.
  James William Thomas Diary.
Wayne L. Wiltfang. Morocco, Indiana.
  George D. Buswell Diary.
Rockingham County Public Library. Harrisonburg, Virginia.
  "Location of Madison Hall Near Port Republic."
Society of Port Republic Preservationists. Port Republic, Virginia.
  P. C. Kaylor Letter to George E. May, December 6, 1929.
  George E. May, "Harrison Bateman," two-page typescript.
  Miscellaneous Manuscript Notes.
  "Some Historic Soil; Madison Hall," anonymous five-page typescript.
  Spellman Family Notes.
  Clara V. Strayer Scrapbook.
  Tenth Virginia "Reminiscences," anonymous typescript.
Stonewall Jackson House. Lexington, Virginia.
  Thomas M. Wade Letters.
Tennessee State Library and Archives. Nashville, Tennessee.
  Brown-Ewell Papers.
Tulane University Library. New Orleans, Louisiana.
  "Cross Keys and Port Republic" by Capt. William R. Lyman.
  William P. Harper Diary.
  "Historical Memoranda, The Opelousas Guards," in "Record Roll, Eighth Regiment."
  "Historical Memorandum" signed by Major William H. Manning in "Record Roll, Sixth Regiment."
  William R. Lyman Memoir.
  "Port Republic Killed." Nominal list of 6th Louisiana casualties in Collection 55-B, Box 24, Folder 3.
  George P. Ring Papers.
  Scrapbooks in the Louisiana Historical Association Collection.
  "The 16th Mississippi Regiment" (anonymous), Collection 55-B, Box 24, Folder 12.
United States Army Military History Institute. Carlisle Barracks, Pennsylvania.
  Anonymous 66th Ohio Memoir, Harrisburg CWRT Collection.

S. Z. Ammen Compilation in Clemens Papers.

A. J. Barrow Diary.

52nd Virginia Letter (by "J.J.H."), Lewis Leigh Collection.

Isaac Gardner Diary.

Benjamin A. Jones Memoir.

Luther B. Mesnard Memoir, Civil War Miscellaneous Collection.

John F. Neff Letter, CWTI Collection.

Francis A. Reader Memoir.

V. W. Southall Letter, Harrisburg CWRT Collection.

University of Michigan. Historical Collections, Bentley Historical Library. Ann Arbor, Michigan.

Nina L. Hess Collection.

D. C. Wright Letter, June 16, 1862.

University of North Carolina. Southern Historical Collection. Chapel Hill, North Carolina.

William Allan Memoir.

Joseph Franklin Kauffman Diary.

Joseph M. Kern Papers.

Harry Lewis Papers.

Edward Hitchcock McDonald Reminiscence.

Samuel J. C. Moore Papers.

Polk-Brown-Ewell Papers.

University of Texas. Barker Texas History Center. Austin, Texas.

James J. Kirkpatrick Diary.

University of Virginia. Alderman Library. Charlottesville, Virginia.

John Warwick Daniel Papers.

Wilbur Fisk Davis Memoir.

Jedediah Hotchkiss war-dated notes on blank pages of printed 1857 Mossy Creek Academy catalogue.

James Fontaine Minor Papers.

Micajah Woods Papers.

Virginia Historical Society. Richmond, Virginia.

Robert P. Carson Memoir.

Joseph H. Chenoweth Diary.

Joseph F. Harding, "Memoir of Major Chenoweth."

George K. Harlow Letters.

Abner Crump Hopkins Diary.

J. Ambler Johnston Papers.

Watkins Kearns Diary.

George McCulloch Mooney Memoir.

William F. Randolph Reminiscences.

William E. Trahern Memoir.

"The Life of General James A. Walker, by his daughter."

Charles Copland Wight Memoir.

James Harrison Williams Diary.

Virginia Military Institute. Lexington, Virginia.

Alumni Personal Files.

Joseph Hart Chenoweth Collection.

Records of the Superintendent.

Virginia Polytechnic Institute and State University. Blacksburg, Virginia.

Dr. Harvey Black Papers.

Virginia State Archives. Richmond, Virginia.

James Dinwiddie Letters.

James W. Orr Recollections.

"Register of Deaths, Rockingham County, 1862-1870."

William H. Ropp Letters.

West Virginia University Library. Morgantown, West Virginia.

Jeremiah Church Memoir.

Roy Bird Cook Papers.

John S. Hoffman official report of Cross Keys, June 12, 1862.

Alfred H. Jackson letter and two unidentified memoirs, in 31st Virginia File.

William L. Jackson Letters.

John J. Polsley Letters.

Roll Book, Co. A, 32nd Ohio, in the Pinnock Papers.

George P. Wallace Letters.

Western Reserve Historical Society. Cleveland, Ohio.

James Barnett Papers.

Richard S. Ewell letter to John Esten Cooke, February 10, 1864.

James Hewes Memoir (1st Maryland).

Royce Family Papers.

Published Primary Sources

"About the Fight at Front Royal." Indianapolis *Daily Journal*, June 23, 1862.

Allan, William. *Jackson's Valley Campaign: Address of Col. Wm. Allan.* Richmond, 1878.

――――. *History of the Campaign of Gen. T.J. (Stonewall) Jackson in the Shenandoah Valley of Virginia.* Philadelphia, 1880.

Arehart, W. H. "Diary of W. H. Arehart." *Rockingham Recorder,* vol. I, no. 2 (December 1946).

"Arrival of Sick and Wounded Soldiers." Washington *Evening Star,* June 16, 1862.

Ashby, Thomas A. *The Valley Campaigns.* New York, 1914.

"The Ashby Boys." New York *Tribune,* June 12, 1862.

Baldwin, Thomas. *A New and Complete Gazetteer of the United States.* Philadelphia, 1854.

Baldwin, W. E. "Port Republic." *National Tribune,* September 25, 1884.

"The Battle at Port Republic." Washington *Evening Star,* June 16, 1862.

"The Battle Near Port Republic." Richmond *Dispatch,* June 21, 1862.

"The Battle of Cross Keys." New York *Tribune,* June 19, 1862.

"Battle of Port Republic." Richmond *Whig,* June 18, 1862.

"Battlefield Memorials." *Rockingham Register* 2 (1959): 186.

Bean, William G., ed. "The Valley Campaign of 1862 as Revealed in Letters of Sandie Pendleton." *Virginia Magazine of History and Biography* 78 (1970): 326-64.

Becker, Carl M., and Ritchie Thomas, eds. *Hearth and Knapsack: The Ladley Letters, 1857-1880.* Athens, Ohio, 1988.

Beirne, Rosamond R. "Three War Letters." *Maryland Historical Magazine* 40 (1945): 287-94.

Booth, George W. *Personal Reminiscences of a Maryland Soldier.* Baltimore, 1898.

Boyd, David French. "Major Bob Wheat." New Orleans *Daily Item,* August 25, 1896.

――――. *Reminiscences of the War in Virginia.* Austin, Texas, 1989.

Brown, W. S. "The Mistake That Was Made in Not Burning the Bridge." *National Tribune,* June 2, 1887.

Brunk, H. A. *Life of Peter S. Hartman.* N.p., privately printed, 1937.

Buck, Samuel D. "Gen. Joseph [*sic*] A. Walker." *Confederate Veteran* 10 (1902): 34-36.

――――. *With the Old Confeds.* Baltimore, 1925.

Burnett, Edmund Cody, ed. "Letters of Barnett Hardeman Cody and Others." *Georgia Historical Quarterly* 23 (1939): 362–80.

Buschbeck, Adolphus. "Official Report of the Battle of Cross Keys." *Pennsylvania Daily Telegraph* [Harrisburg], June 30, 1862.

Caffey, Thomas E. *Battle-Fields of the South*. New York, 1864.

Camper, Charles, and J. W. Kirkley. *Historical Record of the First Regiment Maryland Infantry*. Washington, 1871.

Carrington, James M. "Distinguished Confederates Call." *Shenandoah Valley* [New Market], September 10, 1908.

"Casper W. Boyd." *Alabama Historical Quarterly* 23 (1961): 291–99.

Chamberlayne, John Hampden. *Ham Chamberlayne, Virginian*. Richmond, 1932.

Clark, Van Buren. "Jackson at Cross Keys." Atlanta *Journal*, October 26, 1901.

Clark, Walter. *Histories of the Several Regiments and Battalions from North Carolina in the Great War*. 5 vols. Raleigh and Goldsboro, 1901.

Clarke, James. "Some One Has Blundered." *Civil War Times Illustrated* 19 (Nov. 1980): 30–33.

Clement, H. C. "With Jackson in the Valley Campaign," in Maud Carter Clement, ed., *War Recollections of the Confederate Veterans of Pittsylvania County* (Berryville, 1961).

Coles, Isaac. "War Reminiscences of Capt. Isaac Coles," in Clement, *War Recollections* (see Clement, H. C.).

Confederate States Almanac and Repository of Useful Knowledge for 1862. Vicksburg, Mississippi, 1861.

Conner, James. *Letters of General James Conner*. Columbia, S.C., 1950.

Cooke, John Esten. *Wearing of the Gray*. New York, 1867.

Couper, William. *One Hundred Years at V.M.I.* 4 vols. Richmond, 1939.

Crawford, J. H. "Took Him Prisoner." Winchester *Evening Star*, February 22, 1910.

Crisman, Jacob. "Crisman Claims It." Winchester *Evening Star*, February 25, 1910.

———. "Gave Yell and Charged Enemy." Winchester *Evening Star*, January 25, 1910.

Crose, J. A. "Letter from the Shenandoah Valley." Indianapolis *Daily Journal*, July 2, 1862.

Culp, Edward C. *The 25th Ohio Vet. Vol. Infantry*. Topeka, Kansas, 1885.

Culpepper, Benjamin F. "The 15th Alabama with Trimble in the Shenandoah Valley." Atlanta *Journal*, September 21, 1901.

Cunningham, F. M. "Port Republic." *National Tribune*, June 2, 1904.

Dabney, Robert L. "Stonewall Jackson." *SHSP* 11:145–58.

———. *Life and Campaigns of Lieut.-Gen. Thomas J. Jackson*. New York, 1866.

Davis, John Staige. "Death of Lieut. Mack." Rome [Georgia] *Tri-Weekly Courier*, July 17, 1862.

Dixie [pseud.]. "Letter from the 7th Regiment." Aurora [Indiana] *Commercial*, June 19, 1862.

Dorsey, F. "Percy Captured?" Winchester *Evening Star*, March 12, 1910.

Douglas, Henry Kyd. *I Rode with Stonewall*. Chapel Hill, N.C., 1940.

Dyer, Gustavus W., and John T. Moore. *Tennessee Civil War Veterans Questionnaires*. 5 vols. Easley, S.C., 1985.

Edmonds, Amanda V. *Journals of Amanda Virginia Edmonds*. Stephens City, Virginia, 1984.

"The 8th Louisiana Brigade." Richmond *Whig*, June 24, 1862.

Ewell, Richard S. *The Making of a Soldier*. Richmond, 1935.

"Extract of a Letter from an Officer of Jackson's Army to His Wife." Richmond *Whig*, June 18, 1862.

"The 15th Alabama." Columbus [Georgia] *Weekly Sun*, July 8, 1862.

[Fifty-Second Virginia.] *Notice to members of the 52nd Regiment ... a list of the killed and wounded in the battles of Port Republic*. Staunton, Virginia, 1862.

"Fight at Port Republic, Va." *Ontario Repository & Messenger* [Canandaigua, N.Y.], June 18, 1862.

"Fighting Them Over." *National Tribune,* October 30, 1884.

"The First Maryland Regiment." Richmond *Dispatch,* June 19, 1862.

Fishburne, Clement D. "Historical Sketch of the Rockbridge Artillery." *SHSP* 23:98-158.

Fisk, Wilbur. *Anti-Rebel.* Croton-on-Hudson, N.Y., 1983.

Fonerden, Clarence A. *A Brief History of the Military Career of Carpenter's Battery.* New Market, Virginia, 1911.

Fontaine, Lamar. *My Life and My Lectures.* New York and Washington, 1908.

Fortson, Roderick S. "Stonewall Jackson at Port Republic." *Confederate Veteran* 9 (1901): 266-67.

Fravel, John W. "Jackson's Valley Campaign." *Confederate Veteran* 6 (1898): 418-20.

"Fremont's Army in Rockingham." Undated clipping from *Rockingham Register* in M. J. Solomons Scrapbook, Duke University (see manuscript listing).

French, S. Bassett. *Centennial Tales.* New York, 1962.

"From Front Royal." Washington *Evening Star,* June 16, 1862.

"From Gen. Fremont's Army." Washington *Evening Star,* June 16, 1862.

"From Stonewall Jackson." Rome [Georgia] *Tri-Weekly Courier,* June 24, 1862.

Frye, Rose W. *Recollections of the Rev. John McElhenney, D.D.* Richmond, 1893.

Fuller, J.F.C. *The Army in My Time.* London, 1935.

Garber, Alexander M. *A Sketch of the Life and Services of Maj. John A. Harman.* Staunton, Virginia, 1876.

Gill, John. *Reminiscences of Four Years as a Private Soldier.* Baltimore, 1904.

Goldsborough, William W. *The Maryland Line in the Confederate States Army.* Baltimore, 1869.

———. *The Maryland Line in the Confederate States Army.* Baltimore, 1900.

Gordon, William F. "Under Sentence of Death." *Southern Bivouac,* new series, 1 (1885-86): 589-92.

Green, Brian and Maria. "Letters and Cover Discovered." *North-South Trader's Civil War,* vol. XVI, no. 3 (1990).

Hadley, John V. "An Indiana Soldier in Love and War." *Indiana Magazine of History,* 59 (1963).

Hall, James E. *The Diary of a Confederate Soldier.* N.p., 1961.

Hamilton, A. S. "The 21st Georgia at the Battle Near Port Republic." Atlanta *Daily Constitutionalist,* July 4, 1862.

———. "Occasional Correspondence." Rome [Georgia] *Tri-Weekly Courier,* July 28, 1862.

———. "Private Dispatch." Atlanta *Southern Confederacy,* June 15, 1862.

Hays, Ebenezer Z. *History of the Thirty-Second Regiment Ohio ... Infantry.* Columbus, 1896.

Heneberger, E. R. Grymes, ed. *Harrisonburg, Virginia: Diary of a Citizen.* Harrisonburg, 1961.

Herndon, John G. "Infantry and Cavalry Service." *Confederate Veteran* 30 (1922): 172-74.

Herst, Herman, Jr. "Unrecorded 'Stonewall' Jackson Turns Up." *Confederate Philatelist,* November-December 1975, 169-70.

Hewes, Michael Warner. "Turner Ashby's Courage." *Confederate Veteran* 5 (1897): 613.

Hotchkiss, Jedediah. *Make Me a Map of the Valley.* Dallas, Texas, 1973.

Houghton, W. R. and M. B. *Two Boys in the Civil War and After.* Montgomery, Alabama, 1912.

Howard, McHenry. *Recollections of a Maryland Confederate Soldier and Staff Officer.* Baltimore, 1914.

Huffman, James. *Ups and Downs of a Confederate Soldier.* New York, 1940.

"Humor in Battle." Randolph [West Virginia] *Enterprise,* January 15, 1914.

Huntington, James F. "Operations in the Shenandoah Valley, from Winchester to Port Republic," in *Papers of the Military Historical Society of Massachusetts* 1:301-37.

Hurst, Samuel H. *Journal-History of the Seventy-Third Ohio Volunteer Infantry.* Chillicothe, Ohio, 1866.

Imboden, John D. "Stonewall Jackson in the Shenandoah," in *Battles and Leaders of the Civil War* 2:282-98.

"An Incident After the Battle of Cross Keys." *National Tribune,* June 10, 1886.

Jackson, Mary Anna. *Memoirs of Stonewall Jackson.* Louisville, Kentucky, 1895.

"Jackson Believed to Be Reinforced." *New York Times,* June 18, 1862.

"Jackson's Latest Victories." Richmond *Whig,* June 17, 1862.

Johnson, Thomas Cary. *The Life and Letters of Robert Lewis Dabney.* Richmond, 1903.

Johnston, Joseph E. "The Purpose of It." Washington *Evening Star,* June 14, 1862.

Jones, B. F. "Battle of Port Republic." *National Tribune,* December 11, 1884.

Jones, J. W. *The Story of American Heroism: Thrilling Narratives of Personal Adventures during the Great Civil War.* Springfield, Ohio, 1896.

Jones, John William. *Christ in the Camp.* Richmond, 1888.

Keesy, William A. *War as Viewed from the Ranks.* Norwalk, Ohio, 1898.

Kelly, Henry Brooke. *Port Republic.* Philadelphia, 1886.

Kennedy, Joseph C. G. *Preliminary Report on the Eighth Census, 1860.* Washington, 1862.

Kephart, Simon, and George M. Conner. "Shenandoah Valley." *National Tribune,* February 24, 1887.

Krzyzanowski, Wladimir. *The Memoirs of Wladimir Krzyzanowski.* San Francisco, 1978.

Lacy, William S. *William Sterling Lacy: Memorial, Addresses, Sermons.* Richmond, 1900.

"Latest from Front Royal." Washington *Star,* June 20, 1862.

Lathrop, J. M., and B. N. Griffing. *An Atlas of Rockingham County.* Philadelphia, [1885].

LaTourette, G. S. "War Time Incident of Stonewall Jackson." *Fayette* [County, West Virginia] *Tribune,* May 5, 1926.

Lee, Mrs. Hugh H. "An Extract from the Journal of Mrs. Hugh H. Lee." *Maryland Historical Magazine* 53 (1958): 380-93.

"Letter from the Army of the Shenandoah [7th Indiana]." Indianapolis *Daily Journal,* July 4, 1862.

Lewis, Lunsford Lomax. *A Brief Narrative Written for His Grandchildren.* Richmond, 1915.

Liddell Hart, Basil H. *The Remaking of Modern Armies.* London, 1927.

Lightsey, Ada Christine. *The Veteran's Story.* Meridian, Mississippi, 1899.

Lostutter, David. "Port Republic." *National Tribune,* December 25, 1892.

"The Louisiana Brigade." Richmond *Whig,* June 18, 1862.

McCarthy, Carlton. *Detailed Minutiae of Soldier Life.* Richmond, 1882.

McClendon, William A. *Recollections of War Times.* Montgomery, Alabama, 1909.

McDonald, Edward H. "Says That Wyndham Was Not Captured." Winchester *Evening Star,* March 8, 1910.

McDonald, William N. *The Laurel Brigade.* Baltimore, 1907.

McGuire, Hunter H., and George L. Christian. *The Confederate Cause and Conduct.* Richmond, 1907.

McGuire, Judith W. *Diary of a Southern Refugee During the War.* New York, 1867.

McIlwaine, Richard. *Memories of Three Score Years and Ten.* New York, 1908.

McKim, Randolph H. *A Soldier's Recollections.* New York, 1911.

Martin, Joseph. *New and Comprehensive Gazetteer of Virginia.* Charlottesville, 1835.

Mathis, Ray, ed. *In the Land of the Living.* Troy, Alabama, 1981.

Max, Jimmie. "Port Republic." *National Tribune,* March 17, 1887.

Moore, Cleon. "General Jackson at Port Republic." *The Sunny South* [Atlanta], August 1, 1896.

———. "Stonewall Jackson at Port Republic." *Confederate Veteran* 22 (1914): 511.

Moore, Edward A. *The Story of a Cannoneer Under Stonewall Jackson.* New York and Washington, 1907.

Moore, Frank, ed. *The Rebellion Record.* 11 vols. New York, 1861-68.

Moore, Samuel Scollay. "Through the Shadow." *Proceedings of the Clarke County Historical Association,* December 1990.

"More About the Battle at Port Republic." Richmond *Whig,* June 20, 1862.

"More Secesh Prisoners." Washington *Evening Star,* June 16, 1862.

"The Most Brilliant Action of the War." New York *Tribune,* June 16, 1862.

Munford, Thomas T. "A Confederate Cavalry Officer's Reminiscences." *Journal of the U.S. Cavalry Association* 4 (1891):276-88.

———. "Reminiscences of Jackson's Valley Campaign." *SHSP* 8:523-34.

Myers, Franklin M. *The Comanches.* Baltimore, 1871.

Nachtigall, Herrmann. *History of the 75th Regiment, Pa. Vols.* North Riverside, Illinois, 1987.

"A Near View of the Yankees." *Religious Herald,* July 10, 1862.

Neese, George M. *Three Years in the Confederate Horse Artillery.* New York and Washington, 1911.

Nisbet, James Cooper. *Four Years on the Firing Line.* Chattanooga, Tennessee, [1915?].

———. "From Stonewall Jackson." Macon [Georgia] *Daily Telegraph,* June 27, 1862.

O. T. "The Battle at Port Republic." Indianapolis *Daily Journal,* June 19, 1862.

Oates, William C. *The War Between the Union and the Confederacy.* New York and Washington, 1905.

O'Bannon, J. H. "Honor to Whom Honor." Richmond *Dispatch,* June 21, 1891.

O'Ferrall, Charles T. *Forty Years of Active Service.* New York, 1904.

Official Register of the Officers and Cadets of the U.S. Military Academy. New York, 1856.

Osborn, Hartwell. *Trials and Triumphs.* Chicago, 1904.

Paulus, Margaret B., ed. *Papers of General Robert Huston Milroy.* N. p., 1965.

Paver, John M. *What I Saw from 1861 to 1864.* [Indianapolis, 1906?]

Pile, George C. "The War Story of a Confederate Soldier Boy." Bristol [Tennessee] *Herald-Courier,* January 23-February 27, 1921.

Poague, William T. *Gunner with Stonewall.* Jackson, Tennessee, 1957.

"Port Republic." *National Tribune,* June 2, 1904.

Pryor, Shepherd G. *A Post of Honor.* Fort Valley, Georgia, 1989.

[Quitman Guards]. *A Historical Sketch of the Quitman Guards, Company E, Sixteenth Mississippi Regiment.* New Orleans, 1866.

Randolph, Isham. *Gleanings from a Harvest of Memories.* Columbia, Missouri, 1937.

Ray, B. "The Unburned Bridge at Port Republic." *National Tribune,* July 28, 1904.

Ray, George B. "Journal of George B. Ray . . . 5th Ohio." *Historical and Philosophical Society of Ohio Publications,* 1962, 57-73.

Richardson's Almanac 1862. Richmond, 1861.

Roberts, John N. *Reminiscences of the Civil War.* N.p., 1925.

Robson, John S. *How a One-Legged Rebel Lives.* Charlottesville, 1891.

Roll of Honor. No. XV. Washington, 1868.

Room, Carl [pseud.]. See Cleon Moore.

Schurz, Carl. *The Reminiscences of Carl Schurz.* 2 vols. New York, 1907.

SeCheverell, J. H. *Journal History of the Twenty-ninth Ohio Veteran Volunteers.* Cleveland, 1883.

"Sixteenth Mississippi Regiment." Richmond *Dispatch,* June 19, 1862.

Skidmore, Richard S., ed. *The Civil War Journal of Billy Davis.* Greencastle, Indiana, 1989.

Slaughter, Philip. *A Sketch of the Life of Randolph Fairfax.* Richmond, 1864.

Smith, Glenn C., ed. "Diary of a Virginia Schoolmistress, 1860-1865." *Madison Quarterly,* vol. IX, no. 2 (1949).

"The Squarest Battle of the War." Detroit *Free Press,* March 4, 1882.

Stratton, Robert B. *The Heroes in Gray.* Lynchburg, 1894.

Strother, David Hunter. Cecil D. Eby, Jr., ed. *A Virginia Yankee in the Civil War.* Chapel Hill, N.C., 1961.

Taliaferro, William B. "How History Is Written." Richmond *Dispatch,* June 26, 1891.

Taylor, George Braxton. *Life and Letters of Rev. George Boardman Taylor.* Lynchburg, 1908.

Taylor, Richard. *Destruction and Reconstruction.* New York, 1879.

"Taylor's Louisiana Brigade." New Orleans *Daily Picayune,* June 10, 1866.

Thomson, O. R. Howard, and William H. Rauch. *History of the "Bucktails."* Philadelphia, 1906.

Thomson, Orville. *Narrative of the Service of the Seventh Indiana Infantry.* Privately printed, 190—.

Tracy, Albert. "Fremont's Pursuit of Jackson."*Virginia Magazine of History and Biography* 70 (1962):332-43.

"The Twenty-Seventh Virginia Regiment." Richmond *Dispatch,* June 19, 1862.

Underwood, John L. *Women of the Confederacy.* New York and Washington, 1906.

U.S. War Department. *War of the Rebellion: A Compilation of the Official Records of the Union and Confederate Armies.* 128 vols. Washington, 1880-1901.

"A Visit to the Country." *Rockingham Register,* December 12, 1873.

W.C.F. "Letter from the Thirteenth Regiment." Indianapolis *Daily Journal,* June 25, 1862.

Waddell, John. "The Battle of Cross Keys." *National Tribune,* January 1892(?).

Walker, Charles D. *Memorial, Virginia Military Institute.* Philadelphia, 1875.

"War News—Fight at Port Republic, Va." *Ontario Repository & Messenger* [Canandaigua, N.Y.], June 25, 1862.

Wayland, John W. *Virginia Valley Records.* Strasburg, 1930.

Webb, Charles Henry. "The Battle of Cross Keys, between Fremont and Jackson." *New York Times,* June 16, 1862.

———. "Gen. Fremont's Command." *New York Times,* June 17, 1862.

———. "Overtaking the Enemy." *New York Times,* June 14, 1862.

[West, Beckwith]. *Experience of a Confederate States Prisoner.* Richmond, 1862.

"Wheat's Battalion." Richmond *Dispatch,* June 19, 1862.

Wheeler, William. *In Memoriam.* Cambridge, Mass., 1875.

White, William S. *Sketches of the Life of Captain Hugh A. White of the Stonewall Brigade.* Columbia, S.C., 1864.

Whitehead, Paul. "An Historic Scene: Stonewall Jackson at the Battle of Port Republic." Richmond *Dispatch,* July 12, 1891.

———. "Stonewall Jackson's Escape at Port Republic." Richmond *Dispatch,* June 16, 1891.

Wilder, Theodore. *The History of Company C, Seventh Regiment, O.V.I.* Oberlin, 1866.

Willis, Edward. "Letter of Colonel Edward Willis." *SHSP,* 41:161-65.

Wilson, Daniel A. "The Battle of Port Republic." Macon [Georgia] *Daily Telegraph,* June 24, 1862.

Wingfield, Henry W. *Two Confederate Items.* Richmond, 1927.

Winscott, Elliott. "From the 7th Regiment." Lawrenceburg [Indiana] *Democratic Register,* June 18, 1862.

Winters, Joshua. *Civil War Letters and Diary of Joshua Winters.* Parsons, West Virginia, 1991.

Wood, George L. *The Seventh [Ohio] Regiment.* New York, 1865.

Wood, James H. *The War.* Cumberland, Maryland, 1910.

Yancey, Mary Gibbons. "A Civil War Letter." *Rockingham Recorder,* April 1988, 34–38.

Yeary, Mamie, comp. *Reminiscences of the Boys in Gray.* Dallas, Texas, 1912.

Periodicals

Atlanta *Daily Constitutionalist,* 1862.

Atlanta *Journal,* 1901.

Atlanta *Southern Confederacy,* 1862.

Aurora [Indiana] *Commercial,* 1862.

Bristol [Tennessee] *Herald-Courier,* 1921.

Civil War Times Illustrated, 1980.

Columbus [Georgia] *Weekly Sun,* 1862.

Confederate Veteran [Atlanta], 1890.

Confederate Veteran [Nashville], 1893–1932.

Fayette [County, West Virginia] *Tribune,* 1926.

Georgia Historical Quarterly, 1939.

Harrisonburg *Daily News-Record,* 1929, 1953, 1960, 1992.

Indiana Magazine of History, 1963.

Indianapolis *Daily Journal,* 1862.

Journal of the U.S. Cavalry Association, 1891.

Lawrenceburg [Indiana] *Democratic Register,* 1862.

Lexington [Virginia] *Gazette,* 1862.

London *Times,* 1879.

Lynchburg *Virginian,* 1862.

Macon [Georgia] *Daily Telegraph,* 1862.

Madison Quarterly, 1945, 1949.

Magazine of American History, 1886.

Maryland Historical Magazine, 1945, 1950.

Mobile *Register and Advertiser,* 1862.

Muzzle Blasts, 1992.

National Tribune, 1884, 1886, 1887, 1889, 1892, 1904.

New Orleans *Daily Item,* 1896.

New Orleans *Daily Picayune,* 1866.

New York *Daily News,* 1865.

New York Times, 1862.

New York *Tribune,* 1862.

Ontario Repository & Messenger [Canandaigua, N.Y.], 1862.

Our Living and Our Dead, 1875.

Randolph [W.Va.] *Enterprise,* 1914.

Religious Herald, 1862.

Richmond *Dispatch,* 1862, 1891, 1902.

Richmond *Whig,* 1862.

Rockingham Recorder, 1879, 1946, 1959, 1988.

Rockingham Register, 1873.

Rome [Georgia] *Tri-Weekly Courier,* 1862.

Shenandoah Valley [New Market], 1908.
Southern Historical Society Papers, 1876-1959.
Staunton *Vindicator,* 1863, 1867.
Sunny South [Atlanta], 1896.
Virginia Magazine of History and Biography, 1962, 1970.
Washington *Evening Star,* 1862.
Washington Post Magazine, 1993.
Winchester *Evening Star,* 1910.

Secondary Sources

Alexander, Margie H. *The Story of Port Republic.* [Elkton, 1970].
Armstrong, Richard L. *7th Virginia Cavalry.* Lynchburg, 1992.
——. *11th Virginia Cavalry.* Lynchburg, 1989.
——. *25th Virginia Infantry.* Lynchburg, 1990.
Ashcraft, John M., Jr. *31st Virginia Infantry.* Lynchburg, 1988.
Barnes, Joseph K., comp. *The Medical and Surgical History of the War of the Rebellion.* 6 vols. Washington, 1875-83.
Bassford, K. S. *The Evolution of Harrisonburg.* Harrisonburg, 1945.
Bates, Samuel P. *History of Pennsylvania Volunteers, 1861-5.* 5 vols. Harrisburg, 1869-71.
"The Battle at Cross Keys." Richmond *Whig,* June 19, 1862.
"The Battle at Port Republic." New York *Tribune,* June 18, 1862.
Beautiful Thornrose. Staunton, 1921.
Bilby, Joseph G. " 'Rashly Led Forward': Percy Wyndham and the First New Jersey Cavalry." *Muzzle Blasts,* March 1992, 17-19, 61-62.
Bohannon, Keith S. *The Giles, Alleghany, and Jackson Artillery.* Lynchburg, 1990.
Booth, Andrew B. *Records of Louisiana Confederate Soldiers.* 4 vols. New Orleans, 1920.
Booty, Kent. "Jackson's Battle of Port Republic." *Curio,* vol. I, no. 1 (1978): 31-33.
Cartmell, Thomas K. *Shenandoah Valley Pioneers.* Winchester, 1909.
Chapla, John D. *42nd Virginia Infantry.* Lynchburg, 1983.
——. *48th Virginia Infantry.* Lynchburg, 1989.
Chase, William C. *Story of Stonewall Jackson.* Atlanta, 1901.
Cook, Anna Maria Green. *History of Baldwin County, Georgia.* Anderson, S.C., 1925.
Cooke, John Esten. "The Battle of Port Republic." Staunton *Vindicator,* February 15, 1867.
——. "Southern Generals in Outline." New York *Daily News,* October 24, 1865.
——. *Stonewall Jackson: A Military Biography.* New York, 1876.
"Coolness of Jackson." Richmond *Whig,* June 17, 1862.
Cunningham, H. H. *Doctors in Gray.* Baton Rouge, Louisiana, 1958.
Davis, Julia. *The Shenandoah.* New York, 1945.
"Destructive Fire." Staunton *Vindicator,* November 13, 1863.
Driver, Robert J. *The 1st and 2nd Rockbridge Artillery.* Lynchburg, 1987.
——. *52nd Virginia Infantry.* Lynchburg, 1986.
——. *58th Virginia Infantry.* Lynchburg, 1990.
Evans, Clement A., ed. *Confederate Military History.* 13 vols. Atlanta, 1899.
Fisher, Lewis F. *The Family of John Lewis, Pioneer.* San Antonio, Texas, 1985.
Foster, John Y. *New Jersey and the Rebellion.* Newark, 1868.
Freeman, Douglas Southall. *Lee's Lieutenants.* 3 vols. New York, 1942-44.
Frye, Dennis E. *2nd Virginia Infantry.* Lynchburg, 1984.
Hardesty's Historical and Geographical Encyclopedia. New York and Richmond, 1884.
Havron, W. H. "Stonewall Jackson's Valley Campaign." *Confederate Veteran* [Atlanta], 1 (1890): 193-205 and 319-22.

Heinl, Robert D. *Dictionary of Military and Naval Quotations.* Annapolis, 1966.

Henderson, George F. R. *Stonewall Jackson and the American Civil War.* 2 vols. London, 1898.

Henderson, Lillian, comp. *Roster of the Confederate Soldiers of Georgia.* 6 vols. Hapeville, Georgia, 1959–64.

Hess, Nancy B. *The Heartland: "Rockingham County."* Harrisonburg, 1976.

Hopley, Catherine C. *"Stonewall" Jackson, Late General of the Confederate States Army.* London, 1863.

Hutton, Ralph B. *The History of Elkton.* N.p., 1958.

Indiana Adjutant General. *Report of the Adjutant General of the State of Indiana.* 8 vols. Indianapolis, 1865–69.

Johnson, John Lipscomb. *The University Memorial.* Baltimore, 1871.

Kearsey, Alexander H. C. *A Study of the Strategy and Tactics of the Shenandoah Valley Campaign.* Aldershot, England, 1953.

King, W. C., and W. P. Derby. *Camp-fire Sketches and Battle-field Echoes.* Springfield, Mass., 1889.

Krick, Robert K. *Lee's Colonels: A Biographical Register of the Field Officers of the Army of Northern Virginia.* Dayton, Ohio, 1991.

———. *Stonewall Jackson at Cedar Mountain.* Chapel Hill, N.C., 1990.

Lee, Alvid E. "The Battle of Cross Keys." *Magazine of American History* 15 (1886):487–91.

———. "Battles of Port Republic and Lewiston." *Magazine of American History* 15 (1886): 590–93.

Lossing, Benson J. *Pictorial History of the Civil War.* Hartford, 1868.

McNeer, Rembert D. *Port Republic Methodist Church.* N.p., 1943.

Macrae, David. *The Americans at Home.* New York, 1952.

Malone, Dumas, ed. *Dictionary of American Biography.* 20 vols. New York, 1936.

Martin, David G. *Carl Bornemann's Regiment, the Forty-First New York Infantry.* Hightstown, N.J., 1987.

Mauzy, Richard. *The Descendants of Henry Mauzy.* Harrisonburg, 1911.

May, George E. "The Battle of Port Republic." *Madison Quarterly* 7 (1947): 95–101.

———. "The Early Days of Port Republic." *Madison Quarterly* 5 (1945): 119–29.

———. "Port Republic Writer Reveals Error." Harrisonburg *Daily News-Record,* December 2, 1929.

Mellott, Jeff. "Heavy Metal." Harrisonburg *Daily News-Record,* February 4, 1992.

Merchant, Thomas E. *Eighty-Fourth Regiment, Pennsylvania Volunteers.* Philadelphia, 1890.

Miers, Early Schenck, ed. *Ride to War: The History of the First New Jersey Cavalry.* New Brunswick, N.J., 1961.

Miller, Gordon W. *Rockingham: An Annotated Bibliography.* Harrisonburg, 1989.

Moon, William A. *Historical Significance of Brown's Gap in the War Between the States.* Waynesboro, Virginia, 1937.

Moore, Alison. *The Louisiana Tigers.* Baton Rouge, 1961.

Moore, James. *June 1862, Civil War Battles of . . . Cross Keys [and] Port Republic.* Harrisonburg, n.d.

Moore, Robert H. *The Charlottesville . . . Artillery,* Lynchburg, 1990.

Murphy, Terrence V. *10th Virginia Infantry.* Lynchburg, 1989.

Musick, Michael P. *6th Virginia Cavalry.* Lynchburg, 1990.

Neff, Ray A. *Valley of the Shadow.* Terre Haute, Indiana, 1989.

New York Adjutant General. *Registers of New York Regiments in the War of the Rebellion.* 43 vols. Albany, 1894–1906.

Ohio Roster Commission. *Official Roster of the Soldiers of the State of Ohio.* 12 vols. Cincinnati, 1886–95.

"Old Mill at Lynnwood." Harrisonburg *Daily News-Record,* March 5, 1960.

Paris, John. "The Soldier's History of the War." *Our Living and Our Dead,* vol. II, no. 4 (June 1875).

Parrish, T. Michael. *Richard Taylor, Soldier Prince of Dixie.* Chapel Hill, N.C., 1992.

Pennsylvania at Gettysburg. 2 vols. Harrisburg, 1893.

Phisterer, Frederick. *New York in the War of the Rebellion.* 5 vols. Albany, 1912.

Pohanka, Brian C. "Myles Walter Keogh." *Greasy Grass,* May 1988, 5-11.

Pula, James S. *For Liberty and Justice: The Life and Times of Wladimir Krzyzanowski.* Chicago, 1978.

Randolph, Sarah N. *The Life of Gen. Thomas J. Jackson.* Philadelphia, 1876.

Rankin, Thomas M. *37th Virginia Infantry.* Lynchburg, 1987.

Rawling, Charles J. *History of the First . . . Virginia [Union] Infantry.* Philadelphia, 1887.

Reader, Frank S. *History of the . . . Second Virginia [Union] Infantry.* New Brighton, Pa., 1890.

Reidenbaugh, Lowell. *27th Virginia Infantry.* Lynchburg, 1993.

———. *33rd Virginia Infantry.* Lynchburg, 1987.

Riggs, David F. *13th Virginia Infantry.* Lynchburg, 1988.

Ruffner, Kevin. *44th Virginia Infantry.* Lynchburg, 1987.

———. "Civil War Desertion from a Black Belt Regiment," in E. L. Ayers and J. C. Willis, eds., *The Edge of the South: Life in Nineteenth-Century Virginia* (Charlottesville, 1991).

Showalter, Noah D. *Atlas of Rockingham County.* Harrisonburg, 1939.

The Soldier of Indiana in the War for the Union. Indianapolis, 1866.

"Some Historic Soil." Richmond *Dispatch,* October 19, 1902.

[Sparkman, Achilles Pearson]. Obituary in *Confederate Veteran* 21 (1913):452.

Stafford, G.M.G. *General Leroy Augustus Stafford.* New Orleans, 1943.

Svenson, Peter. "Backyard Battlefield." *Washington Post Magazine,* January 24, 1993, 12-16 and 23-26.

Switzer, George F. *The Descendants of Dr. George Whitfield Kemper, Jr.* [Harrisonburg, 1951?]

Tanner, Robert G. *Stonewall in the Valley.* Garden City, New York, 1976.

Terrell, Isaac Long. *Old Homes in Rockingham County, 1750 to 1850.* Verona, Virginia, 1983.

Thomas, Henry W. *History of the Doles-Cook Brigade.* Atlanta, 1903.

Walker, Charles D. *Memorial, Virginia Military Institute.* Philadelphia, 1875.

Wallace, Lee A., Jr. *5th Virginia Infantry.* Lynchburg, 1988.

———. *A Guide to Virginia Military Organizations, 1861-1865.* Lynchburg, 1986.

Wayland, John W. "The Battle of Port Republic." Harrisonburg *Daily News-Record,* July 31, 1953.

———. *A History of Rockingham County, Virginia.* Dayton, Virginia, 1912.

———. "Wayside Taverns." Harrisonburg *Daily News-Record,* June 12, 1953.

West Virginia Adjutant General. *Annual Report of the Adjutant General of the State of West Virginia.* Wheeling, 1865.

Wharton, Henry M. *War Songs and Poems of the Southern Confederacy.* [Philadelphia?, 1904]

Wilson, Lawrence. *Itinerary of the Seventh Ohio Volunteer Infantry.* New York, 1907.

Wise, Jennings Cropper. *The Long Arm of Lee.* 2 vols. Lynchburg, 1915.

"Wyndham, Percy, 1833-1879." London *Times,* February 3, 1879.

INDEX

(continued from front flap)

vivid color to this canvas. Krick draws striking portraits of Jackson, John C. Frémont, Robert E. Lee, Richard S. Ewell, and Erastus B. Tyler. Maps show exactly where and how the battles were fought, and the book's many vintage photographs and illustrations make the scenes leap from the pages.

Minutely detailed sketches of topography emphasize the importance of the Valley's landscape; Krick quotes one soldier's letter home: "Either army can surround the other, and I believe they both can do it at the same time." The movements of individual units, and the identities and fates of countless officers, ranks, and civilians conjure up the time, place, and characters of these thrilling, pivotal battles.

Photograph by *The Free Lance–Star*

Robert K. Krick is the author of numerous books, including *Stonewall Jackson at Cedar Mountain, The Fredericksburg Artillery,* and *Lee's Colonels.*